Crusading at the Edges of Europe

This book is the first to compare Denmark and Portugal systematically in the High Middle Ages and demonstrates how the two countries became strong kingdoms and important powers internationally by their participation in the crusading movement.

Communication in the Middle Ages was better developed than often assumed, and institutions, ideas and military technology were exchanged rapidly, meaning it was possible to coordinate great military expeditions across the geographical periphery of Western Europe. Both Denmark and Portugal were closely connected to the sea and developed strong fleets, at the entrance to the Baltic and in the Mediterranean Seas respectively. They also both had religious borders, to the pagan Wends and to the Muslims, that were pushed forward in almost continuous crusades throughout the centuries.

Crusading at the Edges of Europe follows the major campaigns of the kings and crusaders in Denmark and Portugal and compares war technology and crusading ideology, highlighting how the countries learned from each other and became organized for war.

Kurt Villads Jensen is Professor of Medieval History at the University of Stockholm, Sweden.

Crusading at the Edges of Europe

Denmark and Portugal c. 1000 – c. 1250

Kurt Villads Jensen

LONDON AND NEW YORK

First published 2017
by Routledge
2 Park Square, Milton Park, Abingdon, Oxon OX14 4RN

and by Routledge
711 Third Avenue, New York, NY 10017

Routledge is an imprint of the Taylor & Francis Group, an informa business

© 2017 Kurt Villads Jensen

The right of Kurt Villads Jensen to be identified as author of this work
has been asserted by him in accordance with sections 77 and 78 of the
Copyright, Designs and Patents Act 1988.

All rights reserved. No part of this book may be reprinted or reproduced or
utilised in any form or by any electronic, mechanical, or other means, now
known or hereafter invented, including photocopying and recording, or in
any information storage or retrieval system, without permission in writing
from the publishers.

Trademark notice: Product or corporate names may be trademarks or
registered trademarks, and are used only for identification and explanation
without intent to infringe.

British Library Cataloguing-in-Publication Data
A catalogue record for this book is available from the British Library

Library of Congress Cataloging-in-Publication Data
Names: Jensen, Kurt Villads, author.
Title: Crusading at the edges of Europe : Denmark and Portugal,
    c. 1000 – c. 1250 / Kurt Villads Jensen.
Other titles: Korstog ved verdens yderste rand. English
Description: Milton Park, Abingdon, Oxon ; New York, NY : Routledge,
    2017. | Includes bibliographical references.
Identifiers: LCCN 2016020422 | ISBN 9781472469380 (hardback :
    alkaline paper) | ISBN 9781315575216 (ebook)
Subjects: LCSH: Denmark—History—To 1241. | Portugal—History—To
    1385. | Crusades. | Denmark—History, Military. | Portugal—History,
    Military.
Classification: LCC DL167 .J4613 2017 | DDC 946.9/01—dc23
LC record available at https://lccn.loc.gov/2016020422

ISBN: 978-1-4724-6938-0 (hbk)
ISBN: 978-1-315-57521-6 (ebk)

Typeset in Times New Roman
by Apex CoVantage, LLC

Contents

	List of maps and figures	vi
	Preface	viii
1	The letter to chief librarian Bruun	1
2	Were there any crusades in the periphery?	14
3	The missionary wars of the 11th century: precursors of the crusades	51
4	Is the edge of the world far away?	91
5	The extending of Jerusalem	104
6	Afonso and Valdemar: the victorious crusader kings	130
7	The struggle for land and history	186
8	The rise and fall of the crusader kingdoms	260
9	Syncretism and regimentation	311
10	Coordinated crusades in north and south?	324
11	Conclusion	333
	Literature	339
	Index	371

Maps and figures

0.1	The Baltic Area © Johnny Grandjean Gøgsig Jakobsen	xi
0.2	Denmark © Johnny Grandjean Gøgsig Jakobsen	xii
0.3	Portugal © Johnny Grandjean Gøgsig Jakobsen	xiii
0.4	Iberian Peninsula © Johnny Grandjean Gøgsig Jakobsen	xiv
0.5	Place names with "snekke" in Denmark © Johnny Grandjean Gøgsig Jakobsen	xv
0.6	Wendish place names in Denmark © Johnny Grandjean Gøgsig Jakobsen	xv
0.7	Cistercians in Denmark © Johnny Grandjean Gøgsig Jakobsen	xvi
0.8	Cistercians in Portugal © Johnny Grandjean Gøgsig Jakobsen	xvii
1.1	"The head was altogether complete and of a most beautiful shape, with an oval face, prominent nose bone, and with complete rows of teeth of a rarely even and beautiful shape." Description of Berengaria from the archaeological report, 1855. Here a cast in the church of Sankt Bendt in Ringsted. © Mona Bager Jensen	2
2.1	Erik Arup, 1876–1951. © University of Southern Denmark Press	24
2.2	Alexandre Herculano, 1810–1877. © Coimbra University Press	33
3.1	Jellingstone, 980s. Christ the Victorious on the cross, which is depicted with branches and leaves as the tree of life. © Anne Pedersen, National Museum, Copenhagen	61
4.1	Relief above the Cat's Head Door at the cathedral of Ribe. The crosses are held up towards omega, the last letter of the alphabet, the end of time and the heavenly Jerusalem, which is inscribed in alpha, the beginning, the Word. The dating is uncertain: from around 1170 to the middle of the 13th century. Who the individuals are is equally uncertain. That it has something to do with crusades seems obvious. © John H. Lind	98
7.1	Dormitory, Alcobaça. The monastery of Alcobaça was established in 1153 by Bernard of Clairvaux. It was from the beginning closely attached to the Portuguese crusades. The nave and large parts of the monastic area dates to the middle of the 13th century. © Kurt Villads Jensen	193

Maps and figures   vii

7.2   The round church of Bjernede on Zealand – one
of the Danish copies of the Holy Sepulchre in Jerusalem.
© Kurt Villads Jensen   204
7.3   The mortal remains of St. Vincent arrive in Lisbon on a
ship with only the ravens navigating it. In the margin of the
Portuguese manuscript from the early 13th century, a scribe
has added a quote from St. Paul's letter to the Philippians
(1,29): "For unto you it is given in the behalf of Christ, not
only to believe on him, but also to suffer for his sake."
© University of Southern Denmark Press   226
7.4   The knight Domingos Joanes from Oliveira. Statue,
presumably from his funeral church; 65 centimetres tall,
14th century. © University of Southern Denmark Press   237
8.1   Fighting between a Christian crusader and a heathen rider?
Or two crusaders paying homage to the cross before they set
out? Relief in granite above the entrance to the church of
Nødager in Djursland, Denmark, around 1200. © University
of Southern Denmark Press   266
8.2   *King Valdemar and Queen Berengaria on the morning after
their wedding.* Painting by Agnes Slott-Møller, 1931.
© University of Southern Denmark Press   285
11.1 The plait of Berengaria, now on display in the church
in Ringsted. © Worsaae, *Kongegravene* . . ., 1858.   337

Preface

On names and sources

This book deals with Denmark and Portugal during the High Middle Ages and it contains many names. This is deliberate. History is created by people who interacted with and against each other; sometimes they were closely connected, often through family lines. Nevertheless, only a small fraction of all the people I have come to know from Danish and Portuguese sources through the years are mentioned. And they are only an infinitesimal fraction of the many people who lived in Denmark and Portugal during the 12th and 13th centuries.

This book is loaded with references to medieval sources. Some are direct quotes; many are rephrased with slightly different wording from the original. This is a deliberate attempt to let the sources themselves speak directly to the modern reader. Now, most professional historians – at least in Scandinavia – would loudly proclaim that the sources cannot speak! They say nothing by themselves but can solely answer the questions which historians formulate and put to the sources.

If the question has not been formulated, the answer cannot be found in the sources. This book is built on the presumption that earlier Danish historians neglected the crusades in their reading of medieval sources from the North simply because they did not pose the questions and did not look for them. However, it is also my experience that we always find something unexpected and surprising when we go to the sources themselves and not just refer to them by co-opting the footnotes of other historians. And – most importantly – though I have attempted to describe events and institutions, first and foremost I attempt to understand how individuals in medieval Denmark and Portugal thought and felt about themselves and about the infidels, "the other." Thoughts and emotions are closely connected with the language in which they are expressed. Therefore it is important to give the reader a first-hand impression of the language by quoting extensively from the original sources.

This book is concerned with ideas and mentalities; it is some sort of medieval cultural history. It therefore becomes necessary to include many different types of sources: detailed descriptions from the time of kings and their battles, the yellowed stiff parchment documents with set formulas that meticulously note transfer of property and purchase prizes and obligations, theological tracts on sin and

Preface   ix

rebellion and mercy and the enthusiastic descriptions of mass killings. Sources also include material remnants such as ships and horses. No individual can be an expert in all this, and it is easy to misconstrue something. We will have to live with that. I have chosen to attempt to create a comprehensive picture rather than to hide in the narrow hole of the specialist.

Quotes from sources are normally my own translations from Medieval Latin, Danish, Old Norse, French, German, Portuguese and Spanish. Bible quotes are translated as they appear in the sources and their scriptural context is examined with reference to the Latin Vulgata, which often differs from modern, authorized Bible translations.

Reading sources and the works of earlier historians has been a pleasure over many years. It is first of all made possible by favourable conditions and good colleagues at the Institute for History at University of Southern Denmark. A grant from the Danish National Research Council for the Humanities made it possible in 1999–2001 to concentrate on a project on Denmark and the crusade movement together with John H. Lind and Carsten Selch Jensen, soon to be joined by post-graduate student Ane L. Bysted. Later, I had the great pleasure of working with Janus Møller Jensen and Johnny G.G. Jakobsen. Participating in discussions, travel and conferences with all of you has been immensely inspiring. This also, and not least, goes for the many discussions about everything that I have had with my good friend and colleague Torben K. Nielsen. I had an opportunity to cultivate my special interest in Portuguese matters during a three-month stay at the University of Coimbra in 2000, financed by the Organization of Danish University Rectors. I was allowed to use the many beautiful, old and well-equipped libraries and enjoyed great hospitability and helpfulness from many, not least Saul António Gomes, João Gouveia Monteiro, Maria Helena da Cruz Coelho and Agostinho Ribeiro Mendes. I have visited Coimbra since and every time I have been received with similar friendliness. "Portugal was born in Guimarães" is written in tall letters on the city wall when one drives into the charming and well-preserved medieval city, where the first King of Portugal allegedly was born. The mayor of Guimarães has very kindly donated to me many volumes of publications of papers from historical conferences in the city.

During the years 2001–2002, I could continue the work at the Danish Institute for Advanced Studies in Humanities; September and October 2005 were spent at the Centre for Medieval Studies in Bergen, Norway, which gave me inspiration to carry on. That same year, I was unlucky to be assigned as a member of the National Research Council, which was an exciting, though a bit of a time-consuming, task.

All in all, it has taken a long time to finish this book, but I have been in great company with medieval crusaders and their sources. However, it has meant that perspectives and questions have changed over the years. When I began, there was only very little crusade research in Denmark. This has most certainly changed. Thus, the aim of this book has also changed somewhat. Originally, the idea was to encourage new research on crusade history in a Danish context. The aim now is rather to create a larger, comprehensive picture and to demonstrate that it is

x   *Preface*

indeed possible to shed new light on medieval Nordic history by working with the crusades. This, on the other hand, has made neither the labour nor the volume of this book any smaller.

Several people have read the Danish manuscript at different stages and have shared valuable commentaries and thoughts: Bodil Heiede, Merete Harding, Brian P. McGuire, John H. Lind, Tore Nyberg, Benedicte Fonnesbech-Wulff and Michael Kræmmer. Kirsi Salonen's help and encouragement was invaluable for completing the book. Johnny G. G. Jakobsen made the maps and Mona Bager Jensen took many lovely photographs. Fernando Coelho Kvistgaard translated the book from Danish into Portuguese and sent me loads of helpful comments and corrections, as did João Gouveia Monteiro and Miguel Gomes Martins while reading the Portuguese version. A warm expression of thanks is due also to Anders Nygaard who translated the book into English. Thank you to you all for your great effort. And finally, warm thanks to the foundations and institutions whose kind support has made it possible to publish this book.

Kurt Villads Jensen
Stockholm, July 2016

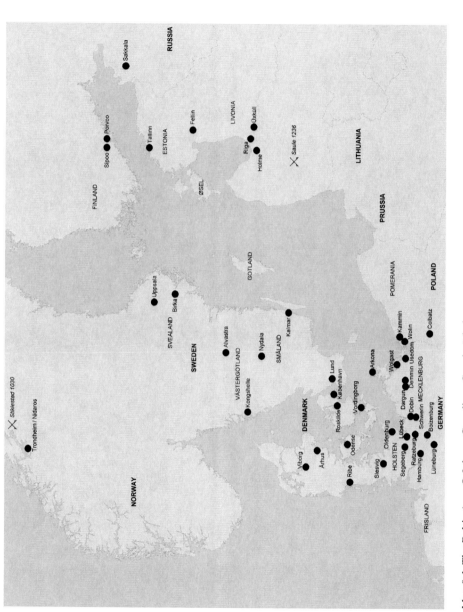

Map 0.1 The Baltic Area © Johnny Grandjean Gøgsig Jakobsen

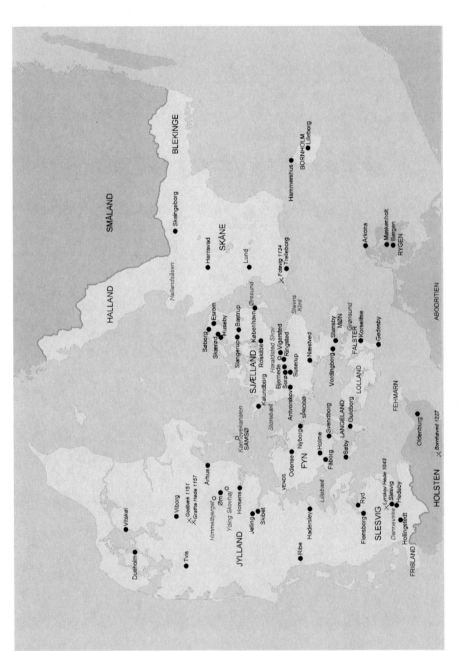

Map 0.2 Denmark © Johnny Grandjean Gøgsig Jakobsen

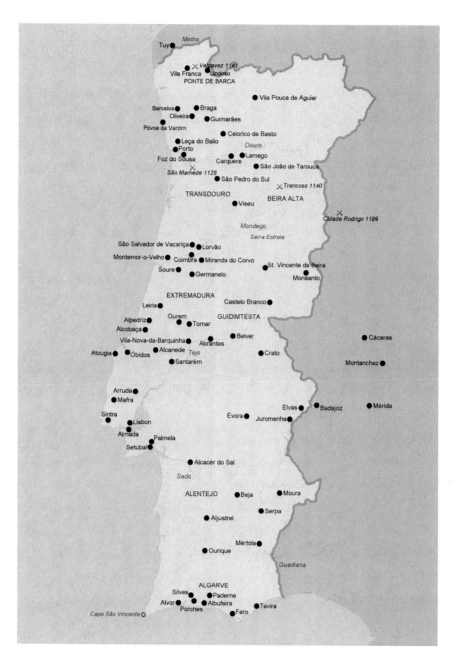

Map 0.3 Portugal © Johnny Grandjean Gøgsig Jakobsen

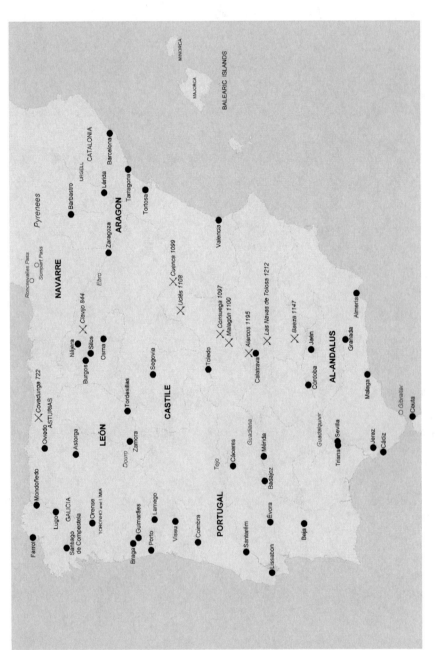

Map 0.4 Iberian Peninsula © Johnny Grandjean Gøgsig Jakobsen

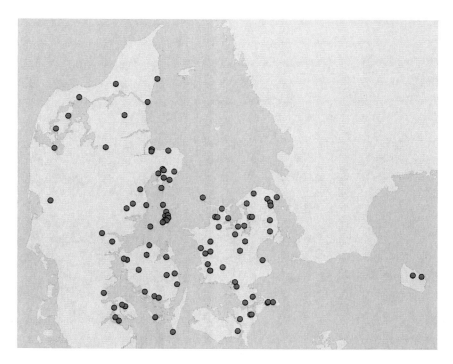

Map 0.5 Place names with "snekke" in Denmark © Johnny Grandjean Gøgsig Jakobsen

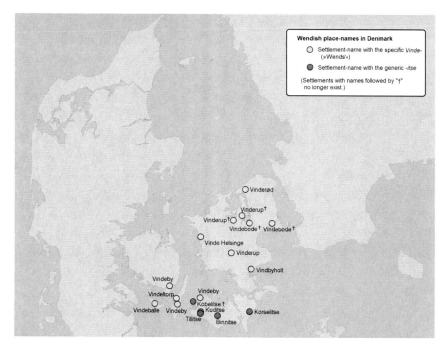

Map 0.6 Wendish place names in Denmark © Johnny Grandjean Gøgsig Jakobsen

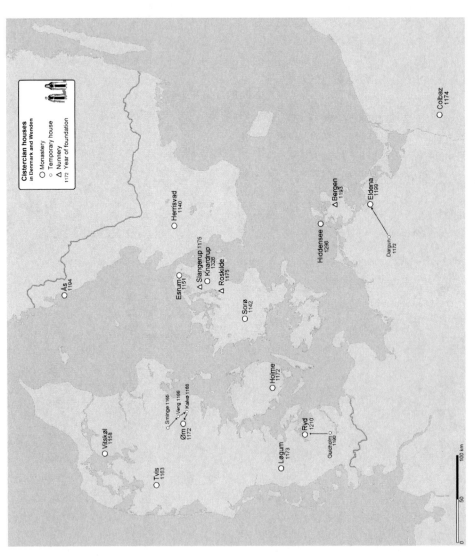

Map 0.7 Cistercians in Denmark © Johnny Grandjean Gøgsig Jakobsen

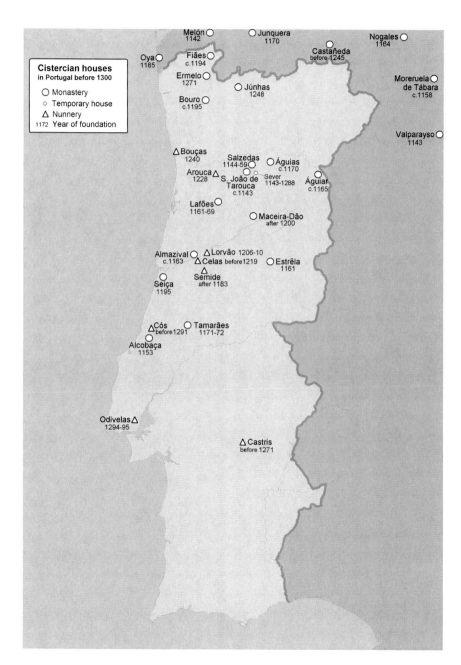

Map 0.8 Cistercians in Portugal © Johnny Grandjean Gøgsig Jakobsen

1 The letter to chief librarian Bruun

In March 1892 Luciano Cordeiro, the secretary at the Geographical Society in Lisbon, wrote a letter to the scholarly and well-informed Chief Librarian at the National Library in Copenhagen, Christian Bruun. The letter was written in French, the obvious and courteous language at the time, even though Bruun most probably was able to read Portuguese. Cordeiro had met Bruun at an orientalist conference in Lisbon,[1] and he now asked for information about the Portuguese princess Berengaria, who in the year 1214 had married the famous Danish King Valdemar the Victorious, and about Leonora, who was married to his son. In Portuguese sources, the facts are exceedingly sparse. As the two princesses left Portugal, they disappeared from domestic sources – was there anything to be found in Danish medieval sources that could explain why a royal princess from the warm South was married to a king in the far and distant North?[2] Bruun approached the matter with his usual efficiency. Thanks to his eminent grasp of the sources, he was able to send a quick and lengthy reply to Cordeiro in September. With the letter came a copy of *Kongegravene i Ringsted* (*The Royal Tombs in Ringsted*),[3] which was donated to the Geographical Society of Lisbon. It is a beautifully laid out report from the excavations in 1855 under the auspices of King Frederic VII. The exquisite prints show the medieval royal skulls, and in his letter, Bruun emphasized the anatomist Ibsen's characterisation of Berengaria's skull: "The head was altogether complete and of a most beautiful shape, with an oval face, prominent nose bone, and with complete rows of teeth of a rarely even and beautiful shape. . . . [T]he other parts of the skeleton, that is, the arms and the legs . . . were finely and beautifully shaped to a high degree." Leonora's skeleton, on the other hand, had been disturbed and she had had cavities in her teeth.[4] On January 31, 1893, Bruun gave a lecture about Berengaria during a meeting at Royal Nordic Society for the Study of Antiquities.[5] Also in 1893, Luciano Cordeiro published his own book *Berengaria and Leonora, Queens of Denmark*. Bruun had apparently read the book in manuscript and used long passages from it in his article.

Cordeiro's question has never been answered adequately. Historians have for a long time wondered why King Valdemar II the Victorious chose to marry Berengaria, the sister of King Afonso II the Fat of distant Portugal. For Danish historians, Portugal is not only far away, it also belonged to a completely different culture with different values and a different geographical orientation from

Denmark during the Middle Ages. For Portuguese historians, Denmark is even further away and has a short history spanning not more than a thousand years. The country is inhabited by tall, Viking-like people, who find it difficult to speak a cultured Romanesque language. During the 1800s, Danish historians explained the strange royal marriage between two representatives from such different cultures as something "purely personal" regarding the Danish King. Berengaria was

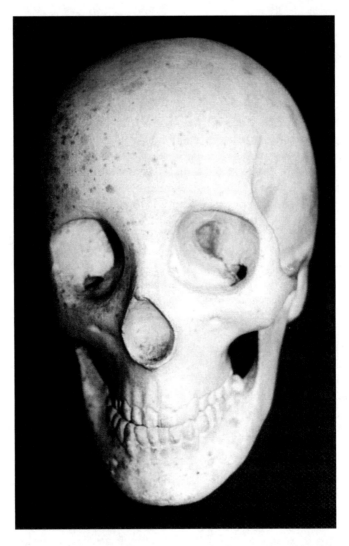

Figure 1.1 "The head was altogether complete and of a most beautiful shape, with an oval face, prominent nose bone, and with complete rows of teeth of a rarely even and beautiful shape." Description of Berengaria from the archaeological report, 1855. Here a cast in the church of Sankt Bendt in Ringsted. © Mona Bager Jensen

an outstanding beauty and some thought that Valdemar had seen her during an expedition to Portugal and the Holy Land and had decided – twenty-five years later – to marry her. Others thought that he had heard about her person and her character and was impressed. Yet others were of the opinion that he had seen her in Flanders and had fallen helplessly in love. Amongst some Portuguese historians, Berengaria's beauty is still mentioned as an explanation.[6]

There is, however, another and altogether much more interesting explanation: Valdemar and Afonso were both great crusader kings, just as their fathers and grandfathers, also called Valdemar and Afonso respectively, had been. During their reigns, the frontiers were moved gradually further into the lands of the infidels, and Denmark and Portugal became independent, strong kingdoms that gained their special positions as guardians of the frontiers of the world of Latin Christendom. The thesis in this book is that a comparable mental background and common horizon was developed in the two countries. This led to the creation of parallel institutions and could even lead to royal weddings. It happened in the aftermath of the capture of Jerusalem during the First Crusade in 1099 and with inspiration from the general European crusading movement in the Middle East. Considered from this crusade perspective, the differences between Denmark and Portugal in the 12th and 13th centuries were not crucial.

A synthesis and a thesis

There are many reasons for investigating Danish and Portuguese medieval history. It began with curiosity regarding the distance between the two countries and Berengaria's beauty, but it became part of something larger that has preoccupied me for some time. How do you get a holistic view of the medieval period in the two countries? How can piecemeal information change an established image – be it conscious or unconscious? It developed into an attempt to create a synthesis in which many well-known pieces, as in a mosaic, were being joined together to form a new overall picture.

Many historians have been more attracted to writing about precisely defined topics in which limited number of questions are being raised and answered. That is analysis. If the historian then combines all these analyses together to form a coherent picture into something that is larger than the sum of its parts, you have a synthesis. In the second half of the 20th century, Danish historians have been accused of lacking the initiative to make syntheses and have instead kept themselves to safe areas – the small analyses – where the risks are fewer. The disadvantage, it is claimed, is that the historian then only writes for his colleagues and not for a broader audience, which is not interested in reading highly specialized work. Another disadvantage is that a coherent view of a period or a certain domain in history is rarely given. The historians are just walking in the footsteps of their predecessors.[7]

In reality, any historical investigation must include both an analytical and synthesizing part. In general, it is also unfounded to accuse Danish historians of not writing syntheses. During the last decades, several excellent overviews have been published of whole eras or institutions – history of Denmark, foreign policy and

4   *Letter to chief librarian Bruun*

artillery. With regard to volume, it is probably still markedly less than what Portuguese historians produce. They publish one large general history of Portugal after the other, written by a single individual or by groups of authors, tightly edited and lavishly put together. Nevertheless, Danish syntheses are far from rare. As far as this is concerned, there is nothing special in this book. Rather, what is different and new is 1) the attempt to view the history of Denmark as being closely tied up with missionary wars and the crusades and as part of a common European history; and 2) the close comparison with Portugal.

The overall thesis is that missionary wars and crusades can explain everything – or, put the other way round, that most individuals by far in both Denmark and Portugal during the period from the 11th century onwards were intensely engrossed in God's war against the infidels and organized their societies in order to wage this war. From around 1100, they perceived their missionary wars as a form of crusade and as attempts to imitate the conquest of Jerusalem in 1099. To a larger or lesser extent, this tendency continues all through the medieval period and far into the 16th century, but I have chosen to stop this investigation in the middle of the 13th century. At that point the crusades had become well established, and changes in mentality and practice through the following centuries did not lead to anything fundamentally new.

Comparison in history

All historical writing is comparative. We must assume that the past is comparable with the present, that there are similarities and differences which we can perceive and realize as being similarities and differences. However, in practice it is complicated. It is also possible to assert that the only things we can see in the past are those that resemble the present and our contemporary experiences.[8] The unpleasant conclusion is that there must be an awful lot from the past that we cannot catch sight of any longer.

There are many metaphors for this chronological contraction of all perception. One is the street lamp. To search for something in the past is like looking for a lost coin at night under a street lamp. It is possible to see what the lamp casts its light on. One can change position and search in another direction for the coin, but still one can only see what is within the reach of the light, whereas we are blind to what lays outside the cone of light. Reality might be even worse than this metaphor. Perhaps there is great wealth directly under the light. We are just unable to perceive it as such because we have never seen such things before. There is not much to do about it, apart from recognize that no historical analysis will ever be complete. The following is also just one of many possible suggestions on how to interpret the past in a way that makes sense in the present. Other historians can put other suggestions forward.

Narrative

Comparison is not only a basic condition for all historical writing about which one does not need to speculate too much on a daily basis. It can also be a chosen method of work, pedagogically and cognitively.

Letter to chief librarian Bruun 5

Comparison can make a pedagogical point by relating something in such a way that it appeals to the reader emotionally. The reader is compelled, subconsciously, to draw parallels to something entirely different. It is possible, for example, to write about the dreaded Mongols of the Middle Ages in a subtle and discreet way and to choose words which make the reader automatically think about the barbaric dictatorship of the Nazis. They could also be described differently and make everybody think about their childhood books about free and proud Indians in the American West. Or one can write about the Mongols using words taken directly from everyday stories about officials and law making in the EU. Whether this is good or bad depends on the reader. The same wording can lead to different associations, depending on time and place and on the reader. It is rhetoric and is concerned with how the historian subconsciously or deliberately spreads associations through the text and lays out discreet pointers, which lead the reader in a certain direction. It concerns the narrative method in historical research, which arranges the tracks in the narrative in such a way that they fit in with contemporary experience.[9]

It can be done in so many different ways. It is probably possible to write a study of the crusades without quoting a single source directly, which would be quite boring. However, that might even be the purpose, because the study then gets a touch of objectivity and resembles a collection of tables or formulas that nobody can contradict. The individual agent gets completely lost in the structures. I have chosen to do the opposite: to quote in large measure in order to recreate the spiritual climate that was a necessary requirement for the crusades. That is obviously not fully possible, because we have different experiences today. Few readers have had a sword in their hand and cut off the head of another human and rejoiced in a fountain filled with blood; few have seen devils and demons or heavenly lights in the sky. My quotes and my way of retelling the past, however, ought hopefully to inspire readers to recollect the scent of the great narratives of which there is still a faint echo in our modern culture: narratives about death, shame, honour, duty, resurrection, hope and God. The quotes have the indisputable advantage that they are all genuinely medieval. We cannot get any closer to the people who lived a thousand years ago.

Comparison as a perceptual tool

Comparison can, however, have an altogether different purpose, which is making something visible for oneself that one would otherwise not perceive.[10] A comparison can be a vantage point wherefrom the world can be turned anew, an opportunity to step out of one's own experience and observe one's own tradition in a new light. Comparison in history is just like journeying very far away; when you get back home, it is possible to acknowledge things about your own country that you were not aware of before.

In practice, it seems as if there have been two predominant ways of drawing deliberate comparison: searching for differences and searching for similarities.[11] During the 18th and 19th centuries, most sciences were probably particularly

6 *Letter to chief librarian Bruun*

interested in finding similarities in order to deduct general laws, i.e. regularities, which could be employed in several different areas within the field. Sometimes it was rather simple, such as the idea that geographical conditions determined the political conditions. Hot countries were underdeveloped and poor because the natives couldn't work in the heat. This was a common idea amongst the philosophers of the Enlightenment during the 18th century but has its roots all the way back to Aristotle.[12] Cultural geography was comparative and searched for similarities, as did some of the social sciences. From the late 18th century, they operated with theories of development in stages, i.e. that all societies necessarily had to go through the same development and through the same stages in order to reach their contemporary form.[13] The idea of development in stages was given its most influential expression in the writings of Karl Marx and Friedrich Engels, but caught on far wider and gripped good and proper conservative historians too. "The matter of history is the handed-down tradition about the development of humanity," the conservative Danish historian Caspar Paludan-Müller wrote in 1874.[14] A third example of comparison for finding similarities is linguistics. From a somewhat obscure search for the language of God in the 17th century, this field quickly developed the methods that are still of fundamental importance in modern comparative linguistics today.

Within historical research, the tendency during the 19th century was clearly to search for differences because history never repeats itself and every period is distinctive, *unmittelbar zu Gott*, as expressed by the father of historical criticism, Leopold von Ranke.[15] The differences were also intended to emphasize the specific national character and were to be used in arguing that the historian's own land and people were something peculiar. Usually, comparison was employed in order to characterize all other countries as having something in common – for example, that they all were feudal during the Middle Ages – and then demonstrate that one's own country was never feudalized, or never really feudalized.

There were exceptions from this urge to find differences. From the late 19th century and through the 20th century, some of the great cultural historians saw a cyclical pattern in the birth, growth and demise of great cultures – for instance, Johan Huizinga's autumn of the European Middle Ages, A. J. Toynbee's twenty-six selected civilizations through the ages, or most recently, Huntington's seven or eight selected civilizations.[16] Some historians began in the 20th century to look for similarities between societies at the same stage of development, both in economic-social history during the early part of the century and in Marxist-influenced research in the latter half. Nevertheless, historical research through the 20th century has, by and large, been tremendously national and mostly focused on the differences. In reality, this has led to a fundamental problem: the comparison becomes impossible because the countries which have been researched have, from the outset, been defined as different and as such as incomparable.[17] It therefore becomes very important to decide deliberately which elements it is at all possible to compare.

Until the middle of the 20th century, historians had mostly compared institutions or cultures, i.e. singular phenomena, on which, despite the complexity, it

Letter to chief librarian Bruun   7

was possible to get a grip and characterise qualitatively: a strong or a weak royal power, many or few sons inheriting their father's estate, suppressed peasants near the royal centre and free peasants at the frontiers. From the middle of the 20th century, economic and social historians, and soon the French historians of mentalities, joined in with new quantifiable material. They compared immense amounts of source evidence – the use of language in thousands of testaments, yield of grain or cattle prices.[18] This quantitative comparison aimed to attain objectivity, an approximation to what many historians thought must be scientific precision. The volume of data replaced the experiments of the scientific laboratory.[19]

Today, both the quantitative and the qualitative comparison are alive and well. There is counting and there is thinking. In some cases, historians from the two traditions even converse and in practice succeed in combining both methods. However, this applies in particular to those who research the early modern period from the late 15th century to the 19th century. With regards to the High Middle Ages, the 12th and 13th centuries, it is simply not possible to create large batches of numbers and data to support statistical comparison, especially not from Scandinavia. When researching the High Middle Ages, comparison is qualitative.

It is possible to compare structures and changes.[20] In the real world, structures have both a mental and a physical aspect at the same time. The mental structures that interest me especially in this context are the ideas about propagating and defending religion, by military means if necessary. That refers to the ideas concerning the early missionary wars and, from around 1100, the crusades and other religious wars which had the conquest of Jerusalem as their model. It is a mental structure consisting of smaller units: the idea of dying for the truth, the idea of the inhuman opponent, an active rewriting of prehistory, etc.[21] The physical aspect is all the structures or institutions that appeared in order to support this idea of spreading the religion: castles, ships, weapons and knightly orders. In which ways did they resemble each other in Denmark and Portugal and in which ways did they differ?

Did Denmark and Portugal have anything to do with each other at all? Are the two historical societies alike because there has been a close connection between them for centuries? Or have they been isolated from each other so that we, in advance, can rule out that those similarities are due to mutual influence? Similarities could perhaps stem from common structures; the same solution could have been found to parallel problems. The explanation is then, as the French historian Marc Bloch phrased it, "the human intellect's monotonous and astonishing poverty through history."[22] We simply do not possess a great imagination when it comes to organizing societies.

If two societies might have had something to do with each other, it becomes far more interesting: one might have borrowed from the other and vice versa, they might have borrowed directly or through an intermediate institution or they might have developed something common from a common background. In that case, comparisons help to make the historian aware of features in one society that have been overlooked in the other but which actually turn out to have been there all the time. It is therefore not necessary to account entirely for whether there happens to

8 *Letter to chief librarian Bruun*

be a direct connection between the two or not, if it is possible to point to a common focal point or frame of reference. The intention with this book is to argue that Jerusalem and the religious wars and crusades in this way served as a point of orientation for both Denmark and Portugal in the High Middle Ages.

The comparison of Denmark and Portugal has three purposes. First, it should hopefully serve as an entry to understanding the contacts between the two countries and their respective connections to a common European crusading world, with its centre in France, the Curia and, not least, Jerusalem.

Second, comparison shall help to fill out the holes in the scattered medieval source material. Perhaps it is possible to find something in the Portuguese material that is similar to some of the few fragments in the Danish sources, and vice versa. In this way, the few jigsaw pieces that constitute the sources should obtain a new frame, a new background into which to be set, where some of them hopefully fit better and make more sense.

The third aim with this comparison is to contribute to the understanding of the common European history of the crusade. The idea of war, for the sake of God and to imitate the crusade to Jerusalem, was received enthusiastically all over Europe and played a part in shaping the societies locally. They were of course shaped by many other things as well (climate, economic development, state building, law and theology) which could be relevant to include and which could explain parallel developments. However, the intention in this book is thus to stay strictly with the crusades and attempt to see the influence they actually had.

E silentio conclusions and the silence of the sources

The function of comparison in historical research has been discussed in recent years, and an important change seems to happening. Earlier, comparisons were made in order to find differences, but today more and more compare in order to find similarities between countries and cultures in the Middle Ages. This is due to a different conception of what medieval societies looked like and how they actually functioned. However, there is also increasingly a perception that the search for differences has rested on a very flimsy basis, from a methodological viewpoint. Many historians have, since the late 19th century, been operating with their very own definition of *e silentio* conclusions – that is, conclusions derived from the silence of the sources. *Quod non in actis, non in mundo* – "what is not mentioned in the sources does not exist in reality." This is, of course, nonsense because if we do not have any sources, we cannot know whether something existed or not. The reason why this tenet has gained such a gravitas amongst historians is really quite odd and based on a misunderstanding. The sentence stems from medieval law, where it makes sense as a normative statement and marks the defining boundary between an oral and a written legal culture – if something has not been written down, it does not count.[23] However, the sentence cannot be applied as a descriptive statement regarding how to make sense of the past.

To make it all worse, historians have often been so hypnotized by the few remaining sources that they have committed what one might term a "double *e silentio.*" They have assumed that the contents of the sources must cohere and give us a comprehensive and reasonably complete picture. This is not necessarily correct; however, it has led to many attempts to see connections between sources, which are widely separated in time because there simply are no sources covering the intermediate period. This might easily convey an impression of the past as being static and unchangeable. The comparison between Denmark and Portugal is hopefully an attempt to find some of the holes by showing a pattern, a correlation, which leads to opportunities for ideas and changes to which there are no sources any longer.

One of the crucial problems for Danish medieval history is the frightening scarcity of sources. Portugal's case is slightly better documented, but not much. This book rests, therefore, on a very slender basis. It does not, however, turn it into pure, postmodern fiction, because at no point does it go against the sources that we do possess. This is what Christian Bruun voiced in his own congenial and rather ironic way when he warned Luciano Cordeiro of how uncertain the sources to the history of Berengaria in Denmark actually were: "Due to the silence of the sources regarding Berengaria, it has often been necessary to take to hypothesises and combinations, though only in such a way that these usually have some fact to rely upon."[24] Especially the term "usually" is a precise description of the circumstances under which the researcher of medieval Denmark works. It is, therefore, of paramount importance to be aware of the linguistic nuances in the few sources that we do have.

Modern and medieval language

Modern society is organized in a very practical way. Above all, things have a practical purpose, according to which they are described and identified. If they in addition are beautiful to behold, they have been designed or branded. This, however, is something extra, added in order to signal a certain lifestyle with the owner. A vase is a vase to stand flowers in and it might be a designed vase of a specific brand. Apart from that it is nothing. A vase has a practical function and signals a certain lifestyle. That is all. The only real attempt in the 20th century to attribute meaning to things other than function and lifestyle, the only attempt at typological thinking, was Freudianism, which saw sexuality in everything – male sexuality in pointed items, female sexuality in rounded or hollow things.[25]

The Middle Ages were more refined. The fourfold method of interpretation taught the theologians that any text might contain firstly a literal statement about what happened in historical time. At the same time, it gives a key to understanding the present. Finally, the text can point out a direction for the future, a purpose for everything, for both the individual and for the whole world as such. We know this way of interpretation from the writings of the theologians[26]. It permeated medieval society and was common in all sorts of communication, but especially significant in written sources from the Middle Ages. An object did not only have a practical function or a symbolic meaning, it had both and therefore connected this world with the beyond.[27] A sword is not only a pointed object with a practical function but a symbol of death, too, which entered the world with the Fall, and

10 *Letter to chief librarian Bruun*

simultaneously as a symbol of the justice, *justicia*, God shall manifest when He as judge on the Day of Judgement separates the righteous from the unrighteous. Therefore, the sword is also a symbol of how man shall live here and now, that is, with justice always in his heart. Everything is a sign, as St. Augustine put it in around 400 CE.[28] Every object points towards something else and possesses a spiritual meaning.[29] The 12th-century man had a "symbol mentality."[30]

Today, we live according to an Aristotelian ideal, which says that things either are or are not, and if something is white, it cannot be black. During the Middle Ages, things could be both simultaneously, depending on the perspective and the questions they were asked. We think more in terms of contrast of "either-or," whereas many in the Middle Ages thought in categories of "both-and." At which time this shift took place is impossible to say with any precision. The first tentative step was the urge of the scholastics of the 12th and 13th centuries to define and find contrast; this was a new method compared to earlier, when the monks tried to find a common denominator in apparently contradicting statements. They were ruminating (i.e. chewing the cud) on the text, they themselves said.[31] They were harmonizing, historians would say today, and this is not meant positively any longer.

Medieval research of the 20th century has been characterized by modern language. An institution was either meant for defence, or it was for attack, to mention just one amongst several obvious examples from the discussions of Scandinavian historians. It was either a crusade, or the participants reaped an economic yield. If money played a role, it could not be termed a crusade, several historians have insisted, not least in the puritanical Scandinavia. In the Middle Ages, institutions could be for both defence and attack at the same time, and the same word could mean defence in certain contexts and attack in others. "Signed with the Cross" could refer to a newborn baby with wet hair above the baptismal font, but it could also signify the professional, religious warrior who had taken the cross. The designation made the contemporaries think of both at the same time, and to be signed by the cross as a crusader was almost like being born again; at least it was a serious attempt to confirm one's baptism.

The intention with the following is to present the most significant events and some of those institutions that were established in Denmark and Portugal during the 12th century. In this context, it is important to be mindful of the ambiguity of medieval language. Several of these institutions can be found in countries that did not conduct crusades, or only did so rarely. Castles were built, even if no heathen was near. However, when these universal institutions were applied in the crusades against the heathen, they gained an added significance. A castle then became not only a fortification but an image of God as the mighty fortress, shielding us from the Devil's attacks.

Notes

1 Luciano Cordeiro, *Berengela e Leonor rainhas da Dinamarca* (Lisbon, 1984).
2 Chr. Bruun, 'Berengaria af Portugal, Valdemar II Sejers Dronning. En Historisk Undersøgelse', *Aarbøger for nordisk Oldkyndighed og Historie* II, 8 (1893), pp. 46–120.

Letter to chief librarian Bruun 11

3 J.J.A. Worsaae, *Kongegravene i Ringsted Kirke aabnede, istandsatte og dækkede med nye Mindestene ved Hans Majestæt Kong Frederik Den Syvende* (Copenhagen, 1858).

4 Cordeiro, *Berengela e Leonor*, p. 75; quoting from Worsaae, *Kongegravene*, pp. 64, 68.

5 Bruun, *Berengaria*.

6 Fr. Hammerich, *Danmark i Valdemarernes Tid (1157–1375). En historisk Skildring* (Copenhagen, 1860), p. 132: "She was lovely shaped, brave and magnanimous but also avaricious and hard. The People hated her," Johannes C.H.R. Steenstrup, *Danmarks Riges Historie* (Copenhagen, 1898–1905), vol. 1, p. 751; Cordeiro, *Berengela e Leonor*, with Mattoso's introduction; Alexandre Herculano, *História de Portugal desde o começo da monarquia até o fim do reinado de Afonso III* (Lisbon, 1846–53), vol. 1, pp. 238–2399; Maria Josefina Andersen, 'Princesas portuguesas D. Berengária e D. Leonor, Rainhas da Dinamarca', *Congresso do Mundo Português* II (Lisbon, 1940); Maria Teresa Nobre Veloso, *D. Afonso II. Relações de Portugal com a Santa Sé durante o seu reinado* (Coimbra, 2000), pp. 73–74.

7 Claus Møller Jørgensen, 'Patterns of Professionalization and Institutionalization in Denmark from 1848 to the Present', in: Frank Meyer and Jan Eivind Myhre (eds.), *Nordic Historiography in the 20th Century* (Oslo, 2000), pp. 114–148, describes Danish historical writing at the end of the 1900s with the keywords empiricism and specialization. In general, Bernhard Eric Jensen, *Historie – livsverden og fag* (Copenhagen, 2003), pp. 140–161.

8 Koselleck treats the *experience* of the observer or the historian as a prerequisite for telling histories and to understand the experiences of others and to analyse them. Koselleck distinguishes between direct personal experience, the narrated and collective experiences and, finally, the experience based interpretations of the world, which cover generations and are not immediately realized as experience by those who share them. Koselleck thinks that the understanding of the importance of experience is by and large a feature of modernity and did not exist earlier. This is unlikely. See Reinhart Koselleck, *Zeitschichten. Studien zur Historik* (Frankfurt a.M., 2000), especially "Erfahrungswandel und Methodewechsel", originally from 1988.

9 "Ganz ohne den Vergleich kommt die Sprache des Historikers offenbar selten aus," writes Haupt and Kocka about the subconscious ability of the historian to make comparisons as he writes; Heinz-Gerhard Haupt and Jurgen Kocka, 'Historischer Vergleich: Methoden, Aufgaben, Probleme. Eine Einleitung', in: Heinz-Gerhard Haupt und Jürgen Kocka (eds.), *Geschichte und Vergleich. Ansätze und Ergebnisse international vergleichender Geschichtsschreibung* (Frankfurt, 1996), pp. 9–45, here pp. 10–11. On narrative elements of historical writing and research, see Hayden White, *Metahistory: The Historical Imagination in the Nineteenth Century in Europe* (Baltimore, 1973) and his later books. Lawrence Stone, 'The Revival of Narrative. Reflections on a New Old History', *Past and Present* 85 (1979), pp. 3–24, created a greater interest in exposing the narrative in historical writing itself; see also *The History and Narrative Reader*, ed. Geoffrey Roberts (London, 2001). The discussions in the wake of White forced historiography out of the strongly descriptive and detail-ruled black hole where "historiography became, like theology, the study of error;" Michael Bentley, 'General Introduction: The Project of Historiography', in: Michael Bentley (ed.), *Companion to Historiography* (London, 1997), pp. xi–xix, here p. xiii.

10 Haupt and Kocka, 'Historischer Vergleich'; A.A. van den Braembussche, 'Historical Explanation and Comparative Method: Towards a Theory of the History of Society', *History and Theory* 28 (1989), pp. 1–24; Jürgen Kocka, 'Comparison and Beyond', *History and Theory* 42 (2003), pp. 39–44; Michael Werner and Bénédicte Zimmermann, 'Beyond Comparison: Histoire Croisée and the Challenge of Reflexivity', *History and Theory* 45 (2006), pp. 30–50. For medieval history specifically, see Michael Borgolte, 'Perspektiven europaischer Mittelalterhistorie an der Schwelle zum 21. Jahrhundert', in: Michel Borgolte (ed.), *Das europäische Mittelalter im Spannungsbogen des Vergleichs* (Berlin, 2001), pp. 13–27.

12   *Letter to chief librarian Bruun*

11   John Stuart Mill, *Method of agreement* and *method of difference*, in: John Stuart Mill, *A System of Logic* (London, 1872) [1843], vols. 1–2, p. 448.

12   Montesquieu, *De l'esprit des lois* (Genève, 1748), book 14.17; see E.H. Price, 'Voltaire and Montesquieu's Three Principles of Government', *Publications of the Modern Language Association of America* 57, 4 (1942), pp. 1046–1052.

13   For Portugal, Luís Reis Torgal, José Amado Mendes, and Fernando Catroga, *História da história em Portugal. Séculos XIX–XX*, vols. 1–2 (Lisbon, 1998), vol. 1, pp. 137–140 and ff.; for Denmark, Jens Chr. Manniche, 'Historieskrivningen 1830–1880', in: Aksel E. Christensen, H.P. Clausen, Svend Ellehøj, and Søren Mørch (eds.), *Danmarks Historie* (Copenhagen, 1992), vol. 10, pp. 199–266; Jens Henrik Tiemroth, 'Professionalisering og demokrati 1880–1991', in: ibidem, vol. 10, pp. 267–285.

14   Mads Mordhorst and Jes Fabricius Møller, *Historikeren Caspar Paludan-Müller* (Copenhagen, 2005), here p. 271.

15   Leopold von Ranke, *Über die Epochen der neueren Geschichte*, lecture 1854, in: Leopold von Ranke, *Weltgeschichte*, vols. 1–9 (Leipzig, 1881–1888), here vol. 9, p. 537.

16   Johan Huizinga, *The Waning of the Middle Ages: A Study of the Forms of Life, Thought and Art in France and the Netherlands in the Fourteenth and Fifteenth Centuries* (Harmondsworth, 1955) [1919]; Arnold J. Toynbee, *A Study of History* (London, 1935–1961), vols. 1–12; Samuel P. Huntington, *The Clash of Civilizations and the Remaking of World Order* (London, 2002) [1996]. It is problematic to label Huntington a great cultural historian, but he was obviously inspired by the cultural historical tradition of comparing civilizations.

17   Braembussche's 'Historical Explanation' distinguishes between contrasting and universalizing comparative history (pp. 13ff.) but holds that both approaches necessarily have to be more descriptive than analysing and explanatory. This is probably wrong.

18   Haupt and Kocka, 'Historischer Vergleich', pp. 32–34.

19   "[T]he comparative method is an adaptation of experimental logic to investigations in which actual experimentation is impossible." William H. Sewell Jr., 'Marc Bloch and the Logic of Comparative History', *History and Theory* 6 (1967), pp. 208–218, here p. 209.

20   Werner and Zimmermann, 'Beyond comparison' claim that *comparison* always tends towards becoming synchronous (p. 35), whereas *transfer*, i.e. transfer of culture, which they distil as a specific methodological approach developed from comparison, can almost not avoid becoming diachronic (p. 36). It seems unnecessary to distinguish between comparison and transfer in this way; both structures and changes, synchronous and diachronic, must be included in a comparison.

21   In Denmark, the interest in mental structures became obvious only during the 1980s, expressed for example in *Dansk Identitetshistorie*, ed. Ole Feldbæk (Copenhagen, 1991–1993), vol. 1–4 and in an interest in nationalism and national symbols; Inge Adriansen, *Nationale symboler i det danske rige 1830–2000* (Copenhagen, 2003). It is also an expression of the anthropological influence on medieval history and the new cultural history, Hans-Werner Goetz, *Moderne Mediavistik. Stand und Perspektiven der Mittelalterforschung* (Darmstadt, 1999), pp. 262–370. Lastly, it clearly coincides with a new interest from the 1970s in the theology and ideology of the crusades.

22   Marc Bloch, 'Toward a Comparative History of European Societies', in: F.C. Lane and J.C. Riemersma (eds.), *Enterprise and Secular Change. Readings in Economic History* (Homewood, IL, 1953), pp. 494–521 [originally 1928].

23   Detlef Liebs, *Lateinische Rechtsregeln und Rechtssprichwörter* (Munich, 1998), p. 197. The maxim apparently does not stem from ancient Roman law. As early as in 1921 the Danish historian Erik Arup criticized Aage Friis for arguing that "the sources says nothing thereof" and therefore get "worryingly close to the basic tenet of the old written legal procedure: quod non est in actis, non est in mundo. This sentence is, of course, especially unjustifiable in historical research." If it is otherwise possible to

Letter to chief librarian Bruun   13

extract "facts" from the sources, which Arup was convinced was possible, "is it for the historical researcher altogether indifferent" whether these facts "are expressly stated in a source statement or not." Quote from Inga Floto, 'Erik Arup og hans kritikere', *Historisk Tidsskrift* 78 (1978), pp. 474–498, here p. 476.

24 Bruun, 'Berengaria af Portugal', p. 48.

25 It is bordering on the absurd to attempt to characterise the use of language and the readings of whole cultures, and it is certainly possible to find numerous modern examples of metaphorical and analogue understandings of texts. It is, however, my impression that these today belong in literature in a broad sense, but have left historical writing and most of the practical world we inhibit. Besides, they are different from the medieval readings by being open. There is no common standard or frame of comprehension. "Therefore, literature's connection to reality is often left to the individual's frame of comprehension. This weakens the possibility of literature to enter a dialogue with our common reality." Helle Munkholm Davidsen, *Litteratur og Encyklopædi. Semiotiske og kognitive aspekter af den litterare teksts mening* (Odense, 2006); Umberto Eco, *The Role of the Reader* (Bloomington, 1979).

26 Beryl Smalley, *The Study of the Bible in the Middle Ages* (Oxford, 1952); Henri Lubac, *Exégèse Mediévale* (Paris, 1959), vol. 1–2; Gilbert Dahan, *L'exégèse de la Bible en occident médiéval* (Paris, 1999).

27 "The Middle Ages never forgot that all things would be absurd, if their meaning was exhausted in their function and their place in the phenomenal world, if by their essence they did not reach into a world beyond this." Huizinga, *The Waning*, p. 194.

28 Augustinus, *De doctrina christiana*, PL 34, cols. 15–122; especially book 2.

29 Beverly Mayne Kienzle, *Cistercians, Heresy and Crusade in Occitania, 1145–1229. Preaching in the Lord's Vineyard* (York, 2001), pp. 64–67.

30 M.-D. Chenu, *Nature, Man and Society in the Twelfth Century. Essays on New Theological Perspectives in the Latin West* (Chicago, 1968).

31 J. Leclercq, *The Love of Learning and the Desire for God. A Study of Monastic Culture* (London, 1978), p. 90.

2 Were there any crusades in the periphery?

There are numerous problems involved in writing about crusades in the countries in the geographic periphery of Europe. Their sources preserved only a fraction of what has been handed down from England, France, Germany and the Spanish kingdoms. Furthermore, the sources have an in-built lop-sidedness when it comes to crusades. The Scandinavians and the Portuguese went by ship when travelling to the Holy Land, whereas most Germans and French walked overland. The sea-travellers were only noticed when they landed in order to take in water and provisions, whereas the walkers' journey could be noted down in each and every town and city they travelled through. For that reason alone, we should expect the peoples in the periphery to be underrepresented in the sources.[1]

There are, however, other and more serious reasons to why it is difficult to write about crusades in the periphery, namely the long historical tradition regarding how the crusades are described and understood – that is, historiography. This concerns both the general European tradition and the local traditions in Denmark and Portugal. Initially, it is necessary to try to get an impression of the historiography before it is at all possible to even begin to research Danish and Portuguese crusades in any detail. It is especially important to realize what one actually means by the word *crusade*.

Pope Urban on climate

The historical treatment of the crusades, that is the intellectual attempt to describe, understand and explain what actually happened, probably began sometime in the afternoon of July 17, 1099, in Jerusalem.[2] The same morning, a three-day-long carnage was coming to an end, Muslims and Jews were all killed. The crusaders' horses had been wading in blood to the bridles, the contemporary Latin sources wrote enthusiastically, because the Latin conquest was then entirely like the description of God's just wrath in the Revelations.[3] All later descriptions of religious wars, also from Denmark and Portugal, have had this image of currents of blood as a literary background and as an example for the justification of the struggle.

After the siege had lasted a couple of weeks, the first crusaders had increased their efforts. Barefooted and fasting, they had walked around the Holy City; they

Were there crusades in the periphery?   15

sang and prayed and hoped that the walls would crumble, as the walls of Jericho did when Joshua attacked. On Friday, the first crusaders jumped from the siege tower to the city walls – on the same day and hour as the Saviour drew his last breath.[4] The conquest of the city and the massacre of its inhabitants continued until Sunday morning, until the day and hour that He rose again and ascended into heaven. The crusaders then went to church and thanked God for the victory. After this, they began to organize themselves in practical terms, with a church leader and a temporal leader. Not least, however, they were trying to understand what had actually happened. At first, they were simply amazed and did not know what to do and why. Soon, however, two general explanations were formulated which have guided crusading research ever since. One was that it was the will of God. The other, that it was first and foremost a French undertaking. The countries at the edge of the world, such as Denmark and Portugal, were placed at the intersection of these two explanations. It is possible to follow this development closely in the very first accounts of the crusade which were written between 1099 and the early 1120s.

The will of God was important and remained so to these crusade historians. This is clear from a series of details and explanations, from the references to the winepress of the wrath of God in the Revelation to the hordes of white, dead riders from heaven – the dead crusaders, who during the struggle had joined living ones, fought on their side and secured victory for them.[5] Nevertheless, it seems that the direct intervention of God was soon toned down and modified. This can be seen directly in Fulcher of Chartres, whose account is known from an early version – commenced just short of a year after the conquest in 1099 – and a later, corrected version from around 1124–1127. It is unusual to have several versions of texts from around 1100, and this gives us an opportunity to see how Fulcher changed his opinion as time passed. He participated in the first crusade as a chaplain for Baldwin, who became king of Jerusalem in 1101. During the early fervour over the fall of Jerusalem to the Christians, Fulcher described the events as the result of a direct intervention of God. In the later versions, which were finished in around 1126, God disappeared almost imperceptibly and was replaced everywhere with Baldwin or a more general "we" or "our people."[6] The changes reflect a different mental climate, from the euphoria of the early conquest to the drawn out and complicated process of making a new society function at even the most basic, practical administrative level. The changes also reflect a problem for the earliest historians: they were almost all clerics, for whom everything ultimately must have a theological explanation. They were, however, at the same time employed by noblemen to write the history of these noblemen and their families – they were employed to write the history of the crusade, as if it was part of a French family's history. How can the crusade at one time be the will of God and simultaneously be carried out by the French? The authors explained this by embellishing and commenting on who took part and what they actually did during the expedition. A remarkable development of the understanding of the crusade took place; this can be followed closely in the sources from the first twenty years after the conquest.

16   *Were there crusades in the periphery?*

One of the earliest accounts of the first crusade is the anonymous *Gesta francorum*, written by someone in the entourage of the Norman nobleman Bohemund before 1100. According to the *Gesta*, the crusade began as a great movement in all areas of France. After Urban's sermon in Clermont on November 27, 1095, the French joined enthusiastically. They sewed crosses on their clothing and decided to follow Christ.[7] They formed three main groupings, which chose three different roads to Constantinople and then to the Holy Land. And here the use of language begins to get blurred. At first, the term *franci* in the chronicle designates those living in France, but they go on to form groups consisting of people from France, Southern France, Flanders and Southern Italy. The author simply changes the connotations of the word and lets *franci* slip unnoticed from designating the French to denote all those who followed the French.[8] This was on purpose and reflects a certain view of the crusade as a French undertaking, which was followed by Normans and Flemish princes. The same use of the words can be found in the writings of those who themselves took part in the first crusade or wrote immediately after the conquest of Jerusalem – Fulcher of Chartres, Peter Tudebodis, Raymund of Aguilers. Fulcher of Chartres wrote of an army that came from everywhere, from the islands in the sea and from all the kingdoms of earth, so that the prophecy of David was fulfilled: *All nations whom thou hast made shall come and worship before thee, Oh Lord.* Men leave their loving wives and their children, fathers and mothers to travel to Jerusalem, and weeping and admonitions were heard everywhere. Then Fulcher continues directly with "we Franks in the west." In spite of his mention of Normans, Germans and all the others, he combines them all with the designation *franci*.[9]

Albert of Aix has the same introduction as Fulcher. He wrote very shortly after the first crusade but had a broader notion than the *Gesta francorum* of what really was at stake. Again, it all began with Pope Urban's sermon, after which the noblemen took an oath before God to walk the holy road to the grave of the Lord. As a confirmation of the oath, a powerful earthquake shook the earth – in reality, it was nothing but the trampling of the thousands of participants from all the different kingdoms: from France but also from Lorraine, from Germany, England and Denmark. Even though the initiative remained French, Albert stressed already in his introductory chapter that the crusade was tremendous and with adherents from all countries. It is a theological point that a crusade willed by God cannot be a French expedition alone. And with that began a historical tradition, which was to include more and more participants in the first crusade.[10]

This is the case with Baldric of Dole, who wrote in 1108. His work depends to a large degree on the anonymous *Gesta francorum,* but his introduction is completely different. It begins in a rather elevated rhetorical way: "Who has ever heard of so many princes and dukes and noblemen and foot soldiers, who fought without a king, without an emperor to lead them?" This could only be explained as the inspiration of the Holy Spirit, which was now introduced as one of the driving forces behind the crusade. Baldric went on to describe how Urban's sermon stirred the French and Flemish leaders and that he would now describe their deeds. This he does in the rest of the book, but before that, he concludes the introduction with a description of how the rumour of Urban's sermon reaches all of Christendom. "It came to England and the other isles, which are separated from France by the abyss of the ocean with thundering waves." It came to Brittany and Gascony, to Galicia in Spain, and to the city states of Venice, Genoa and Pisa, who delivered ships for the crusade, and to all who lived by the shores of the Mediterranean or the Ocean, that is, the Atlantic or the North Sea. Thus, Baldric has an understanding of the crusade as a phenomenon with its centre in France but, at the same time, it was a mass movement that included all of Christendom in the periphery. This differentiation between centre and periphery is only mentioned briefly in the introduction – Baldric does not embellish the theme, such as later historians would do.[11]

One of them was Guibert of Nogent, who also wrote in 1108 and in Northern France too, just like Baldric. He called his work *Gesta Dei per francos*, The Acts of God by the French, and it was they who were the heroes of his story. As opposed to the Germans and the Italians, the French were, as the name suggests, rather lively, and if they were not reined in, they could be unreasonably wild towards other nations.[12] By way of conclusion, Guibert summed up that the conquest of Jerusalem did not happen due to military tactics, such as the victories of antiquity had done, but rather it was thanks to faith and strength, and to French courage and bravery. However, in his introduction, Guibert had emphasized how the crusade began as a mass movement without leaders. The crusaders were like grasshoppers, without a king but covering all of Earth with their swarm. When it is cold, they do nothing, but when they are being heated by the sun – the crusaders by the sun of righteousness – they begin to swarm. Urban's call for crusade came to the French people alone, but the heat of the French attracted all other nations. They swarmed towards the French, tried to emulate them and to communicate with them. People came from the furthest shore of the ocean. One could see groups of Scots coming out from the mists and their swampy borderlands, with naked legs and dirty coats, wild and terrifying at home but peaceable in other places. The Scots were carrying their ridiculous, old-fashioned weapons in large quantities, "but they assisted the French with their piety and devotion."[13] Guibert himself had met great multitudes of the barbaric peoples who were unable to speak even a single known language. All they could do when travelling through Europe was to raise their hands and cross their index fingers to show that they were on their way to Jerusalem.[14]

Guibert did not only think in terms of a French centre and a general Christian periphery. He also introduced a completely new differentiation between a French centre, which conquered Jerusalem militarily, and a barbaric periphery – and a barbaric North in particular – which participated and contributed spiritual support but did not have any military significance.

This "barbarification of the periphery" became a huge success. Later historians adopted it unhesitatingly and embellished it even further. Just one example, William of Malmesbury, who wrote in the early 1120s; "Not only people around the Mediterranean but also those on the furthermost isles and the barbarian nations were touched by love of God. The fields lay deserted; the houses were without

18   *Were there crusades in the periphery?*

their inhabitants. The Welsh left their poaching, the Scots their usual lice and flies, the Norwegians their gorging on fish, the Danes their unceasing drinking.[15] So the peoples of the periphery did take part – but as barbarians.

William had an almost scientific explanation of this difference, which he attributed to Pope Urban. In his long rendering of the Pope's sermon in Clermont, William has him explaining that nations live in different climates. In the South, under the burning sun, people dry out and have only very little blood in their bodies, but they are very knowledgeable. They are wise but not good warriors; the proof is the Turks' tactics of fleeing and avoiding open battles. The military success of the Turks in Spain and Northern Africa are due to their cunning and their use of poisoned arrows, not their bravery. In the North, on the contrary, it is cold; people live far from the sun, their large bodies are filled with blood in abundance and they fight willingly and with bravery, but they are a bit primitive and not particularly clever. "But you" – and here Urban addressed the French audience – "You live in the temperate zone, you do not lack intelligence and you have enough blood in you to show contempt for death and wounds, you are brilliant in both knowledge and strength, you shall go on this glorious expedition."[16] With William's explanation, the barbarification of the periphery is completed and is no longer a question of different cultural background but a geographical and scientific fact. And it was especially valid for the northern periphery: "The third climate of Earth is Europe, and what a small part of it do we Christians inhabit! For who would call all the barbaric nations on distant isles, who navigates the icy ocean and lives like animals, Christians?"[17]

Regarding the southern periphery, it was different. According to Urban's sermon, we ought to expect that those living in the South did not bother to go on the crusade because it was too hot. This is not the case. On the contrary, the Iberian Peninsula was a necessary precondition for the proper crusades, because here a series of religious wars took place – a kind of proto-crusades, or crusades before the crusades – which created certain military alliance and theological ideas and institutions that became important for the crusade to Jerusalem. In practice, however, it turns out that the early crusading chronicles with few exceptions do not mention anyone at all from Spain or Portugal as participating in the first crusade. Baldric speaks of participants from Galicia, "the furthermost amongst men" from the home province of the popular pilgrimage site of Santiago de Compostela. Apart from that, he does not mention anyone from the Iberian Peninsula. Guibert of Nogent referred to Guillaume, known as the carpenter, because, while fighting, he chopped the enemies as if they were sticks, but who, apart from that, was mostly all talk. He had participated in a French expedition to Spain to stop the Muslims that came swarming in from Africa but had lost his faith.[18]

The result of these early writings about the first crusade was obviously a common European historiographical tradition, which emphasized the French contribution and neglected any participation from the periphery or spontaneously did not take it into account.[19] This tendency has been accepted and taken on by national, historiographical traditions in the countries of the periphery; and these, from the middle of the 1800s, evolved along certain tracks in which the crusades

Were there crusades in the periphery? 19

simply did not fit. It concerns perceptions of their own lands and peoples but also of such fundamental categories as the origin of the white race. This will be dealt with shortly, but first it is necessary to discuss how to understand the word, or the concept, "crusade."

What was a crusade? – the struggle about a definition

A new concept of the crusades has had a breakthrough in Scandinavia during the latest decade. This is due to the efforts of hard-working Scandinavian historians but is obviously connected with the great changes in international crusade research, which have taken place during the latest generation too. Since 1970 interest in the crusades in Western Europe has grown tremendously, not only with regard to literature and movies,[20] but amongst professional historians too. Many more historians work within the field now than during the rest of the 1900s, and the period from 1970 to 2010 was a golden age for crusade research internationally, best compared to the very dynamic environment amongst British, French and German historians during the latter part of the 19th century.[21] The large amount of new research has led at times to a rather heated debate about what a crusade really was during the Middle Ages. The answer is complicated, not least because there was no unambiguous term for the phenomenon before around 1200.[22] At that time, the first sources mentions *croisade*, *cruzada* and similar words in French, Spanish and Italian,[23] and soon the word was in use in Latin, usually as *cruciate*. It was not particularly widespread until very late in the Middle Ages. The most common term for crusade is *peregrinatio*, but also *iter* and a little later *passagium* were quite common. One of the most frequently used designations alongside peregrination was *expeditio*. Each of these words carries at the same time different meanings – pilgrimage, journey or military expedition. This can sometimes lead to misunderstandings of the Latin sources, but often the context is quite unambiguous. A peregrinatio to the Holy Land with 200 ships filled with heavily armed warriors is most likely to be understood as a crusade rather than a peaceful pilgrimage.[24] It is more interesting to note that the problems with understanding and translating the imprecise terms reflects that the crusades were an extensive, wide-ranging and common phenomenon, which had both a military and a spiritual angle. There were so many aspects attached to the medieval understanding of a crusade that it was difficult to contain in a single word.

Until around 1970, most historians agreed that the crusades were armed expeditions with the purpose of liberating and later defending the Holy Grave in Jerusalem. In this sense, the crusades began in 1099 and led to the establishment of the Kingdom of Jerusalem, which lost its capital and the Holy Grave to Saladin in 1187. The remnants of the Middle Eastern kingdom fell with the loss of the last Christian fortress, Acre, in 1291, and with this, the history of the crusades ended. This definition became increasingly under discussion and attack from around 1970, not least by the many British and American members of the Society for the Study of the Crusades and the Latin East, founded in 1980. The traditionalists, undauntedly represented by the German historian Hans Eberhard Mayer,[25]

20 *Were there crusades in the periphery?*

have been designated *exclusivists* by their disagreeing colleagues, because they exclude all other forms of crusades than those to Jerusalem. The *inclusivists* or *pluralists*, however, operate with a completely different definition. According to them, the crusades were those medieval wars that were fought against the enemies of the Church, that had papal authorization, or that gave the participating soldiers indulgence or spiritual merit. This last definition is obviously much broader. The geographical borders become markedly extended – the wars against Muslims on the Iberian Peninsula and against heathens in the Baltic become real crusades, as do the wars against heretics anywhere in Western Europe. At the same time, the chronological frames are being similarly extended. The crusades continued after the fall of Acre in 1291, in Northern Europe up until the Reformation and later, in Southern Europe all the way up towards the 1700s.

When the crusades began is all of a sudden a rather more complicated question. Wars against the enemies of the Church, papal authorization and spiritual merit existed before Pope Urban's sermon in Clermont, which made the British historian Christopher Tyerman[26] deny that there was anything new in the crusades. Everything was there before, all the way back to the Carolingians in the 9th century, and the so-called crusades were only a continuation of earlier forms of holy war. This is an opinion that has a striking resemblance to the views of both Danish and Portuguese historians of the wars in their own lands during the 12th and 13th centuries. They were only a continuation of the Viking raids, it has been claimed, or of the centuries-old Christian dream of a *reconquista*,[27] of winning the Iberian Peninsula back from the Muslims. Their arguments suffer from a fundamental flaw; that the contemporaries evidently perceived the conquest of Jerusalem in 1099 as being qualitatively different from all previous wars. A new era, a new epoch in the history of man, was heralded with the conquest of Jerusalem. "After the creation of the world, nothing more wondrous happened, apart from the mystery of the saving cross, than what took place in the present day with the conquest of Jerusalem by our people,"[28] Robert the Monk wrote in the Middle Ages' most widely known account of the first crusade.[29]

It is also a starting point for understanding the Danish and Portuguese wars of that time in a new way. With the few sources at our disposal, it can be difficult to establish whether the participants in a particular battle were promised spiritual merit or not and whether a Pope authorized it or not – personally or via a delegated authority to a local archbishop. This kind of discussion easily ends up in barren formalism and debate about definitions, where the viewpoints stand unwavering in opposition to each other: papal bull or not? Crusade or not?[30] It is much more important to maintain that the conquest of Jerusalem was perceived as something decisively new and that after 1099 one could not fight a war against infidels anywhere in Western Europe without comparing it to the first crusade.[31] Jerusalem became a guiding principle for later warriors, a motive or a frame of reference, which could be transferred straight away to both the Baltic and the Iberian Peninsula. It is from this new interest in Jerusalem, not from a formalistic definition of crusades as such, that Denmark and Portugal are to be compared in the following pages.

The crusades did not emerge out of the blue but gathered together many different experiences into an effective mass movement that journeyed to Jerusalem in 1096: a long tradition of holy war and the use of violence in missionary efforts,[32] an even older tradition of pilgrimages,[33] a new theology on indulgence[34] and the whole papal reform movement of the latter half of the 11th century,[35] which eventually gave the Holy see a completely new and until then unknown political influence. Furthermore, during all this, slow economic growth took place everywhere in Western Europe, which created the material surplus which was to pay for sending the crusaders to Jerusalem.

The conditions accumulated quietly until everything was unleashed in a dramatic military expedition that affected all parts of Europe. Pope Urban's crusade was something quite new because, only twenty years before, Gregory VII had attempted to organize a similar military expedition but without any response.[36] Yet, the crusades were only possible because of the Christians' long-time experience in using warfare in the service of religion. The earlier missionary wars in the Frankish region, including Denmark, and in the Iberian Peninsula were thoroughly tested, but they had functioned well without any central papal direction. The new idea of a crusade to Jerusalem did not fall on stony ground in the periphery of Europe but could be immediately incorporated into the existing tradition. The innovation after 1099 was that the Popes were much more directly involved than before and especially that Jerusalem became the object of comparison and the ideal of all the missionary wars that were fought in the periphery, too. The crusading idea permeated both the rhetoric of war and the practical organization of the wars in both Denmark and Portugal.

It has nevertheless been difficult for Danish, and to a certain degree Portuguese, historians to integrate the crusading movement into their countries' history. It simply felt outside the frame of understanding established by a long tradition.

Professor Arup and the white race in Denmark

Writing history begins with sitting down and trying to perceive, not *what* others wrote, but *why*. What were their conscious or – more often – unconscious purposes with historical research, what was their concept of the surrounding world and which frames for the understanding of the past did this establish? It is only with a sense for all of these underlying notions that it becomes possible to take a position: which notions does one share, with which does one disagree and what does this mean for one's own approach to writing history?[37]

This may sound straightforward but it leads to a problem, which is actually rhetorical in nature. In order to characterize an individual historian or his collected output, one needs to simplify drastically and concentrate on a few significant sentences, which summarize a complete outlook and make it stand out. Such characterization approaches caricature. There is probably not much else to do about it than to emphasize, from the very beginning, that any historiographical survey is a coarse simplification and that it only observes a limited segment of a tradition from a very particular viewpoint, and that it is in no way intended to discredit

22   *Were there crusades in the periphery?*

the whole tradition as such. Without the tradition, we would be nowhere. In this sense, all historians are dwarves sitting on the shoulders of giants – they continue to build on the great labour of earlier historians.

Danish historical tradition has since the middle of the 19th century been nationally centred to quite an extreme degree.[38] There are old historical precedents for this. Around 1200, Saxo Grammaticus wrote in his account of the deeds of the Danes that the Danish kings had emerged from Denmark; the dynasty was not founded by immigration from the outside world, as almost all the other European historians of his time wrote. This had a huge influence on all later Danish attempts to understand medieval Denmark, despite the severe criticism of Saxo's reliability that was raised in the 20th century.[39] The criticism, which concerned details in Saxo's account, completely failed to notice Saxo's perspective, that the history of Denmark was depicted as unaffected by anything from outside. This tradition of viewing everything from the inside became amplified in the 19th century, initially after the secession of Norway from the union with Denmark in 1814 and later – and especially – after the national trauma of 1864 when Denmark lost about 20% of its territory to Prussia. The historians turned inwards; "The old Danish school of history did not readily cross the national border," Ellen Jørgensen wrote in 1943.[40] This had an impact on which subjects the historians chose to work with. To a very large degree, it was Danish history within the borders of modern Denmark.[41]

This choice of subjects also had a crucial significance for which type of explanations Danish historians employed to account for causal relations. If nothing of interest happened to Danish history outside of Denmark, all Danish history must necessarily be explained by something older – something older *in Denmark*. The explanations of causal relations therefore becomes *diachronic*, they are drawn from further back in time. They do not become *synchronic*, simultaneous. Through the years, this has led to explanations which, given closer inspection, are quite illogical. Danish laws from the 12th and 13th centuries have been scoured and analysed in order to distil even older layers from the 11th century and from a distant past without written sources in the 8th and 9th centuries. These again are explained as a further development of some older Germanic tribal laws – for which no sources actually exist but have been constructed from yet other high medieval law codes, which are several hundred years later than these alleged Germanic primordial laws. Danish research in this field was completely dependent on German research in legal history and its great interest in Scandinavian material, and Danish research did not differ from research into law history in the other Scandinavian countries. What has been missing until very recently are comparisons between Danish and foreign laws from the 12th and 13th centuries.[42] Indeed, this shows that there was often an obvious relation between generally European and Danish material. Nevertheless, most Danish history has been written from the tacit understanding that all development in Denmark has grown from something older in Denmark and not been influenced from the outside.

It might seem odd that historical research has been able to maintain this image of an isolated Denmark, as indeed a series of institutions came to that country

Were there crusades in the periphery? 23

during the Middle Ages that could not be interpreted as having developed from something older in Denmark. The Christian Church is an obvious example. However, this has been possible by employing two tricks that are closely connected. One is to claim that these foreign phenomena were never really integrated in Danish society but remained on the surface or were parasites, which did not really mean much to the Danes at the time or for the course of history. That Denmark was not really Christian until the Lutheran Reformation in 1536 and that the Catholic church of the Middle Ages was merely an instrument used by the sons of the nobility to squeeze money out of the peasantry can be found as an undercurrent in much Danish historical writing in the 20th century. Feudalism never reached Denmark. This was claimed by the father of historical criticism in Denmark himself, Kristian Erslev, in an article in 1899, which has been termed possibly the most damaging article to Danish medieval research ever.[43] It closed off an important discussion and cemented the view that comparative research was only to seek differences between Denmark and the rest of Europe; similarities were out of the question.

The other trick is that historians have operated with the *people*, the primordial, uncontaminated people, which stayed pure despite the pressure of all things foreign. During the 19th century ethnology emerged in Denmark as in the other European countries, and this study engaged in the question of immigration into Denmark. Many historians did consider immigration in one form or the other into Denmark, but this took place a long way back in a very distant past. The earliest Stone Age peoples were so primitive that they must have belonged to a Finnish people, wrote C. F. Allen in his handbook *Haandbog i Fædrelandets Historie* (*A Handbook to the History of the Fatherland*), which was published in 1840 and went on to become one of the most well-known historical works. The Bronze Age arrived with the immigration of another people, which Allen was unable to locate any further. The third immigration wave was a Gothic–Germanic people, who brought the Iron Age to Denmark, Allen asserted. With this, we are still about half a millennium before Christ, and since then there was apparently no immigration into Denmark. Many other historians assumed that the latest immigration was even further back in time, to the emergence of agriculture at the transition between the Palaeolithic and Neolithic eras. As Vilhem la Cour wrote in 1941:

> This much ought to be certain, that the bulk of the people even today are the same as for about 4000 years ago, when the Neolithic Era broke through. If other elements have arrived with later immigration, they were neither sufficiently strong nor numerous to displace the older inhabitants from its old villages. Society itself is much older. It has grown organically from exactly this soil and has borne witness to this in matters large and small through the Ages.

This was during the German occupation of Denmark, when there were good reasons to mark oneself out as a separate nation without any immigration from the south. However, the idea did not owe its existence solely to the war. It was widespread before that and actually highly inspired by German research.

24 Were there crusades in the periphery?

In 1925, Erik Arup, the famous and controversial professor of history, contributed the flightiest and most extraordinary example of Danish nation and soil thinking – *Blut und Boden*, as it was termed in contemporary German writings.[44] He wrote that the entire white race had emerged from a mutation, a leap in evolution, in the area around the Baltic Sea. The white race is characterized by two things: a willingness to multiply as great as that of the Chinese, and a strong urge to wander, "which has made possible its triumphal progress through the whole world in such a relatively short space of time." The white race began to wander over the Russian steppes all the way to Northern India, where it returned and wandered back towards Europe, to the Mediterranean. Everywhere the white race went, it mingled with the local population – it forced its language upon them, but it is impossible to be certain to what degree the ideas of the locals had time to influence the roaming Aryans. The old tribes of the white race still live pure and uncontaminated in their old habitat. They are the Germanics in Northwest Germany (Arup is perhaps referring to the formerly Danish Schleswig and Holstein?), the Slavs of Poland, the Balts in the Baltic provinces and the Danish people in Denmark.

Figure 2.1 Erik Arup, 1876–1951. © University of Southern Denmark Press

The Danes are, Arup wrote, *autochthonous*, they are indigenous in their own country.[45] *Autochthonous* means something that has grown from the soil, such as vegetables. It is obvious that Arup consciously but indirectly polemicized against the much more moderate Professor Johannes Steenstrup, who thirty years before had argued against the new racial theories and sarcastically had remarked that "[t]here is, of course, something grand in the idea that we Danes are supposed to be one of the most autochthonous peoples on Earth." But there was a complete lack of sources, and archaeology could not say anything about nation and nationality, which to Steenstrup "is mostly decided by the language."[46]

Arup did not care. He was obviously inspired by the lengthy discussions amongst contemporary German archaeologists regarding the primordial home of the white Aryan race, for example the trend-setting Gustaf Kossinna in Berlin. Arup actually thought he had good arguments from the Danish material in itself: the skeletons and especially the crania of the Stone Age peoples. They were "so close to us living now with regard to type and character that there can be no doubt that they are our ancestors," he wrote in his *History of Denmark*. One might imagine Arup examining a Stone Age cranium in his hands until he ascertains with satisfaction that it has a close resemblance to his own and concludes that it is impossible that there was ever any immigration into Denmark. They were close to us in type *and* character, he wrote. Consequently, it is not just a superficial similarity; it means that they were thinking the way that we do.

Arup's faith in the testimonial powers of the crania was rather strong as it was common during that time. In 1931 he wrote a biography of the great Danish King Svend II Estridsen, who died in 1076[47] and of whom we shall hear more later on in this book. Arup began with some thoughts regarding the cerebral volume of Svend's skull, which had been examined during excavations in the Cathedral of Roskilde, where he lies buried together with his mother Estrid[48] and the bishops Asser and Vilhelm. Luckily, Svend had a rather large brain volume, 1665 cubic centimetres as opposed to the modern average of 1500 for men. Bishop Asser only had a volume of a sorry 1320 cubic centimetres, which caused Arup to remark that, "at that time, too, it was possible to reach the highest positions, within the Church, with a very modest brain volume." Estrid was a remarkably intelligent woman; her volume was 1460 cubic centimetres as opposed to the female average of 1300. Unfortunately, she had protruding teeth and a crooked back. "With her, as with so many outstanding women, mental superiority was not combined with physical beauty," Arup concluded forthright. It was presumably a sarcastic remark aimed at Arup's student Astrid Friis, who went on to became the first female professor at the University of Copenhagen and a colleague of Arup, who was rather critical of his methodological basis. Astrid Friis was outstandingly gifted but did not quite live up to the ideals of female gracefulness of that time.

Arup was not a Nazi and would never have argued in favour of genocide. He was thinking in racial terms because this was considered good science at the time and because he was fascinated by skeletons and skulls, as this was a relatively new area of research that was considered a way in which to take history even further back in time.[49] The lasting result of Arup's fascination with bones is not

26 *Were there crusades in the periphery?*

racial thinking, either. This disappeared for good reasons after World War II; it has only surfaced during the last few years and only amongst extremist, confused youth with internet access, who like to quote Arup, and amongst geneticists with an interest in history. What was left after 1945 was not Arup's argument but his perspective. If everything, even the white race itself, began in Denmark, there is no reason to concern oneself with anything outside the Danish borders. Subsequent historians settled the problem of Arup's racial thinking by keeping completely silent about it, but, unconsciously, they kept his perspective. What should be treated in historical research are "the concepts that constitute the Danish kingdom: The people and the land, Denmark and the Danes," according to one of the subsequent generation's greatest and most influential medieval historians and a student of Arup's, Aksel E. Christensen, in 1969.[50]

There are several other characteristic traits in Danish historical writing that caused the crusades to disappear. In around the middle of the 19th century a strong anti-aristocratic sentiment arose in historical writing, which was very likely to have had something to do with the introduction of a parliamentarian system but which was nevertheless strong in comparison to the neighbouring countries. Possibly in Sweden and certainly in Prussia and Northern Germany, the aristocracy obtained political roles during the 19th century and were secured a place in modern historical writing, which could be critical, where they were seen as an important part of society. In Danish history they disappeared or were actively disliked. The nobility was "[w]ithout strength and core . . . a frail, inwardly rotten, badly founded building, which only one single hard push was sufficient to overturn."[51] The nobleman "let himself, first and last, be led by the thought of his own personal advantage."[52] The noblemen "were greedy and shortsightedly self-made";[53] and one historian wrote about "the wild robbery of land by the exalted lords and ladies . . . with violence, chains, coercion and a knife on the throat."[54] These quotes come from 1840 to 1997 and demonstrate the tenacity of the aristocratic horror image.[55] This image has no room for the crusades and none at all for the crusaders' ideals of fighting for truth and justice. There is only room for detailed research on a fragile documentary basis on the aristocracy as landowners and, as such, as parasites on the good Danish medieval peasant,[56] and not for consideration as to whether they actually held more spiritual and religious interests.[57]

Danish historical writing never liked the aristocracy and it certainly never liked warfare.[58] A general survey of medieval military history has never been written,[59] and actual warfare itself takes up remarkably little space in all accounts of medieval history. The only really good rendering of how to kill in medieval Denmark is, characteristically, written by an English historian.[60] Besides, several of the historians at Danish universities, Arup among them, were avowed pacifists. Therefore, there was no room for the crusades, and if they were mentioned, they had no significance, as opposed to the more peaceful pursuits of the peasants. "It was men such as Bjørn and his sons who in those days made the country richer through their toil. And their work deserves to be mentioned just as much as those who went on crusade against the Wends and the Estonians with Absalon or Andreas

Were there crusades in the periphery? 27

Sunesen," Arup wrote on the peasant Bjørn, who cleared new land for cultivation in the early 13th century.[61]

All in all, the contrasting of war and the peaceful cultivation of the soil was dear to Arup. In the lapidary sentences of the runic stones of the 9th and 10th centuries, Arup saw "the human and natural, good and sincere feelings,"[62] that were not in any way coloured by the contemporary blood-drenched wars and the raids abroad. In Denmark proper, we were peasants, and this was human and natural as opposed to waging war. Arup ended his chapter on runic stones by quoting the Søndervinge Stone: "Tovi raised this stone after his brothers Yre and Kade. Blessed be the one who ploughed and sowed in his youth, this will surely provide a good yield." This could stand as a policy statement of all of Arup's historical writings, as it neatly sums up his view on the Danish Middle Ages. Views on history change over time, from generation to generation, and often even faster. Today war is again – unfortunately one might add – considered quite a natural condition for all human societies at all times, even in Denmark. Interpretation of sources changes as well. The last line of the Søndervinge Stone is read like this by runologists today: "sowed and practiced 'sejd'. A 'ræte' is the man who devastates this memorial."[63] It is about "sejd," sorcery, which punishes the "ræte," the knave who has the audacity to destroy the runic stone – or maybe even just to read it wrongly? It is a brutal threat of death and destruction and has nothing about sowing and harvesting in peace.

Finally, Danish historical research has been completely governed by material approach. Agriculture or trade, these were the two fields one could work with, and everything was explained as economics or as a result of social changes. The fact that these factors only rarely figure in the medieval sources has in no way shaken the conviction of the explanations. Perhaps it is a deliberate attempt on behalf of the medieval source to hide the truth, which now at last is revealed by the methodological work of the critical historian? Or put another way, there has been a solid tradition in Danish historical writing to assert that much medieval activity was probably mere pretence, a veiled attempt to get money and power. The saintly miracles were the monasteries' attempt to fool money from gullible local people, pilgrimages were a type of camouflaged trade journeys and the Danish so-called crusades were royal attempts to assemble more power and, therefore, more money. There are exceptions amongst Danish historians, but the know-all economic model of explanation has had a solid foothold until quite recently.[64] A more neutral way of putting it would be that most historians have been modernist. They understood the Middle Ages simply and directly from modern assumptions regarding economics and power and have far more difficulty understanding the past on other premises.[65]

The crusades have been interpreted as a form of imperialism. Hal Koch, one of the leading Danish church historians in the mid-20th century, wrote: "The fantastical and scandalous spectacle of the crusades began shortly before 1100. Initially, Denmark did not participate. True, up here they were eager to regard the fight against the Wends as 'crusades'; however, such an interpretation of the Danish raids across the Baltic is rather sympathetic. Many of the Wends, the

28   *Were there crusades in the periphery?*

fighting was directed at, were long since christianized, and, moreover, the Danish endeavours had by no means any intention of converting anyone to Christianity but rather to ravage and pillage."[66] He makes a quick reservation regarding the raid of Rügen, in which case there actually was a Christian mission that came from Denmark; otherwise, the crusades are obviously only a pretext for improving the economy. The expeditions of King Valdemar II the Victorious against Estonia in 1219 are dismissed briefly with the explanation that they were "outwardly in the form of a crusade but in actual fact with a view to create a colonial empire." This attitude of ideology as a stalking-horse for politics was neatly summed up by another historian: "Behind the ideas lay most often the real struggle for power, which brilliantly exploited the ideas as they saw fit."[67] The sentence must have been written in 1945, and today one can only wonder why someone – in precisely that year – would dismiss the notion that ideas can create history.[68]

The narrative of the Danish crusades does exist, despite everything, but one has to look for it – and it is a complete coincidence if one, as a Danish historian, finds it. International crusade historians, on the other hand, are quite familiar with the narrative. This is due to the French Count Paul Riant's monumental work on Scandinavians on crusade and pilgrimage to the Holy Land, published in part with his own money in 1865, when he was only twenty-nine years old. Before that, he had spent some years absorbed in studies of the sources and had familiarized himself with Danish language and culture. For the rest of his life, Riant was able to write letters in eloquent Danish language, employing a slightly rigid Gothic fracture handwriting, which was otherwise unknown in France.[69] All sources known at the time were examined and included in the book, which still today is a treasure trove of information. This was planned to have been only the beginning. It was Riant's plan to continue with a book on the Scandinavian crusades in the Baltic and then to continue with a book on their crusades in Africa and Asia. Unfortunately, it came to nothing, partly because Riant returned to Paris and became a busy historian in scholarly societies and, probably worse yet, he began publishing medieval texts, which was exceedingly meritorious but frighteningly time absorbing as well.

Riant believed that the Scandinavians were obvious crusade participants due to the great Nordic tradition of bravery, *l'ésprit nordique*. At the same time, he showed in concrete detail how many of the Middle Eastern crusaders could be traced back to Scandinavia. Riant was immediately accepted and praised by his Scandinavian colleagues. The book was published in 1865; that same year he was admitted to the Swedish Royal Academy of Science; two years later, he was admitted to the Royal Nordic Society for the Study of Antiquities.[70] One year after that, his book was published in a Danish translation. Riant corresponded with Danish historians until his death in 1888, especially those affiliated with libraries, and once a letter from Riant concerning the find of an interesting source was read out at a meeting of the Royal Nordic Society for the Study of Antiquities.

However, no one ever read Riant's book. It is astonishing, but there is no trace of Riant at all to be found in any of the many general histories of Denmark or the

Were there crusades in the periphery? 29

specialized studies published between 1865 and 2004. He is not to be found in the bibliographies, not mentioned in the historiographical surveys, and no historian wrote about crusades. If they mention the word, it happens in a way that makes it hard to imagine that they had ever opened Riant's work.

Riant's book was simply published at the worst possible time. He fell victim to the 1864 syndrome among Danish historians – they all closed in on studying the history of modern Denmark back in time, independent from outside influences, isolated, without space for anything as exotic as crusades, which went against the idea of being a little, humble country. This is possibly the reason Riant was totally neglected in exactly that country where his research ought to have evoked the most interest.

Few nevertheless read Riant's book, but these were typically not the historians at the university among them was Chief librarian Christian Bruun. Equally, there was the pastor A. Fabricius, who published a little book in 1882 on the connections between Scandinavia and the Iberian Peninsula, which, to a large extent, was based on Riant.

During the 20th century, the crusades were rarely considered a factor that was to be taken seriously in order to understand Danish medieval history.[71] The most interesting example is a study by Thomas Riis from 1977 of Danish political institutions, where the crusading ideology is included as a means to strengthen royal power. The Danish crusades are not placed in a context together with the other European crusades; this lies outside the scope of the book. Another Danish historian, Tore Nyberg, has in a series of articles treated the crusades as a general background to Danish expansion in the Baltic and researched among other things the extension of the Order of St. John in Denmark and the other Scandinavian countries.[72] The crusades have in no way become an integrated part of our understanding of the history of that period. Among the most striking examples of them being omitted is a history on Danish foreign policy from 2001, where the inclusion of them would have been obvious.[73]

In 1998, a research project on Denmark and the crusading movement was initiated. The collaborators were four historians of different ages and backgrounds but had one thing in common: they came to Danish medieval history from without. They had begun their studies and research by specializing thoroughly in other subjects – Germany, Russia and Eastern Europe, the scholarly environment at the Paris University, the Mediterranean. Perhaps this explains why they found it natural to search for similarities between Denmark and the rest of Europe in their research of the crusades.[74] An additional explanation could be that there was simply a reorienting of Danish medieval research taking place, which was a result of changing views on the role of history and of a topical discussion of the role of the nation state henceforth. Impressions of this shift materialized as themes at meetings and conferences, for example at the 24th Nordic Meeting of Historians in 2001, where one of the topics was the Nordic countries and Europe in the Middle Ages.[75] In 2003, Nils Hybel published a book on medieval Denmark as a part of Europe, which actually included the crusades. More recently further books on Danish and Baltic crusades have appeared,[76] and the subject has

30   *Were there crusades in the periphery?*

begun to surface in broader and more general accounts.[77] In this way, the comparative perspective has gradually begun to manifest in books and in summaries and broader writings.

Herculano's peasants and his crusader kings

From a crusade perspective, Portuguese historiography seems to have striking parallels with the Danish.[78] Like Denmark, Portugal cultivated a narrative in the 19th century of being a small country, oppressed by a powerful, hostile neighbour, but also of having had a glorious past. It was a country which during the 19th century became proud of being somewhat backward. Not only did it feel marginalized and disregarded in Europe, it actually perceived this as a distinction, an exceptional ability to hold on to something primordial. This gave rise to discussions regarding Portugal's position in the history of Europe and of the world.[79]

During the Napoleonic Wars, Denmark chose sides with the French emperor, whereas Portugal turned against him. This did not help much. Portugal was occupied by Spanish–French forces in 1807. This was expected, so King João VI and all of the royal family fled to Brazil, followed by administrators and the top of the Portuguese society, perhaps as many as 10,000 people. In 1808, the British liberated and also occupied Portugal; they were led by Wellington, who was to become rather famous later on. In 1815, only a year after Norway had gained independence from Denmark, Brazil became independent from Portugal. The Portuguese king, however, had to stay in Brazil, with little prospect of returning. The motherland had become a colony. There was a real danger that Portugal would disappear as an independent nation. This contributed to creating a national trauma amongst historians which has striking similarities to the Danish experience after the catastrophe of 1864, when Denmark lost one fifth of its territory and had to live in the shadow of an expanding and aggressive Prussian great power.

In 1820, a revolution attempted to introduce a constitutional monarchy with a constitution and a parliament, and the king returned to Portugal. Several counterrevolutions followed, reintroducing absolute monarchy. Brazil seceded as an independent Empire in 1822. In 1832 and again in 1846, Portugal was the scene of civil war. The result was the final dissolution of the old monarchy, widespread unrest where scattered gangs plundered the country, extensive land reforms with the seizure of estates belonging to monasteries and the Church and a split into sharply opposed factions, where one supported the Church and another aimed to liberalize it and curtail its power significantly.[80]

During the 19th century, Alexandre Herculano (1810–1877) influenced Portuguese historical research tremendously, due to both his extensive publishing of critical text collections according to the most up-to-date historical criticism and through his great historical and literary achievements. Herculano stood squarely within romanticism; one of the driving ideas behind his great *História de Portugal* was to uncover the Portuguese national spirit – *índole*.[81]

Were there crusades in the periphery? 31

Portugal, since the 16th century, had traditionally been described as a unique polity, favoured by God, founded as the first king, Afonso Henriques, witnessed a cross in the heavens during the battle of Ourique in 1139. The miracle is mentioned for the first time in a text from 1416,[82] and in 1599, a document was discovered in the monastery of Alcobaça, which supposedly contained King Afonso's oath of allegiance to Christ in return for Christ promising that Portugal was to remain as a nation forever. Herculano, being a liberalist and a practitioner of historical criticism, dismissed the miracle as a late invention and the document as a hoax, and as a good romanticist, he instead emphasized the importance of the people as the creator of Portugal. This caused some stir. Actually, Herculano had only written briefly about the miracle in a footnote in his *História de Portugal* from 1846, but it resulted in a year-long feud between historians with different convictions and a very harsh condemnation of Herculano by the Church, and he had to explain his viewpoints in several refutations and pamphlets.[83] This might have been the direct inspiration for Herculano to later write *The History of the Inquisition in Portugal*. In this context, it is more interesting to take a closer look at the concept of the people, as Herculano expressed it, and which framed Portuguese historical writing until this day.

Herculano and his successors employed the concept of race. However, the Portuguese word *raça* is usually understood in a less concrete way than in its Germanic usage, and it can be used today with connotations more like in English. Crucial to Herculano was the *vontade* of the people, its will to be a people. This is a much more refined and nuanced view than Arup's, one that is much closer to that of the Danish historian Steenstrup.[84]

To Herculano, the apex of Portugal was absolutely the Middle Ages, when Portugal became Portugal. It was a period characterized by growth and progress, of ripening in an almost biological sense, but from 1480 the decline began. From then on, it was downhill for Portugal, all the way to the modern constitution of his own time. According to Herculano, the era of discovery from the late 15th century, which generally takes up much space in general writings on Portugal, was therefore a period of decline too, because it was characterized by political centralization and religious fanaticism. The Middle Ages, on the contrary, was indeed a period of opportunity for the people to assert themselves and to express their desire to become a nation. There was unity in diversity and freedom together with authority.[85] It is quite logical, from Herculano's standpoint in romanticism and his view of the Middle Ages, that his writings were to herald a mythologizing of the fatherland and a longing after *o tempo perdido*, the lost or bygone time. This longing was given a literary form by some of Portugal's great writers, among them Almeida Garrett with his novel *Viagen na minha terra* (*Travels in my Country*) in 1846. It takes place as a journey from Lisbon to Santarém and depicts national types and their life, all the time against the background of castles and buildings from the medieval golden age. Ruins, dust and life – which has come to a standstill and rests in itself. There is nothing comparable in Denmark. The closest would be to join Steen Steensen Blicher's depictions of people on the moors of Jutland and Fritz Reuter's *Landmandsliv* (*Rural Life*) with B.S. Ingemann's

32   *Were there crusades in the periphery?*

figurative descriptions of the rapid and heroic life of the Middle Ages. There is, nevertheless, a difference.

In Denmark, the Middle Ages were incorporated as something alive and contemporary, which was possible to emulate and follow – most energetically expressed in the cooperative movement and the folk high schools, where rural youths were educated with stories from the Middle Ages to take active part in politics. The Middle Ages had not gone away; they were indeed highly relevant. In Portugal however, the Middle Ages were lost, which might have had something to do with political factors – the liberal revolutions were defeated or were in jeopardy, and the right balance between people and government, which Herculano had found in the Middle Ages, was difficult to implement in practice in the modern 19th century. From the 1870s, if not earlier, this led to the widespread belief amongst the Portuguese that their country had been marginalized in relation to the rest of Europe.

One great synthesis-making historian among Herculano's successors was Oliveira Martins, who in his later works cultivated the nation into a mythical figure, with an almost independent being and development throughout history. He operates with a more straightforward racial concept than Herculano. In his great history of Portugal, Martins criticizes Herculano for not taking modern science seriously. "That the original character traits of the people remain constant is today an incontrovertible fact," he wrote in 1886. This was only two years after the Swedish archaeologist Montelius had expressed the same ideas in an article, which heralded the introduction of racial thinking in the Nordic countries. The folk character can be used in a scientific context, Martins thought. It is – among other things – possible to infer back from modern people to historic times and extract certain specific characteristic traits of the people in earlier times.[86]

The Portuguese were, according to Martins, a part of the Iberian peoples but were different nevertheless.

> "The individuality of the Lusitanian character is attributable to a larger share of Celtic blood that runs in our veins and mixes with our Iberian blood." What characterizes this particular mix of races is something vague and elusive, as opposed to the resolute determination of the Castilian. The Lusitanian heroism contains a tinge of nobleness, as opposed to the rage of the neighbouring Spaniards. In Portuguese literature, one finds a tone of depth and sentimentality, irony and trust. The Spaniards, on the other hand, are brutal without depth, can be impudent but do not understand irony, they love but do not evince trust. Martins continues the comparison and concludes by writing that Spanish history is always tragic and passionate whereas Portuguese history is fundamentally more epic, and "the differences in history are derived from the differences in folk character."

With Herculano and Martins, certain important themes for later Portuguese historical research were established which have been of critical importance to Portuguese crusading history until very recently. One is Herculano's idea of the will of the people as the creator of the country. In some way, this probably had an

Figure 2.2 Alexandre Herculano, 1810–1877. © Coimbra University Press

influence on the perception of the peaceful coexistence between Christians and Muslims in the areas conquered by the Christians. Part of the picture of medieval Portugal is that in spite of the inquisition, despite occasional persecutions of Jews, the confrontation between Christianity and the two other religions was less severe than in Spain. The conquests were less bloody if the Portuguese led the effort than

34 *Were there crusades in the periphery?*

if it was other crusaders, especially the Spaniards with their rage. This claim is highly debatable when confronted with medieval sources, but it is a stable component in modern Portuguese writings on the Middle Ages.[87]

Another theme in historical writing is the heroic nature and, at the same time, the sentimental depth of the Portuguese mind. Bravely fighting in the service of a higher cause, for faith and for truth, is a natural part of the understanding of the Portuguese Middle Ages, which differs from the Danish understanding of history during the 19th and 20th centuries. The heroic element was relegated to a rather inferior place in Denmark during the 19th century, and if it appears at all among historians or, more likely, literary writers, it was as ancient heroic deeds for the hero's own sake to win himself a good name. Danish warriors did not fight in the service of a higher cause and certainly not for Christianity, whereas this was an inevitable part of the life of a Portuguese hero. In this way, Danish historians faithfully continued to further Pope Urban's claim regarding the Northern warriors being great fighters but not particularly clever and without a greater purpose.

A third theme is the Portuguese special development compared with the rest of Europe and particularly to Spain, whether this was perceived as an expression of the will of the people or directly as the result of a particular racial makeup. Portuguese historians have, just like Danish historians, searched for differences compared with other countries rather than similarities. Just as in Denmark, Portuguese historians concluded that there was no feudalism in Portugal during the Middle Ages. The Portuguese kings did not have a feudal relationship with the Spanish emperor in the High Middle Ages, just as the Danish king did not have a relationship with the German emperor.[88] And just as in Denmark, this claim began to be queried during the 1980s; these days, several historians believe that it is indeed possible – with due precision and reservation – to speak of a form of Danish or Portuguese feudalism.[89] Incidentally, this happens at the same time that several historians in international forums suggest giving up the term *feudalism* completely, because it is a late and imprecise concept.[90]

Finally, the idea that Portugal has a particular purpose permeates traditional Portuguese historical writing. In a sense, this is already quite obvious in *Os Lusíadas* from 1572, the Portuguese national epic *par excellence*, written by Luís de Camões. With regards to time and outlook, it somewhat corresponds to that of the Danish court historiographer Arild Huitfeldt, who wrote ten volumes on the history of Denmark over ten years from 1595. The works of both writers were much read during their own time and have had a tremendous effect on later views on the history of their nations. Camões's work, however, was a literary masterpiece and can still move the reader, whereas Huitfeldt's is only read by historically interested specialists today. Perhaps it is fairer to compare *The Lusiads* with the Danish Saxo from around 1200, which was translated from Latin into Danish for the first time by Anders Sørensen Vedel only three years after the first publication of Camões's epic. Saxo's work has had a similar role in defining Danish national character ever since; it has been published in many editions and is still read widely, due to its literary qualities too. Camões was known and highly esteemed by poets all over

Europe. The Danish poet Johannes Ewald invoked the great Portuguese poet in his declaration of love to the smiling Louise, to whom he was inspired to write during walks in the North Zealand countryside: "Hvor Rungsted indhegner den reeneste Lyst, der fyldte Camoenen mit bryst" ("Where Rungsted encloses the purest delight, there the Camoen filled my breast")."[91] The poem was written in 1773, and Ewald had probably just read *Os Lusíadas* in some anniversary edition. Perhaps the work even inspired him to write one of the two Danish national anthems, *Kong Christian stod ved højen mast* (*King Christian stood by the lofty mast*), which was premiered as part of the vaudeville play *Fiskerne* (*The Fishermen*) in 1780. The lyrics are maritime and heroic, entirely in the spirit of Camões; they feature naval battle upon naval battle and Denmark closely connected to the fateful sea: "Du danskes vej til ros og magt, sortladne hav" ("The path of you, Dane, to glory and might, dark-rolling wave"). *The Lusiads* were only translated into Danish in 1828 by H. V. Lundby, who was the Danish charge d'affaires in Tunis, but Ewald had been able to read them in Portuguese or in one of the many translations to other European languages.

The Lusiads are about crusades. They consist of ten songs, which extol the Portuguese kings for having "spread dominion and faith" from North to South and to the farthest East. One main figure in the story is Vasco da Gama, who rounded the Cape of Good Hope in 1497 and opened the sea route to India, south of Africa, for the Portuguese. Before this the Lusiads depicts colourfully, and in great detail, the long history of the constant struggle by the Portuguese against the Muslims, all the way back to the time of the first king, Afonso Henriques. Everything, however, has a certain twist. Not content to laud the Portuguese, Camões wishes at the same time to ridicule and diminish everyone else. The English are incompetent and the French sit back ineffectual, whilst the Portuguese perform great feats.[92] When it comes to chauvinism, Camões is not unlike the medieval Danish Saxo but the grounds are different nevertheless. Saxo writes during the intellectual renaissance of the 12th century, when the rediscovered Fortuna, the classical goddess of fortune, was still unpredictable, and the wheel of fortune could turn and make the greatest into the smallest.[93] During the times of Camões, Fortuna had become far heavier and more difficult to turn. That the Portuguese were to discover the whole world and lead it to a new and better age had been planned from the beginning of time and was inevitable. With Camões, the history of the Portuguese became an expression of a cosmic narrative for the predestined dispensation of God. After the Assyrians, the Persians, the Greeks and the Romans, the Portuguese had now taken over ruling the world and founded the 5th empire, which had been prophesied in the Book of Daniel in the Old Testament.[94] Through Camões, the Portuguese received a special mission in the history of the world, an idea that was developed by later historians.

The special mission was a notion that was further strengthened with the mythical Sebastião figure, which emerged soon after Camões had finished *Os Lusíadas*. In 1578, King Sebastião led a Portuguese crusader army against the Muslims in Alcácer Quibir in Morocco but fell in the battle. His body was not found, and soon

36   *Were there crusades in the periphery?*

rumours arose that he had not died but would return and demand his throne back and lead his people to further, great victories. Sebastião became sort of a Messiah figure in Portuguese history, who was to arise and return during the last days when Portugal was in danger and must be saved, just as another kind of Ogier the Dane figure. What is interesting is that whereas Ogier the Dane, to Danish historians, mostly belongs to folklore and has been referred to the tourist industry and as a rallying point for nationalist groupings and resistance fighters, Sebastião was used much more actively and positively by Portuguese historians, even in the 20th century. Whether they individually actually believed that he would return in flesh and blood must be discussed in each instance, but most understood him as an adequate and still effective symbol of all Portuguese history.[95] King Sebastião demonstrates how the most resounding defeat in Portuguese history is turned into a mystical prophecy about future greatness, and he ends up being able to "represent the incarnation of the qualities of the Portuguese nation."[96] The miracle in Ourique, Portugal as the 5th kingdom and Sebastião as a Messiah or Ogier the Dane figure, has been woven together in later Portuguese historical writing and has laid the foundation for the perception of a peculiar Portuguese national genius or a peculiar Portuguese race.

Luciano Cordeiro, who wrote to Christian Bruun regarding Berengaria, was obviously inspired by the ideas of a special Portuguese historical mission and stands as an important transition figure in imparting them onwards to the 20th century. He belonged to a circle of famous students around Herculano who deliberately led historical research into its new, positivistic and – they believed – very scientific path. Cordeiro continued his studies of the Portuguese connections northwards with a book on Countess Mahaut or Mathilde of Flanders, whose name was originally Teresa. She was a daughter of Afonso Henriques and in 1183 was married to the Count of Flanders.[97] Cordeiro furthermore became a great historian of the Age of Discovery and wrote about the Portuguese in Africa, in Asia and in America in a series of exhaustive books, which are still well worth going through because of the great amount of concrete information they contain. Of greater impact was that, in 1875, Cordeiro founded the Geographic Society in Lisbon. The plan was for it to gather geographical and geodetic studies from several regions and had as its declared background the large Portuguese colonial empire, which was to be studied not only scientifically but historically as well. The Society became a forum of debate, but since its founding it has also organized conventions and seminars which have influenced Portuguese historical writing and has been more internationally oriented than the more strictly historical research environments.[98] Cordeiro must have been an altogether rather active person, as he in 1873 together with his brother founded the Portuguese Tramway Company in Lisbon, which is still responsible for public transport in the capital.[99]

While Cordeiro was writing, the British Ultimatum arrived in 1890. This was a downright British ban on the Portuguese connecting the two colonies Angola and Mozambique by taking control of the vacant land between them, because that would include the narrow strip of land that the British railway from Cairo to Cape Town was intended to run on. The railway was one of the great ideas of Cecil Rhodes,

Were there crusades in the periphery? 37

dictator of the Cape Colony, but was never actually realized. Nevertheless, the plan alone was enough to halt the Portuguese and prevented them from creating an African colonial empire running from coast to coast. King Carlos, who had accessed the throne only a short time earlier, had to give in to British pressure, and the Portuguese reaction to the humiliation was strong. A rebellion broke out in Porto and the city was declared a republic. It did not last long but during the declaration of the republic on January 31, 1891, a newly written revolutionary hymn was sung. It later became the national anthem of Portugal, which it still is. The song draws on the tradition from Camões and the colonial mind-set and is about the sea:

> Heroes of the sea, noble race,
> Valiant and immortal nation,
> Now is the hour to raise up on high once more
> Portugal's splendour.
> From out of the mists of memory,
> The fatherland becomes tangible to you
> Through your great forefathers
> That have lead you to victory!
> To arms, to arms
> On land and sea,
> To arms, to arms
> To fight for our fatherland,
> To march, march against the guns!
> Unfurl the unconquerable flag
> In the bright light of your sky!
> Cry out to all Europe and the whole world:
> Portugal has not perished.
> Kiss your happy ancestral land
> And the Ocean, to make it roar with love.
> And your conquering arm
> Shall show new worlds to the world!
> To arms, to arms, . . .

The British ultimatum had profound consequences. Politically, it was the beginning of the end of the monarchy. The republican forces became stronger and stronger, and the king attempted to include them in the government during the following years. However, in 1908, King Carlos dissolved parliament out of fear of a republic and had the leaders of the republicans arrested. On February 2, Carlos, together with his son Luís Filipe, was shot on the street in Lisbon by the teacher Manuel Buiça and the shop assistant Alfredo Costa.[100] Large-scale unrest followed and Portugal became a republic in 1910. In 1926, the army intervened and asked António de Oliveira Salazar to take over the economic direction of Portugal. He was a professor of Economics at the law faculty of the University of Coimbra, and from 1933 he was virtually leading the Portuguese dictatorship, which lasted until the Carnation Revolution of 1974.

38   *Were there crusades in the periphery?*

The British Ultimatum and the introduction of the republic had a decisive influence on Portuguese historical writing too. Initially, the international political humiliation strengthened the perceptions of Portugal's decline from the greatness of fore to the present humble and dependent position. This, however, was soon replaced by insistence on Portugal's mythical, world historic mission – which is expressed in the national hymn. The still large colonial empire justified this, and historical research took it up and developed it. The soul of the people, which Herculano had written about, was transformed into both a racial concept and especially into a nation concept. The strict demands of an almost objective and scientific positivism gave way to very strong inspiration from the French philosopher Henri Bergson.[101] He held that the humanities are empathic and deal with what is alive, whereas the exact sciences can only deal with what is abstract and static. According to Bergson, human consciousness is able to simultaneously contain the memory of the past and an anticipation of what is coming, and Portuguese historians could easily transfer this concept from the individual consciousness to history as such. The dividing line between past and present was effaced in empathic historical research, and acts of the past gave strength to the present. One result of this mind-set was that the role of great men in history was given greater emphasis, which most often fit well with the ideology of the dictatorship, while that of social history was given less. The result was history written in the shadow of the dictatorship. Whereas this could emphasize the medieval *reconquista* as an important step in the development of a specific Portuguese nation quite well, and resulted in many excellent studies of individuals and single institutions, it was research fundamentally driven for the sake of the nation.[102] It also led to isolation in relation to foreign research, something later Portuguese historians have pointed out as being a shortcoming.

The period from around 1950 to the fall of the dictatorship in 1974 was characterized by a slow struggle to expand the categories of subjects that medieval researchers could work with. The laborious philological work of publishing texts continued and has resulted in several publications of very high standards, but simultaneously, social history and the economic history of the High Middle Ages were cultivated – there are actually sources for this in Portugal unlike in Denmark. Even such a politically charged subject as the internal political administration of the medieval cities received some attention. After 1974, several historians returned from exile and, especially from the 1980s, more and more have begun researching the role of Portugal in Europe generally and not least the importance of the crusades for an understanding of Portuguese history. This has not been unambiguous in the Portuguese research tradition.

Already in 1853, Jose Barbosa Canaes de Figueiredo Castello Branco protested during a meeting in the Royal Academy of Science in Lisbon against a historian who had researched the influence on the first crusade of the Spaniards but had concluded that the crusade idea only arrived in Portugal after the fall of Constantinople to the Turks in 1453.[103] This was completely wrong: Castello Branco asserted and referred to a letter from 1110 from Pope Paschal to the city of Coimbra, which clearly called for crusade in Portugal. Castello Branco's view on the

Were there crusades in the periphery? 39

crusades was followed by Alexandre Herculano in his great history of Portugal, and many Portuguese historians after Herculano did take Portuguese crusades into account. Exactly how close the connection was between the Portuguese and the general crusades was debated though. Some tried to differentiate, and they operated with Portuguese religious wars against the infidel, which were supposed to have been different from the crusades to Jerusalem in many ways. The Portuguese crusades or religious wars have been explained with reference to religion and with Portugal's special mission in history as opposed to the Danish crusades, which have been explained in economic and political terms. The result, however, is the same in that not many believed in a connection between the general and the local crusades, neither Danish nor Portuguese.

The crusade sceptical approach was articulated most clearly by the great crusade historian Carl Erdmann in 1930 in an article in German, which was translated into Portuguese ten years later. Erdmann became one of the most influential figures of international crusade history when he published his book in 1935 on the emergence of the international crusade idea, which is still an important starting point for present day attempts to understand what crusades actually were. Before this, however, he had studied Portuguese medieval history intensely and with Teutonic thoroughness carried out the publication of an edition of papal letters to Portugal. Erdmann wished to settle with the idea that Portuguese overseas expansion was a continuation of the crusades of the High Middle Ages and, with that, that Portugal had a special mission in world history. Erdmann's views are not always clear. First, he brushes off the question of whether it was a religious or an ethnical conflict on the grounds that "[f]aith and race were closely connected and we are most likely not able to decide when and where the two concepts were perceived as different at all by the medieval Spaniards."[104] Therefore, one would expect that the Spaniards were always Christians, but Erdmann continues by stating that the contrast between Islam and Christianity was not severe and irreconcilable. In the real world, it was possible to ally oneself with the religious enemy. "It is a reasonable thought that it was first and foremost a profane war," Erdmann continued. In defence, one fought for home and land, in attack to extend the borders. Therefore, the war was fundamentally economic, not religious, and in this way, Erdmann approaches a way of explanation which is not far from that of Danish historians. In addition to that, Erdmann defined *crusades* as crusades to Jerusalem only. Very few Portuguese took part in the expeditions to Jerusalem because they stayed at home and fought the Muslims in their own country and these were, by definition, not crusades. Besides, the fighting in Portugal lacked one of the important elements in the crusades, papal indulgence. This only came later, and Erdmann considers whether 1197 or 1217 was the first real Portuguese crusade, involving indulgences and everything.

After Erdmann had become a famous crusade historian, his article was translated into Portuguese and reviewed courteously and with much irony by the famous and influential historian Torquato de Sousa Soares. He wrote that Erdmann "has been unable to understand the character of the Reconquista movement in its completeness and complexity." Not actually on methodological grounds but

40 *Were there crusades in the periphery?*

because Erdmann had chosen to ignore some of the crucial elements of the *recon-quista*. "The fragility of his whole construction stems from this."[105] It was normal for the time to be rather blunt when criticizing other historians, and Erdmann himself had described the argumentation of the great Alexandre Herculano as being "haltlos und phantastisch."[106] Perhaps it was only the distinguished Portuguese historian's way of returning the compliment. Torquato Soares had been through the great doctoral ceremony a few years previously, was allowed to bear the traditional Portuguese university insignia, and he had just contributed to a great work on Portuguese overseas expansion. He had become a member of the ultra-national society *Friends of Olivença*, which is still fighting to reclaim a very small border area which Spain did not return to Portugal despite promises to do so at the peace of 1817. And he was a cofounder of a new historical periodical, the profile of which he was to raise together with raising his own profile.

Torquato Soares pointed out, correctly, that all of Erdmann's conclusions were narrowly dependent on his definition of a crusade – so that the argumentation came close to a self-affirming circularism. Soares dismissed the idea that race and religion were in any way connected and added that at least this was certainly never the case in Catholic Christendom. Only a little more than five years earlier, the Protestant church in Germany had disgraced itself by paying tribute to Hitler as a new German prophet and including the Nazi theory of Aryan world dominion as part of modern, Lutheran theology.[107] Erdmann's idea felt natural at the time and very German,[108] but – as Soares wrote – it was unlikely to represent the medieval point of view in any way. Soares also mentioned that papal indulgence to Christian warriors was fundamental to the definition of a crusade and that it was also given to the Portuguese who fought the Muslims in Portugal. Besides, it was possible to have crusades without drawing a cross: "The fact that the Portuguese did not take the cross in order to fight the Saracen, does not deprive the war of its character of a religious war." The differences between the Portuguese and the general crusades are attributable to the very different concrete contexts in which they were fought. The crusades to Jerusalem were waged by Western Europeans, who had a particular conception of Muslims but who had rarely met any. The Portuguese crusades were waged in a society where the opponents knew each other across the religious divide and where they had to live amongst each other after the conclusion of the war. This, however, did not mean that the wars were any less motivated by religion. All in all, Soares was rather critical of Erdmann's idea of a profane war, but concluded his review with the words: "But apart from these divergences regarding views, I consider the thesis of the eminent German historian to be proven, by and large." This was meant ironically.

Torquato Soares could find support in new books that were published around the same time as his review of Erdmann's article. One of them was the thorough *História de Portugal*, written by the Jesuit Luíz Gonzaga de Azevedos and published in six volumes in the years 1935–1940 after the death of the author. This is still one of the most detailed, modern treatments of Portuguese medieval history. Azevedo includes the crusades as an important key to Portuguese history and mentality in the Middle Ages and, at times, he attempts to fit them into a larger

European context even though his problems with access to sources and European research literature obviously made it difficult for him.

Since then, the crusades have constituted an important part of Portuguese medieval history up until the latest comprehensive works, but there is still some disagreement as to how integrated the Portuguese crusades were with general European crusades. "Respublica Christiana created a shared room, where individuals could move about, settle down and get a position and where only few barriers were known. The fight against the heathen, The Church, and the common language, Latin, made this movement possible, which the Papal see supported and gave its blessings to,"[109] Oliveira Marques summarized in 1996 and thus emphasized the open European society of the Middle Ages. In 2003, this opinion was strongly underlined and became available to a larger international audience in the American historian Joseph F. O'Callaghan's well-argued book on *Reconquest and Crusade in Medieval Spain*, which includes Portugal as well. Oliveira Marques and others exemplify that Portuguese historical writing has also increasingly moved from being dominated by exclusivists, who excluded the Portuguese wars as being not real crusades, to become inclusivists, who compare the Portuguese crusades with the Middle Eastern and other crusades.

There are decisive differences in the working conditions that historians in Denmark and Portugal have had in recent times. Portugal was, until 1974, a dictatorship with censorship laws that could ban or obstruct research within certain fields. During the dictatorship, modern history was a subject that one simply should not delve into. And even medieval researchers could be hit with political bans. Oliveira Marques and other historians had to find employment for several years at universities in America and in other countries abroad before they were able to return in 1974. Antóino Sérgio's very personal take on the history of Portugal had to be published in Spain in 1929 but was banned in Portugal for more than forty years.[110]

Nevertheless, if one were to make an overall comparison between Danish and Portuguese historical traditions, the similarities are striking. In both places, the idea of having a peculiar historical development can be found, and this stems from a conviction of having a special mission, which found its expression in writings on Danes or Portuguese as a specific race or a specific national character. This idea goes back a long way in both countries and draws on medieval sources and classics, such as Saxo or Camões, and was hammered out during the romanticism of the 19th century. The 19th century put its stamp in a decisive way on modern historical writing in the 20th century and later in both countries, where it continued along those general lines. This is probably most easily recognized in Portuguese tradition for two reasons. One is almost rhetorical. Portuguese historical writing is allowed to be elegant and well formulated, and it is allowed to contain grand gestures and to issue general statements about nation and destiny, even today. Danish historical writing has been more puritanical and increasingly so, all the way up through the 20th century. The ideal was value-free historical writing that only spoke of subjects that the researcher had studied in depth and in which he was a specialist. The other reason is perhaps a part of the explanation of

42   *Were there crusades in the periphery?*

the first one: in Portugal there has never been the same sharp boundary between history together and the fine arts, as it was the case in Denmark. Danish historical writing has been almost monopolized by professional historians, who delimited themselves from everybody else by insisting that only they themselves mastered the correct critical methodology, such as it had been introduced by Erslev. In Portugal, Herculano wrote novels and contributed to public debate, too. Oliveira Martins was an engineer and built railroads at the same time as he wrote about the Lusitanian race; and Jaime Cortesão and José Saraiva were men of letters and philosophers as much as they were historians. That too meant that great general questions found their way into historical research in a much more direct way than in Denmark. This certainly does not, however, mean that Danish historians were not influenced by their tradition and the debates of their time, even if they tried to give the impression that this was the case.

Notes

1 This difference is rarely discussed in crusade research; map in Richard W. Unger, 'The Northern Crusaders: The Logistics of English and Other Northern Crusader Fleets', in: John H. Pryor (ed.), *Logistics of Warfare in the Age of the Crusades* (Aldershot, 2006), pp. 251–273.

2 Regarding the first crusade and the conquest itself, see *The First Crusade. Origins and Impacts*, ed. Jonathan Phillips (Manchester, 1997); *La Primera cruzada, novecientos años después: el concilio de Clermont y los orígines del Movimiento cruzado*, ed. L. Garcia-Guijarro Ramos (Madrid, 1997); *From Clermont to Jerusalem: The Crusades and Crusader Societies, 1095–1500*, ed. Alan V. Murray (Turnhout, 1998) with an excellent bibliography and list of sources. On sources for Christian's massacre and their afterlife, see B. Z. Kedar, 'The Jerusalem Massacre of July 1099 in the Western Historiography of the Crusades', *Crusades* 3 (2004), pp. 15–75. Historiography of the crusades since 1099, see Kurt Villads Jensen, 'Introduction', in: Tuomas M.S. Lehtonen and Kurt Villads Jensen with Janne Malkki and Katja Ritari (eds.), *Medieval History Writing and Crusading Ideology* (Helsinki, 2005), pp. 16–33; Christopher Tyermann, *The Debate on the Crusades, 1099–2010* (Manchester, 2011). Christopher Tyerman, *God's War: A New History of the Crusades* (London, 2006), pp. 124–164 is comprehensive and balanced on the first crusade. Interpretation of motives and mentality of first crusaders in J. Riley-Smith, *The First Crusade and the Idea of Crusading* (London, 1986); Sini Kangas, *Deus vult: Images of Crusader Violence ca. 1095–1100*, Unpublished PhD-dissertation, Department of History, Helsinki University (2007); William J. Purkis, *Crusading Spirituality in the Holy Land and Iberia* (Woodbridge, 2008).

3 The descriptions of the crusaders wading through blood draws on the description in the Revelations of the winepress of the wrath of God that was trodden until blood reached the "horse bridles, by the space of a thousand and six hundred furlongs from Jerusalem" (Revelations, 14.20).

4 Peter Tudebodis, *Petri Tudebodi seu Tudebovis sacerdotis Sivracensis historia de Hierosolymitano itinere*, RHC Historiens Occidentaux III, pp. 1–117; here 15, 3.

5 Baldric, *Baldrici episcopi Dolensis Historia Jerosolimitana*, RHC, Historiens Occidentaux, IV, pp. 1–146; here 3, 17; *Gesta Francorum et aliorum Hierosolimitanorum*, The Deeds of the Franks and the Other Pilgrims to Jerusalem, ed. by Rosalind Hill (London, 1962), here cap. 29; Robert the Monk, *Historia Hierosolimitana*, PL 155, cols. 667–758; here 5, 8; 7, 13.

6 Verena Epp, *Fulcher von Chartres: Studien zur Geschichtsschreibung des ersten Kreuzzuges* (Düsseldorf, 1990), pp. 49–51.

Were there crusades in the periphery?   43

7 Gesta franorum, Cap. 1: motio valida per universas galliarum regions; Cap. 2: Fecerunt denique galli tres partes. Una pars francorum. . .

8 Regarding *franci* as a general term for crusaders, see also Marcus Bull, 'Overlapping and Competing Identities in the Frankish First Crusade', in: André Vauchez (ed.), *Le concile de Clermont de 1095 et l'appel à la croisade* (Rome, 1997), pp. 195–211; here pp. 195–203.

9 Fulcher of Chartres, *Historia Iherosolymitana . . . auctore domno Fulcheri Carnotensi*, RHC Historiens Occidentaux III, pp. 311–485; here 1, 6.

10 Albert of Aix, *Historia Expeditionis Hierosolymitanae*, PL 166, cols. 389–716. RHC, Historiens Occidentaux, IV, pp. 300–713; here 1, 5–6: "terraemotus . . . quam ex regno Franciae quam Lotharingiae terrae, teutonicorum simul et anglorum et ex regione danorum."

11 Baldric, 1, 8.

12 Guibert of Nogent, *Dei gesta per Francos et cinq autres textes*, ed. R.B.C. Huygens. Corpus Christianorum Continuatio Mediaevalis; 127A (Turnhout, 1996), here 2, 10.

13 Ibid., 1, 1: suae fidei ac devonitis nobis auxilia praestare.

14 Ibid.

15 William of Malmesbury, *Gesta regum Anglorum* = The History of the English Kings, ed. R.A.B. Mynors, Rodney M. Thomson and Michael Winterbottom (Oxford, 1998), vols. 1–2, here 348, 2.

16 Ibid., 347, 7–8.

17 Ibid., 347, 6.

18 Guibert of Nogent, *Dei Gesta*, 4, 7. The text is not entirely clear regarding who actually lost faith in Christianity during the French expedition to Spain. The carpenter is also mentioned by Robert the Monk, 4, 12, but is not connected to the Spanish expedition.

19 E.g. Robert the Monk, prologue: "nam quis regum aut principum posset subigere tot civitates et castella, natura, arte seu humano ingenio præmunita, nisi francorum beata gens, cujus est Dominus Deus ejus, populum quem elegit in hereditatem sibi."

20 Susan B. Edinton, 'The First Crusade in Post-War Fiction', in: Marcus Bull and Norman Housley (eds.), *The Experience of Crusading, Western Approaches* (Cambridge, 2003), vol. 1, pp. 255–280, is a well-written introduction to crusading novels from the second half of the 20th century. It is also thought provoking thanks to the discussion of the differences between historical research and fiction during the Middle Ages and today.

21 Definition of crusade, and historiography, Jean Flori, *La guerre sainte. La formation de l'idée de croisade dans l'Occident chrétien* (Paris, 2001); J. Riley-Smith, 'The Crusading Movement and Historians', in: J. Riley-Smith (ed.), *Oxford Illustrated History of the Crusades* (Oxford, 1995), pp. 1–12; Giles Constable, 'The Historiography of the Crusades', in: Giles Constable (ed.), *Crusaders and Crusading in the Twelfth Century* (Aldershot, 2008), pp. 3–44; Janus Møller Jensen, 'War, Penance, and the First Crusade. Dealing with a "Tyrannical Construct"', in: Tuomas M.S. Lehtonen and Kurt Villads Jensen with Janne Malkki and Katja Ritari (eds.), *Medieval History Writing and Crusading Ideology* (Helsinki, 2005), pp. 51–63; Jensen, 'Introduction'; Tyerman, *God's War*, pp. 27–57; Norman Housley, *Contesting the Crusades* (Oxford, 2006), pp. 1–23; José Manuel Rodriguez García, 'Historiografía de las Cruzadas', *Espacio, Tiempo y Forma*, Ser. 3, H.a Medieval 13 (2000), pp. 341–395, is thorough and considered and with a special emphasis on the Iberian Peninsula.

22 Medieval terms for crusades, see James A. Brundage, 'Cruce Signari: The Rite for Taking the Cross in England', *Traditio* 22 (1966), pp. 289–310; M. Markowski, 'Crucesignatus: Its Origin and Early Usage', *Journal of Medieval History* 10 (1984), pp. 157–165; Giles Constable, 'Medieval Charters as a Source for the History of the Crusades', in: Peter Edbury (ed.), *Crusade and Settlement: Papers Read at the First Conference of the Society for the Study of the Crusades and the Latin East and Presented to R.C. Smail* (Cardiff, 1985), pp. 73–89, here p. 7; Christopher Tyerman, 'Were

44   *Were there crusades in the periphery?*

There Any Crusades in the Twelfth Century?', *English Historical Review* 110 (1995), pp. 553–577; Christopher Tyerman, *The Invention of the Crusades* (Houndmills, 1998), pp. 49–55.

23 According to Rodríguez García, 'Historiografía,' p. 570, the Spanish word *crozada* was used for the first time in 1212.

24 On the transition from unarmed pilgrims to armed pilgrims to crusaders and about ceremonies in connection with the taking of the cross, see James A. Brundage, *Medieval Canon Law and the Crusader* (Madison, 1969), pp. 3–29; Markowski, 'Crucesignatus'; Giles Constable, 'The Place of the Crusader in Medieval Society', *Traditio* 29 (1998), pp. 377–403, here pp. 384–390. The example of 200 ships refers to the Danish King Erik Ejegod's *peregrinatio* in 1103, which Danish historical tradition stubbornly sticks to referring to as a pilgrimage.

25 H.E. Mayer, *Geschichte der Kreuzzüge* (Stuttgart, 1995).

26 Tyerman, *The Invention*. Tyerman was not the first to call attention to the problems of defining a crusade at the time of the first crusade, see e.g. E. Christiansen, *The Northern Crusades: The Baltic and the Catholic Frontier 1100–1525* (London, 1980), p. 48. Richard A. Fletcher, 'Reconquest and Crusade in Spain ca. 1050–1150', *Transactions of the Royal Historical Society* 37 (1987), pp. 31–47, calls the first crusade "a muddy affair" (p. 42).

27 Definition of *reconquista*, and whether there is continuity between the 700s to the 1100s, is debated. One problem is that there was no single, precise term for *reconquista* in the Middle Ages, just as was the case with the term *crusade*. See Odilo Engels, *Reconquista und Landesherrschaft. Studien zur Rechts- und Verfassungsgeschichte Spaniens im Mittelalter* (Paderborn, 1989); Patrick Henriet, 'L'idéologie de guerre sainte dans le haut moyen âge hispanique', *Francia Forschungen zur westeuropäischen Kultur* 29 (2002), pp. 171–220, here p. 173.

28 Robert the Monk, prologue: "Sed post creationem mundi quid mirabilius factum est præter salutiferæ cruces mysterium, quam quod modernis temporibus actum est in hoc itinere nostrorum Iherosolimitanorum."

29 The innovative aspect of the crusades is emphasized by far the most historians, e.g. Cowdrey in the very first sentence in a paper on Christianity and warfare: "Few would disagree that the experience of the crusades had profound and indelible effects upon the views of western Christians about the morality of warfare and, indeed, upon the character and culture of western Christianity." H.E.J. Cowdrey, 'Christianity and the Morality of Warfare During the First Century of Crusading', in: Marcus Bull and Norman Housley (eds.), *The Experience of Crusading* (Cambridge, 2003), vol. 1, pp. 175–192, quote p. 175.

30 Well presented by Anders Bøgh, 'Korståge? Om den nyere korstogsbevægelse i dansk historieskrivning – samt en anmeldelse', *Historie* 108 (2008), pp. 175–187. The call for clarity and over-simplification has difficulties in breaking through. The research is on the contrary marked by a certain gentle treatment of the concepts, described aptly by Alexander Pierre Bronisch, ' "Reconquista und Heiliger Krieg". Eine kurze Entgegnung auf eine Kritik von Patrick Henriet', *Francia Forschungen zur westeuropäischen Kultur* 31 (2004), pp. 199–206, on p. 201: "Eine Analyse wichtiger historischer Arbeiten zum Themenkreis 'Heiliger Krieg und Kreuzzug' zeigt, dass – verkürzt dargestellt – jeder etwas anderes unter 'Heiliger Krieg' versteht aber keiner seine Vorstellung exakt definiert. Wir haben somit ein terminologisches Problem mit der Folge, dass wir uns nie sicher sein könne was der andere eigentlich meint, wenn er vom 'Heiligen Krieg' spricht."

31 Purkis, *Crusading Spirituality*, 59: "The impact of the liberation of Jerusalem on western Christian mentalities was so profound that one contemporary even compared its significance to Christ's redemption of mankind on the cross." see also Jonathan Phillips, *The Second Crusade: Extending the Frontiers of Christendom* (New Haven,

2007), pp. 17–36 on the first crusade as the backdrop for the wars of the following generations everywhere in Western Europe.

32 The literature on holy war and crusades is rather extensive; important surveys are F.H. Russell, *The Just War in the Middle Ages* (Cambridge, 1975); Peter Partner, *God of Battles: Holy Wars of Christianity and Islam* (London, 1997); *The Church and War*, ed. W.J. Sheils, (Oxford, 1983); good backgrounds in Erdmann Carl, *Die Entstehung des Kreuzzugsgedankens* (Stuttgart, 1935); E.-D. Hehl, *Kirche und Krieg im 12. Jahrhundert. Studien zu Kanonischem Recht und Politischer Wirklichkeit* (Stuttgart, 1980); Riley-Smith, *The First Crusade;* Flori, *La guerre sainte;* Cowdrey, 'Christianity and the Morality'; John France, 'Holy War and Holy Men: Erdmann and the Lives of the Saints', in: Marcus Bull and Norman Housley (eds.), *The Experience of Crusading, Western Approaches* (Cambridge, 2003), pp. 193–208; Tyerman, *God's War*, pp. 27–57. Kathleen Cushing has treated some most interesting discussions of Anselm of Lucca (died 1086) on violence for the furthering of the Church's cause, which she interprets as a result of the attempts of the reform movement to free themselves from the secular princes. They could, however, also be used directly in crusade theology. See Kathleen Cushing, 'Anselm of Lucca and the Doctrine of Coercion: The Legal Impact of the Schism of 1080?', *Catholic Historical Review* 81 (1995), pp. 353–372; Kathleen Cushing, *Papacy and Law in the Gregorian Revolution: The Canonistic Work of Anselm of Lucca* (Oxford, 1997).

33 Constable, 'The Place of the Crusader'; Purkis, *Crusading Spirituality*, especially 30–58.

34 Nikolaus Paulus, *Geschichte des Ablasses im Mittelalter* (Paderborn, 1922–1923), vols. 1–3. Jessalynn Bird, 'Innocent III, Peter the Chanter's Circle and the Crusade Indulgence: Theory, Implementation and Aftermath', in: Andrea Sommerlechner (ed.), *Innocenzo III: urbs et orbis. Atti del congresso internazionale Roma, 9–15 settembre 1998*, 2 vols. (Rome, 2003), vol. 1, pp. 503–524; Ane L. Bysted, *The Crusade Indulgence: Spiritual Rewards and the Theology of the Crusades c. 1095–1216* (Leiden, 2015).

35 Colin Morris, *The Papal Monarchy: The Western Church from 1050 to 1250* (Oxford, 1989); H.E.J. Cowdrey, *Pope Gregory VII, 1073–1085* (Oxford, 1998). The reform movement is also connected to the Peace of God movement; see H.E.J. Cowdrey, 'The Peace and Truce of God in the Eleventh Century', *Past and Present* 46 (1970), pp. 42–67; *The Peace of God: Social Violence and Religious Response in France Around the Year 1000*, ed. Thomas Head and Richard Landes (Ithaca, 1992); Marcus Bull, *Knightly Piety and the Lay Response to the First Crusade: The Limousin and Gascony, ca. 97a. 1130* (Oxford, 1993). On the influence of the reform movement on rhetoric and argumentation and on the creation of the first European public, see Leidulf Melve, *Inventing the Public Sphere: The Public Debate During the Investiture Contest (ca. 1030–1122)* (Leiden, 2007).

36 H.E.J. Cowdrey, 'Pope Gregor VII's "Crusading" Plans of 1074', in: B. Kedar, H.E. Mayer and R.C. Smail (eds.), *Outremer* (Jerusalem, 1982), pp. 27–40; Cowdrey, *Pope Gregory VII*; Uta-Renate Blumenthal, *Gregor VII. Papst zwischen Canosa und Kirchenreform* (Darmstadt 2001), pp. 123–136.

37 Historiography can be a simple description of how a particular environment wrote history, and historiography can be a more systematic analysis of which fundamental categories influenced a particular environment and established the framework for its historical writing. The latter concerns 'Grundlagenreflexion' (Jörg Rüsen, *Grundzüge einer Historik* (Göttingen, 1983–1989), vols. 1–3, especially vol. I: *Historische Vernunft. Grundzüge einer Historik I: Die Grundlagen der Geschichtsgewissenschaft*; or subject matrices; Thomas S. Kuhn, *The Structure of Scientific Revolutions* (Chicago, 1970).

38 For the following, see Kurt Villads Jensen, 'Den hvide race og den danske jord', *Historie* (1998), pp. 92–103; Ellen Jørgensen, *Historiens Studium i Danmark i det 19.*

46   *Were there crusades in the periphery?*

Aarhundrede (Copenhagen, 1943); Floto, 'Erik Arup'; Manniche, 'Historieskrivningen'; Jensen, *Historie – livsverden.*

39 Research on Saxo is extensive. An excellent and scholarly survey is given by Niels Henrik Holmqvist-Larsen, 'Saxo Grammaticus in Danish Historical Writing and Literature', in: Brian P. McGuire (ed.), *The Birth of Identities. Denmark and Europe in the Middle Ages* (Copenhagen, 1996), pp. 161–188. The Saxo edition from 2005 contains an extensive introduction and bibliography. Saxo as a historian, see Inge Skovgaard-Petersen, 'Saxo. Historian of the Patria', *Medieval Scandinavia* 2 (1968), pp. 54–77; Inge Skovgaard-Petersen, *Da Tidernes Herre var nær. Studier i Saxos historiesyn* (Copenhagen, 1987). Most recent general introduction to Saxo's work is Thomas Riis, *Einführung in die Gesta Danorum des Saxo Grammaticus* (Odense, 2005).

40 Jørgensen, *Historiens Studium.* Already in 1911, history professor Kristian Erslev in his speech as rector of the University of Copenhagen emphasized that "all the [historians] that were to lead the new generation only became men under the impression of our defeat in 1864 and its consequences;" (Kristian Erslev, *Vort Slægtleds Arbejde i dansk Historie. Rektortale ved Københavns Universitets Aarsfest 16. November 1911* [Copenhagen, 1922]), p. 13; and that "the interest has shifted from the Kingdom's outer history to the inner" (p. 21). At the same time, he rejected the national historical writing of the 19th century and praised as a step forward the fact that Danish historians now engaged themselves in world history more than previously (pp. 25–26). For the generations of historians following Erslev, this only applied to a very limited degree.

41 The concept of an isolated Denmark did exist earlier. In the very first issue of what is still the leading historical journal in Denmark, Christian Molbech wrote that Denmark had for 600 years been almost "outside any contact with state affairs and politics of the rest of the world" except Scandinavia ('Om Historiens nationale Betydning og Behandling: Om historiske Arbeider og Formaalene for en historisk Forening i Danmark', *Historisk Tidsskrift* 1 [1840], pp. 1–41).

42 The difference between the old and the new approach is obvious when comparing Poul Johs. Jørgensen, *Dansk Retshistorie. Retskildernes og Forfatningsrettens Historie indtil sidste Halvdel af det 17. Aarhundrede* (Copenhagen, 1940), with Per Andersen, *Legal Procedure and Practice in Medieval Denmark* (Leiden, 2011).

43 Cf. Michael Gelting, 'Europæisk feudalisme og dansk 1100–1200-tal', in: Poul Enemark (ed.), *Kongemagt og Samfund i middelalderen. Festskrift til Erik Ulsig*, udg. m.fl. (Aarhus, 1988), pp. 3–17; Michael Gelting, 'Det komparative aspekt i dansk højmiddelalderforskning. Om Familia og familie, Lid, Leding og Landevarn', *Historisk Tidsskrift* 99 (1999), pp. 146–188. Portugal has had exactly the same discussion regarding feudalism or not during the 19th and 20th centuries. The first step in a reexamination of the Danish tradition is Aksel E. Christensen, 'En feudal periode i dansk middelalder?', *Scandia* 16 (1944), pp. 45–68; and his *Kongemagt og aristokrati. Epoker i middelalderlig dansk statsopfattelse indtil unionstiden* (Copenhagen, 1945), esp. pp. 143–178. However, he ends up concluding that "Denmark never became a proper feudal state, as the constitutional law remained more or less unaffected. The process of feudalization was nevertheless so advanced that the country developed exceedingly strong feudal characteristics in political as well as social terms" (pp. 145, 177). The tendency of feudalization itself was very brief and not implemented fully but abandoned by the new regime under Valdemar IV Atterdag in 1340. And "the feudal elements were only loose extensions to the old Danish legal constitution" (Ibid.).

44 The expression Blut und Boden was presumably used for the first time in Oswald Spengler's *Der Untergang des Abendlandes* from 1922.

45 Erik Arup, *Danmarks Historie 1 (til 1282)* (Copenhagen, 1925), pp. 45–46. See also Thyge Svenstrup, *Arup – En biografi om den radikale historiker Erik Arup, hans tid og miljø* (Copenhagen, 2006). Svenstrup, however, does not mention Arup's thoughts concerning the white race at all and only tries to assess Arup's influence on later Danish historical writing to a limited extent.

Were there crusades in the periphery? 47

46 Steenstrup, *Danmarks Riges Historie.*
47 The Danish chronicle tradition from Lund gives 1074 as the year of Svend's death; the tradition from Roskilde and Icelandic and Anglo-Saxon sources gives it as 1075 or 1076. Pope Gregory VII wrote to Svend in 1075 and likely would have been aware of Svend's death, if this had taken place already in 1074.
48 Erik Arup, 'Kong Svend 2.s Biografi', *Scandia* 4 (1931), pp. 55–101. DNA investigations in 2003 have shown that the two skeletons in Roskilde Cathedral cannot be mother and son, which Arup could of course not know in 1931.
49 For more information on racial thinking in Denmark, see Poul Duedahl, 'Når begreber dræber. En begrebshistorisk analyse af racebegrebet', in: Per H. Hansen and Jeppe Nevers (eds.), *Historiefagets teoretiske udfordring* (Odense, 2004), pp. 107–127.
50 Aksel E. Christensen, *Vikingetidens Danmark på oldhistorisk baggrund* (Copenhagen, 1969).
51 Molbech ('Om Historiens nationale Betydning', pp. 9–10). With the Reformation, the Catholic ecclesiastical hierarchy, which for a long time had been the only counterweight to the nobility, was dissolved: "Now that the Aristocracy or the nobles, after it for a long time ago had suppressed the free peasantry and elevated itself above the burghers, no longer had a counterweight, it expanded well, judging by how it looked, with regards to outward power and material strength. And after the Reformation of the Church it was able, unimpeded, to share with the king the rich, with unimaginable swiftness and carelessness squandered loot from the secularized ecclesiastical lands. But exactly through lack of counteracting forces, the nobility weakened in its inner strength and core and became a frail, inwardly rotten, badly founded building, which only one single hard push was sufficient to overturn." The hard push was to be the introduction of absolutism in 1660.
52 Kristian Erslev, *Danmarks Riges Historie* (Copenhagen, 1898–1905), vol. 2, p. 222: "One could also ask the question whether these privileged classes who stood forward as the ones who were to speak on the behalf of all Danes, had a complete moral right to do this; whether they really felt the duties that such a position entailed; whether they were led by a thought of the common Fatherland and its benefit; or whether their own class interests to them stood at the forefront, or the individual nobleman firstly and lastly let himself be led by the thought of his own personal advantage."
53 Christensen, *Kongemagt*, p. 185. A.E. Christensen writes about the royal succession in 1376: "the popular-democratic tone from earlier times had to give way to an aristocratic tendency. . . . the popular element have been without any importance. . . . so poorly was the people and old constitutional practice valued" (1945, 227).
54 Niels Skyum-Nielsen, *Fruer og Vildmand* (Copenhagen, 1997), p. 93, and several similar wordings in his other publications.
55 Alternatives to this tradition do certainly exist, e.g. Lars Bisgaard, *Tjenesteideal og fromhedsideal. Studier i adelens tankemåde i dansk senmiddelalder* (Aarhus, 1988); Lars Hermanson, *Släkt, vänner och makt. En studie av elitens politiska kultur i 1100-talets Danmark* (Göteborg, 2000), but they have been few.
56 It is quite remarkable that A. E. Christensen's well-thought-out and thorough book on royal power and aristocracy from 1945 only mentions the aristocrats as warriors very, very briefly, and that he does not employ the word *crusade* at all.
57 Lars Bisgaard, 'Det religiøse liv i senmiddelalderen. En tabt dimension i dansk historieskrivning', in: Per Ingesman and Jens Villiam Jensen (eds.), *Danmark i Senmiddelalderen* (Aarhus, 1994), pp. 342–362. A similar blind spot for the aristocracy's spiritual side is found in German research, despite the more positive assessment overall, see e.g. Werner Paravicini, 'Rittertum im Norden des Reichs', in: W. Paravicini (ed.), *Nord und Süd in der deutschen Geschichte des Mittelalters* (Sigmaringen, 1990), pp. 147–191, specifically p. 148.
58 Per Ingesman, 'Radikalisme og religion i dansk middelalderforskning. En fagtraditions magt i historiografisk lys', *Fønix* 16 (1992), pp. 45–62.

48   *Were there crusades in the periphery?*

59 The period is, however, mentioned in *Danmarks Krigshistorie*, ed. Ole L. Frantzen and Knud J. V. Jespersen (Copenhagen, 2008), vols. 1–2, which was the first on this topic more than a century.

60 Christiansen, *The Northern Crusades*.

61 Arup, *Danmarks Historie*, pp. 277–278.

62 Ibid., p. 109.

63 DR 83, already pointed out by Lis Jacobsen in a fierce review of Arup's *Danmarks Historie*; see Svenstrup, *Arup*, p. 374.

64 This is without any empirical basis, at least as far as the crusades are concerned. Riley-Smith's statement on the Middle Eastern crusades fully covers the Nordic ones as well: "the fact remains that no compelling case, based on evidence, for the prevalence of the profit-motive among crusaders to the east has ever been made." Jonathan Riley-Smith, 'Some Modern Approaches to the History of the Crusades', in: Torben Kjersgaard Nielsen and Iben Fonnesberg-Schmidt (eds.), *Crusading on the Edge. Ideas and Practice of Crusading in Iberia and the Baltic Region, 1100-1500* (Turnhout, 2016), pp. 9–27.

65 Anders Bøgh, 'Mellem modernisme og middelalder. Dansk middelalderhistorie før og nu', in: E. Christiansen and J.C. Manniche (eds.), *Historiens Ansigter* (Aarhus, 1991) pp. 35–52.

66 Hal Koch, *Kongemagt og Kirke 1060–1241* (Copenhagen, 1963), pp. 339–340.

67 John Danstrup, 'Træk af den politiske magtkamp 1131–82', in: Astrid Friis og Albert Olsen (eds.), *Festskrift til Erik Arup* (Copenhagen, 1946), pp. 67–87, here p. 72.

68 This goes for A. E. Christensen as well. His book was published the same year the war ended: "Does all this [involving canon law in the treatment of the 13th century struggles between kings and archbishops] actually anything about the true character of the struggle? Are these researchers not guilty of a serious methodological error when they conclude directly from the form of the process and the legal dressing of the disputes to the core and causes of the dispute? Have not all great politicians and men of the Church not least, at all times mastered camouflaging their efforts to gain power in fine principles?" (Koch, *Kongemagt*, p. 77).

69 Riant, letters in the Royal Library, Copenhagen.

70 Ane L. Bysted Jensen, Kurt Villads Jensen, Carsten Selch Jensen, and John Lind, *Jerusalem in the North: Denmark and the Baltic Crusades, 1100–1522* (Turnhout, 2012), pp. 11–14.

71 Knud Hannestad, *Korstogene. Et møde mellem to kulturer* (Copenhagen, 1963) is the only book in Danish on the crusades from the 20th century and only deals with the Middle Eastern crusades. Christiansen, *The Northern Crusades*, is a brilliant book on the Baltic crusades; it includes Denmark on par with the other powers around the Baltic Sea.

72 Tore Nyberg, 'Kreuzzug und Handel in der Ostsee zur dänischen Zeit Lübecks', in: O. Ahlers, A. Graßmann, W. Neugebauer, and W. Schadendorf, (eds.), *Lübeck 1226. Reichsfreiheit und frühe Stadt* (Lübeck, 1976), pp. 173–206; Tore Nyberg, 'Deutsche, swedische und dänische Christianisierungsversuche ostlich der Ostsee im Geiste des 2. und 3. Kreuzzuges', in: Zenon Hubert Nowak (ed.), *Die Rolle der Ritterorden in der Christianisierung und Kolonisierung des Ostseegebietes* (Toruń, 1983), pp. 93–114; Tore Nyberg, 'Zur Rolle der Johanniter in Skandinavien. Erstes Auftreten und Aufbau der Institutionen', in: Zenon Hubert Nowak (ed.), *Die Rolle der Ritterorden in der mittelalterlichen Kultur* (Toruń, 1985), pp. 129–144.

73 Esben Albrectsen, '700–1523', in: Carsten Due-Nielsen, Ole Feldbæk and Nikolaj Petersen (eds.), *Dansk Udenrigspolitiks Historie* (Copenhagen, 2001), pp. 10–215.

74 Bysted et al., *Jerusalem in the North;* also Carsten Selch Jensen, 'Valdemar Sejr, korstogsbevægelsen og den pavelige reformpolitik i 1200-tallets første halvdel', *Historisk Tidsskrift* 102 (2002), pp. 23–54. Janus Møller Jensen began, independently of this project, during the same years to work with Danish crusades, see his, 'Danmark og den hellige krig. En undersøgelse af Korstogsbevægelsens indflydelse på Danmark ca. 1070–1169', *Historisk Tidsskrift* 100 (2000), pp. 285–328. The changes in Nordic

crusade research have been noticed internationally; see e.g. Housley, *Contesting the Crusades*, pp. 114–115.

75 *Norden og Europa i middelalderen. Rapporter til Det 24. Nordiske Historikermøde, Århus 9–13. august 2001*, ed. Per Ingesman and Thomas Lindkvist (Aarhus, 2001).

76 Thomas Riis, *Das mittelalterliche danische Ostseeimperium* (Odense, 2003); Janus Møller Jensen, *Denmark and the Crusades, 1400–1650* (Leiden, 2007); Iben Fonnesberg-Schmidt, *The Popes and the Baltic Crusades 1147–1254* (Leiden, 2007).

77 Michael Kræmmer, *Kongemordernes slægt* (Copenhagen, 2007).

78 Historiographical surveys of Portuguese history are A. H. de Oliveira Marques, *Ensaios de historiografia portuguesa* (Lisbon, 1988); Torgal et al., *História da história*; José Jobson Arruda and José Manuel Tengarrinha, *Historiografia Luso-Brasileira Contemporânea* (Bauru, 1999); Armando Luís Carvalho Homem, 'O medievismo em Liberdade: Portugal, Anos 70/Anos 90', *Signum* 3 (2001), pp. 173–207; Isabel de Barros Dias, *Metamorfoses de Babel. A istoriografia ibérica (secs. XIII-XIV): Construções e estratégias textuais* (Lisboa, 2003).

79 José Mattoso, 'Portugal e a Europa', *Communio. Revista internacional católica* 3 (1985), 114–125, in José Mattoso, *A Escrita da Historia. Teoria e Métodos* (Lisbon, 1997), pp. 129–141; and António Martins da Silva, 'A ideia de Europa no período entre as duas guerras. O Plano Briand e o posicionamento português', *Revista de História da Sociedade e da Cultura* 2 (2002), pp. 85–151, are interesting examples of how the historic special development was employed in the heated discussions of the interwar period on Portugal's participation in Europe and at the same time its preservation of a unique spirit and unique mission.

80 James M. Anderson, *The History of Portugal* (London, 2000).

81 see generally Torgal et al., *História da história*, vol.1, pp. 45–48, pp. 80ff.

82 Duarte Galvão, *Crónica de el-rei D. Afonso Henriques* (Lisbon, 1995), cap. XIV.

83 Ana Isabel Buescu, *O Milagre de Ourique e a História de Portugal de Alexandre Herculano. Uma Polemica Oitocentista* (Lisbon, 1987).

84 Jensen, 'Den hvide race'.

85 Fernando Catroga and P.A. de Carvalho, *Sociedade e Cultura Portuguesas*, vols. 1–2 (Coimbra, 1996), vol. 2, p. 71.

86 Joaquim Pedro de Oliveira Martins, *História de Portugal*, vols. 1–2 (Lisbon, 1886), vol. 1, pp. 3ff.

87 For a general critique of the Iberian idea of peaceful coexistence in the Middle Ages, see Maya Soifer, 'Beyond Convivencia: Critical Reflections on the Historiography of Interfaith Relations in Christian Spain', *Journal of Medieval Iberian Studies* 1 (2009), pp. 19–35.

88 Alexandre Herculano, *História de Portugal desde o começo da monarquia até o fim do reinado de Afonso III* (Lisbon, 1846–53), vol. 1, pp. 238–2399; Paulo Merêa, *Introdução ao problema do feudalismo em Portugal* (Coimbra, 1912); Paulo Merêa, *O poder real e as Cortes* (Coimbra, 1923). Discussion excellently summarized in Marcelle Caetano, *História do direito portugues: Fontes – direito publico (1140–1495)* (Lisbon, 1992), pp. 149–175; for Denmark Kristian Erslev, 'Europæisk Feudalisme og dansk Lensvæsen', *Historisk Tidsskrift* 7. Rk. 2 (1899), pp. 247–305.

89 José Mattoso, 'Sobre o problema do feudalismo em Portugal (Reposta a Robert Durand)', *Revista Portuguesa de História* 21 (1984), pp. 13–19; José Mattoso, 'O feudalismo português', Lecture at the Academia Portuguesa de História 19th of July 1985, in José Mattoso, *Fragmentos de uma Composição Medieval* (Lisbon, 1987), pp. 115–123; Gelting, 'Europæisk feudalisme'.

90 Susan Reynolds, *Fiefs and Vassals. The Medieval Evidence Reinterpreted* (Oxford, 1994); *Die Gegenwart des Feudalismus*, ed. Natalie Fryde, Pierre Monnet and Otto Gerhard Oexle (Göttingen, 2002). Historians in northern Spain have also, during the same period, switched from rejecting to accepting feudalism; see Simon Barton, *The Aristocracy in Twelfth-Century Leon and Castile* (Cambridge, 1997), pp. 67ff.

50 *Were there crusades in the periphery?*

91 Printed in several editions of Ewald's works, now on the internet as well: http://www. kalliope.org/digt.pl?longdid=ewaldandrea4

92 For example *Os Lusíadas* III, 37.

93 Thyra Nors, 'Slægtsstrategier hos den danske kongeslægt i det 12. århundrede. Svar til Helge Paludan', *Historie* 2000 (2000), pp. 55–66; fortuna in the 12th century, Tuomas M.S. Lehtonen, *Fortuna, Money, and the Sublunar World. Twelfth-century Ethical Poetics and the Satirical Poetry of the Carmina Burana* (Helsinki, 1995).

94 Camões, Os Lusíadas I, 24. The idea of Portugal as Daniel's fifth kingdom of the world was taken up and much extended during the period right after the restoration of the Portuguese kingdom in 1640.

95 Ruth Tobias, *Der Sebastianismo in der portugiesischen Literatur des 20. Jahrhunderts: zur literarischen Konstruktion und Dekonstruktion nationaler Identität am Beispiel eines Erlösermythos* (Frankfurt a.M., 2002).

96 Inge M. Larsen, *Sem Poder et sem Renome. Den parallelle nationale diskurs i Portugal – dens opståen, udvikling og kulmination hos* Renascenca-*generationen.* Unpublished PhD-dissertation, University of Copenhagen (1998).

97 Luciano Cordeiro, *A Condessa Mahaut* (Lisbon, 1899).

98 Torgal et al., *História da história*, vol. 1, p. 129. The homepage of the Society is http://socgeografia-lisboa.planetaclix.pt/index.html.

99 http://www.carris.pt/index.php?area=empresa_historia

100 Anderson, *The History of Portugal*, p. 139.

101 Torgal et al., *História da história*, chapter 7.

102 Actually quite parallel to the Spanish tradition under Franco, illustrated by R. Menédez Pidal, *Los españoles en la historia y en la literatura* (Madrid, 1947), strongly criticized in Fletcher, 'Reconquest and Crusade', pp. 32–33.

103 Jose Barbosa Canaes de Figueiredo Castello Branco, 'Apontamentos sobre as relações de Portugal com a Syria no seculo 12', *Memorias da Academia real das sciencias de Lisboa. Classe de sciencias moraes, politicas e bellas lettras, nova serie*, tom. 1, parte 1 (1854), pp. 49–97.

104 Carl Erdmann, 'Der Kreuzzugsgedanke in Portugal', *Historische Zeitschrift* 141 (1930), pp. 23–53, here p. 24.

105 Torquato de Sousa Soares, 'Review of Carl Erdmann: A idea de cruzada em Portugal', *Revista Portuguesa de História* 1 (1941), pp. 305–311.

106 Erdmann, 'Der Kreuzzugsgedanke in Portugal', p. 25, note 3. He put it somewhat more positively in the introduction to the source edition Papsturkunden from 1927, where Herculano "in einem psykologish merkwürdigen Masse den Dichter und den strengen Forscher in sich zu vereinigen vermocht," so that one without hesitation can count him amongst "die grossen Historiker" (Papsturkunden, p. 18).

107 "Christus ist zu uns gekommen durch Adolf Hitler," the Deutsche Christen proclaimed in 1933 (http://www.landtag-sh.de/oeffentlichkeit/publikationen/sr-heft-7_kirche-christen-juden.pdf; p. 30). "In Adolf Hitler ist die Zeit erfüllt für das deutsche Volk. Denn durch Hitler ist Christus, Gott der Helfer und Erlöser, unter uns mächtig geworden," a synod in Thuringia declared in 1934 (http://www.freiberger-dom.de/gemeinde/sondertext/bonhoeffer.html). Shelley Baranowski, 'The 1933 German Protestant Church Elections. *Machtpolitik* or accommodation?', *Church History* 49 (1980), pp. 298–315; Kurt Meier, *Kreuz und Hakenkreuz. Die Evangelische Kirche im Dritten Reich* (Munich, 2001).

108 Which, of course, does not imply that Erdmann was a Nazi. There is nothing to suggest that he was.

109 A. H. de Oliveira Marques, 'O poder e o espaço', in: Maria Helena da Cruz Coelho e Armando Luís de Carvalho Homem (eds.), *Nova História de Portugal* (Lisbon, 1996), vol. 3, pp. 11–163, here p. 15.

110 Arruda and Tengarrinha, *Historiografia*, pp. 111–114.

3 The missionary wars of the 11th century

Precursors of the crusades

Al-Andalus

A strait only sixteen kilometres wide separates North Africa from the Iberian Peninsula and connects the Atlantic Ocean with the Mediterranean. In 711, the Berber commander Jabal Tariq crossed the strait and landed on the promontory that was later named after him, Tariq's mountain, Gibraltar. The Arabic conquest of the dry plateaus to the south went quickly, and in less than ten years, Tariq's armies had reached the more mountainous and difficult terrain in the North. Here, they suffered their first defeat to the Christian king Pelágio in the battle of Covadunga in 722.[1] The Arab expansion continued nevertheless all the way to Poitiers, only about 300 kilometres from Paris, where the Muslims were halted by the Frankish ruler Charles Martel in 732 in a battle that made him famous in later historical writing as the saviour of Europe. Perhaps the Muslims only retreated because there was nothing of interest to them so far to the north in Europe. Nevertheless, the result was that the strong Arab empire became confined to the south of the Pyrenees. Almost all of the Iberian Peninsula came under the rule of successive Umayyad regents, who, in 929, finally formalized the prevailing political state of things when Abd al-Rahman III proclaimed himself a caliph, independent from the original caliph in Baghdad. *Al-Andalus*, the Arab term for the Muslim empire on the Iberian Peninsula, was in both military and cultural terms a strong power, and independent in relation to the rest of the Muslim world.

Al-Andalus, including the later Portugal, was a mixed society with large, immigrated Muslim groups together with Mozarabs, descendants of the original Visigothic Christians, who were allowed to a large degree to preserve their original way of life and especially their religion.[2] They spoke a form of Latin, but without links to the attempts in the rest of Western Europe to standardize Latin after classical patterns, it developed gradually into the Spanish languages and Portuguese. Besides, the Mozarabs used Arabic as everyday language and – with time – as liturgical language, too; many had Arab or Arab-Visigothic double names. Christian churches and monasteries continued to function under Muslim rule, although a slow reduction in the number of Christians probably took place. Mostly, things went well between the two religions, even though there were examples of bloody confrontations.

52 *Missionary wars of the 11th century*

In the middle of the 9th century, a martyr movement emerged in Córdoba. In just a few years it managed to produce fifty-four Christian martyrs as members of the local Christian community, and especially of one particular monastery in that area, deliberately sought martyrdom by publicly attacking the Prophet Muhammad and Islam with harsh and blasphemous words. When they refused to withdraw their blasphemy, even after prolonged interrogations and negotiations, they were beheaded.[3] The fanatical movement was, however, an exception and a problem for both the Muslim and the Christian populations. It is characteristic that a Christian synod in Córdoba in 852 directly rejected this form of provoked martyrdom and declared that it should not be counted as genuine martyrdom.[4] The stories about these martyrs of Córdoba only began to become widely known, to the north of the Pyrenees as well, after the year 1000.[5] Until then, there was no unified, determined Christian attempt to conquer or reconquer the peninsula from Islam – the concept of a centuries-old *reconquista* is a construction that belongs to a later period – the crusading era of the 12th century.[6] This, of course, does not preclude that there was constant warfare between different rulers on the Iberian Peninsula, and that some of them at times were perceived as being waged for religious causes.

After year 1000, decisive changes took place. With the death in 1002 of Al Mansur and that of his son Abd al Malik in 1008, the Umayyad dynasty in Al-Andalus was broken up, and, through the 11th century, a series of Muslim petty kingdoms, *taifas*, emerged.[7] Politically, the landscape became tremendously unstable. The individual taifa kingdoms only existed for fifty years on average before they were swallowed up by neighbouring kingdoms. One of them was the kingdom centred on the powerful city of Badajoz in the southwestern part of the peninsula, which seceded from the Caliphate of Córdoba around 1012 and soon included all of present day Portugal south of the River Douro. The alliances between the small Muslim and the small Christian kingdoms on the northernmost part of the peninsula often crossed religious barriers; Muslim rulers quite often allied themselves with Christian neighbours against other Muslim kings and vice versa.[8]

At times, the cooperation took place in decidedly military alliances between two equals, at other times one part had to buy peace from the other. During the first half of the 11th century, Zaragoza on the Ebro, known as the "white city" because of its brilliant walls and the riches stemming from irrigated agriculture, every year paid the formidable sum of 10–20,000 gold dinars to the Christian King Fernando I of León. Some of this gold was forwarded to Cluny, the greatest monastery and spiritual centre of Latin Europe, in order to embellish the main altar there.[9] Other Muslim cities bought themselves peace in the same way by paying *párias*, annual protection money. During the 11th century, this applied to as large cities as Toledo, Badajoz and Sevilla.[10] In 1074, Abd Allah of Granada consented to paying 30,000 dinars for protection. That el Cid was able to collect a yearly amount of 144,000 dinars for not conquering the area around Valencia almost sounds too much.[11]

During the 11th century, a Christian expansion began, led by Sancho III the Great of Navarra, who subjugated Aragon and Castile and *de facto* León. At his death in 1035 this relatively large kingdom was shared between his sons. The oldest, García, received Navarre, Fernando got Castile, Gonçalo was given some lesser principalities and the illegitimate son, Ramiro, got Aragon. The subsequent bloody wars between the sons and their descendants left two great rulers in the region by the end of the 11th century, Alfonso VI of León-Castile and Sancho I of Aragon, who was succeeded by Pedro I in 1094.

These Christian kingdoms expanded, and from the middle of the 11th century this happened by way of warfare, which apart from possible economic and political causes was also perceived as religious acts and had a connection with papal reform movements. Bands of especially French knights arrived on the peninsula to fight the Muslims in return for indulgence. The first ones were Guillaume VI (or VIII) of Aquitaine – a son of a good friend of the Danish King Canute the Great – and Robert Crespin from Normandy. In 1064, they went across the Pyrenees through the most popular pilgrimage route and the access way to the Iberian Peninsula since Roman times, the Somport pass, which led from Aquitaine down to the broad plains to the north of the Ebro. The aim was to assist Count Ermengold III of Urgell in his attempt to conquer Barbastro in Aragon.

Guillaume of Aquitaine was associated with the Cluniac reform movement and donated several estates to daughter monasteries of Cluny. He had problems regarding the canonical legality of his marriage, which were then fixed by the direct decision of Pope Gregory VII, and he continued his engagement in the Spanish region after Barbastro by having his two daughters married to Alfonso VI of León-Castile and Pedro I of Aragon. In a similar fashion, Ermengold of Urgell had had his daughter Isabella married to Pedro's father, Sancho I, but apart from that, Ermengold could have played a more decisive role for the conceptual basis of the missionary wars in a much larger perspective. It seems that the idea of indulgence – so that the penitent could exchange some or all of the penance that was imposed by the Church by another penance – was first used consistently by the Bishop of Urgell in 1035.[12] It has been much discussed whether Pope Alexander II was directly behind this campaign against the Muslims at Barbastro with promises of indulgence.[13] It is at least certain that Alexander in 1063 had promised indulgence and absolution to "those who travels to Spain to fight against the Muslims," and that same year, he wrote to Bishop Wilfred of Narbonne, that according to all laws it was forbidden to shed human blood, except for punishing criminals or in the defence against the Muslims.[14] Furthermore, in the same year, in 1063, Alexander sent to Roger Guiscard a papal standard, which should be raised in the war to show the papal support, and at the same time, the Pope promised indulgences to the warriors in Roger's army. The idea was spreading.[15]

Henceforth, indulgences were still given to support the Christians and fight the Muslims in Spain, and it seems that more people were willing to take on the task. The metropolitan over the northernmost archdiocese in Christendom, Adalbert of Hamburg-Bremen, had also decided to travel to Spain and preach Christianity. He had to delay the journey, however, when he became enthusiastic about the progress of the mission in Iceland and Greenland and promised to go there instead.[16] Adalbert died in 1072, and his wish to travel to Spain could have arisen

54　*Missionary wars of the 11th century*

in connection with the battle of Barbastro. Contact did exist between the Iberian Peninsula and the centre of the Danish Church, and ideas concerning indulgences for fighting against the infidel were known in both places.

Another participant at Barbastro was Count Evulus of Roucy, about whom Pope Gregory VII wrote to the French nobles in 1073. Evulus had decided to liberate Spain from the Muslims and therefore placed his army in the service of St. Peter. The land that he wanted to conquer from the Muslims he would hold on behalf of St. Peter. Furthermore, Gregory emphasized, all of Spain had belonged to St. Peter since the time of the early Church. The fight against the Muslims was in this way only an attempt to re-establish the correct state of things and to return to the status quo.[17]

This interest from the outside world in helping Spain was grist to Gregory's mill. One of the great projects in his programme for reforming the Western Church was to extend, as well as to defend, Christendom – he had plans of leading a missionary war against the Turks in the Byzantine Empire himself [18]– and to control it. Therefore, in 1074 he wrote to Alfonso VI of León-Castile and to Sancho IV of Navarre and described how the Spanish kingdom had been Christian since the apostles Peter and Paul dispatched seven bishops from Rome to Spain. But the region had been separated from the Roman rite, at first by the Arians and later by the Muslims. Three years later, he wrote of how the Muslim conquest had interrupted the payment of Peter's pence to Rome from Spain.[19] Now was the time to change this, to reintroduce to Roman rite and to get Spain back under the protections of Peter the Apostle.

On the May 6, 1085, Toledo fell to Alfonso VI of León-Castile, who then took the title "Emperor over the three religions."[20] In Western Europe, this was proclaimed a huge Christian victory, and it is a pivotal event which could justifiably be used to mark the beginning of the Christian *reconquista*. "Due to the sins of the people, the city was taken by the Saracens, and with force had the freedom of the Christian religion been destroyed, and for almost 370 years, the archiepiscopal dignity there had to yield. But in our time, divine gentleness has again looked favourably upon its people." So wrote the new Pope, Urban II, when he congratulated Alfonso with the victory and reinstated Toledo as an archdiocese with primacy over all of Spain and installed Bernaldo as its new archbishop. Now Toledo was to be the starting point of a targeted mission amongst the Muslims, which Bernard was to convert with his words and his example.[21] Alfonso won himself a reputation as a brilliant king with great power and "almost a wonderful counselling angel and truly Catholic," because he had raided the land of the Saracen for so long.[22] It is the powerful words from Isaiah 9, 6 (the prophecy of a virgin who gives birth to a son, whose name shall be Wonderful Counsellor, and so on) that are used to describe him: Alfonso VI is here being placed on equal footing with Christ himself.

At first, however, the conquest of Toledo was disastrous for the Christians on the Peninsula. After Alfonso's victory, the surrounding Muslim petty kingdoms felt seriously threatened. Umar al-Mutawakkil, who had a realm around Évora and Lisbon, was one of many who found it necessary to request assistance from the Almoravids in Northern Africa. The Almoravids were a Berber dynasty with a touch of fanaticism from the founder, Ibn Yasin, who had conquered most of Morocco in religiously motivated wars. The Almoravids now initiated a counterattack, a real jihad, under the founder's successor, Yussuf Ibn Tashufin, who landed in Spain in June 1086.[23] Already in October that year, he defeated Alfonso VI for the first time, and during the following years, he returned to the Iberian Peninsula several times and incorporated the many taifa kingdoms in the Almoravid Empire, too. Umar al-Mutawakkil now felt the threat from the Almoravids more serious than that from the Christians; he changed sides quickly and surrendered the Portuguese cities of Lisbon and Santarém and the castle of Sintra to the Christian King Alfonso VI in 1093. The year after, however, the whole area was quickly conquered by the Almoravids, and Umar was executed. Only the Muslim Zaragoza and the Christian el Cid in Valencia held out against the Almoravids for some time yet, Zaragoza as long as until 1110, whereas Valencia fell in 1102, three years after the death of el Cid. The Almoravids turned out to be a much more difficult opponent for the Christians to break than the Muslim petty kings, and they contributed to a decisive change in the political landscape on the Iberian Peninsula. In the wake of the conquest of Toledo and during the intensified struggle against the Almoravids, Portugal emerged.

The Portuguese county

The region between Douro and the River Tagus is bordered on the east of a high mountain range, which could only be crossed via a few passes. It forms a large triangle that is parted on the middle by the River Mondego and the massif of Serra Estrela, the Starry Mountains, because of the glittering dust of quartz. According to a folk legend, a beautiful princess lived there. She was in love with Diego, who rode out with her father to fight the Muslims. One day, Diego did not return from an expedition, and she wandered about in the mountains, shouting "My Diego, my Diego" – mon Diego. Hence the name of the river is Mondego, and wherever she shed a tear, it is glittering and gleaming even today.

The region "on the other side of the Douro," Transdouro, was a frontier area between Christendom and Islam, and saw constant warfare during the 11th century. Perhaps it was sparsely populated because of these never-ending wars – which is a greatly discussed topic.[24] When Alfonso VI had prevailed over his two brothers and rivals – Sancho died, García was in chains for eighteen years – he united the rule over Castile and León and Galicia, and from there he attempted to press further into Transdouro. From latest 1075, Alfonso had some kind of an alliance with Sisnando Davidiz, the lord of Coimbra, the most important city on the banks of the Mondego.

The creation of Portugal as a kingdom is a good example of how foreigners came to the Iberian Peninsula and, by involving themselves in the unstable political situation and taking part in the religious wars of the 11th century, were able to create new positions for themselves. Two French cousins from Burgundy, Henrique and Raimundo, arrived in León and placed themselves in the service of

56   *Missionary wars of the 11th century*

King Alfonso VI. They were of the finest of families.[25] Raimundo was the fourth son of William I Bravehead, who was duke of Burgundy 1059–1087. Henrique was a brother to two other dukes of Burgundy, Hugh I (duke 1076–1079), who renounced the duchy and became a monk in Cluny, and Eude I, who succeeded him as duke and died in 1102. Both cousins were related to the powerful abbot Hugh of Cluny and to the later Pope Calixtus II, and both were staunch supporters of the reform movement that originated from Cluny. It seems that Raimundo had participated in an expedition on the Peninsula against Tudela for the first time in 1086 or the year after under the leadership of Duke Eude I,[26] and in 1090, he returned and stayed in Galicia. The two foreign knights married a princess each, Raimundo married the legitimate daughter of Alfonso VI, Urraca, in 1091; Henrique received Alfonso's illegitimate, but exceedingly beautiful, favourite daughter, Teresa.

In 1093, Raimundo received all of Galicia as a fief from his father-in-law, and from here he initiated the successful raid to the south – as far as Santarém and Lisbon – that Alfonso had been invited to by Umar al-Mutawakkil of Badajoz. As mentioned, it was a short-lived success in the fight against the Almoravids, who without difficulty reconquered it all the year after. This might have been the background for Alfonso's thinking – the region from the north coast of Galicia to the River Tagus was too large for one count, and, therefore, he chose to divide it by the Minho River. The region south of the Minho, Portugal proper, was given to Alfonso's new son-in-law, Henrique, who had arrived to the Peninsula from Burgundy at the latest by 1094 and presumably was married to Teresa that very year. Henrique received Portugal in 1096;[27] for that reason, it would be appropriate to choose that year as the date of the birth of modern Portugal. It has been discussed for a long time amongst historians whether Henrique received it as a fief that the king could revoke, or as a hereditary fief or almost as a property that he could hand down without any restrictions.[28] Most importantly, however, is the fact that Portugal at the time was a very poorly defined region that was almost completely ruled by Muslims. It was up to Henrique himself to see what he would be able to get out of his title.

The division of an area into two counties could easily lead to mutual rivalry, and a certain level of regulation must have taken place between the two cousins. At the same time, their father-in-law was without male offspring, and the two sons-in-law and powerful counts were by now closest to him. Therefore, at some point between 1095 and 1107, before the death of Alfonso VI, Raimundo and Henrique entered an agreement on the division of the inheritance. If Henrique conquered Toledo first, he promised that Raimundo was to have a share of it. If Raimundo came first, he promised to give Toledo and all its lands to Henrique when Alfonso was dead, on the condition that Henrique was to hold it as a vassal of Raimundo. In return, Raimundo was to have all of León and Castile. If Raimundo was not capable of giving Henrique Toledo, he was to have Galicia instead. The agreement must have been exceedingly important, not only to the two counts, but also in order to create a mutual peace for the fight against the Muslims. For that reason, it was negotiated with the assistance of the envoy Dalmatius Geret from Cluny.[29]

The foundation of Portugal was laid in connection with the many wars on the Iberian Peninsula during the 11th century; through the century, these were increasingly justified with reference to religion. The Pope and the extremely important ecclesiastical institution of Cluny entered actively and supported secular princes both with promises of spiritual merit and indulgence and also in practical terms by assisting in diplomacy between contending parties. Family connections were of decisive importance, and a good marriage could be the entry to a warring career and to land. Henrique had the right background and arrived to the right place at the right time, and possibilities were great in a religious frontier like the county of Portugal. This was a region which despite many differences had several features in common with the distant Denmark, not least with regard to religious wars.

The Danish marches

Around the same time as Charles Martel's victory over the Muslims at Poitiers, the first Danish trees, which were to strengthen the sides on the long earthwork across Jutland and block the entry from Northern Germany to Denmark, were chosen for felling. The earthwork was to be around ten kilometres long, not much less than the Straits of Gibraltar. The trees were felled in 737, in total around 30,000 oak trees. The earthwork Dannevirke seems to have been built very quickly. There were some precursors from the 7th century, and the work maintained its military function; it was extended and strengthened several times until the 13th century. It was the largest fortification in Northern Europe in the early Middle Ages.[30]

Denmark is completely divided in islands, Adam of Bremen wrote around 1075.[31] The country was in every way characterized by water, and all transport of goods and soldiers must have been frequently reloaded onto ships. The mainland consists of a single peninsula roughly 400 kilometres long, but is so narrow at its southern foot that it could be closed off by the relatively short earthwork by the Dannevirke. In addition there are many large and small islands; during medieval times it was difficult to move across them because of the many small rivers and marshy areas. The total coastline of modern Denmark is about 7,300 kilometres. It is a flat landscape – the highest point is Yding Skovhøj at 173 metres, with the so-called Himmelbjerg ("Mountain of Heaven") at an impressive 147 metres above sea level as a close contender. The former Danish provinces of Scania, Halland and Blekinge cannot boast of a much higher elevation, around 210 metres for the highest spot on the Halland Ridge, but that part of Denmark was much more impassable than the rest of the country. Denmark is like a low-lying delta, where the North Sea, with its connections to the cultures of the Atlantic and the Mediterranean, is connected via narrow sounds with the Baltic, which gave access to Eastern Europe, to Russia and, through the great rivers, to the worlds of Byzantium and Arabia.

We know terribly little about the history of Denmark in the Middle Ages, compared to the rest of Europe. The oldest preserved document from Denmark dates from 1085, and before that, Denmark is mentioned in a few papal letters and in a few notes in foreign annals. Therefore, archaeology, which has an old and

58 *Missionary wars of the 11th century*

illustrious position in Denmark, is of paramount importance to the early history. However, it is difficult for archaeology to shed a light on problems of political or ideological nature, such as warfare and Christianity.

In the early 700s, the construction of great military works was undertaken in Denmark. The earthwork of Dannevirke is an impressive monument and is still an obvious feature in the landscape. Only a few years before, in 726, the Kanhave Canal was constructed. This is a canal, half a kilometre long, that cut through the strategically placed island of Samsø so that a fleet was able to sail quickly from the eastern to the western side of the island and dominate the waters between Jutland and Funen.[32] The size of all these works alone has been considered a proof of a unified Danish kingdom in the early 8th century – only a powerful king could have disposed of sufficient resources to build such constructions.[33] As such, the argument is correct, but nothing can be said of how large an area such a powerful king has ruled.

The overall impression, however, is that there existed an area called Denmark, where there were mostly several petty kings at the same time, who fought amongst themselves in attempts to extend their power base. One important feature in the struggles was obviously alliances with neighbouring kings – Christians or non-Christians, but we know most of alliances with Christians, as it is from them that we have the written sources. In the early 8th century, the missionary Willibrord was sent from the king of the Franks to "the tremendously wild people of the Danes" and was admitted to the presence of the Danish king Angantyr, "a man crueller than a beast and harder than stone." Willibrord gave up trying to convert Angantyr but bought thirty boys and took them with him home, taught them Christianity and baptized them.[34]

In the early 9th century, there were several kings in Denmark, and some of them sought the assistance of the German emperor against the others. Often, one condition in these alliances was that a Christian mission was to be allowed in Denmark. Around 822, Archbishop Ebo of Reims was missionizing in Denmark, and he succeeded in converting several persons. In 826, King Harald Klak was again driven out of his kingdom. Again, he sought help with Emperor Lothar I, who argued that his people would be more eager to help Harald and his men if they were Christian. Harald, his wife and his son were then baptized in Mainz, and Harald had Lothar himself as godfather, and received rich christening presents, such as horses and weapons.[35] He returned to Denmark followed by the missionary Ansgar, but was not able to recapture his Danish lands and was given a fief by the emperor to the north of the Elbe near Denmark. In this way he was to act as an imperial margrave.[36] His competitor in Denmark, King Horik,[37] seems to have allowed Ansgar to continue the mission for some time, but later rulers in the 9th century apparently returned fully to heathenism.

The reports about conversions, missionaries and church building over more than 200 years show that Danish petty kings abandoned Christianity again when it was politically opportune or when they were driven out by their heathen rivals. Despite the seemingly fierce conflict that the sources imply, the result was a kind of syncretistic religion. Shortly before 900, the archbishop of Reims wrote to the

Pope to ask what he was to do with the newly converted Scandinavians, who had been baptized and baptized again, but continued to live as heathens, killing Christians and priests and eating the offerings for the idols. Pope John IX (898–900) replied that because their faith was still crude and unpolished, the bishop had to move carefully and just make sure to maintain the contact with them, so that they were not burdened with heavy demands on how to live properly and therefore perhaps abandoned the faith again. Besides, one should rejoice that those who formerly found pleasure in spilling human blood now were redeemed by drinking the sweet blood of Christ.[38]

This form of syncretism among the Danes was depicted by the contemporary Widukind in his chronicle of the Saxons in a chapter from the 960s about their final conversion: "The Danes have been Christian since times immemorial but they nevertheless worship heathen idols. Once it happened at a feast, where the king was present, that there was a discussion about the worship. The Danes confirmed that Jesus truly is God but there are other gods who are greater than Him, namely those who give mortals more powerful signs and wonders."[39] A priest, Poppo, now stood up and volunteered to carry red-hot iron to prove the truth of Christianity, and with this, he convinced the king, Harald the Good,[40] who in the annals of the 12th century received the epithet Blåtand (Bluetooth). Harald was baptized together with his wife and his son Svend, who was given the baptismal name of Otto, after the Holy Roman Emperor Otto I the Great. Heathenism was now banned in Harald's kingdom.

Harald Bluetooth was baptized around 965 and initiated a large-scale ideological and military Christianization of Denmark. Harald's program involved, among other things, building a church in his town Jelling, right in the middle between the two enormous burial mounts that had been erected in memory of his parents.[41] After this, it is possible that he moved his heathen father, Gorm, from his tumulus and gave him a Christian burial in the church – a kind of post mortem baptism. As many other newly converted Christians in the periphery of Europe, Harald had coins struck with crosses,[42] and in around 981, he had four completely symmetrical castles built, the Trelleborg-type ring castles.[43] Their ground plan is an exact copy of the medieval world map, with Jerusalem in the centre, and they repeat the same motif as Harald's cross coins in large format.

The castles and other great construction projects must have been part of a seemingly successful conquest of the surrounding petty kingdoms in the rest of Denmark, which now came under Harald's rule. The conquest was followed up by the foundation of churches, a bishopric in Odense on the island of Funen and one in Roskilde on the distant Zealand. Whether there were similar castles in Scania is debated,[44] but the church in Lund – the later archiepiscopal see – dates from 990 or earlier and could have been founded by Harald. In 2014, one more fortress of the Trelleborg-type was discovered near Køge in Eastern Zealand. It had been totally unknown till then but its location fits well into the general pattern of a large-scale conquest of Denmark.[45] When it was completed, Harald had a runic stone erected in his new Christian grounds in Jelling along with an enormous figure of Christ, a lion that stamps down the snake of evil and a runic inscription

60　*Missionary wars of the 11th century*

in which Harald proudly proclaimed that he had "won for himself all of Denmark and Norway and made the Danes Christian."

The interpretation of the images on the Jelling Stone has been much debated, and the lion has been perceived both as an image of the evil one and as a symbol of Christ.[46] With horizontal bands of runes instead of the traditional vertical ones, the stone is obviously an imitation of an illuminated manuscript. The only biblical verse where a lion and Christ appear together is Genesis 49, 8–10, Jacob's prophesy to his sons and his blessing of them on his deathbed. The son Judah is a lion's whelp, which the brothers must praise, and who shall be in the neck of his enemies. Jacob then prophesies of Judah in verse 10: "The sceptre shall not be taken away from Judah, nor a ruler from his thigh, till he come that is to be sent, and he shall be the expectation of nations." The one who nations expect is of course Messiah, Christ. The Lion of Judah is thus a precursor of Christ, the one who rules until Christ arrives. This was a well-known passage in medieval biblical exegesis, also because it was a standard quote in polemics against the Jews. The passage was an important link between the modern Christian rulers and the ancient Jewish kingdom over God's chosen people. Through Jacob, Judah received a blessing and thus a share in the covenant God had entered with Abraham. In this way, secular rule obtained divine authority. The point is that even though Christian rule replaced Jewish rule, it could only derive legitimacy by originating from Jewish rule. The new does not make the old obsolete, but instead completes it.

By choosing Genesis 49, 10, Harald made it clear that he now perceived himself to be a Christian king with a share in Old Testament divine legitimization of righteous rule. The play of the old and the new pact in the lion and Christ must also have made onlookers think of how the Christian Harald succeeded the heathen Gorm, and how in this way he had legitimacy not only as a Christian conquering king but also as the descendant of the local ruling family.

The lion is depicted together with a snake. There is no similar obvious biblical passage to point to as with Christ and the lion, but in the Book of Revelations, the lion of Judah is identified with the lamb of Christ which fights the dragon, the great beast of the Apocalypse (Revelations 5, 5). The audience at the unveiling of the stone may have understood the image to mean that Harald as a new Lamb of God has fought and vanquished the dragon of heathenism. Perhaps the motif from the Revelations also relates that Harald was convinced that the Day of Judgement was to happen soon. It has been discussed extensively by historians, but many are of the opinion that in the latter half of the 900s a belief that Jesus would return, hold judgement and establish his new kingdom in the year 1000 became widespread amongst Latin Christians.[47] If Harald was gripped by these ideas, it would have been even more important to him to convert before this happened. It would have also been natural for him to embellish the Jelling Stone with a motif from the Apocalypse and with it, refer to both the first and the last books of the Bible.

Harald's wholehearted conversion to Christianity set the framework for Danish history all the way through the 11th century. It became one of the most important tasks for the Danish king henceforth to lead missionary wars from a unified Denmark and to convert heathens – at roughly the same time that Sancho the Great

Missionary wars of the 11th century 61

Figure 3.1 Jellingstone, 980s. Christ the Victorious on the cross, which is depicted with branches and leaves as the tree of life. © Anne Pedersen, National Museum, Copenhagen

began to unify the northern Christian Spain, and the Spanish *reconquista* gradually began. However, it is also certain that the conversion to Christianity was a gradual process in Denmark. After the mid-900s, Christian tombs became numerous in Western and Southern Jutland, whereas they only became more common in the eastern part on Zealand and in Scania during the first few decades after 1000,

62 Missionary wars of the 11th century

one to two generations later.[48] After Harald's death, Bishop Odinkar of Schleswig led a large-scale missionary drive in Funen, in Zealand, in Scania and in the rest of Sweden, and many were converted.[49] Some noblemen continued to be heathens until at least the middle of the 11th century, for example the founder of the mighty Hvide family of Zealand, Toke Trylle (Toke the Magician).[50] Archbishop Adalbert of Hamburg-Bremen complained that many continued the heathen customs up to his own time – this is probably until his accession to his see in 1043 – and did not keep the fast on Fridays, that they soiled the religious festival days and Lent with gluttony and sex and that they rejoiced in shedding blood. Some were given to fornication and incest and other unnatural acts, and many had two or three or countless wives. They ate animals that had died from accident or disease and blood and meat from draught animals.[51] They were not yet proper Christians.

Harald himself had a sad ending. His son Svend spearheaded a heathen uprising by those who had been forced to convert to Christianity, whilst Harald "put all his trust in God" and fought for Christianity. In this way, Harald is compared to the prototype of a righteous king, the Old Testament King David of the tribe of Judah. Just as he had been forced to fight against his son Absalom, Harald went to war against Svend. However, he was hit by an arrow and had to flee on a ship to the Slavic town of Wolin where he was well received, "which he could not have hoped for, because they are heathens." Harald died in Wolin, presumably in 987, but his remains were brought back and buried in Roskilde. Almost one hundred years later, Adam of Bremen summarized Harald's life with these words, which show that there must have been ongoing efforts to depict Harald as a true Christian martyr for the faith:

> But this Harald, who was the first to force Christianity upon the nation of the Danes, and who filled all the northern world with churches and preachers, this Harald was wounded innocently and cast off for Christ, and he shall not, I hope, lack the palm leaves of martyrdom. . . . And some testify that healings happen through Harald, both when he was alive and after his death, at his grave and in other places. The blind often regain their sight, and other miracles have supposedly taken place.[52]

Harald had waged war against the Norwegians in order to convert them to Christianity, successfully, according to his own narrative on the Jelling Stone. Harald gained supremacy over the southern part of Norway, Viken, and in 974, he accepted Haakon Sigurdson as a vassal and supported him, in return for Haakon agreeing to be baptized.[53] This had a favourable effect on the way that the king of the rest of Norway, Olav Tryggvason, initiated an effective and brutal conversion to Christianity, probably as a reaction to the Danish attempt to combine mission and military expansion. Olav fell in the year 1000 in the battle of Svold, the location of which is unknown. Fifteen years later, he was succeeded by Olav II (St. Olav), who fell at Stiklestad in 1030; he was transferred to the cathedral of Trondheim, which became one of the most important pilgrimage sites in Northern Europe. St. Olav became one of the great missionary and crusading

Missionary wars of the 11th century   63

saints, both in the Baltic region and in the Holy Land. The conversion at the time of Harald extended further than just to Denmark, and newly converted Christian kings began eagerly to propagate their new faith through warfare.

Harald's successor, Svend Otto or Svend Forkbeard, has had a somewhat shady afterlife in historical writing because some of the oldest sources, and Adam of Bremen particularly, vividly portrayed him as an apostate. It is difficult to establish whether this is true or not. Probably in 991, Svend launched his first raid against England, which he followed up with regular expeditions during the following two decades. Large sums were extracted as protection money from the English, and in 1013 Svend conquered all of England. We know very little of the reason for the conquest; an excuse might well have been to protect the Danes who lived in England, or to "avenge old outrages."[54] The Danish attacks were, on the contrary, perceived as just, at least by nearby Hamburg-Bremen. When Svend's son Canute killed Æthelred during the siege of London, it was "God's just judgment," because, thirty-eight years previously, Æthelred had killed his own brother and martyred him. God's punishment now came in the form of the Danish king.[55]

Canute the Great inherited one of the largest realms in Northern Europe from his father, Svend, and in his diplomas he alternated between the titles *rex* and the Byzantine sounding *basileus*,[56] emperor, which he had taken over from his English predecessor, the very Christian King Edgar, who died in 975.[57] Canute once referred to himself as *imperator*, installed by the King of Kings, Christ, to rule over all the English on the island.[58] Canute's contemporary court minstrels emphasized his background as a scion of both the Jelling dynasty and of Ivar the Boneless, who had conquered York in 866, and therefore had a much more legitimate claim on the Northern English region than King Edgar's family.[59] Canute spent much time in England, but he had good connections to the German Emperor Conrad as well. Conrad let Canute participate in his coronation in Rome in 1027.

According to Canute himself, the journey to Rome was a pilgrimage, which he undertook for three reasons: partly to redeem himself from sin, partly for the salvation of his kingdoms and partly to pray specifically for the protection of St. Peter.[60] Whether the need to redeem himself from sin had a specific cause, we can only guess. There were several unfortunate incidents during Canute's rule in England. One of his most important vassals had earlier killed the Archbishop of Canterbury when he was unable to squeeze him for protection money. Canute himself might have killed his brother-in-law, Ulf, who was married to his sister Estrid.[61] Canute's journey may have had many causes, but the most important reason in this context is that it would give absolution.

Canute established a closer association with the Western European Church and the Papal see. Two important monasteries, St. Michael in Schleswig and All Saints in Lund, probably date back to Canute's time. Both monasteries were Cluniac,[62] and particularly the round church of St Michael was to play a role in the 12th century in the sacral topography of Schleswig, as it constituted the top of the exact east-west oriented cross, which the five churches of the city formed;[63] it was actually the same pattern as the earlier King Harald's ring castles. Thus, it seems that Canute deliberately supported the reform-friendly monastery of Cluny. As part

64 *Missionary wars of the 11th century*

and parcel of this presumed association, Canute also took on the ideological concept of the ruler as protector with the support and command of God. His Nordic bards did not praise him for his fortunes in war, as was usual in Nordic tradition, but as "the greatest lord under the sun." "Canute protects the land, just as the Lord of the whole world protects the brilliant hall of the mountains (Heaven)," Canute was "dear to the Emperor, near to St. Peter." "Canute protects the land, just as the guardian of Byzantium – God – protects heaven."[64] The last stanza, which divides Earth and Heaven equally between Canute and God, almost seems like an attempt to outdo Emperor Conrad, who at his coronation as German king in 1024 was hailed as "the vicar of Christ" with the explanation that as Christ ruled in heaven, so the King was to rule on Earth.[65]

It is likely that it was Canute who was the first introduced Peter's pence from Denmark, just as he emphasized that Peter's pence ought to be paid from England as well.[66] Peter's pence was originally a voluntary gift to St. Peter in Rome, which was laid on the altar.[67] Later, it became a fixed yearly tax, which simultaneously became a formal sign of a particular vassal status in relationship to the Pope. Therefore, the fact that Peter's pence were paid from Denmark from the 11th century indicates an attempt to establish a very close connection with the Pope.

A few years before his journey to Rome, Canute had sent a magnificent manuscript with gold letters, images of saints and a list of the apostles to the Duke of Aquitaine. We know this because the abbot of the monastery of St. Martial in Limoges referred to precisely this manuscript at a synod in Limoges in 1031, which discussed, among other things, whether Martial had been an apostle of Jesus or not. Some were of the opinion that it was he who held the towel for Jesus during the Last Supper.[68] According to Canute's list of the apostles, Martial was a real apostle. The recipient of the manuscript was Duke Guillaume V (or VII; there are two ways of counting Aquitaine counts) the Great of Aquitaine, who died 1030. How the two rulers knew each other is uncertain. Perhaps it was through the Duke's grandfather, the Nordic Rollo, who was installed as Duke of Normandy in 911 to protect the Frankish kingdom against raids by Scandinavians, from whom also Canute's English wife descended. Canute's purpose in presenting this extravagantly fine gift to the Duke is unknown today. In the coming generations, however, the trails of their descendants were to cross each other again and again. It began as early as in 1035. That year, Canute's daughter Gunhild was married to the new German Emperor, Henry III. She died three years later, and was succeeded as Empress in 1043 by Agnes of Aquitaine, the daughter of Duke Guillaume V. Canute's descendants became kings of Denmark. Guillaume's descendants were married to the kings of León and Castile and were married into the noble houses in Flanders and Burgundy, which again made connections with the Danish royal house.

In 1042, Magnus became king of Denmark. He was a son of the Norwegian martyr St. Olav and appears to have been an eager missionary king. One of his very first acts was to attack eastern Slavic land at the mouth of the River Oder and in a large battle to conquer Jomsborg, and he burned down the town to drive out the heathens there.[69] He proved to be "dear to the Danes and terrible to the

Slavs."[70] The same year, Magnus held a synod in Schleswig with the bishop of Bremen and the duke of the Saxons, presumably to plan the mission amongst the Slavs in more detail. Magnus now began to strike coins with the heavenly Jerusalem and his saintly father with a cross in one hand and in the other, his distinct attribute as a saint, the Nordic long axe.[71] In 1043, Magnus defeated a Slavic pagan army at Lyrskov Heath in South Jutland. According to Adam of Bremen, this was the largest battle in the history of Denmark, leaving 15,000 dead. On the eve of the battle, Magnus saw his father in a dream, promising him victory, even though the heathens outnumbered Magnus. When the day broke, the air filled with the sound of the church bell *Glad* in Trondheim 1100 km further north, where Olav lay buried. As the fighting began, Magnus took off his chain mail. Wearing only a red silk shirt, he swung his father's colossal axe, Hel, with both hands and mowed down the enemy before him.[72]

In the eastern part of Denmark, on the island of Falster, Magnus founded two churches, dedicated to St. Olav nearby two fortifications, which possibly date to that period. The churches are situated on the northern and the southernmost part of the elongated island, and in a way they divide the island between them. Falster was probably still an area were missionary work took place in the middle of the 11th century, whether the population was traditional Nordic heathens or predominantly pagan Slavs.[73]

The armed mission on the Danish frontier regions continued, also after Magnus around 1047 was succeeded by Svend Estridsen, the son of Canute's sister. In 1052–1053 the Archbishop of Hamburg-Bremen decided to summon Svend Estridsen to a synod in Schleswig in order to repair the relationship between the two after the bishop had forced Svend to divorce his wife, to whom Svend was too closely related. The meeting went well. The Archbishop and the King vied with each other in presenting gifts, and finally they concluded the meeting – as it was the custom amongst the barbarians in Denmark – with a feast that lasted for eight days. The subject matter discussed at the meeting, however, was the extension of the peace of Christianity and the conversion of the heathens, resulting in the Bishop of Hamburg-Bremen procuring an agreement of friendship between Svend Estridsen and the German Emperor and in plans for a joint expedition against the Slavs. Apparently, mass conversion amongst the Slavs was extensive, not least because of the efforts of Sven's son in law Gotskalk, who descended from a Slavic princely family. The Archbishop installed new bishops in the Slavic areas, among them Johannes from Scotland in Mecklenburg, and in Ratzeburg Aristo, who had arrived from Jerusalem. The Bishop now held a meeting in Hamburg with Svend Estridsen and Gotskalk, who received encouragement that "without yielding any ground should he complete the task he had begun for Christ, and the bishop promised him that he would be victorious in everything, and then, if he had suffered any misfortune for the sake of the name of Christ, he would be blessed. Many rewards awaited him in Heaven because of the conversion of the heathens, and he would receive many [martyr] crowns for the salvation of every single one." The Archbishop gave the same encouraging sermon to the Danish king, with expert use of many convincing passages from the Bible – although not those warning

66   *Missionary wars of the 11th century*

against gluttony and women, because those sins are inseparable from the nature of the Danes.[74]

Thus by the middle of the 11th century, the mission from Denmark had, as an ideological phenomenon, reached the same point as in Spain. In one place, the Archbishop – and in the other, the Pope – promised absolution and martyrdom to those fighting the heathens.

In the Slavic areas, the course of mission and politics happened differently from Scandinavia. In the eastern part of the Baltic, Poland was converted to Christianity during the 10th century, whereas between Poland and all the way to the region of Holstein in the West, the peoples stayed mostly heathen. Local heathen princes were able to gather support for uprisings against Christian rulers, Slavic or foreign. No unified, large, territorial state emerged under a heathen prince, something which earlier in the 20th century gave occasion to claims that Christianity had a civilizing effect and that the transition to Christianity resulted in a societal development leading to a more advanced state. This is a model that only makes sense from a certain perspective, where the appearance of the national state is the purpose of all history. It would be just as reasonable to claim that the social organization of the heathen Slavs was exceedingly effective, as they were able to hold their ground against missionary attempts and crusades from their Christian neighbours for a couple of hundred years yet.

From the 11th century, the heathen Slavic peoples on the other side of the Baltic were subject to more systematic attempts to mission and conversion from both the archdiocese in Hamburg-Bremen and from the Danish king. There was nothing new in that. The mission amongst the Slavs dates back to at least the 9th century, but towards year 1000 it seems to have been intensified and to have had greater success when measured in conversions. Churches were built everywhere in the Slavic lands, and out of twenty-two earlier heathen areas, only three were left around year 1000.[75]

Brandenburg and Havelsberg in the Slavic areas became bishoprics in the middle of the 10th century, at the same time as the establishment of the first Danish missionary bishoprics. This parallel development was soon to change again, however, because of several powerful and successful heathen reactions amongst the Slavic peoples. This happened in 983 in an uprising against Emperor Otto II of Germany – incidentally in cooperation with the Christian Danish King Harald! – and again around 1000, in 1018 and in 1066. A member of King Svend's family, the dean Oddar, was missionizing amongst the Slavs at the River Elbe but was killed in Oldenburg under the Slavic rebellion in 1018.[76]

Throughout the 11th century, Danish kings predominantly waged war against the heathen Slavic peoples. It happened partly as independent initiatives, and partly in cooperation with local Slavic princes, who allied themselves with, and often married into the Danish royal family. The wife of Harald the Good, Tove, was a daughter of the Obotrite prince Mistivoi. Harald's son Svend married Gunhild, daughter of Duke Mieszco of Poland; Harald's daughter was married to Mistivoi's son Uto, who fell during a heathen rebellion in 1018. Uto's son, Gotskalk, was brought up as a Christian but nevertheless decided to recapture the land of his father with massive support from heathen groupings. When he finally lost an important battle, he returned to Christianity and followed Canute to England.[77]

Gotskalk became involved in the power struggle between two Danish kings, Magnus and Svend Estridsen; he supported the latter, whose daughter he married.[78] He received support from Svend Estridsen to retake his father's land in the middle of the 11th century, and "no one faster or stronger or more zealous champion for Christianity ever emerged from the Slavic lands. If his life had been longer, he would have succeeded in forcing all heathens into Christendom."[79] Gotskalk fell during another heathen uprising in 1066. His young son, Henrik, had to flee with his mother to the court of his grandfather in Denmark, where he was brought up. In the 1090s he was able to return on Danish ships from his maternal uncle, the new Danish king, and recapture his father's land in the Obotrite region. He secured his position by building a strong fortress in the area of Old Lübeck.[80]

Taken together, these examples give a sense of how closely connected the Danish kings were to the Slavic princely houses. They also show the dynamics of mission in a religious frontier area. Change of religion was a constant option for local princes in order to obtain valuable Christian allies from abroad, and Christian neighbouring princes, who were eager for missions, could only hope for lasting results if they involved and allied themselves with the local elite. This pattern was repeated everywhere in religious frontier lands, on the Iberian Peninsula too, and it continued into the following century and into the proper crusade era. Just as in Portugal and other places on the Iberian Peninsula, in Denmark and the Baltic region too, there was a shared Christian mission field, an open area where the new papal reform movement entered with active support in the latter half of the 11th century. This happened with promises of indulgence and martyrdom, and by forging personal ties of friendship between the Pope and chosen, particularly Christian, princes.

Gregory's friend Svend Estridsen

The very first letter by Gregory VII after he had been chosen as Pope was sent on April 28, 1073, to a small group: Duchess Beatrice of Upper Lothringia, the bishops of Ravenna and Reims, Abbot Hugh of Cluny and the Danish king, Svend Estridsen. Gregory told of his election to Pope and of the rebellion of the people of Rome; he asked for the support of the recipients of the letter and that prayers would be said for him in their churches.[81] On January 25, 1075, the Pope wrote again to Svend Estridsen, regretting that he had received no letters from Svend since his appointment to Pope in 1073.[82] Before that, Gregory felt, Svend had been well-disposed towards him. This implies that Svend had supported the Church reforms Gregory had initiated when he was still Cardinal Hildebrand, and which had had him elected Pope.

The situation was now somewhat different, because Gregory was aware that his care should extend not only to kings and princes but to all Christians. Therefore he turned to Svend, who was allegedly superior to princes of other realms

68   *Missionary wars of the 11th century*

in learning and eagerness to support the Church. Firstly, Gregory reminded him of his responsibility as king and that he should demonstrate, "that justice always ruled in his heart." All flesh hurries towards its end, death spares no one, and kings and paupers live under the same condition: they turn to dust and ashes but shall be called to account for their deeds on Judgement Day. Gregory's admonishing introduction emphasizes that Svend must show the justice in his heart and so let his good intentions lead to concrete actions, which are discussed in the rest of the letter. Justice, *justicia*, is a key term, central to Gregory's theology and to his understanding of his office as the successor of St. Peter.[83] *Justicia* should rule the conduct of the individual ruler, but at the same time, *justicia* should be supported actively and spread by clerical and secular means. In this way, *justicia* became the very concept that in Gregory's worldview united princes and Pope in a joint project of importance to all of Christendom.

To Gregory's predecessor, Alexander II, Svend had asked for an archdiocese to be established "as an honour to his kingdom." If he still wished for this, and if he wished to surrender himself and his kingdom to Peter, the apostolic saint, and to be supported by his authority, Svend should send emissaries to the Pope to negotiate these matters. If Svend in addition would place his military might to assist the Holy Mother Church against heretics and the enemies of God, Gregory would like to receive a positive message concerning this. A Danish bishop had told Gregor that Svend would let a son with a faithful following fight in the Pope's household, his *aula*. Near Rome, there was a fertile locality by the sea that was plagued by heretics. Svend's son could have this to govern as a duke and defender of Christendom.

The letter raises several questions: about what it really concerns, which perceptions and actual political circumstances it reflects and about the reason, or rather reasons, for its writing. First, it is worth noting that the letter is not a reply to letter from Svend Estridsen, or the granting or refusal of a request, such as most medieval papal letters. The letter was written on the initiative of Gregory, even though it takes positions on matters which Svend had raised earlier with Gregory's predecessors. For this reason alone, the letter must be seen primarily in a papal and European context and only that it gives information on Danish matters. The letter is part of the Gregorian reform policy, and the earnest call on Svend to remember death and to seek justice are thematic and sometimes word-for-word similar to what Gregory wrote to other rulers with a special religious responsibility, for example the kings on the Iberian Peninsula.[84]

Gregory had a very tangible goal: to ask for military help, partly from Svend and his people generally, partly from Svend's son and his men. Help for the Roman Church from Svend and the Danes was to be used against "those who profane God, and the enemies of God," against *profanes et inimicos Dei*. These are rather vague terms, as far as it goes, which according to circumstances might cover many different religious and political groupings. However, the fact that an expression with two segments is used, and not only "the enemies of God," presumably means that Gregory was thinking of internal as well as external enemies of Christianity, both heretics, who did not recognize papal authority, and Muslims.

Missionary wars of the 11th century   69

The heretics Gregory had in mind could very well have been bishops and archbishops in England and Germany who considered his Church reforms too excessive. It could have been the North Italian cities and it could have been the people of Rome who had rebelled when he was elected Pope. Primarily though, he was presumably thinking of the Normans in Southern Italy who conquered Bari in 1071, the last Byzantine territory on the Italian Peninsula, and who the Pope must have felt were an obvious, political threat.[85] Concerning the enemies of God, it is likely that Gregory was thinking of the Turks who – also in 1071 – defeated a Byzantine army in the decisive battle of Manzikert in Eastern Anatolia, whereupon the Byzantine emperor had asked for help in the West. Gregory probably had of all these enemies in his mind when he wrote to Svend Estridsen. At least it does not seem that he was considering his problems with the Northern German Church in particular.[86]

Gregory's mention of Svend's son entering the service of the Pope is somewhat more tangible. According to the letter, Svend had suggested via a bishop that the son should serve in "the apostolic aula," that is, in the papal palace. If this is correct, then Svend Estridsen was probably thinking of an organization similar to the Varangian Guard of the Byzantine emperor. They were a group of Nordic warriors who served as the emperor's bodyguard, and simultaneously had a function as elite troops in regular battles. They had served bravely, but in vain, at Manzikert in 1071.[87] Gregory, however, had a different suggestion: to let the son become duke of a heretic-infested but fertile area near Rome by the sea. Which area he had in mind, we do not know, but it may well have been a part of Apulia under Norman control or another of the South Italian areas known for heavy, spicy, quality wine.

The Normans were in conflict with the Papal see during the 11th century. In 1053, Leo IX even led an army which, having been promised martyrdom, fought the Normans at Civitate under the banner of St. Peter and lost.[88] Leo was held capture at Benevento until one month before his death, an event that Gregory must have remembered clearly. In 1059, an understanding was reached between Pope Nicholas II and the Normans Richard and Robert Guiscard, who took Aversa and Apulia, and Calabria and Sicily (which still had to be taken from the Muslims), respectively, as fiefs from the Pope and became papal vassals. Shortly after Gregory's accession, it came to a new head, after which Gregory sought to mobilize other Norman princes in Italy against Robert Guiscard.[89]

In spring 1074, Gregory wrote to the papal vassal William I Bravehead of Burgund – the father of the Danish King Canute's sister-in-law – and asked him, together with other papal vassals such as Raymund of Saint-Gilles (brother-in-law of Henrique of Portugal) and Richard of Capua to come to assistance; first to defeat the Norman Robert Guiscard and then to continue to Byzantium to help the emperor and the suppressed Christians there. The justification was that Robert Guiscard, through his conduct, had broken his oath of fealty to the Pope and thereby threatened Christianity in the same way that Jews and Muslims did.[90] The friends and vassals of the Pope were intending to play important roles in the struggle against the enemies of the Pope and, thus, the enemies of the Church. The group of friends included both Danish and Portuguese rulers.

70   *Missionary wars of the 11th century*

Cluny and the papal vassals in the 11th century

Part of the Church reform movement of the 11th century was the establishment of a network of personal relations between the Pope and several noblemen, which the letter from Gregory to Svend Estridsen exemplifies. The network collects the threads of other reform movements, such as the Peace of God movement in the beginning of the century, the liturgical unification under the spiritual leadership of Cluny, and the prioritizing of Rome as the centre of Western Christendom and with that a movement away from independent bishop churches to a decidedly papal Church. This reform network was created when several princes placing themselves under the Pope as his vassals, or rather, as vassals of St. Peter. In some cases, they gave their lands to the Pope and then received it again as fiefs from him. In some cases, but not all, this handover was followed by a financial obligation to pay Peter's pence to the Papal see.[91]

In 1068, King Sancho I Ramírez of Aragon went to Rome and "surrendered myself and my kingdom to the power of God and St. Peter." This was presumably a repeat of what his father, Ramiro I, had already done, more or less at the same time as when the Danish King Canute travelled to Rome.[92] Apparently, this did not have any practical significance in the short term; Gregory ceased to refer to it his subsequent letters. Count Bernard II of Barcelona's vassal relationship was more substantial. In December 1077, he reformed seven monasteries and removed abbots accused of simony. He laid down that Peter's pence was to be paid in the future, and he decided to personally pay a further 100 mancus in gold as an installation gift for becoming a special warrior of St. Peter, *peculiaris miles sancti Petri*. It is still not clear, however, whether this payment ever reached Rome.

The monastery of Cluny played a decisive role in the papal reforms on the Iberian Peninsula. The monastic movement was introduced in Navarre, Aragon and Castile early in the 11th century under Sancho the Great, but from the middle of the 11th century a swift movement to the West took place. Cluny became closely connected to León and the "imperialism" of its rulers; the dream of establishing a Spanish empire, which was to lead the fight against the Muslims.[93] Fernando I and Alfonso VI of León-Castile were the driving forces behind this connection to Cluny.

Cluny prayed for its benefactors on special occasions – after a great victory or when they were in danger. The monks constantly sent up prayers, dedicated with all their hearts, Abbot Odilo wrote just after 1035, that Aragon might be liberated from attacks by the heathens and persecutions from false Christians, and that there may be peace and harmony between the children of the late King Sancho. They prayed especially for the son Ramiro I, who like his fathers was bound to Cluny by an unbreakable chain of love. Daily, they prayed two of David's Psalms; one was "To thee have I lifted up my eyes" so that the Lord would sweep Ramiro's soul and body away from evil and protect his entrance and his exit, now and in all eternity. The other Psalm was "Lord, how are they increased that trouble me! Many are they that rise up against me."[94] Nevertheless, that was the least part of it. From the second half of the 11th century, the kings of León and Castile were

Missionary wars of the 11th century   71

included in the regular liturgy at Cluny; magnificent and extended services were held, where the only prayers were for their benefit. Fernando was included in "the great annual celebration," which otherwise only included prayers for the two German Emperors Henry II and Henry III and for the Empresses Adelaide (married to Emperor Otto I, died in 999) and Agnes. The latter was the second wife of Henry III; she died in 1077. It might as well have been his first wife, Kunigunde or Gunhild, daughter of the Danish King Canute the Great, but she had died in 1038, only three years after her marriage to Henry. At the great annual celebration in Cluny, all the bells rang, including the two large ones, the High Mass was extended, there were candles at the altar and a feeding of the poor afterwards. During the week after Christmas, the officium was not to be celebrated at night, with one exception only, the prayer for Fernando due to his good deeds for Cluny. He was celebrated with the liturgy that was otherwise reserved to the memory of Cluny's own abbots, and in a more celebratory way than even the Holy Roman emperors.[95] Apart from these special celebrations for Fernando, he and the governing kings of Spain – this means León and Castile – were mentioned in several prayers and when handing out food to the poor. Seen from Cluny, the region of interest was no longer Aragon and the other areas in the eastern part of the peninsula but the northwestern corner.

The magnificent liturgy at Cluny was due to Fernando's great gift to the monastery in around 1063, to the value of 1000 dinars in gold yearly, but must also have been due to the steady support Cluny received during the following years from Fernando's son, the "burning clunifiliac,"[96] Alfonso VI. He himself received help and support from Cluny in the shape of prayers, as well as direct diplomatic assistance in negotiations with the Pope and with other princes on the Iberian Peninsula. In January 1072, Alfonso was defeated by his brother Sancho II of Castile and was sent to confinement in Burgos. He was set free six months later and was allowed to reside in Toledo, presumably thanks to the direct miraculous intervention of the first Abbot Hugh of Cluny.[97] Perhaps it was also due – a later source claimed – to the fact that St. Peter himself had appeared in Burgos and demanded Alfonso's release.[98] In turn, Alfonso became the prince in all of Europe who supported Cluny with the largest sums by far, and in 1077, he doubled the gift of his father and promised, for all eternity, to send 2000 dinars in gold every year. After his death too, Alfonso received help from Cluny. One of his loyal soldiers, Pedro Engelbertiz, had become a monk in his old age in the monastery of Nájera, and in 1142, he told Abbot Peter the Venerable of Cluny that he had had a vision. He had seen Alfonso VI tormented by devils together with all the other sinners until he was freed, thanks to the prayers of the Cluniac monks. Abbot Peter relates the story in his book on miracles as an argument against heretics and doubters who deny that intercessory prayers can be of any good to the deceased.[99] Behind the somewhat unusual name Pedro Engelbertiz hides obviously the good Nordic name Peter Engelbrektsen, one tangible example of the ties between Scandinavia and the Iberian Peninsula.[100]

During the 11th century, a network of noblemen who supported the new reform movements emerged via connections to Cluny, and many of them entered into a

72   *Missionary wars of the 11th century*

special dependency to the Pope and became vassals of St. Peter. There were many of those in France, on the Iberian Peninsula and around the edge of Europe. On the other hand, there were only a few German noblemen from the Empire, which probably should come as a surprise, the conflict between Emperor and Pope taken into consideration. The vassals of St. Peter appear to be part of a papal attempt to surround the Emperor with princes loyal to the Pope. Simultaneously, thorough research of the individuals in question shows that the vassals of St. Peter stuck together. A distinctive number of their children were married to other children of St. Peter's vassals, often through several generations.

Svend Estridsen was a vassal of St. Peter,[101] and the marriages of several of his children linked the Danish royal family to princely houses friendly to the papal reform in many places in Western Europe, among them Portugal. The next interesting point is that the great leaders of the first crusade in 1095–1099 were completely dominated by vassals of St. Peter.[102] Under these circumstances it was almost unavoidable that the vassals in both Portugal and in Denmark felt obliged to go on crusade. Together with the obvious ideological obligation, however, there was a series of practical matters that had to be taken into consideration, and they were completely dependent on local affairs. At times, religious wars took place in perfect agreement with religious opponents – against other religious opponents, of course.

Missionary strategies

In the 11th century, missions were carried out by missionaries with a massive backup of armed warriors. However, in order to be able to function in a religious frontier region and to penetrate into the other side of the frontier, it was necessary for the Christians to know about the region and to be motivated. A fixed and uniform pattern emerges in both Denmark and Portugal. The success of the missionary wars depended completely on whether the Christians were facing an opponent that might be united by a common faith but simultaneously divided into conflicting petty kingdoms or tribes. Therefore, the Christian kings allied themselves to changing groupings of their opponents, either through short-lived military ad hoc alliances or through more long-term dynastic political marriage arrangements. Both solutions were put to use in both Denmark and Portugal in the 11th century. In Portugal, we have several sources for the military alliances, and in Denmark the dynastic connections are better known.

The Muslim king of Granada recounts that Alfonso VI of León-Castile, during their negotiations in 1074, was to have said: "Conquest is expensive in men and money, and will cost more than I can ever hope to regain, even if I was to win. And if I win, I shall have a population that I cannot trust because of their religion, and it is practically impossible to kill them all and settle the land with Christians. For this reason, it is better for me to set up one Muslim ruler against the other and demand protection money from all of them. In the end, they will be so weak from their mutual fighting that they will surrender themselves voluntarily to me, and I will reach my goal without straining myself."[103]

Missionary wars of the 11th century 73

This policy of alliance with princes of the other religion was possible because some on the other side of the religious frontier viewed it as being opportune. Some who, whether they themselves converted or not, saw an advantage in fighting together with the Christians – or simply were in such trouble politically that they could see no other way out. Raimundo's expedition against Santarém in 1093 was only possible because Umar of Badajoz had summoned him out of fear of the Almoravids, as mentioned above. The Danish expeditions against the Obotrites in 1019, and again in the 1090s, were only possible because they had the support of a local pretender, Uto at the beginning of the century and Henrik Gotskalksen at the end.

When a region was conquered one way or the other, it had to be secured for Christianity. This was achieved by building churches and establishing monasteries, and in the coming passages we shall take a closer look at how this worked in practice in the 12th and 13th centuries. However, since ancient times a particular way of monastic organization existed on the Iberian Peninsula, so-called *pactism*, which was extended with the conquest of the Christian areas. Pactism considered monastic life a mutual contract between an abbot and a community of monks, who had specific obligations towards each other, which were specified in detail in a written pact. Any monk who broke the pact was to be whipped and excluded from the Communion; any monk who fled the community should be tracked down and brought back, and those who had assisted him, whether secular or priests, were to be excommunicated. A monk who conspired against the abbot was to be severely whipped. In return the abbot promised to rule fairly, and if he became a tyrant, the community of monks could remove him. The pact was entered and sealed at the same time that the abbot presented a gift to the community of monks, usually landed property.[104] These pact monasteries differed from traditional Western monasticism with an all-powerful abbot who could not be deposed and where the monks enter as single individuals. The Iberian pact monasteries were collective and mutual. One possible explanation of this specific way of organization is that it harks back to some Germanic, Visigoth sense of community. Another and reasonable explanation, which does not exclude the first one, could be that it is a way of organization that is well suited to a religiously disputed frontier area. The abbots here also had to make political decisions, which in reality could mean life or death for the monks and, for that reason, it was important to have some control over the abbot. For the same reason, it was important to be able to act as a strong community and punish those who broke away. The collective monastery could also arise from some form of noblemen's private monasteries, for family and friends. The collective organization would indeed have been important for the settling and cultivation of newly conquered land.

The earliest known such monastic pacts are from the 8th century. In 959, the Duchess Mumadona Dias founded the monastery of São Salvador in Guimarães as a pact monastery. From 1045, we have a pact with the pledges of both the monks and the abbot from São Salvador de Vacariça, which later came under the cathedral of Coimbra.[105] The monastery was founded in around 990 and received very substantial landholdings as gifts in the 1020s, and even though the abbot fled

74   *Missionary wars of the 11th century*

from the Muslims to another monastery, São Salvador de Vacariça apparently continued to function under Christian, Muslim and then later again Christian political rule. Unfortunately, we know nothing about how the monasteries were organized in the North during this early period, and there do not seem to be signs of any form of pactism. This might only be down to the lack of sources, because it is certain that the earliest missionary work in the disputed frontier lands was hard and called for special ways of organization.

The shared reason for the military expeditions was to convert the heathens or at least to fight them and limit their extension. And the incentive for the individual participant was to gain indulgence or, as a last resort, to become a martyr and enter Heaven directly. In 1063, Pope Alexander II promised absolution to those fighting in Spain. A few years earlier, the great patriarch of Northern Europe, the Archbishop of Hamburg-Bremen, had promised both Gotskalk and the Danish king Svend Estridsen absolution and the martyr crown of victory if they fought the good strife against the heathens. Thus, the missionary, political and ideological backgrounds were identical in Denmark and Portugal. In both countries there were connections to the papal reform monastery of Cluny, even though older monastic forms continued to exist on the Iberian Peninsula, which were apparently unknown in Scandinavia. The question is whether it is possible to point to any direct connection between Denmark and Portugal in this period and – in a broader perspective – between Scandinavia and the Mediterranean world.

Connections between the Nordic countries and Portugal in the 11th century

The parallel development in Denmark and Portugal is unlikely to be a coincidence. There were regular and close connections throughout the whole of the 11th century and earlier, both between the two countries directly and indirectly, via the Papal see and the Byzantine Empire.

South of the River Tagus the landscape is completely flat with broad views, but spread out over the flat plain are a few isolated hills. One is Palmela, about thirty kilometres south of the river on the peninsula of Setúbal, which is part of a short chain of small, strongly fortified hills. Because of the wide vista, it was an important relay station in military communications long into the 20th century. The hill was fortified during the Muslim era, and one of the extensions of the castle took place in connection with an attack from Scandinavians – *northmanni, lomani, leodemances, piratae* in the Latin sources, *madjus* in the Arab sources. Usually, they cannot be located any more precisely than to somewhere in Scandinavia, but their presence along the western shores of the Iberian Peninsula is stated in the sources, and in order to counter them, both Christian and Muslim rulers strengthened their castles and built strong navies.[106]

The first known attack that is mentioned in the sources took place in the middle of the 9th century. After having raided in France, a group of Scandinavians continued their expedition to Galicia in 844, where they were at first defeated by the Christian King Ramiro of Asturia, and 70 of their 100 ships were burned. The

King and his Queen Urraca celebrated the victory with great gifts to the church in Santiago. However, the Scandinavians were apparently not completely defeated, or maybe they received reinforcements from their compatriots. In either case, they continued southwards, attempted an attack on the Muslim city of Lisbon despite Abd al-Rahman II's strong navy and in the end, they even attacked Seville and plundered its surroundings. Soon after they were put to flight, many were killed and their ships were burned. Some of them where encircled by the Muslim relief armies; they had to convert to Islam and settled in the river valley of the Guadalquivir, where they specialized in producing quality cheese for the markets in Seville and Córdoba.[107] Others managed to flee and went to Africa or back to Scandinavia.

In those years, it seems that the connections between Scandinavia and the Iberian Peninsula were good, and despite differences in religion, there was communication across long distances. When the Scandinavians lost the battle at Seville, their king back in Scandinavia asked for peace. This indicates that it was not just random groups who went plundering, but an expedition initiated and commanded from Scandinavia. Abd al-Rahman therefore chose to send one of his seasoned diplomats, Al-Ghazal, to Scandinavia.[108] Earlier, he had negotiated on behalf of the sultan with the Byzantine emperor. By then he was around fifty years of age and, despite his grey hair, he still lived up to his epithet, which means "the handsome one." Together with his retinue he sailed out from Silves, where two magnificently fitted Northman ships were waiting for them. Off Cape Finis Terre they sailed into a fierce storm but were able to ride it out and reached the land of the Northman, where the ships were repaired. After another three days sail they arrived at the residence of the king, where they received an honourable welcome and many gifts. In his speech of praise, Al-Ghazal wished the king power, a long life and reward in the next life, which lasts for eternity under the protection of the living and eternally one God, without Whom "everything will be destroyed, and His is the judgement, and to Him you will be returned." The last sentence is a quote from the Quran[109] and somewhat subtle, because just before the same verse says: "And do not invoke with Allah another deity. There is no deity except Him." This is an obvious passage to quote against the Christian doctrine of the Trinity. Al-Ghazal and his Arab readership knew this, but the Nordic king possibly did not; at least he was impressed with the praise. The Northmen had been heathens but were Christian now, even though there were still a few adherents of the old faith left on the many islands in the sea. They were fire worshipers – either this was an Arab standard term for heathens or it could have referred to the custom of burning the dead – and they still practised marriage between siblings and other abominations. The Christian Northmen fought the heathens and made them slaves, Al-Ghazal tells us. He also recounts that he spent much time in discussion with their learned men, and that he defeated them with his arguments. This must obviously have concerned God, whether Christianity or Islam was the true religion, and demonstrates clearly that Scandinavia at that time was open to different religious currents. During the reign of King Horik in the 9th century, Denmark shifted between persecutions of Christians and inviting Christian missionaries.

76 *Missionary wars of the 11th century*

During the middle of the 840s, Horik again allowed missionary work and was taught the Christian faith, which he discussed eagerly with the bishop of Hamburg, Ansgar, who had been dispatched to Denmark.[110] Perhaps Ansgar was one of those floored by Al-Ghazal in a theological dispute at the court of Horik, even though the Danes ended up being Christian rather than Muslim.

Al-Ghazal stayed for some time at the royal court, where Queen Nud became rather enthralled by the handsome Arab. He improvised a beautiful Arab love song to her:

> You are weighed down, my heart, by an unsettling passion,
> That you fight, as with a lion.
> I am in love with a Northern woman;
> Who does not want the sun of beauty to set,
> Although she lives on the edge of God's world,
> Where the one who wants to reach her, cannot find a path.

Perhaps Al-Ghazal was blinded by the Northern beauty, perhaps he only exploited the excitement of a slightly naïve queen to obtain diplomatic advantage, as he himself hinted to an acquaintance. However, he promised her that the poem would be disseminated all over Al-Andalus, so that all would get to know the beauty of the Nordic queen and praise her and dream of her. Then he began his journey home. At first, he went to Shent Ya'qub, Santiago in Compostela, where Al-Ghazal delivered a letter from the Scandinavian king to the ruler of Galicia. Then he continued home via Toledo. The content of the letter is not specifically mentioned in the Arab narrative, but its very existence demonstrates at least direct contact between King Ramiro and a Scandinavian king, who might have been King Horik I of Denmark.

Ramiro would have received the letter from the Scandinavian king in the summer of 846, and Latin sources mention that in the same year there were attacks again from Scandinavian ships at Mondoñedo, which were averted thanks to the prayers of the holy Bishop Gundisalvus.[111] A later tradition from Galicia tells us that a ship went down every time he raised his arms towards heaven in prayer. This later tradition also tells us that it was a group of Danes led by Regner, who had just been dispatched to Spain by their king, Horik.[112] Regner's fleet must have accompanied Al-Ghazal home, or their movements were at least coordinated. At first, it is perhaps tempting to see an alliance between Horik and Abd al-Rahman against Ramiro, but this does not fit well with the simultaneous Arab mobilization against the Scandinavians with a naval build-up and fortification of the coast. Perhaps Horik had actually decided to support Christianity and had sent a Christian army on a pilgrimage expedition to Santiago, and then something went wrong.

In 854, Scandinavians were in Galicia again, and three or five years later they were followed by a large new army in seventy ships under the leadership of Bjørn Ironside and Hasting. They were repulsed in Galicia and then continued as far south as Morocco, where after a few bloody battles they took prisoners and then continued eastwards along the Spanish coast to Catalonia and Italy. Over a few hundred years, the stories about Hasting's raid developed into the narrative of how

Missionary wars of the 11th century 77

he had pretended to be a newly converted Christian and dead and in this way was carried inside the city of Luna to be buried. Then he jumped up from the bier and began a massacre and plunder of the city. And how he, to his immeasurable regret, discovered that this was not after the all the city of Rome they had conquered but only a small port city.[113]

The story is a fanciful mix of many other narratives and incidentally wrong – Luna had been plundered and destroyed one hundred years before Hasting arrived in Italy – but there are no reasons to doubt that the famous Scandinavian commander, Hasting from England, also led an army to Galicia.[114] These expeditions put together meant that there was considerable knowledge in Scandinavia on the situation on the Iberian Peninsula. All sorts of items must have found their way from the South to Scandinavia, among them a small number of Muslim coins, dirhems, from Córdoba.[115] Perhaps more people came north than the few diplomats, such as Al-Ghazal, whom we know by name. One Irish source tells about Ragnhnall (Ragnar Lodbrok?) who had been driven out of the Orkney Islands. His three sons wished to win fame and glory so as to be able to return to Scandinavia and win political positions there. Therefore, they first plundered among the Franks and the Saxons. Then they crossed the "Irish Sea" to Spain, where they pillaged and destroyed. Then they crossed the Strait of Gibraltar to Africa and fought the Mauritanians. After having had his hand cut off, the king of the Mauritanians fled, and plundering and massacres followed. More than two out of three Scandinavians were killed, but the rest returned north with many black slaves – *maur* means *black*, the chronicle tells us – "and these black men were in Ireland for a very long time."[116] There must have been a reasonable number of southern and black slaves in Scandinavia, in the same way as large, light-skinned Scandinavian slaves – *saqaliba* – were in demand at the Arab courts.[117]

For approximately one hundred years, the infrequent sources do not mention Scandinavians carrying out raids on the Iberian Peninsula. From the 960s, however, the Scandinavian attacks increase again. In 966, thirty Danish ships sailed into the Bay of Sado to the south of Lisbon and up the river to Alcácer do Sal, where they went ashore and pillaged the Muslim region all the way to Lisbon. Here they were repulsed, but they continued along the coast southwards to Silves, where they were decisively defeated by a Muslim fleet. This group hailed from an army of Danes who had been in the service of Duke Richard of Normandy. Some of them he had managed to get baptized, but those who wanted to keep their heathen religion, he had sent to Spain.[118] As early as in 968, another fleet with 100 ships arrived in Galicia, led by a certain Gundered. They plundered, attacked Santiago and the region far around the city and during Lent, on March 29, they killed Bishop Sisnando of Santiago. They continued to ravage Galicia and the region between the rivers Minho and Douro for some time and were only defeated by Count Gonçalo Sanches, in 970.

The invasions continued. In 1008, the Scandinavians killed Count Mendo Gonçalves in Galicia and continued south up the River Minho all the way to Tuy, indeed almost to Braga. In 1014 or 1015, an expedition arrived under the leadership of Olav, who later became king of Norway and a crusader saint. They too

78 *Missionary wars of the 11th century*

attacked the area along the Minho and all the way to Braga, where the army stayed for nine months and took prominent prisoners, who were to be ransomed by their families. Amarelo Mestaliz, who was ill and frail, went bankrupt and had to sell all his belongings in order to be able to pay the ransom for his three daughters from the Scandinavians.[119] After many months of plundering, Olav's army continued south all the way to Cádiz before it returned to Scandinavia. Later on, there are reports of a Scandinavian army on the coast south of Douro in 1026, but subsequently the sources dry up regarding the remainder of the 11th century. This does not mean that there were no connections between the North and the Iberian Peninsula. The famous warrior Ulf Jarl received the epithet Galicia-Ulf because of his expeditions to Galicia, and they must have taken place after the middle of the 11th century.[120] The objective was probably to participate in the fight to liberate Santiago de Compostela, which had been under Muslim rule since 997.

One individual with the rather Danish name Esbern[121] had been to the region in the late 11th century, at least long enough to have a son. There is a testament from 1117, drawn up by Rodrigo Esberniz, i.e. Rodrigo Esbernson. He made decisions on giving away some of his estate and concludes, as was common in testaments of the day, with a cursing formula against those who would interfere with his decisions, but with a rather unique formulation that is not found in any other Portuguese testament: "If some of my people come from near or afar to try and subvert my testament."[122] Esbern's son Rodrigo considered it feasible that some of his Danish family would come to Portugal to demand an inheritance from him. There were others.

The liberator of Toledo, the defender of Christianity Alfonso VI of León had the aforementioned Pedro Engelbertiz among his soldiers. One of his highest officials was the notary Pelagius Eriquez with the strange epithet Botan, perhaps a son of the Erik who in 1078 laboriously copied a large manuscript with the etymologies of Isidor in his monastery in Silos.[123] We do not know how they were related, but the names Erik and Erikson are obvious signs of a continued connection with Scandinavia through the 11th century. However, there were probably not many individuals, let alone a large and systematic settlement of Scandinavians. For example, there is a lack of place names with a Nordic origin. The only ones that have a slight taste of something Nordic are the two town names *Lordemanos* in León and *Lordemão* near Coimbra in Portugal, which presumably are named after one of the Latin designations for the Scandinavians, *lomani*.[124] That is all.

It is suggestive that there is a temporal coincidence between this second wave of Scandinavian expeditions and the conversion of Harald the Bluetooth. It begins in the 960s. Mostly, Scandinavian historians have viewed these expeditions as pure plundering – if they have dealt with them at all. This goes for Portuguese historians as well; they have also emphasized how the expeditions led to countermeasures from the Muslim side, such as the strengthening of the navy by Abd al-Rahman II and later, and to the fortification of strategic sites, Lisbon, Palmela, among other places. The Christians were also preparing against the Scandinavians. Oviedo in Galicia was fortified in around the year 900, and the church later had an inscription that said that it happened to protect valuables when "the fleet of

Missionary wars of the 11th century   79

the heathens, as it usually does, comes as pirates."[125] Contemporary with the Scandinavian raids, the Duchess Mumadona built the first castle in Guimarães around 970. The Scandinavians came, and the locals defended themselves.

In reality, things were probably somewhat more complicated. At the same time as Scandinavian expeditions, local Christians raided the Muslims and Muslim rulers led expeditions against the Christians both at land and at sea. Sometimes the Muslims supported Christians and vice versa. Usually, the same regions were exposed to attacks again and again. So, we can discern the same pattern of changing alliances across the religious frontiers, as in the Danish and Slavic region during the 10th and 11th centuries.

In 997, al-Mansur began an expedition northwards to the same region that Olav later went to, and he continued all the way to Santiago. He thrust his way ahead with an army on land and was supported by a fleet off the coast. The Christian Count Veila Gonçalves supported al-Mansur and assisted him with an army consisting of Muslims and Christians, but later "God infused in his heart that he should turn to Christianity." Erik Gonçalves surrendered the fortress Maia to his relative Veila and with that to al-Mansur. However, on the way, he took care of himself by taking the estate of Dona Zalamiz and her son Didago, which he had to hand back and compensate later when al-Mansur's expedition had finished and the Muslims had withdrawn. It is from here we know the details of the incident,[126] but it seems to have been typical for the period.[127] Alliances criss-crossed religious frontiers, but individual outrages and individual replacements of political alliances were nevertheless perceived as part of a religious war. When Veila turns away from al-Mansur and reconciles himself with the Galician Counts, it is because God infused him. Similarly, we can surmise that the engagement of the Scandinavians in Galicia and Portugal was connected to the slow advance of Christianity in their home countries. Many of the Scandinavians would have been Christians and, presumably, they perceived fighting the Muslims as a religious obligation. Most of the fighting after the middle of the 10th century took place in Muslim Portugal rather than in Christian Galicia. At the same time, there were Scandinavian raids, plundering and slave hunts in the Christian regions too, which were not necessarily committed by heathen Scandinavians. The Iberian Peninsula in this era demonstrates very clearly that Christians could fight Christians in religious frontier lands too.

The road to the East

Another link, and a very well established one, between Scandinavia and the Mediterranean world went through the Baltic Sea and the great Russian rivers to the Black Sea and Constantinople. Here, the Byzantine emperor had a special force consisting of Scandinavians – the Varangian Guard – loyal elite soldiers armed with the dreaded Nordic battle-axe.[128] In some Byzantine sources they were referred to as the "wine skins," which probably says something about their lifestyle; most contemporary Nordic translations discreetly changed this term to the "friends of the emperor."[129] From the early 12th century, and possibly before, the

80 *Missionary wars of the 11th century*

Varangians had their own church, dedicated to the Virgin Mary and St. Olav. One of the most famous members of this group of soldiers was the Norwegian Harald the Brutal, Hardrada, who received the nickname *Bulgar-burner* for his efficiency in the service of the Byzantine emperor at the northern border of the empire. Harald had fought together with his brother Olav at the battle of Stiklestad in 1030 but had gone to Byzantium after the defeat. He served in the capital but also in many other places in the empire. He pillaged several Muslim cities – where is not known – and in the late 1030s he went to Jerusalem. Two years later, he fought Muslims and rebels in Sicily under the command of the famous Byzantine general and rival emperor Georgios Maniakes. In 1046, Harald returned home and became king of Norway, after having married a princess from Kiev. Through her two sisters, he became brother-in-law to King András I of Hungary and Henry I of France. It seems that he maintained the connections to Byzantium until his death.[130] He fell in England in 1066 at the battle of Stamford Bridge.

Quite a few Scandinavians were in Byzantium and in the Middle East, as one can see from the relatively large number of runic stones in Scandinavia dedicated to the memory of those who died in the South or amongst the Greeks.[131] The presence, however, was spiritual as well. St. Olav's sword was kept in the Varangian church in Constantinople, his helmet was in Antioch and his chain mail in Jerusalem. There was talk amongst the Scandinavians that he had not died at Stiklestad but had been seen in Syria fighting the Muslims.[132] These stories are legends included in the Scandinavian sources and demonstrate that the Holy Land had an exceedingly prominent position in the Scandinavian imagination. This is confirmed in one of the holiest places of Christendom. At some time during the 12th century,[133] the Church of Nativity in Bethlehem was restored and the Byzantine images of saints on the columns were repainted. However, two of them were replaced by new saints. One was St. Olav, the other, the Danish St. Canute.

The Varangian guard consisted of Scandinavians – Danes, Norwegians and Swedes – and of Anglo-Saxons. It seems to have been rather common for young aristocrats to enter the emperor's service for some years and fight in several places, perhaps visit Jerusalem and then return to Scandinavia. This implies that many in Scandinavia had excellent knowledge about the situation in the Byzantine Empire and thus the Holy Land. When the Seljuk Turks were victorious at Manzikert in 1071, a considerable number of Varangians fell as well, despite their long axes. Soon after, people in Denmark would have been aware of the Byzantines' precarious situation. When the first crusade was announced in 1095 to help the Greek brothers against the Turks, it must have resonated widely in Scandinavia.

Apart from direct links between Scandinavia and Byzantium, many indirect connections existed, of which only a few are known today. One of them evidently went through Flanders. The year after King Canute of Denmark was killed in 1086, his father-in-law, Robert I the Frisian of Flanders, went on a pilgrimage to Jerusalem. One direct reason might have been that he had killed Godfrey of Lorraine, the uncle of Godfrey of Bouillon, who later became a famous crusader.

Missionary wars of the 11th century 81

A more overriding reason was his deep faith, for which he was praised at the time. On his way back in 1089, Robert visited the Byzantine emperor, who asked for help. He immediately promised to dispatch a contingency of 500 Flemish knights to fight the Turks. The Knights arrived in Byzantium in 1090 and were brought into action in the campaign at Nicomedia.[134] Due to the close Danish-Flemish connections, Svend Estridsen and his sons were very aware that assisting the Byzantines was a meritorious and a natural thing for a good Christian prince to do.

Who was married to whom?

Through several hundred years there was regular contact between Scandinavia and the Iberian Peninsula, and between the Mediterranean and the Holy Land via two routes, an eastern and a western. There would have been a common Christian ideology in north and south regarding warfare to convert heathens and Muslims. Moreover during the 11th century, Spanish, Portuguese and Danish rulers supported the Cluniac reform movement and they supported papal reform, especially under Gregory VII. Many rulers in these areas became papal vassals and held newly conquered land directly under St. Peter.[135] This was the case for Sancho I of Aragon in 1068 and Alfonso VI of León-Castile; for the counts of Barcelona during the 11th century, presumably for Canute the Great of Denmark, and without doubt for Svend Estridsen and perhaps some of his sons. In this way, they entered into a network where they not only supported the Pope but each other as well through marriages between the princely houses. If one takes a closer look, there is a close connection between the Danish and the Portuguese family lines in the late 11th century.

In around 1080, King Canute IV of Denmark (St. Canute) was married to Adele, who was a daughter of Count Robert I of Flanders, one of the vassals of St. Peter. Exactly at this time, the important monastery of St. Bertin in the city of St. Omer had the brilliant idea of rewriting their annals so that the progenitor of the Flemish counts, Baldwin from the 9th century, became a son of one of Charlemagne's heroes, Ogier the Dane.[136] Adele's brother, Robert II, became one of the main leaders of the first crusade. After King Canute was killed in St. Alban's church in Odense in 1086, Adele returned to Flanders with their son, Carl. The daughters stayed in Denmark and were married off to Swedes; Adele was later married to another of St. Peter's vassals, the Duke Roger Bursa of Apulia, a brother of Bohemund the Norman, another of the heroes of the first crusade.

Adele's sister Gertrude ended up becoming the second wife of Thierry of Lorraine and ancestress of a long dynasty of crusaders all the way through the 12th century; she is one of more examples of how connections to the crusade movement were often established through the women.[137] Adele was named after her paternal grandmother, Princess Adele, a sister to the French King Henry I and a sister to Robert, the first duke of Burgundy, who was married to a sister of Abbot Hugh of Cluny. The grandchild of Robert I of Burgundy was Count Henrique of Portugal. In this way, the Portuguese Henrique and the Danish Adele had great

82 *Missionary wars of the 11th century*

grandparents in common. However, there is an even closer dynastic connection between Portugal and Denmark.

Count Henrique of Portugal was brother to Count Eude I of Burgundy. Eude had a daughter, Florina, who had been married to a prince of Fillipenses, but had been widowed. It was intended that the niece of Henrique was to be married to a Danish prince, Svend, so she followed him on the first crusade, where both of them fell in Anatolia during the summer of 1097.

The connections between Denmark, Flanders, Burgundy and Portugal were closer still. Robert II of Flanders and Eude I of Burgund were married to two sisters. The brother of these sisters was Raimundo, Count of Galicia and cousin to Henrique of Portugal. Or put another way: Robert II had a brother-in-law who was king of Denmark and a son of Svend Estridsen, another brother-in-law who was Count of Galicia and a third brother-in-law who was Duke of Burgundy and a brother to the Count of Portugal and father-in-law to a prince of Denmark, who was a son of Svend Estridsen. Through these two brothers-in-law, the Danish royal house was connected to another of the great heroes of the first crusade, for Raimundo and Henrique were married to the sisters Urraca and Teresa, who had a third sister, Elvira, who was married to Raimund IV Saint-Gilles, Count of Toulouse and the first to take the cross after Urban's sermon in Clermont. Through this network in Flanders and Burgundy, the Danish royal house became related to the most famous crusader of them all, Godfrey of Bouillon, who after 1099 was to become the first ruler of the new, Christian Jerusalem. One sister of Robert II of Flanders was married to the Danish king; another sister was married to the brother of Godfrey the Bearded, the maternal grandfather of Godfrey of Bouillon.

The Danish royal house and the Dukes of Burgundy were so closely intermarried that one can imagine them meeting over a good Christmas lunch discussing how they should rule their lands and extend them. They were at least aware of what each other was doing in political terms. And directly through the family members and via intermediaries, they exchanged thoughts and ideas. The ideological climate in the two countries became analogous. This was the background for the rulers in both places to wholeheartedly join the crusading movement after 1099, and for a parallel development in Denmark and Portugal that took place during the next century or so. This has never really been noted by modern Danish and Portuguese historians, partly for the many historiographical reasons mentioned above but also because the perception of distance and geographical centre and periphery has changed since medieval times. Without this perspective – without becoming medieval again, so to speak – the Danish–Portuguese connections would remain difficult to comprehend and seem improbable.

Notes

1 For the conquest and the immediate aftermath, R. Collins, *The Arab Conquest of Spain 710–797* (Oxford, 1989); the whole Muslim period, Richard A. Fletcher, *Moorish Spain* (London, 1992); Thomas F. Glick, *Islamic and Christian Spain in the Early Middle Ages* (Leiden, 2005) connects conquest with economic and cultural changes.

Missionary wars of the 11th century   83

2 A. H. de Oliveira Marques, 'O "Portugal" islâmico', in: Jean Pierre Leguay, António Henrique R. de Oliveira Marques e Maria Ângela V. da Rocha Beirante (eds.), *Nova História de Portugal* (Lisbon, 1993), vol. 2, pp. 121–249, here pp. 208–211; José Mattoso, *Identificação de um país: ensaio sobre as origens de Portugal, 1096–1325*, vols. 1–2 (Lisbon, 1995), vol. 1, pp. 320–340.

3 Kenneth Baxter Wolf, *Christian Martyrs in Muslim Spain* (Cambridge, 1988); Jessica A. Coope, *The Martyrs of Córdoba: Community and Family Conflict in an Age of Mass Conversion* (Lincoln, 1995).

4 Fortunato de Almeida and Damiao Peres, *História da Igreja em Portugal* (Porto, 1967), p. 74.

5 B. Z. Kedar, *Crusade and Mission: European Approaches Toward the Muslims* (Princeton, NJ, 1984).

6 Literature on the *reconquista* and when it began is huge. See e.g. Maria Ângela Beirante, 'A "reconquista" Cristã', in: Jean Pierre Leguay, Antonio Henrique R. de Oliveira Marques e Maria Ângela V. da Rocha Beirante (eds.), *Nova história de Portugal*, 2 (Lisboa, 2003), pp. 253–263, here pp. 253–255, which after some consideration perceives the reconquista as continuous since the Muslim conquest in 711. For a critique of this idea, e.g. Jose Maria Mínguez, *La Reconquista* (Madrid, 1989); Eduardo Manzano Moreno, *La frontera de al-Andalus en época de los Omeyas* (Madrid, 1991); L. Krus, *Passado, Memoria e Poder na Sociedade Medieval Portuguesa* (Redondo, 1994), pp. 103–127; Eduardo Manzano Moreno, 'The Creation of a Medieval Frontier: Islam and Christianity in the Iberian Peninsula, Eighth to Eleventh Centuries', in: Daniel Power and Naomi Standen (eds.), *Frontiers in Question: Eurasian Borderlands, 700–1700* (New York, 1999), pp. 32–54; Isabel de Barros Dias, 'Cronística afonsina modelada em português: um case de recepção activa', *Hispania* 67 (2007), pp. 899–928, here p. 911; whereas this is cautiously argued for in Alexander Pierre Bronisch, *Reconquista und Heiliger Krieg. Die Deutung des Krieges im christlichen Spanien von den Westgoten bis ins frühe 12. Jahrhundert* (Münster, 1998), (strongly criticized by Patrick Henriet, 'L'idéologie de guerre sainte'; answered briefly by Alexander Pierre Bronisch, 'Reconquista und Heiliger Krieg') and vigorously by J. F. O'Callaghan, *Reconquest and Crusade in Medieval Spain* (Philadelphia, 2003). Regarding the Spanish area, see also Peter Linehan, 'Religion, Nationalism and National Identity in Medieval Spain and Portugal', in: Stuart Mews (ed.), *Religion and National Identity* (Oxford, 1982), pp. 161–199; Fletcher, 'Reconquest and Crusade'; Richard A. Fletcher, *Saint James' Catapult: The Life and Times of Diego Gelmirez of Santiago de Compostela* (Oxford, 1984); Peter Linehan, *History and the Historians of Medieval Spain* (Oxford, 1993) with the chapter "The Invention of the Reconquista." When the *reconquista* actually began, is perhaps a question of how it is defined; in any case, so many changes took place in history writing and liturgy after 1100 inspired by the first crusade that it is difficult to maintain the idea of continuity.

7 David Wasserstein, *The Rise and Fall of the Party-Kings: Politics and Society in Islamic Spain 1002–1086* (Princeton, NJ, 1985); Clay Stalls, *Possessing the Land: Aragon's Expansion Into Islam's Ebro Frontier Under Alfonso the Battler, 1104–1134* (Leiden, 1995). For the taifa kingdoms as a prelude to confrontation and crusades, see Hanna E. Kassis, 'Muslim Revival in Spain in the Fifth/Eleventh Century. Causes and Ramifications', *Islam* 67 (1990), pp. 79–83.

8 Several examples in Fletcher, 'Reconquest and Crusade', p. 35, who uses them as an argument against the idea of a continuous *reconquista* from the 9th century.

9 Stalls, *Possessing the Land*, p. 10.

10 Beirante, 'A "reconquista" Cristã', p. 264.

11 Simon Barton, *The Aristocracy in Twelfth-Century Leon and Castile* (Cambridge, 1997), p. 109.

84   *Missionary wars of the 11th century*

12 Paulus, *Geschichte des Ablasses*, vol. 1, pp. 138–140; Ane L. Bysted, *The Crusade Indulgence. Spiritual Rewards and the Theology of the Crusades c. 1095–1216* (Leiden, 2015), pp. 79–80.

13 Barbastro has been singled out as a kind of a proto-crusade by Carl Erdmann, *Die Entstehung des Kreuzzugsgedankens* (Stuttgart, 1935), pp. 124–127, a point which Fletcher, 'Reconquest and Crusade', p. 43 clearly rejects. Bull, *Knightly Piety*, pp. 72ff. argues against the view that the Pope should have given indulgences for fighting against the Muslims at that time. Bull's arguments are scrutinized and rejected by Jean Flori, *Croisade et chevalerie: XIe-XIIe siécles* (Bruxelles, 1998), pp. 54–59. Riley-Smith argues that the indulgence was given to pilgrims, not to warriors (*The First Crusaders, 1095–1131* (Cambridge, 1997), p. XX). See also Alberto Ferreiro, 'The Siege of Barbastro 1064–65: A Reassessment', *Journal of Medieval History* 9 (1983), pp. 129–144.

14 *Epistolae pontificum romanorum ineditae*, ed. Samuel Loewenfeld (Graz, 1959), no. 82 and no. 83.

15 Erdmann, *Die Entstehung*, p. 123.

16 Adam of Bremen, *Adami Gesta Hammaburgensis ecclesiae pontificum*, ed. J.M. Lappenberg (Hannover, 1876), lib. 4, cap. 35.

17 Reg. Greg. VII: *Das Register Gregors VII*, ed. Erich Caspar, vols. 1–2 (Berlin, 1967) [1920], I, 7.

18 Ibid., I, 46. In 1074, Gregory reacted to an appeal from Byzantium and called for the Christians in the West to help. They were to assist militarily and free Byzantium from the infidel, and Gregory would lead the expedition himself. It came to nothing because of problems with the Holy Roman Emperor and because there was nothing like the same reaction as to Pope Urban II's sermon twenty years later. The immediate cause of Gregory's plan must have been the Seljuk victory at Manzikert in 1071. For Gregory's plans of leading a war against Muslims, see H.E.J. Cowdrey, 'Pope Gregor VII's "Crusading" Plans of 1074', in: B. Kedar, H.E. Mayer and R.C. Smail (eds.), *Outremer* (Jerusalem, 1982), pp. 27–40; Uta-Renate Blumenthal, *Gregor VII. Papst zwischen Canosa und Kirchenreform* (Darmstadt 2001), pp. 123–136; for the Seljuks, see Claude Cahen, *Orient et Occident au temps des croisades* (Paris, 1983), and his *The Formation of Turkey. The Seljukid Sultanate of Rūm* (Harlow, 2001) [1988]; as the background for Urban's speech in Clermont, see Christopher Tyerman, *God's War. A New History of the Crusades* (London, 2006), pp. 49–50.

19 Reg. Greg. VII, IV, 28.

20 Muslim sources state that Alfonso took the title "Emperor over the religions;" quoted in Fidel González Fernández, 'El contexto historico de la "reconquista" española y la Orden trinitaria (Ordo Sanctae Trinitatis et Captivorum)', in: Giulio Cipollone (ed.), *La liberazione dei 'captivi' tra cristianità e islam. Oltre la crociata e il ğihād: Tolleranza e servizio umanitario* (Città del Vaticano, 2000), pp. 131–159, here p. 134. Alfonso named himself "Emperor over two religions," Kassis, 'Muslim Revival', p. 98. Already in 1077, Alfonso had taken the title imperator totius hispaniae, which in different formulations goes back to the 10th century; O'Callaghan, *Reconquest and Crusade*, p. 29.

21 PL 151, cols. 289–290.

22 Annales Compostellani. "vir illustris et magnæ potentiæ et quasi magni consilii Angelus et catholicus." The place is a quote from Isaiah 9, 6, but rendered according to the Latin retranslation of the Greek Septuaginta, and not to the Latin Vulgata (which uses the expression admirabilis consiliarius). The Latin Septuaginta was probably far better known on the Iberian Peninsula than in the rest of Western Europe because of a greater linguistic awareness in the discussions with Jewish communities. The expression magni consilii angelus, however, was known and quoted from Petrus Comestor (Historia scolastica, PL 198, col. 1500; PL 198, col. 1723) to Bernard of Clairvaux (In circumcision, PL 183, col. 134; in Cantica canticorum, PL 183, col. 1038), and it was

Missionary wars of the 11th century 85

used in the liturgy for the ordinary Christmas service; see Heinrich Husmann, 'Sinn und Wesen der Tropen veranschaulicht an den Introitustropen des Weihnachtsfestes', *Archiv für Musikwissenschaft* 16 (1959), pp. 135–147.

23 For the earliest Muslim dynasties in Al-Andalus, see 'Abdulwahid Dhanun Taha, *The Muslim Conquest and Settlement of North Africa and Spain* (London, 1989), relying on Arab historical writing. Almoravids and Almohads, see Fletcher, *Moorish Spain*; Bernard F. Reilly, *The Contest of Christian and Muslim Spain 1031–1157* (Oxford, 1992); Hugh Kennedy, *Muslim Spain and Portugal: A Political History of al-Andalus* (London, 1996). Kassis, 'Muslim Revival', connects the arrival of the Almoravids to the Iberian Peninsula with an increased conflict between Christians and Muslims. Glick, *Islamic and Christian Spain*, pp. 184–219 (the section Ethnic Relations, esp. pp. 202ff.) emphasizes the differences in the Muslim population internally and how Muslims with Arab background feared a berberization from the Almoravids and earlier.

24 Bernard F. Reilly, *The Kingdom of Leon-Castille Under King Alfonso VI, 1065–1109* (Princeton, NJ, 1988), pp. 116–117.

25 The many family connections in the remainder of this book are based on António Caetano de Sousa, *História Genealógica da Casa Real Portuguesa* (Lisbon, 1748); national biographies from several countries, and general reference works.

26 Luíz Gonzaga de Azevedo, *História de Portugal*, vols. 1–6 (Lisboa, 1935–1944), vol. 3, pp. 33ff.

27 Ibid., vol. 3, p. 178, dates the takeover to 1097. The uncertainty is attributable to, among other things, the fact that Henrique acted as lord or governor of Coimbra, Braga and Tordesillas, respectively, during the years of 1095–1097; see also Ibid., 177.

28 The discussion is summarized in Marcelle Caetano, *História do direito portugues: Fontes – direito publico (1140–1495)* (Lisbon, 1992), pp. 136–147.

29 DPM I: 1, no. 2. The dating of this agreement is disputed. Reilly, *The Kingdom of Leon-Castille Under King Alfonso VI*, p. 276 says 1094–1095; according to Charles Julian Bishko, 'Count Henry of Portugal, Cluny, and the Antecedents of the Pacto Succesorio', *Revista Portuguesa de História* 13 (1971), pp. 155–188, it is 1104–1105; see also Jose Maria Soto Rabános, '¿Se puede hablar de un entramado político religiose en el proceso de independencia de Portugal?', *Hispania* 67 (2007), pp. 795–826, here pp. 799–802.

30 Classical is Hellmuth H. Andersen, *Danevirke og Kovirke. Arkæologiske undersøgelser 1861–1992* (Aarhus, 1998); see also Andres Minos Dobat, 'A contested heritage – the Dannevirke as a mirror and object of military and political history', in: Michael Bregnsbo and Kurt Villads Jensen (eds.), *Schleswig Holstein – Contested Region(s) Through History* (Odense, 2016), pp. 193–218. Research history in Jørgen Jensen, *Danmarks Oldtid*, vols. 1–4 (Copenhagen, 2001–2004), vol. 4, pp. 244ff. Whether the Dannevirke was Northern Europe's largest fortification in the early Middle Ages depends on the definition of fortification and of early Middle Ages.

31 Adam of Bremen, 4, 1.

32 Anne Nørgård Jørgensen, 'Naval Bases in Southern Scandinavia from the 7th to the 12th Century', in: Anne Nørgård Jørgensen, John Pind, Lars Jørgensen, and Birthe L. Clausen (eds.), *Maritime Warfare in Northern Europe* (Copenhagen, 2002), pp. 125–152.

33 Esben Albrechtsen, '700–1523', in: Carsten Due-Nielsen, Ole Feldbæk, and Nikolaj Petersen (eds.), *Dansk Udenrigspolitiks Historie* (Copenhagen, 2001), pp. 10–215; Jensen, *Danmarks Oldtid*, vol. 4, p. 251.

34 Alcuin, *Vita sancti Willibrordi, Monumenta Alcuiniana*, ed. Wilhelm Wattenbach and Ph. Jaffé (Berlin, 1873), pp. 39–61, cap. 9. Early mission in Northern Europe generally, Ian Wood, *The Missionary Life: Saints and the Evangelisation of Europe, 400–1050* (Harlow, 2001); *The Cross Goes North: Processes of Conversion in Northern Europe, AD 300–1300*, ed. Martin Carver (London, 2003). Early mission in Denmark, see Jensen, *Danmarks Oldtid*, pp. 500–512; *Kristendommen i Danmark for 1050*, ed. Niels Lund (Roskilde, 2004).

86   Missionary wars of the 11th century

35 Ermoldus Nigellus, *In Honorem Hludovici Elegiacum Carmen*, ed. Edmond Faral (Paris, 1932), 1882–2513.
36 Rimbert, *Vita Anskarii*, ed. Georg Waitz (Hannover, 1977), 1, 7.
37 Niels Lund, 'Horik den Førstes udenrigspolitik', *Historisk Tidsskrift* 102 (2002), pp. 1–20.
38 Epistola ad Heriveum, PL 131, cols. 27–29.
39 Widukind, 65.
40 The epithet "the Good" comes from his wife, Tove Mistivojsdatter's rune stone to the memory of her mother, Sønder Vissing I; DR 55.
41 Jensen, *Danmarks Oldtid*, vol. 4, pp. 371–381. Excavation history in Knud J. Krogh, *Gåden om kong Gorms grav. Historien om nordhøjen i Jelling* (Herning, 1993), who argues that Gorm has been moved from a heathen to a Christian burial. This has been vigorously criticized, e.g. Harald Andersen, 'The Graves of the Jelling Dynasty', *Acta Archaeologica* 66 (1996), pp. 281–300; Knud Ottosen and Michael H. Gelting, 'Kong Gorms mulige begravelse', *Svundne tider* 10 (2007), pp. 42–48.
42 Robert Bartlett, *The Making of Europe: Conquest, Colonization, and Cultural Change, 950–1350* (London, 1993), pp. 280–288; Brita Malmer, 'Kristna symboler på danske mynt ca. 825–1050', in: Niels Lund (ed.), *Kristendommen i Danmark for 1050* (Roskilde, 2004), pp. 75–85.
43 Jensen, *Danmarks Oldtid*, vol. 4, pp. 381–392. The Trelleborgs have been interpreted as assembly points for the Viking army before the raids against England, but with dendrochronology they could with certainty be placed under Harald when there were no known raids against England; N. Bonde and K. Christensen, 'Trelleborgs alder. Dendrokronologisk datering', *Aarbøger for Nordisk Oldkyndighed og Historie* 1982 (1984), pp. 111–152. It was then suggested that they were constructed to support Harald's conquest of all of Denmark; Tage E. Christiansen, 'Trelleborg og Pine Mølle', *Aarbøger for nordisk Oldkyndighed og Historie* 1989 (1989), pp. 9–98. The castles might have had several purposes at the same time but their distribution across Denmark fits best with the interpretation of Tage E. Christiansen.
44 The circular castle excavated at Trelleborg in Scania is not as regular as the other ring castles and is likely older; Martin Borring Olesen, 'Trelleborg eller ej? – om den skånske trelleborgs tilknytning til de danske ringborge', *KUML. Årbog for Jysk Arkæologisk Selskab* 2000 (2000), pp. 91–111.
45 Søren Sindbæk, 'Enigmatic Viking Fortress discovered in Denmark', 2014, at http://www.danmarksborgcenter.dk/sites/default/files/mediearkiv/pdf/pm_eng_csi_3_9_2014_hg.pdf, accessed 20 May 2015.
46 Lise Gotfredsen and Hans Jørgen Frederiksen, *Troens Billeder. Romansk kunst i Danmark* (Copenhagen, 2003), pp. 145–148 and passim.
47 *The Apocalyptic Year 1000. Religious Expectation and Social Change, 950–1050*, ed. Richard Landes, Andrew Gow and David van Meter (Oxford, 2003).
48 Leif Chr. Nielsen, 'Hedenskab og kristendom. Religionsskiftet i vikingetidens grave', in: Peder Mortensen and Birgit M. Rasmussen (eds.), *Høvdingesamfund og Kongemagt* (Aarhus, 1991), pp. 245–267.
49 Adam of Bremen, 2, 34.
50 Nielsen 'Hedenskab og kristendom'. The source for Toke Trylle is *Genealogica Absalonis*.
51 Adam of Bremen, 3, 55.
52 Ibid., 2, 25–26. Adam's description of Harald was repeated unchanged in the annals of Lund in the 12th century.
53 Wolfgang Seegrün, *Das Papsttum und Skandinavien* (Neumünster, 1967), p. 49.
54 Adam of Bremen, 2, 49.
55 Ibid., 2, 53.
56 DD 1:1, no. 395 from 1019; no. 405 from 1020–1035; 407 from 1021–1023; 414 from 1023; 416 from 1024; 424 from 1027–1035; 429 from 1031; 430 from the same

year; 434 from 1032; 436 from 1033. In other letters, Canute used the title rector or gubernator.

57 PL 138, the years 964, 966, 974.

58 DD 1:1, no. 386 from 1018.

59 Roberta Frank, 'King Cnut in the Verse of His Skalds', in: Alexander R. Rumble (ed.), *The Reign of Cnut: King of England, Denmark and Norway* (London, 1994) pp. 106–124; here pp. 110–113.

60 From William of Malmesbury, *Gesta regum Anglorum* = The History of the English Kings, ed. R.A.B. Mynors, Rodney M. Thomson and Michael Winterbottom (Oxford, 1998), vols. 1–2, 183, 1–9.

61 Skovgaard-Petersen, Inge, 'Oldtid og Vikingetid', in: Aksel E. Christensen, H.P. Clausen, Svend Ellehøj, and Søren Mørch (eds.), *Danmarks Historie* (Copenhagen, 1977), vol. 1, pp. 15–209, here pp. 187–188; E. Christiansen, *The Northern Crusades: The Baltic and the Catholic Frontier 1100–1525* (London, 1980), pp. 199–200.

62 Seegrün, *Das Papstum*, p. 65; Tore Nyberg, *Monasticism in North-Western Europe, 800–1200* (Aldershot, 2000), p. 89, considers that St. Michael was presumably founded under Bishop Radulf (1026–1047) and presumably with Cluniac inspiration. He concludes nevertheless that during the first half of the 12th century there are no signs of monastic life in Scandinavia, and that there is nothing to support the notion that Canute the Great was to have introduced Benedictine monastic life in Denmark (pp. 169, 173).

63 Christian Radtke, 'Die Entwicklung der Stadt Schleswig: Funktionen, Strukturen und die Anfange der Gemeindebildung', in: Erich Hoffmann and Frank Lubowitz (eds.), *Die Stadt im westlichen Ostseeraum: Vorträge zur Stadtgründung und Stadterweiterung im hohen Mittelalter* (Frankfurt a.M., 1995), pp. 47–91, here p. 68.

64 Frank, 'King Cnut', p. 116.

65 In the sermon of the Arcbishop of Mainz, see also Franz-Reiner Erkens, 'Vicarius Christi – Sacratissimus Legislator – Sacra Majestas. Religiöse Herrschaftslegitimierung im Mittelalter', *Zeitschrift der Savigny Stiftung für Rechtsgeschichte: Kanonistische Abteilung* 89 (2002), pp. 1–55. The title of Vicarius Christi dates back to the Ottonians.

66 William of Malmesbury, 183, 8. In 1104 Pope Paschal II wrote to the Danish bishops about the Peter's pence, which had been set up by the bishops' predecessors.

67 Herluf Nielsen, 'Peterspenge', *KLNM* 13 (Copenhagen, 1956–78), pp. 249–252.

68 DD 1:1, no. 428, cf. M.J. Toswell, 'St Martial and the Dating of Late Anglo-Saxon Manuscripts', *Scriptorium* 51 (1997), pp. 3–14; also Richard Landes, *Relics, Apocalypse, and the Deceits of History. Ademar of Chabannes, 989–1034* (Cambridge, 1995).

69 *Magnúss saga ins góða*, in Snorri Sturluson. *Heimskringla*, IF 28, pp. 3–67, chapter 27–28.

70 Adam of Bremen, 2, 75.

71 C.J. Becker, 'Magnus den Godes Hedeby-mønter – De første danske erindringsmønter', *Nordisk Numismatisk Unions Medlemsblad* 1983 (1983), pp. 42–47.1983.

72 Magnúss saga ins góða, chapter 27–28.

73 Morten Pedersen, *Det tidlige kirkebyggeri og sognedannelsen på Falster*, unpublished dissertation, University of Southern Denmark (Odense, 1999).

74 Adam of Bremen, 3, 21.

75 Ibid., 2, 24.

76 Ibid., 2, 43.

77 Ibid., 2, 66; Helmold of Bosau, *Helmoldi presbyteri Chronica Slavorum*, ed. G.H. Pertz (Hannover, 1868), cap. 19.

78 Adam of Bremen, 3, 19.

79 Ibid., 3, 18.

80 Michael Müller-Wille, *Mittelalterliche Grabfunde aus der Kirche des slawischen Burgwalles von Alt Lübeck: zu dynastischen Grablegen in polnischen und abodritischen Herrschaftsgebieten* (Stuttgart, 1996).

88 *Missionary wars of the 11th century*

81 DD 1:2, no. 10.
82 DD 1:2, no. 11.
83 Morris, *Papal Monarchy*, pp. 109ff.; Cowdrey, *Pope Gregory VII*, pp. 559–560.
84 Reg. Gre. VII, I, 75; 13.4.1074, to Phillip of France; I, 83; 9.5.1074, to Alfonso VI of León-Castile; IV, 28; 28.6.1077, to kings and nobles in Spain. On Gregory and kings and nobles, see also Rudolf Schieffer, 'Gregor VII und die Könige Europas', *Studi Gregoriani* 13 (1989), pp. 189–211; Blumenthal, *Gregor VII*, pp. 290–298.
85 In January 1075, Gregory was probably not thinking of the German Emperor Henry IV, with whom he entered into a conflict only in the summer of 1075; Blumenthal, *Gregor VII*, p. 151, p. 162, pp. 290–298. For the battle of Manzikert, se Cahen, *Orient et Occident*; Cahen, *The Formation of Turkey.*
86 As interpreted by Koch, *Kongemagt*, pp. 51–55.
87 For the history of the Varangian Guard in general, see Sigfús Blöndal, *The Varangians of Byzantium* (Cambridge, 1978).
88 Erdmann, *Die Entstehung*, pp. 108–110.
89 Kenneth Baxter Wolf, *Making History: The Normans and Their Historians in Eleventhcentury Italy* (Philadelphia, 1995).
90 Reg. Greg. VII, I, 46; cf. Wolf, *Making History*, pp. 26–27, pp. 48–56.
91 About the roles of vassals of St. Peter during the first crusade, see Riley-Smith, *The First Crusaders.*
92 Cowdrey, *Pope Gregory VII*, p. 470. He refers to P. Ewald, 'Die Papstbriefe der Brittschen Sammlung', *Neues Archiv der Gesellschaft für ältere deutsche Geschichte* 5, 2 (1880), pp. 277–596, here no. 2, pp. 359–360.
93 Charles Julian Bishko, 'Liturgical Intercession at Cluny for the King-Emperors of Leon', *Studia Monastica* 3 (1961), pp. 53–76, p. 55.
94 Odilo, epistola 2; PL 142, col. 941 (Psalms 122, Psalms 3). Both are short, and especially Psalm 3 is a strong testimony about the persecuted king who puts all his faith in the Lord.
95 Bishko, 'Liturgical Intercession', pp. 57–58.
96 The expression is from Ibid., p. 61.
97 Charles Julian Bishko, 'Fernando I and the Origins of the Leonese-Castilian Alliance with Cluny', in: C.J. Bishko (ed.), *Studies in Medieval Spanish Frontier History* (London, 1980), pp. 1–136 [1968/69]; Bishko, 'Liturgical Intercession', p. 65.
98 *Crónica Najerense*, ed. Antonio Ubieto Arteta (Zaragoza, 1985), pp. 111–113.
99 Petrus Venerabilis, De miraculis, PL 189, cols. 903–907.
100 According to verbal communication with the Institute for Onomastics, University of Copenhagen, Engelbrekt is a purely Nordic form and is unlikely to relate to any name with roots in the Iberian Peninsula.
101 DD 1:2, no. 17. That Svend always exhibited "oboedientie reuerentiam circa beati Petri apostoli honorem" must mean that he was a vassal of St. Peter.
102 Riley-Smith, *The First Crusaders.*
103 Abd Allah. *El siglo XI en 1a persona: Las "Memorias" de Abd Allah, último Rey Zirí de Granada destronado por los Almorávides (1090)*, traducidas par E. Lévi-Provençal y Emilio García Gomez (Madrid, 1980), p. 163.
104 Charles Julian Bishko, 'Portuguese Pactual Monasticism in the Eleventh Century: The Case of São Salvador de Vacariça', *Estudios de História de Portugal*, vol. ecs. X–XV. Homenagem a A.H. de Oliveira Marques (Lisboa, 1982), pp. 139–154.
105 LP 153, cf. 137, 148 and 150.
106 A.H. de Oliveira Marques, *História de Portugal: Das Origens ao Renascimento* (Lisbon, 1997), vol. 1; Jaime Ferreiro Alemparte, *Arribadas de normandos y cruzados a las costas de la Península Ibérica* (Madrid, 1999).
107 Évariste Lévi-Provencal, *Histoire de l'Espagne musulmane*, vols. 1–3 (Paris, 1950–1967), vol. 1, p. 224.

Missionary wars of the 11th century 89

108 W.E.D. Allen, *The Poet and the Spae-Wife. An Attempt to Reconstruct Al-Ghazal's Embassy to the Vikings* (London, 1960). Contrary to most early researchers, Allen thinks that Al-Ghazal's diplomatic mission went to a Scandinavian king in Ireland. However, his arguments are not convincing. Judging by the distances by ship, we are probably dealing with a king in contemporary Denmark rather than Norway or Sweden.

109 The Quran, 28, 88.

110 Rimbert, Vita Anskarii, 24. His mission to Horik took place in around 845, not around 850, see introduction to chapter 24.

111 Liudprand (?), Adversaria, in PL 136, col. 1145.

112 A. Fabricius, *Forbindelserne mellem Norden og den Spanske Halvø i ældre Tider* (Copenhagen, 1882), p. 56.

113 Dudo. *Dudonis de moribus et actis primorum Normanniae ducum*, PL 141, cols. 609–758; on Hasting cols. 621–625. Dudo wrote in around 1015–1030.

114 Angelo Forte, Richard Oram, and Frederik Pedersen, *Viking Empires* (Cambridge, 2005), pp. 62–63.

115 Anne Kromann, 'Finds of Iberian Islamic Coins in the Northern Lands', in: Mario Gomes Marques and D.M. Metcalf (eds.), *Problems of Medieval Coinage in the Iberian Area. A Symposium Held By the Sociedade numismática scalabitana and the Instituto de Sintra on 4–8 October, 1988* (Santarem, 1988), pp. 243–253.

116 Fragmentery Annals of Ireland, FA 330.

117 On the northern European slave trade through Dublin, see Poul Holm, 'The Slavetrade of Dublin, Ninth to Twelfth Century', *Peritia* 5 (1988), pp. 317–345.

118 Dudo, col. 740–747.

119 Rui Pinto de Azevedo, 'A expedicão de Almançor a Santiago de Compostela em 997, e a de piratas normandos à Galiza em 1015–16', *Revista Portuguesa de História* 14 (1973), pp. 73–93.

120 Knytlinga saga, chapter 75; Saxo 12.1.1.

121 According to Institute of Onomastics, University of Copenhagen, Esbern is a Danish form of the name, neither Swedish nor Norwegian.

122 DMP IV:1, no. 47: "si quidem quod fieri negauero aut aliquis homo uenerit de gente mea tam de propinquis quam de extraneis qui hunc testamentum meum inrumpere quesierit, . . . Another testament (or a different version of the same) of Rodrigo's has a more common wording: si nos, aut aliquis homo venerit, tam propinquis quam extraneis" LP 44.

123 Historia Silense, Introduction, p. 87.

124 Vicente Almazán, 'Vikingerne i Galicien', in: Christopher Bo Bramsen (ed.), *Vikingerne pa Den Iberiske Halvø*, udg. Christopher Bo Bramsen (Madrid, 2004), pp. 41–51, here p. 51.

125 Fabricius, *Forbindelserne*, p. 68.

126 Azevedo, 'A expedicão de Almançor'.

127 Another example is Osorio Díaz, who was reproached by King Bermudo II for having followed Al-Mansur "contra gentem et patriam nostrum;" Amancio Isla, 'Warfare and Other Plagues in the Iberian Peninsula Around the Year 1000', in: Przemysław Urbańczyk (ed.), *Europe Around the Year 1000* (Warsaw, 2001), pp. 233–246, here p. 237.

128 On the Road to the East and Scandinavians in Byzantium, see R. M. Dawkins, 'The Later History of the Varangian Guard: Some Notes', *The Journal of Roman Studies* 37 (1947), pp. 39–46; *Varangian Problems. Report on the First International Symposium on the Theme "The Easter Connections of the Nordic Peoples in the Viking Period and the Early Middle Ages"*, ed. Knud Hannestad, Knud Jordal, and Ole Klindt- Jensen (Copenhagen, 1970); Ellis Davidson, *The Viking Road to Byzantium* (London, 1976); Blöndal, *The Varangians*; Simon Franklin and Jonathan Shepard,

90 *Missionary wars of the 11th century*

The Emergence of Rus, 750–1200 (London, 1996); Krijnie Ciggar, 'Denmark and Byzantium from 1184–1212. Queen Dagmar's Cross, a Chrysobull of Alexius III and an "ultramarine" Connection', *Mediaeval Scandinavia* 13 (2000), pp. 118–143. Until 1204 there was a permanent guard of Varangians in Byzantium, presumably around 5000 men, from around 1100 probably half Scandinavian, half English. Service in the imperial guard was apparently a family tradition, and Byzantine emperors wrote directly to Scandinavian kings to ask for more men, for example in 1195; see the summary in Donald E. Queller and Thomas F. Madden, *The Fourth Crusade: The conquest of Constantinople* (Philadelphia, 1997), p. 107. The connections to Denmark were good and frequent. When Bishop Absalon defeated Prince Bugislav in Pomerania in 1185, the rumour of his victory spread to Byzantium with lightning speed, as Absalon was later told by some of his own knights, who did service there; see Saxo, 16.5.11.

129 Davidson, *The Viking Road*, p. 191.
130 Until his death, he continued to show loyalty and to be a friend of the emperor, according to Byzantine sources; see Ivan Dujčev, 'Les Normands a Byzance et dans la peninsule des Balkans', in: Knud Hannestad, Knud Jordal, and Ole Klindt-Jensen (eds.), *Varangian Problems. Report on the First International Symposium on the Theme "The Easter Connections of the Nordic Peoples in the Viking Period and the Early Middle Ages"* (Copenhagen, 1970), pp. 201–208, here p. 205.
131 Else Roesdahl, *Vikingernes verden* (Copenhagen, 1993), p. 213, p. 315. In Sweden, around twenty-five runic stones were erected to the memory of those who participated in Ingvar's ill-fated expedition around 1040. One of them ends: "Tola raised this stone after his son Harald, Ingvar's brother. Valiantly, they travelled far for gold, and in the east, they gave food to the eagle. They died in the south in Serkland."
132 Gerd Wolfgang Weber, 'Saint Olafr's Sword. Einarr Skulason's *Geisli* and Its Trondheim Performance AD 1153 – A Turning Point in Norwego-Icelandic Scaldic Poetry', in: Gerd Wolfgang Weber (ed.), *Mythos und Geschichte – Essays zur Geschichtsmythologie Skandinaviens in Mittelalter und Neuzeit* (Trieste, 2001), pp. 145–151. For Olav as a crusader in the Nordic skald tradition, see also Hans-Peter Naumann, 'Nordische Kreuzzugsdichtung', in: Hans-Peter Naumann, Magnus von Platen and Stefan Sonderegger (eds.), *Festschrift für Oskar Bandle zum 60. Geburtstag am 11. Januar 1986* (Basel, 1986), pp. 175–189, here pp. 178–180.
133 Jaroslav Folda, 'Art in the Latin East, 1098–1291', in: J. Riley-Smith (ed.), *Oxford Illustrated History of the Crusades* (Oxford, 1995), pp. 141–159, dates it to around 1130 (p. 143); Niels Skyum-Nielsen, *Kvinde og Slave* (Copenhagen, 1971), p. 82, to the 1160s.
134 M.M. Knappen, 'Robert II of Flanders in the First Crusade', in: Louis J. Paetow (ed.), *The Crusades and Other Historical Essays Presented to Dana C. Munro by His Former Students* (New York, 1928), pp. 79–100.
135 Reg. Greg. VII, I, 7; Flori, *Croisade et chevalerie*, p. 36.
136 Knud Togeby, *Ogier le danois dans les littératures européennes* (Copenhagen, 1969), p. 49; refers to Chrétien César Auguste Dehaisnes, *Les annales de Saint-Bertin et de Saint-Vaast: suivies de fragments d'une chronique inédite, pub. avec des annotations et les variantes des manuscrits, pour la Société de l'histoire de France* (Paris, 1871), p. 298.
137 see generally Thérèse de Hemptinne, 'Les épouses des croisés et pèlerins flamands aus XIe et XIIe siècles: L'exemple des comtesses de Flandre Clémence et Sibylle', in: Michel Balard (ed.), *Autour de la première croisade. Actes du Colloque de la Society for the Study of the Crusades and the Latin East (Clermont-Ferrand, 22–25 juin 1995)* (Paris, 1996), pp. 83–95; Jonathan Riley-Smith, 'Family Traditions and Participation in the Second Crusade', in: Michael Gervers (ed.), *The Second Crusade and the Cistercians* (New York, 1992), pp. 101–108.

4 Is the edge of the world far away?

Distance is a geographical as well as a mental notion. To the very first crusaders in the early 12th century, the centre was France. Thus the countries around France mentally occupied the periphery, far away, at the edge of the ocean. The same image was used by successive Popes in both the 12th and 13th centuries; they designated both Denmark and Portugal as being placed by "the outermost edge of the world." This, however, reflects a mental geography centred on Rome in a Christian continent surrounded with water. It is a written tracing of the graphical image of the whole world, as it is known from circular maps or T maps.[1] One of the most famous is the Hereford mappa mundi from the middle of the 12th century, which shows Jerusalem as the centre of the world and the three parts of the inhabitable world, the continents Europa, Asia and Africa. This image is in turn a magnification, an extension of the image of the Holy City, the heavenly but also the earthly Jerusalem, which is circular and separated into four parts by a cross that consists of the four great roads from the four city gates. The Holy Sepulchre and Golgotha are at the centre of Jerusalem, and thereby the centre of the whole world. A beautiful rendering of this Jerusalem is from an illustration for an early copy – from the middle of 12th century – of Robert the Monk's crusading history and of the anonymous Gesta Francorum, which has been in Danish ownership and is now kept at the University Library at Uppsala.[2]

During the Middle Ages the world was perceived as a circle with a centre and a periphery, but this was a mental image. At times it meant that the periphery was far away, perhaps barbaric and primitive. On some world maps, the periphery was home to monsters on the frontier between human and demonic. The periphery was dangerous. However, this also made the periphery an exceedingly important area, because here was a frontier that needed defence or to be moved further out. Spiritual as well as military defence was especially important in the periphery. Here it was possible to cross the frontier to the non-Christian and demonic world but for this very reason, it was here too that people with greater spiritual energy journeyed to fight for Christianity. There was simply more holiness at the periphery than at the centre, generally speaking.[3] In this way, the comments of the earliest crusader historians, about the barbarians helping out with their prayers, become not only an empty phrase to barbarize those from the North and ridicule their efforts. It also reflects the medieval perception, that it was on distant islands

92   *Is the edge of the world far away?*

and in dark forests or wild deserts amongst the heathens that most holy men and hermits lived. "You came from the borders of the earth but filled with faith and dedication," the Cistercians in Clairvaux wrote of the Danish Archbishop Eskil in 1153.[4] From a spiritual point of view and in a missionary context, it became an absolute necessity to have a deserted land in the periphery, which was penetrated slowly by the pious hermit, the spiritual equivalent to the armed knight, "the spiritual adventurer, gripped by the allure of the desert."[5] Again, the deserted and dangerous land was more of a mental than a physical quality. On the other hand, this has cheated modern historians, who took the medieval descriptions at face value. They believed, for example, that large areas on the Iberian Peninsula lay waste and uninhabited after the Muslim conquests or – in smaller measure – that large parts of Denmark were deserted after attacks of the heathen Wends. To the medieval writers, deserted meant heathen, without Christian worship, not empty of people. Most often it turns out – and more and more, as archaeology begins to supplement the written sources – that the medieval sources do not point to material but to spiritual poverty.

The periphery was also the military frontier where heathen peoples from the "outside" should be halted. The countries in the periphery were the "Gate to Christendom," as the Hungarian kings perceived themselves during this period.[6] The kings in these countries were given a special role as the defenders of Christendom. This applies to both Denmark and Portugal as well as to other countries with a religious frontier; Hungary and Poland for example. This does not mean that the countries in the centre did not have any military importance, because the warriors could move. Often they had a tradition of being Christian that was much older than the peripheral countries. France had a successful mission as early as in the 4th century, and it continued to be exceedingly important to activate both Germany and France for the papal, centrally led crusades. Due to their special position, however, the peripheral countries were possibly just as important. They simply had another function, which was to conduct the perpetual crusades. This also means that the mental distance between centre and periphery in medieval Europe was not so great, even though the countries in the periphery were situated at the outermost edge of the world. Thus it was precisely here that it was necessary to defend Christianity, or even better, to extend Christianity by pushing the frontier between Christians and heathens further and further into heathen land. When it came to the struggle for faith, the periphery became central.

Frontier societies

In 1893, the American historian Frederick Jackson Turner suggested that American history should be perceived as a result of the frontier between the civilized East and the Wild West, which was pushed further and further westwards during the 1800s by the collective efforts of settlers, solitary trappers and the US Cavalry.[7] Turner dealt with the area to the east of the Mississippi, but his successors soon transferred this idea to the American expansion on the prairie. Turner asked what would happen when the civilized European suddenly had to survive by himself in the wilderness, surrounded by savages with a social order which was completely different from the centuries-old European social order. Adaptation to nature was an important precondition – if one did not adapt, one went under. Solidarity and group communities, and in the end democracy, were formed, when there was no state with established institutions to take care of things. Most important was the freedom, the inviolable right, of the individual to create his own future, to own his own gun, or to just travel a little further west if too many neighbours and public institutions established themselves where one was already living. With freedom came efficiency, because no constricting guild ties or old social differences prevented the capable from developing fully.

Turner's thesis became very popular because it gave a simple explanation for the emergence of a specific American culture and because it could apparently be applied to very different fields. It also fitted well with some of the traditional perceptions of the strong individual's struggle against nature and savages that were widespread through the 19th century in boys' novels such as J. F. Cooper's *The Last of the Mohicans* (1826) and western pulp novels by the hard-working German writer Karl May (died 1913), which were first in the line for adaption when German immigrants settled in Hollywood and began to make movies. At the same time, there were old European precursors of Turner's thesis going back all the way to the Roman Tacitus. There was especially a solid tradition, from the 18th century, of writing of the noble savage who can teach the old civilization certain values which church and state had caused to be lost. The reason that Turner's thesis became popular around the year 1900 is perhaps that the Wild West had almost gone. Turner himself had formulated his question during a famous talk in 1893 at the American Historical Association in this way: what was America to do now that the frontier had gone? What then, could define American culture? This nostalgic looking back, this yearning for what had been lost, secured the wide circulation of Turner's thesis in America.

With time, Turner's frontier thesis was criticized in the USA[8] but became popular amongst historians all over the world and was extended to other regions and periods than America in the 19th century. The thesis was discussed and modified in countless ways, of which two were especially important. One was that several historians moved the focus from the frontier region itself to the old hinterland – what did the Wild West frontier mean to the old American states to the East, to England, to Europe as such? One important result, which was even more obvious with regard to Central and South America, was the massive import of valuables from the new to the old countries in the form of precious metals, foodstuffs and markets. The old lived off the new. The other important change to the frontier thesis was when it was extended to deal with clashes between great cultures. Turner's starting point had been the clash between civilized and savage, but with Owen Lattimore's studies from the 1940s to the 1960s, frontier studies also dealt with clashes between different but equally powerful cultures.[9] Lattimore's own interest was Central Asia, where an ancient and flexible nomadic culture clashed with – and co-existed

94 *Is the edge of the world far away?*

with – the world's oldest and most stable empire, China. Central Asia, however, was also the meeting point of Chinese Confucianism, Indian Buddhism, Middle Eastern Islam and North Eastern Christianity. How did people behave in such surroundings where not only individuals but also whole cultures had to adapt to each other in order to survive or otherwise destroy each other? Lattimore's extension of the term has had enormous influence on frontier studies and is an inspiration to many influential studies. Despite all their differences, there is a direct inspiration from Lattimore to Samuel P. Huntington's much debated *Clash of Civilizations* from 1996.

Within medieval studies,[10] this form of frontier history began to appear in some works from the 1920s about the German desire to extend eastwards – *Drang nach Osten*. Here it was possible to combine the idea of a specific German, expansive, national character with a claim that living in the frontier area between Slavic and orthodox peoples led to a distinct frontier culture. The word for *frontier* or *border* in languages such as German or Danish (*Grenze* and *grænse*, respectively) is actually Slavic – *graniza* – and entered the Germanic languages during the crusades of the Teutonic Order to the East among Slavic-speaking heathens along the Baltic shores in the 13th century.[11] Later in the 20th century, frontier studies have been applied to many different countries in Eastern Europe, to the crusader states in the Holy Land and to the relationship between centre and periphery in compounded states in the Middle Ages, e.g. Scotland or Wales as a frontier region in the medieval French–English empire, and not least for the countries in the Iberian Peninsula. Iberian historical writing was Turnerized from the 1960s onwards.[12] The frontier land – between Christian Europe and the heathen world – was a wonderland where young nobles and enterprising peasants were able to carve out careers in greater freedom than at home in the centre.

The very definition of a frontier has been discussed and refined, not least by medieval researchers. In short, it is possible to distinguish between a frontier as a line and a frontier as a zone: either as something established and defined, which divides two regions, cultures or political units from each other, or as something undefined and undefinable, where elements of two cultures are being mixed. The same differentiation lies behind the difference in "separation frontiers" and "coalescing frontiers" – in one instance, the two cultures exclude each other, in the other, they grow together and might even in time form a third, distinct culture. In the same way, it is possible to differentiate between real frontiers and mental frontiers. In the Middle Ages, there could easily have been good contacts in practice across the frontiers between two cultures, for instance between Christians and Muslims in the Holy Land, together with upholding an ideology on severe opposition. The same is probably the case for the Dane Saxo, who depicts the relations between Danes and Wends as being perpetually characterized by violent clashes, whereas archaeology points to a high degree of peaceful co-existence in the Middle Ages.

Frontier societies were different from those at the centre. Most obviously they were "organized for war," which was the title of a famous article by Lourie from 1966, later reused by Powers in a book on medieval Spain.[13] Frontier societies

Is the edge of the world far away? 95

were militarized to a high degree, a greater proportion of the population than elsewhere was armed and organized in protection guilds or societies. They defended home as well as raided enemy lands in order to steal cattle and enemy heads, which were raised triumphantly on poles at home to deter enemies and encourage their own people. The level of freedom was high, there were fewer autocratic nobles and fewer subjugated peasants. More peasants displayed the sign of a free man, a fluttering beard, which the nobles cut off when the frontier had moved further ahead and the free peasants were subjugated and forced to pay taxes.[14] There are more castles and fortresses, large and small, in the frontier region than in the centre. Literature in frontier societies is more implacable towards the others, those on the other side of the frontier, whether it is Spanish Dominican monks writing about the Muslims or the Danish medieval chroniclers' writings about the Wends. Finally, frontier societies have been compelled to develop specific institutions that make it possible to communicate across the frontier.

In historical writing, frontier societies were used for two things in the 20th century. Some historians were able to use them in a national context and emphasized their own country as a leader in the struggle against the others, those on the other side of the frontier. This applies to, among others, Hungarian and Polish historians, who perceived their countries as Europe's bulwark against the destructive forces from the East during the Middle Ages – Mongols, Turks, Islam and Russians. It applies to many Spanish and Portuguese historians, who interpreted their countries as leaders in the European expansion, in the *reconquista*.[15] Other historians used the frontier thesis to emphasize the tolerance in their countries and the ability and tradition for having different religions and nations living side by side.[16] This applies to other historical traditions on both the Iberian Peninsula and in certain countries in Eastern Europe.

Frontier history has thus many uses and is often able to create a more dynamic picture of medieval history than other traditions. It is food for thought then that there is no Danish tradition for perceiving Denmark as a frontier region during the Middle Ages. It would have been obvious, but it clashes with the widespread perception of Denmark as the centre for everything and as a unity with borders that have been settled and beyond dispute from time immemorial. This raises some questions relating to how centre and periphery have functioned in historical writings in general from an overall European perspective.

Centre and periphery – the diffusion model

A periphery is only a periphery in relation to a centre, and, with regard to the Middle Ages, this is perceived geographically as well as mentally. There is, however, a danger in the use of language itself of overlaying the sources from the past with a value-laden judgement. What is located at the centre is central, what is located in the periphery is peripheral. This is a problem with almost all general histories of Europe. Broadly, they deal with what took place in France; for certain, delimited periods, England is involved, for others, Northern Italy. Scandinavia is only mentioned with regard to the Viking Age, Portugal gets at most half a page, a

96 *Is the edge of the world far away?*

bit more when the Portuguese discover the seaway south of Africa. This way of looking at European history is connected with – and strongly furthers – a particular way of explaining historical change: the diffusion model. If there is a centre, then everything new must have emerged there and then spread to the periphery – diffusedoutwards. Therefore, it is quite natural to consider a certain diffusion period, a certain time lag in the periphery. They were behind and only later gained the institutions and ideas that were to be found in the centre of Europe. This is a traditional way of understanding history which has been dominant in Danish historical writing and which is indeed still around, despite written sources and archaeological finds that demonstrate that the countries in the periphery adopted precisely what they wanted from other regions immediately after it had been invented. In the 200s and over the following centuries, one large army after another was slaughtered in Southern Jutland, and the weapons were sacrificed by being thrown into a bog. These were state-of-the-art Roman weapons, which had been replaced as fast as the Roman arms developers invented new models.[17]

The diffusion model is also pre-eminent in one of the most popular books on medieval Europe, Robert Bartlett's excellent *The Making of Europe* from 1993. Everything simply originates from the 9th-century Carolingian Empire and then diffuses outwards to the periphery from around 900 to around 1300. This is the case for economic matters, especially coinage. It is the case politically, in the way that almost all royal families in Western Europe can trace themselves back to Charlemagne. It is the case culturally, with common systems of writing and formulas that are spread from France and especially from Paris. It is the case for religion, as local saints over time are replaced by common European saints, either from the early Church or later from France. It is the case militarily, as new technology such as trebuchets and cavalry spread from the centre of Europe to the periphery with travelling knight or mercenaries.

It is not at all impossible that many of these phenomena can actually be proven to have existed in France before they were found in other countries. That is not the problem with the diffusion model. The problem is rather that it is a one-way model – from centre to periphery, not the other way. With that, the diffusion model does not take the dynamism between centre and periphery into account – things were developed at the centre as an answer to a demand in the periphery, or the other way round, institutions from the centre were developed further and kept alive in the periphery and then returned to the centre in a new and stronger version, so to speak. The crusades are an obvious example indeed. The European centre in France, and in time also in Rome, is impossible to envision without Jerusalem which was located in the periphery of Europe and was simultaneously central to European thinking. And further: when the crusades had been initiated, they were kept alive by the countries in the periphery that had religious frontiers. It was here that the crusades actually took place, and it was here that institutions and ideas and a substantial amount of historical writing and theology on crusades and the non-Christians were developed. All this later returned to the centre where it had a solid standing, for example at the University of Paris during the 12th century.

Is it far to Portugal?

Both Denmark and Portugal were frontier countries at the edge of the world, on the outermost periphery of Latin Western Europe. From the point of view of a diffusion model, they ought to be developmentally hopelessly behind, compared to the European centres, especially France. In reality, there was no delay. On the contrary, there was a high degree of simultaneity between centre and periphery in medieval Europe, and there was good communication between the individual countries in the periphery. This is a claim that runs counter to both the Danish and the Portuguese tradition for historical writing on the 12th century.

Were there really such good connections between Denmark and Portugal and other countries in the Western European periphery, such that it is possible to imagine some form of coordinated effort in the joint European crusades? And how, then, were these military initiatives agreed in practical terms? Who brought messages from one crusader king to another? How far was it from Denmark to Portugal? Did the two countries really have anything to do with each other? One of the important sources to these questions – mentally and practically – is a travel guide from Ribe in Denmark to Acre in the Holy Land, originally from Adam of Bremen's chronicle from the 1070s. It was considered of such importance that it was included in both King Valdemar's Cadaster from around 1230 and in Albert of Stade's chronicle of the world from the mid-1200s.

> From Ribe it is possible to sail to Flanders to Cincfal in two days and two nights. From Cincfal to Dartmouth in England two days and one night. This is the outermost point of England to the south, and the route to there from Ribe is in the south-easterly direction. From Dartmouth to Brittany to Saint Matthieu one day. From there to Farrol at Saint Jacob three days and three nights. From there to Lisbon two days and two nights, and this route is south-westerly. From Lisbon to the Straits of Gibraltar three days and three nights in south-easterly direction.[18]

Cincfal is possibly a place in the bay at Sluis in Flanders. Dartmouth, with the peninsula Start Point, was the traditional medieval disembarkation port in England for crusaders and pilgrims.[19] Saint Matthieu is the westernmost promontory in the peninsula of Brittany; Farrol is in Galicia. The route continues via Tarragona, Barcelona, Marseille, Messina in Sicily and from there directly to Acre in the Holy Land. The whole journey from Ribe to Acre is estimated at forty days. It was possible to get from Ribe to Lisbon in only ten days and eight nights, a little less than a week and a half. That was all – if one sailed fast and at night time as well.[20]

In practice, the travellers would have been dependent on the wind and the weather and the journey would often have taken quite much longer. The anonymous German description of the conquest of Silves in 1189 begins with a description of the journey. The fleet consisting of eleven ships departed from the island of Walcheren in the southernmost part of the Netherlands; the following morning

98 *Is the edge of the world far away?*

Figure 4.1 Relief above the Cat's Head Door at the cathedral of Ribe. The crosses are held up towards omega, the last letter of the alphabet, the end of time and the heavenly Jerusalem, which is inscribed in alpha, the beginning, the Word. The dating is uncertain: from around 1170 to the middle of the 13th century. Who the individuals are is equally uncertain. That it has something to do with crusades seems obvious. © John H. Lind

they had to leave one of the ships behind as it got stuck in the sand. Reportedly, it took eight days to reach the English coast, where they apparently arrived on April 24.[21] The following day, they arrived at Sandwich and lost three ships that ran aground during a storm. They put in and waited for twenty-three days and managed to repair one of the ships and buy a new one in London. Other ships joined from other countries, amongst them probably a group from Denmark, but at a different pace depending on the weather and on procuring provisions.

From Sandwich they sailed into a headwind and did not arrive at Dartmouth until around May 23. They found new companions here and departed the next day for Brittany, but at first there was no wind, then it was a head-on breeze, and they were floating around on the sea for six days. Strong gales then carried them to the small island of Belleisle near Brittany, where they had to wait for eight days. Finally, the wind turned and they sailed day and night to La Rochelle and on past Saint Matthieu. Then the wind was playing up again, and they drifted about for

Is the edge of the world far away?   99

nine days. Finally, they reach Galicia and visited Santiago on Midsummer Day, June 25. Eight days later, they travelled on and, having a favourable wind, reached Lisbon around July 2. After a stay of eleven days, they continued to Alvor and from there to Silves after three further days of sailing. So the journey from southernmost Netherlands to southernmost Portugal took three months, from mid-April to late July. Around six weeks were periods of waiting to repair ships or to have a closer look at Santiago or Lisbon, but the rest of the time was spent sailing. These crusaders thus spent much more than forty days completing the distance that King Valdemar's Cadaster estimated to be ten days. It was all down to the sailing ships' nearly complete dependency of the weather.

King Valdemar's Cadaster includes another account of a journey, appearing in the manuscript just before the description of the route to Lisbon and Acre. It goes in a completely different direction, from the south-eastern point of Blekinge in present day Southern Sweden through the Baltic Sea along the Swedish coast to Tallinn in Estonia.[22] It is rather more detailed than the route to Acre and contains 101 place names on the way. The distance between them is given in "ukaesiones," which indicates how long a team of rowers can row at one time before it needs to be replaced or to rest. This depends on certain circumstances, especially the current in certain waters, and this is very difficult to calculate how far this might be in modern units. Eventually one will reach a distance of roughly 8.3 kilometres, give or take a few hundred metres. This is, however, a rather uncertain and average result for many reasons.[23] The distance from the starting point in Blekinge to Tallinn is around 1000 kilometres and that is given as roughly 125 ukaesiones.[24] No time estimate is given in this description; the reader is only told that the rowers have to be replaced more than 125 times. At the same time, it is not a single, direct route but several parallel or alternative routes.

The two Danish descriptions of these journeys cannot be compared directly, and they might have been recorded under very different circumstances. However, it is immediately striking that the one to Portugal is short, simple, and very fast, perhaps unrealistically so. People at the time would have known that only in the rarest cases would a traveller with a good deal of luck manage to get to Portugal in ten days. The other description of the journey to Tallinn is very detailed and records, matter-of-factly, how far it is in terms of work performance. It can be done faster if sails are used instead of oars and one has fair wind, but ukaesiones are probably the most reliable way to record distances at sea. An important difference in the two descriptions is that one records a mental distance: Portugal is close to Denmark. The other one records a very reliable and detailed physical distance.

At the same time, there was presumably some sort of affinity amongst the countries in the geographical periphery, which would have also been conditioned by them using the same transport route, the sea. When sailing, it would have been a very long way to inner France but not that far between Denmark and Portugal. Mentally, the distance would not have been too great. This appears on the oldest map of the world known from Danish and Nordic Middle Ages, a relatively primitive T map in the Colbatz Annals.[25] Jerusalem is right in the centre of the map, with Bethlehem to the south – to the right – and Antioch to the north. Space on

100 *Is the edge of the world far away?*

the map is very limited and there was only room for a modest number of names. The selection is telling.

Asia has the usual cities that were known from returning crusaders – Damascus and Tyre, Escalon. Troy was well-known from history, and the names of the most important countries appear as well: Upper and Lower Egypt, India and Babylonia – the latter was geographically unwieldy during the Middle Ages, and presumably it commonly covered the area that the Caliph in Baghdad (Babylon) ruled, i.e. the Muslim world in Asia. Furthermore, the "Caspian Gate" is labelled; the iron gate which Alexander the Great had built in antiquity between the civilized world and everything outside, especially in order to keep the people of destruction, Gog and Magog – which have been described in such lively and ominous terms by both Ezekiel and in the Apocalypse of St. John – away from the West. Behind the Caspian Gate on the Colbatz map live not the horse-riding people Gog and Magog but the Amazons. Perhaps this is because Adam of Bremen in his account, which was fifty years older at most, had described the Amazons in the eastern part of Scandinavia several times but only mentioned the apocalyptic Gog and Magog once in passing – whom he, by the way, thought were Swedes.[26] The other continent, Africa, is represented on the map by Ethiopia and the Ethiopian desert, alongside Mauretania, Libya, Carthage and several other places.

In Europe, several places by the sea are mentioned: Sweden, Denmark, England, the Iberian Peninsula, Rome, Bari, the principality of Achaia in the Peloponnese, Greece and Constantinople. In the Mediterranean are Sicily and Crete. Finally, Cologne is included as the only place in Europe not directly by the sea, although it was possible to sail there via the Rhine. On this map, Europe is obviously viewed from the sea and it is made by – or for – someone used to sailing. At the same time, it mentions carefully, one after the other, the places where one would call when sailing to the Holy Land. From this perspective, the Iberian Peninsula and Portugal would not have been far from Denmark. It was part of the mental map of Europe in Denmark during the 12th century and only one stop on the way to the centre.

A much larger and more detailed world map was made at the monastery in Ebstorf in Lüneburger Heide, a rich area due to large salt deposits, over which Danish kings tried to gain control during the 12th and the 13th centuries, in the interest of the Danish exports of herring.[27] The map is large and round and has a reasonable degree of geographical usefulness due to the many names of cities and rivers. At the same time, it is a theological map in the sense that the world is inscribed in Christ. At the top, furthest to the East, is His head. Portugal and Galicia are His right foot.

If we move north from Galicia, the distance to Scandinavia is very small indeed. Southern England is almost on a level with Galicia and from there it is only a narrow strait to Flanders and the area around Lüneburg, which takes up a disproportionate amount of space, and from there to Scandinavia. Prussia comes just after Scandinavia, next are Alexander's iron gates and behind them Gog and Magog.

The maps of Colbatz and Ebstorf are Christian maps, where geography and theology merge.[28] The centre is Jerusalem but the periphery is just as important.

Is the edge of the world far away? 101

The periphery includes the head of Christ and His body's limbs, hands and feet. The map not only reflects a Christian dream of making the whole world Christian, but also a claim that the whole world is contained in Christ and lives though Him. Not a single one of the limbs can be amputated without Christ losing His perfect, circular shape. The shape of the circular world maps were deliberately chosen to convey a message because there were other ways to draw maps during that time. The best known is probably the exceedingly detailed world map of Al-Idrisis, made in Sicily during the middle of the 12th century.[29] It is centred in the Mediterranean and is much more like what we perceive to be a scientifically accurate geographical map. However, this was exactly why the Christians of the High Middle Ages found it inadequate. It depicts a physical world but not the mental world. In the physical world, it might have been a long way to Portugal from Denmark. In the mental world, they were bound together in Christ, and in both countries, the faithful fought the infidels; they were working as limbs on the body of Christ. In the mental world, both countries were closely bound to the ocean that went around the earth, which they navigated and which connected them despite the many physical kilometres separating them. And both countries were connected by being the same distance from the centre of the world, Jerusalem.

Notes

1 For the following, see Evelyn Edson, *Mapping Time and Space. How Medieval Mapmakers Viewed Their World* (London, 1997); Michael Gaudio, 'Matthew Paris and the Cartography of the Margins', *Gesta* 39 (2000), pp. 50–57; Naomi Reed Kline, *Maps of Medieval Thought. The Hereford Paradigm* (London, 2005); catalogue over maps and their inscriptions, Leonid S. Chekin, *Northern Eurasia in Medieval Cartography: Inventory, Text, Translation, and Commentary* (Turnhout, 2006). About the Hereford mappa mundi, see also Valerie I.J. Flint, 'The Hereford Map: Its Author(s), Two Scenes and a Border', *Transactions of the Royal Historical Society* 6. ser. 8 (1998), pp. 19–44.
2 Ellen Jørgensen, 'Fra svenske Biblioteker', *Kirkehistoriske Samlinger* 5. Rk., 5. Bd. (1909–1911), pp. 771–786.
3 "Periphery, as applied to medieval history by Jacques Le Goff, acquires a geographical, cultural and religious meaning, instead of denoting economic and social structures. It carries the ambivalence of liminality: it can be a place where danger lurks or, alternatively, a place of access to the divine. To be on the fringes of the medieval Christian world could be regarded as a barbarian; it could also be seen as a source of holiness." Nora Berend, *At the Gate of Christendom: Jews, Muslims, and "pagans" in medieval Hungary, ca. 100a. 1300* (Cambridge, 2001), p. 54.
4 DD 1:2, no. 114.
5 José Mattoso, *Portugal Medieval. Novas interpretações* (Lisbon, 1992).
6 Berend, *At the Gate of Christendom.*
7 Frederick Jackson Turner, *The Frontier in American History* (New York, 1921).
8 E.g. Richard Hofstadter, *The Progressive Historians. Turner, Beard, Parrington* (London, 1969).
9 Owen Lattimore, *Nomads and Commissars. Mongolia Revisited* (Oxford, 1962); Owen Lattimore, *Studies in Frontier History. Collected Papers 1928–1958* (Oxford, 1962).
10 Nora Berend, 'Preface', in: David Abulafia and Nora Berend (eds.), *Medieval Frontiers: Concepts and Practices* (Aldershot, 2002), pp. x–xv; David Abulafia, 'Introduction. Seven Types of Ambiguity, c. 1100–c. 1500', in: David Abulafia and Nora Berend (eds.), *Medieval Frontiers: Concepts and Practices* (Aldershot, 2002), pp. 1–34;

102   Is the edge of the world far away?

Daniel Power and Naomi Standen (eds.), *Frontiers in Question: Eurasian Borderlands, 700–1700* (New York, 1999); Robert I. Burns, 'The Significance of the Frontier in the Middle Ages', in: Robert Bartlett and Angus MacKay (eds.), *Medieval Frontier Societies* (Oxford, 1989), pp. 307–330; Carlos de Ayala Martínez, Pascal Buresi, and Philippe Josserand (eds.), *Identidad y representatión de la frontera en la España medieval (siglos XI–XIV)* (Madrid, 2001); William Urban, 'The Frontier Thesis and the Baltic Crusade', in: Alan V. Murray (ed.), *Crusade and Conversion on the Baltic Frontier 1150–1500* (Aldershot, 2001), pp. 45–71; (1997), pp. 3–14; Pierre Toubert, 'Le concept de frontière. Quelques réflexions introductives', in: Carlos de Ayala Martínez, Pascal Buresi and Philippe Josserand (eds.), *Identidad y representación de la frontera en la España medieval (siglos XI–XIV)* (Madrid, 2001), p. 1–4; Giles Constable, 'Frontiers in the Middle Ages', in: O. Merisalo (ed.), *Frontiers in the Middle Ages. Proceedings of the Third European Congress of Medieval Studes, Jyväskylä, 10–14 June 2003* (Louvain-la-Neuve, 2006), pp. 3–28.

11 Power and Standen, *Frontiers*, introduction.

12 Toubert, 'Le concept de frontière'.

13 E. Lourie, 'A Society Organized for War: Medieval Spain', *Past and Present* 35 (1966), pp. 54–76; Powers, James F., *A Society Organized for War. The Iberian Municipal Militias in the Central Middle Ages, 1000–1284* (Berkeley, 1987).

14 Thomas Bisson, *Tormented Voices* (Cambridge, MA, 1998). The beard was a badge of honour everywhere in Europe. When some in Northern France in around 1190 imagined the Danish King Gudfred's outrageous and contemptuous behaviour towards Emperor Charlemagne, it was suggested that Gudfred had pulled the beards of Charlemagne's ambassadors. It was impossible to go any lower (*La Chevalerie d'Ogier de Danemarche. Canzone di gesta*, ed. Mario Eusebi (Milano, 1963), verse 23).

15 E.g., José Honório Rodrigues, 'D. Henrique e a abertura da Fronteira Mundial', *Revista Portuguesa de História* 9 (1960), pp. 45–62.

16 For an excellent summary of frontier theory, tolerance and the specific idea of Iberian convivencia, see Soifer, 'Beyond convivencia'.

17 Jørgen Ilkjær, *Illerup Ådal* (Højbjerg, 2000).

18 Codex ex-Holmiensis A 41 ("King Valdemar's Cadaster") fol. 127r, printed SRD V, 622; cf. KVJ: *Kong Valdemars Jordebog*, vols. 1–3, ed. Svend Aakjær (Copenhagen, 1926–1945), 1, *25; also in a (younger?) scholion to Adam of Bremen, scholion 99.

19 The route to England broadly agrees with Adam stating that Canute the Great with 1000 ships sailed across the dangerous North Sea, which "seafarers say can be crossed in three days if the wind is in south-east." – "*per quem, sicut nautae referunt, a Dania in Angliam, flantibus euris, triduo vela panduntur.*" Adam of Bremen, 2, 50.

20 Overland travel took much longer, as described by the Icelandic abbot Nikulás of Munkathvera, who travelled from Iceland via Denmark to Rome in 1154; see Francis P. Magoun Jr., 'The Pilgrim-Diary of Nikulas of Munkathvera: The Road to Rome', *Mediaevel Studies* 6 (1944), pp. 314–354.

21 Charles Wendell David, 'Narratio de itinere navali peregrinorum Hierosolymam tendentium et Silviam capientium A.D. 1189', *Proceedings of the American Philosophical Society* 81, no. 5 (1939), p. 175. There are problems with the dating in the beginning of the text; the company was to have left on May 1 and arrived in England on April 24, which is hardly the case.

22 Jarl Gallén, *Det "danska itinerariet." Franciskansk expansionsstrategi i Östersjön.* (Helsinki, 1993); Christer Westerdahl, 'Transportvägar. Itinerariet och forntida transportsystem', in: Gerhard Flink (ed.), *Kung Valdemars Segelled* (Stockholm, 1995), pp. 24–32. 1995; Henrik Breide, 'Itinerariet. Det historiska dokumentet – en översikt', in: Gerhard Flink (ed.), *Kung Valdemars Segelled*, udg. Gerhard Flink (Stockholm, 1995), pp. 11–23.

23 N.E. Nørlund, *De gamle danske Længdeenheder* (Copenhagen, 1955), pp. 64–69.

24 This is the number Nørlund builds his average number upon. However, the travel route itself mentions a series of place names without any distance between them being mentioned. This is probably an error in the manuscript. The number of ukaesiones should probably be higher than 125, and therefore they must have been less than 8.2 kilometres each.

25 Original in Berlin, photo in the Royal Library, Copenhagen, Bjørnbo's cartographic collection, St.fol. 29. Lars Hemmingsen, 'Middelaldergeografien og Historia Norwegie', in: Inger Ekrem, Lars Boje Mortensen and Karen Skovgaard-Petersen (eds.), *Olavslegenden og den latinske historieskrivning i 1100-tallets Norge* (Copenhagen, 2000), pp. 26–53, has a reconstruction of the map with its names on page 52, which are not entirely satisfactory. Damascus has for example been turned into Manasseh.

26 Adam of Bremen, 1, 26.

27 Nils Hybel and Bjørn Poulsen, *The Danish Resources ca. 1000–1550. Growth and Recession* (Leiden, 2007), e.g. p. 362.

28 Edson, *Mapping Time and Space*; Gaudio, 'Matthew Paris'; Kline, *Maps of Medieval Thought*.

29 Konrad Miller, *Weltkarte des Arabers Idrisi vom Jahre 1154* (Stuttgart, 1981).

5   The extending of Jerusalem

The sermon of Pope Urban in Clermont in 1095 was spread to the outermost edge of the world and to the ocean and the other side of the sea. This also included Denmark and the rest of Scandinavia and the Nordic region. Danish, Icelandic and other annals report how the Scandinavians "went to Jerusalem," how there "was a great movement towards Jerusalem." In these sources, the word "movement" – *motio* – is used; it resembles the contemporary French writers' description of the crusade as an earthquake that shook the whole Christian world.[1] Urban's message must have been distributed by clerics and preachers who were dispatched, but who they were, we do not know. The Scandinavian sources are too few to have handed down any names but they report, in unmistakeable terms, on the massive backing for the crusade, in Denmark too. *Dane fore mange thill Ierusalem att stride gen hedinge* (many Danes went to Jerusalem to fight against heathens), the annals of Lund narrate for 1096. With regards to the Iberian Peninsula we know a little bit more but not much. The Archbishop of Toledo took part in the synod in Clermont; he heard Urban's sermon and could have passed it on to bishops and priests in all of Spain when he got back. Gripped by the general mood, he himself took the cross but was relieved by Pope Urban because he was needed more at home than in the Holy Land.[2] Not until 1105 was Archbishop Bernaldo able to travel on a pilgrimage to Jerusalem.[3] The Bishop of Coimbra was presumably also present at Clermont, but this is not entirely certain.[4]

Coincidentally, with this broad popular mobilization, practical political matters had to be settled. Princes had to be involved, alliances established, supplies safeguarded. This was organized by prominent noblemen belonging to the circle of vassals of St. Peter, who went on recruitment drives.

In 1096, Godfrey of Bouillon began his campaign to create support for the crusade. In 1099, he was to become the third Christian who jumped from the siege tower to the city wall of Jerusalem[5] and a few days later, he was the first ruler of Christian Jerusalem. Later in the Middle Ages, he became an icon, an example of the perfect knight, on par with Alexander the Great and Charlemagne. He had, thus, been involved in the planning of the expedition right from the beginning at the very highest level. After an agreement with both the German Emperor Henry IV and the Hungarian King Kálmán, Godfrey gained access to Eastern Europe. He travelled through Romania and Bulgaria to recruit supporters. Furthermore, he

The extending of Jerusalem   105

entered a pact with the Byzantine Emperor – presumably about procuring assistance and provisions for the crusader army. He entered "military alliances[6] with Sicily, Byzantium, the Danes and the Norwegians as well as with the other armies on the other side of the sea, indeed with all nations that worship Christ."[7] Apparently, this information cannot be confirmed by other sources, but it was written by Ekkehard in his chronicle of the world, which he produced in three revised editions between 1107 and 1117. Ekkehard himself took part in a crusade in 1102 together with the Welf princes, and he was closely connected to Otto of Bamberg, the missionary of the northern Baltic coast.[8] Ekkehard was most certainly very well informed about what happened in Denmark.

The participation of the Norwegians and the Danes in this early and crucial phase of the crusades was remembered and emphasized as being important in the next generations, both internally amongst the primary organizers of the crusader movement and publicly in crusader narratives and songs. In 1147, Abbot Peter of Cluny gave a great and very, very long crusade sermon for the monks in the monastery, *A Praise of the Lord's Grave*:

> What else [than the hope of salvation] made you assemble from the unknown east and the distant west, from the outermost northern and southern remote areas by this grave, that once hid a deceased man? . . . What else made you assemble, Frenchmen and Germans, and you, Danes and Norwegians with your furious barbarism and strength. The first among you journeyed over land, the last across the sea and, with the strain of war and by spilling your blood you won a brilliant victory and tore the grave loose from the yoke of the Persians and the Arabs. Which other pay, say I, did you receive for such strains, other than salvation itself?[9]

At the monastery of Cluny, one of the most important cultic and political centres of Western Christendom and the very source of the crusade idea, the efforts of the Danes, during the first crusade, were specifically remembered half a century after the event.

From around 1180, we have an interminably long poem about the conquest of Antioch and the first crusade, almost 10,000 alexandrine verses in Old French. It was a great success at the time and became widely known. The more important of the crusade leaders have leading roles, but in addition there are multitudes of heroes who all come from the region north of the Loire, most of them from the Flemish area and were vassals of Duke Robert, the brother-in-law of the Danish king St. Canute. After a long rattling-off of heroes, the poem mentions nations, of which there are only three: "Then came those from Denmark, Lorraine and Friesland,/ as fast as horses can run when driven by spurs,/ and the Turks assembled from everywhere,/ all trembled at the sound of their fierce screech,/ the cleaving swords made such a kill,/ that blood and brains covered the sand."[10]

The efforts of the Norwegians and the Danes during the first crusade were specifically emphasized in internal theological interpretations, and in sermons to monks and in public, widely known ballads of chivalry. This makes it so

106   *The extending of Jerusalem*

much stranger that they slipped out of modern historical writing in their own countries.

Prince Svend of Denmark

Godfrey's mission proved effective and had tangible results. Also in 1097, the Danish Prince Svend – son of Svend Estridsen – journeyed towards the Holy Land. He did not get that far. The rumour of his unhappy destiny reached the great crusader army as it went through Asia Minor after the conquest of Nicaea. The noble and handsome Svend, together with his army of 1500 knights, was delayed and had been further held up by the splendid reception they had received from the Byzantine Emperor. They now continued through Asia Minor to join the rest of the army and believed themselves to be safe in the newly conquered territory, but Sultan Soliman lay in ambush in a thicket of reeds and rush.

Svend "was killed in a swarm of arrows, and all of his following accomplished the same martyrdom of the hands of the malevolent butchers." This was not particularly strange, Albert of Aix wrote, because the Turkish Sultan had received reinforcement from the treacherous Greeks. Nevertheless, Svend defended himself valiantly and struck many Turks to the ground with his sword, as his men also did. In the end, they were completely exhausted and could not lift their weapons and could no longer resist the enemy. They were nailed to the ground by the Turks' arrows and they perished.

Svend had been accompanied on the march by Florina, daughter of Count Eude of Burgundy. She had recently been widowed and now hoped to be married to this important man after the victory of the faithful at Jerusalem. But the "savagery of the Turks put this hope to shame." She tried to flee to the mountains on her mule, was hit by six arrows but managed to stay in the saddle. The Turks caught up with her, they took her to the Sultan and she was decapitated together with her fiancée Svend.[11]

The story was taken from Albert of Aix by William of Tyre, who mentioned it in his history of the Crusader Kingdom of Jerusalem from the early 1180s.[12] After that, it became immensely popular, not least after the new account by Torquato Tasso in his heroic cycle of poems from 1581, *Gerusalemme Liberata*, which was translated into several European languages. Torquato had the faithful squire Rinaldo taking up Svend's sword and with that, he entered the city wall of Jerusalem as the first crusader.[13] This further embellishment of the story is pure imagination, but it became very popular in Europe, including in Denmark, where the Danish historian Anders Sørensen Vedel knew of it and referred to Svend's example in his draft to a publication of the crusading chronicle by Robert the Monk.[14] In the 17th century, the Danish King Christian IV had his court artist Karel van Mander paint a very large and impressive painting of the heroic death of Prince Svend.[15]

Doubts over whether Svend was a historical person at all were raised with the ascent of the school of historical criticism in the 19th century; at first in 1841 by the student of Leopold von Ranke, von Sybel, and then by Paul Riant in 1865.[16]

The arguments against centre around the fact that 1) a Burgundian Princess Florina is not to be found on any medieval Burgundian genealogical tree – she is known only from Albert of Aix – and 2) that Sultan Soliman (Kilij Arslan) ought to have been away from Anatolia when Svend and his army were mowed down. The most important argument, however, is that the great Danish historian Saxo from around 1200 would not have omitted to tell the story of his patron King Valdemar's famous ancestor, if it had any foundation in reality.

The criticism is overstated. There are many women, also from the princely houses, whom we only know from one single source. Kilij could very well have had an army in Anatolia at the same time as he himself was far away. And Saxo was – as research from the 20th century has increasingly shown – a most eclectic writer, who only raised issues that suited his agenda, which was to emphasize the line of Valdemar's right to the throne above all the collateral branches.[17] This Svend, who died in 1097, was no direct ancestor of Valdemar and could therefore justifiably be used by other claimants to the throne as well. This could have been a reason for Saxo to omit him. Taking all factors into account, there is no reason to doubt that Svend participated in the first crusade, even though he did not make it to Jerusalem, or to doubt that his participation was the result of the negotiations led by Godfrey in 1096.

Henrique in Portugal

During the same year that Svend went on a crusade, the paternal uncle of his fiancée was on an expedition against the Muslims in Portugal. In 1096, Henrique took over ruling the region south of the River Minho while his cousin, Raimundo, continued to be the Count of Galicia including Santiago de Compostela. Raimundo's wars against the Almoravids during the preceding years had been victorious, but he was unable to remain in control of the lands as far south as Lisbon, which were soon retaken by the Muslims. Santarém, on the other hand, remained under Christian control, at first under Raimundo and then under Henrique until 1111. The overall military situation was influenced by the well-organized Almoravid troops that had arrived from North Africa after Alfonso VI's conquest of Toledo in 1085. Now they were engaging in a determined re-conquest of the whole of the central part of the Iberian Peninsula, from Lisbon in the West to Valencia in the East. Both Raimundo and Henrique received great military assignments as vassals of Alfonso, in several places of his kingdom.

In 1097, Alfonso suffered a defeat to the Almoravids in the battle of Consuega, not far from Toledo. At the same time, the Almoravids lay siege to Valencia, which was defended by el Cid. The crusader year of 1099 was militarily disastrous for the Christian rulers on the Iberian Peninsula. Alfonso VI again suffered a defeat near Toledo, and near Cuenca Ibn Aisha was victorious in a battle that turned into an unusually bloody slaughter of the Christian warriors. On July 10, 1099, el Cid died in Valencia[18] while the crusaders in the East were only five days away from the final conquest of Jerusalem. The defence of Valencia was continued by the widow of el Cid, Donna Ximena, who was relieved by Alfonso VI despite

108   *The extending of Jerusalem*

the earlier conflict between him and el Cid. As part of that expedition, Henrique and Raimundo attempted an attack on the Almoravids at Malagón in the area of Toledo, which ended up as a huge defeat for the two cousins.[19] This happened in September 1100. In the spring of 1102, Henrique suffered yet another great defeat, now at Vatalandi near Santarém[20] where his forces apparently tried to halt a Muslim army from Lisbon that attempted to extend the Muslim territory northwards. The sources are few, but the Muslim attacks were clearly quite regular, and they were presumably initiated every spring.

We only know of Vatalandi in 1102 from the sources because this turned into "a very great misfortune" to the Christians. However, this does not imply that the battle as such was a singular event. The fight against the Almoravids was presumably one of Henrique's most important duties and, therefore, it would have been quite natural for him to go on a crusade to Jerusalem as well. He left his duchy right after a great defeat to the Muslims. This cannot, as suggested by an American historian,[21] be due to the fact that Henrique was indifferent with regard to the Muslims and that everything was peaceful in Portugal. On the contrary, when things went wrong during religious wars in Portugal, it was an obvious idea to go on a crusade to the Holy Land to obtain indulgence and absolution. Just as this was an obvious idea in Denmark too.

Erik I of Denmark and Henrique of Portugal on their way to the Holy Land

After the conquest of Jerusalem in 1099, things went fast. Returning crusaders talked enthusiastically about the wondrous miracle in which they had participated but also about the new Christian kingdom's glaring need for immediate and large-scale help. The lukewarm ones were convinced, new ones joined in and those who had been delayed now finally went on their way. This became the first great reverberation of the first crusade: the crusade of 1101, which was fought in vain in Eastern Anatolia to free Baldwin, the new King of Jerusalem, from Turkish captivity. One of the most famous participants was the undaunted old veteran of the fights against the Muslims in Northern Spain, Duke Eude I of Burgundy, the brother of Count Henrique of Portugal. He had fallen out with the Pope by plundering land belonging to Cluny and now did penance by going on a crusade.[22] Eude achieved what was to become the old crusader's greatest wish during the coming centuries, to end a long warrior life in the service of religion by dying on a crusade, although he died not in the Holy Land but near Tarsus in Cilicia,[23] not so far away from where his son-in-law, Svend of Denmark, had fallen.

During the same period, the young Carl of Flanders went on crusade.[24] He was a son of the Danish King Canute IV and thus the nephew of Eude's son-in-law. After the killing of his father in 1086, Carl went to Flanders and was raised by Eude's brother-in-law. Presumably Carl followed Eude on the crusade and probably listened to the veteran warrior's stories and advice. Eude and Carl probably discussed when they were to go. Whether other people were involved in these plans is not known.

The extending of Jerusalem   109

Two years later, in 1103, Emperor Henry IV decided to go to Jerusalem after all. The investiture contest with the Papal see and the political unrest with obstinate princes had made it impossible for him to participate in 1099. However, Henry decided now was the time, and he let his new bishop proclaim the news at a meeting in Magdeburg over Christmas.[25] He called on his princes and his people to participate. It all came to nothing, not least because of Henry's son's rebellion against his father. The preparations were nevertheless ongoing, and somehow they involved the Danish King Erik the Good (Erik Ejegod).

As the first Western European King, Erik went on a crusade in 1103 with an army, which according to a much later source sailed in 200 long ships. He was followed by his wife, Bodil. "On the journey, she shared his crusade vow but not his bed and thus she let chastity heighten the honour of the glory."[26] Their son Erik Emune probably joined him as well.[27] The journey secured Erik a place in all Danish annals for the rest of the Middle Ages, even the most lapidary ones. In the more extensive narratives, however, his journey is described rather differently. In around the year 1200, Saxo recounted how Erik had been gripped by "mad savagery" because of a harp player and had killed four of his own men. As an act of penance, he had promised to go to Jerusalem. Thus he went, even though the Danish people wanted to give a third of their fortunes to collect a penance with which he could commute his crusade vow. The idea of commuting the crusade vow to financial support was well developed in Saxo's time but unknown during Erik's reign a hundred years earlier. The story is pure fantasy but elegant because it gives an internal, personal and Danish explanation of Erik's decision. It does not mention the German Emperor at all, which fits in well with Saxo's overall anti-German inclination.

Saxo describes in detail how Erik was received by the Byzantine Emperor. After some initial hesitation – the Emperor was worried that Erik would turn the Danish constituent of the imperial guard against him – the Danish army was allowed to enter the city and was received by the Emperor in person in a triumphal procession through streets decorated with flowers. As a memorial of the event, the Emperor had a portrait painted of the giant and legendarily strong Erik, and gave him a splendid silk robe with woven imperial eagles (which later came to embellish the reliquary of Erik's brother, Canute, in Odense).[28]

As a parting gift, Erik wanted relics, not riches. He was presented with a splinter of the True Cross and relics of St. Nicholas, which he sent back to the church in his native town, Slangerup. Here the altar had been built on the exact spot where Erik's mother had given birth to him.[29] A nativity cult based on Denmark's first royal crusader was clearly being established when Saxo wrote a little less than a century later. A nunnery was founded to attend to the cult at the church, and, during the latter half of the 12th century, it was under the supervision of eager crusading Cistercians in Esrom. What they told in Slangerup about Erik's crusade, in the liturgy at the grave of St. Nicholas and in homiletic stories, we sadly do not know any longer.

The Icelandic Knýtlinga saga was written in the middle of the 13th century but is based on older material now lost. It contains long verses by Erik's

110 *The extending of Jerusalem*

contemporary, the famous skald Markús Skeggjason. His Eiríksdrápa – praise of Erik – is presumably rendered unchanged in the Knýtlinga saga. Here Erik's crusade is described rather differently from Saxo. It is clearly a continuation of Erik's role as defender of the faith and the propagator of Christianity in the Baltic region. Erik is the "destroyer of the heathen Wends." Therefore, he journeyed to Jerusalem as a real Christian king "with a large army." Even though it is not mentioned directly, it is suggested here by Markús that the crusades in the Baltic and to Jerusalem really were two sides of the same coin. Erik proclaimed his decision to go Jerusalem far and wide, and many men joined him, both from Denmark and from other countries. Many nobles assisted him financially. There is nothing in the Knýtlinga saga about a killing needing repentance but it says: "The King, valiant in strife, set out from the north with his warriors to heal the wounds of his soul. He prepared for Paradise and wished for the peace of Jerusalem to obtain a pure life."[30] Despite the taciturn Icelandic formulation, it sounds like an echo of Urban's sermon in Clermont.

When Erik left – and this is where the perspective is extended – it happened with the understanding of two mighty rulers in his vicinity. "The King of the Franks was helpful to the brother of King Canute, with gifts, shining silver." This must refer to the French King Philip I, whose brother had participated in the first crusade and whose son-in-law was the Norman Bohemund of Antioch. Why he should have particular interest in supporting a Danish crusade is not known. It would have been easier to comprehend if the old, Icelandic text had said the "Flemish King" or ruler. This would also explain why Erik in this context is described as the brother of Canute – Canute was the saint-father to the future Count of Flanders, Carl, and particularly interesting in this context. However, this suggestion of an emendation is based solely on a sense that this reading would suit the context better.

The reference to another ruler is more obvious. It says directly in the Knýtlinga saga that Emperor Henry sent expensive gifts as well as regular troops and men to accompany Erik all the way to Byzantium.[31] This must be read such that Erik was involved in Henry's plans – perhaps they had arranged to travel together – and that Henry then chose to support Erik with provisions and men when he himself was prevented from going. Thus, this was a joint Danish–German crusade which ended up with only Erik going. Erik did not make it all the way to Jerusalem. He died en route in Cyprus and was buried there. Bodil reached Jerusalem and died on the Mount of Olives; she is buried in the Church of St. Mary there.[32] We do not know what happened to the rest of the Danish crusader fleet. Perhaps remnants of it participated in the very large fleet at Jaffa in 1106, which consisted of 7000 Flemings and Englishmen "who had been reinforced by many Danes."[33]

At the same time as Erik and Bodil, Count Henrique of Portugal went on a crusade too. He reached Jerusalem and was back in Portugal, probably around 1104. This is known from a single document written in Coimbra in 1103.[34] It refers to certain decisions that "shall be ratified by our Lord Henrique when he is back from Jerusalem." That is all. The rest is guesswork or very late narratives. Perhaps he followed the Genoese fleet that took Baldwin to Holy Land

The extending of Jerusalem 111

in 1103. Perhaps Henrique had just been called upon to go on a crusade by his relation Emperor Henry, as the Portuguese historian Azevedo thought in 1940.[35] We do not know for sure, but we can imagine it to be the case. In the same way, we might also imagine that Henrique must have known about the crusade of his relative, Erik the Good. Perhaps they met or perhaps they attempted to coordinate their movements. This is likely if Emperor Henry had connections to both of them. On his way, Henrique visited Rome and presumably tried to strengthen his newly established archdiocese Braga in relation to Santiago de Compostela and Toledo. Pope Paschal II issued several letters in favour of Braga in 1103.[36] This parallels Erik the Good succeeding in having Lund established as an archiepiscopal see in 1103–1104, and the attempts, only four years later, by the Norwegian King Sigurd the Crusader (Sigurd Jorsalfar) to have Nidaros established as an archiepiscopal see. Sigurd had even sworn publicly in the Holy Land that he would work towards that.[37] Thus, establishing archdioceses and participating in crusades were connected. Cynically, we could say that the first was a reward for the latter; however, it was probably down to the fact that a region engaged in a crusade needs an archbishop. In 1103, Braga became an independent archdiocese and was freed from its subordination to Toledo, which had traditionally held primacy over all of Spain and had attempted to assert its primacy by force since the Christian conquest in 1085. At the same time, Braga had new bishoprics transferred to its authority; not just the originally Galician Astorga, Orense, Mondoñedo and Tuy on the border by the River Douro but also Porto, Lamego, Viseu and Coimbra in the frontier region, where the religious wars were raging during these years.[38]

Portuguese chronicles from the 15th and 16th centuries have much more to tell about Henrique's crusade than the meagre, contemporary records. Henrique, too, used the journey to obtain several relics and bring them back to Portugal, amongst them an arm from St. Luke the Evangelist, which the Byzantine Emperor presented him on his return journey because of his fame and chivalry and because he was a son of the King of Hungary.[39] Actually, he was not, but it does not make the story any worse. In addition, the Emperor gave him St. Giraldo's mantle, which he passed on to the Archbishop of Braga.[40] Whether there is any historical background to these stories is impossible verify today.

Henrique was accompanied by the canon Teotónio from the archdiocese of Coimbra, who probably officiated as a kind of chaplain priest to Henrique – and this is a fact. He settled in Jerusalem and lived with the priests at the Holy Sepulchre for several years until he returned and founded the convent Santa Cruz in Coimbra, with the specific liturgy used at the services at the Holy Sepulchre.[41] Teotónio presumably accompanied his bishop, Maurício Burdino, who had come to Portugal from Limpoges in Southern France and who was to have a notable clerical career as a relic hunter and Pope and ended up an imprisoned fool in Rome.

After 1103, Portuguese and Danish rulers, it appears, did not go on crusades to Jerusalem anymore. There is possibly one exception, the Danish King Erik Emune.[42] Others took an oath to go on crusade to Jerusalem but were prevented

112   *The extending of Jerusalem*

from leaving, as we shall hear more about in the following sections. This does not mean, however, that the crusades were no longer important, quite the opposite. The explanation is that both the Baltic region and the Iberian Peninsula became centres for crusades in themselves. Here the Danish and Portuguese rulers had a role to fulfil that was important to the crusading movement at large. The fighting in the local regions became in actual fact a sort of support to the Jerusalem crusades. This does not mean that Jerusalem was forgotten. With regards to prestige, Jerusalem was a high priority and usually higher than local crusading aims, and large groups of Scandinavians and Iberians went to the Holy City. Rarely the kings, however. They continued the Jerusalem crusades at home.

"Like going to Jerusalem . . ." – crusader privileges and salvation

The crusade to Jerusalem in 1099 was effective because it resonated with the missionary wars and the general atmosphere of danger and doom in the 11th century. The conquest of the Holy City itself was perceived by contemporaries as something unique, historically as well theologically. Nevertheless, parallels were soon drawn between this unique phenomenon and the wars that were in some ways local, 12th-century continuations of the missionary wars of the 11th century. Local clergy in the Nordic countries and in the Iberian Peninsula recognized the potential in the crusade concept – it actually worked, and convincingly so in 1099 – and soon after they tried to introduce something similar in their own lands. The conquest of Jerusalem was unique, but definitions were still vague, and other wars could be considered at least somehow inspired by and compared to the Jerusalem crusade. This applies to two crusade proclamations very early in the 12th century, one with Danish participation, directed against the Slavic heathens, the other to the Prior Martin and the nobleman Martin Muniz in Coimbra in Portugal, and directed against Muslims.

Magdeburg 1108 – and from there to Småland and Obotritia

In 1108, perhaps even the year before, Archbishop Adelgoz of Magdeburg with his bishop colleagues from Merseburg, Naumburg, Meissen, Havelsberg and Brandenburg and other noblemen sent out an appeal for help.[43] The recipients were several other bishops and clerics, including the Abbot of Corvey, but also as far west as Cologne, Aachen and Brügge, and to Duke Godfrey of Lower Lorraine and Robert II of Flanders, and to all believers in Christ of every rank and everywhere. It is an appeal to all dear brothers in Saxony, Franconia, Lorraine and Flanders, and it is a plaintive cry. Magdeburg and the other bishoprics have for a long time been pestered and hard pressed by the manifold attacks and unrest of the heathens and now ask for help to raise "your Mother Church" from the ruins. Thus, the letter writers in the North counted on a particular dedication amongst the princes of the North to a particular Northern "Mother Church." The letter begins with a long description of the cruelties committed by the heathen Slavs, which

The extending of Jerusalem   113

does not fall short of the earliest crusade historians' descriptions of the Muslims in vivid detail. "The cruellest heathens have risen against us and defeated us without mercy while they, in their inhuman evil, boast of having desecrated the churches of Christ with their idols." They pillage, rape, kill, torture and decapitate. They draw out the innards of some Christians, cut off their hands or feet and ask: "Where is your God?" The God of the heathens is named Pripegala, allegedly a compound of Priapus and Beelphegor – the Greek and the Old Testament Moabit idols with enormous phalluses. The identification of those two might have been made by the Magdeburg bishop himself; but he could also have borrowed it from a work on virginity by the contemporary crusade historian Guibert of Nogent.[44] It is interesting and perhaps not only a coincidence that Moabites was also one of the expressions of the Pope then in office for the Muslims on the Iberian Peninsula. "Pripegala wants heads," say the heathens, and they decapitate Christians in front altars of the idols, where they also keep large vessels with Christian blood for their rituals. All in all, it is a description that is quite close to particularly Robert the Monk' rendering of Urban II's crusade sermon, which also elaborated on the cruelty of the heathens.[45]

The letter continues by directly encouraging the audience to follow the example of the good ones and to imitate the French: spread the message in the churches, purify yourself by fasting, invoke heaven, assemble the nations and let it be preached in the outermost frontiers of your ecclesiastical provinces, make the war holy and mobilize the strong warriors. Rise up, princes, against the enemies of Christ, gird on your swords – writes the Bishop, using the same words as Urban II in his sermon.[46] "Prepare yourself, just as the French did to liberate Jerusalem. Our own Jerusalem, which was free from the beginning, has now become a slave woman because of the cruelty of the heathens.[47] Her walls crumble because of our sins." The region in question here was Christian before but has now been retaken by the heathens.

The Danish King Niels had already offered his assistance and that of his people in this war, just like other princes in the region. The German King Henry V was the initiator and swiftly made himself available, along with everyone he was able to call upon. To the recipients of the letter, the Bishop exclaims: "I speak to you – no, through me Christ speaks to you" – also one of Urban's phrases[48] – and says: "Rise up, hurry, my female friend, my dove, come." "Rise up, bride of Christ and come." The heathens here are the very worst but their land flows with the best of meat and of milk and honey and corn and all kinds of poultry, and if only it was tilled, it would give much higher yield than anywhere else.[49] The participants in this war against the Slavs would thus be able to save their souls and – if they felt the urge – acquire the best land to colonize.[50] Finally, it is promised that God himself will assist the warriors. "He who vanquished his enemies in the distant Orient with those Frenchmen[51] who ventured with strong arms, He will also give you will and power to subdue the inhuman nations who live by these frontiers and to have progress in everything." The letter is full of biblical references and formulations, which could form a basis for the preaching of a crusade in Northern Europe, which it directly encouraged the recipients to initiate.

114 *The extending of Jerusalem*

The Christian war against the heathen Slavs is equated in every way to the expedition to Jerusalem, directly by comparison, theologically by promising salvation, and in details such as utilizing the same themes and Bible passages as Pope Urban. The letter draws on common crusading themes and the narratives of Pope Urban's sermon at Clermont. If one was to point to a single original source, Robert the Monk's depiction draws the closest similarities. This was almost contemporaneous with the Magdeburg letter, and was widely distributed in Flanders, the German lands and Denmark.[52]

Since then, the assessment of the importance of this letter has varied but it has mostly been considered an isolated occurrence, an exception. Doubts have been raised about the authenticity of the letter, most consistently by the Belgian historian Henri Pirenne during his anti-German period, written while Pirenne was a German prisoner-of-war in Jena in 1916.[53] However, there is no reason to believe that the letter is a forgery.[54] This suspicion has nevertheless remained, not least because the publisher of the letter – in the text edition that is best known – identified it as "without official characteristics, more likely the work of a private person, presumably a Flemish cleric." This edition was published in Magdeburg in 1937, on the anniversary of one thousand years of German Eastern Europe. The German colonization of Eastern Europe was "the greatest cultural effort of the German Middle Ages," the publishers wrote in the preface to this scientific collection of medieval documents.[55] In this there was evidently no room for Flemish and Danish initiators, not to mention the Pope. The Danish edition of the text contains the same addition, saying that the letter probably was written by a private person.[56] This goes completely against the testimonies of the text itself. It states clearly that the letter was issued by the Bishop of Magdeburg and his closest colleagues in their role as bishops, thus not as private persons. The confusion and the suspicion of the author being a Flemish private person[57] occur because the letter mentions several clerics from Flanders, which is situated rather far away from Magdeburg. However, considering the contemporary crusader networks, there is nothing at all unusual about the recipients of the letter. The nearby heathen island of Rügen on the Baltic coast had been placed under the newly established archdiocese in Lund as a missionary field.[58] Thus, the Danish King Niels had missionary interests on Rügen and his sister's son, Henrik Gotskalksen, fought to re-establish a Christian kingdom amongst the Western Slavs. To the Bishop of Magdeburg, King Niels was the nearest and most obvious prince to turn to, to ask for help against the heathens. It would have been just as obvious to King Niels to try to involve his brother's brother-in-law, the veteran crusader Robert II of Flanders. He in turn would have referred to Godfrey of Lower Lorraine, a relative to Godfrey of Bouillon, with whom Robert had fought at the walls of Jerusalem.

There is nothing strange about the letter from Magdeburg. It describes a concrete attempt to raise a crusade – with spiritual merit and direct comparison with the first crusade. At the same time, it reflects a tremendous extension of the term *crusade*, from being directed at Jerusalem to being fought against the heathen Slavs as well, precisely to defend "our Jerusalem" in the North. Unfortunately,

The extending of Jerusalem 115

we do not know whether this crusade materialized, and if it did, how much came out of it.

The Slavs were not the only heathens or infidels in the Baltic region against whom crusades were fought. In 1123 or 1124, King Niels of Denmark initiated a crusade against the heathens in Småland. It was to be a joint undertaking between Niels and his neighbour King Sigurd Jorsalfar of Norway. The two of them had had the opportunity to discuss crusades before. In 1110 or 1111, when Sigurd travelled home via Byzantium and Eastern Europe from his successful crusade to the Holy Land, he was received in Schleswig by Niels, who welcomed him with a great celebration. Niels honoured Sigurd by accompanying him all the way through Jutland, until Sigurd could sail directly to Norway.[59] Perhaps Niels had just returned from a crusade on Magdeburg's behalf – at least the negotiations must still have been fresh in his memory. Sigurd continued his crusade at home in Norway by fortifying Kongshelle, on the eastern frontier towards the heathen Västergötland in Sweden, with a castle built in peat and stone and surrounded by a moat. The local population was called upon to deliver stones or sharp-pointed stakes for the defence of the castle. As a matter of precaution, he kept the relic of a large splinter of the True Cross that he had brought back from Jerusalem at Kongshelle, even though he had promised to give it to the Cathedral of St. Olav in Trondheim.[60] The Cross was deemed more necessary in the struggle for the extension of Christianity at Kongshelle at the border with Sweden. It turned out to be a mistake to keep such a valuable relic in a disputed frontier castle. Heathens from Wendland attacked and took the castle and the relic after a long and hard struggle during the 1130s. Eventually, the heathens let the Christians buy back the Cross and contented themselves with burning the castle church, which, after having been saved miraculously twice, finally burned to the ground.[61]

The expedition of 1123–1124 was to be directed at Småland in order to Christianize the population, "because those who live there do not hold on to Christianity, even if they had received it. Because at this time in Svealand, there were many heathen peoples and many who were bad Christians, and some of their kings renounced Christianity and continued to make blót (pagan sacrifices)."[62] King Blót Svend and one person named Erik are mentioned by name. King Niels and Sigurd arranged to meet in Øresund. The Danes arrived first and waited and waited and finally decided that the Norwegians had let them down; the Danish crusader army was dissolved and returned home. Shortly thereafter, Sigurd Jorsalfarer arrived with 300 ships and discovered with fury that the Danes had apparently let the Norwegian army down by not showing up. In order to take revenge, he decided to pillage Danish areas. He began in Tummatorp and continued as far east as Kalmar. He took 1500 heads of cattle in tribute, "and then the Småland peoples took on Christianity." Later, King Sigurd returned to his kingdom with much plunder, *ok var þessi leiðangr kallaðr Kalmarnaleiðangr* – "and this crusade was called the Kalmar crusade." Another way to propagate Christianity, that King Niels' son Magnus practised with great success, was to plunder the heathen areas for cultic objects. The heathens believed that thunder happened because of great hammers striking in the sky and therefore they worshiped colossal copper

116　*The extending of Jerusalem*

axes: great hammers of the pagan god Thor. Magnus had these taken away from their sanctuary on an island and brought them to Denmark. Magnus was remembered for several generations in the heathen areas as "the robber of the heavenly plunder."[63]

The crusade of the Danish and Norwegian kings presumably had a third participant: Duke Boleslaw of Poland, with whom Niels was probably already an ally. At this time, a Danish–Polish marriage alliance between Boleslaw's daughter Richiza and Niels' son Magnus must already have been formed. According to Polish annals, Boleslaw went on an expedition in 1123 "across the sea," where he supposedly conquered several castles.[64] Boleslaw's expedition took place at the same time as he finally subjugated Pomerania by conquering Szczecin in 1121, after almost two decades of bloody crusades. After that, he could go "across the sea," towards Kalmar, which in this way became the local, Baltic Outremer.[65]

The Danish–Norwegian–Polish crusade to Småland and Kalmar was highly praised by none other than the venerable Abbot Peter of Cluny in a letter to Sigurd.[66] Peter thanks the Lord of Ages – *saeculorum dispositor* – who has placed Sigurd at the outermost frontier of Earth and under the frozen North Pole, but with the southern warmth of His Spirit, has melted his northern wind and loosened the ice of doubt and of the body. "About you one can truly sing: 'Arise, O north wind, and come, O south wind, blow through my garden, and let the aromatical spices thereof flow.'"[67] Sigurd exchanged the sceptre of power for the yoke of Christ and fought the enemies of the Cross in both his own lands and in the distant southern and eastern lands – another instance of putting crusades in the Baltic region on equal footing with crusades to Jerusalem – and Sigurd fought on land as well as on the sea. Peter concludes by thanking God for the thoughts of crusade He inspired in Sigurd and asks Sigurd to complete what he began. This indicates that the letter was written before Sigurd actually left together with Niels and Boleslaw. Thus, the plans of a crusade against the people of Småland were discussed with Cluny beforehand. There would have been close connections between Denmark and Cluny. Eskil, later to become Archbishop, had perhaps already at this time been admitted to the Cluniac brotherhood – "As he loved this place very much."[68]

We know nothing about the extent to which the expedition to Småland would have been sanctioned by the Pope and whether the participants received indulgence. Peter of Cluny's comments are excited but vague and do not mention indulgence. Perhaps it was not necessary, perhaps the participants received indulgence from the archdiocese in Lund, which at some point, between its establishment in 1103 and 1127, received all of the Nordic countries and the heathen Slavic regions by the Baltic shores as a missionary field by papal decision.[69] We cannot resolve this with certainty, but perhaps this is only interesting in the context of a very formalistic discussion of the definition of the term *crusade*. Most importantly: the Kalmar expedition was a religiously motivated war against apostates, and it was compared with the crusades to Jerusalem, as it is clear from Peter's letter to Sigurd.

During the same years as the crusade to Småland, several missionary wars took place in the Wend areas between South Jutland and Poland. Canute Lavard played

The extending of Jerusalem 117

a decisive role in those. Canute was the younger son of King Erik the Good. When the father went on a crusade in 1103, he let the minor son stay at home to be reared, according to Saxo, by the Zealand nobleman Skjalm Hvide.[70] According to Helmold of Bosau,[71] Canute soon fled to the German Lothar, Duke of Supplinburg, later the German King and later yet the Holy Roman Emperor. Meanwhile, Erik the Good's brother Niels took over the throne in Denmark.

Shortly before 1120, Canute was installed as Prefect of Schleswig by King Niels and, during the 1120s, he expanded from the West into the Wendic area with the support of Lothar and had churches and castles erected. From the East, the Polish Dukes extended further and further westwards, and between them was Canute's cousin, Henrik Gotskalksen near Rügen. All of them waged crusades, mutual feuds and proper wars, although the finer details of their alliances can be difficult to reconstruct today because the few sources have different leanings and give different depictions of the political situation. Nevertheless, one thing is certain: the balance of power changed significantly when Henrik Gotskalksen died in 1127. In return for a large amount of money, Lothar installed Canute Lavard as Prince of the Obotrites (*knese*). Canute moved in from the West to fight Henrik's two sons; his ally Duke Vartislav moved in from Pomerania in competition with Poland; and different noblemen must have sailed the short distance from Zealand to the Wendic regions to participate in the fighting.

Perhaps it was due to the rivalry of these groups in the religious wars or perhaps a dispute with regard to the Danish royal succession, that King Niels's son Magnus lured Canute into an ambush at the Haraldsted forest near Ringsted on Zealand on January 7, 1131, and killed him. The murder was widely condemned in medieval sources, even by the otherwise Magnus-friendly *Roskilde Chronicle*,[72] and could only be explained as an act committed by the encouragement of the Devil. The murder led to bloody wars between Magnus's and Canute's networks of family and allies.[73] Magnus fell together with a large army in the battle of Fotevig on June 4, 1134. His father, King Niels, fled from the battle all the way through Denmark to Schleswig, where he was killed by the townsmen of Canute Lavard's city on June 25.

The main opponent of Niels and Magnus was Erik Emune, a half-brother of Canute Lavard and apparently a crusader.[74] After having strengthened his position by killing eleven out of twelve nephews, he turned against the heathens on Rügen. This presumably happened in 1135. Erik Emune was the first to take horses on his ships when he crossed the Baltic, Saxo claims, which is certainly a gross exaggeration. The fortress Arkona on Rügen had been fortified, but the Danish army isolated the town from any heathen relief expeditions by digging a moat through the isthmus that connected Arkona with the rest of Rügen and built a wall across the isthmus. Despite successful sorties by the defenders of Arkona, they eventually had to surrender. Their lives were spared in return for converting to Christianity.[75] According to the conditions of the surrender, they were allowed to keep their idol, which depicted St. Vitus. Saxo commented a generation later that this was only something that the Rügians had claimed, but it must have been accepted as a satisfactory explanation during the times of Erik Emune, as the idol was not

118   *The extending of Jerusalem*

destroyed. Saxo continued to write that the Rügians only let themselves be baptized because they were thirsty and, after the long siege, wanted a refreshing bath in the lake used for the mass baptism. It was not out of faith in the truth of Christianity and as soon as Erik Emune's army withdrew, they drove out the priest they had been given to teach them Christianity. Without worrying about the hostages they had been forced to send to Denmark, they returned to worshiping their idol.

It is doubtful how much we can trust Saxo's account in detail. His aim was obviously to depict the people of Rügen as having been baptized and then abandoning Christianity again. Theologically and according to Canon law, this placed the Rügians in a different category. They were no longer heathens, who were, in principle, not to be forced into Christianity, but apostate, who had to be forced back with any means possible. Their apostasy, only mentioned in a couple of lines in Saxo's great work, was the theological justification for the many Danish expeditions against the Wends, which he described in detail in numerous following pages of his narrative.

There is, however, no reason to doubt that Erik Emune actually had led a missionary war against Rügen and that this fitted into his policies as a crusader king. Erik had supported Sigurd Jorsalfarer's religious building in the frontier castle of Kongshelle with a shrine.[76] Knýtlinga saga mentions furthermore that Erik already as a very young man was to have accompanied his father, Erik the Good, on the crusade to Jerusalem in 1103.[77] It is certain that in 1135 he presented the monastery in Ringsted with lavish gifts in memory of his "cruelly killed brother," Canute Lavard, and that he commissioned the earliest biographies of Canute and his miracles, which emphasized the depiction of Canute as a crusader who spread Christianity amongst the Wends. The gift to the monastery in Ringsted, which was to develop into the most important Danish sepulchral monument for successful crusader kings for almost 200 years, was an expression of gratitude because Erik Emune had been victorious during the confrontation with King Niels the year before at the battle of Fotevig. At the same time, the gift was associated with the conquest of Rügen. It was either a preparation for the expedition or it was given in gratitude to celebrate the apparently successful conversion of the Rügians.

At the time of Canute Lavard's killing in 1131, his son had not yet been born. In the following years he was probably raised at his maternal grandfather's place in Russia.[78] When the son, Valdemar, returned to Denmark as a young man, he could thus point to a well-established family tradition for participating in crusades and missionary wars. He was active in a region which had been compared to the Holy Land in a crusading context since 1108, and his father was increasingly perceived as a crusader saint. We will return to these matters in the following chapters but, before that, we shall look at how the idea of the crusade in the meantime had also taken root in Portugal shortly after the conquest of Jerusalem in 1099.

Coimbra 1110

Pope Urban died on July 29, 1099, two weeks after the conquest of Jerusalem by the crusaders but without knowing anything about the great success of his

The extending of Jerusalem   119

initiative. He was succeeded by Paschal II, who as a cardinal had been Urban's legate to Spain. As one of his first official acts, Paschal appointed the Cardinal Bishop of Porto (in Italy), Maurício, as papal legate to the Holy Land, and he sent a long letter of congratulations to the crusaders in Jerusalem. However, Paschal's knowledge of the situation on the Iberian Peninsula soon forced him to take a decision on the relationship between the Jerusalem crusades and the struggle against the Muslims on the peninsula.

In letters to European rulers, Paschal generally impressed upon them that those who had earlier taken a vow to go on crusade now had to fulfil their vow. Those who didn't go and those who absconded en route to Jerusalem now had to go all the way and fight to protect the new Christian kingdom in the Holy Land, as it was under threat.[79] However, he made an exception for warriors from Northern Spain.

It pained Paschal to hear of Alfonso VI of León and Castile's tribulations with the Muslims and of what the King had written about captured Christians. Therefore, Paschal wrote to Alfonso's soldiers and directly forbade them from going to Jerusalem, stating that if they fought in Alfonso's kingdom or in his duchies – this must refer to Galicia and Portugal – they would receive remission of sin.[80] The following spring, on March 25, 1101, Paschal wrote to everybody living in Alfonso's kingdom, both clerics and laypeople, and impressed upon them his earlier commands. He had forbidden them from going to Jerusalem because Spain was attacked daily by the hordes of Muslims and Moabites – here, Paschal uses the same term as the Magdeburg letter – and because of the noblemen's expedition to the Middle East there were reasons to fear the tyranny of the heathens. Paschal thus had the noblemen forbidden from going and called on those who had left Spain to return home at once. Muno, Diego and Nuño were forced home in this way, and thus Paschal now called on their compatriots not to mock and ridicule them because of this – what apparently must have been the usual fate of a crusader who gave up halfway. On the contrary, Paschal recommended that everyone should stay at home and participate in the struggle against these Moabites and Moors as an act of penance, and in this way they would "receive the absolution and grace of the Apostolic Church."[81] The context is telling.

There is no doubt that Paschal supported the newly won Jerusalem and encouraged everybody who had taken the cross to go. At the same time, he made an exception with regards to the Iberian Peninsula, because the danger from the Muslims there was just as great as in the Holy Land. The spiritual merit of fighting in Spain and Portugal were comparable to that given to the crusaders to Jerusalem. The wars on the Iberian Peninsula were real crusades, just like the one to Jerusalem.

Unfortunately, one of the crucial letters from Pope Paschal to Coimbra cannot be dated. It was issued on January 12, but without mention of the year, so in principle it could be from any year during the whole of Paschal's time in office, 1100–1118. Carl Erdmann suggested in 1927 that it was possibly from 1110.[82] Paschal wrote to the Prior Martin and the Chapter of the Cathedral and Martin Muniz and all Christians in Coimbra. Initially, he thanked Count Henrique for having "torn the church in Lorvão from secular hands" and presented it to the

120   *The extending of Jerusalem*

Cathedral in Coimbra.[83] Paschal now confirmed this donation. Lorvão is situated in the mountains, only fifteen kilometres from Coimbra and on the northern side of the River Mondego, but at that time, the area must nevertheless have been insecure for the Christians. Paschal continues his letter by writing that he gives "his children in Coimbra and the knights of Christs – *milites Cristi* – who fight the Moors indulgence for the sins which they have confessed. Blessed are those who suffer persecution for the sake of justice – *propter justiciam* – and with confidence, they shall protect the Church of God and win His glory."[84] The church in Lorvão is thus donated to the Cathedral in Coimbra, and those who defend it against the Muslims shall receive absolution.

Pope Paschal's letters from 1101 and 1110(?) are important because they demonstrate the instantaneous spreading of the crusade idea immediately after the conquest of Jerusalem. This is worth keeping in mind because there has been a long-established tradition amongst historians of claiming that the crusade idea only arrived later on the Iberian Peninsula; the wars before that were only just wars or defensive wars, but not proper crusades. The crux of the matter then is often the papal promise of indulgence. Starting from their individual definitions, historians have dated the first "real" Iberian crusade differently. Many[85] have referred to 1123, when Pope Calixtus II – whose family was closely connected with Portugal and León-Castile – wrote to all kings, counts and princes in Spain asking them to support to the troubled Iberian Church. He promised those who put crosses on their clothes to fight against the heathens "the same absolution of sins as we have given those who defend the Church in the East."[86] Those who had taken the cross and had not fulfilled their promise to go to war before the coming Easter were to be excommunicated and excluded from the flock of the Church until they had done penance – that is, until they had participated in the Iberian crusade.[87] That same year it was emphasized at the First Lateran Council that everybody who had taken the cross for the Holy Land or for the Iberian Peninsula should travel before Easter of the following year.[88] There is no doubt that Calixtus, with his wording in 1123, deliberately wished to emphasize that a crusade was the same in the East as in the West – exactly as Peter of Cluny did in his letter to the Norwegian King Sigurd Jorsalfarer in the same year. However, this was the same idea that Paschal had expressed more than twenty years before. Paschal used the words "do your penance (in the Iberian Peninsula)" – *poenitentias peragatis* – and promised that the warriors in return would "receive the remission and grace of the Church" – *ecclesiae remissionem et gratiam percipiatis* – or the absolution of their sins – *peccatorum absolutionem*. Calixtus promised them "the same absolution of sins" as those who went to Jerusalem – *eamdem peccatorum remissionem*. The difference is small and in practice without significance.[89] The crusades arrived on the Iberian Peninsula two years after the conquest of Jerusalem by the first crusade, and Calixtus' letter from 1123 only confirmed the prevailing and already existing papal indulgence policy.

The similarity between Jerusalem crusades and those on the Iberian Peninsula was expressed even more directly one year later, in 1124.[90] Archbishop Diego of

Santiago de Compostela wrote: "Just as the knights of Christ and the faithful sons of the Holy Church opened the road to Jerusalem with great toil and bloodshed, so shall we become knights of Christ and vanquish his malevolent enemies, the Muslims, and in this way open the road to the same Holy Sepulchre through Spain, which is a shorter and less burdensome road."[91] Together with bishops of Braga, Toledo, Osma, Burgos, León, Tuy and of other places, Diego proclaimed almost at the same time that, "with God's consent, the road to Jerusalem has been opened in this part of the world, and the Church of God, which had been held in the chains of slavery, was set free."[92] It cannot possibly be expressed any more clearly. The road to Jerusalem went through the wars against the infidels not only in the Holy Land but also on the Iberian Peninsula and in the Baltic region. The concept of crusade, with indulgence and all the rhetoric and the perception of the infidels, had been extended from Jerusalem in the centre to the countries in the periphery, where they must do battle as well. Count Henrique reacted to this and took part in this extension of the crusades in Portugal, just as Canute Lavard and his cousin and his paternal uncle did in Southern Denmark and in the Baltic. However, it was the sons of the two rulers who systematized and streamlined the war against the infidels, and who used their participation in crusades to create positions for themselves as very powerful kings.

In the power of the enemy – captives and ransoms

In these religious frontier regions, falling into the enemy's hands was always a realistic possibility. Anytime, when on the field or at home on the farm or in the castle, there was a risk of being attacked, defeated and taken away as a captive. If one participated in one of the many raids far into enemy territory with the intention of plundering and taking prisoners, it could go wrong. Slave raiders always exposed themselves to risk, not only of being killed but also of becoming slaves themselves. Some were set to work, the rich ones were held until an agreement on ransoming was negotiated.

In around 1130, a young nobleman from Denmark was captured by heathen Wends and held in iron chains, and he was chained to a peasant at night to prevent him from cutting through the chain and escaping.[93] The unfortunate captive feared a life in slavery as he knew that his family would not pay a ransom – they had already done that twice! During night-time, he therefore killed the peasant and sawed off his leg so he himself could escape into the forest, still wearing the chains. However, when it became day, he was found by dogs and brought back. The Wends had specially trained bloodhounds to track down runaway slaves, which says something about the extent of slave raiding and slave escapes.

The young man was thoroughly beaten and lost his hearing and some use of his limbs. He was then placed in a more secure prison together with sixteen other Christian prisoners. There he sat until he in a dream had a vision of St. Olav, who took off his chains, opened the door for him and hid him from the bloodhounds so he could escape back home. He travelled on to Trondheim and went into the service of St. Olav, presumably by entering a monastery.

122   *The extending of Jerusalem*

In a similar way, Santiago helped Christians in Muslim captivity – the narratives were written down and kept in the account of his deeds at Santiago de Compostela. When the Almoravids counterattacked after Alfonso VI's conquest of Toledo in 1085, a count was captured together with twenty men and one priest, taken to Zaragoza and put in a dungeon, which was reportedly as dark as Hell. The priest suggested praying to Santiago, who suddenly appeared as a shining figure that lit up the room, and the captives who were sitting bent from their aches threw themselves at his feet. Santiago broke their chains and led them through the dark night to the city gates, which quietly opened when he made the sign of the cross in front of them. They closed silently when they had walked out into freedom. Another time, Santiago saved a prisoner by letting him jump from a very tall tower without getting hurt. A third prisoner, who had been freed, went on the pilgrimage trail to Santiago de Compostela and gave his chains to the main altar in the church, where they were displayed when the miracle stories were written down.[94]

The other great Portuguese saint, Vincent, also freed a captive from Muslim imprisonment.[95] This was an unfortunate monk, Sancho, from Mallorca, who had been captured together with his abbot and taken to Malaga. Here, they met a canon from Córdoba, who had abandoned his faith and become a Muslim. The abbot tried to convince him to return to Christianity "because there is no faith if it is not the faith in Christ; everything else is infidelity, which does not save but leads to perdition." The apostate mentioned it to the king of Malaga and the abbot was flogged to death "with these whips that the Muslims call azoutes." Sancho was sold to Ceuta, where Vincent arrived at night in a brilliant light and freed him. He lifted Sancho from the ground and the chains fell from his hands and feet. Sancho wondered why no one else in the cell was woken up by the noise of the chains falling to the floor. Nor did anyone see how the shining Vincent and Sancho put a boat out and it sailed so quickly that it felt as if it was being drawn with a rope, and they arrived in Córdoba. Sancho was led across the great square in front of the mosque without anyone noticing him. The Muslims nevertheless took their bloodhounds out to search for him. St. Vincent led him to a little cave where the dogs went all the way up to Sancho's feet, sniffing but without finding him. Sancho eventually reached Lisbon and the cathedral where Vincent is buried. The next day, a large procession was organized outside the church, with sermons and songs of praise. Sancho then stood with his chains around his neck and his hands – he evidently carried them all the way – and testified that Vincent freed him, and the crowd entered the cathedral with him and hung the chains by the saint's grave.

The Danish crusader saint Canute Lavard helped a Swede who was captured by the heathens. Just like Santiago, Canute came at night, shining brilliantly, released the prisoner from his chains and led him out through the locked doors of the dungeon. In gratitude, the emancipated Swede gave 144 pounds of incense to Canute's tomb in Ringsted.[96]

Freeing Christian prisoners from heathen captivity became an important activity of crusader saints. The narratives of how they did so helped crusaders' families and brought hope and lessened the fear of those venturing out to fight in enemy

The extending of Jerusalem   123

lands. The pious gifts, chains and the enemy's weapons could be seen in the main church of the saint and served as a guarantee of the authenticity of the narratives.

At the same time institutions were established in the frontier regions to collect money to ransom the captives.[97] This was to relieve the families so they did not have to face this task on their own, as it could be difficult to fulfil if young, foolhardy warriors were so unfortunate as to get captured several times. On the Iberian Peninsula, wealthy individuals early on began to leave a sum in their testament to ransom prisoners, either in money, a plot of land or their Muslim slaves, who could be exchanged for Christian slaves. Similar practices became widespread on the Muslim side as well. The money was administered by the executor of the will, in some cases it was probably left to the local cathedral to collect the sums from different testaments and to decide who was to be ransomed. It is reasonable to assume that it would have been those whose families were unable to pay. Whether they also considered who would be able to take part in the wars against the infidels in the future is unknown. The actual exchange of prisoners across the religious frontier on the Iberian Peninsula was, from the beginning of the 12th century, handled by traders who traded on both sides, often Jews. They became known under the Arab designation *alfaqueque*, and their fee was normally 20% of the ransom.[98]

The ransoming of Christian slaves did play a military role, but the primary objectives in the testaments were predominantly charitable. The issuer wished to perform a good act which could help in the afterlife. Therefore, it is not uncommon that the testament contains clauses saying that the Muslim or heathen slaves were to be emancipated after the death of the owner. The Danish Archbishop Absalon freed several slaves in 1201 in his testament. This concerns "the formerly free women, whom the Marshal Niels received in slavery, together with their children, wherever they are." Not an especially precisely defined group but apparently large. There is also the slave woman whom Absalon received from Scania, together with her children. Finally it is the Christian cook, or Christian the cook – this is not entirely clear – who "unjustly had been taken prisoner and made a slave." It almost sounds as if it was a mistake, which must have been rather depressing for the good cook.[99]

The composition of the household could be mixed and consist of slaves as well as former slaves, and they were often treated quite differently. In 1116, João Gondesendes and his wife drew up a will in which they gave property to their emancipated slaves Martin, son of Cid, and Peter Palaiz, and this was to go to the archdiocese of Coimbra when the two of them died; a lifelong pension to two old, loyal slaves, who already had been rewarded with their freedom. Additionally, they freed all the slaves and slave women who were in their possession at their death. The wording suggested that the number of slaves in the household could fluctuate. Finally, all their Muslim men and Muslim women were to be exchanged with Christian captives.[100] There is thus a clear distinction between slaves and Muslim slaves. The first group was emancipated, the second one exchanged for Christian slaves.

From the late 12th century, monastic orders emerged whose special duty was to release money and ransom Christian captives from the heathens.[101] In special

124   *The extending of Jerusalem*

cases, the friars should offer to exchange themselves and become slaves in return for having another Christian set free. The largest of them was the Order of the Holy Trinity, which was recognized by Innocent III in 1198. The friars were supposed to divide all income into three portions. One was to be used for the upkeep of hospitals, the other portion was to support the friars and the third was to be used for ransoming Christians or, for a suitable payment, to ransom Muslim slaves from Christian masters so they could be exchanged for Christian captives. Normally, the Trinity friars should only live in groups of six persons, of whom three should be lay and three clerics. The Trinity Order arrived in Santarém in 1208 at the latest and in Lisbon in 1218. The Mercedars, the Friars of Our Lady of Mercy, was a similar but somewhat smaller ransom order; it was established in 1218.[102] There is no mention in the sources of these or similar orders in Denmark.

Widespread slavery would have been a natural consequence of living in a society which waged war constantly. Slavery and trade in human beings was well established far back in time, a long time before Christianity arrived in Scandinavia. Both phenomena continued uninterrupted into the crusade era but now with the sometimes troublesome detail that slaves belonging to another religion might convert to Christianity and then find support for the idea that they ought to win freedom as well. It came very slowly and nothing indicates that slavery was abolished quickly in Denmark for religious reasons. The importance and extent of slavery has probably been underestimated generally in Danish historical research. It is difficult to estimate with any certainty because of the scarcity of sources, but a comparison with Portugal indicates that slavery would have been rather widespread in Denmark and Scandinavia.

Notes

1 Fuit mocio cristianorum euncium Ierusalem super paganos; the annals of Lund and Colbaza for 1096; again, under 1101: Item mocio facta est euncium Ierusalem, DMA p. 9 and p. 55; see also DMA p. 17: Dane fore mange thill Ierusalem att stride gen hedinge. DMA p. 108. The Icelandic annales regii: hófz Iorsalaferð af norðrlöndum – there was journeying to Jerusalem from the countries in the North; *Islandske Annaler*, p. 110; cf. Lögmann annals, Ibid., 251.

2 Luíz Gonzaga de Azevedo, *História de Portugal*, vols. 1–6 (Lisboa, 1935–1944), vol. 3, p. 60, that refers to Rodrigo de Toledo.

3 Annales Toledanos 1105, p. 386.

4 Azevedo, *História de Portugal*, vol. 3, pp. 46ff.

5 Alan V. Murray, *The Crusader Kingdom of Jerusalem: A Dynastic History 1099–1125* (Oxford, 2000), pp.60–61.

6 Sociatis sibi . . . auxilis.

7 Ekkehardus Uraugiensis, Chronicon universale, PL 154, col. 959–960.

8 He became the first abbot at the monastery of Aura, founded by Otto; see the biographical introduction in Schmale and Schmale-Ott's edition of Ekkehard, pp. 19–31.

9 Petrus Venerabilis, *De laude dominici sepulchri*, in Giles Constable, 'Petri Venerabilis sermones tres', *Revue Benedictine* 64 (1954), pp. 224–272, here p. 246.

10 *La Chanson d'Antioche*, ed. Suzanne Duparc-Quioc (Paris, 1977–1978), vols. 1–2, p. 355, lines 9004–9009. "Tot cil de Danemarce, Loherenc et Frison, Tant com cevals puet corre a coite d'esperon, se fierent tot ensanble es Turs par tel randon. De son espiel

The extending of Jerusalem 125

trençant cascuns abat le son; As espees trençans font tele occision, Li sans et li cervele en gist sor le sablon."

11 Albert of Aix, *Historia Expeditionis Hierosolymitanae*, 1, 54, PL 166, col. 469, Annalista Saxo, 730. Kurt Villads Jensen, 'Denmark and the Crusading Movement. The Integration of the Baltic Region Into Medieval Europe', in: A.I. Macinnes, T. Riis and F.G. Pedersen (eds.), *Ships, Guns and Bibles in the North Sea and the Baltic States, ca. 1350–c.1700* (East Linton, 2000), pp. 188–205.

12 William of Tyre, IV, 20.

13 Torquato Tasso, *Gerusalemme liberata*, ed. Luigi Bonfigli (Bari, 1930), chan. 8, st. 2–42; *Gierusalemme conquista*, lib. 9. Actually, the first to scale the wall were two Flemish knights, Letold and Gilbert of Tourney, quickly followed by Godfrey of Bouillon; see Murray, *The Crusader Kingdom*, pp. 60–61.

14 Jørgensen, 'Fra svenske Biblioteker'.

15 Steffen Heiberg, *Christian IV og Europa: Den 19. Europarådsudstilling Danmark 1988* (Copenhagen, 1988), p. 76, pp. 102–103.

16 Heinrich von Sybel, *Geschichte des ersten Kreuzzugs* (Düsseldorf, 1841), 78–79; Paul Riant, *Expéditions et pèlerinages des Scandinaves en Terre Sainte au temps des Croisades* (Paris, 1865), pp. 146–152.

17 Demonstrated in Thyra Nors, 'Ægteskab og politik i Saxos Gesta danorum', *Historisk Tidsskrift* 98 (1998), pp. 1–33.

18 For the life of el Cid, Richard A. Fletcher, *The Quest for el Cid* (Oxford, 1989), which also describes the cult that emerged after the death of el Cid and how el Cid had been embalmed to keep him fresh and ready to participate in the last, decisive battle against the Almoravids.

19 Charles Julian Bishko, 'The Spanish and Portuguese Reconquest, 1095–1492', *A History of the Crusades* 3 (1975), pp. 396–456, here p. 406; Azevedo, *História de Portugal*, vol. 3, p. 62; A.H. de Oliveira Marques, 'O poder e o espaço', in: Maria Helena da Cruz Coelho e Armando Luís de Carvalho Homem (eds.), *Nova História de Portugal* (Lisbon, 1996), vol. 3, p. 19. However, Mário Jorge Barroca, 'Da reconquista a D. Dinis', in: Manuel Themudo Barata and Nuno Severiano Teixeira (eds.), *Nova História militar de Portugal* (Lisbon, 2003), vol. 1, pp. 22–161, here p. 35, thinks that the Almoravids were defeated. The battle is mentioned in Annales Toledanos II, in España Sagrada 23, p. 403, but only with Henrique as leader.

20 Barroca, 'Da reconquista a D. Dinis', p. 35 dates it to the first half of 1102; Marques, 'O poder e o espaço', p. 19 to 1103.

21 Bishko, 'The Spanish and Portuguese Reconquest', p. 406.

22 Cartulaire de Cluny, *Recueil des chartes de l'abbaye de Cluny*, ed. A. Bernard and A. Bruel, vols. 1–6 (Paris, 1876–1903), vol. 5: no. 3809, pp. 156–159. The peace with Cluny cannot be dated any nearer than 1101. See also James Lea Cate, 'The Crusade of 1101', *A History of the Crusades* 1 (1958), pp. 343–367, here pp. 349–350; J. Riley-Smith, *The First Crusaders, 1095–1131* (Cambridge, 1997), pp. 121–122.

23 Jean Richard, *The Crusades ca. 1071– ca. 1291* (Cambridge, 1999), p. 73. Several of the early narrative sources confuse Eude with Stephen of Burgundy (Cate, 'The Crusade of 1101', p. 350), so it is not certain if Eude fell in 1101 or rather in 1102.

24 Mentioned in Galberti Brugensis 20; in PL 166, col. 955. It has been debated whether Carl went crusading in 1101 or 1107–1108; cf. Murray, *The Crusader Kingdom*, pp. 139–146; Jonathan Phillips, *Defenders of the Holy Land. Relations Between the Latin East and the West, 1119–1187* (Oxford, 1996), p. 274 who insists on the later dating. Riley-Smith (*The First Crusaders*, p. 159) argues that Carl went on crusade just after 1100 and presumably stayed in the Holy Land until near 1111. He refers to Gualter of Thérousanne's vita of Carl: Hic autem noster Carolus annis pueritiae transactis adultus, postquam militiae cingulum accepit, Hierusalem sanctam sepulcrum Dominicum visitaturus, devotus adivit; ibique adversum paganos fidei nostrae inimicos arma ferens, Christo Domino aliquanto tempore strenue militavit, et ei, cui prae

126   *The extending of Jerusalem*

omnibus serviendum esse prudenter advertebat, suorum primitias laborum et actuum dedicavit: mox divina ordinante dispositione, ad avunculum suum Robertum juniorem marchionem, in Flandriam revertitur, et ab illo eo, quo talem juvenem decebat, honore suscipitur (Gualterus Tarvanensis 5, PL 166, col. 905). Carl cannot have left until after November 1, 1101, when he was witnessing a letter in Paderborn, see DD 1:2, no. 61.

25 Ekkehardus Uraugiensis Chronicon, PL 154, col. 987.

26 Saxo, 12.6.5. Crusade vow is translation of eodem voto.

27 According to Knytlinga saga, chapter 79.

28 P.J. Riis and Thomas Riis, 'Knud den Helliges ørnætappe i Odense Domkirke – et forsøg på nytolkning', *KUML* 2004 (2004), pp. 259–273. The eagle silk is still on display today in the cathedral of Odense.

29 Saxo, 12.7.4.

30 Knytlinga saga, chapter 81. On Nordic skaldic poetry, see Hans-Peter Naumann, 'Nordische Kreuzzugsdichtung', in: Hans-Peter Naumann, Magnus von Platen and Stefan Sonderegger (eds.), *Festschrift für Oskar Bandle zum 60. Geburtstag am 11. Januar 1986* (Basel, 1986), on Markús pp. 175–178. Markús's poem about Erik is considered the turning point when the Christian Middle Ages entered Nordic skaldic poetry, Naumann, 'Nordische Kreuzzugsdichtung', p. 176, note 6.

31 Knytlinga saga, chapter 79.

32 In modern Danish historical literature, Erik's journey is often termed a "pilgrimage." That it was supposed to be a crusade is normally not mentioned. Exceptions from this are, amongst others, Tore Nyberg, *Die Kirche in Skandinavien. Mitteleuropäischer und englischer Einfluss im 11. und 12. Jahrhundert. Anfange der Domkapitel Børglum und Odense in Dänemark* (Sigmaringen, 1986), p. 12, which refers to Erik as filled with crusading zeal. Bodil was the daughter of Galicia-Ulf's son (Knýtlinga saga, chapter 75; Saxo, 12.1.1); however, only Knýtlinga saga mentions that she was a half-sister to Emperor Henry.

33 Albert of Aix, 10, 1–4.

34 LP 80, from May 1103, which mentions that Henrique is in Jerusalem. Whether he returned later in 1103 or the year after is not known.

35 Azevedo, *História de Portugal*, vol. 3, p. 57.

36 Papsturkunden, no. 3–7. Jose Maria Soto Rabános, '¿Se puede hablar de un entramado político religiose en el proceso de independencia de Portugal?', *Hispania* 67 (2007), pp. 805–809, points out that Braga actually was not established as an archiepiscopal see but was recognized as such like in antiquity after the area had been retaken and re-Christianized around 1070.

37 Magnussona saga, chapter 11.

38 José Mattoso and Armindo de Sousa, *A Monarquia Feudal (1096–1480)* (Lisbon, 1993), p. 37.

39 The Hungarian background was later adopted by Camões, Os Lusíadas 3, 25.

40 Duarte Galvão, *Crónica de el-rei D. Afonso Henriques* (Lisbon, 1995), cap. XIX–XX.

41 Francisco Marques de Sousa Viterbo, *O mosteiro de Sancta Cruz de Coimbra* (Coimbra, 1914). For the extension of convents that lived according to the same rule and liturgy as the Holy Sepulchre in Jerusalem, see Nikolas Jaspert, *Stift und Stadt. Das Heiliggrabpriorat von Santa Anna und das Regularkanonikerstift Santa Eulàlia del Camp im mittelalterlichen Barcelona, 1145–1423* (Berlin, 1996), about Santa Cruz in Coimbra pp. 119–120; their extension on the Iberian Peninsula Nikolas Jaspert, 'Die Ritterorden und der Orden vom heiligen Grab auf der iberischen Halbinsel', *Militia Sancti Sepulcri: idea e instituzioni; atti del colloquio internazionale* (Citta del Vaticano, 1998), pp. 381–410. For imitations of the Holy Sepulchre, his 'Vergegenwärtigungen Jerusalems in Architektur und Reliquienkult', in: Dieter Bauer, Klaus Herbers and Nikolas Jaspert (eds.), *Jerusalem im Hoch- und Spätmittelalter. Konflikte und Konfliktbewältigung – Verstellungen und Vergegenwärtigungen* (Frankfurt, 2001), pp. 219–270, here pp. 223–225; Colin Morris, *The Sepulchre of Christ and the Medieval*

West. From the Beginning to 1600 (Oxford, 2005), esp. 180–253. For Santa Cruz, see António Cruz, *Santa Cruz de Coimbra na cultura portuguesa da Idade Media* (Porto, 1964); Saul António Gomes, *In limine conscriptionis. Documentos, Chancelaria e Cultura no mosteiro de Santa Cruz de Coimbra (Séculos XII a XIV)* (Viseu, 2007).

42 A very late tradition says that Erik later in his life "supposedly went to Jerusalem/ and saw the Holy Sepulchre, wherefrom he soon came back healed." ("skal haffue reyst to Jerusalem/ oc beset den hellige Graff, huorsaare hand kom helbred tilbage.") (Huitfeldt 1603, 216) Huitfeldt had access to much medieval material that has later been lost. See Janus Møller Jensen, 'King Erik Emune (1134–1137) and the Crusades. The Impact of Crusadig Ideology on Early Twelfth-Century Denmark', in: Kurt villads Jensen, Kirsi Salonen and Helle Vogt (eds.), *Cultural Encounters During the Crusades* (Odense, 2013), pp. 91–104.

43 *Urkundenbuch des Erzstifts Magdeburg*, vol. 1, no. 193, pp. 249–252.

44 Guibert of Nogent, *Opusculum de virginitate*, PL 156, col. 587.

45 Robert the Monk, *Historia Hierosolymitana*, PL 155, cols. 667–758, 1.

46 Baldric of Dole, 2. *RHC*, p. 17.

47 Cf. Robert the Monk, PL 155, col. 671.

48 Fulcher of Chartres, 3.

49 The same words as Urban's regarding the Holy Land according to Robert the Monk, PL 155, col. 672.

50 "Hic poteritis et animas uestras saluificare et si ita placet, optimam terram ad inhabitandum acquirere."

51 Here the more precise term *galli* is used, not *franci*.

52 Peter Knoch, 'Kreuzzug und Siedlung. Studien zum Aufruf der magdeburger Kirche von 1108', *Jahrbuch für die Geschichte Mittel- und Ostdeutschlands* 23 (1974), pp. 1–33, here pp. 20–21; Jørgensen, 'Fra svenske Biblioteker'.

53 Henri Pirenne, 'Un appel à une croisade contre les Slaves adresse à l'évêque de Liège, au duc de Lotharingie et au comte de Flandre au commencement du XIIme siècle', in: *Mélanges Camille de Borman. Recueil de Mémoires relatifs à l'histoire, a l'archéologie et à la philologie offert au Baron de Borman et publié par ses amis et admirateurs* (Liège, 1919), pp. 85–90.

54 Giles Constable, 'The Place of the Magdeburg Charter of 1107/08 in the History of Eastern Germany and of the Crusades', in: Franz J. Felten und Nikolas Jaspert (eds.), *Vita religiosa im Mittelalter: Festschrift für Kaspar Elm zum 70. Geburtstag* (Berlin, 1999), pp. 283–299.

55 "Magdeburg . . . wurde . . . zur Metropole des gesamten Ostens, dessen Kolonisierung, das größte Kulturwerk des deutschen Mittelalters, hier seinen Ausgang genommen hat." Einleitung, VII.

56 DD 1:2, no. 39: "The present letter has no official characteristics. It is a call to arms, written by a private person, to participate in the fight against the Wends," it is claimed without any argumentation.

57 Which is also mentioned in one of the latest treatments of the letter, Constable, 'The Place of the Magdeburg Charter'.

58 At least, Otto of Bamberg had to ask the permission of the Danish Archbishop Asser to missionize on Rügen in 1127. Whether Rügen was placed under Lund by the establishment of the archiepiscopal see or at a later time before 1127 is impossible to say for sure.

59 Magnussona saga, chapter 13; Gary B. Doxey, 'Norwegian Crusaders and the Balearic Islands', *Scandinavian Studies* 68 (1996), pp. 139–160, who discusses the chronology on pp. 144–150. Dowey discusses whether Sigurd's expedition was a crusade (pp. 156–159) and concludes: "Despite the ambiguity of the evidence regarding whether Sigurds's journey was a pilgrimage or a crusade, it is hard to imagine how the expedition could possibly fall outside the crusading movement as a whole." On the skaldic tradition's depiction of Sigurd as a crusader, see Naumann, 'Nordische Kreuzzugsdichtung',

128   *The extending of Jerusalem*

pp. 182–186. Against the Norwegian expeditions to the Holy Land Being crusades, Arnved Nedkvitne, 'Why Did Medieval Norsemen Go on Crusade?', in: Tuomas M.S. Lehtonen and Kurt Villads Jensen with Janne Malkki and Katja Ritari (eds.), *Medieval History Writing and Crusading Ideology* (Helsinki, 2005), pp. 37–50.

60 It was quite common for crusading kings to bring a splinter of the True Cross back, not least because it was a sign of military power; they were often carried at the head of the army; see Jaspert, 'Vergegenwärtigungen Jerusalems', pp. 253–255; Alan V. Murray, 'Might Against the Enemies of Christ: The Relic of the True Cross in the Armies of the Kingdom of Jerusalem', in: John France and William G. Zajac (eds.), *The Crusades and the Sources. Essays Presented to Bernard Hamilton* (Aldershot, 1998), pp. 217–238.

61 Magnussona saga, chapter 19; Magnúss saga blinda ok Haralds gilla, chapter 10–11.

62 Magnussona saga, chapter 24. Tore Nyberg has suggested that the crusade is connected with a great, regular sacrificial feast that occurred every eight years; Nyberg, *Monasticism*, p. 129. Discussed by Nils Blomkvist, *The Discovery of the Baltic. The Reception of a Catholic World-System in the European North (AD 1075–1225)* (Leiden, 2005), pp. 307–334, who argues against it being a crusade, as Småland had been Christianized at that point. Thus, he does not consider that the crusade was directed exactly against apostates.

63 Saxo, 13.5.5. It is not clear from Saxo whether this expedition was part of the raid against the Småland peoples or whether it happened slightly later.

64 Pomniki Dziejowe Polski, vol. 2, p. 832; Ane L. Bysted, Kurt Villads Jensen, Carsten Selch Jensen, and John Lind, *Jerusalem in the North: Denmark and the Baltic Crusades, 1100–1522* (Turnhout, 2012), pp. 36–37.

65 This appears from the chronicle by the so-called Gallus Anonymus authored before 1118. Here it is described how Prussians, Pomeranians and other Slavs further to the west took refuge in baptism in difficult situations, but as soon as they had regained their strength, they fell from Christianity and attacked the Christians. Whether this description of the heathens is true or not remains undecided but the wording was to become a classic justification for crusades against heathens, and was thus used to justify the Kalmar crusade as well, cf. Gallus Anonymus, *Chronik*, 48.

66 Diplomatarium Norvegicum, vol. XIX, no. 25; also published in LPV: *The Letters of Peter the Venerable*, vols. 1–2, ed. Giles Constable (Cambridge, MA, 1967), I, no. 44, 140–141; notes LPV II, 128. Virginia G. Berry, 'Peter the Venerable and the Crusades', *Petrus Venerabilis, 1156–1956, Studies Commemorating the Eighth Centenary of His Death*, ed. G. Constable and J. Kritzeck, *Studia Anselmiana* 40 (1956), pp. 141–162, holds (on p. 144) that Peter's letter was issued in the context of a crusade that Sigurd was to have planned in 1130, shortly before his death. Her arguments do not seem convincing.

67 Peter quotes Song of Songs 4, 16.

68 Fuit enim hujus loci magnus amator. PL 166, cols. 841–842, which tells us that Abbot Pontius (dismissed 1122) admitted Archbishop Bernard of Toledo in the community of Cluny and likewise Archbishop Eskil of Lund. Chronologically, something is wrong – Eskil was either admitted as a very young man and a long time before he became a bishop, or the note has been backdated; Cowdrey, 'Two Studies'.

69 DD 1:2, no. 50–52.

70 Saxo, 12.6.5.

71 Helmold, 49.

72 Chronicon Roskildense, XIV.

73 Hermanson, *Släkt, vänner och makt*.

74 The battle of Fotevig was led as a religious war with Communion and in the name of God at the behest of Archbishop Asser, according to Knytlinga saga, chapter 97. This is not a contemporaneous tradition, but Janus Møller Jensen ('King Erik Emune') has argued convincingly for its reliability with regard to this question by reading it in the context of the contemporaneous European crusade policy.

The extending of Jerusalem   129

75 Saxo, 14.1.6.
76 Magnussona saga, chapter 32.
77 Knytlinga saga, chapter 79. This is inconsistent with Saxo (12.6.5), who vaguely mentions that Erik was placed in the care of some less important people while his father went on his pilgrimage.
78 John Lind, 'De russiske ægteskaber. Dynasti- og alliancepolitik i 1130'ernes danske borgerkrig', *Historisk Tidsskrift* 92 (1992), pp. 225–263, here pp. 230ff.
79 Paschal, letter XXII, PL 163, col. 44. For the participation in the first crusade of Spanish noblemen, see Margarita C. Torres Sevilla-Quiñones, 'Cruzados y peregrinos leoneses y castellanos en Tierra Santa ss. XI–XII', *Medievalismo* 9 (1999), pp. 63–82.
80 Paschal, letter XXVI, PL 163, col. 45. Paschal employs here the term *venia peccatorum*, which may or may not be the same kind of absolution that the crusaders to Jerusalem had been promised by Urban.
81 Paschal, letter XLIV, PL 163, col. 63.
82 Papsturkunden, commentary to no. 11, p. 164.
83 Probably refers to LP 59 of July 1109.
84 Paschal, littere, in Castello Branco, 'Apontamentos', p. 73; LP 625.
85 Richard A. Fletcher, *Saint James' Catapult: The Life and Times of Diego Gelmirez of Santiago de Compostela* (Oxford, 1984), pp. 297–299, with further references.
86 Calixtus, letter CCXLIX, PL 163, col. 1305.
87 "si ab hoc Paschate usque ad aliud votum suum persolvere non sategerint, a gremio sanctae Ecclesiae, donec satisfaciant, submovemus."
88 Canon 13; COD, 167–168.
89 Ane L. Bysted, *The Crusade Indulgence. Spiritual Rewards and the Theology of the Crusades c. 1095–1216* (Leiden, 2015), pp. 164–167; pp. 177–178.
90 Often dated 1125 but probably erroneously; see William J. Purkis, *Crusading Spirituality in the Holy Land and Iberia* (Woodbridge, 2008), p. 131, note 85.
91 Historia Compostellana, lib. 2, cap. 78.
92 Peter Rassow, 'La cofradía de Belchite', *Anuario de historia del derecho español* 3 (1926), pp. 220–226, here p. 225.
93 From Magnussona saga, chapter 39.
94 Liber Sancti Jacobi, vol. 1, p. 261, p. 273, p. 275.
95 Miracula Vincentii, lib. 2, cap. 6.
96 VSD, pp. 242–245.
97 James William Brodman, *Ransoming Captives in Crusader Spain. The Order of Merced on the Christian-Islamic Frontier* (Philadelphia, 1986).
98 Ibid., p. 7; Amancio Isla, 'Warfare and Other Plagues in the Iberian Peninsula Around the Year 1000', in: Przemysław Urbańczyk (ed.), *Europe Around the Year 1000* (Warsaw, 2001), p. 240, mentions a case from 986, where Jewish middle men received fifty silver solidi to ransom Christian captives.
99 DD 1:4, no. 32.
100 DMP IV:1, no. 1.
101 *La liberazione dei 'captivi' tra cristianità e islam. Oltre la crociata e il ğihād: Tolleranza e servizio umanitario*, ed. Giulio Cipollone (Cittá del Vaticano, 2000); rule of order in BP 35.
102 Brodman, *Ransoming Captives;* Saul António Gomes, 'A produção artesanal' and 'Grupos étnico-religiosos e estrangeiros', in: Maria Helena da Cruz Coelho and Armando Luís de Carvalho Homem (eds.), *Nova História de Portugal* (Lisbon, 1996), vol. 3, p. 337; José Mattoso, *Identificação de um país: ensaio sobre as origens de Portugal, 1096–1325*, vols. 1–2 (Lisbon, 1995), vol. 1, pp. 429–431.

6 Afonso and Valdemar
The victorious crusader kings

Afonso Henriques

Count Henrique and his beautiful wife Teresa, who always remembered to emphasize her imperial pedigree in her letters, clearly had great expectations of their first child, who was to continue the family line and extend Henrique's county yet further into Muslim territory. Teresa gave birth to the child at the castle in Guimarães or at Viseu. It was a boy, larger and more beautiful than any other child one could imagine. Apart from the stunted lower legs. He would never be able to walk or ride, and the doctors that were summoned agreed that he could never be cured. Count Henrique's disappointment was immense. His good friend and closest adviser, Egas Moniz, asked to have the child handed over so he could raise it, as agreed beforehand, but Henrique answered bitterly that he would never put such a burden on Egas. The child was a cripple because of the sins of its father, and "it would never become a human."[1] Thus, one was only human during the Middle Ages if one was able to ride and wage war, otherwise not.

Egas Moniz nevertheless insisted and was of the opinion that it was because of his own sins that he was to raise a cripple, not because of Henrique's. In the end, he took the child with him to his castle. When the young Afonso had reached the age of five, Egas saw a beautiful woman in a dream. She turned out to be the Virgin Mary. She commanded Egas to excavate an old church, founded in her honour but never completed. It had been forgotten and overgrown, but inside the church he would find an image of Maria. Egas believed the dream, found the image, completed the church and placed the miracle-working image on the altar. Then he laid Afonso with the crippled legs on top of the altar. The miracle happened. The legs straightened and grew and he was completely healed. This happened, Maria explained in the dream, "because my Son needs him to destroy many enemies of the faith." The great monastery of Carquere was built around this church and Egas raised Afonso "with even greater care." He followed Afonso for the rest of his life as his special advisor, his *aio*, which in meaning is close to the Danish title *marsk* or the English *constable*, that is, supreme commander of the royal forces.

The story is known only from chronicles from the 15th and 16th centuries, at least 300 years after the birth of Afonso. Is it true? Could the late medieval chroniclers have had access to sources or royal family traditions which are now

Afonso and Valdemar 131

lost? Or is it simply a good story, an "urban legend" that someone at some point in time thought applied well to Afonso, which others later passed on faithfully? We cannot decide that with any degree of certainty. However, maybe that is not so important because even though the content of the story might be wrong – viewed from a historian's cynical, critical point of view – it still transmits to us today a morale or an atmosphere that very well might hark back to Afonso's own time. We see something similar in Danish source material about Valdemar, and there are several other examples from high medieval historical writing and knightly literature. The great heroes became heroes against all odds. Many heroes had a difficult childhood, they were orphans, cast-offs, prisoners or they had been cripples, just like Afonso. In many cases it is true, from a critical historical point of view, for example in the case of the fatherless Valdemar. In other cases, it is an invention. In all cases, it was part of the hero mythology genre.[2]

Actually, Afonso experienced many troubles during his childhood. We do not possess any detailed information, but the circumstances surrounding the young son of a Count were at least as chaotic and bloody as in Denmark during the times of the young Valdemar. Afonso's father, Count Henrique, died in April 1112.[3] His cousin Raimundo in Galicia had died in 1107, their shared father-in-law, the great warrior Alfonso VI, had died in 1109, perhaps of grief. The year before, in 1108, Sancho was just seventeen years old when he fell in a battle at Uclès against the Almoravids. Sancho was Alfonso's only, albeit illegitimate, son, whom he had begotten with the Muslim Princess Zaida of Seville as she fled to León from the Almoravids. This means that one ruler and three obvious heirs to León and Castile and the rich city of Toledo died within just a few years of each other, and they left a vacuum of power, which ambitious noblemen, distant members of the royal family and enemy forces from the outside immediately tried to fill.

Raimundo's widow, Urraca, married King Alfonso I of Aragon in 1109, but apparently not from love alone. Already in 1110 the married couple was in open war against each other. They both tried to control land in Portugal; they switched between laying siege to Henrique in Coimbra and allying themselves with him. Internal wars continued in Aragon until 1126. At the same time, in 1111, a year-long rebellion broke out amongst the people of Coimbra against Count Henrique and particularly the enforced Roman liturgy of the Church. The French knights had with the use of sheer force ensured that the old Mozarab rite was replaced by the Roman Catholic one. Whether or not there is a direct connection between the new rite and this rebellion is uncertain, but on May 26 that year, Santarém was retaken by the Caliph of Morocco himself, Ali Ibn Yussuf, whom the Christian annals called Cyrus and compared with the ancient Persian ruler.[4] Coimbra was besieged several times over the following years, and, under his personal leadership, the suburbs were razed to the ground and thousands of Christians were murdered. Muslim pressure on the lands around the River Mondego intensified. In 1116, the Christians in Soure burned down their castle and fled to Coimbra, the strongholds of Miranda do Corvo and Montemor-o-velho were lost and fell to the Muslims again.[5]

The news of King Alfonso's VI death in 1109 was not the only reason for the fighting; it was perhaps also an offshoot of Sigurd Jorsalfarer's expedition to

132   *Afonso and Valdemar*

Portugal. Sigurd first arrived in Galicia in 1108. He spent the winter there but fell afoul of Urraca and plundered the region; he "gave the raven plenty to eat," the sagas explained, referring to dead bodies on the battlefield.[6] From there, the Norwegian fleet sailed southwards and defeated eight large Muslim ships en route. Sigurd arrived at Sintra, conquered the strong Muslim castle there and killed the heathens who refused to convert. Then he conquered and pillaged first Lisbon, then Alcácer, and took much plunder in both places. The victories lasted only for a short time. Sigurd was on his way to the Balearic Isles and to the Holy Land, but his strong fleet of Norse longships would have constituted quite a decisive force.[7] Whether he attacked the Muslims together with Count Henrique is uncertain. It is not mentioned in the saga. However, this was meant to glorify Sigurd and would not have found it particularly important to mention some Portuguese ally. In any event, Sigurd's presence shifted the balance of power in the area between Mondego and Tagus and could, therefore, have played a part in provoking Muslim counterattacks.

For several years, Henrique's widow, Teresa, met with demands from her sister, Urraca, for an oath of fealty. This was to recognize the supremacy of a badly defined and struggling Galicia-León-Castile-Aragon over Portugal. At the same time, the Portuguese noblemen in Coimbra also speculated on the possibility of changing loyalties, and some of the most important of them actually submitted to Alfonso I of Aragon.[8] Perhaps this was a protest against the increased influence of Galician noblemen on Teresa. On the other hand, Teresa attempted to convince Alfonso I, by using a secret messenger, that he was in the process of being poisoned with herbs by his own wife, her sister.[9] A contemporary chronicle tells us that Urraca governed *tyrannice et muliebriter*, tyrannically and as a woman.[10] This was not meant as praise. The powerful Bishop of Santiago de Compostela, Diego Gelmírez, operated in these troubled waters; he was possibly behind Teresa's imprisoning of the Archbishop of Braga in 1122, which led her to be excommunicated by the Pope.

In this somewhat complex situation, it is perhaps not so strange that Teresa looked around for a strong protector. She found him in the guise of the mighty Galician nobleman Fernão Peres de Trava, with whom she lived for around ten years until her death in 1130. The Trava family probably considered trying to get control over an independent Galicia, and as a guardian of the future ruler of Castile-León, they were well placed for this.[11] Fernão Peres's relationship with the dowager countess brought many advantages. He received castles and land in Portugal, he became lord of Coimbra and he acquired the title of Duke.[12] Fernão and Teresa's open cohabitation – without being married – attracted attention and possibly caused scandal, and it is difficult to understand completely why they had chosen that sort of relation. Perhaps Teresa had actually married Fernão's brother, Bermudo Peres, and afterwards changed her preference?[13] If this was the case, she was not only living in sin but in a prohibited family relationship.[14] In 1122, Bermudo was married to Teresa and Henrique's daughter, Urraca, so if Teresa had been married to Bermudo, it would have been an illegitimate marriage on two counts. Later medieval sources are not without strong criticism. In the vita of the founder of Santa Cruz it is recorded that one day in Viseu, Teotónio preached so pointedly and with such great authority that Teresa and Fernão blushed from shame and left the church in a hurry. As Teresa later wanted revenge and waited outside the church, she sent a messenger saying that Teotónio should hurry up in finishing the mass. He replied that he had another Queen in heaven that was much better and much more noble than Teresa.[15] Perhaps this construction only reflects that the marriage in the early 12th century was still considered a private, political and non-ecclesiastical act in the Iberian Peninsula, which it most certainly was not when the narrative about it was written in the monasteries at the end of the century.[16] What Afonso thought about his mother's behaviour is unknown. A modern Portuguese biography depicts it as a strain on Afonso, which almost traumatized him.[17] It is impossible to say, but the criticism of Teresa's conduct and her love for a Galician Duke was so important that Afonso was able to raise a Portuguese army of noblemen against his mother.

During Whitsun 1125, the sixteen-year-old Afonso Henriques entered public life for the first time. In front of the noblemen in the church, he girded his sword and knighted himself. This is mentioned in the Afonso Annals, which were written sixty years later, in around 1185, and they place the event at the Church of São Salvador in Zamora,[18] a peculiar place and somewhat remote. Coimbra, Guimarães or Braga would have been more obvious choices, so perhaps something has been confused over the years. The meaning of the act itself though cannot be mistaken. Afonso showed character, and by girding his sword himself, he demonstrated that he was independent of his mother and Fernão Peres de Trava. He was ready to take over the legacy of his father, and he was willing to front the old, Portuguese noble families who, through the preceding five years or longer, had more or less disappeared as witnesses in Teresa's letters and had been replaced by the vassals of the Trava family. What role the Church had in Afonso's ceremony is not known. Just as Valdemar's attempt to canonize his father in 1146, it is depicted as an almost private undertaking, which of course would not have been the case. Afonso would have found some support from the Church, but how broad it was it this stage is unknown. The cooperation of the Archbishop of Braga is not unlikely, considering his strained relationship with Teresa and in light of the fact that his closest competitor, Archbishop Diego Gelmírez, had in 1124 assisted at a similar ceremony in Santiago de Compostela. Raimundo's seventeen-year-old son Alfonso had also girded his sword himself and had become the ruler of Castile and León as Alfonso VII.

The rebellion did come, albeit slowly. Not until 1128 was Afonso strong enough to enter an open battle against Fernão's and his mother's army, which he defeated at São Mamede to the northeast of Guimarães on St. John the Baptist's Day, June 24. This was probably not an accidental date. St. John was the patron saint of the Order of St. John, and he was the precursor of Christ: a positive sign of Afonso's future career. The immediate result was that Fernão and Teresa withdrew to Galicia. Teresa died in 1130. She had by then given birth to two of Fernão's children without being married to him. Fernão later went on crusade to Jerusalem at least twice. The last time was in 1153, perhaps the same year as the

134 *Afonso and Valdemar*

Danish Bishop Svend of Viborg reached the Holy City together with his brother Eskil, a tyrannical nobleman with much experience in spilling blood.[19] Both of them had taken the cross and received the grace of dying near the Holy Sepulchre.

One of Afonso's first acts after the decisive victory over his mother was to confirm her extensive donations to the Knights Templar, and furthermore, Afonso joined the order himself. We shall take a closer look at this act in a later section; however, it is characteristic for Afonso and for the period that a new ruler in an area with religious frontiers had to engage himself immediately in the crusades in order to safeguard his powerbase.

During the first few years, Afonso was tied up militarily in the north and had to fight to gain control over some castles, especially the Galician counties of Toronho and Límia.[20] This brought him into open conflict with his cousin, Alfonso VII, which initially ended in 1137 with a peace settlement in the frontier town Tuy, which amongst other things meant that the Portuguese ruler had to swear fealty to Alfonso VII.[21] This turned out to be inadequate, and the wars continued, perhaps because powerful frontier barons such as the counts Rodrigo Peres Veloso of Líria and Gomes Nunes of Toronho saw an advantage in having their overlords engaged in mutual conflict, or perhaps because the two cousins were both too proud to compromise. This only changed after the battle at Valdevez in 1141. The terrain was rough and the two rulers were positioned on each their own ridge, able to see each other but unable to move forward with their armies. Instead of a massed attack, the army was disintegrating through a series of skirmishes, during which the noblemen rode down to the bottom of the valley and fought in small groups or individually against each other. Many were taken prisoner. Protracted negotiations about exchanges and ransom money loomed, and a decision was not immediately forthcoming. Instead of continuing the war, the two rulers agreed to find a solution through a *bafordo*, a duel between two warriors, one from each side.[22] Afonso Henriques' man lost and now they could settle for peace. All prisoners were set free and all conquered land on both sides was handed back. The wavering Count Gomes Nunes had made himself equally unpopular on either side and had to flee to the north of the Pyrenees, where he became a monk in Cluny. Most interesting though, is the reason for the necessity of a peace agreement. Afonso Henriques' oldest warriors persuaded him, arguing that the conflict between Portugal and Castile made Portugal vulnerable to Muslim attacks. They had already ravaged badly and were likely to move further ahead if Afonso did not make peace with Alfonso, and thus would be able to concentrate his forces for the defence of the faith.[23] Those wars were already well under way; many of them were proper Christian wars of expansion and it was simply impossible for the Portuguese to continue a war on two fronts. The peace of Valdevez demonstrates something typical of medieval religious frontier societies, namely that crusades could make peace between mutually fighting Christian princes – or perhaps rather that the main purpose of a peace agreement between Christian princes was to wage war, that is, wars against Muslims or other infidels.

The expansion southwards was realized through regular military expeditions and by establishing strongholds within the Muslim area, and Afonso must have started doing this right after the victory at São Mamede. In 1135, the castle of Leiria was founded as far as seventy kilometres from Coimbra and in a mountainous and difficult terrain. "As the first, I erected a castle from the ground in the wasteland," Afonso recalled some years later.[24] It seems like an exposed position but perhaps the area actually was rather empty. Some sources at least suggest that although the Muslim armies were able to pillage in the area, they did not have enough manpower to establish a permanent garrison. It was nevertheless a dangerous place to be and Leiria suffered attacks from the Muslim forces. In 1140, the lord of the castle was captured and more than 250 knights were felled by the sword, "and there was great sadness and outcry in the house of the Portuguese King."[25] At Veldevez, Afonso's advisors referred directly to the disaster at Leiria when arguing for a peace settlement with Alfonso VII.[26] In 1144 came the next big attack on Leiria. The Christian population in the area sought refuge behind the castle walls with their cattle and belongings.[27] Both humans and cattle were slaughtered on a large scale or led south as spoils of war. This, however, was not going to put a stop to the Christian crusade. On the contrary.

In 1145, the city council of Coimbra with permission of the King took an unusual step. It decided that "anyone who wishes to go Jerusalem does not have permission to go but shall come to the help of the castle of Leiria and the whole of the Extremadura region, and anyone who dies during this shall receive the same absolution as those who go to Jerusalem."[28] The ban against travelling to Jerusalem is issued by the city council, as is the promise of indulgence, although the latter in the most positive interpretation at the most can be the secular authority's proclamation of the Bishop's decision. In practice it seems rather like an attempt by a city council to stiffen its authority by investing itself with the authority of the bishop. The point, however, is obvious. The expansion southwards in Portugal was still equal to a crusade to the Holy Land.

In the meantime, Afonso had been active in other battles, of which the battle at Ourique in 1139 was to become the most famous and was to have enormous influence on the shaping of the Portuguese self-image. Precisely how it was perceived at the time we do not know and we are not sure where Ourique actually is either. Some have suggested the area south of the Mondego, others the region south of the Tagus, or even somewhere in Castile. According to contemporary sources it was an important battle,[29] but it was not until later historical writing that it was described as the decisive turning point, the battle of fate, where God Himself intervened and promised victory through a miracle, and where Portugal was born. The battle took place on the day of St. James, July 25, which was probably a deliberate choice of Afonso's and a precursor of how enormously popular Santiago was becoming as a crusader saint, in Portugal as well as in the Spanish lands. The later royal chronicle from around 1185[30] reports in detail on the enormous army the Muslim King Ismar had assembled, both from the Iberian Peninsula and from the land across the sea, from Morocco. All joined his army, even women, who fought as the Amazons did. The Christians only discovered this after the battle as they were having a closer look at some of the fallen and discovered that they were not men. Afonso was encircled on a hill amongst a sea of Muslims; he fought from

136   *Afonso and Valdemar*

morning until the evening, but "protected by the divine grace" Afonso eventually won an overwhelming victory, and "from that moment, the strength and audacity of the Muslims was seriously weakened." Thus, Afonso's victory was attributed to divine intervention as early as in the 12th century, though without making it clear what God precisely did. This came later.

At the beginning of the 15th century it was told how the noblemen had tried to convince Afonso to retreat and abandon the unequal fight – there were one hundred Muslims for every Christian. Then Afonso gave one of history's great inflammatory speeches: "We fight for God, for Faith, for Truth. The apostates, whom you are looking at, fight against God and for falseness. We fight for our land; they fight to take our land." The Portuguese fight for the *samgue e uimgamça*, blood and revenge, of their ancestors and for the freedom of their women and children. Emphatically, he summarized his speech: "If we kill them, we shall win land and worldly glory, if we die, we shall win heaven and eternal glory."[31] Later that same evening, Afonso was visited by a hermit who had had a revelation: "Prince Afonso, God has commanded me to say to you that because of your great will and your great wish to serve Him, He wishes you to be comforted and strengthened, and tomorrow He will let you defeat King Ismar and his great forces, and He commanded me to say to you that when you hear a bell from my hermitage, you shall go outside, and God will appear for you in the sky."[32] Half an hour before daybreak the next morning, the bell began to chime, as the hermit had said, and Afonso went outside his tent and saw Our Lord Himself on His cross in heaven. He fell on his knees and thanked God with tears in his eyes, because he had "been assured by God that Portugal was to remain a realm for ever." Then he arranged his warriors in battle order, he rode back and forth in front of the ranks and encouraged them with cheers and called them by name. However, when they saw the overwhelmingly large Muslim army, it occurred to all the warriors that this was going to be the most honourable day of their generation, and so they wished to proclaim Afonso a king before the battle. He answered his "friends, lords, brothers," that he had no other wish than to remain their brother and comrade – *irmaão e conpanheiro*. Nevertheless, the soldiers raised him and cried "Reall, Reall, por el Rey dom Affomsso Hamrriquez de Portugall."[33]

After the victory, Afonso remained in the camp for three days, "as a king usually does." In the memory of He who had given him victory, Afonso decided to introduce a new bearing. Because he had witnessed the Lord Himself on a cross in heaven, he resolved that his white shield was to be embellished with a red cross. The red cross was to consist of five shields, in remembrance of the five Muslim kings he had defeated. On each shield were to be thirty pieces of silver in the memory of the death and suffering the Lord had suffered for thirty pieces of silver. Later Portuguese kings kept this bearing, the chronicle tells us, although it was difficult to find space for this many silver pieces on the small shields, so they put five pieces on each shield and five in a cruciform.[34] Other chronicles said that the cross consisting of five shields was to recall the five wounds Afonso had received during the battle which he was able to show to a cardinal, who was a papal legate, just as Christ had received five wounds on the cross.[35]

Afonso and Valdemar   137

All this is according to Duarte Galvão's chronicle from the early 15th century. The depiction is elegant and alive, with a fine and intuitive portrayal of Afonso's actions and thoughts, but it is certainly much later than the battle of Ourique. How much we ought to trust its narrative is debated. The miracle in the sky was, as already mentioned, rejected as a late legend by Alexandre Herculano in 1846, and it is true that the miracle cannot be confirmed by earlier sources. However, as is the case in general for medieval history, much information could have survived for centuries in sources that are now lost. It cannot be dismissed that Afonso had a vision on these grounds alone, but we cannot be sure. On the other hand, we are on much firmer ground when it comes to his election as a King by acclamation. During the first months of 1140 the Portuguese chancellery changed its practice; Afonso was no longer addressed as Prince or Lord but as King.[36] It was to be another generation before Afonso's royal title was acknowledged by the Pope in 1179, but he began to use it himself around the new year of 1139–1140. At that time, the Portuguese kingdom was born.

The context is obvious. The title of King must have been a direct consequence of the battle of Ourique, and this suddenly lends more credence to the depiction from the much later chronicle than if we did not have the statements of a few, contemporary letters. Then it is probable that Afonso on the battlefield itself had been raised on a shield by his loyal soldiers before the decisive battle and proclaimed King.[37] Whether this was very important at the time depends on the perspective. It was important to Afonso, and he used the title straight away. It must also have been considered important by Afonso's cousin, Alfonso VII of Castile. In 1135, he had taken the same, proud title as his maternal grandfather, *totius Hispanie imperator*, Emperor of all Spain. After a quarter of a century, the empire had been re-established; on one hand the new emperor would have been wary of rivals and attempted to limit the power of his neighbours; on the other hand his prestige and political impact increased with mightier vassals. Emperors ideally rule over kings. After the battle at Valdevez in 1141, peace was re-established between Afonso and Alfonso, and the peace settlement must have involved the beginning of some form of formalization of a feudal relation. It was extended and strengthened two years later at a meeting between the cousins in Zamora where the papal legate Guido was present as well. We cannot tell what happened from the very brief references to the meeting but Alfonso VII must have recognized Afonso as a King. At least it ends with the imperial chancellery in Castile from then on addressing Afonso of Portugal as a King in the Emperor's official letters to him.[38]

The Popes, on the other hand, do not seem to have been in any hurry to recognize Afonso's royal title. They continued addressing him as a Duke and Portugal as a *terra*, a region, and not as a *regnum*, a kingdom. This does seem somewhat odd. The relations with the Papal see ought to have been excellent during those years. At the meeting at Zamora, Afonso entered an agreement with Guido about becoming a St. Peter's vassal. He had "decided to have that St. Peter as patron and defender – *patronus et advocatus* – to whom the keys of Heaven have been entrusted by Jesus Christ." Afonso, therefore, handed his lands over to St. Peter and the Holy Roman Church. He was to pay a yearly tax of four ounces of gold,

138   *Afonso and Valdemar*

which his descendants had to pay too, in return for always having the protection and consolation of the Church and never in the future having to endure any other ecclesiastical or secular rule in his lands, apart from that of the apostolic see.[39] It did not help. Sure, Afonso was recognized as a papal vassal but the papal letters still did not recognize him as king. Ten years later, after the conquest of Lisbon in 1147, Afonso had become one of the great crusader heroes of Western Christendom, and he wrote proudly to Pope Hadrian IV: "It is not unknown to Your Highness, Holy Father, that I decided to become your knight and dedicated son, as I was to your predecessors." Afonso therefore asks for papal protection and for privileges for the monastery of Santa Cruz in Coimbra, where he wanted to be buried and to which he donated the church estates of Leiria. Afonso named himself King of Portugal in his letter. Hadrian sent a reply to his very beloved son, the Duke of the Portuguese.[40]

There might be two rather different issues behind the difference in Portuguese and papal language. One is that the title King – *rex* – would have been perceived differently. On the Iberian Peninsula, the use was somewhat looser. *King* would at times have been used as an almost honorific title and would not necessarily have designated an independent ruler of a kingdom. Afonso's own parents are a good example. They issued several letters under the title "Henrique Count of Portugal and Teresa, Queen and daughter of Emperor Alfonso.[41] Teresa's title of Queen was to show her fine pedigree, not that she was an independent regent or married to a King. This kind of inaccuracy was difficult to imagine from the Church, where a King was installed by the Church and anointed and crowned in a particular ceremony, whereby he actually belonged to the clergy and became a Priest-king, a successor of David. On the Iberian Peninsula, the ecclesiastical ceremony was of course the most common way of becoming a King, but there was probably an ancient alternative: being raised up on a shield, which seen from the perspective of the Church had no sacred content and no legitimacy at all.[42] Thus, the title of King could of course not be used for Afonso in the papal letters. Of course, the Popes could just have recognized the title anyway and arranged for the necessary ceremony to be held, but this did not happen.

Another explanation for the papal reluctance was perhaps that they wished to keep the crusades on the Iberian Peninsula under one leadership only, that of the Spanish Emperor. This, at least, is the explanation Portuguese historians have called attention to since Erdmann in 1935.[43] On the other hand, the crusades on the Iberian Peninsula were normally not placed under a single leader but took place simultaneously on several fronts. There might have been coordination, but a single leader was rare. The best example of this is the so-called second crusade, which was initiated in 1144 by events in the Middle East almost precisely one year after Afonso Henriques had become a papal vassal.

1147: Damascus, Dobin and Lisbon

On Christmas Eve in 1144, December 24, the Christian principality Edessa fell to the Muslim ruler 'Imad ad-Din Zenghi of Aleppo and Mosul. When news of

Afonso and Valdemar 139

this disaster reached the Papal Curia late the next spring, steps were immediately taken to organize a crusade to liberate Edessa. However, it very soon developed into a crusade on many different fronts at the same time.[44] "Those who commanded the crusade decided that one part of the army should be dispatched to the Middle East, another to Spain and a third to the Slavic peoples."[45]

Ambassadors from the Holy Land – the only one known by his name today is Bishop Hugh of Jabala – roused the Pope to indignation with their reports, and at the same time, other emissaries from the King of Jerusalem went directly to the French King Louis VII. At a Christmas meeting in Bourges, he took an oath to come to the relief of the Holy Land. At that time, the Pope was only beginning the issue on December 1, 1144, of the crusade bull *Quantum predecessores*, which was reissued in March 1146. The Pope referred to the terrible danger and to the great success of the first crusade after Urban's sermon; now it was necessary but also possible to do the same again. Abbot Bernard of Clairvaux was at the same time given papal authorization to preach the crusade, a task that he took up with impressive zeal and effort on journeys around most of Northwestern Europe. His legendary oratory worked wonders: "The earth shakes, for the Lord is losing his land! The enemies of the cross raise their heads and sullies with their swords the blessed land, the promised land." One result of Bernard's efforts was that the German King Conrad III took the cross and departed together with his nephew, the later Emperor Fredric I Barbarossa. At the same time, the French King also went on crusade to the Middle East. The movements of the two great armies were coordinated, not least for the very simple reason that it would be impossible to supply everybody with provisions if they happened to be in the same area at the same time. Communication and coordination was high.[46] The armies were large; both the German and the French King were accompanied by many noblemen. One of them was Amadeus III of Savoy, who left in 1147. One of his sisters was married to the French King, the other sister was married to the German Emperor Henry IV. The previous year, his daughter Mathilde was married to Afonso Henriques of Portugal. Another one was Thierry II of Lorraine. His brother-in-law was Robert of Flanders, who was married to Raimundo of Galicia's sister. He was also a brother-in-law to Adele, who had been married to Canute of Denmark, and in 1128 he had succeeded Canute's son Carl as Count of Flanders. There were thus several close connections between the participants from Portugal and Denmark during the second crusade to the Middle East.

Militarily, the crusade of Louis and Conrad ended in disaster, something the participants ought to have known in advance. One evening while travelling through Europe, the tents of the army were shrouded in a strange mist and completely drenched in blood.[47] They continued nevertheless and managed to participate in a futile siege of Damascus, which at least demonstrated that they had made an effort. Thereafter, King Conrad returned home while Louis stayed for some time in the Kingdom of Jerusalem, although without waging war against the Muslims. Contemporary chronicles judged this crusade negatively. It had been fruitless, even counterproductive, as it had given the Muslims hope of being able to be victorious also in the future and had disheartened the Christians. The sins of

140   *Afonso and Valdemar*

the Christians demanded divine punishment, and sons of Belial and the precursors of Antichrist had seduced the Christians and, with their hollow sermon, made them go on the ill-fated expedition against the Saracens, Gerhoch of Reichersberg wrote.[48] Bernard of Clairvaux, on the other hand, defended the crusade as a great success in the spiritual sense. The worse militarily, the better spiritually: the more Christians who fell, the more entered heaven as martyrs. The more Christians who had participated, the more had received indulgence.[49]

When the news of Edessa reached the Papal Curia in 1145, some of those present would have been emissaries from King Alfonso VII of León-Castile with accusations against the Portuguese Archbishop João of Braga for not recognizing the primacy of the archdiocese of Toledo.[50] They were at the same time probably informed about the renewed attacks from the North African Almohads, a reform movement within Islam that had begun a conquest of Al-Andalus and now threatened the Christian areas in the Iberian Peninsula. During the shock after Edessa, Alfonso's emissaries succeeding in having a papal bull issued that promised indulgence to those who helped fighting the Muslims in Spain.[51] With that, it became possible for Alfonso to initiate the conquest of the valley south of the Ebro, in 1145–1148, in the form of a real crusade.

On January 9, 1147, the Almoravid's strong castle Calatrava at the River Guardiana fell. On October 17, Alfonso succeeded in conquering Almería on the south coast with auxiliary armies from Navarra, Barcelona and Montpellier and with the support from a fleet of sixty-three ships from Genoa, which had continued south after a series of successful small crusades against Minorca. Almería held out until the end and the Muslim population was massacred after the conquest.[52] Alfonso VII's fight against the Muslims had special support from God, Pope Eugene III wrote on hearing the news of the fall of Almeíra.[53] In the tribute *Poema de Almería*, the secretary of the venerable Abbot Peter of Cluny, Peter of Poitiers depicted King Alfonso as the just warrior of heavenly wrath, who fought a holy war, acceptable to God. This was actually prophesied already at Alfonso's birth, when a bleeding star was visible in the sky for thirty days.[54] After Almería, Alfonso continued with a new crusade against Jaén in 1148, this time without success.[55] For a long time afterwards, Alfonso dated his letters with reference to the number of years after the fall of Almería.[56]

After the conquest of Almería, the Genoese fleet continued back north towards the important city of Tortosa, "The key of the Christians."[57] It finally fell on December 31, 1148, after a seven-month siege by Castilian and Leonese, English, Flemish, Aragonese, Catalan, Southern French and not least Genoese auxiliaries under the leadership of Count Ramon Berenguer IV of Barcelona.[58] He continued the crusades and conquered Lérida in October 1149. The area around the Ebro was now wholly in Christian hands. It went so well that, in 1151, Alfonso VII and Ramon Berenguer shared the rest of Al-Andalus between themselves; apparently, they anticipated that the Muslim presence on the Peninsula would soon be over. However, it was to be a long time yet – almost three and a half centuries.[59]

In Northern Europe, Bernard's preaching had mobilized great crowds. Some of the German princes, however, had been less willing to go to the Holy Land and mentioned that many heathens lived in their close vicinity. In March 1147, Bernard gave them permission to fulfil their crusade commitment by fighting the Slavic peoples to the east of the River Elbe. The theological reason was that the Devil had become nervous because of the Christian success in the Holy Land – with the fall of Edessa and the overall fear for the future of Jerusalem taken into consideration, this remark should be considered an aphorism at best. The Devil was afraid, Bernard claimed, and therefore he had decided to attack in the North. Fighting against the heathens at the Elbe was therefore in reality to come to the assistance of Jerusalem.[60] Bernard thus operated with some form of a pincer strategy, both from the Devil's perspective and in order to counter the Devil. Most importantly, he very clearly depicted the wars in the East and in the North as one single war with two fronts. Bernard's ideas caught on. Duke Henry the Lion of Saxony went on a crusade against Dobin. Margrave Albert the Bear of Brandenburg together with Wladislaw of Bohemia went on a crusade – he had first taken the cross to go to the Holy Land but changed his mind after Bernard's sermon. They went against the Pomeranians and laid siege to the main city of Szczecin, where the Christian population raised crosses on the walls and sent their Bishop Albert out to negotiate. He pointed out that they had been Christians since the mission of Otto of Bamberg in around 1120 and thus logically should not be the object of a crusade. The Bohemian contingent then went back home.[61]

In Denmark, a cardinal had travelled all the way from Rome to participate in a church synod in Odense in 1146, probably in the early summer.[62] This was rather soon after Pope Eugene III received the news of the fall of Edessa, and whether at first it had any direct connection with Bernard's sermon in German is probably unlikely. The cardinal's task was to preach a crusade, which he proceeded to do for the Danish King. The King's reaction must have astounded the cardinal. King Erik Lamb abdicated, entered a monastery and died shortly after. He was followed by two kings, Canute, chosen in Jutland, and Svend, chosen on the islands, and what was to develop into a ten-year-long civil war began. The first task of the rival kings, however, was to cooperate by going on a joint crusade against the heathen Wends at Dobin, a town at the Bay of Wismar, not far east of Lübeck. A truce was negotiated between the two kings, presumably on the initiative of the rural dean Keld of Viborg, who in vain had sought permission from the Pope to go and preach amongst the Wends so that he would be killed for the sake of Christ and become a martyr.[63] Pledges were given, hostages exchanged and the two kings sailed off.

When Canute and Svend reached the Wendish area, they joined forces with a Saxon cavalry army. Other heathens from Rügen arrived to assist their co-religionists in Dobin, but after a long siege the town of Dobin was taken, the inhabitants were forced to be baptized and to release their many Christian captives. After this, the Danish army could not hold together any longer, and the two kings parted ways and travelled home separately. According to Saxo, this happened because the contingents from different Danish regions quarrelled amongst each other and because the two kings did not trust each other.[64] According to Helmold of Bosau it happened because "the Danes are mighty warriors at home but completely useless

142   *Afonso and Valdemar*

in real warfare."[65] The result of this crusade was short lasting. The Wends of Dobin fell back to their old beliefs as soon as the crusader army had disappeared, and anyway the Christian slaves, whom they had been forced to let go, were only weak and old people, with almost no value as labourers, Helmold added.

In the Scandinavian sources, the expedition to Dobin was perceived as a real crusade according to all criteria. It is claimed directly by Saxo in around 1200 and in the Knýtlinga saga from the 13th century, which contains older material, that King Canute and King Svend took the cross and left – as the Pope had commanded all Christians – to fight the heathens closest to their own frontiers. "[I]n order to be better able to do this, they made a temporary peace – *pax* – and withdrew the sword from their own bowels to turn to revenge for Christianity."[66] As soon as they had taken the cross, they would have received absolution for all the sins they had confessed. The Pope had promised this "on God's behalf." The Knýtlinga saga adds that the Pope had also promised that if they fell, their souls would be in heaven before their blood cooled on the ground.[67] Two years after the attack on Dobin, a large expedition or crusade followed against Arkona on Rügen.[68] At the same time as the Nordic crusade against Dobin, another crusade, which also had a connection with Bernard, took place in Portugal.

Bernard's preaching tour in the North had continued with a several-month-long campaign through the Rhineland and the Low Countries, and Bernard assembled a large army, which was to come to the assistance of the Portuguese King. This happened as a response to an approach from Afonso Henriques, who had sent his brother Pedro to Bernard in France and informed him "about all necessary things." Pedro now wished to continue with the great crusader army to the Holy Land while his brother, with Bernard's assistance, was going to fight in Portugal.[69] This was not the first time that Afonso had tried to get assistance from the North for his fight against the Muslims. He had tried to get French and Nordic help in 1140 or 1142; the warriors had turned up in Portugal and followed the King on a large attack on Lisbon, but without success.[70] The crusaders continued to Jerusalem and left Afonso Henriques without having taken control of Lisbon. In 1147, it succeeded at last. Earlier, historians have believed that the participation of the crusaders in the wars in Portugal was a coincidence, and that they had been persuaded to help the Portuguese King as they were passing through on their way to Jerusalem anyway. This, however, seems very unlikely. Everything indicates that it would have been a meticulously planned expedition agreed upon with Afonso Henriques.[71]

In May 1147, the army assembled at Dartmouth: including men from Flanders, the Rhineland, especially Cologne, and from Boulogne, Normandy, Scotland, England and other countries in the North. Some had participated in the expedition five years earlier and most had taken an oath to go to Jerusalem as well. In total there were between 170 and 200 ships, the number of men was probably around 10,000–13,000.[72] The whole enterprise was described in detail by an English-French priest, Raol.[73] In order to maintain mutual peace between so many different people, a council was established, he wrote, which consisted of two representatives for every thousand men; they were to pass sentences and distribute money. These councillors were called judges and sworn brothers – *conjurati*. At the same time, solemn coalition agreements were concluded with mutual securities given, and they agreed to harsh punishments – life for a life and tooth for a tooth. No one was allowed to try and take the men from another crew. All warriors should confess and receive communion every Sunday as long as the expedition lasted. The individual contingents of the army had their own leaders – one a lesser nobleman, but the rest were mostly unknown individuals from one of the big cities. One of them, however, had a very special connection with the crusades: Arnald of Aerschot, a nephew to Godfrey of Bouillon. He led the contingents from Cologne and Lorraine. The council was obviously meant as a joint war command: it was to make decisions after public meetings that were open for all and with an open debate.

After having taken these precautions, the fleet sailed out from Dartmouth on May 23. Five days later, they could see the peaks of the Pyrenees in the far distance. But at night a terrible storm broke; the impenetrable darkness echoed from the songs of the sirens who tried to lure the crusaders, but they repented and confessed their sins and prayed to God, and by His mercy all were saved from the sirens' temptations. After yet more delays and storms, which scattered the fleet, they reached Santiago de Compostela at Whitsun, on June 7.

The crusaders were expected in Portugal. Afonso Henriques was busy in the south with preparations for the attack on Lisbon after his surprise conquest of Santarém in March. In a letter Afonso ordered Bishop Pedro of Porto to be ready to receive them with friendship and to accompany them to Lisbon. The main contingent of crusaders had reached as far as Porto on June 16.[74] Bishop Pedro gave a fiery speech to these crusaders from the outermost frontiers of the earth, *terre finibus*. He told them of the plunder awaiting them but mostly about the spiritual merit in the fight against the Muslims in Portugal, which was just as great as in continuing to Jerusalem. He furthermore encouraged them and praised them with many Bible quotes for having left property and family and the alluring embraces of their wives in order to follow Christ. He sketched the unhappy fortune of the Iberian Peninsula, wholly in the hands of Moors and Moabites: only a few cities held out, but for how much longer? Porto itself had been attacked and the cathedral pillaged only seven years previously, he claimed – an event for which we have no other sources than this narrative about the conquest of Lisbon. It might only have been a part in argumentation at the time for just wars, that they were waged in defence as a reaction against the aggression of others. Pedro continued: "The Mother Church cries unto you, with severed arms and disfigured face and demands the blood of her children and revenge from your hands. She cries and cries aloud; 'Take revenge on the heathens, punish the nations.' Therefore, you shall not hurry on to Jerusalem, because what is praiseworthy is not to have been in Jerusalem but to have lived righteously on the way there."[75] Those who live by the sword shall die by the sword, that is, if he carries the sword without the permission of a higher authority. These crusaders, however, carried with the permission from God the sword of justice, by which robbers and adulterers shall be punished, and the impious shall be wasted on the ground. If they fight with this

144   *Afonso and Valdemar*

sword, the crusaders will not be reproached for anything or be accused of murder. "Truly, there is no cruelty when it concerns piety for God."

The army continued south in order to join Afonso Henriques. On June 28, it arrived at the River Tagus, where one can collect gold on the shores during early spring, still according to Raoul. The river consists of two thirds of water and one third of fish, and the shellfish are as numerous as the sand. Fish and shellfish are more delicious than anywhere else, and it keeps without beginning to rot. Lisbon itself is on the top of a hill. Founded by Ulysses, it is the richest trading city in all of Africa and most of Europe. The land surrounding Lisbon abounds in gold, silver, iron and an abundance of olives and all kinds of fruit and wine; at Sintra there is wondrous spring water, which cures all coughs so if the locals hear some-one cough, they know that it is a stranger. On the wide pastures, the horses are unusually fertile because the mares are being impregnated by the western wind, and only after they have conceived are they served by the stallions.

The whole narrative has a mythical quality: a fantastic travelogue, a fairy tale. At the same time, it reflects both Portugal's economic capacity compared with most countries in Northern Europe as well as the contemporary perception in the north of Portugal as a fertile country, rich in precious metals. Finally, it is an image with a striking similarity to our reports on Pope Urban II's sermon in Clermont, where he described the Holy Land as the land that flows with milk and honey, the promised land, where it is possible to not only fight for God or justice but also to hope for financial gains. This is one aspect that the author of this narrative does not make any secret of. The participants expected to get money and that was also an overall necessity, simply to provide for the army on the journey.

King Afonso was presumably relieved to see the crusaders arrive, and the negotiations about the partition of the spoils seem to have been concluded quickly, if this English source is to be believed. Afonso promised that the foreigners could have all the plunder from the city and ransom money from the prisoners, and that they and their heirs in all eternity were to be exempted from a particular customs duty known as *pedatica*. Afterwards they were to hand over the control of the city to Afonso, so in the longer term it was not a financially disadvantageous arrangement for the King. In return, Afonso promised that he would not withdraw from the fighting before the city was conquered, unless he became terminally ill – perhaps he had let down allies from the North during an earlier crusade?[76] To confirm the arrangement, hostages were exchanged, twenty from each side – high ranking secular participants and even some bishops.

The siege of Lisbon dragged out for more than four months. The initial negotiations took place with the crusaders just beneath the city wall and the Muslim lord of the city and the Mozarab Bishop of Lisbon on the wall itself. The Muslims were told that their possession of Lisbon was unjust, as it was originally a Christian city. However, as they had been living there for such a long time, 358 years altogether, they would be allowed to remain in the city if they just handed it over to Afonso. They would also be allowed to retain their customs – this presumably means that they would have a right to keep their religious services and their own internal jurisdiction in civil law cases. The argumentation is interesting, because

Afonso and Valdemar   145

here it is almost acknowledged that Muslims could have a prescriptive right to a city, that they might have been there for so long that it does not make sense to make an original Christian claim to it. This would have been very unusual, not least in the 12th century, when theologians and jurists otherwise agreed that land that had been Christian once should always belong to the Christians, no matter how long it might have been ruled by others.[77]

Of course, Afonso's offer might have been practically motivated. It would have been unrealistic to envisage that the whole population was to be driven out or killed or converted to Christianity by force, but the argumentation was nevertheless a legal one, that they had been in possession for a long time. The Muslims were apparently aware of which way the wind was blowing and that it was unlikely that they would be able to pay off the Christian besiegers, because they knew that the crusaders were driven not by lack of things but by the ambition of their souls – *mentis ambitione*. In one forest there is room for many elephants and lions, but the earth and the sea is not enough for the Christians, they would say.[78] The discussion between the Christians and the Muslims turned harsher, and it was ended with the words of the Bishop of Porto: "When we part, I shall not greet you farewell, and you will probably not greet us, either." The Muslims turned down the offer to surrender the city and the battle began.

The fighting began with trebuchets that had stones hailing down upon the opponents from both sides, and so it continued all through the siege. We must imagine that there were constantly stones in the air and that there was a constant risk of being hit by projectiles. At the same time, the parties began working each other up psychologically through mutual insults and mockery. From the city wall, the Muslims made faces at the crusaders and insulted them by shouting that their wives did not in any way miss them, as they were whoring away randomly and had lots of children – and that the crusaders should not care about that, as they would not get back home anyway, but were to die here. And if a single one of them were to survive and get back, he would be destitute and defeated. They mocked Mary and Jesus by saying that He could not be God, because God could not be human, as He then would not be almighty. They spit on the cross, wiped their behinds with it and threw it down to the crusaders. The Christians replied humbly by offering the Muslims freedom to leave with all their belongings, if they would only surrender the city, the Christian writer of our main source writes, but the Lord punished the Muslims for their wickedness by blinding them and making them say no. At the same time, a miracle happened. A bleeding host was found in the Flemish camp – it continued to bleed until after the conquest. The miracle was difficult to interpret. Some thought that it revealed that the Flemings, despite their crusade vows, were thirsting more after blood than after justice.

It soon became obvious why Afonso Henriques had been so keen to get help from the North. The English and Flemish crusaders and particularly a tower builder from Pisa possessed a superior siege technique and were able to build large siege towers. The first were soon put to the torch by the encircled Muslims during quick sorties, but those that came after were successfully defended by the crusaders. The foreigners furthermore had great experience in building mines, that

146   *Afonso and Valdemar*

is, long shafts that went under the city walls; they were supported by a wooden construction that was finally burnt away. Several times the attempts were warded off by the defenders, and sometimes the mines collapsed by themselves. But when it did work, the walls above the mine would collapse, as happened in Lisbon on October 16 over a distance of about fifty metres.

The siege was interrupted several times by sorties and small battles. At one point, a group of English crusaders had crossed the river to go fishing on the other shore, but they were attacked and killed by the Muslims south of the Tagus. Revenge was arranged and it turned out successfully. The English went back to the Christian camp with 200 prisoners and eighty Muslim heads, which were put on spikes below the city wall so the encircled people in the city could see them. The Muslims in Lisbon negotiated and the heads were handed over for burial, and that whole night the crusaders heard loud wailing and lamenting from the city, "and since then, the English were especially admired by the Flemings and Portuguese and by those from Cologne."

A new siege tower was built, blessed with holy water by the Archbishop, and with a splinter of the true cross held aloft, a priest gave a fiery sermon to the crusaders. Every person has his own guardian angel, he said, but it is possible to turn away from one's guardian angel and then one can only get it back by reconciling with God and making penance – whereby the priest obviously thinks that the audience must participate in that act of penance, which constitutes a crusade. The sermon continues for a long time; the listeners are promised martyrdom and that they will gain a better life by losing this present one. Bishop Pedro of Porto also encourages the crusaders to fight to defend the fatherland – *patria* – that means to conquer Lisbon from the Muslims. Encouraged in this way, the Christians continued the fighting with more luck, and despite hard resistance, they succeeded in slowly moving the siege tower right next to the wall. The defenders realize that the city is now lost, and on October 21 they enter a truce with exchange of hostages.

Then everything turns to panic, and the actual chain of events is difficult to unravel from the sources, which each have their own view regarding which of the participants were the real winners. The Muslims will only surrender to Afonso and the Portuguese but not to the foreign crusaders, because they are faithless and cruel. Some of the foreign crusaders are obviously afraid that they are going to miss out on the plunder and that a political solution, rather than a military one, will be found. One group breaks away and proclaims that they do not need any leader other than the Holy Spirit and that things always go wrong anyway when the noblemen interfere and take command. They were obviously serious about that. Citizens from the great cities and free men from the Flemish marshlands had been able to fend for themselves without the leaders from the old families. Coincidentally, the narrative contains a distant echo of the stories from the first crusade, when it was the people who forced the noblemen to continue the march towards Jerusalem after the conquest of Antioch, even though the leaders had tired from the fighting. At Lisbon, a large group of Flemings and people from Cologne directly attacked Afonso's camp during his negotiations with the Muslims; they were soon called to order by their leaders and in the end had to swear loyalty to Afonso. That oath did not last for long.

Conditions were agreed upon. Each of the groups in the crusader army were to put a number of men forward who were to enter the city and occupy the most important sites. Afonso himself came last with his men and all of the clergy, who with incense and holy water walked in procession and sang the liturgy used at the purification and re-consecration of desecrated churches. However, the Flemings and those from Cologne cheated and smuggled more of their people inside the city than agreed, and they now began large scale pillaging and massacre of the Muslim population. During the slaughter, they also killed the Mozarab Bishop of Lisbon, probably by accident.[79]

After the conquest of Lisbon came God's punishment of the Muslims. They were hit by the plague and their bodies lay in their thousands, rotting along the River Tagus. The few survivors roamed about pale and ill, but had at least learnt to sing "Hail Mary." This is mentioned by the English source; perhaps they were Mozarabs and not Muslims. However, the year after, it rained blood through the whole of April over the Muslims' land in Extremadura.[80] The crusaders chose the Englishman Gilbert as the new Bishop of Lisbon. He took up his post immediately and was to attend to his office as the spiritual head of a newly conquered city. As early as 1150 or 1151,[81] he was on a tour of England preaching to raise a new crusade to Portugal, which was to concentrate on Seville and perhaps Alcácer do Sal.

Several of the foreign crusaders settled in Lisbon and the surroundings and never returned to their original lands. "The colony of crusaders still lives in Lisbon," Helmold of Bosau wrote in the North, almost astounded, judging by the tone of his voice. This was around thirty years later. It was also he who summarized the great war on three fronts like this: "Of all the efforts made by the crusader army, there was only a happy outcome in Lisbon."[82]

After the conquest of Lisbon – Afonso crosses the Tagus

The second crusade had been a joint effort for all of Western Europe; participants had moved from one religious frontier to the other, and the contemporaries rightly viewed it as one and the same war, led on several fronts. The result was mixed, not least because of the defeat in the Middle East. Plans for immediate, new crusades were faced with fierce criticism of both the course of the second crusade and of the crusading idea as such. The terrible numbers of fallen Christians touched everybody, also those who, according to Bernard, ought to have rejoiced the very high harvest of new martyrs for heaven. "When we consider the vehement loss of prestige for the name of Christ, which the Church of God has suffered in our time, and that so many men recently spilled their blood, we tremble in great fear." It was none other than Pope Eugene III who wrote this to the French Abbot Suger. He added that Louis' firm decision to take the cross again "relieved his pain slightly," and he promised the absolution of sins to those that took part.[83] However, it was not an expression of a great enthusiasm for crusades. The experience in the Middle East made them wary. This, however, was not the case in the Iberian Peninsula.

148 *Afonso and Valdemar*

During the months after the conquest of Lisbon, the crusade continued in Portugal, where it conquered Sintra with the strong fortress Castelo do mouros. Then Afonso crossed the Tagus and was able to capture the castle of Palmela, standing isolated on a rocky outcrop in a completely flat landscape. He then continued towards Alcácer do Sal, one of the strongest Muslim fortifications on the Peninsula. It was arrogant and unrealistic, even though the sources perhaps overstressed the difference in strength somewhat. According to them, Afonso and his sixty knights from Santarém, who had even lost their heavy armour, were attacked by 500 well-equipped and armoured Muslim knights and 40,000 foot soldiers. They had repulsed the attack and fought so bravely that the Muslims had been forced to withdraw and seek shelter behind the strong walls of Alcácer do Sal. During the siege, Afonso was wounded in the shin by a lance. "I shall relate in a moment how this happened," a narrative reports, collected soon after his death. Sadly, we are never told. The manuscript ends here and do not contain that particular story.[84] Despite the descriptions of Afonso's courage and excellent qualities as a general, there is no reason to doubt that he had a lucky escape from an attack on a superior opponent, even though he had support of many ships from the North.

This first attack on Alcácer do Sal was considered "a much more prominent miracle of the Lord than anything God ever did in the world with any of the kings of antiquity" by contemporaries. Thereby it was directly compared with the conquest of Jerusalem during the first crusade in 1099, which Robert the Monk had claimed to be greater than anything any earlier general had ever accomplished. The result was that the River Tagus now not only was the border between Christendom and Islam but also the starting line, the point of departure for Afonso's attacks further and further in the South.

There were many Muslim petty kingdoms, and they fought amongst themselves, and the Almoravids' centralized supremacy over Al-Andalus was to be short-lived. Contemporaneous with Zenghi's conquest of Edessa, several cities in Al-Andalus were objects of radical rebellions, led by Sufis. It might have been some form of social unrest, with demands of poverty and asceticism directed at the propertied classes, but how the following of these Sufis was actually constituted is uncertain.[85] From Mértola, the rebellions spread to Beja and Silves during 1145, and perhaps both Alcácer do Sal, Lisbon and Santarém had been threatened or directly attacked by Muslim rebels. In Silves, Ibn Qasi was deposed, and he sought help from the Almohad Caliph in Morocco. In February 1147, the Almohads crossed the Strait of Gibraltar and began a systematic conquest of Al-Andalus, which might briefly have included Lisbon and Santarém. Not taking account of the assistance of the foreign crusaders, this could be an explanation for Afonso Henriques' brilliant victories in 1147. The rebellions seriously weakened the local Muslim dynasties on the Iberian Peninsula, and the Almohads delivered the decisive push, which prevented a Muslim rallying to the defence of Lisbon.

Ibn Qasi was installed as Almohad governor in Silves but the more subordinate position does not seem to have pleased him. In 1150, he rebelled against the Almohads and was followed by the governors in Badajoz and Cádiz. Ibn Qasi sent a messenger to "the lord of Coimbra" asking for help.[86] Afonso jumped at the chance immediately. As a sign of his good will and as a pledge for the alliance, he sent a gift to Ibn Qasi in the form of a war horse, a shield and a lance. This would have been fitting for a defence alliance between two warriors. However, the fact that it was also a threat from Afonso would have been difficult to overlook. The alliance must have given Afonso new hope of being able to lead the crusade further south, and this is presumably the explanation for Gilbert of Lisbon's journey to England to recruit crusaders at this very time. The success of 1147 was to be repeated but things turned out differently this time. Before Afonso's plans materialized, the population of Silves rebelled against Ibn Qasi, presumably at least in part because of his alliance with the Christians. In any case, his severed head was spiked on the very spear that Afonso had presented to him and was carried around the city in triumph. Afonso suffered yet another defeat in an attempt to conquer Alcácer do Sal in 1151. It seems that Afonso then suspended the crusades for some years. The crusading mood in Western Europe was somewhat dull and became even more so after the death of Bernard of Clairvaux in 1153.

In 1157, the Emperor of Spain, Alfonso VII, died and his large empire was divided between his two sons. Sancho III was given Castile with Toledo, and Fernando inherited León. The two brothers were not particularly well disposed towards one another, but at a meeting the year after they were at least able to agree on sharing the Muslim parts of Spain equally, as they conquered it, and in the same way they divided Portugal between themselves. Whether the plans to conquer Portugal were realistic was never discovered because of the sudden death of Sancho in 1159.[87] After a few border skirmishes, Afonso and Fernando made peace in 1165, which was sealed with the marriage between Afonso's daughter, Urraca, and Fernando the year after. True, the marriage was annulled again in 1175 after pressure from the Papal see, because the two were too closely related. Before this, however, Urraca had given birth to the heir to the throne, Alfonso IX, who was to continue the family line after Fernando's death in 1188. Due to the close family relations, he was to become an important figure in creating peace between Portugal and León and Castile for a period.[88]

The death of the Emperor became an occasion for Afonso to resume the crusades. This was going to happen in cooperation with both the German King Conrad III and the French King Louis VII, who in 1157 had decided to go on a joint crusade to the Iberian Peninsula. In the end, they did not cross the Pyrenees, as Pope Hadrian was against the expedition and refused to give indulgence on the grounds that the expedition did not take place in agreement with the local kings.[89] Hadrian obviously put his trust in Sancho and Fernando to continue the crusades with local forces. It was the same year that Afonso wrote his letter to the Pope to remind him that he was the Pope's most loyal vassal and that he had always supported him and his predecessors. Afonso wrote as a proud and self-aware king; he could do so justly after the conquest of Lisbon, but in his reply, Hadrian still only addressed him as a duke. The interest of the crusaders did not abate completely. It turns out later that a great many ships "from the north, from France and adjoining regions" had arrived in Portugal on two occasions and helped Afonso with

150　*Afonso and Valdemar*

the siege of Alcácer do Sal, but in vain.[90] This must have happened in 1147 and in 1151.

The attempts to expand to the south of the Tagus were intensified after Afonso resumed the crusades in 1158. Raid after raid pushed still further south and each spring a new expedition began. To begin with, the goal was again Alcácer do Sal, which after the conquest of Lisbon had become the most important Muslim port city to the North. Just as the Christian attacks came regularly from Lisbon, Alcácer do Sal was the point of departure of regular Muslim raids against the Christians. In 1158, Afonso Henriques headed a large army; after the attempts during preceding years to attract crusaders from other parts of Western Europe, this army seems to have consisted solely of Portuguese forces. The castle of Alcácer do Sal was besieged for two months, where the walls were attacked daily, and on the Day of St. John, June 24, it fell at last, and all Muslims were driven out from it.[91] The expansion continued however over the following years, though Afonso did not personally lead the army. It was completely different groups that won the spectacular victories. In 1162, Beja fell after a four-month siege to a group of town knights – *plebeis militibus* – from Coimbra under the leadership of Fernão Gonçalves, a son of the castle bailiff in Coimbra. They rode about 350 kilometres through difficult terrain to fight the Muslims, and they must have constituted an effective force since they were able to take Beja, even though it happened during a night attack.[92] Three years later, Évora fell to Geraldo Geraldes "the Fearless" and his band of freebooters, also during a night raid. They gave the city to Afonso and continued the conquests – they were soon able to take Cáceres and Montanchez and Serpa and finally Juromenha, all in less than a year.[93] Geraldo the Fearless became feared amongst the Muslims for his surprise night attacks with large scaling ladders,[94] mostly during winter nights, in fog and pouring rain. Geraldo was the first one on the wall; he would catch the watchman and with a sword on his throat force him to shout his usual cry of a watchman: "Nothing new, everything is quiet." Meanwhile the rest of Geraldo's men climbed the wall, and with a loud and frightening cry, they penetrated into the town, killing everyone they met. "The Demon" and "The One cursed by God" were some of the epithets used for Geraldo by the Muslim chroniclers, or simply "the Dog."

All these castles lay in a ring around Badajoz and protected the access roads to the stronghold, which was now the key to controlling all of Alentejo. In 1169, the conquest of Badajoz had been initiated by Geraldo the Fearless, but this time Afonso took part. In the fighting between Portuguese and Muslims from several places, the Leonese began to interfere, and the son-in-law Fernando came to the relief of the Muslims against Afonso! The background and course of the battle will be explored in closer detail in the next chapter and compared to the Danish King's conquest of the greatest heathen castle in Northern Europe during the same year. For now it suffices to say that Afonso suffered a disabling accident at Badajoz when galloping back into the castle. This was to have a decisive effect on the fate of the crusades on the Iberian Peninsula. Afonso was taken prisoner by Fernando and had to ransom himself with twenty-five towns, gold and twenty large warhorses. After that, he had to spend at least three months at the spas at São

Afonso and Valdemar 151

Pedro do Sul before he was able to slowly return to Coimbra, where he spent the rest of his life until his death fifteen years later. The warrior Afonso was never to ride a horse again and thus was no longer a full human being.

From now on, the crusades had to be organized differently since Afonso no longer could lead in person. On August 15, 1170, he knighted his son Sancho in the Church of Santa Cruz in Coimbra, and he buckled the weapons and insignia on Sancho himself. Fittingly, this took place on the day of the Assumption of Mary, the day she was taken up to heaven and crowned by Christ himself. Sancho was fifteen or sixteen years old and was soon able to lead armies against the Muslims and against his brother-in-law, Fernando of León.

As part of the preparations for the expedition against Badajoz, Afonso had attempted to involve the Knights Templar and gave them extended privileges if they would cross the Tagus and support his crusade, but to no avail. Afonso reacted by leaning on other military orders, which he established or called upon from the outside during the years after his defeat at Badajoz. In 1172, he invited the Order of Santiago to Portugal. It had been established only two years previously by Fernando of León. Afonso donated the Castelo de Monsanto and the year after Castelo de Abrantes to the Order of Santiago, and during the next decade, it was to control the strongholds south of the Tagus, especially Palmela. In the same year,[95] Afonso established a completely new military order, which was to have the special favour of the royal family henceforth. This was the Knights of Évora, who had their main seat in the royal castle of Évora. In 1211, it changed its name to the Order of Avís, and in 1385 its Grand Master became Portuguese King and founder of the Avís dynasty. The investing of power on the military orders was tactically motivated because the members were highly trained, efficient troops, but it was part of a long-term strategy as well. The orders were permanently mobilized and did not go home again after having conquered a castle, as ordinary crusaders tended to do. On the contrary, they followed up the conquests by building new castles further inside enemy territory, and as a next step, they tried to utilize the land by having it cultivated by slaves or Christian colonists. The military orders became indispensable in the crusades everywhere, and Afonso's use of them was comparable to what other rulers did in the same period.

In the year of 1178, Sancho succeeded in advancing all the way to Seville, to which he laid siege. He also pillaged and burned the suburbs of the neighbouring town of Triana. After a few years of respite, the war against the infidel resumed. The reaction from Pope Alexander III came immediately. On May 23, 1179, he issued a document that finally recognized Portugal as an independent kingdom.[96] Portugal had in practice been a kingdom since the battle of Ourique in 1139, but only now was Portugal recognized by the Pope, and Afonso was recognised as an equal member in the group of European kings. It happened because of Afonso Henriques' crusades:

> With obvious arguments it has been proven that you by martial efforts and military battles as an unyielding extirpator of the enemies of the name of Christ and as a loving defender of the Christian faith, as a good son and

152 *Afonso and Valdemar*

catholic ruler in many ways have shown obedience to the holy Mother Church, and that you leave behind a name worth remembering, and an example for your descendants to follow. And it is right and just that the Apostolic see shall love what the heavenly dispensation has already chosen as a kingdom and the salvation of the people, and that the Church also in practice lends an ear to its reasonable requests. As we then look closer at your person, which is embellished by wisdom, dedicated to justice, and well suited to rule the people, we shall take under the protection of the Holy Peter and ourselves the kingdom of Portugal with full honours and with the dignity, kings demand, and likewise, all the land that you with assistance from the divine grace may tear from the hands of the Saracens, of which the surrounding Christian rulers cannot claim any right, those we grant your excellency and confirms it with apostolic authority.

Portugal became an independent kingdom in 1179 because Afonso Henriques during his whole life had been an "unyielding extirpator of the enemies of the name of Christ." This was to be remembered for a long time. Pope Innocent III reissued the bull to Afonso's grandson Afonso II on April 16, 1212, with almost identical wording.[97] This was to be expected. It is perhaps more striking that Pope John Paul II on the 800th anniversary for the issue of the bull gave a speech to the Portuguese in the church of Sant'Antonio dei Portoghesi in Rome. Here, he emphasized the exceptional position of the Portuguese in relation to the Holy see on the basis of that Afonso Henriques had extended the frontiers of the Christian faith.[98] The crusades are still to this day an important and dignified thing to mention when the birth of Portugal and its first king are being celebrated.

When Afonso Henriques died, he had for years been weak and only a shadow of his former self. The heavy blow that he received during the siege of Badajoz in 1169 might have been detrimental. Whether he was capable of perceiving his own weakness and whether he was able to rejoice in the unreserved papal recognition of his royal status in 1179 is not known. Thus, we do not know either how much influence he had on the design of his last resting-place. However, no matter who was behind it, the epitaph summarized precisely what all of Afonso's long life had been about:[99]

> *Alter Alexander iacet hic, aut Iulius alter*
> *Belliger invictus, splendidus orbis honor.*
> *Pacis & armorum cauto moderamine doctus*
> *Alternare vices tempora tuta dedit*
> *Quid pietas Christi, vel quantum debeat isti,*
> *Ad fidei cultum Regna subacta docent.*
> *Post Regni fastus fidei moderamine pastus,*
> *In miseros inopes accumulavit opes.*
> *Quod cruces hic tutor fuerit, necnon cruce tutus,*
> *Ipsius clipeo crux clipeata docet.*
> *Vivax fama licet tibi tempora longa reserves,*

Digna suis meritis dicere nemo potest.
Here lies buried a new Alexander, or a new Caesar,
The invincible warrior, a splendid honour to the world,
With his moderate government he created secure times
By wisely alternating between the path of peace and weapons
What constitutes the piety of Christ, and how much it is owed,
He taught the kingdoms that were forced to the faith.
After having been unhappy with royal power, he was strengthened by faith
And accumulated all his means for the poor.
That he was the guardian of the cross, and guarded by the cross,
Is demonstrated by the cross, which is marked on his own shield.
Vivid fame, even if you spend as much time as you please,
No-one can praise his deeds in a fitting way.[100]

Valdemar the invincible

King Valdemar was referred to as *Invictissimus* in a letter shortly after his death – not only the invincible, but the utmost invincible.[101] In later historical writing, he is known as Valdemar the Great, and he has lent his name to a whole era in the Middle Ages, the Valdemarian Era, covering from about 1157, when he became the only king, until about 1241, when his son, Valdemar the Victorious died. Under Valdemar the Great, Denmark became unified and powerful, and was able to hold its own during the rest of the Middle Ages and after. For this reason, and because we know relatively much about the Valdemarian Era thanks to Saxo's chronicle from around 1200, Valdemar has become one of the great, mythical, national figures in Danish historical writing. Valdemar succeeded. And he did so, this book suggests, because he linked himself to the crusades and supported them. However, it was not at all a given from the outset that he was to end up the utmost invincible. Just like Afonso, Valdemar only became a hero after he had been through a terrible lot and had overcome all difficulties on his way.

Valdemar grew up without his father, Canute Lavard, who had been killed on January 7, 1131, even before Valdemar was born. According to Saxo, the powerful Hvide family on Zealand cared for Valdemar as a foster son; he grew up together with Absalon and thereby established a lifelong friendship with the future Archbishop. This does not seem the most probable story, at least not for Valdemar's earliest years, when the situation in Denmark was very complicated. Because of the killing of Canute Lavard, Prince Magnus and King Niels were attacked by Erik Emune and many noblemen in an open rebellion, so at the time the King and his son would presumably have gone to great lengths to remove the young Valdemar and his claim to the throne. It simply would not have been safe for Valdemar to stay in Zealand. It is more likely, as the later Knýtlinga saga states, that he began his life in exile in Kiev with his maternal grandfather, Mstislav Vladimirovich.[102] The years after the murder of Valdemar's father were characterized by constant warfare between the members of the royal family. Prince Magnus fell in a great battle at Fotevig at Whitsun in 1134, where five bishops and perhaps up to sixty

154 *Afonso and Valdemar*

clerics were also killed.[103] His father, King Niels, fled and went, strangely enough, to Canute Lavard's main city of Schleswig, where he was killed on June 25, 1134, by the burghers who were organized in some form of city guild, which might already at that time have had Valdemar's murdered father as a patron saint.[104]

Wars continued. They were inevitable political wars about power between members of the royal family, but the contemporaries also pointed to a deeper religious cause in the struggle between good and evil. On the very day of the battle at Fotevig, shepherds on Iceland saw the souls of Niels and Magnus and the dead bishops and all their allies flying in the sky in the shape of black ravens and other birds, wailing: "Woe, woe betide us, what are we doing. Woe, Woe betide us, what shall happen to us!" The answer came immediately in the form of a group of immensely large griffins that caught the ravens and threw them down to hell through the opening in Mount Hekla. One of the shepherds – presumably shaken – joined the Cistercian order and was admitted to a Swedish monastery, where the abbot took the case so seriously that he reported it and had it discussed at the highest level, at the general chapter of the order. From there it spread to the European chroniclers.[105]

Concomitantly, there was a serious setback for the Christian mission in Holstein during the latter part of the 1130s. The heathen Pribislav attacked from Lübeck against Segeberg, which had been fortified by Canute Lavard,[106] and plundered and burned the newly built monastery there. Furthermore, people in Holstein began to suffer from spirit possessions. The priest and exorcist Vizelin expelled a devil by the name Rufinus from the body of a young woman and forced it to speak. It said that it now was on the way to Denmark. Earlier, two devils had failed to reach that destination, and as a punishment Rufinus himself was now dispatched by the Prince of Hell personally. Rufinus did make it to Denmark, presumably in 1137, because "After the killing of King Erik [in 1137] such a disturbance occurred in Denmark that anyone can see with their own eyes that a great devil must have come to harass that nation. For war and plagues and other misfortunes for mankind is the work of demons, as everybody knows."[107] In the subsequent wars between several Danish kings and pretenders, Canute Lavard was an important fellow player. His half-brother Erik Emune gave large gifts to the monastic community in Ringsted "To the memory of my brother Canute, blessed memory, who was cruelly murdered, and whom I loved uniquely above all other mortals."[108] This happened in 1135, and that same year or the year after, Erik Emune conquered Rügen and Christianized the people there; this turned out to be a short-lasting joy, as they quickly fell back to heathenism again.

The fatherless Valdemar reappeared in history in 1146. Together with his cousin, Svend, he attempted to perform a private canonization of his father by placing his bones in a reliquary on the high altar in the church in Ringsted. It did not succeed due to the opposition of Archbishop Eskil, presumably for formal reasons because his authority and that of the Pope had been infringed, as they had not been involved beforehand.[109] The most important in this context, however, is that the canonization attempt must have been grand and public. It would of course have been a religious act, but it was a ritual, political manifestation too. At the age

Afonso and Valdemar 155

of fifteen, Valdemar appeared in public for the first time and thus demonstrated that he intended to take on the responsibilities of a royal family member and the son of a religious warrior. This corresponds to the ceremony when Afonso Henriques girded himself and put on his sword in 1125. It is, of course, possible that the young Valdemar was used cynically in a political game by the older cousin. Notwithstanding who actually took the initiative for the canonization, the older Svend and the younger Valdemar had a joint interest in a religious and political manifestation.

Very soon after the failed attempt to canonize Canute Lavard, Svend was chosen as King by the Zealanders, whereas the Jutlanders chose Canute, who was a son of Canute Lavard's killer Magnus. Svend and Canute began the first of a long series of wars against each other, but in 1147, they were briefly reconciled in order to go on a crusade together against the heathen Wends at Dobin, as already related above. Neither Helmold of Bosau nor Saxo mention the young Valdemar as participating in the expedition. Nevertheless, he was immediately entangled in the wars between King Svend and King Canute, which were to last for more than a decade. Valdemar was installed by King Svend as Duke of Schleswig, his father's old position. He was sure of a positive reception here. The wars during the following years are vividly described by Saxo, including many heroic details; however, Saxo evidently had problems with making all the events form a harmonic, coherent whole. The most likely reason for his occasionally somewhat vague statements is that Valdemar ruthlessly changed sides and only had his own political goals in mind, and Saxo subsequently had to lay all the blame and the wavering on Canute and Svend.

Both Svend and Canute sought alliances with strong neighbours. Count Adolf of Holstein ended up becoming an ally of Canute, perhaps due to simple political resentment against having Valdemar as Duke in Schleswig. Adolf had the backing of Duke Henry the Lion and was thus able to repel an attack from Svend. With the assistance from a Saxon mercenary army, Canute attempted to conquer Jutland, and it came to a battle at Viborg, which Svend had just fortified with a rampart. Valdemar now turned out to be an experienced knight. He broke a lance with the brave and battle-hardened Saxons, he held the only ford at an important river against several horsemen and he stayed in his saddle and kept control of his horse as it was forced onto its rear in the water – forced backwards by four spears that hit Valdemar simultaneously. One spear pierced his helmet, penetrating between the helmet and his forehead, but Valdemar just broke it off, threw it away, and fought on.[110] That this is an act of a true hero is clearly Saxo's opinion. In the end, Canute's men had to withdraw.

Soon after 1050, both Svend and Canute sought help from King Conrad III of Germany. They both styled him as a father and emperor of the Romans, even though he in reality was only king, and Svend ended his letter by asking Conrad to let his princes subjugate the Wends and offered his assistance in this undertaking whenever the emperor wanted him to.[111] Offers of Danish assistance in crusades had become a powerful political basis for negotiation. When Conrad died in 1152, the two Danish kings turned up to an assembly meeting with the successor,

156 *Afonso and Valdemar*

Fredric Barbarossa, who gave the Danish crown to Svend and apportioned parts of Denmark to Canute and a part too to the young Valdemar.[112] The future emperor's supremacy over the Danish kings was quite obvious and recognized by them.

This, however, did not secure peace. The wars continued and were waged with widely diversified troops. In around 1152, Canute had to flee, first to Sweden and later to Russia, from where he managed to assemble an army of Saxons and march up through Jutland, where he was defeated by Svend.[113]

Canute now fled to Friesland and tried to recruit support there. By promising lower taxes, he managed to talk the Frisians into helping him build a castle by Milde River. The Frisians were savage by nature but supple. They had spears and light weapons, and they jumped over the ditches between their low-laying fields using long poles,[114] which made the area exceedingly difficult to manoeuvre for cavalry. Then Svend went to Schleswig with the whole Danish war fleet and had the ships pulled over land all the way to Hollingsted, a distance of about a dozen kilometres alongside the 400-year-old Dannevirke earthworks.[115] Then he was able to lay siege to Canute's castle and devastate Friesland with fire, as a medieval annals laconically report it.[116]

Saxo describes in more detail how young warriors on both sides challenged each other, how Canute hid himself for Svend, how the fighting lasted into the night and how Valdemar, during the confusion of darkness, accidentally mowed down a group of his own soldiers, believing they were Frisians. According to Saxo, the fighting ended with Svend and Valdemar being victors, and Canute had to flee yet again. Coincidentally, Saxo has the Frisians asking Valdemar for permission to restart the war and try to fight once more. It is a strange story; according to Saxo, it was almost like a wager. It might signify that the Frisians did not think that they had been defeated. The somewhat later Annals of Ryd has a different version. According to this, "Canute went against Svend, and together with the Frisians, he defeated him in battle."[117]

In any case, the battle in Friesland became a decisive turning point, because Valdemar now chose to become engaged to Canute's sister Sofie. This is what the annals laconically tells us, whereas Saxo has great difficulty in cobbling a plausible narrative together. Svend has all of a sudden become a bad king who goes back on his word and likes to dress according to foreign Saxon fashion, and who, by and large, has gone soft. Canute's advisors systematically praise the Princess's great beauty to Valdemar. This might have some truth in it; the medieval historian Svend Aggesen later wrote that nature had embellished her with such exceedingly beautiful curves as a true masterpiece of beauty that even Ovid would lack the words to describe her.[118] However, at the time that Saxo has Valdemar fall for her beauty, she was a minor, and only when Canute promised him one third of his possessions did Valdemar become engaged to the girl; he immediately sent her into the care of a woman by the name of Bodil, who was to take her in hand until she was mature.[119] A direct alliance between Valdemar and the son of his father's killer ought to have raised some moral questions, but it was conducive to his career. That same year, Canute and Valdemar were chosen by "all Danes"[120] as their kings, and Svend had to flee to his in-laws in Meissen. Saxo's inconsistent

Afonso and Valdemar 157

story of the battle in Friesland, his blackening of Svend, and the emphasis on the beauty of the underage girl was simply to blur the fact that his great hero Valdemar betrayed his king and cousin in order to manoeuvre himself in position to something bigger than just Duke of Schleswig.

The occasion was to arise soon. In 1157, Svend, Canute and Valdemar agreed to share all of Denmark between themselves. Valdemar got Jutland, Canute Zealand, and Svend Scania. In order to mark peace and the introduction of the triple monarchy, Canute invited the two others to a celebration in Roskilde, which was held August 9. Mutual suspicion was ripe and heavy security in place. The host had arranged for a German singer of satire who, in front of them all, mocked Svend for his bad luck. Later in the evening, one of Svend's noblemen, Thetlev, entered the hall and nodded almost indiscernibly towards Svend.

Canute sensed that something was amiss; he embraced the surprised Valdemar and kissed him. Then Svend's men jumped at Canute and Valdemar, while Svend sneaked away in the twilight. Valdemar leaped from his seat, wrapped his cloak around his arm and averted the worst blows. He suffered a deep wound in his thigh but managed to get out. The windows were covered from the outside and there was total confusion in the darkness. Thetlev cleaved Canute right through the forehead, and the later Bishop Absalon softly rocked him in his lap, believing the dead king to be his friend Valdemar. Everyone who managed to get through the doors was cut down, no matter which party they belonged to. Only Absalon walked resolutely and with determination towards the guards and escaped unhurt, having found out that the cleaved head in his lap did not belong to Valdemar.[121]

The Feast of Blood in Roskilde, as it is known in Danish historical tradition, is a high point in Saxo's narrative and in the later historical tradition, it is retold in all history books and was a popular motive for historical paintings. The outrage is unequivocally directed against Svend as the villain and traitor. It is, however, a rather peculiar story. Canute was the host and on his home ground. It is odd that he was unable to secure himself against assassination attempts from Svend's party. However, the one who gained the most from the killing of Canute was Valdemar. The detailed description of Svend's actions and of his devious motives is only known from Saxo, whose sympathy is unequivocally on the side of Valdemar and Absalon. Saxo even goes as far as to accuse Svend of having been provoked to the atrocity by a woman who had chaffed him with only possessing one third of the land that he ought to have had by himself. Ruled by a woman! It could hardly be any worse for Saxo.[122] As far as it goes, it would make sense if Valdemar and Absalon were behind the bloody celebration in Roskild as an attempt to come up with a radical solution to the problem of having three kings at once.[123]

It almost went wrong for Valdemar, whether the Feast of Blood was his idea or not. He had to flee and hide in Zealand because Svend had ordered that holes be drilled in all boats on the island. In the end, the hero Esbern Snare succeeded in forcing a carpenter to repair a boat so that Valdemar could be brought to Jutland, where he immediately married his young fiancée, Canute's sister, in order to gain support from his men. A final showdown between Valdemar and Svend was now unavoidable.

158   *Afonso and Valdemar*

In the autumn, the two armies assembled on a moor near Viborg. Large flocks of ravens were circling so close above Valdemar's men that they could have hit them with their spears. To excite the warriors, a bard rode in front of the army and sang songs about Svend's perfidious deed. At the battle of Grathe Moor Valdemar was victorious. Svend's men were captured and executed; Thetlev from the Feast of Blood wept and whimpered, unable to hold back his tears he "revealed that his manly body was only a convent for a woman's soul."[124] Svend himself fled further into the moor but was recognized and decapitated by a peasant. He was buried without any religious ceremony;[125] that is, he was just shoved underground as an animal or a heretic. This might suggest that Valdemar perceived his war against Svend as a kind of religiously just war or as a crusade. It took place on October 23, 1157. The location of the battlefield is known precisely because of the battle axes that archaeologists have found on the site.[126]

Valdemar won all the royal power and ruled for twenty-five and a half years. That is how one annals summarized the impact of the battle at Grathe Moor.[127] He won the kingdom and became a *ruler of peace* and *son of peace – moderator pacis et filius pacis*, another annals reported.[128] To show his gratitude, Valdemar established a Cistercian monastery in Vitskøl, after the faithless had attacked him, even though he was unarmed and had feared no evil, and they attempted to pierce him with swords. But divine mercy had protected him, even though he did not carry a sword, and had snatched him from the midst of the swords of the enemy warriors.[129] Now, with even greater justification than before, Valdemar could call himself "King of the Danes, by the Grace of God."

These struggles between several Danish kings took place at the same time as constant Wendish attacks on the Danish shores, Saxo claims. This is a problematic statement, but there was probably some truth in it; the Wends were likely to have exploited the general unrest and attacked Danish settlements, just as the fighting Danish kings did. The point, however, is that Saxo obviously has the fight against the Wends as an intrinsic part of the duties of a Danish king. The increasing danger from the Wends leads to a logical conclusion: it was good that Valdemar became king, so that he was able to put a stop to the disorder. Earlier, Svend had attempted to do it but with much less success than Valdemar. Svend led several expeditions to the Wendish lands but without much luck because he was too impetuous and was not a real strategist. He then got scared and hurried down to his boat before his men, Saxo tells us.[130] Valdemar would never have acted like this, we are to understand. Svend also built two castles at the Great Belt, one on Funen and one on Zealand, but both were later destroyed by the Wends;[131] in contrast to the strong castle measuring twenty-six by thirty-two metres[132] that Valdemar later built on the island of Sprogø in the middle of the Great Belt. In Saxo's time, this still stood as a powerful demonstration of Valdemar's ability to control Danish waters and keep them free from the heathen Wends.

On several occasions, Svend had fought bravely against the Wends in Denmark, especially on Funen, where his men in one instance slaughtered so many Wends that the skin wore off their palms, and they had to wield their swords with the bleeding flesh of their hands. This would have been around 1150. Seven years

Afonso and Valdemar 159

later, the situation was rather different, as Svend now invaded Funen leading a Wendish force. This was soon after the island had been exposed to yet another heavy and destructive attack from the Wends. One more attack like that, and Funen would have been lost for Christendom.[133] If we are to believe Saxo, the Wendish presence was strong on Funen at this time. Perhaps the Wendish agricultural systems along the Little Belt date back to this period, and maybe the present day name Vends for one of the counties on Funen indicates that the population here at some time has been Wendish. The field structure around Little Belt and on the island of Lolland is markedly different from the rest of medieval Denmark. A two-course system is characteristic, as opposed to the much more common three-course system.[134]

Svend returned from his exile with the Margrave of Meissen and was able to promise the people of Funen peace – *pax* – and freedom from taxes, both promises guaranteed by his Wendish forces. Svend persuaded many, and they now decided on their own free will to defend him. Strangely, Saxo does not mention by name the Wendish prince who was leading Svend's troops. It was Niklot, the king of the Obotrites, who had a fragile alliance with Duke Henry the Lion of Saxony. The Duke now commanded the Wends in Oldenburg and Obotritia to assist Svend. At that time some of the Wends in the West would have been Christians, but Niklot himself was a stout heathen. The year before, during an imperial assembly meeting in the late winter of 1156, he had commented drily on one Duke Henry's conversion attempts with the words: "Let the God who is in heaven be your God, then you can be our God, and that is enough for us. Worship Him, and we shall worship you." The Duke was understandably shocked and reproached Niklot for his blasphemous words. But actually he had no time for the mission, as he had just returned from Italy and was mostly concerned about his treasure chest, which was "empty and waste," just like earth before creation.[135] The head of Niklot the Heathen later ended on a spike, triumphantly taken to Valdemar's camp and shown to all – including his son Prislav, who had changed sides and had become a Christian and one of Valdemar's faithful vassals.[136] Perhaps it was during negotiations with Niklot about military assistance that Svend presented a fine drinking cup to the heathen god Svantevit in Arkona on Rügen. Anyway, it is proof that important alliances could be made across religious frontiers in Denmark as well.[137]

When the Wends could not be defeated or used in military alliances, it may have been necessary to buy them off. The people on the large island of Lolland were in an exposed position, and they chose to pay the Wends to be left in peace, and many of them would have had a Wendish background themselves. It was worse that King Svend chose to pay for peace when he saw that the country was close to its breaking point because of the constant pirate attacks. The prize was 1500 silver marks, which he had to pay to Duke Henry the Lion in order to get him to command the Wends to stay at home and not attack the Danes. Henry seems to have had a strong hold over the Wends who lived to the North and Northeast of his duchy, whether they were Christians or heathen. "He put his foot on the neck of the rebels, dismantled their castles and punished traitors, made peace – *pax* – in

160 *Afonso and Valdemar*

the land and built new castles. . . . He was the only one whom the Wends feared. He put bits in their mouths and could lead them wherever he wanted. If he called for peace, they obeyed; if he called for war, they said: We are ready."[138]

Svend's payment of protection money did not work, however. Henry took the money but did not keep his promise. On top of the military troubles now came the humiliation, Saxo wrote, and the Danes were bitter with Svend. The common fatherland had been cheated because of the King's mistake, and they thought it completely wrong to pay tax and not obtain peace by the use of weapons.[139] This would have been in around 1154.

The popular outrage might not have been that tangible though. After having become sole King, Valdemar did exactly as Svend. In the spring of 1159, he paid more than a thousand marks to Henry the Lion to make peace with the Wends. Henry now called on Niklot and the other Slavic princes and commanded them to swear that they would not attack Denmark. To be on the safe side, he ordered them to bring their warships to Lübeck so they could be registered and kept under surveillance. The Wends dutifully handed over a number of small and old, derelict ships at the port of Lübeck but kept the good ships at home.

As Henry became preoccupied in Northern Italy with the wars of the Emperor, the Slavs from Oldenburg and Mecklenburg attacked Denmark nevertheless, and in the Duke's lands, people now feared counterattacks from the enraged Valdemar. The detailed narrative continues by relating how it ends with a joint crusade by Henry and Valdemar against the Wends – and Niklot only succumbs after having attempted to conquer Lübeck.[140] Saxo does not mention any of this; it is known solely from Helmold's description. However, the point is that both Svend and Valdemar paid protection money to Henry to obtain peace from the Wends. Thus, it seems to have been a rather common phenomenon and demonstrates how crusades and religious wars in frontier areas had, in practice, to adapt to the balance of power and only could be carried out if Christian princes were prepared to negotiate with pagans and vice versa.

After Valdemar had become sole King, he immediately plunged himself into the fight against the pagans. During the following fifteen years he led religious wars against the Wends eighteen or twenty-two times – depending on the sources – that is, more than one expedition every year.[141] The Englishman Radulphus Niger, who most certainly was not a great admirer of Valdemar, summarized it such: "After having killed Svend, Valdemar ruled alone, cruel and powerful, but a good propagator of the Christian faith nevertheless."[142]

Valdemar's good friend Absalon was elected bishop in 1158 by the canons at the Roskilde Cathedral at an election which the new king honoured with his presence while carefully emphasizing that he in no way would put any pressure on anybody or try to influence events. Valdemar got with Absalon a dedicated crusader bishop who "was as much admiral as bishop, because he thought it was poor if the religion was protected inwardly but allowed to perish outwardly. It is not a lesser duty of the priests to repulse the enemies of religion than to perform the sacred acts," Saxo wrote,[143] a very clear formulation of the duty of the Church in the crusade ideology of the time.

Afonso and Valdemar 161

By and large, the cooperation between the King and Church in Denmark seems to have proceeded with the best possible mutual understanding in respect of missionary wars. Bishop Absalon of Roskilde became a constant participant in one expedition after the other together with his close relatives, the seasoned Hvide family. Bishop Eskil of Aarhus fell at a battle in Wendish areas in 1165, but his body must have been boiled or salted down, as he was buried with the Cistercians at the monastery he had established at Øm at home.[144] His successor, Bishop Svend of Aarhus, also participated in several crusades; he stood upon the idol to mock it further after the wooden statue had been toppled in the town of Karenz on Rügen.[145] Bishop Frederik of Schleswig followed Valdemar's crusading command and sailed out with a fleet despite strong winds from the south. His ship went down and Frederik drowned, but his body was washed ashore on the coast of Zealand much later at Whitsun; it was well preserved and sweet-smelling, which was a sign of his holiness. The miracle highlighted the expedition's status as a crusade, where the participants were promised full indulgence and martyrdom – even if they died en route and never reached the actual fighting.[146] Archbishop Eskil proclaimed in 1159 that anyone who did not follow the King on crusade against the Wends would be excommunicated[147] and deprived the means of grace. This threat is only known from a single comment in Saxo and gives rise to some questions regarding the relationship between theology and obedience to the king: was the threat of excommunication only valid for this specific crusade or did it come into force if the participants failed to appear on a later crusade? Were the warriors obliged to participate by their king's crusading vow or had they also taken the cross individually? Unfortunately, we are unable to conclude anything from the Danish source material.

When not concerning religious wars, the relationship between King and Church was not always smooth. In 1159, two Popes were chosen, Victor IV, who had support from Emperor Fredric Barbarossa, and Alexander III, who as a cardinal had insulted Fredric by claiming that he had received benefits from the Pope. Benefits could refer to something quite innocent, such as good deeds, good will and the like. However, it could also refer to something more exact: enfeoffments from an overlord to a vassal, and it could be understood in such a way that the Emperor received his power from the Pope. Alexander's statement was made in 1157, when he was the envoy of his papal predecessor to the Emperor, to convince him to interfere and release the imprisoned Archbishop Eskil of Lund, who had been taken prisoner on his way back from Rome. The details of the case are uncertain, but Eskil insisted fervently that he did not want help in any way, as he would rather die for Denmark than rule in Denmark.[148] In spite of this, he was in the end released and was soon back home. When the great schism was a reality in 1159, Eskil supported his spokesman in front of the Emperor, Alexander III, and King Valdemar supported the candidate of his imperial overlord, Victor IV. In 1161, Valdemar attacked Eskil's castle Søborg and confiscated much of the estate belonging to the church in Lund; Eskil went into exile in 1161 and only returned to Denmark in 1167. He travelled to Jerusalem and Rome and spent much time with Pope Alexander III, for example at Sens in France. There he met several interesting crusade advocates.

162 *Afonso and Valdemar*

While Eskil was in exile, Valdemar continued his expeditions against the Wends. In 1160 and 1164, they were organized in cooperation with Duke Henry the Lion. These were plundering expeditions and brief disruptions for the enemy, raids that were repeated year after year. However, at the same time, Valdemar was aiming at a more permanent conquest of those lands. In 1162, he initiated a renovation and strengthening of Dannevirke, which was fitted with an impressive brick wall, eight metres high and fortified with a watchman's gallery and stockades on the top. It spanned over four kilometres and was presumably the first structure in Denmark to be built in brick. The construction lasted for the rest of Valdemar's twenty-year-long reign. The highly nationalistic and anti-German Annals of Ryd note that "Valdemar wished to be ahead of the evils of the Germans and surrounded the fortification of Dannevirke with a wall of stones. Earlier it had only been fortified with stockades of wood."[149] Dannevirke might well have been in use for defence against forces from the South, possibly even Germans, but it was predominantly a support base for further Danish expansion down into Schleswig and Holstein, where large areas were still heathen. It formed part of a deliberate securing of the frontier further and further into enemy territory.

Further to the East, Valdemar attempted to establish a similar military bridgehead at the town of Wolgast, which he considered the most strategically important town for the domination of the Eastern Wendic lands. In 1164, the town was abandoned by the Wends, fearful of the rumours of the Danes' cruelty against the neighbouring towns and that the renowned admiral Vetheman, who had established a crusading city militia in Roskilde, was installed as the commander of the town. At the same time, Valdemar commanded Bishop Absalon of Roskilde, Bishop Svend of Aarhus and his own cousin Buris to populate the town with their subordinates, who were to receive privileges in return for performing military duties in the frontier land. It came to nothing, because only Absalon's Zealanders dared to move that far out.[150] This was probably a correct assessment by the more timid people from Funen and Jutland, who had also been designated as volunteer colonists. At the time when the large Danish army arrived, the Wends were attacked by Count Adolf of Holstein and Count Reinald of the Ditmarshes with their numerous warriors, but they were killed to the last man by the Wends.[151] The relative strength of the adherents of the two religions was far from settled in advance.

At some time in this tense crusading environment, the Knights of St. John arrived in Denmark. From the 1160s, King Valdemar gave them an especially privileged position by donating to the Order a tax of one denarius from every household in Denmark, a tax that was to go to crusading purposes.[152] It is also possible that the Knights of St. John had a special ideological significance for the Danish King after his conquest of Rügen, and that the Danish flag is actually a banner of the Knights of St. John.[153] Finally, it is also possible that King Valdemar, in around 1170, attempted to create a local Danish order of chivalry, the Knights of St. Canute, with his father as the dedicated guardian saint.

Valdemar's original attempt to canonize his father in 1146 had been delayed but not prevented. He worked meticulously to support a cult, which must have already been quite vigorous, even though it was not officially recognized yet. In

1160, Valdemar received a sum of one or two marks in gold from the Monastery of Esrom for the gilding of Canute Lavard's reliquary in Ringsted, a large sum in a Danish context.[154] At the same time, a new and gigantic church was being built around the shrine. It was the first large-scale construction of a church in brick, a worthy setting for a royal cult of a saint and place for remembrance and for royal burials for almost 200 years. Both in its idea and in its precise architectural design, the church in Ringsted is clearly inspired by Emperor Lothar's similar church in Königslutter.[155] It was being prepared for official canonization, reports of miracles were collected and a vita was written which emphasized Canute Lavard's achievement in the mission amongst the Slavs.

The militarization of society

The restorer of peace and father of the Fatherland

War was ubiquitous in the Middle Ages, and there were variations in how much individual societies as a whole were organized in anticipation of warfare. In frontier societies, militarization reached a higher level, they became "Societies organized for war." This militarization became increasingly sustained and extensive during the 12th century, both in Denmark and in Portugal. More individuals were involved in warfare, new methods of warfare were introduced and more effective warfare institutions were established.

With militarization, an ideological rearmament took place in which one of the important elements was to emphasize the idea of the King as a guarantee for peace. In this context it meant that he extended Christendom and secured peace for the missionaries to preach, if necessary by war. This was usually necessary. The greatest warlords in Denmark and León-Castile in this period both styled themselves as the "Restorer of Peace"; they thus took on Pope Urban II's title of honour, which he received because he succeeded in calling for a crusade.[156] *Pacis restaurator* was one of the honorific titles which Alfonso VI of León used about himself in his letters after he had conquered Toledo in 1085. And *pacis conseruator* was one of the titles that Valdemar the Great had written on a lead tablet, which was placed by the head inside his grave in 1182. This was after he had conquered Rügen and converted all the heathens there to Christianity. The most adequate translation of *pacis conseruator* is possibly "the Resumer of War," the one who successfully turned the tide from heathens attacking Christians to Christians attacking heathens. *Pacis conseruator* does not mean absence of war and bloodletting, on the contrary.

We are used to translating *pax* as peace, as was the meaning of the word during the reign of Emperor Augustus, when the gates to the temple of Janus were closed because all war had stopped in the empire, that is, in the world. During the Middle Ages, *pax* meant something different, because a society without warfare was inconceivable. In a medieval text, *pax* is often to be translated as "war," meaning crusade. When Valdemar had defeated his last rival in the battle of Grathe Moor, he was called the *son of peace* – he was now able to concentrate all his efforts on

164   *Afonso and Valdemar*

crusades.[157] The son of peace is one whom Jesus Himself blesses with a permanent blessing and who is one of the workers sent to the field of mission to reap the harvest.[158]

In Santa Cruz, the ideological crusade centre of Coimbra, the special prayer for Good Friday said: "We pray to the almighty God and Father that he cleanses the world for all errors and heresies, that He receives the dead, that He fights back hunger, that He opens the prisons and loosen the chains, that He takes pity and allows the crusaders to return, the ill to be healed, and the seafarers to reach the port of salvation, that He bestows peace in our time, defeats those enemies who rise up against Him and that He tears us from the hand of hell because of His Name."[159] Peace in our time and fight against those who rise up against God. These were strong words during the worship of Good Friday, with the altarpiece closed and all the figures hidden in black and even the priest himself in a black cope, and said on the very day that the first crusaders began the sanguineous conquest of Jerusalem.[160]

Just as complicated as *peace* is the term *fatherland*, which these warrior kings protected or liberated. On the same lead tablet, Valdemar is called the "liberator of the fatherland," *patrie liberator* and Saxo described him as the "restorer of the fatherland," *patrie reparator*.[161] Saxo called Bishop Absalon the "father of the fatherland," *parens patrie*.[162] Apparently, this was not a problem to modern historians, who translate *patria* as "fatherland" and suppose that it simply refers to Denmark. In the same way, many Portuguese historians have until now reckoned that the word *patria* in their medieval sources referred to present-day Portugal or at least to the old duchy of Portugal, to the north of the River Tagus. To fight and die for the fatherland was supposedly an expression of a medieval nationalism, similar to the modern one. It is unlikely to be this simple.

There seem to have been two fundamental meanings of the term *patria* in the Middle Ages. The first is the place where one comes from and where one's fathers had lived before oneself. The other is the territory ruled by one's overlord. The last view means that the fatherland was not really a country but rather an idea or a series of peoples who happened to be ruled together by the same king. The king figure is central to the concept of *patria*; the fatherland was defined on the basis of the father of the fatherland.[163] In the first sense, on the other hand, *patria* is the place where one was born, the ancestral soil or, perhaps, the ancestral spirit, because the place of birth was not necessarily something physical. To peasants and noblemen, the fatherland could be the village or the estate they cultivated after their fathers. To monks, the fatherland might be their monastery, where they continued the lives of their fathers. Not their biological fathers, however, but the life and deeds of their spiritual fathers, and they felt a long continuity all the way back to the desert fathers of late antiquity – some of them even felt that their *patria* stretched all the way back to the patriarchs of the Old Testament. Physical and spiritual matters were – as always in the Middle Ages – deliberately combined. At the same time, peasants and monks alike knew that they had inherited a much greater *patria* than village and monastery, namely the whole Christian *patria*, and they also knew that their real fatherland was ultimately in heaven and

Afonso and Valdemar 165

not on earth, that is paradise. "We fell from our fatherland and live as prisoners and outcasts in exile in this world," Portuguese monks wrote in a text on one of their crusade saints.[164]

To die for the fatherland became a notion in the Middle Ages which many tried to live up to and realize. It is, however, only in very rare circumstances that it is to be perceived in the modern, nationalistic sense. Often it means to die for the king but usually it refers to death in the service of a higher cause. Mostly it implied leaving one's home country behind. Kings or historians in the 12th century would not use the word "fatherland" without thinking of Urban II's great sermon in Clermont, which is full of appeals to leave one's present country and travel to the real fatherland, that is Jerusalem, and through martyrdom towards the heavenly fatherland. Death takes the good person to his fatherland faster, Urban had promised. He ended this theme with the urgent words: "Drive the un-pious from the sanctuary of God and do not let love to your home hold you back because to a Christian, the fatherland is exile and the exile is the fatherland."[165] Defending the fatherland meant leaving one's own country to go on a crusade. In this way, kings eager for crusades all over Europe imitated those rulers who, as another Judas Maccabeus, actually defended the earthly Jerusalem and thus created a hope of reaching the heavenly Jerusalem. The kings of Jerusalem were *spes patrie*, the hope of the Fatherland.[166]

The King was the defender of the fatherland but during the crusades, his position stretched even further. He was to be a distant and inaccessible world ruler, who fitted into God's plan for salvation and carried out His wishes. However, he was also to be an active member of the band of warriors, taking part in the fighting and being comrade with the ordinary soldiers. He was exalted because it "had pleased the foresight of the Creator of all to put us in a place that is more prominent than that of anyone else," as Valdemar the Great wrote in the 1170s, even though the days of men are filled with sorrow and their number are as the months of the flower to the Lord.[167] Canute VI spoke of his *monarchia*, his absolute rule, which he exercised "cum sederem in solio ciuitate Lundensium," "when I sat on my throne in Lund."[168] The wording shows that Canute perceived himself as the new Solomon, whom David prophesized was to rule after him and "sit upon my throne."[169] And furthermore, Canute organized the affairs of the Danish church provinces "and I saw and realized that it was good" – just as the Lord God Himself during the first six days of the creation of the world had seen that all that he had created was good. A mortal ruler cannot place himself higher.

Apparently, the Portuguese kings did not use quite such bombastic terms to describe themselves as did the Danish. The introductions in their letters are generally rather brief and only emphasize that it is important to have things put into writing, so that posterity shall not doubt what was decided. At one time only, Sancho I compared himself to Solomon, who had said that "those who judge earth must love justice."[170]

While emphasizing their exalted status, the warrior kings maintained that they were equal to their soldiers. After a magnificent and unexpected victory, Valdemar the Great disbanded the naval personnel, but first he showed them a special

166 *Afonso and Valdemar*

favour by kissing them all, presumably on the mouth.[171] The Valdemar symbolically made all the conscripted warriors his personal vassals – and thus made himself their equal. It must have been the rowers, the ordinary crusaders, with whom Valdemar equalized himself at this occasion, not the noblemen. He had kissed them earlier in their career, when they made a personal vow of loyalty to him. The equal relationship between ruler and warriors was institutionalized with the establishment of the royal military organization or guard, the "Vederlag." In this guard, all members were *commilitiones*, "co-soldiers," and the King was a member on an equal footing with the other warriors.[172]

Afonso Henriques cultivated a relationship with his soldiers. On the eve of the attack on Muslim Santarém in 1147, Afonso gave a pep talk to his soldiers:

> You know my co-soldiers (*commilitiones*), that you during my time and before have had to endure many attacks and burdens from this city, which we now stand before. You know the destruction it has brought to our land, to you and to my whole realm and how it has restricted our movements. You have known for a long time the threat from its heathens. But now, I could have assembled all the strength of my army, I could have called on all the help that I could get. But I did not wish to. I chose you alone. You, who have always followed me; you, who are experienced warriors, even in the most desperate conditions. I confide my plans in you because I am certain that you share my view. Have confidence in me, my soldiers, because what I wish to do together with you is easy and useful.

Afonso reveals his battle plan to capture Santarém and concludes: "Therefore, fight for your children and your grandchildren. I shall be one of you, in the vanguard and no one shall ever separate me from your company, neither alive nor in death.[173]

Peace, fatherland and king – as a world ruler or a fellow soldier – were fundamental concepts in the descriptions of the crusades at the time, in Denmark as well as in Portugal. They were ritualized and came to feature as an established part in ceremonies for the reception of high-ranking ecclesiastic and secular rulers, when all of the local clerics were lined up to sing: "The compatriots of the apostles and God's servants come to us today, and they bring peace and light up the fatherland by giving peace to the heathens and liberating the people of the Lord."[174] The terms crop up time and again in many different types of sources, and each term had more layers of meaning than today. Sometimes, some of them meant the exact opposite of what we would immediately think. Peace to the heathens meant war and bloodstained crusades.

The cruel necessity of war – warfare in practice

Wars were usually waged with a high degree of cruelty but also in very different ways, depending on the immediate circumstances. When Fernando I of León-Castile captured Viseu and Lamego in 1055, the Muslims in Viseu were sold as slaves to Christian masters, whereas the Muslim population of Lamego were

Afonso and Valdemar   167

mostly killed and the few survivors were enslaved.[175] After Fernando had laid siege to Coimbra for six months in 1064, the Muslim population managed to negotiate a surrender, according to which they were allowed to live in return for surrendering the city, leaving all their belongings to the Christians and travelling south to live on the far side of the River Mondego.[176] When Alfonso VI captured Toledo in 1085, he planned to tear down the mosque, but the Mozarab Count Sisnando recommended that he show mercy to the Muslims and the Muslim princes so he could win their loyalty.[177] When Afonso Henriques initiated the Portuguese part of the second crusade in 1147, he first captured Santarém on March 15 and had all Muslims killed or exiled.

"Everything else, man can do against his will, but man can only believe willingly," St. Augustine wrote in his commentary to the Gospel of St. John,[178] and is frequently quoted by theologians during the whole of the medieval period. Thus, forced baptism was in principle not possible, and discussions amongst theologians could then turn into questions of when there is force and when there is heavy-handed, but theologically acceptable, persuasion. Presumably, the theological ban against forced baptism was adhered to in principle and in broad terms. It existed, however, at the same time as a completely different, direct perception that it was possible and indeed desirable to force the infidels into becoming Christians. Turpin's *History of Charlemagne* was a very popular text during the Middle Ages and recounts the conquest of the whole of Spain. Charlemagne prayed to the Lord to be allowed to capture Pamplona "for the sake of the honour of Your Name" and the walls crumbled. "Those Saracens who wished to be baptized, he let live, and those who rejected baptism, he put to the sword." This might be perceived as a manifestation of a knight's mentality, which was separated from the official theological discourse. This distinction cannot be maintained, however, for the reason that Turpin's narrative was included in the official collection of miracles and liturgy of St. James in Santiago de Compostela. At one of the most important pilgrimage sites in Europe, it was represented, without any reservations, as natural that Muslims are to be converted or killed.[179]

War was emotionally charged. The ideas behind warfare were not only cool, strategic considerations or logically and textually unimpeachable theological elucidations. The very idea of war was painful on a deep, personal level, because it hurt Christ. A priest on the Danish island of Als celebrated Mass – this would have been around 1170 – and when he held the chalice up high to receive the Eucharist, he saw inside the chalice real flesh and blood. He "was not used to seeing this," so he took the chalice to the Archbishop. Many believed that it was a divine sign to strengthen the people in the Faith but the Archbishop reckoned that there would be a deeper meaning. The miracle forebode a threatening and serious persecution of the Church and much shedding of Christian blood. "Because every time the blood of the martyrs is shed, Christ is crucified in his limbs again."[180] Thus, every time a heathen spear pierced a Christian, Christ himself would have felt the pain and, in a way, die again. It is not possible to gather how widespread this notion was, but it should not be dismissed as simply a pious propaganda, designated to attract crusaders. At a time when men could feel love because Christ loved them

168 *Afonso and Valdemar*

first, they would have been able to feel pain and anger so much more strongly if they were convinced that Christ too, felt the pain.

The physical pain of Christ's sufferings has justified the most brutal retribution and revenge over the enemies of Christ, which the Christians of the time made no attempt to hide. "They separated into plundering groups and went around pillaging far and wide in the area for several days. They burned all the villages they came across, tore down the synagogues[181] and tossed all Muhammad's books on the fire. Every single Muslim theologian they found was put to the sword. They had all the Muslims' vines, olive trees and fig trees chopped down, and where their feet tread, the earth was barren."[182]

These are the words of the official imperial chronicle about the expedition of Alfonso VII in May 1138, south of the River Gualdalquivir: terror and plunder. Saxo relates how the Danes under the leadership of Valdemar the Great attacked the Wends yet again and pillaged so thoroughly that the swallows built their nests in the rigs of Danish ships – there were simply no thatched roofs left in the Wendish area, everything had been burned down. Valdemar continued towards the city of Wolgast and pillaged the area with iron and fire and plundered the enemy for everything.[183] Valdemar was "guided by his desire for spilling blood."[184]

Before the crusaders set out, they assembled in the church for worship, prayer and Communion. In Roskilde, they "anticipated that everything would fare better if they had reconciled themselves with God before they went to war."[185] The communion just before the crusade was meant to ensure that the warrior went straight to heaven if he fell during fighting, but it also reduced the risk of being killed.

Records have been preserved from the Iberian Peninsula containing the special liturgy that was used at springtime to send the crusaders off for raids into the territory of the infidels. Strangely, the liturgy books dating to the end of the 12th century from Santa Cruz in Coimbra have not preserved any specific crusade liturgy,[186] but it is known from other collections. Large parts of the liturgy went back to Visigothic times in the first century after the Arab conquest in 711, but it has been debated whether it had been in use continuously until around 1100. The earliest consisted of sung quotes from the Maccabees and from the Book of Judith. "Guide our paths to free your people." "We bid you this sacrifice, Oh Lord, and pray that you will visit your people." "Turn our hearts towards your law and your commandments, and create peace, and hear our prayers and reconcile us with you, and do not leave us during evil days."[187] Again, the peace of the Lord meant going to war against the infidels.

Medieval warfare presents us with a series of apparent paradoxes. This is perhaps not so strange. Warfare is not logical but has to be adapted to fast-changing circumstances. It is nevertheless striking how little logic there seems to be in the individual battles of the religious wars. Some ended as massacres, others in surrender on relatively easy terms. Some rulers and theologians adhered to a kind of a freedom of religion, where those belonging to another faith could continue their worship in some form. At other times, those same individuals would demand conversion or death. Religiousness could further the fortunes of war and peace meant crusade. Some of the explanation for these paradoxes is perhaps that they are due to emotions and that a modern, analysing and causally consistent scheme is simply not applicable.

Control with the weapons production – iron in Minho and Halland

Access to iron became of decisive importance to societies that were as dependent on warfare as Denmark and Portugal. The extraction was systemized by kings or great ecclesiastic landowners, and access to iron was closely regulated and monopolized. Everywhere in Europe, a technological revolution in iron ore extraction took place during the 11th to the 13th centuries.[188] On the Iberian Peninsula, a slow arms build-up took place among the Christians, who in the 11th century seemed to become better at producing weapons than the Muslims, which presumably had something to do with better extraction and manufacturing techniques with regards to iron.[189] The earliest mention of watermills used for iron manufacturing in Portugal stems from 1010,[190] the mills probably worked the bellows. Only in the 13th century were mills used to drive the hammers to beat the iron clean from slag. The iron ore deposits belonged to the King, but exploitation was delegated out to specialists in extraction or manufacture of iron. From 1145, this was closely regulated in Coimbra. Trade in iron was strictly forbidden, except for the blacksmiths. Prices were fixed: four denarius for a set of horseshoes for horses, two for a set for asses, six denarius for spurs to knight and all the way up to fifteen denarius to put tin on the bridle for the warhorse.[191]

Some of the largest and most accessible iron ore deposits in Portugal are in Minho and Douro, where the re-conquest began. There is the area around Vila Pouca de Aguiar near Vila Real, Celorico de Basto near Braga, where Henrique chose to be buried, or Foz do Sousa near Porto. In 1220, each blacksmith in Vila Pouca was obliged to pay six pieces of iron to their overlord, the mine workers had to pay one piece each. In Celorico, every household was obliged to pay twelve iron hammers and two pieces of iron, each the width of a hand. In Foz do Sousa, every blacksmith had to pay one ploughshare to the King, the tax records of 1258 inform us.[192] The control of iron was a royal monopoly. The towns could have all kinds of royal rights transferred in the great town charters, but the kings usually made an exception with mining. That was too important to leave to the towns.

There was one crack in the King's tough monopoly, however, and an important one at that: the religious orders. The Cistercian order in particular received all the royal rights over their land, including iron ore extraction. On an overall European level, the Cistercians became mining specialists during the 12th and 13th centuries and developed new techniques and ensured fast dissemination of both technique and products. Alcobaça had four mines just in its holdings to the north of the Tagus and a special house for the ironworkers, on whose land the "Ironworkers' brook" flowed through. The Cistercians were obviously the most efficient but they were not the only ones. The monastery of Santa Cruz in Coimbra had an iron mill in the district of Leiria, and at some point, probably in the 13th century, the monastery bought the nearby iron ore mine in Cornegainha.[193]

170   *Afonso and Valdemar*

There is iron all over Europe. Sometimes it had to be extracted from mines that were dug, carved or blown deep into the mountains. Mine digging was in itself a complex technique, which could also be used during sieges to undermine the city walls. In other places, iron ore might gather on the surface at wet meadows or by little brooks, where the iron ore in the ground water gets into contact with the air, oxidizes and precipitates as rust. This "bog iron" is found as red dust or small lumps of metal and was the most accessible type of iron ore since prehistoric times. In Scandinavia, bog iron was gathered all through the Middle Ages, even though it was less pure than the iron ore from the mines, which meant a larger wastage during production.

During the 12th century, a revolution in iron production took place all over Western Europe, with increased extraction, increased trade and new technology for the processing of the iron.[194] The use of small traditional forges were built for a single process and then abandoned because it was too cumbersome to remove the slag. They could produce a bloom of around forty kilograms of iron, half of which had to be beaten off by the blacksmith. They left around 200 kilograms of slag. During the 12th century, forges were developed in the Mediterranean region, including in Catalonia, which could produce 150 kilograms of iron at each burn and, at the end of the 13th century, four-metre-high forges in Germany could make 900 kilograms. This would have demanded an enormous amount of wood, which first had to be turned into charcoal and then used for fuel in the forges. One single burn in one of the old-fashioned forges supplied forty kilograms of iron but cost twenty-five cubic metres of fuel. From the 1190s, it became necessary to mine coal in Germany for the forges, but systematic use of the forests continued elsewhere.

The demand from the crusaders was an important impetus to this iron revolution. Iron was, of course, useful in many places in society but for the crusaders it was of paramount importance, and the amounts were huge. When Richard the Lionheart prepared for his crusade in 1188, he bought, among other things, 50,000 new horseshoes.[195]

In Denmark, bog iron was collected and iron was extracted since before the Common Era, and the simple technique probably implies that it took place everywhere in Denmark during the Middle Ages. Iron ores were found everywhere, but North Jutland and especially Halland had large deposits of bog iron and endless forests for fuel. The Cistercians quickly discovered this. In 1197, Archbishop Absalon donated the distant village of Toager in Halland to the Cistercians in Sorø, "where they will have sufficient wood for making salt, to extract iron from the soil, and as timber for their buildings."[196] Soon a mill was erected on the property to process the iron ore, presumably a large central smithy with mill power. It is often described as the earliest known iron mill in Europe,[197] which it obviously cannot be, as we have sources for one in Portugal almost two centuries earlier. Søndre Jernvirke (Southern Ironworks) in Halland is known from written sources,[198] and the name only makes sense if there was a Nørre Jernvirke (Northern Ironworks) too. Søndre Jernvirke was examined by archaeologists during the first half of the 1990s. They excavated a nine-by-six-metre large hillock, which turned out to consist of slag from the iron extraction process. Also found were

Afonso and Valdemar 171

two small circular forges made from clay and stone, only twenty centimetres in diameter on the inside.[199] This was all, but evidently enough to ensure the largest or second largest monastery in Denmark had iron for its own use and for export.

The Cistercians in Esrom also had large holdings in Halland, the first of which they received in 1176 from Valdemar I, who had put emphasis on the right to felling within these areas.[200] This was disputed by the locals, but the King and the Archbishop intervened and secured Esrom's access to the wood.[201] Later, Valdemar II re-confirmed the Cistercians' full and unlimited rights over the land in Halland where they were able to freely utilize the rich iron ore deposits.[202] Finally, also the Order of St. John had holdings in Halland, and the people living on the order's land were exempted from royal taxes in 1216.[203] At that time, Halland was in no way a missionary field, and the Hospitallers' interest in the area is probably best explained by their desire to get iron ore for the production of weaponry in order to continue the crusades. Through the 13th century, the region continued its iron production, which was paid as tax to the Archbishop in Lund – this must be the explanation for the King's official being able to steal 300 pieces of iron from the Bishop's stock in 1257.[204]

Extraction and manufacture of iron were important elements in the economy and in production in the widest sense of medieval societies, and technological development is demonstrated in all European countries in the period from 1000 onwards, and with a new, qualitative leap in around 1200. By comparing Denmark and Portugal it is easier to perceive how ramified iron production really was, how it was of great royal interest to control it, how the Cistercians developed it in different ways, and it all suggests how iron production was closely connected to warfare and crusades.

1168: Badajoz, Jerusalem and Rügen

Twenty years after the conquest of Lisbon, the second attempt to coordinate large, simultaneous Western European crusades in several places along the religious frontier took place. In 1168, Valdemar of Denmark and the somewhat older Afonso Henriques decided to perform a large attack directly against the strongest heathen fortress in their regions, against Badajoz in the disputed area between Castile and the Almohads, and against Arkona on Rügen, respectively.

Afonso's expedition in 1168 against Badajoz had been well prepared. Initial raids had been conducted by the loyal Geraldo the Fearless, the Portuguese el Cid. Afonso Henriques arrived next year, leading the main force. He succeeded in conquering the city, but the Muslims were relieved by none other than Afonso's son-in-law, Fernando II of León. Now the Portuguese themselves were besieged.

During one of the Portuguese sorties, Afonso fell to the ground and was taken prisoner by Fernando. As mentioned before, Afonso never fully regained his mobility, and one consequence was the crowning of Sancho in 1170. Another was an eight-year-long truce with the Muslims. When war was resumed in 1178, the recognition from Pope Alexander III arrived immediately; the bull *Manifestis probatum*[205] with papal recognition of Afonso as King of the Portuguese. If Afonso

172   Afonso and Valdemar

had not been injured, this recognition would have presumably arrived in as early as 1170 – at the same time that Valdemar of Denmark received great privileges from the Pope, also as a crusader.

Geraldo, who had prepared the conquest of Badajoz, had been taken prisoner together with Afonso. After they were both set free, Geraldo quarrelled with Afonso, apparently because he was not allowed to plunder a newly conquered city. He went to Morocco therefore, where he entered into the service of the Caliph and became governor of Sus. He was executed a few years later when it was revealed that he had negotiated in secret with Afonso about surrendering Morocco to him in preparation for a large crusade in North Africa.[206]

In 1169, the threat from the growing power of Saladin was felt so impending by the people in the Kingdom of Jerusalem that a high-ranking delegation was sent from the Holy Land to Western Europe. Amongst its members was the Archbishop Frederic of Tyre. The aim was to convince Alexander III to organize a new, large and universal crusade. The envoys arrived in Italy in July and received full papal backing, and they began a preaching and recruiting tour to the Western European rulers. By September, they were in Paris, where they offered the keys of Jerusalem to King Louis VII.[207]

Earlier that year, an understanding had been reached between Louis of France and Henry II of England after several years of conflict and strife. A peace agreement was conditional upon the rulers participating in a crusade to the Holy Land together. Another element of the agreement was that Henry was to reconcile himself with Archbishop Thomas of Canterbury and let him return to England after several years of exile. Everything fell in place and it was decided that the crusade would begin at Easter in 1171. Among the preparations was the crowning of Henry II's son, the fifteen-year-old Henry the Young during a solemn ceremony in Canterbury Cathedral by Archbishop Frederic of Tyre and other high-ranking ecclesiastics on June 14, 1170. The crowning and the present noblemen's swearing of allegiance to Henry the Young were obviously aimed at securing succession of the son if the father was to die during the crusade.[208]

While the delegation from the Holy Land slowly made its way northwards, another delegation travelled south to meet the Pope in Benevento, which it did during the autumn of 1169. There is no proof that the two delegations met, but they may have done so, for example in Paris or in Northern Italy. At least they were envoys at such a high ecclesiastic and diplomatic level, and with such important business that they must surely have known of each other's existence. The delegation from the North consisted of bishops and high-ranking ecclesiastics and other envoys from the Danish King Valdemar I the Great. They were to relay the good news of Valdemar's victory over the heathens, of his conquest of Rügen, to the Pope.

In the early summer of 1168, the Danish crusader fleet once again set sail towards Rügen, a land rich in crops, fish and game.[209] The goal was Arkona on the northernmost point of the island, the greatest heathen place of worship in Northern Europe. Arkona was a strong fortress, protected on three sides by steep cliffs that were higher than a crossbow arrow could shoot, and on the fourth side

Afonso and Valdemar 173

was a high earthen rampart with palisades.[210] Inside the town was the temple of Svantevit, a magnificently carved wooden building with an inner sanctum, into which only a high priest was allowed to enter. The idol of Svantevit had four heads, cleanly shaven and with short hair, a drinking horn and a sword inlaid with silver. He was worshiped with offerings of cattle, wine and honey cakes the size of a man. In an adjacent stable stood the god's sacred, white horse, which, some mornings, was steaming white with sweat as if the god had been riding in a battle all night. Before they went to war, the high priest led the horse forwards and took auguries from its gait to see whether they were to win or whether they ought to postpone the war to another day. All the heathens paid a tax to the temple and handed over one third of all their war booty to the god.

The Danish crusaders placed a contingent of soldiers to cut off any assistance to Arkona from the outside and then the trebuchets were set to bombard the palisades. The wooden gates had been strengthened with earth and turf at the front to prevent them from catching fire. It became apparent that the turf had subsided a little at one of the gates, and one of the young crusaders could crawl up and enter the cavity between turf and gate. Sheltered by the tower above the gate, he was able to ignite a fire, which spread fast and began to consume the tower. Simultaneously, the Danish crusaders and their reinforcements from the Pomeranian vassals Kazimir and Bugislav attacked, and it was soon clear for the Wends that the battle was lost.

The Wends surrendered, accepted handing over their idol and the temple treasure, and becoming Christians "in the same way as in Denmark." All the temple's belongings were to fall to the Church, and in the future the Wends themselves were to supply troops for the King's continued crusade. In return, their lives would be spared. This almost led to a mutiny in the Christian army, which lost out on the plunder as well as "the wonderful revenge" they could have taken on the heathens.[211] Bishop Absalon and Archbishop Eskil argued that if all the inhabitants were slaughtered, the other Wendish towns would fight back to the last man, whereas if the inhabitants of Arkona were spared, it would become much easier to conquer the rest of Rügen. The objections of the army were ignored because "the people shall obey their masters, not the master the people," as Archbishop Eskil remarked.[212]

The conquest happened on July 15, the day of St. Vitus; it was explained by Saxo that the saint was no longer prepared to tolerate the heathens' misuse of his name. The idol in the heathen temple was turned over, pulled out of the temple and chopped into kindling that was used for the cooking of the soup for the army. The humiliation of the god was complete and the people of Arkona were baptized. When the rest of Rügen had surrendered, the island was divided into twelve parishes, churches were erected and the whole area was put under the authority of the see of Roskilde. Then a delegation was dispatched to Pope Alexander III with the news of the fall of Arkona, which reached Italy during the autumn of 1169.[213]

The Pope's response came in November. A bull praised Valdemar as the shield of faith and commended him for having created peace and extended Christendom. The formulation is different but the thinking quite the same as in the papal

174   *Afonso and Valdemar*

bull *Manifestis probatum* to Afonso of Portugal. Pope Alexander acknowledged Valdemar's conquest and placed Rügen under the see of Roskilde, even though the island had belonged to the missionary field of the archdiocese in Lund since the beginning of the century. Another bull gave permission to the canonization of Valdemar's father, Canute Lavard,[214] because he too had been a shield of the faith and created peace with his crusades.[215] This took place the year after, when Valdemar's son, the seven-year-old Canute the Young, was also crowned.[216] The direct succession was secured and members of the collateral branches of the royal family had been pushed aside. It is obvious from the preserved liturgy from the canonization that Valdemar perceived a direct correlation between his own luck as a crusader and his father's help as a saint.

Alexander apparently decided to initiate yet another large, unified crusade on several fronts, at least both against the Middle East and in the Baltic region, and he wished to coordinate them closely. The preparations began in the summer of 1170 with the Danish and the English coronation ceremonies, and it was agreed that Henry of England and Louis VII of France were to begin their crusades at Easter, in 1171.[217] However, five days after Christmas, in 1170, Henry was so unfortunate as to have had Archbishop Thomas Becket killed in front of an altar in Canterbury Cathedral. The great Middle Eastern crusade came to nothing. Henry was immediately excommunicated and England was laid under interdict; thus he was unable to participate in the crusade.[218] As Henry was unable to go, Louis ventured not to go alone. Some of the others who had taken the cross did actually participate, for example the Saxon Duke Henry the Lion went to the Holy Land via Byzantium in 1171, but the crusaders were too few to make a difference militarily.[219]

The Danish conquest of Rügen took place without any direct assistance from Duke Henry the Lion, who nevertheless invoked an agreement about the two rulers dividing the lands which they conquered during crusades. He gained nothing from that, however, and furiously he commanded the Wends in his lands to attack Denmark from the West. "They obeyed happily, opened the gates that earlier had closed off the ocean, and poured over the Danish islands as a wave, and conquered several of them and held them. After a long fast, they satiated themselves on the Danish riches and became stout, fat and strong. On market day, there were 700 Danish slaves in the market place in Mecklenburg, who were for sale, if only there had been enough buyers."[220] This happened in 1171 but was met with Danish counterattacks east of Mecklenburg. Valdemar and Henry met and made peace on June 24, 1171. Then, the Duke went on a crusade to the Holy Land, and when he returned home, he fell into disfavour with Emperor Fredric Barbarossa; on January 1, 1180, he was dispossessed of all his fiefs and had to go in exile to his English father-in-law, Henry II. He was no longer a realistic competitor to the Danish expansion in the Baltic.

The Danish crusades received new strength from the conquest of Rügen. As early as the spring of 1170, some Danish ships undertook a raid further to the east, against a grouping of Curonians and Estonians, apparently as a kind of a festive prelude to the canonization of that summer. It almost went wrong. Several fell, but

Afonso and Valdemar 175

Esbern Snare fought single-handedly against an untold number of heathens and succeeded in warding off a great disaster.[221] In the spring of 1171, King Valdemar continued with a crusade further eastwards, against Pomerania, and pillaged the region around Wolin. The town itself was conquered and burned down two years later.[222]

New Cistercian missionary monasteries were established in the frontier lands between Rügen and Pomerania and were consecrated on Canute Lavard's saint's day, June 25.[223] From September 1171, a whole new missionary field was opened up, as Alexander III issued several bulls, calling in the Danes and the other Scandinavians to continue the crusades all the way to Estonia and to support the Bishop Fulko, who earlier had been consecrated as missionary bishop. The participants were promised one year's indulgence, just like those who went to Jerusalem to fight for the Holy Sepulchre, and those who fell in the fight against the Estonians would receive full indulgence for their sins and thus go straight to heaven.[224] However, it does not seem like many heeded the call; the crusades to Estonia and Finland only began in earnest ten to twenty years later.

There was continued religious warfare against the Pomeranian lands during the 1170s, and the Danish force now included the new Christians from Rügen. Plunder was often taken in kind, but sometimes the Pomeranians had to pay for peace, e.g. in 1178 against the sum of 2000 marks.[225] A proper mission followed in the area with the establishment of churches,[226] albeit slowly to begin with.

There is a lack of written evidence but there is a striking conjunction of coincidence between Henry and Louis's crusades to the Middle East – which came to nothing – and Valdemar's crusade to Pomerania and further eastwards in 1171 and the following years. Alexander's letters show that the Pope followed the crusades in the Baltic region closely. The papal crusade plans in 1171 seem to have been an attempt to repeat the pincer movement from 1147 and to attack the Devil both in the North and in the Middle East.

When Valdemar died in 1182, his body was sewn into a leather cover, and by his head a lead plate was placed which proudly summarized his long career as a crusader and mentioned the acts that he should be remembered for: "Here lies the King of the Danes, Valdemar the First, the fighter and master of the Slavs, the liberator of the fatherland, the preserver of peace, who as son of St. Canute fought the inhabitants of Rügen and, as the first, converted them to the Christian faith. He died in the year 1182 after the incarnation of the Lord, in the 26th year of his rule, on the 12th of May."[227]

Valdemar was only fifty-one years old, but despite his background as exiled and fatherless, he became one of the powerful and recognized kings of his time, precisely because he had engaged himself successfully in the crusades in the Baltic region, just as Afonso Henriques had engaged himself in the crusades on the Iberian Peninsula. The crusades were of great importance for the personal lives and destinies of the two kings, but they also signified a decisive restructuring of the lands that they governed: old as well as newly conquered lands. During the rule of Valdemar and Afonso, Denmark and Portugal were increasingly organized for war and the art of killing; technologically and organizationally,

176   *Afonso and Valdemar*

they became more refined as the decades went by. At the same time, theology and historical writing were developed, which glorified and furthered the crusades. The wars were given an ideological expression, or the ideology was put into practice, depending on which angle one chooses, but the two phenomena were closely connected.

Notes

1 Duarte Galvão, *Crónica de el-rei D. Afonso Henriques* (Lisbon, 1995), cap. XV–XVI. The birth of Afonso is dated to 1094 in this source, whereas everything suggests that it more probably took place in 1109, fifteen years after the marriage of Henrique and Teresa; A.H. de Oliveira Marques, 'O poder e o espaço', in: Maria Helena da Cruz Coelho e Armando Luís de Carvalho Homem (eds.), *Nova História de Portugal*, vol. 3 (Lisbon, 1996), p. 20. Afonso's life and destiny is the basic narrative in all modern depictions of how Portugal came to be as an independent kingdom, and his effort is described and analysed in all these works. An excellent synthesis is given in José Mattoso, *D. Afonso Henriques* (Lisbon, 2006).

2 J. Campbell's Jungian-inspired work (*The Hero with a Thousand Faces* [Princeton, NJ, 1949]) has the peculiar birth as an important criterion of an archetypical hero. See also Isabel de Barros Dias, 'Ares, Marte, Odin. . . .', in: A. Ward (ed.), *Teoria y practica de la historiografía medieval* (Birmingham, 2000), pp. 80–93, for the legendary traits of the Afonso figure.

3 José Mattoso and Armindo de Sousa, *A Monarquia Feudal (1096–1480)* (Lisbon, 1993), p. 37. Others place Henrique's death in 1112–1114, for example A.H. de Oliveira Marques, *História de Portugal: Das Origens ao Renascimento* (Lisbon, 1997), vol. 1, p. 77.

4 Chronica Gothorum, short version, era 1149; Pierre David, *Études historiques sur la Galice et le Portugal du VIe au XIIe siècle* (Lisbon, 1947), p. 302.

5 Mário Jorge Barroca, 'Da reconquista a D. Dinis', in: Manuel Themudo Barata and Nuno Severiano Teixeira (eds.), *Nova História militar de Portugal* (Lisbon, 2003), vol. 1, pp. 35–56; Marques, 'O poder e o espaço', p. 21.

6 Magnussona saga, chapters 4–5. Sigurd took revenge on the earl who ruled the country because he had broken an agreement about providing provisions. The earl must have referred to Raimundo and, after his death in 1107, presumably Urraca.

7 On Sigurd's expedition, Doxey, 'Norwegian Crusaders and the Balearic Islands'.

8 Mattoso and de Sousa, *A Monarquia*, pp. 18–35.

9 Anónimo de Sahagún, 29.

10 Chronicon ex historiæ compostellanæ 1109, p. 328.

11 The Trava family were eager crusaders, see Margarita C. Torres Sevilla-Quiñones, 'Cruzados y peregrinos leoneses y castellanos en Tierra Santa ss. XI–XII', *Medievalismo* 9 (1999), pp. 73–74 and passim.

12 Simon Barton, *The Aristocracy in Twelfth-Century Leon and Castile* (Cambridge, 1997), p. 241.

13 As suggested by Mattoso and de Sousa, *A Monarquia*, p. 48.

14 Family relations – *affinitas* – between two persons were prohibited in canon law from the middle of the 12th century in up to the seventh degree. See Jean Gaudemet, *Le mariage en occident: les moeurs et le droit* (Paris, 1987).1987.

15 Vita sancti Theotonii, 5–6.

16 Mattoso and de Sousa, *A Monarquia*, p. 48.

17 Diego Freitas do Amaral, *D. Afonso Henriques. Biografia* (Lisboa, 2000).

18 Annales D. Alfonsi, Era 1163.

19 *Exordium magnum cisterciense* III, XXVII; also in SM II 437–442.

Afonso and Valdemar 177

20 Chronica Adofonsi Imperatoris i, 74.
21 Jose Antunes, 'A versão portuguesa do "Tratado" de Tui (1137). Uma interpretação diferente da de Paoulo Merêa e de outros historiadores', *Actas do 2º Congresso Histórico de Guimarães* 4 (Guimarães, 1996), pp. 33–43.
22 Barroca, 'Da reconquista a D. Dinis', p. 41. Not in Chronica Adefonsi Imperatoris.
23 Chronica Adefonsi Imperatoris i, 84.
24 LS 12, p. 128.
25 Saul António Gomes, *Introdução á história do castelo de Leiria* (Leiria, 1995).
26 Chronica Adefonsi Imperatoris i, 84.
27 Gomes, *Introdução á história do castelo de Leiria*, p. 29.
28 LP 576.
29 Luíz Gonzaga de Azevedo, *História de Portugal*, vols. 1–6 (Lisboa, 1935–1944), vol. 4, pp. 211–218.
30 Annales D. Afonsi, Era 1177.
31 Galvão, *Crónica*, XIV.
32 Ibid., XV.
33 Ibid., XVI. "Verily, verily, Afonso Henriques shall be King of Portugal." In this context, the meaning of *Reall* is closer to "verily" than "royal."
34 Ibid., XVIII. Em aspa – in the shape of a saltire.
35 The development of the tradition of Afonso's five wounds is examined in Maria de Lurdes Rosa, 'O corpo do chefe guerreiro, as chagas de Cristo e a quebra dos escudos: caminhos da mitificação de Afonso Henriques na Baixa Idade Média', in: Camara municipal de Guimaraes (ed.), *Actas do 2º Congresso Histórico de Guimarães* (Guimarães, 1996), vol. 3, pp. 85–91. The cardinal does not seem to have been named in the sources and might well have been a pious invention.
36 José Mattoso, 'A realeza de Afonso Henriques', *Histórica & Crítica* 13 (1986), 5–14. in José Mattoso, *Fragmentos de uma Composição Medieval* (Lisbon, 1993), pp. 213–232.
37 Mattoso and de Sousa, *A Monarquia*, pp. 62–64.
38 Mattoso, 'A realeza de Afonso Henriques', p. 219.
39 António Brandão, *Terceira parte da Monarchia lusitana* (Lisboa, 1632), p. 136. Brandão also reproduces a reply letter from Pope Innocent II that supposedly recognized Afonso as a king but that is a later forgery; Papsturkunden, no. 32.
40 LS 1,XII; 1,XIV, p. 94 and 98.
41 DMP I, various.
42 Peter Linehan, 'Utrum reges Portugalie coronabantur annon', *Actas do 2º Congresso Histórico de Guimarães* 2 (1996), pp. 387–401.1996 is an updated treatment of the question of whether Afonso was anointed and crowned or not, and concludes he was not. Linehan mentions as an "ancient practice" (in France, amongst other places), that the noblemen raised the King on a shield; 1996, 400–401.
43 Carl Erdmann, *Das Papsttum und Portugal im ersten Jahrhundert der portugiesischen Geschichte* (Berlin, 1928), which was translated into Portuguese in 1935. Cf. Marcelle Caetano, *História do direito portugues: Fontes – direito publico (1140–1495)* (Lisbon, 1992), p. 205; Marques, 'O poder e o espaço'; Jose Maria Soto Rabános, '¿Se puede hablar de un entramado político religiose en el proceso de independencia de Portugal?', *Hispania* 67 (2007), pp. 795–826.
44 Giles Constable, 'The Second Crusade as seen by Contemporaries', *Traditio* 9 (1953), pp. 215–279, is still one of the most important analyses of the medieval perception of the many crusades as one, joint expedition. A.J. Forey, 'The Second Crusade: Scope and Objectives', *Durham University Journal* 86 (1994), pp. 165–175, argues against and emphasizes the local outlook of most contemporary historians and crusaders, not the joint European or Christian. Jonathan Phillips, *The Second Crusade: Extending the Frontiers of Christendom* (New Haven, 2007), p. xxiv and passim takes more or less a centre position; he rejects talk of an overall plan behind the second crusade and

178　*Afonso and Valdemar*

considers Bernard of Clairvaux and Eugene III more reactive than proactive (p. xxvii). In my context, the most important feature is that there was close contact between various crusade areas rather than whether there was an overall plan behind the simultaneous crusades. My opinion, however, is that the close contact must reflect some developed form of coordination and thus a plan, which of course might have been flexible and could have been changed on the way.

45　Helmold of Bosau, *Helmoldi presbyteri Chronica Slavorum*, ed. G.H. Pertz (Hannover, 1868), cap. 59.

46　Jonathan Phillips, *Defenders of the Holy Land. Relations Between the Latin East and the West, 1119–1187* (Oxford, 1996), pp. 73–99; Jonathan Phillips, 'Papacy, Empire and the Second Crusade', in: Jonathan Phillips and Martin Hoch (eds.), *The Second Crusade. Scope and Consequences* (Manchester, 2001), pp. 15–31; Virginia G. Berry, 'The Second Crusade', *A History of the Crusades* 1 (1958), pp. 463–512; Rudolf Hiestand, 'The Papacy and the Second Crusade', in: Jonathan Phillips and Martin Hoch (eds.), *The Second Crusade. Scope and Consequences* (Manchester, 2001), pp. 32–53; Phillips, *The Second Crusade*.

47　Helmold, 60.

48　Kelly DeVries, 'God and Defeat in Medieval Warfare: Some Preliminary Thoughts', in: Donald J. Kagay and L.J. Andrew Villalon (eds.), *The Circle of War in the Middle Ages. Essays on Medieval Military and Naval History* (Woodbridge, 1999), pp. 87–97.

49　Peter Dinzelbacher, *Bernhard von Clairvaux: Leben und Werk des berühmten Zisterziensers* (Darmstadt, 1998), pp. 284–307. Bernard, *De Consideratione Libri Quinque*, II, 1, PL 182, esp. cols. 741–745. The reasons for the failure of the crusade are discussed in Graham A. Loud, 'Some Reflections on the Failure of the Second Crusade', *Crusades* 4 (2005), pp. 1–14.

50　Erdmann, *Das Papsttum und Portugal*, p. 34.

51　J.F. O'Callaghan, *Reconquest and Crusade in Medieval Spain* (Philadelphia, 2003), p. 42.

52　Charles Julian Bishko, 'The Spanish and Portuguese Reconquest, 1095–1492', *A History of the Crusades* 3 (1975), pp. 396–456; Bernard F. Reilly, *The Kingdom of Leon-Castille Under King Alfonso VI, 1065–1109* (Princeton, NJ, 1988), pp. 88–103; John Williams, 'The Making of a Crusade: The Genoese Anti-Muslim Attacks in Spain, 1146–48', *Journal of Medieval History* 23 (1997), pp. 29–53.

53　PL 180, cols. 1203–1204.

54　Annales Toledanos, p. 386.

55　Simon Barton, 'A Forgotten Crusade: Alfonso VII of Leon-Castile and the Campaign of Jaen (1148)', *Historical Research* 73 (2000), pp. 312–320.

56　Urkunden Kaiser Alfons VII; 11th of January 1050, and others.

57　Nikolas Jaspert, 'Capta est Dertosa, clavis Christianorum: Tortosa and the crusades', in: Jonathan Phillips and Martin Hoch (eds.), *The Second Crusade. Scope and Consequences* (Manchester, 2001), pp. 90–110.

58　Rudolf Hiestand, 'Reconquista, Kreuzzug und heiliges Grab. Die Eroberung von Tortosa 1148 im Lichte eines neuen Zeugnisses', *Gesammelte Aufsätze zur Kulturgeschichte Spaniens* 31 (1984), pp. 136–157, goes through the existing sources in detail regarding who participated in the conquest of Tortosa. Some of his identifications have been criticized by Antonio Virgili, '*Angli cum multis aliis alienigenis*: Crusade Settlers in Tortosa (second half of the twelfth century)', *Journal of Medieval History* 35 (2009), pp. 297–312; but this does not significantly change the main impression of the conquest of Tortosa as a joint crusade with participants from many places. Cardinal Nicholas Breakspear, later legate to the Nordic countries and still later Pope Hadrian IV, also participated and continued the tradition of his monastery to support the crusade movement; Damian J. Smith, 'The Abbot-Crusader: Nicholas Breakspear in Catalonia', in: Brenda Bolton and Anne J. Duggan (eds.), *Adrian IV The English Pope (1154–1159)* (Aldershot, 2003), pp. 29–40, here pp. 32–33.

Afonso and Valdemar 179

59 Reilly, *The Kingdom of Leon-Castille Under King Alfonso VII*, pp. 112–113; Barton, *The Aristocracy*, pp. 17–18.
60 Bernard, Opera, vol. 8, no. 457.
61 Vincent of Prague, year 1147.
62 DD 1:2, no. 86.
63 VSD, 268–269.
64 Saxo 14.3.6–14.3.9.
65 Helmold, 65.
66 Saxo, 14.3.5.
67 Knytlinga saga, chapter 108.
68 According to the Annals of Ryd; AD, p. 79.
69 Bernard, Epistolae, in Opera, vol. 8, no. 228; Harold V. Livermore, 'The "Conquest of Lisbon" and Its Author', *Portuguese Studies* 6 (1990), pp. 1–16; Jonathan Phillips, 'St Bernard of Clairvaux, the Low Countries and the Lisbon Letter of the Second Crusade', *The Journal of Ecclesiastical History* 48 (1997), pp. 485–497; Susan B. Edginton, 'Albert of Aachen, St Bernard and the Second Crusade', in: Jonathan Phillips and Martin Hoch (eds.), *The Second Crusade. Scope and Consequences* (Manchester, 2001), pp. 54–70. A. J. Forey, 'The Siege of Lisbon and the Second Crusade', *Portuguese Studies* 20 (2004), pp. 1–13, on the other hand, argues for the traditional view, that the presence of the Nordic crusaders at Lisbon was a coincidence and not discussed or planned beforehand; see also Forey, 'The Second Crusade'. Sources from the German area in Bruno Meyer, 'El papel de los cruzados alemanes en la reconquista de la Península Ibérica en los siglos XII y XIII', *En la España Medieval* 23 (2000), pp. 41–66; F. Kurth, 'Der Anteil Niederdeutscher Kreuzfahrer an den Kämpfen der Portugiesen gegen die Mauren', *Mitteilungen des Institutes für Österreichische Geschichtsforschung* Appendix 8 (1909), pp. 131–252. Stephen Lay, 'The Reconquest as Crusade in the Anonymous *De expugnatione Lyxbonensi*', *Al-Masāq* 14 (2002), pp. 123–130, is short and general.
70 Chronica Gothorum; Harold V. Livermore, *A History of Portugal* (Cambridge, 1947), p. 71, n. 2. Chronica Gothorum mentions the attack under 1140; according to De expugnatione Lyxbonensi, it happened five years before 1147, that is, in 1142. Perhaps they were two different expeditions.
71 Phillips, 'St Bernard of Clairvaux'; cf. De expugnatione Lyxbonensi, introduction by Jonathan Phillips.
72 Such calculations are extremely uncertain and only make sense if we knew the size of the ships in the fleet. That probably varied significantly.
73 De expugnatione Lyxbonensi, introduction.
74 The date according to the letter from Vinand the priest, cf. Susan B. Edginton, 'The Lisbon Letter of the Second Crusade', *Historical Research* 69 (1996), pp. 336–339.; Edginton, 'Albert of Aachen'.
75 De expugnatione Lyxbonensi, 78. The idea of revenge was part of the crusades from the beginning but only became more widespread in crusader narratives from the 1170s; Susanna Throop, 'Vengeance and the Crusades', *Crusades* 5 (2006), pp. 21–38; Philippe Buc, 'La vengeance de Dieu. De l'exégèse patristique à la réforme écclésiastique et à la première croisade', in: D. Barthélemy, Francois Bougard and Regine Le Jan (eds.), *La vengeance 400–1200* (Rome, 2006), pp. 451–486.
76 This was the opinion of Alexandre Herculano, *História de Portugal desde o começo da monarquia até o fim do reinado de Afonso III* (Lisbon, 1846–53), vol. 1, p.496.
77 James Muldoon, *Popes, Lawyers, and Infidels. The Church and the Non-Christian World 1250–1550* (Philadelphia, 1979), pp. 3–28.
78 De expugnatione Lyxbonensi, 120.
79 The Bishop and not the Muslim cadi, see José Mattoso, *Identificação de um país: ensaio sobre as origens de Portugal, 1096–1325*, vols. 1–2 (Lisbon, 1995), vol. 1, p. 322.

180 *Afonso and Valdemar*

80 Annales Toledanos 1148, p. 388.
81 Charles Wendell David, 'Narratio de itinere navali peregrinorum Hierosolymam tendentium et Silviam capientium A.D. 1189', *Proceedings of the American Philosophical Society* 81, 5 (1939), pp. 592–675, here p. 594.
82 Helmold, 61.
83 Azevedo, *História de Portugal*, vol. 4, p. 94.
84 Annales D. Alfonsi, Era 1185.
85 Marques, 'O poder e o espaço', pp. 66–68.
86 Azevedo, *História de Portugal*, vol. 4, pp. 93–95.
87 Marques, 'O poder e o espaço', p. 31.
88 Mattoso and de Sousa, *A Monarquia*, p. 94.
89 O'Callaghan, *Reconquest and Crusade*, p.50.
90 Annales D. Alfonsi, Era 1196.
91 Ibid.
92 Ibid., Era 1200; Barroca, 'Da reconquista a D. Dinis', p. 46.
93 Annales D. Alfonsi, Era 1204; Barroca, 'Da reconquista a D. Dinis', p. 46.
94 Azevedo, *História de Portugal*, vol. 4, p. 125; Barroca, 'Da reconquista a D. Dinis', p. 46.
95 The year was 1175 according to Barroca, 'Da reconquista a D. Dinis', p. 47; but according to others, it was in the late 1160s.
96 *Manifestis probatum:* published in PL 200, cols. 1237–1238.
97 BP 176.
98 http://www.vatican.va/holy_father/john_paul_ii/homilies/1979/documents/hf_jp-ii_hom_19790522_santonio-portoghesi_it.html#top.
99 Brandão, *Terceira parte*, p. 267.
100 The text is transmitted late and the date of it must therefore be assessed using internal criteria. Verses 5–8 have a tone that fits well with the poetic arts of the late 12th century, whereas the rest, to a greater or lesser degree, seem later and might have been written in the 16th century. Thanks to Fritz Saabye Pedersen, University of Southern Denmark, for his assistance in assessing and understanding the poem.
101 DD 1:3, no. 103, 1182–1185, issued by Absalon. Incidentally almost the same designation that Alfonso VII used of himself in 1156, *invictus*; see Fletcher, *Saint James' Catapult*, pp. 253.
102 Knytlinga saga, chapter 93; Lind 'De russiske ægteskaber'.
103 Annales Magdeburgenses, 1134, mentions 60 clerics.
104 This is debated, cf. Christian Radtke, 'Kommune og gilde i Slesvig i højmiddelalderen', in: Lars Bisgaard and Leif Søndergaard (eds.), *Gilder, lav og broderskaber i middelalderens Danmark* (Odense, 2002), pp. 41–62.
105 Albert of Trois-Fontaines to 1131 (p. 829).
106 Helmold, 54.
107 Ibid., 55.
108 DD 1:2, no. 65.
109 VSD, pp. 216–217.
110 Saxo, 14.5.8. The battle of Viborg took place in 1151; AD, pp. 78–79.
111 DD 1:2, no. 103 and no. 104.
112 DD 1:2, no. 110 and no. 117; Niels Skyum-Nielsen, *Kvinde og Slave* (Copenhagen, 1971), p. 140.
113 In 1153; AD, p. 79.
114 Saxo, 14.7.1.
115 Annals of Ryd, AD, 79: "adductis inde [sc. Sleswic] nauibus per terras usque Huchlstiæth," which makes sense if the idea was to attack Northern Friesland. Saxo claims that Svend took the ships overland from Schleswig to the Eider, which would have been far and monstrously difficult and strangely pointless too: "nonnullas naves Sleswici subductas ad Eidoram usque solo tenus pertrahendas curavit," Saxo 14.7.3.

Afonso and Valdemar   181

Long-distance transport of ships overland was not a solely Nordic phenomenon. During the first crusade, ships for 50–100 men were tied to three, four or more wagons and pulled by animals and men seven miles up to the lake by Nicea, William of Tyre reports. Ronnie Ellenblum, 'Frankish and Muslim Siege Warfare and the Construction of Frankish Concentric Castles', in: Michel Balard, Benjamin Z. Kedar and Jonathan Riley-Smith (eds.), *Dei gesta per francos. Etudes sur les croisades dédiées à Jean Richard* (Aldershot, 2001), pp. 187–198.

116 Annals of Ryd; AD, pp. 79, 81.
117 Ibid., p. 81.
118 Sven Aggesen, Brevis historia, cap. XIX.
119 Saxo, 14.14.2.
120 Annals of Lund, AD, p. 81.
121 Saxo, 14.18.1–7.
122 Nanna Damsholt, *Kvindebilledet i dansk højmiddelalder* (Copenhagen, 1985).
123 Interestingly discussed in Michael Kræmmer, *Den hvide klan. Absalon, hans slægt og hans tid* (Copenhagen, 1999).
124 Saxo, 14.19.16, convent is a loose translation of muliebrem animum virili corpore clausum confiteretur.
125 Saxo, 14.19.15.
126 Skyum-Nielsen, *Kvinde og Slave*, p. 143.
127 Annals of Lund, AD, p. 83.
128 Helmold, 85. Son of peace is from Luke 10, 6.
129 DD 1:2, no. 120.
130 Saxo, 14.5.1.
131 Saxo, 14.6.1.
132 Vilhelm la Cour, *Danske borganlæg til midten af det trettende århundrede*, 1–2 (Copenhagen, 1972), p. 154.
133 Saxo, 14.17.7. "cultu vacua mansisset resque eius non afflictae modo, verum etiam perditae fuissent." *Cultu vacua* can be translated to *uncultivable, waste*, such as the translator Peter Zeeberg has done. However, it might also refer to *worship*, and Saxo may have been referring to both phenomena at the same time.
134 Karl-Erik Frandsen, *Vang og tagt. Studier over dyrkningssystemer og agrarstrukturer i Danmarks landsbyer 1682–83* (Esbjerg, 1983), pp. 209, 259.
135 Helmold, 84.
136 Saxo, 14.25.8–9. Helmold, 88 tells a different story about Niklot's death.
137 Saxo, 14.39.8.
138 Helmold, 102, 109.
139 Saxo, 14.15.6.
140 Helmold, 87.
141 Curt Weibull, 'Saxos berättelser om de danska vendertågen 1158–1185', *Historisk Tidsskrift* 83 (1983), pp. 35–70.
142 Radulphus Niger, 89.
143 Saxo, 14.21.3. Admiral is a translation of *pirate* in Saxo, which has caused problems for translators and historians alike. "Pirate" and "Viking" are the most common suggestions, but both bear derogatory connotations today, which is not the case in Saxo's text. "Admiral" is chosen to convey the meaning of a powerful leader of a fleet.
144 Exordium monasterii Caræ insulæ, cap. 1; cap. 12.
145 Saxo, 14.39.44.
146 Saxo, 15.1.1. Saxo does not mention directly whether the participants had been promised indulgence and martyrdom.
147 Saxo, 14.23.2. "non solum consilium probavit, sed etiam, qui regi comites deessent, admodum exsecratus" In Saxo's archaizing language and in this context, excratus presumably means "excommunicate" rather than just "condemn" or similar. Against this interpretation, see Niels Lund, 'Leding and Crusading', in: Birgitte Fløe-Jensen

182   Afonso and Valdemar

and Dorthe Wille-Jørgensen (eds.), *Expansion – Integration? Danish-Baltic Contacts 1147–1410 AD* (Vordingborg, 2009), pp. 39–43, here pp. 42–43. For excommunication to force crusaders actually to go on a crusade; see James A. Brundage, *Medieval Canon Law and the Crusader* (Madison, 1969), pp. 128–131.

148   DD 1:2, no. 119.

149   AD, p. 85.

150   Saxo, 14.30.7.

151   Helmold, 100.

152   DD 1:7, no. 156.

153   Thomas Riis, *Les institutions politiques centrales du Danemark 1100–1332* (Odense, 1977), pp. 187–189.

154   DD 1:2, no. 122 mentions one mark of gold; DD 1:2, no. 126 mentions two marks of gold.

155   Michael Müller-Wille, *Mittelalterliche Grabfunde aus der Kirche des slawischen Burgwalles von Alt Lübeck: zu dynastischen Grablegen in polnischen und abodritischen Herrschaftsgebieten* (Stuttgart, 1996), p. 47.

156   Fulcher of Chartres, 1, 4: "Nam pacem renovavit, ecclesiæque jura in modos pristinos restituit, sed et paganos de terris cristianorum instinctu vivaci effugare conatus est."

157   Helmold, 85.

158   Luke 10,6.

159   Ritual de Santa Cruz, p. 39.

160   Amnon Linder, *Raising Arms. Liturgy in the Struggle to Liberate Jerusalem in the Late Middle Ages* (Turnhout, 2003).

161   Saxo, 14.22.4.

162   Saxo, 14.21.3; 14.28.23. In 13.7.6, Saxo employs this title for Archbishop Asser. Abbot Suger of Paris was addressed *pater patrie*, cf. Halvdan Koht, 'The Dawn of Nationalism in Europe', *The American Historical Review* 52 (1947), pp. 265–280.

163   Inge Skovgaard-Petersen, *Da Tidernes Herre var nær. Studier i Saxos historiesyn* (Copenhagen, 1987); Ernst Kantorowicz, 'Pro Patria Mori in Medieval Political Thought', *American Historical Review* 56 (1951), pp. 472–492.Alexander Pierre Bronisch, *Reconquista und Heiliger Krieg. Die Deutung des Krieges im christlichen Spanien von den Westgoten bis ins frühe 12. Jahrhundert* (Münster, 1998), pp. 55–56; Thomas Eichenberger, *Patria. Studien zur Bedeutung des Wortes im Mittelalter (6.-12. Jahrhundert)* (Sigmaringen, 1991); Thomas Riis, *Einführung in die Gesta Danorum des Saxo Grammaticus* (Odense, 2005), pp. 95–102; Ariel Guiance, 'To Die for Country, Land or Faith in Castilian Medieval Thought', *Journal of Medieval History* 24 (1998), pp. 313–332. "The primary sense of belonging [in the Middle Ages] was to a natio rather than to a regio, and territory only gradually replaced descent as the main principle of identity"; Giles Constable, 'Frontiers in the Middle Ages', in: O. Merisalo (ed.), *Frontiers in the Middle Ages. Proceedings of the Third European Congress of Medieval Studes, Jyväskylä, 10–14 June 2003* (Louvain-la-Neuve, 2006), p. 5.

164   Vita Martini, 11.

165   William of Malmesbury, *Gesta regum Anglorum* = The History of the English Kings, ed. R.A.B. Mynors, Rodney M. Thomson and Michael Winterbottom (Oxford, 1998), vols. 1–2, 347, 15. According to Guibert of Nogent, *Dei gesta per Francos et cinq autres textes*, ed. R.B.C. Huygens. Corpus Christianorum Continuatio Mediaevalis; 127A (Turnhout, 1996), 2, 3, Urban compared the crusaders to the Maccabees, who had fought for liturgy and temple, whereas the Christians fought to preserve the freedom of the fatherland, *libertatem patriae*. Crusaders use of the Maccabees; Mary Fischer, 'The Books of the Maccabees and the Teutonic Order', *Crusades* 4 (2005), pp. 59–71.

166   "Hic est Balduwinus alter Judas Machabaeus/ Spes patriae, decus ecclesiae, virtus utriusque", epitaph of Baldwin II of Jerusalem (d. 1131); *Itinera Hierosolymitana Crucesignatorum (saec. XII–XIII)*, ed. S. de Sandoli, vols. 1–4 (Jerusalem, 1978–1984);

Afonso and Valdemar   183

vol. 2, p. 330. In Santa Cruz, Afonso was referred to as another Macabee; Armando de Sousa Pereira, 'Motivos bíblicos na historiografia de Santa Cruz de Coimbra dos finais do século XII', *Lusitania Sacra* 2a sér 13–14 (2002), pp. 315–336, here p. 321.

167   DD 1:3, no. 50.

168   DD 1:3, no. 134.

169   1 Kings 1,13.

170   DDS, no. 48.

171   Saxo, 15.1.6.

172   Sven Aggesen, lex castrensis.

173   De expugnatione scalabis. José Mattoso, *Ricos-homens, infanções e cavaleiros: a nobreza medieval portuguesa nos séculos XI e XII* (Lisbon, 1982), pp. 188–190, employs the term *companheirismo* on Afonso's relationship with his warriors; Maria dos Anjos Brandão Maurício Guincho, 'Le premier roi de Portugal, prisonnier de ses premiers mots: essay d'analyse du recit *De expugnatione scalabris*', in: Danielle Buschinger (ed.), *La Guerre au moyen age: Réalité et fiction* (Amiens, 2000), pp. 69–81.

174   *Die Prufeninger Vita Bischof Ottos I. von Bamberg nach der Fassung des Grossen Österreichischen Legendars*, ed. Jürgen Petersohn (Hannover, 1999), II, 1, p. 82. Ernst Kantorowicz, 'The "King's Advent": And the Enigmatic Panels in the Doors of Santa Sabina', *The Art Bulletin* 26 (1944), pp. 207–231, shows how the reception of secular lords were perceived as a parallel to the reception of the soul of the deceased in heaven (p. 208), and how peace to the heathens could express the wish for concrete acts of war as well as a spiritual struggle.

175   Historia Silense, cap. 86–87.

176   Ibid., cap. 87–90.

177   According to Ibn Bassam from Santarém; R. Menédez Pidal, and E. García Gómez, 'El conde mozárabe Sisnando Davídiz y la Política de Alfonso VI con los taifas', *Al-Andalus* 12 (1947), pp. 27–41; here pp. 31–32; or al-Maqqari; Julie A. Harris, 'Mosque to Church Conversions in the Spanish Reconquest', *Medieval Encounters* 3 (1997), pp. 158–172, here p. 158. According to Rodrigo Ximénes de Rada (6, 24), it was the Queen who wished to turn the mosque into a church, whereas Alfonso VI wished to let it continue as a mosque.

178   Augustinus, Tractatus in Ioannis Evangelium 26, 2; Pl 35, col. 1607.

179   Liber Sancti Jacobi, vol. 1, pp. 303–304.

180   Helmold, 103.

181   Synagogues here mean mosques. Harris, 'Mosque to Church Conversions', pp. 159–160, emphasizes that destroying mosques was rare, as they were usually converted to Christian churches and dedicated to St. Mary.

182   Chronica Adefonsi Imperatoris ii, 36. Barton, *The Aristocracy*, p. 167.

183   Saxo, 14.57.4–5.

184   Saxo, 14.39.1.

185   Saxo, 14.6.2. Mentioned as a common practice in the narratives on the first crusade, e.g. Gesta francorum, 29.

186   David, *Études historiques*, p. 552.

187   *Missa de hostibus*; Bronisch, *Reconquista und Heiliger Krieg*.

188   Peter Carelli, *En kapitalistisk anda. Kulturella förändringar i 1100-talets Danmark* (Stockholm, 2001), pp. 80ff.; Bjørn Poulsen, 'The Widening of Import Trade and Consumption Around 1200 A.D.: A Danish Perspective', in: Lars Berggren, Nils Hybel and Anette Landen (eds.), *Cogs, Cargoes, and Commerce: Maritime Bulk Trade in Northern Europe, 1150–1400* (Toronto, 2002), pp. 31–52, here pp. 45–46; Nils Hybel and Bjørn Poulsen, *The Danish Resources ca. 1000–1550. Growth and Recession* (Leiden, 2007), p. 218.

189   Ricardo Luiz Silveira da Costa, *A guerra na Idade Média. Estudo da mentalidade de cruzada na Península Ibérica* (Rio de Janeiro, 1998), pp. 95ff.

184   *Afonso and Valdemar*

190   Mattoso, 'A realeza de Afonso Henriques', p. 379.

191   Saul António Gomes, 'A produção artesanal' and 'Grupos étnico-religiosos e estrangeiros', in: Maria Helena da Cruz Coelho and Armando Luís de Carvalho Homem (eds.), *Nova História de Portugal* (Lisbon, 1996), vol. 3, p. 337.

192   Saul António Gomes, '"A produção artesanal" and "Grupos étnico-religiosos e estrangeiros"', in: Maria Helena da Cruz Coelho and Armando Luís de Carvalho Homem (eds.), *Nova História de Portugal* (Lisbon, 1996), vol. 3, pp. 309–383, 476–486, here pp. 476–477; Henrique da Gama Barros, *História de administrão publica em Portugal nos seculos XII a XV*, vols. 1–4 (Lisbon, 1885–1922), vol. 6, pp. 121–122; also Robert Durand, *Les campagnes portugaises entre Douro et Tage aux XIIe et XIIIe siècles* (Paris, 1982), pp. 201–205.

193   Gomes, 'A produção artesanal', pp. 477–478.

194   R. Sprandel, *Das Eisengewerbe im Mittelalter* (Stuttgart, 1968); John France, *Western Warfare in the Age of the Crusades, 1000–1300* (Ithaca, 1999), pp. 30–31; Carelli, *En kapitalistisk anda*, p. 80.

195   France, *Western Warfare*, p. 31.

196   DD 1:3, no. 223; cf. Bo Fritzbøger, 'Esrum Klosters landskaber', in: Søren Frandsen, Jens Anker Jørgensen and Chr. Gorm Tortzen (eds.), *Bogen om Esrum Kloster* (Frederiksborg, 1997), pp. 79–97.

197   Medeltida danskt järn, *Framställning av och handel med järn i Skåneland och Småland Under medeltiden ed. Sven-Olof Olsson* (Halmstad, 1995).

198   DD 1:4, no. 67; DD 1:4, no. 99.

199   Jens Vellev, 'Jernfremstilling', in: Else Roesdahl (ed.), *Dagligliv i Danmarks middelalder. En arkæologisk kulturhistorie* (Copenhagen, 1999), pp. 221–226; Vagn Fabritius Buchwald, *Iron and Steel in Ancient Times* (Copenhagen, 2005); Vagn Fabritius Buchwald, *Iron, Steel and Cast Iron Before Bessemer* (Copenhagen, 2008).

200   DD 1:3, no. 55.

201   DD 1:3, no. 103.

202   DD 1:4, no. 55.

203   DD 1:5, no. 84.

204   APL, 28.

205   *Manifestis probatum.*

206   Bishko, 'The Spanish and Portuguese Reconquest', p. 415.

207   On the events in 1169, see Phillips, *Defenders of the Holy Land*.

208   Ibid., pp. 195–200; Henry the Young, see W.L. Warren, *Henry II* (London, 1973).

209   Helmold, 108, end of chapter.

210   Saxo, 14.39.1–34.

211   Throop, 'Vengeance and the Crusades', has examined the motive of revenge in crusader narratives and shows that this became much more prevalent during the 1170s than before. On the long prehistory of the motive of revenge in Christianity from Antiquity to the first crusade, see Buc, 'La vengeance de Dieu'. On use of the theme in Baltic crusades, see Kurt Villads Jensen, 'Bring dem Herrn ein blutiges Opfer. Gewalt und Mission in der dänischen Ostsee-Expansion des 12. und 13. Jarhunderts', in: H. Kamp and M. Kroker (eds.), *Schwertmission. Gewalt und Christianisierung im Mittelalter* (Paderborn, 2013), pp. 139–157.

212   Saxo, 14.39.28.

213   On the treatment of Svantevit, see Ane L. Bysted, Kurt Villads Jensen, Carsten Selch Jensen, and John Lind, *Jerusalem in the North: Denmark and the Baltic Crusades, 1100–1522* (Turnhout, 2012), pp. 36–37.

214   DD 1:2, no. 189 and 190.

215   In festis 87.

216   The same summer as Henry the Young of England and Sancho of Portugal were crowned as joint rulers.

217   Phillips, *Defenders of the Holy Land*, pp. 202–204.

218 Henry was required to go on a crusade as a penance for the murder, which in practice he commuted to a large sum of money; cf. A.J. Forey, 'Henry II's Crusading Penances for Becket's Murder', *Crusades* 7 (2008), pp. 153–164.

219 Phillips, *Defenders of the Holy Land*.

220 Helmold, 109.

221 Saxo, 14.40.3.

222 Saxo, 14.42.1–22.

223 Stella Maria Szacherska, 'The Political Role of the Danish Monasteries in Pommerania 1171–1223', *Medieval Scandinavia* 10 (1977), pp. 122–155.

224 DD 1:3, no. 27. The dating is disputed. See also Iben Fonnesberg-Schmidt, *The Popes and the Baltic Crusades 1147–1254* (Leiden, 2007), pp. 54–65.

225 Saxo, 15.1.4.

226 DD 1:3, no. 64.

227 Drawn in Worsaae, *Kongegravene*, plate XI and XII.

7 The struggle for land and history

Taking the land in possession

When the crusaders extended Christendom, they moved the frontier between Christendom and heathenism further and further into heathen territory. The frontier was not a fixed line but a zone, an area with constant wars and mixed populations, and the crusades rarely consisted of a large, unified military expedition, which determined in a single battle whether the area was to be heathen or Christian. Such battles did take place, but that was only one form of a crusade amongst many other initiatives. It is easy to get lost in a barren and very technical discussion concerning when it is possible to consider the wars real crusades and when they were some other type of war. The most important thing, however, is that all the struggles in the frontier regions were perceived, in one way or the other, in religious terms. They were all part of the common Christian duty to disseminate the cross, even though the individual wars were fought differently.

At one end of the scale were the regular terror attacks and raids a long way into heathen territory in order to plunder and cause as much disturbance as possible, and then to return home. At times there were arrangements concerning tribute and protection money. At times there were large-scale wars. Large armies were mobilized, troops came to assistance from outside and the warriors went through solemn ceremonies, took the cross and became true crusaders. At the other end of the scale was the establishment of a permanent Christian presence with military centres of power and a church structure together with a general religious education of the people. This happened in different ways, depending on local circumstances. Nevertheless, several common features keep recurring and make comparison between North and South possible.

It was a drawn-out process, which never took place in a religious vacuum where the participants suddenly were presented with something completely novel. On the contrary, the followers of the two religions knew about each other very well and would have had a sense of what their opposites thought and stood for. On the Iberian Peninsula, the Muslims had been living side by side with the original Christian communities from the beginning of the 8th century. In the Slavic areas along the Baltic coast there had been missionary activities since the 9th century, and churches and Christian communities had existed since at least the

The struggle for land and history   187

10th century. At times, the Christian communities were persecuted and had to give up living as Christians. In the South, "they fell from faith," in the North, "they turned back to heathenism," as contemporary documents and narratives tell us again and again. The religiously mixed society in the North, against which the Danish crusades were directed, was described thus by the Saxon Duke Henry the Lion, in 1158:

> The heathen peoples in our duchy of Saxony are called Wends, and since the earliest times under Charlemagne,[1] they have always been rebellious against God and destroyed the holy Church, and after they finally had bowed their tough necks under the Christian faith, it often happened that they fell back into the vomit of idolatry. We have inherited them as tributary peoples from our ancestors, although in such a way that we have very often had to break their slaves' necks with the sword even in our own time, and we have increased their taxes much more than before due to their evil.[2]

The idea of an original Christendom, which was under pressure now, had an important legitimizing function in both the North and South. If there had been a Christian presence, it was permitted to defend it. If the Wends had been Christians in the past, it was permitted to force them back into the faith, as opposed to the Muslims and heathens who never before had been Christians. Those latter could be forced to hear the preaching of the Word, but only the apostates could be forced to convert. On the other hand, the mosques of the Muslims were reconquered and rechristened; the idea was that most of them had probably been built as churches originally and had been taken over by the Muslims.[3]

Henry the Lion took over the Slavic castle of Ratzeburg about twenty kilometres to the south of Lübeck in 1143. He strengthened its fortifications and installed his own bailiff to strengthen his military power. In 1154, it was raised to episcopal residence; a Premonstratensian from Magdeburg was installed as bishop and, in 1158, Henry the Lion continued to give large gifts to Ratzeburg to safeguard the extension of the Church.

> One servant is the group of scholars who for a long time have preached the Word and called the rejecters to the table of God, the other servant is the group of princes whose place it is to force the savage people by drawing the sword. We considered money lower than winning a reward for the soul, and those whom we earlier fought on behalf of the Emperor we now fought for the Saviour's sake. . . . with many expenses to soldiers and with great loss of life, we have got the savage peoples back to Christianity, so that we and our helpers have deserved the eternal dinar as a reward.[4]

The establishment of a Church structure with priests was followed up by a deliberate settlement policy where Christian colonists were invited to settle in the newly conquered areas, in order to control them as well as to make the whole populace Christian. That too was a lengthy process. On the Iberian Peninsula there

188 *The struggle for land and history*

continued to be Muslim populations throughout the Middle Ages. In the Wendish areas the sources are fewer, but it seems that the Wends in some areas only gave up heathenism for good in the middle of the 14th century. This might have been because they were economically hard-pressed during the late medieval agricultural crisis. If that is the case, we may assume that the princes in the region favoured the Christians legally and economically to persuade them to convert. Perhaps the final conversion of the Wends happened because the religious climate became harsher during the crisis and due to mass death from the late medieval plague. Then they might have been finally forced to convert to Christianity.[5] The earliest evidence that the craft guilds discriminated against the Wends and demanded its members must be of pure German descent in the Wendish area stems from 1353. This immediately spread to Lüneburg, Magdeburg, Brandenburg, West Pomerania and other areas that had been conquered by the crusades during the 12th and 13th centuries,[6] but where religious divisions seem to have been reduced to a question of descent eventually in the 14th century.

Church structure and settlement had been established by rulers and clerics at all levels, but a special role is attributable to the Cistercians, who might also have served as a connecting link between Denmark and Portugal. During the 12th century, they had an exceedingly important function in formulating a crusade ideology and propagating it to the noblemen.

The Cistercian link?

The Cistercian Order combined three features that were decisive in the success of the crusades on a local level: a thoroughly organized utilization of the landscape, a well-argued theological justification of war against evil, which had a tremendous appeal amongst secular noblemen and a Europe-wide organization. On the common European level, the Order created an international and effective network over just a few years; the abbots of the individual monasteries met on a yearly basis, ideas were exchanged fast and plans that may involve countries even very far from each other were made.[7]

The Cistercian Order arose as a reform order amongst the Benedictines precisely during the years of the first crusade and in Burgundy, one of the core regions of the crusade. Reform movements and Cluny had been sufficient for the 11th century, but now real crusades and Cistercians were needed. Bernard entered the Order in 1113 and in 1115, he was sent from Cîteaux to establish Clairvaux and to become the abbot of the new monastery. During the following almost forty years until Bernard's death, about 350 Cistercian monasteries were established all over Europe, all built according to the exact same architectural design, all with the same liturgy and the same daily routine, and all of them were connected via the yearly general chapter in Cîteaux. Every single monastery originated from another, as a daughter from a mother, and it was the duty of the abbot of the mother monastery to inspect, visit and critically examine all the daughter monasteries. Sometimes this was practically impossible. From Clairvaux, Bernard founded sixty-eight new Cistercian monasteries in Northern England, Ireland, Wales, Sweden, Denmark

The struggle for land and history   189

and Portugal. It would have been impossible for him to visit them all himself so he had to rely on inspections carried out by deputies.

The oldest Cistercian monastery in Denmark[8] is Herrisvad in Scania, established in 1144 as a daughter monastery of Cîteaux. Later in the 12th century, Herrisvad gained a couple of daughter monasteries on Funen (Holme 1171) and in Jutland (Tvis 1163). Nydala and Alvastra in Sweden were both established directly from Clairvaux, in 1143. More interesting in this context, though, is the monastery of Esrom, established directly from Clairvaux in 1150/51. Earlier, there had been a Benedictine monastery on the site, but this was reformed with monks from Clairvaux. It happened on the initiative of Achbishop Eskil after he had received a vision. Once as a young man in Hildesheim, Eskil fell ill and was close to death and the doctors had given up on him, but then Eskil was led in spirit to a dwelling, which was as hot inside as a burning furnace. The flames came out of the furnace and dragged him inside. He immediately began to burn and believed that only death and eternal fires were left for him. Then he saw the merciful God, who showed him a narrow path out of the sea of flames to the great palace where the Queen of heaven, the mistress of the angels, sits on her throne. The narrative continues by recounting how Eskil prayed for mercy and was both teased and mocked by the Virgin Mary because he tried to ransom himself with his own money – it was simply not adequate. She agreed to let Eskil promise that he will sow five kinds of grain and harvest five measures of them, one of each, and give them to the Virgin Mary. Then he will be sent back to life, not because he ransomed himself but out of mercy. During the first long while after his return, those present only heard him say again and again; "Thank you, God, that I shall not burn. Thank you, God, that I shall not burn." When he regained his composure a little, he spoke about the vision; he realized that that he must establish five new monastic orders to the glory of the Virgin Mary in his archdiocese.[9] This he does and one of the orders was the Cistercians in Esrom.

The frightening tale must stem from Eskil himself; he passed it on to his new brothers during his last years. He had then abdicated the archiepiscopal see and entered the monastery of Clairvaux, where he died in 1181. It is included in the collection of miracles by Herbert of Clairvaux from around 1180 and the great history of the Cistercians *Exordium magnum cisterciense* from around 1200. It would have been edifying and would have demonstrated that the Virgin Mary had given the Order special attention. However, it is not mentioned in the official history of the Order that Eskil had a background which made it quite natural for him to support an order such as the Cistercians. He was part of the international chivalrous culture, to which the Cistercians in particular directed their attention. Eskil quoted the *Chanson de Roland* in his letter to "his master and special friend," the French King Louis,[10] he went on a pilgrimage or crusade to Jerusalem in the 1160s and supported the crusades against the Wends after his return by participating personally. He had close connections to one of the greatest magnates of the country, Peder Bodilsen, who took great interest in church reform. In addition, Eskil was a close friend of Bernard and visited him in Clairvaux in 1153. A short time after his return to Denmark, he received the sad notification that Bernard had

190   *The struggle for land and history*

"not passed away, but gone ahead; not gone under, but gone over; not suffered death, but escaped it."[11]

Eskil summed up his own efforts during the establishment of Esrom in this way:

> We wish that all shall know the care and assiduity with which we fought to extend Christian religion and the worship of the divine majesty to all of Denmark's frontiers. Therefore, we also assembled believers from different monastic orders and installed them in different areas within this region, and in order to not lack in Cistercian brothers, we went – despite great troubles and expenses – to the blessed abbot of Clairvaux, Master Bernard, and we brought a seed of his children, from which a harvest of souls of the believers later will sprout, back with us to our land.[12]

The document continues by enumerating the costly gifts which Eskil and his closest relative Count Niels gave to Esrom. In the process of donating his gift, the Count entered the Cistercian order and was admitted to Esrom. The monastery continued to receive numerous and great gifts and soon grew in size. Right from the beginning, it received support from the kings, from both Canute and Valdemar, who at first were allies and later fought each other. It seems that Esrom had a special relationship to Valdemar. At a very early point in time, Valdemar gave an estate to Esrom in order to save his soul; at the same time, the monks gave one or two marks in gold to embellish the reliquary of his father.[13] Thus, right from the beginning, the Cistercians in Esrom contributed to the cult of Canute Lavard, who was to become the great Danish crusader saint. All this taken together indicates that Esrom was intended, right from the beginning, to play a role in the Danish crusades.

Esrom became rich and a mother monastery to five direct daughter monasteries and seven in the next generation. In 1158, King Valdemar gave land to the establishment of Vitskøl in northern Jutland in gratitude for having escaped the assassination attempt at the Feast of Blood and for having become sole king. In 1161, Sorø changed from being a Benedictine monastery to a Cistercian house with monks from Esrom. Sorø was established in around 1140 but was now reformed by Bishop Absalon of Roskilde, who was already deeply involved in the Baltic crusades and later had the conquered lands placed under the see of Roskilde. The enormous Cistercian church in Sorø became the burial church for Absalon's family. He himself was buried there, and so was his brother Esbern Snare, after a long, active life as a crusader. In 1192, the monastery of Ryd in Schleswig was established – the old Benedictine society in the monastery of St. Michael was reformed and the Cistercians assumed responsibility for the church, which was a half-size copy of the Holy Sepulchre in Jerusalem.[14] This happened a short time after King Canute VI had taken the title "King of the Wends" and had continued the expansion along the Baltic shores in a combination of political wars against Christian princes and crusades against heathens. The crusade idea remained alive in Ryd throughout the 13th century. It left its traces in the annals of the monastery, which, amongst other things, extended the tradition concerning Canute the Furry – a mythical great-great-grandfather of Gorm the Old – with a narrative

The struggle for land and history 191

on how he in the distant past had fought in Prussia, Zemgale and the land of the Karelians, all the way next to the Russians, that is, the regions that were crusading targets for Canute VI.[15] In the historical writing and in the ideological shaping of the crusade idea, the effort of the Cistercians was of paramount importance.

In between the establishment of Sorø and Ry, two more new daughter monasteries of Esrom emerged: Dargun in Mecklenburg, in 1172, and Colbatz in Prussia, in 1174. They were founded in newly conquered lands with inhabitants who still to a large degree were heathen; they were established exactly with the aim of Christianizing the lands in depth. We can get a sense of how this went down from the contemporary sources. Before that, we might ask from where Esrom had any ideas on how to organize such a missionary monastery. The most obvious answer is that the abbot of Esrom discussed the problem with his near colleagues from Portugal and especially from the Cistercian monastery of Alcobaça.[16]

The oldest Cistercian monastery in Portugal was established almost precisely at the same time as Herrisvad, in 1143–1144 in São João de Tarouca.[17] How this unfolded is only recorded in a few contemporary sources. The monastery's very large collection of medieval letters was kept at the seminary in Viseu, where everything was lost in a fire in 1841.[18] An extensive narrative about the Cistercians in Portugal was compiled by the Cistercian monk Brito and published as *Cronica de Cister* in 1602. It is based on medieval source material and became rather voluminous; it has been elaborated upon and extended and is generally rather unreliable. In addition there is a late account, but without Brito's additions. This recounts that the establishment of Tarouca took place after a royal initiative and with the support of local noblemen.[19]

Bernard of Clairvaux allegedly sent out a group of eight monks, who went to the Abbot João Cirita – the hermit – in Lamego, one of the strongest Christian fortresses in 11th-century Portugal, just south of the River Douro. They carried a letter of recommendation from Bernard himself; it asked João to receive them kindly and installed him as their principal, their abbot. Carrying the letter with him, João turned to Afonso Henriques in Guimarães and asked for land for the new monastery, which he received in 1139. The group built a simple cell by the River Barosa and prayed, and one night they saw a brilliant light, a sign from God on where to build the new monastery. The light showed itself to them every night for two weeks. It was in a different place to that which Afonso Henriques had originally intended, but the monks received permission to choose it when they promised to pray for Afonso and his parents. They were presented with great gifts by Afonso and by Egas Moniz, Afonso's steward and the most powerful nobleman in the Beira Alta region and, until the death of Afonso, one of his most important advisors.[20]

In the founding legend, the establishment of Tarouca is linked to the fight against the Muslims.

> A few days later, the Moors arrived and laid waste to the region surrounding Trancoso, and the King arrived in Lamego with his troops and rode along the River Barosa. Then he remembered the brothers who lived there, and went to visit them together with his best men to see the place that lived off his gifts.

192 *The struggle for land and history*

But he saw that they were poor and lived in small huts and he felt sorry for them. He asked them to dispatch Brother Adebert to him to implore the Lord to help his army. The brothers sent Adebert to the King together with a cross and a chalice so he could celebrate mass, because he was a priest. The battle began and he prayed, and the King defeated the Moors and entered Trancoso but lost the cross during the struggle. Many other good things happened through Adebert's prayers, and in order to repay him and the brothers and the Lord God, the King promised that he would build a monastery, and by Aldebert's[21] good prayers and the Lord's help once again he defeated many Saracens. Therefore, he came here (to Tarouca), and while the brothers and João Cirita and many others and the bishops of Braga and Lamego witnessed it, the King himself laid the first stone for the monastery while the soldiers and his troops cheered, and he gave Abbot João a letter of donation.[22]

What should we believe? It is most likely a fact that King Afonso Henriques and Egas Moniz presented large gifts to the establishment of a monastery, which was reformed in around 1140 from Benedictine to Cistercian, and there is no reason to doubt the existence of the hermit João Cirita. Perhaps it happened with the dispatch of a group of monks from Bernard of Clairvaux. Perhaps there is a connection between the establishment and the battle of nearby Troncoso, which actually took place in 1140; perhaps this combination is only an expression of the interest for crusades in later Cistercian historical writing. Details besides this, which occur in later narratives about Tarouca, are unfortunately impossible to confirm via other sources. Brito wrote in 1602 that João Cirita had fought side by side with Henrique of Portugal before he became a monk. This is not impossible, but all of Brito's narrative has been dismissed by Portuguese historians as fantasy and a creative combination of incidental sources.

We are on much safer ground when it comes to the establishment of Santa Maria de Alcobaça in 1153, a few years after Esrom, also a daughter monastery of Clairvaux and the last to be established by Bernard before his death in August that year. Alcobaça was presented by Afonso Henriques directly to Bernard with a great charter, which outlines the background to the establishment of the monastery. The goal is stated directly: "As every believer should give the servants of God a share in the boons that he has gathered from the supreme Giver, so that he through these servants of God shall deserve to receive a share of the boots of the heavens, I, Afonso, King of the Portuguese by the mercy of God, give . . . to support you, Master Bernard, abbot in the monastery of Clairvaux, and your brothers and successors in eternity the estate that we own between the two cities of Leiria and Óbidos below the mountain Taicha through the region from Lisbon to the sea."[23] The land was presented to Bernard for a new monastery in order to make useful the land, which the King had conquered from the Muslims, whether cultivated or not, with all vineyards, houses, places and fields, with all its equipment. Everything that had belonged to the royal jurisprudence was to be deleted from the dominion of the King and designated to the Cistercians for all eternity. If the Cistercians were to leave the area again and move elsewhere, the land should

Figure 7.1 Dormitory, Alcobaça. The monastery of Alcobaça was established in 1153 by Bernard of Clairvaux. It was from the beginning closely attached to the Portuguese crusades. The nave and large parts of the monastic area date to the middle of the 13th century. © Kurt Villads Jensen

revert to the King. The establishment of Alcobaça was a result of Afonso Henriques' conquest of Santarém and Lisbon in 1147 with assistance from English and German crusaders, but a pious Cistercian legend, which placed the founding several years earlier, was soon developed in Alcobaça. Thus, the monastery had been there first, and it was, therefore, the monastery and a miracle of St. Bernard that made the conquest of Lisbon possible in 1147.

The argument about who was there first is typical in the Middle Ages – and probably is to this day – and illustrates how closely tied to the crusades and the fight against the infidel the Cistercians perceived themselves to be. This took place in two stages. At first, they assisted with prayers and miracles during the conquest itself, but afterwards came the long haul – cultivating the waste land and converting the defeated peoples to Christianity.

The waste land

Thus, the establishment of Alcobaça was a consequence of the Portuguese crusaders' conquests of large, fortified cities; they could be defended militarily.

194 *The struggle for land and history*

Afterwards, however, the open countryside was to be turned Christian and secured with a permanent, Christian population. This was exactly what the Cistercians were good at. According to their own perception, as well as that of the King, they were to go out and cultivate the desert, the waste land, which had been depopulated after the wars between Christians and Muslims. Whether it really was depopulated and most of the inhabitants were killed or fled elsewhere is an open question.[24] There would have been significant local variations.

In some areas, the crusade zeal got the better of the conquerors; while in others, crusading noblemen held back and protected the local heathen or Muslim population. It has become a part of Portuguese historical self-awareness that the Portuguese crusaders were not as intolerant as others because they knew the region and through generations had experienced being part of a religiously mixed population. There are only a few actual examples in the sources to back up this perception. The only substantial one is a comment in the narrative about the conquest of Lisbon in 1147, where the English and other crusaders wanted to kill the Muslims while King Afonso Henriques wanted to spare them.[25] Likewise, Danish historians have probably assumed that Danish crusaders fought in a civilized fashion and without too much bloodshed; at least, they have only touched upon it lightly.[26] In spite of that Saxo's description of Danish ravaging of Wendish lands is simple and unvarnished ethnic cleansing.[27] Still, it does not seem as if the conquest of heathen lands was followed up by systematic and protracted mass exterminations of the local Muslim or heathen population.[28]

The landscape the Cistercians arrived at was not a complete waste. The idea of the desert, however, was of fundamental importance to the Cistercians; so to them, any new land was by definition a waste land. The desert was not solely a category of demography or cultivation; it was, above all, religious.[29] It conjured up images of the chosen people's wandering in the wilderness for forty years after the exodus from Egypt; it was a place for meditation as well as for diabolical temptations, which Jesus experienced during his forty days in the desert.[30] By walking into the desert to missionize, every Cistercian could have perceived himself as a new John the Baptist (who was "the voice of one crying in the wilderness, Make straight the way of the Lord"), making straight in the desert a highway for our God.[31] In the desert, the air is cleaner, the heavens more open, and God is nearer, Origines wrote. "Rejoice, desert, near to God," Jerome cried.[32]

The desert was also the land of opportunity, the barren soil that could be turned to abundance; the land that could flow with milk and honey, as Urban II had described in his sermon at Clermont,[33] as was repeated everywhere, for example in the Bishop of Magdeburg's call for a crusade in the Baltic in around 1108.[34] And when crusaders and missionaries arrived in the wilderness, it was transformed into the Lord's vineyard,[35] which was fertilized with the blood of the martyrs and the tears of the believers. The harvest was plenty but the labourers few. Thus, one could only ask the Lord of the harvest to send forth labourers[36] so that the earth could deliver a plentiful harvest of souls and ordinary crops.

The Cistercian colonization and cultivation happened in several ways. A number of *granges* were established. They were large farms with enormous, continuous

The struggle for land and history 195

fields, which were cultivated jointly by an effective and disciplined working collective of Cistercian lay brothers or slaves, who received almost no pay and lived on the top floor in the large barns under the leadership of a grange master. We know from Alcobaça that the granges were concentrated around the monastery itself. There were only a few to the North, but more and more were found further in the South, in the territory of Alcobaça.[37] The granges combined all the advantages of large-scale farming and presented an opportunity to experiment with new crops and tools. Their production was so large that it would not have been for self-sufficiency alone; it would have stimulated trade and an early money economy.[38]

The existing villages were furthermore populated with Christians, who were placed under the monastery with regards to jurisdiction and taxation, and new villages were founded. The inhabitants received special privileges in return for moving there, and they were placed under the legal protection of the monastery instead of that of the King. In connection with the repopulation of villages, the monastery issued privileges which gave the inhabitants a high degree of freedom in comparison with other villages further away from the religious frontier.[39] It is not certain who inhabited these villages. Some would have been peasants from Christian regions outside Portugal: from France, León and Castile. Others would have been from Northern Portugal. Yet others were likely to have been local Mozarab Christians, and some were presumably Muslims.[40] Economically, however, the Cistercians' peasants were not in a better position than others. On the contrary.

In general, peasants paid fewer taxes the farther towards the South and closer to the religious frontier they lived. In the North, by the River Douro around Lamego, the peasants paid around a quarter of the yield in taxes. This falls to around one sixth further to the South around Coimbra. In the Serra Estrela mountains, a region that is difficult to access and to conquer, the taxes were no more than one tenth. The taxation level on Cistercian lands under Alcobaça in the southernmost area, however, suddenly goes up and reaches a quarter again. Part of the differences in the taxes between the North and the South can be explained with differences in the fertility between the regions. The yield is simply much larger in the North, which allows for taxes to be correspondingly larger. This is not the whole explanation though. The ability of the landowners to exercise control and their interest in creating money must be included as well. In this regard, the Cistercians were in a strong position.[41]

An economic centre as large as Alcobaça would have also needed to attract specialized artisans, stonemasons, painters and many others. Some of those working inside the monastery seem to have been Muslims. Some were free, many were not, and Alcobaça became one of the largest owners of Muslim slaves in the late 12th century. In around 1300 a template was prepared for Cistercians in Alcobaça, a collection of letters of all sorts that was likely to be of use. The very first model-letter deals with slaves. It demonstrates how to draw up a letter of manumission: "I, Abbot G. of this and this monastery, give this letter of freedom to you, Ali the Muslim, or to you, my slave D., in return for the hundred pounds in Portuguese money, which I have received from you earlier." Muslims are always named Ali in these model-letters, what D stands for is not known, but it has presumably

196   *The struggle for land and history*

been a Christian name: perhaps Diego? "We allow you, and give you power and freedom, to stay on the land of the monastery and to travel away from it and come back to it as often and for any reason, whenever and wherever."[42] Freeing Muslim slaves could be a financial transaction and shows that the slaves of Alcobaça had some kind of ownership of income and could save money to buy their own freedom. Emancipation did not always happen after mutual agreement, however. The same collection of examples from Alcobaça gives detailed instructions on how to advertise and search for runaway slaves. It is the same wording as when other slaves, horses and cows were stolen.

Slaves were used for household work but it is not obvious from the Portuguese sources whether they participated in field labour as well. The monastery could have utilized this relatively large number of specialized artisans to cultivate particular trades. In Alcobaça, the monastery became known for the extraction of iron from the mines in the area and for the manufacture of farm tools, weaponry and other iron objects. The monastery land reached all the way to the sea, where it owned four ports.[43]

In the 12th century, the general chapter of the Cistercian order discussed the slave-holding of Muslims. At several assemblies it was decided that the order was not allowed to trade in Muslims and that Muslims must not be prevented from being baptized. As it was necessary to emphasize this several times, it suggests that it would not have been a remote idea for the abbots of the order to let the Muslims continue their infidelity and as slaves.[44]

In 1195, Alcobaça was almost destroyed in a Muslim attack and then meticulously rebuilt. After forty years and almost two generations, this was still a dangerous, religious frontier land: a potential warzone.[45]

In Esrom, they knew how things worked in Alcobaça, and the daughter monastery in the Wendish area was organized in the same way. The new Cistercian monastery in Dargun was consecrated in 1172 on June 25, the day of the newly canonized crusader saint Canute Lavard. The monastery received large gifts from local, newly Christianized princes, and was from then on to spread Christianity in the large, heathen region. Dargun was consecrated by Bishop Berno of Schwerin, himself a Cistercian. He emphasized that it was the first Christian altar consecrated in this particular part of the Wendish area.[46] The altar was dedicated to God, the Virgin Mary and the holy confessor, Benedict. Berno also gave ten marks from the serving of beer in Lucho and two salt pots in Kolberg and half of the fishing haul from the first part of the River Pene. He had granted the other half to them earlier. He donated all this from his "small and weak bishop's income," he adds, thus underlining how important he perceived the mission to be in the newly conquered areas.

In 1176, Prince Kazimir of Pomerania issued his large privilege to Dargun.[47] He gave it "all power and complete freedom to summon and settle around it, wherever on the estate of the monastery, Germans, Danes, or Slavic peoples or whoever of any ethnicity and trade, and so that the monastery can cultivate the land and divide it into parishes and install priests, and also so that they have a license to serve beer, whether they want to do it our way or in the German or the

The struggle for land and history   197

Danish way." The serving of beer, brewed one way or the other, seems to have been a very important privilege in the northern regions of Europe. It also seems to have been a lucrative business, when a donation from a bishop could consist of simply a yearly beer tax.[48]

Those individuals, whom the Cistercians could persuade to move in and settle in the new lands, were to be free of all service to Kazimir and his noblemen; they were not to pay any of the taxes that others had to pay "according to the customs of our people." What these amounted to is specified straight away: They are not obliged to fortify towns, build bridges or repair them, and they are not supposed to participate in Kazimir's crusades or military expeditions, his *expeditiones*. They shall only exclusively obey their Cistercian abbot. What this means in practice can be reflected on for a long while. The colonists in the frontier regions were quite often exempted from taxes, precisely in return for participating in crusades or raids against the infidels. In 1158, Duke Henry the Lion had established three new dioceses in the Wendish lands in order to propagate the Christian faith: Ratzeburg, Lübeck and Schwerin, and their privileges were reconfirmed in 1174.

Those peasants and colonists who were placed under the dioceses were to be free of all taxes and from *wogiwotniza*, "as the tax to the Duke is called." The new colonists were not to be summoned before the Duke's court. They were nevertheless to supply thirty shields for six weeks for the Duke's crusades, his *expeditiones*, on the far side of the River Elbe; they were to serve by building fortifications at Ratzeburg, just as all other inhabitants in the area. For that use, Henry frees ten *worwercos* to the bishops.[49] Crucial matters in a religious frontier region, and, strangely, precisely what the new colonists at Dargun were exempted from by Kazimir. Perhaps the idea was that the Cistercians were to be responsible for that form of warfare, so that their new colonists could not be commanded by the prince but only by the abbot? Niels Pribislavsen chose a compromise in 1189 when he confirmed his father's gift of land to Dobaran, another Cistercian monastery in the region. The peasants there were exempted from fortifying towns and bridges in front of the towns so they were able to serve the Cistercians better, but there is no mention of war service. This presumably means that the peasants still had to participate in Niels's crusades.[50]

The new colonists came from many different places. Brunswick and Mecklenburg were fortified and the foundations of walls were laid in the marshy land by specialists from the Low Lands and Flanders, who were used to working with damming and in soft soil.[51] Soon after 1100, the Archbishop of Hamburg-Bremen invited the first colonists to settle on and cultivate the waste lands by the delta of the River Weser,[52] the dike builders then quickly moved further and further east. Perhaps the Flemings were also invited to strengthen the local cloth industry; both Brunswick and Mecklenburg later became important centres for the manufacture of wool. The Flemings were brought to the region by the local princes, and the Cistercians presumably used the same kind of specialists. One particular kind of specialized industry was salt production, which the Cistercians were given in donation on a large scale and were able to control. Others came along as well though, among them the Premonstraterians from Lund, who received permission

198   *The struggle for land and history*

to build six new salt cauldrons, in 1177.[53] At times, too many immigrants arrived during those waves of colonization. A heathen uprising in Holstein in around 1130 was specifically directed against the newcomers, who had been attracted "from near and far" to cultivate the land.[54]

Moreover, German-speaking colonists arrived in great numbers, judging from the place names, but this did not mean that the heathen Slavic population was expelled. At times these new settlers would certainly have taken over older Wendish villages; in other instances, a new Christian settlement would have been founded next to an old heathen settlement so dual settlements emerged with the same name. This is known from the Danish conquest of the island of Fehmarn, which was organized with Slavic and Danish villages side by side.[55] This is also known from areas under both Dargun and Doberan, both Cistercian monasteries. They were given the tithe from several towns, among them "Doberan and the Slav town of Doberan," "the two towns Bruno" and "Cuzis and the other Cuzis."[56] Such dual towns continued to exist up until the middle of the 14th century, with the practical problems that followed from this. Earlier, a market was held every Monday in Salzwedel old town, now they had to be held every other week in the old town and every other week in Salzwedel new town.[57] There are only relatively few signs of Danish participation in the colonization of Mecklenburg and West Pomerania. From Eldena, the successor of Dargun, several Danish place names were handed down, for example Ladebow ("ladeplads" or port), Nybow, which may possibly be of Danish origin, and Wampen, which supposedly comes from the Danish word Vandkær. Furthermore, there is one example of a dual town, the Danish and the Slavic Wieck.[58] On the Iberian Peninsula, the crusades also led to a division, so the Christians seized the old towns and the surviving Muslims were placed just outside the town and had to build a new town with the same name.[59]

The colonization of the newly conquered lands in the North has had a peculiar research history because of the scarcity of source material. Furthermore, the historical research has been used to justify on-going policies with crucial implications for millions of people. A German historical tradition has envisaged a massive colonization by immigrant Germans, which stretched from the beginning of the era of the crusades all the way through to the High Middle Ages. At the beginning of the 20th century, this was considered a natural and reasonable expression of the German "Drang nach Osten" and was linked to the idea of the culture bearers: that German expansion was in reality a step on the path towards civilization and economic and political development of the backward Slavic population. Since the Second World War, Polish research has attempted in particular to demonstrate that in reality there was no German immigration; the local Slavic populations only took on the German language because it became the administrative language and carried a high status. Some have envisaged a very extensive colonization, others a very limited one. There are many variants between these theories and definite numbers of population and colonists are impossible to identify for this period.[60] Presumably, it is reasonable to assume that new cultivation actually took place, that the area became more densely settled and that there was an increase in immigration of people from outside. This is consistent with the fact that the 11th and

The struggle for land and history   199

12th centuries were a period of population expansion in all of Europe. Within the borders of present-day Denmark, more and more land was cultivated and new villages were established by local people or by colonists from the outside. This would also have been the case in the newly conquered lands, but there the settlements were necessarily linked to the establishment of the Christian faith.

Spiritual and practical matters went hand in hand, and concerns for one were not to lead to the other being neglected. In 1154, Bishop Gering of Meissen called in Flemings to cultivate the deserted town of Coryn (by Wurzen between Leipzig and Meissen) and gave them the land as an inheritable freehold on favourable conditions. His letter of privilege began with an explanation of why he as a bishop was concerned with such worldly matters as finding people to cultivate the land:

> Although "only one thing is needful," which is, as Mary did, to choose "the best part" and in the sweet contemplation of religious life to choose the blessing of inner quietude, we are nevertheless often forced, as Martha, to deal with the bitter harshness of the active life and "worry about many things." For the tabernacle of the Lord's pact and His Ark of the Covenant would not shine with such splendour if they were not protected by hairy curtains and by red and hyacinth coloured ram's skin against storm and from rain.[61]

Elegantly phrased and richly layered linguistically. The Ark of the Covenant is the visible pledge between God and His chosen people; it should be carried in front during war as a sign that the chosen people have God on their side, such as the crusaders did. The Ark is protected by hairy curtains, which in the Bible text is presumably to be understood as a kind of a fly sheet of a tent. The Latin word *saga*, curtains, also referred to a soldier's coat in Latin – thus, the Christian church amongst the Slavic heathens were to be covered by the warriors' coats. And they were to move beneath ram's skins –*ram* was also a technical term for the most common siege engine, the battering ram. Curtains and skins shall protect against storm and rain, which sounds reasonably prosaic and corresponds with inviting the Flemings from the marshes to the region with their experience in building dikes against flooding. However, the expression "storm and rain" stems from the Book of Isaiah, the brief fourth chapter, which narrates how the Lord descends on the Mount of Zion after having cleansed Jerusalem of sin, such that all the nations can enter the Holy City at last. It is really the Lord God Himself who protects against storm and rain. The scriptural passage immediately passes into the praise "I will sing to my well-beloved a song of my beloved touching his vineyard." To plant a vineyard or to labour in the vineyard of the Lord was possibly the most common expression during this period for mission among the heathens, and the phrase became standard among the missionary-eager Cistercians.[62] None of this is mentioned directly in the letter from Bishop Gering but would have been obvious to most listeners with just a moderate degree of theological schooling. The practical and the spiritual must inevitably go hand in hand, but the conclusion is probably also that seemingly exclusively practical matters have a spiritual aspect or a spiritual meaning to them as well.

The sanctification of landscape

Coincidentally with the colonization and the physical cultivation of the land by the Cistercians, the landscape was taken over spiritually and sacrally. Christianity was physically and visually established by the crusades. This is illustrated in the detailed description by Bishop Berno and Prince Kazimir of the land they donate to the Cistercians. The gift cannot be described using title numbers but has to be localized from distinct fixed points in the landscape, rivers, rocks and hills.[63]

> From the waterfall east of Dargun over Guhtkepole to the tamarisk marsh . . . to the deep salt lake, which in Slavic is known as glambike loug, from there to the west to a great oak, under which there is a large rock of the bedrock. . . . [F]rom there to some mounds, which are known in Slavic as Trigorke and are the burials of peoples from ancient times, . . . from there to the large oak, which is marked with the a cross, that is known in Slavic as knezegraniza (the royal border). From this oak . . . by the line made up by a line of trees marked with crosses.[64]

If there were no other obvious physical features in the landscape, the Cistercians simply cut crosses in the trees in the dividing line, probably at eye level, so that it was noticeable when one left heathen land and entered the Christian area. The Cistercian's idea was obviously that the border between the two religions was a fixed line which could be traced geographically.

It is remarkable how many oak trees act as landscape markers. They are large, by a rock, at a valley, without bark, burnt and much else, but they would have been well-known and sufficiently distinctive to arrange the landscape surrounding them. They were probably the old centres in the sacral landscape. At the beginning of the 12th century, the missionary bishop Otto of Bamberg described his problems in getting the newly converted Christians to fell the old, sacred trees in this very region, and he usually had to give up.[65] The oak trees in the Wendish lands in the 1170s would have been old sacred trees, known to everybody, and they were, as such, useful as markers to describe the landscape. These trees were not felled; they were converted, just as the people. Crusaders and Cistercians cut crosses in them to mark the progress of Christianity, religiously and politically. This was clearly summed up in the term for the cross on the sacred tree, *Knezegraniza*, the royal border. Christianity had come this far.

The trees were to be cleared in order to cultivate the missionary field, Bernard of Clairvaux wrote.

> Because when new fields are established in the forest, the trees must be felled. But they are not thrown away, they can lie on the ground or be collected in heaps, if there are few so that fire can be set to them, and the fire has something to catch hold of, and the old and barren soil can turn new and fertile. So it is, too, with those who hear the Book of Wisdom, that 'the one who cultivates his land is to be satisfied with bread', and they do penance and practice

The struggle for land and history 201

holy obedience and demeanour, and they fell the old forest of their sins from the soil of their heart and body. But they do not throw it to forgetfulness, but assemble on the open land of their memory the sins of their own, of others, and the whole world, and ignite them with the fire of the Holy Ghost, which comes from above.[66]

The trees are the sign of sin, the sins of the heathen, which are to be replaced by eating bread of the Eucharist after conversion. But the trees and sin are conditions under which everyone lives, Christians as well as heathens, and only the purifying flames of the Holy Ghost can help.[67] The Cistercian trees are an obvious example of the medieval way of thinking, where no sharp distinction is made between concrete and spiritual references in language, and where the same object or word could contain a plurality of meanings – the struggle between the heathen gods and Christ, and the universal struggle against sin, but also property boundaries, colonization and the political and military power of the prince.

The crosses on the trees were markings on the landscape of the activity of the Christians, but the crosses themselves participated actively in the crusades as well. The island of Falster had been exposed to attacks from the heathen Wends for years, and the local people piously erected an enormous wooden cross on the beach at Grønsund. When the heathens cut it down in order to win fame, they soon paid for their blasphemy with defeat and shipwreck. Never again did they have any luck with their attacks.[68]

Alcobaça was allowed to erect special markers on the landscape, *coutos* – a kind of a refuge. It was usually a stone, carved with a cross. If a person who had fallen into disfavour with the king or had been sentenced to some punishment were able to reach and touch the stone, he would have refuge and enter the legal protection of the monastery. In return, he was obliged to settle in the village of the monastery and labour for the monastery together with his family. These coutos were meticulously placed in those villages where it was hardest to settle. They were a success for the monastery and led to all of Alcobaça's land becoming known under the umbrella term of *the coutos of the Monastery*. This legal privilege continued until 1672.[69]

The meticulous registration and marking of the landscape had a legal impact. It indicated when a person went from one kind of jurisdiction to another, from the land of one man or institution to another's. At the same time it had a theological background in the biblical narratives of measuring Jerusalem, both the heavenly and the earthly, and of measuring the temple in Jerusalem.[70] By measuring the sacred it was made holy. In the Bible, the act of measuring was directly linked to "wiping Jerusalem clean as a man wipeth a dish, wiping it, and turning it upside down."[71] By measuring the land meticulously, marking it and describing it, the Cistercians cleansed it for heathens.

Not only were the Cistercians to mark the presence of Christianity and organize the new Christian Church in the region, they were also supposed to care for the needs of the new Christian peoples, material as well as spiritual needs, and they were to take care of the spiritual education. The area around Dargun is like

202 *The struggle for land and history*

the area around Alcobaça – it was to be peopled by Christians and was given to the monastery, which could decide for itself what they wished to do with it. Mecklenburg too remained a religious frontier region for a long time. The nearby Cistercian monastery of Doberan was established in 1171; it was destroyed during a heathen revolt in 1179 and was established anew seven years later.[72] Dargun itself fell victim to a heathen revolt at the roughly same time as Alcobaça, in 1198. After this, Dargun moved to Eldena nearer to the bay, where the strong city of Greifswald gradually was established for its protection. However, Dargun was re-established in 1209 by Cistercians from Doberan. The link between Dargun and the mother monastery in Esrom seemed to have weakened during the first half of the 13th century, but it was well established initially.[73]

Very soon after Dargun, Colbatz was founded in 1173–1174 near Szczecin as part of the surrender of that town to Valdemar. Colbatz, too, was a daughter monastery of Esrom. Perhaps it belonged to the missionary area of the archdiocese in Lund, in contrast to Dargun which belonged under Bishop Absalon of Roskilde. Colbatz was to continue the historical annals which had been initiated in Lund, an important example of Cistercian historical writing in Scandinavia.[74] Furthermore, Jarimar established a Cistercian nunnery in the large, central town of Bergen on the island of Rügen in 1193, which was a daughter of a Cistercian nunnery in Roskilde. This is probably typical of the distribution: the nunnery was situated in the formerly heathen area, which was now completely under Christian rule and was organized into twelve parishes and with new churches. The monasteries for the men lay further to the East in the more dangerous religious frontier lands.

Despite the large geographical distances separating them, it appears that both Danish and Portuguese Cistercians approached the matter in the same way when they advanced out into the landscape in order to Christianize it in depth. This is not an accident, but is down to two reasons. One was that the Cistercians generally did what other missionaries and crusaders did, whether they belonged to an order or not – they worked on all levels at once. The other reason is the striking uniformity in everything the Cistercians did because of centralized and strong guidance and because of the high level of internal communication within the order.

Sanctification of the war

The Cistercian monasteries thus played a decisive role in reshaping the frontier land into a Christian landscape: symbolically with monastic buildings, churches and trees with crosses; practically with the cultivation of the land by Christian colonists.[75] But what was their idea with all this? How did they perceive the people, amongst whom the individual Cistercian brothers came out to work, and from whom most of them descended? We know nothing directly about this from any Nordic or Portuguese Cistercian sources. We might, however, gain a reasonably accurate sense of this by anticipating that they thought the same as St. Bernard – or that they at least knew of his views and discussed them when they were going out amongst the heathens. We know Bernard's thoughts on crusades from several texts.

The struggle for land and history   203

Around 1130, Bernard wrote his "Praise of the New Knighthood" – *De laude nove militie*.[76] He wished to support them with his pen, as it was impossible for him to fight with them. It was an important text on war in the service of faith and became an inspiration for later opinions on this matter. The phenomenon is new, Bernard writes. Never before has anyone combined the spiritual life with fighting, but now it has happened in the Holy Land itself, where God walked the earth but where the Devil now attacks with his infidels. Bernard wrote this with great conviction, even though it was not actually the case. The idea of fighting for the faith and of the struggle as a means of giving spiritual merit lies at the heart of Pope Urban II's crusade sermon from 1095. Others had already stressed that the innovation of the first crusade was that it consisted of giving the secular warriors an opportunity to continue their usual occupation by fighting, now in the service of God, and thus gaining a spiritual reward from fighting rather than spiritual punishment.

One of the paramount themes in Bernard's text to the Templars was martyrdom. "Fight with joy, die with joy, because you fight for God." "Rejoice, brave warrior, if you live and are victorious with the Lord, but rejoice even more if you die and follow the Lord," he wrote directly.[77] The new knight serves Christ when he wields his sword, but he also serves himself – his own good – when fighting, and when he falls and goes to heaven.

The Templars could be sure of the spiritual reward, because if one struggles for a good case, it can never be evil, and vice versa. If someone fights another man, he becomes a murderer, no matter who survives the struggle, as if even the will to kill the other man is enough to turn one into a murderer. The knights, on the other hand, do not fight other men, they fight against evil itself. Thus, when they kill, they are not killers of men but killers of evil; they are not *homocides* but *malocides*.[78] Yet, Bernard adds that the heathens are not to be slaughtered – that is the word he uses – if there are other possibilities. It is, however, better to slaughter them than to leave them to rule the just and lead them into injustice. This is exactly what the new knights are to fight against, and Bernard concludes confidently and urgently with a psalm quote: "The Lord is my strength and my refuge, and my salvation."[79] This is how the Cistercians discussed and perceived the infidel enemies, in Esrom as well as in Alcobaça, and it gives some sense of themes – of martyrdom and of genuinely humble and forceful chivalry in the hunt for Muslims or Wends, who have been consigned from the Cistercians to the local noblemen in the area. In Alcobaça, these were families: such as, first and foremost, the Sousa,[80] but also the slightly lesser influential Portocarreiro.[81] In Esrom it was Archbishop Eskil's family and in Sorø the eager crusaders, the Hvide family.[82] Everywhere it was families that were closely connected with the royal family.

Bernard was a nephew of one of the founders of the Knights Templar. He supported the Templars wholeheartedly and wrote a rule on their behalf, which was to become a model for other orders. In the following generations, several chivalric crusader orders emerged that followed the Cistercian rule. The largest and best known is probably the Calatrava order from Castile, which had houses everywhere on the Iberian Peninsula and even one in Prussia.[83] The Portuguese Évora order was founded in Alcobaça and was also organized in the Cistercian way. A later example of a military order with Cistercian rule is the Order of Christ, established in the early 14th century in Portugal on the remnants of the now abolished and banned Templar order; the Order of Christ continued the Knights Templar on the level of the individual knights.[84] All of these military orders sprang from an ideology and a mode of organization that was fundamentally Cistercian and were to be used in the crusades. Do similar local orders exist in Denmark? The sources are few and difficult to decipher, but the Confraternity of Canute, which had Canute Lavard as its patron saint, was militarized, had the king as a brother and his special attention and was spread throughout the Baltic region together with the crusades. The Cistercians would have had a special connection to Canute as they had the monastery in Dargun consecrated precisely on Canute's saint's day. If it is the names of the members of this military order that are preserved in the so-called List of Brethren, the membership included, as one would expect, the Hvide family on Zealand around the Cistercian monastery in Sorø. Perhaps this chapter of the order met in the copy of the Holy Sepulchre, which Ebbe Sunesen had erected shortly before 1170, in nearby Bjernede.[85]

However, Bernard also had a more practical role preaching and planning crusades.[86] After the fall of Edessa in 1144, he began, on the command of the Cistercian Pope Eugenius III, a large-scale tour of Germany and the Low Countries to

Figure 7.2 The round church of Bjernede on Zealand – one of the Danish copies of the Holy Sepulchre in Jerusalem. © Kurt Villads Jensen

The struggle for land and history   205

raise support for the Holy Land. The Saxon counts met him with the argument that there was no reason to travel to the Holy Land to fight the infidel when there were others just as infidel right beside them, that is, the heathen Slavic peoples. The struggle against them was thus placed alongside the crusades and considered just as meritorious as going to Jerusalem. This was not a new idea, but it was exactly what the Archbishop of Magdeburg had pleaded for in 1108, with military support of the Danish King Niels. What was new was Bernard's theological argument. The Devil was enraged because things were going so well for the Christians in the Holy Land that he had conceived a plan to stab Christendom in the back and attack in the North by letting the heathen peoples advance amongst the Christians.[87] This was, as far as it goes, nonsense, as things at that particular time were not going especially well for the Christians in the Holy Land. This did not seem to have made the argument less convincing, however. Because of this pincer movement the Devil had instigated, Bernard thought that fighting in the North in reality was a direct way of assisting Jerusalem. It was the same war on several fronts, including the Iberian Peninsula.

Bernard recruited the German King Conrad to the crusade in the Middle East. He made an intensive preaching tour in the Low Countries and organized an English–Frisian–Colognian expedition, which went to Portugal and joined Afonso Henriques' army and participated in the conquest of Lisbon in 1147.[88] In some way Bernard did prearrange this expedition with Afonso Henriques, so in a sense there is a grain of truth in the legend of the monastery of Alcobaça, which claimed that Bernard's miracle was behind the fall of Lisbon to the Christians, as mentioned earlier. It seems more doubtful whether it was Bernard who was behind the dispatching of a certain Cardinal Hubaldus, who arrived in Odense, Denmark, in 1146, in order to preach and to try to persuade the Danish king to participate in "the crusade of the Holy Bernard."[89] The Cardinal arrived too early for it to have been part of Bernard's preaching tour, but the subsequent Danish participation in the crusade to Dobin must have been influenced by the Bernardian crusade theology, not least by King Svend and King Canute's firm conviction of gaining martyrdom were they to fall fighting against the Wends.[90]

The point of this story of the years 1146–1147 is that it revolves around Bernard. Because of his personal charisma, he was able to persuade people to go on crusade. Thanks to the network of Cistercian monasteries and to supporters such as Eskil, Bernard was able to coordinate what happened in the individual countries and thus involve the whole western periphery of Europe in the crusade in 1147. Thanks to his pincer theology, it was established with great authority that the Baltic crusades were theologically just as meritorious as those to Jerusalem. And with regards to the heathen Wends, they were to be subject to the same treatment as the Muslims whom the Templars fought in the Middle East: they should be exterminated if there was any sign of them being able to harm the Christians.

The second crusade in the Middle East was military disaster.[91] After a futile and only three-day-long siege of Damascus, the Christian crusaders had to retreat without any military accomplishments whatsoever. This was explained in different ways at the time. Some thought that it was because of the Devil. Others

206   *The struggle for land and history*

suggested our sins, that is, that the participating crusaders did not solely intend to do good, that they also took part for more worldly reasons. Bernard argued in a completely different way. It had been a huge success, he thought, because so many Christians had died that the heavens were getting full. And those who had survived had earned hitherto unseen amounts of indulgence.[92]

Among other things, this has caused discussion on whether Bernard was the first to promise the believers indulgence for both penance and guilt, for both *poena* and *culpa*. After the confession, the repentant received absolution, the priest told him that God with this had ransomed him from sin. What remained was poena – the penance, which the Church placed on the sinner as a reminder of the sin – and culpa, the punishment for the sin, which God has measured out for the afterlife as a shorter or longer period in purgatory. By going on a crusade, one would escape the penance of the Church, poena. Bernard was brave enough to stand up and promise, on behalf of God, that the crusade, and the crusade only, would release the participant of culpa (the stay in purgatory).[93] Qualitatively, this is something else entirely. Releasing a sinner from the penance of the Church is something that the Church has the authority to do, without a doubt. Releasing a sinner from the punishment of God is presumably something that only God can do. However, this was the conclusion Bernard had reached, so this was what the Cistercians were able to promise the noblemen. Whether Bernard really was the first person to do so has been much discussed recently. Perhaps Urban II had already had this idea.[94]

Another idea that seems to have been an original innovation of Bernard's was the argument that so many incredibly large amounts of indulgence were given precisely during the second crusade because they were living in the *tempus acceptabilis*. This means they were living during the time that there will be acceptance of sinners by God. To Bernard it is the same as the Old Testament jubilee year with special grace. The idea of tempus acceptabilis was taken up later by Pope Alexander III and particularly by Innocent III, but apparently it cannot be traced back further than to Bernard.[95] Overall, it seems as if Bernard seriously believed that he lived in a time that was especially rich in grace. Therefore, it was also a particularly apocalyptic time, pregnant with the threat of the immediate arrival of the Antichrist and with a joyous expectation for the second coming of Christ. The day of judgement was near perhaps to Bernard and, therefore, it was important to get to Jerusalem now, as quickly and as safely as possible. There were two roads to Jerusalem. The best and the most secure route was still to enter a Cistercian monastery and reach the heavenly Jerusalem through prayer and meditation.[96] However, this was not a road everyone was able to walk. Some lacked the skill, others the will; some had commitments which they could not abandon. For them, the other way was created: the physical road to the earthly Jerusalem, the crusade. It is in the context of these two routes to Jerusalem that we should understand the establishment of many Cistercian monasteries under Bernard during the period from his praise of the Templars until his idea of a special time of grace during and after the second crusade. Both Esrom and Alcobaça were to be safe havens in the wilderness – a New Jerusalem for the many new monks. The others, those who did not have the strength to enter the monastery, should hear about the earthly

Jerusalem and should be persuaded to go on a crusade, which happened through the personal connections between noblemen and Cistercian monks.

With Bernard, a theologization of the noblemen's war took place which was felt not only in scholarly religious works and letters. The same tendency can be found in the secular narratives about the noble feats of warring ancestors, whom the noblemen were keen to emulate and live up to. In the age of the crusades, long dead heroes were transformed into warriors who had fought for the dissemination of the faith.

Sanctification of history – Charlemagne and Ogier the Dane

Charlemagne was the first crusader, and he initiated the *reconquista* of the Iberian Peninsula. This was the image which was cultivated of Charlemagne from the late 11th century and all through the 12th century, and which culminated in his canonization in 1165. Not only that, but there were rumours in the 1090s claiming that he had been resurrected and would lead the crusaders to Jerusalem.[97] From the early 12th century it had been incorporated as a fact in the liturgy at Santiago de Compostela that Charles had cleared the way of Muslims and had been the first pilgrim at the tomb of St. James, and that James had revealed himself in a vision to Charles after a road of stars had shown itself in the night sky, which stretched from the Frisian Sea over Germany and Italy all the way to Galicia. Charles was to march on this milky way with his army, James told him. Afterwards Charles conquered all of Spain and North Africa all the way to Carthage, the 12th-century narrative claims.[98] From the same period we have the first reports of him having been on a pilgrimage to Jerusalem and even having been offered the keys of Jerusalem as defender of the Holy Sepulchre.[99]

The narratives of Charlemagne are, just as many chivalric ballads from the 12th century, something we, with our modern sentiments, would class as pure fiction. During the Middle Ages people probably perceived it differently. There was not such a sharp distinction between what had really taken place and what ought to have taken place. And what ought to have taken place created a code for how to behave and perceive the surrounding world. The British historian Eric Hobsbawm introduced the term *invented traditions*, for which he set out certain criteria: the new "old" traditions must symbolize and create a group community, in this case crusaders; they must legitimize institutions and they must be comprehensive and include conceptions, conventions and social conventions.[100] With the cultivation of Charlemagne and his many feats, the crusading knights gained a mental assembly point, which placed their own participation in the crusades in a larger context and which simultaneously gave them an example to imitate. The ballads of chivalry created a social convention and a behavioural codex that had a strong impact, not least because they were perceived as being old, even though the ballads were actually quite new. This was probably not perceived as a pressing issue for the listeners, because even if Charlemagne's knights perhaps did not behave exactly as the proud knights of the ballads, at least they ought to have done so. And that was just as good.

208 *The struggle for land and history*

Charlemagne's great army in the Iberian Peninsula was made up of contingents from many regions in France and from many other countries. Among them were King Gayferus of Bordeaux with 3,000 heroes, King Gandelbodus of Friesland with 7,000 heroes, Duke Samson of Burgundy with 10,000 heroes and King Ogier of Denmark with 10,000 heroes. This latter is identical to Ogier the Dane from the *Chanson de Roland*. "Songs are still sung about this army today, because it did wondrous things," Turpin wrote in the early 12th century, and it was included in the liturgy at the pilgrimage church in Santiago.[101] Turpin is mentioned as the author in order to lend greater authority to the narrative – it is actually the name of Charlemagne's fighting archbishop from the *Chanson de Roland*, the one who rode a mighty horse, which he took after having defeated and killed the Danish King Grosaille.[102] After many long battles, Charlemagne divided the newly conquered territories between his loyal supporters. Navarre and the Basque country went to the English, the area around Zaragoza to the Greeks and the South Italians, Aragon to those from Poitiers, Al-Andalus in the sea to the Germans and Portugal to the Danes and the Flemings.[103] Denmark, Flanders and Portugal belonged together, and this was decided by Charlemagne himself, it was believed in the early 12th century. In the introduction of the large manuscript from the 12th century with the liturgy of Santiago de Compostela and the miracles of Santiago, it is stated directly that the material is derived from several countries, Denmark among them.[104]

The Danish pilgrims in Santiago would already have known the story of Charlemagne and Ogier the Dane, and most of those who travelled by land would have already visited Ogier's grave in the little town of Belin, not far from Bordeaux, where he lay in a common grave together with the king of Friesland, the king of Brittany and other heroes of Charles. The grave emitted a sweet scent, which healed the sick, one of the most widely known contemporary pilgrim's guides stated.[105] The Danes must nevertheless have been strangely affected by the atmosphere when they finally reached Santiago and inside the enormous building they listened to the story of Charlemagne and Ogier's journey along the starry road to the starry field – *campo stellae*, Compostella – at the outermost point of the world. Perhaps this explains why it seems that the Danes constituted one of the largest groups of pilgrims to Santiago, judging by the number of scallops from Santiago that the archaeologists have excavated in Denmark.[106]

During the 12th century the enthusiasm for Charlemagne grew, and the theme of his resurrection from the tomb and his intention to lead the crusader army to Jerusalem was developed.[107] Before Louis VII went on his crusade in 1147, he had embellished the Church of St Denis in Paris with large, new, stained-glass windows with scenes from the life of Charlemagne, as they were known from the liturgy of Santiago.[108] St Denis housed a collection of items from Charles, including chalices, relics and his own sword. On December 29, 1165, Charlemagne was canonized and his relics were transferred from Aachen, where his grave only recently had been discovered by a miracle, to the Church of St Mary in Cologne. The canonization itself had papal approval, although it came from the antipope, Paschal III, not from Alexander III. The initiative to try and have Charlemagne

The struggle for land and history   209

recognized as a saint came from King Henry II of England and Emperor Fredric Barbarossa. The saint's vita from that occasion was to a large degree based on the legend of Charlemagne, which was known from Santiago. At the same time, the *Chanson de Roland* was translated into German and spiced up with more direct references to crusades, and Henry the Lion was depicted as the new Charlemagne of the Baltic region.[109] The worship of Charlemagne continued. Around 1225, the Cathedral of Chartres was embellished with a series of beautiful stained-glass windows with scenes from the *Chanson de Roland* and with Charlemagne's sin and forgiveness – he had committed incest with his sister and was in reality the father of Roland, a later legend claimed. However, by becoming a crusader, Charles received absolution, even for such a heinous sin.[110]

The character of Charlemagne's loyal knight, Ogier, was developed as a warrior and crusader in literature during the 12th century. He was mentioned for the first time in the Chanson de Ronald from around 1060 or maybe slightly later, and from then he slipped into the liturgy at Santiago de Compostela, into pilgrim's guides to Santiago and, in 1165, into the vita of Charlemagne. In *Chanson de Roland*, Ogier is the Dane "with the short sword" or "the Dane from the other side of the sea," and he gets the command of the vanguard whilst Roland covered the rear guard and fell at Roncevalles. Ogier is only mentioned eight times in the long poem, where he is styled both count and duke but not king. He only became king in the later versions during the 12th century. By the end of the *Chanson de Roland* it is Ogier who urges the leaders of his group to attack the heathens (these leaders are Duke Tierri of Aragon and Duke Geoffrey of Anjou), regions which were amongst the most important suppliers of crusaders in the late 11th century. Ogier is the bravest of Charlemagne's warriors; he personally slays the heathen King Ambure and his dragon, and prevents Muhammad's banner from pushing further ahead.[111]

Ogier entered a monastery shortly after the first edition of the *Chanson de Roland*. This was in 1080. A short narrative about "The Conversion of Ogier the Knight"[112] originated around this year. Ogier had become the mightiest man in the empire of Charlemagne after the Emperor himself it is said, but at the height of his secular power he began to contemplate the frailty of life, and he called to mind the words of Christ: "If any man will come after me, let him deny himself, and take up his cross and follow me." He took up a pilgrim's staff furnished with iron bands. He then walked from monastery to monastery and pounded his staff against the paving in the monastery yard so that the frightened monks jumped up. Only at the monastery Feron in Meaux, about forty kilometres from Paris, were the monks so dedicated that they carried on praying and did not pay attention to Ogier's noise. This was the right monastery for Ogier, who then handed over his weapons as a pious gift to the monastery. He then took the monastic vow and put on a cowl. Before this, he had persuaded his old warrior comrade Benedict to become a monk, "because they had been together in so many killings of men that they now together should seek penance and expiate their sins." Ogier was covered in ash, he went thirsty and fasted in prayer and in tears, his holiness was confirmed by miracles and at his death the angels were jubilant because they are

210   *The struggle for land and history*

more pleased with the conversion of a single sinner than with more than a hundred righteous ones.

The story of Ogier's conversion is an addition from around 1080 to the monastery's miracle narrative about Bishop Faro of Meaux, who lived in the 9th century.[113] At that time, Scandinavians pillaged the Carolingian Empire; they even sailed up the Seine, where they laid siege to Paris and demanded tribute. In 860, "the sea belched forth an even larger wave of Scandinavians," who continued up the Seine all the way to Meaux, where they were pillaged. Earth and air were torn by the lament of the pregnant and of suckling children, and the golden stars perished in the consumption of the greedy flames. The monastery was set alight, but Bishop Faro arrived, extinguished the fire, and all traces of the fire disappeared miraculously. At this point, the narrative continues with the story of Ogier's conversion. In this way, it becomes a success story. The heathen Scandinavians were defeated; Ogier is not only a Christian but becomes a monk and an ascetic who performs miracles.

At the same time, Ogier is obviously a crusader. He received the epithet *preliator fortis et pugnator*, the strong giant and fighter, because of his strength and bravery and he was an *athleta Christi*, a warrior for Christ – all were designations with obvious biblical undertones and standard vocabulary in crusade rhetoric. This is also conveyed with the information about the pilgrim's staff and how he would take up his cross and follow Christ. Perhaps the author of the miracle narrative had heard Pope Urban's crusade sermon with those exact words, or – if the narrative stemmed actually from before Urban's sermon – it was simply in the air.

Ogier remained a popular saint at Feron, and in around 1180, the monastery had an enormous mausoleum made with two statues on top, one of Ogier with his pilgrim's staff and one of Benedict, each about 2.6 metres tall. That Ogier was also said to have been buried in Belin on the pilgrimage route to Santiago does not seem to have worried the monks in Felon. Around the mausoleum stood six stone figures, among them Roland and Bishop Turpin. It must have been a popular pilgrimage destination for Danish students in nearby Paris; perhaps the new sepulchre was admired by the young Anders Sunesen, later Danish archbishop and crusader legate of the Baltic region. Montaigne wrote in his travel diary in 1580 that Ogier's sword was in the mausoleum, bruised and scratched from much use.[114] During the French Revolution this cultural artefact disappeared totally; only Ogier's head was preserved, and today it is exhibited at the local museum.

At the same time, Ogier appeared in more and more chivalric ballads of the period.[115] The *Cycle de Guillaume* from around 1160 consists of three separate ballads. One relates the story of the heathen monster, the giant Ysoré of Coimbra in Portugal, who is killed by the hero Guillame. In another ballad, which is only known from incomplete fragments, Ysoré has become a Saxon and attacks to avenge his father, who was killed by Ogier. Consistency and historical precision are prioritized in these ballads, but as a whole, the Cycle de Guillaume demonstrates that an idea of some kind of a connection between Denmark and Portugal existed during the middle of the 12th century, a connection which went via Ogier the Dane.

The struggle for land and history   211

The earliest ballads of chivalry which have Ogier the Dane as a protagonist originated in around 1195. The very first, which is only known from references in other ballads, concerns the great duel between Ogier and the Muslim Carauel. This must be the Kurdish commander of Acre, with the Turkish name Karakos, "the Black Eagle." After Saladin's victory at Hattin in 1187 and his conquest of Jerusalem, Karakos held Acre for a long time against an army under the King of Jerusalem, Guy de Lusignan, with reinforcements of Sicilians, Italians, Frisians and Danes. It was the preface to the less-than-glorious third crusade which ended with Richard the Lionheart's peace with Saladin in 1192.

The ballads about Ogier originated in Paris, some in Flanders, and were written in around 1200. They recount how Ogier arrived at the court of Charlemagne as a hostage from his father, King Gudfred of Denmark, but also how he grew up to become one of Charles's mightiest warriors, who came to his help in the fight against the heathens. Right from the beginning Ogier is described as a real crusader, *li Danois d'outre mer*, the Dane from Outremer, the French term for the land on the other side of the ocean – the Holy Land.[116] Many themes are developed in thousands of verses of the ballads. One is the conflict between Ogier and Charles's son Karlot, who kills Ogier's son with a chess piece during a game of chess and has to go to the Holy Land and serve the Templars to atone for his sin.[117] Another is the figure of Karakos; having been the commander of Acres he becomes King of India and a prototype of the noble and chivalrous heathen. Karakos' fiancée, Gloriande, falls in love with Ogier but ends up staying with her heathen husband. Most of the story takes place in a distant Rome in the 9th century, which has been conquered by Muslims, just as Jerusalem had been in 1187. Ogier is, rightly or wrongly, accused of having breached his loyalty to Charlemagne and has to fight; he even kills Baldwin of Flanders. He is eventually overpowered and is thrown in prison, and everybody thinks that he has died from hunger and thirst – he eats as much as five ordinary knights and drinks heavily. However, when the empire of Charlemagne comes under threat, Ogier comes forward and fights again for the faith. Every horse he mounts sinks under his weight, but then his faithful horse Broiefort, who had dragged stones in the monastery of Meaux, is found, and he is able to ride out and be victorious.[118] Eventually, Ogier marries an English princess and receives much land in Flanders as a gift from Charles.

Opinion on the literary quality of the ballads about Ogier has been varied. In 1950, one of the great experts of medieval literature compared them to American crime novels: commercial rubbish, which appealed to the lowest instincts of the reader.[119] The figure of Ogier has become almost grotesque with his enormous size, which forces horses to their knees, and with his immense appetite and thirst. A disproportionately large number of the verses in the ballads consist of more and especially less refined descriptions of battles and killings, killings and yet more killings. He represents an ancient Germanic race from the dark forests with his butchery, a French scholar wrote in 1842.

Some literary scholars have even suggested that "the Dane" is not a geographical epithet, but only means "barbarian."[120] This sounds a bit derisory but may have a point in that the size of Ogier perhaps only recounts the common contemporary

212 *The struggle for land and history*

stereotypical perception of Danes or Scandinavians – big and brave but not especially clever warriors, whose bodies are filled with blood because of the cold in the North, as Urban described them in his sermon at Clermont. But all ends well. Ogier ends up helping Charles defeat the infidels. Thus, the Ogier figure does not turn into a parody or become grotesque, rather it turns into a versified and courtly version of the theological perception of the crusades in the early 12th century: They were a joint Christian enterprise, in which everyone participated, no matter how barbaric they were. Now, however, there was the difference that the barbarian actually had a military impact. This comes in contrast to the image that Guibert of Nogent gave in 1108 of barbarians with hopelessly obsolete weapons that were only able to help with their prayers.

The Danes of course knew of the stories about Ogier the Dane, even though it is not until 1260 that he is mentioned in a Danish source, the Annals of Lund, where his name is rendered as Ozsyari.[121] At that time, the narratives about Charlemagne and his warriors had been translated into Icelandic in the form of an anthology, a package deal with all the most important texts in one place. There were excerpts from the French ballads about Ogier, the most important passages from the Santiago liturgy, the story of Charles's pilgrimage to Constantinople and Jerusalem, the battle of Roncevalles from the *Chanson de Roland* and a few others. A Danish translation is known from around 1480, *Karl Magnus' Krønike*, which contains more excerpts than the Icelandic edition, and has been translated in a different way. The idea is the same, however: to create an anthology of texts on Charles. The Danish translation belongs to a different tradition from the Icelandic one and may very well go back much further than the earliest preserved manuscript from the late 15th century.[122]

Ogier the Dane apparently lived to a very old age. This is reported by Albert of Trois-Fontaines, who wrote in the middle of the 13th century and was very knowledgeable about Danish matters. In 1210, "a very frail and ancient knight came from the Iberian Peninsula; he said that he was the Ogier the Dane, about whom is told in the History of Charlemagne, and that his mother was a daughter of Theoderic of Ardenne. He died that very year in the see of Saint-Patrice in Nevers, according to both ecclesiastics and laypeople who saw him."[123] The literature about Ogier the Dane was still being developed nevertheless on a still larger scale. During the Middle Ages, he became a kind of a messianic helper who was to come forth and save the Christian world in the final, decisive apocalyptic battle. Since the 19th century at the latest, he became a figure of national salvation who sleeps so deeply in the bottom of the casemates at Elsinore Castle that his beard has grown through the stone table. When Denmark is in danger, he shall wake up, tear himself loose and save the country.

The many stories about Charlemagne, Ogier the Dane and the other heroes in the chivalric ballads were disseminated far and wide from the middle and the end of the 12th century. They show a deliberate attempt to furnish the crusade movement with a solid historical foundation, and they are interesting due to the fact that they are so very international. The stories have been handed down in complete manuscripts or in fragments from several Western European countries and have contributed to creating a common perception of how a crusading knight was really supposed to be. The fact that one of the greatest heroes was Danish might not be so important in itself but at least it demonstrates that Denmark, from a crusade viewpoint, was not perceived as a peripheral part of Europe. Finally, these ballads are interesting because they crossed literary boundary lines; they were utilized in the liturgy in Santiago de Compostela; they were entertainment at the princely courts; and they were found in crusade sermons and in historical writings about the crusades. Since the stories about Ogier the Dane were so widely known, it is odd that Saxo apparently does not mention him.

Saxo's Ogier the Dane – Starkad?

The greatest Danish narrative by far from this era is Saxo's work on the feats of the Danes from around 1200. It is a meticulous composition. Many issues are skipped or simply discreetly ignored. This applies to the Cistercians, who otherwise were the favourite order of Saxo's patron, Bishop Absalon. Apparently, it also applies to the story of Ogier the Dane, but only seemingly. He appears in a completely different context and under a different name, Starkad or Stærkodder.

There seems to have been two motives behind Saxo's selection and presentation of his material. One is a consistent archaic style, which is – as much as possible – cleansed from Medieval Latin and ecclesiastical terms and rewritten with classical silver Latin expressions. Perhaps Saxo could not come up with a good classical word for Cistercians? The other motive is an attempt to depict Denmark as an expansive and powerful realm which had always been independent: a North European parallel to the classical Roman Empire, all the way down to details such as the elaborate description of the long era of peace during the reign of Frotho (Frode Fredegod), who was a contemporary of Emperor Augustus. Thus, Saxo did not utilize directly the crusader themes of his time, but only referred to them indirectly and rewrote them in classical terms.

Starkad was a giant, just as Ogier the Dane, and he also came from a distant place in the periphery – now as seen from Denmark – so Starkad came from the lands east of Sweden, which are "now inhabited by Estonians and other barbaric peoples."[124] At birth, he was larger and stronger than any other human, and he would yield to no man with regards to bravery. This is why his name is well known until this very day, Saxo wrote, amongst Swedes and Saxons. Starkad was, just as Ogier, an unlucky hero in the contemporary ballads who betrays his master but who is nevertheless there when it is necessary. He has been given an unusually long life, three ordinary human lives, but in each of his lives he is bound to commit an outrage and to kill his master.

Just like Ogier the Dane, Starkad is a roving character who fights and wins glory in Russia, Byzantium, Scandinavia and Ireland. Starkad's many feats are soaked in blood. Innumerable enemies are cut down and at the same time are mocked with insulting poems. "[T]o fight without fear is the most noble conduct; rest and peace is the most bloody shame; to slay, to shed streams of blood, I always perceived the greatest," he admits.[125]

Starkad is as conscious of social class as only a medieval knight could be. During one of his many fights – against nine warriors – he is wounded such that

214   *The struggle for land and history*

his intestines are hanging from his bowel. Slaves and women, one after the other, pass by and offer to bandage him, but he refuses them with contempt. Only when the son of a free man passes by does Starkad have his intestines put back and his wound bandaged.

Saxo's chronology is difficult to follow, but with Starkad, Saxo seems to be in the 5th–6th century, so he is certainly not a Christian knight. Most importantly, however, he is one of Saxo's great moral figures. Starkad must have been somewhat exhausting to be near, as he criticizes everyone for being soft, eating delicious food, dressing too finely, being effeminate or listening to women or for enjoying theatre and entertainment. Meanwhile he praises good old-fashioned virtues: the simple life, tilling the land and simple food. The catalogue of errors is extensive and is in many ways similar to the crusade literature of the 12th century with its depiction of the lack of morals in the crusader army. Defeats during the crusades happened *peccatis nostris exigentibus*, because our sins demand it. With the crusades, warfare had become a moral issue where the military outcome depended on whether the warriors kept to the narrow path of virtue and eschewed sin. Starkad thus clearly reflects the thoughts of the 12th century on warfare, which Saxo places a long way back in history – in a distant past – in order to take possession of history, to sanctify it or at least to make it morally true. And, in this way, he prepares for the narrative's further logical progression, which culminates in the crusade of Valdemar the Great in the Baltic region.

The most important reason for Saxo to simply ignore Ogier the Dane would have been his peculiar nationalism and general dislike of everything German. To write about a Danish hero in the service of Charlemagne would probably have almost hurt Saxo physically. This is why he transplants Ogier to a more distant past and merges him with the Starkad figure, of whom he would at least have known the name, possibly from Icelandic sources. Nevertheless, the widely diffused narratives about Charlemagne also resonated with Saxo and he utilized them elegantly.

Charlemagne is mentioned in three places in all of Saxo's work. The first is under King Gudfred or Gøtrik, who had subdued the Saxons, demanded taxes from them and then marched against Charles, who withdrew to the far side of the Rhine. Charles was called to Rome by the Pope because heathens attacked the city, and luckily for him, Gudfred was assassinated.[126] In the second place, Saxo recounts how Charles and his mighty army, which had won such great and brilliant victories everywhere, had to give up when facing the Danish King Regnar Lodbrok's small and badly equipped band of warriors.[127] The third place is much later in Saxo's account, during the Danish siege of the heathen castle and temple Arkona on Rügen, in 1168. King Valdemar the Great tells his army that the castle will fall soon, sooner than they think. This, he says, is because the "Rügians once long ago had been defeated by Emperor Charlemagne and he had imposed a tax to the sacred martyr Vitus of Corvey on them."[128] When Charles died, they lapsed from the faith and had an idol made of Vitus, which they were worshipping.[129]

This is all that was needed to turn Rügen in the North into a parallel of Spain and of similar religious importance, if the audience happened to be familiar with the *Chanson de Roland*. Charles conquered the Iberian Peninsula in the South and

The struggle for land and history 215

he conquered the Slavic island in the North. In both places, the population was converted to Christianity but lapsed and reverted to worshipping idols of Muhammad or Svantevit. In both places, eager crusader kings walked in the footsteps of Charlemagne and continued or resumed the reconquest, the *reconquista*. And in both cases we are dealing with an invented tradition. Charles did not get any further than the northernmost areas of the Iberian Peninsula, and nothing suggests that he was ever even near to Rügen. But he could have been, and if so, he would have conquered the island and made the inhabitants Christian. Therefore, Saxo probably perceived his narrative as almost true, certainly far from pure fiction.[130] However, it is characteristic of the genre that Saxo writes within that the story of Emperor Charles in Rügen is his very own addition. It is found neither in Adam of Bremen nor in Helmold of Bosau, whose works Saxo knew and utilized in his depiction of early Danish history.

Where did Saxo get it from? He would have been able to hear the *Chanson de Roland* and the ballads of Ogier the Dane anywhere, in Paris and probably in Denmark as well. They constituted part of the *Zeitgeist*. Moreover, it is in fact possible to point to a place where the texts may have been and where Saxo may have visited and collected material. As Starkad is about to fight one of his many unequal fights, this time against a berserker, he rests on a rock, which has had an obvious imprint of him ever since. This is, Saxo writes, at Roliung. This is also the place where Starkad finally died, after having had his head cut off so that it rolled across the ground and bit hard in the grass. Some scholars have suggested that this Roliung is situated near the Cistercian monastery of Herrisvad in Scania, which had been founded by Eskil, the archbishop who was familiar with the *Chanson de Roland*, in 1144. Perhaps Herrisvad was a centre for the traditions of Starkad, and its fine library no doubt had stories of Roland as well as ballads of Ogier the Dane, which it may have loaned to Saxo. He was then able to make his own interpretation and transform the crusade stories in accordance with his own ideas.[131] The Cistercians were important to the crusades, not only with regard to the practical organization but also by recounting the narratives about the crusaders and heroes of the past and having them written down on parchment. This was the case in Denmark, as well as in Europe.

Portuguese crusade history, between God's will and the dragon of the Apocalypse

Portugal lacks a great historical narrative which spans hundreds of pages, such as Saxo's, nevertheless it is obvious that during precisely those years, a deliberate revision of history was undertaken so that it became centred on crusades – very much in the spirit of the time.[132] The writings are relatively short, but when taken together they show an obvious trend: warfare became more sacred and the opponents more implacable.

> Let us sing praise to the Lord, my dear brothers, let us sing Him praise with drums and choir, and let us rejoice in our innermost heart and laud Him with

216   *The struggle for land and history*

voices. The Lord is indeed exalted, when radiantly He threw the heathens who worship Muhammad down before your feet, and He has chosen for us the most precious inheritance, which He loved. And you, you willingly exposed your souls to danger, on bare feet you reach out for spear and shield, you buckle your belt and placed wooden ladders on shoulders, and from the top of the mountains you hurry towards the wall. Call on the people to praise Christ, clap your hands, sing Him a good song and shout with a loud voice: "Listen, you kings, and lend your ear, princes of all the Earth, for the Lord has chosen new wars in our time."

Afonso Henriques conquered Santarém, not with 318 men, as Abraham had, not with 300 as Gideon, but with 125 or even fewer. And it is worth noticing that it is not Afonso but God Himself who, through the Portuguese king, took possession of the most strongly defended city on the Iberian Peninsula. This happened not by the acts of Afonso, but by God to whom all of earth belongs.

In this way begins the history of the conquest of Santarém,[133] written in the monastery of Santa Cruz in Coimbra around 1185, the year of the death of King Afonso, but also contemporary with the Danish history by Svend Aggesen. Not only is the narrative kept in a highly rhetorical style, it also contains many fine minor details, which have made Portuguese historians think that the anonymous author must have participated in Afonso's crusade of 1147 or at least heard the King's description of the events. Danish historians thought the same of Saxo and his description of Valdemar's conquest of Arkona, and of course this is not impossible. On the other hand, it might just be a great writer's dramatic setting of an exciting story. Most important in this context is the perception that the author tries to convey, rather than whether the events unfolded exactly as he claims.

Afonso narrates the description of the strong fortifications of Santarém, which are built by Christian prisoners of war, and of the immense lushness of the region, claiming that is as great as that of Apulia: a land that does not flow with milk and honey but with wine and olive oil. This gave the Muslims a base from which they repeatedly attacked Coimbra and, therefore, it was necessary to wage war against them, as a just defence. With his 120 men from Coimbra, Afonso rides against Santarém to discover from which side it would be easiest to attack. They build ten ladders in order to be able to mount the wall in ten places at once. The first man on the top shall raise the King's banner on the wall and then they shall fight their way to the city gate as quickly as possible, destroy the bar and open the gate for the other warriors. "Tell me, for the love of God, whether it ought to be hard to kill naked and sleepy Muslims? Be sure not to spare anyone, neither because of age nor gender. The baby who clings to the breast shall die, and so shall those old and full of years, and the young woman and the infirm old woman. Trust the labour of your hands, for the Lord is with you and each of you can kill a hundred." Thus, the total extermination of the Muslim population is a good and necessary thing, and when the battle commences, the warriors must remember that at the same time mass and prayers will be said for them in the monastery of Santa Cruz.

The struggle for land and history 217

The battle takes on almost cosmic dimensions, because there shall come, Afonso predicts, a burning star on the right side of the sky, which will fall into the sea and light up the surface of the earth intensely, "and the Lord delivers the city in our hands." Furthermore, the Muslims in Santarém shall receive a marvellous sign as well: In the middle of the day they shall see a snake of iron, which fills half of the sky and is ablaze from tail to head, and their wise men shall predict that Santarém will have a new king. The images of the Apocalypse are turned against the Muslims. Precisely during the final years of the 1180s, there seems to have been a strong interest in the Apocalypse in Portugal, as far as it is possible to assess from surviving manuscripts.

It happened as Afonso had predicted, and while invoking Santiago and the Virgin Mary, they succeed in mounting the wall and opening the city gate, where Afonso fell to his knees and thanked God for the glorious victory.

At the same time around 1185, brief notes were collected from the annals about the life of Afonso Henriques. They were edited and presented in a new and clearer format.[134] This happened at the monastery of Santa Cruz a short time after the death of Afonso, and was conceived as homage to the old warrior. The annals have simply been turned into a long narrative about conquests, wars and constant Muslim attacks, which Afonso heroically averted, a story about Ourique, Santarém and Lisbon. There has always been a war going on against the Muslims – that is the overriding message of the narrative.

During the last years of Afonso's life, one of the canons at the cathedral in Lisbon collected the miracles of St. Vincent. There were many different kinds of miracles, but they were all put into a frame of reference, which was saturated with crusades. "The scripture shows that those kings who rule justly are happy, and nothing it is said, promotes human matters more than if by God's mercy those who have power also lead the people with insight."[135] Thus begins the collection of miracles. What it means to rule justly and to lead the people with insight is explained immediately. "The bravery of King Afonso is glorious, and he has used his power to extend the Church with so many wars that neighbouring kings and the Muslim enemies would rather keep the peace with him than wage war, even though he is now older in age, as well as in mind." The last remark suggests that Afonso's head did not escape unharmed from the incident at the city gate of Badajoz. However, this does not have any consequence for the aim of the miracle collection: it is the duty of a just king to wage constant war against the Muslims and thereby extend Christianity, and it is the duty of the saint to support the king in this undertaking. St. Vincent is described as an *athleta Christi*, a warrior of Christ, one of the common terms for a crusader in the 12th century.

Another crusade text was written in around 1185, the account of the establishment of the monastery of St. Vincent in Lisbon.[136] It recounts the conquest of Lisbon in 1147, when Afonso Henriques "assembled his army against the Muslims, as he used to do every year." There were 180 ships known as barks that arrived for his assistance from the countries in the North, and warriors had come to Portugal to die for Christ by fighting His war and by struggling valiantly against the enemies of the faith. The encircled Muslims were attacked vehemently from land

218   *The struggle for land and history*

as well as from the sea, and at some point, Afonso swore that "if God gives us, His servants, this city and if it pleases Him to exterminate these infidels from the surface of the earth, then He shall know that I, as His servant, will establish two monasteries."[137] In the end, the Muslims of Lisbon have to surrender themselves and the city because the Christian attacks were overwhelming – the defenders did not get a single moment of rest and soon thereafter as many of them fell victim to hunger and thirst as to the Christian swords.[138]

The conquest of Lisbon was depicted strikingly differently by the English–French Raol, who wrote immediately after the event, to the Portuguese account which came almost forty years later. Raol does not make a secret of the major disagreements amongst the different contingents of the crusader army, and especially those from Cologne were difficult. In the hands of the Portuguese author, the story is about a common, Christian front against the Muslims. All the crusaders work together, and there is a unity and solidarity that reaches beyond death. The knight Henry from Cologne was buried at the cemetery of St. Vincent and soon a series of miracles took place by his tomb. Not only did he haunt a priest three times, but he finally had to lay threats before his old squire, who fell in the crusade, was moved and buried right by the side of his master. It was even more wondrous that he healed two young deaf people, who had been mute right from birth and had arrived as pilgrims at his grave, but who were French! Henry had appeared before them and spoke to them. "How much more wondrous, is it not that they, who were from different countries and nations, were now also given the ability to speak another language [than German]."[139] That a German saint could help a French deaf-mute was apparently not something one would expect immediately and thus it made the miracle even greater. And it emphasized the Christian unity in the crusader army.

The crusades implied conquest and domination, of the land and of the heathens who lived there, but also of history. It was peopled with warriors who had waged crusades a long time before the first crusade, and the crusaders could learn from those and emulate them. The historical examples provided confidence and certainty that the crusader was on the right course.

Ships

Scyld of Denmark

Once upon a time, a ship came sailing towards the Danish coast with all sails set but without either rowers or helmsman. Only a little infant was on board on a bed of sheaves and surrounded by gold and treasure. He grew up and became the mighty King Scyld, the ancestor of the Danish royal family known as the Scyldings. He died when he was old and full of years after having fought many wars, earning a reputation as a generous lord who shared gold with his men and who had many strong and proud warriors in his hall. His faithful men laid him on a ship covered in ice near the mast and piled up treasures around him, which were no smaller than those that he had brought with him as an infant. Then they raised a banner woven with gold above him, pushed the ship out to sea and let it sail by itself. "No man in the hall, no man under heaven can say for certain who received such cargo."

Thus narrates the English poem Beowulf from the early 8th century.[140] The story of King Scyld is known by most Danes to this day because of the popular ballad by the romantic poet B. S. Ingemann. It was written in 1834, as the Danes gathered to praise the national past and the memory of great figures which guarded Denmark in troubled times:

> Once upon a time in the olden days,
> The Danish people lacked a king,
> The good people wept and the wicked ones laughed
> Where no fences are, only thorns can grow.
> Then a ship came with all sails set,
> With a lion's-head and hearts a-stern,
> With gold and weapons and treasure on board,
> But not a soul, neither at the mast nor at the helm.

King Scyld arrived on a ship and saved Denmark. So much did people know in Denmark in the 19th and the 20th century and in England in the 8th century. However, it was also known in the 12th century in England, where this part of the story of Beowulf is preserved in English historical works.

The Danish sources from the crusading period knew of King Scyld as one of the first Danish kings. However, they only tell us that he was incredibly strong, but there is no mention of the ship and the little child. That is strange. It fits so well with the image of Denmark as being dependant on the sea and on warships, which permeates the histories of Saxo and Svend Aggesen. The latter quickly continues his short royal history from around 1185 by telling of Scyld's grandson Frode and especially of his exploits leading a fleet that cleansed the Danish waters of pirates. This is a recurring theme with both Svend and Saxo, and it demonstrates how important naval warfare was to the Danes in the Middle Ages.

Because of Denmark's particular geography, the rulers were completely dependent on the constant development of naval technology and of being able to control the social institutions that governed the leadership and the manning of the ships. During the High Middle Ages, naval warfare was well developed and regulated in Denmark. We know of detailed rules concerning equipment and conscription of men, which were written down in provincial laws from the 13th century but presumably date back even further.[141]

Denmark was divided into *skipen*, each of which supplied one ship and each was normally subdivided into forty-two *havne*. The free inhabitants with land and sufficient economic surplus to equip themselves with weapons had a duty to jointly supply one man to the ship. They were organized in a "havne confraternity"; the term alone suggests religious, military content. The physical pulling of oars and fighting was done in turn according to a predetermined rota. A havne brother was required to present himself in person or send his son.[142] If the havne

220   *The struggle for land and history*

brother attempted to cheat by sending just a slave, the slave would immediately be confiscated by the King, or even worse: he could be set free. If it had been agreed beforehand, the havne brother could send his farmhand, but if it had not been arranged, the farmhand would lose his skin. Other provincial laws had simpler rules: anyone other than the havne brother himself or his son would have his ears cut off and be sent back. The ships were nevertheless allowed to carry up to four slaves to cook en route and bale the boat dry, Erik's Zealand Law decided.[143]

The individual ship was commanded by a styresman, who was one of the noblemen; the office was hereditary. The styresman was supposed to pay for his own horse and armour but received some compensation, though only during the years that crusades or other wars were declared. The styresman was required to take all his equipment; besides the horse, this amounted to a crossbow and arrows. If he could not shoot with it himself, it was his duty to take along one man to operate it. When these laws were passed in Denmark, synods and canon law had energetically attempted to ban the use of crossbows against anyone but heathens. In practice, the attempt was a failure, and in practice, Christian princes used their crossbowmen against other Christian princes as well. However, to establish a corps of crossbowmen through public laws and with backing from the Church is almost impossible to imagine, unless this corps was to fight against heathens. This army organization must have been, from its very concept, a crusade organization.

It was also most likely to have been the duty of the styresmen to assemble the warriors and lead them to the fleet's rendezvous point when a crusade was called. Saxo describe how "all those who had responsibility for the crusade confraternity" went so fast to the meeting point that they arrived at the prearranged time or even before.[144] All the havne brothers had to equip themselves with a shield and the three "peoples' weapons," sword, helmet and spear – just as was the case of the members of the town militias in Denmark.[145]

The system of naval warfare also had rules regarding the building of ships, and not least concerning who was to pay, and how. The brothers in a skipen had to defray the expenses of the ship and its equipment and shields but it was to be built by the styresman. If he estimated that there was too little money, the brothers had to build the ship themselves and thus demonstrate that the sum was sufficient – or they would have to cover the shortfall themselves! When the ship was finished, the men were to pull it in the water on a set date and pull it back on land after the expedition. According to the Norwegian Gulating law from the 12th century, each havne brother had responsibilities for his own piece in the puzzle that made up a fully equipped ship – some had the responsibility for the mast, others for the keelson and others for each board plank – and there were rules regarding the cost of each part and each board. The Gulating law also stipulated that the sails were to be stored in the churches. This would have been a practical measure, but it was also a reminder of the connection between warfare and religion.[146] Where the Danish sails were stored for the winter is not known, but church lofts are a reasonable guess. If so, there would have been sails in more than every other church.

Several place names in Denmark contain the word "snekke-" and have been in use during the 12th century, and those names most probably refer to places where

The struggle for land and history 221

the ships were stored.[147] They are spread evenly over the whole country. The crusades therefore were present in a physical and obvious way in even the smallest local communities. Everybody knew where their ship was located, and they would have used winter and early spring to prepare it, repair and tar it; discuss who was to go on a crusade this year and what it would all lead to. This crusade army was a military organization, but to a similar degree, it was an ideological organization too, due to the close geographical coverage and to all the labour that went into keeping a ship ready for action. Crusades were not a distant phenomenon amongst noblemen; they were an everyday feature to most people.

There are examples from the early 12th century that the duty to take physical part in naval warfare was commuted, either as a special privilege or for payment in cash, which could then be used for hiring mercenaries. Presumably, the commutation became increasingly common with time, as seems to have been the case generally in all of Western Europe with the professionalization of warfare in the 13th century. Yet, the detailed rules in Danish laws as late as the Jutland Law from 1241 are evidence that the general fleet under royal command was still an important military machine throughout the 13th century.

The Nordic word for this particular organization of naval warfare is "leidang," which was translated into Latin as *expeditio* – which in the 12th century very often meant crusade – at times it was just a military expedition, but it was always an aggressive undertaking. Saxo used the term *expeditio* ninety-three times in his work, but only five times in the sections concerning the long, heathen prehistory. Eighty times *expeditio* is something which took place during the rule of Valdemar the Great. Thus, *expeditio* is not some loose term for any military undertaking; it is obviously connected to Valdemar and his wars against the heathen Wends. It is a technical term, and it appears to make obvious sense to translate it as *crusade*.

Much calculation has been done to estimate the size of the crusade fleet. If we conservatively estimate that the number of skipen is around 1,000, then the crusader army could have been comprised of perhaps 40,000 men in total. Besides, the 1,000 skipen would have supplied 1,000 horsemen under the command of the King, but would been have paid for by the havne brothers.[148] Then the number of ships and men held by the King and the noblemen as their private fighting force must be added. According to the annals of Ryd and Ribe, King Valdemar II the Victorious conquered Estland in 1219 with a fleet of 1,500 ships.[149] It is not impossible that the figure is correct.

Sea battles

Almost all sea battles took place near the coast, and sometimes it was difficult to simply establish where the enemy ships were located. With a little fog, it was possible for a small ship to sneak around islands and islets, right next to the bank under the foliage of trees, and if the crew was lucky, it might have been possible to get near to the enemy ship without being detected. In this way, the heathen Jomsvikings succeeded in boarding the royal ship in the midst of the fleet and in abducting King Svend, Saxo narrates.[150]

222 *The struggle for land and history*

When two fleets met at sea, the sky became dark with stones. The most important weapon at first was the sling, which was used to send hundreds of stones towards the enemy with great force. The sling was an effective weapon and with some practise, it was very precise, and the thought of David's successful shot at Goliath probably strengthened the medieval crusaders. Importantly, the sling was cheap. Bows and crossbows were probably only used when close up, as the arrows would have been far too expensive to lose in the sea. The sling used only stones of a suitable size, and they could be found in several places. Saxo tells how the Danish crusaders usually put in at the cliffs of Stevns to collect pebbles from the beach. The pebbles there were particularly rounded and were well suited as ammunition for the slings.[151]

When the ships were close, the soldiers would attempt to board the enemy ship. This was a dangerous moment. The manoeuvrability had to be as high as possible in order to moor alongside the other ship at the best place, but at the same time, just a small difference in height could be decisive. This is one reason for the ships getting increasingly larger over time. Another is that the crusades after the Danish conquest of Rügen in 1168 went further east in the Baltic, all the way to Estonia and Finland. That too demanded larger ships, and it particularly demanded ships that were made especially for transporting horses. Finally, ships generally became longer and larger everywhere in Europe during the latter half of the 12th century.[152] From around that time, the first cog-type ships were developed; they were able to hold much more cargo than earlier types. They were conceived and built completely differently from the long ships – broader, larger, more solid and slower.[153] The new, large ships were a precondition for the Danish crusades being able to extend further east from around 1200.

Right from the beginning, there was direct, royal interest in the new war technology, as we know from the launching of one of the earliest large ships. It almost ended in disaster. The ship was built in Schleswig by a society of which King Valdemar the Great was also a member. During the launch – this happened in 1173 at the latest – it simply stood on the sandbanks and could not be brought afloat. It was in danger of breaking up, simply because it was so large. Luckily, the ship builder had the idea of praying to the new martyr of 1171, Thomas Becket, to "lift this machine," and the ship got off the ground. It was one of the earliest miracles of Thomas; hence it was written down and is known today.[154] Archaeology can supplement sparse and random written material. Several ships of the cog type, built between 1150 and 1180, have been found. It has also been established through extensive analysis that at least three of those large ships came from the same place, near Haderslev in South Jutland.

The large ships were likely used for trade, but they were very much military ships too. They were not only able to carry large numbers of horses, soldiers and provisions – and plunder and slaves in enormous quantities – but in open sea battles, they had great advantage over traditional long ships by being taller. In a large, long ship, the gunwale stood roughly ninety centimetres above sea level; on the larger ships, it was almost two metres or even higher.[155] In ship-to-ship fighting, it would have been a huge advantage to fight from large ships. The advantage was

The struggle for land and history **223**

to become greater yet, as the large ships had a tower built on top of the vessel itself.[156]

Demands of both speed and height were incompatible, and the crusaders had to choose between easily manoeuvrable small, fast ships with a low gunwale, or increasingly larger ships with increasingly higher gunwale, which were difficult and slow to move around. The crusaders sometimes chose to go for both solutions at once. In 1210, a small fleet of eight ships with heathen Courlanders came towards a group of crusaders to the north of Gotland, which Bishop Albert of Riga was in the process of taking with him to fight for his Church in Livonia. The crusaders estimated that the decisive factor would be speed so they left their cogs and sailed towards the heathens in their smaller vessels. They were very eager to fight and sailed as fast as they could towards the enemy, who had prepared an unpleasant welcome. The Courlanders had emptied the bows of their ships from ballast, so that the ships lay lopsided in the water with the bows high up. At the same time, they had tied their ships together two by two. The crusaders arrived at full speed in amongst the Courlanders' ships. They were unable to board, however, and were mowed down. Three hundred crusaders fell; they were plundered and thrown naked into the sea.[157]

When the boarding of an enemy ship was successful, there was man-to-man fighting on the deck until all of the ship's crew had been slaughtered or, more rarely, had surrendered. Sometimes the last soldiers chose to jump into the water and drown or hoped to swim to the shore without being killed from above by enemies on a pursuing ship.

The fighting on the deck was a rich opportunity for Nordic heroes to demonstrate their courage and win fame, no matter whether they were Christian or heathen. Esbern Snare and Vetheman were on a patrol together to cleanse the coastline of heathens when their four ships were attacked by seven enemy vessels. The worst, however, was that on board one of them was the hero Mirok, who was completely unable to control his courage, his strength and his thirst for fame. When Vetheman's ship came close, he jumped on to it and soon managed to clear it of men, so that only Vetheman was left to fight him. Only when one of the other ships came to the rescue was Mirok overpowered. In recognition of his great courage, he was allowed to pay his way to freedom rather than being killed, such that "his skill in warfare was honoured more than his misdeeds were punished, and his strength saved him, even if his infidelity ought to have brought him death."[158]

Just as new, special forces were established with the new military orders, it seems that special, effective naval forces were established during the 12th century. When Bishop Absalon in the 1160s fortified Copenhagen with a castle, he established a special corps of mariners to clear Oresund of heathens. They attacked Wendish ships, decapitated everyone on board, and put their heads on poles on the beach in front of the town as a warning to other heathens.[159] The corps was a great success, if we are to believe Saxo. The Wends fled as soon as they saw Absalon's men. A pursuit began and the Wends were often caught up – Absalon's warriors must have had fast, long ships. Most heathens jumped into the sea, and

224 *The struggle for land and history*

some chose to hang themselves from the mast of their ship rather than fall into the hands of the Bishop's soldiers.[160]

Vincent of Lisbon

Once upon a time, a ship slowly entered the harbour of Lisbon all by itself. There were no people on board to navigate it, only two ravens were on the lookout, one at the stem and one at the stern, and they guided the ship safely in. The ship carried the well-preserved remnants of Vincent, who had been a priest in Valencia in the 3rd century, but after unimaginable torment, he became a martyr of the faith in 304, during the Diocletian persecution. He was cut, had salt poured into his wounds, he was roasted on a gridiron, but he had endured it all without complaining. His dead body was first thrown on the ground where two ravens had protected it from being eaten by animals – it was considered one of Vincent's miracles that carrion-eating birds had protected his body.[161] His body was later tied to a millstone and thrown into the ocean, but it had nevertheless washed ashore at Capo São Vincente in the most south-westerly point of Europe: the end of the world.

The cult of St Vincent soon gained extensive popularity, both on the Iberian Peninsula and in England, and in the whole Roman Empire. It was continued by the Mozarabs during Muslim rule, and when the Portuguese crusades had reached far to the south of the River Tagus, Vincent decided to strengthen them and miraculously sailed to Lisbon.

Exactly when this story emerged is not known, but the relics of St Vincent were transferred to Lisbon in 1173 at a time when the Portuguese were under pressure and had managed to get through the truce which King Afonso had been forced to enter into after his unsuccessful crusade at Badajoz in 1168. The relics were transferred to the chapel of St Vincent in the new cathedral in Lisbon, built on the initiative of Afonso a few years after the final conquest.

Vincent became a tremendously popular saint and the patron saint of the city of Lisbon, and, from the 13th century, the seal of the city depicts a ship with a lateen sail and two ravens. Some historians have argued that this was meant to symbolize the city's dependence on the sea as a trade route and food resource.[162] Granted, St Vincent soon became a special saint for sailors and people in distress at sea,[163] but there is more than this behind it. The ship in the seal has a large cross on the mast and is clearly a crusader ship. Vincent's role was to protect the city and to assist in the on-going struggle against the Muslims. In Southern Portugal, he was on an equal footing with Santiago; they were the two saints invoked by warriors before a battle, for instance just before the decisive attack on Alcácer do Sal.[164] In around 1200, Vincent was one of the saints who Charlemagne and Ogier the Dane swore on when mocking the blasphemous Muslim opponents. Santiago and St. Denis were two others whom the heroes supplicated.[165]

In the mid-12th century, the cult of Vincent became popular in Scandinavia too. In 1145, an altar to Vincent and Albanus was consecrated in Lund;[166] in 1161, there was one in Trondheim for St. John the Baptist, Sylvester and Vincent. Several other churches in Scandinavia had altars for Vincent and relics of him; we

The struggle for land and history   225

just do not know how old they are.[167] It seems that the worship of Vincent was on the increase during the latter half of the 12th century and spread significantly geographically – all the way to Scandinavia – and mentally – into the ballads of chivalry. It must have something to do with the new crusading engagement of the old saint when he sailed into the harbour of Lisbon.

How Vincent's ravens should be interpreted is rather more difficult. According to heathen Nordic mythology, they are the messengers of the god Odin. They sit on his shoulders and whisper news from the whole world into his ears. A raven was also the first to be sent by Noah to look for the new, purified earth, which slowly emerged from the flood. Ravens are depicted in several Portuguese city seals, but apparently only in the religious frontier regions, which were slowly captured by the crusaders. The raven was a scout who kept an eye on the enemy and helped the Christians, and the bird was considered a good omen in medieval Portugal. Through St Vincent, it had a special association with the sea – Portugal is the only country with an iconographic tradition of combining Vincent, the ravens and the boat. Vincent's very special position in Portugal only increased as the crusades progressed. At a synod in 1240, all bishops were commanded to request their flock to visit the cathedral and the tomb of Vincent at least once every year.[168]

Portuguese raids from the towns against Muslims, *fossado*, were also undertaken from ships and with the same regularity as land-based raids.[169] The warriors set out during spring or summer and were able to make the most of the predominantly northerly winds to quickly reach their goal, the Muslim coastal towns further to the South. When the coast of the Algarve in the South was captured in 1249, they soon continued to the coast of North Africa as well. The objective was the same as on land, to create fear and prepare for a later, proper conquest, and to take booty: slaves, foodstuffs and easily transportable valuables. The participants in these fossados at sea came from coastal towns and from the towns along the great rivers a long way inland. Participation in these raids seems to have been one of the obligations placed on the townspeople in return for royal charters, certainly from the 12th century. During the first half of the 13th century, this obligation was sometimes commuted to a tax, or it became part of the charter to be free from having to perform warfare duties. It was granted to the people of Setúbal in 1249 that "They shall not take part in war or cavalcade, neither on land nor at sea."[170] However, this did not imply that warfare at sea became less widespread. On the contrary, it seems that kings and noblemen took a more proactive interest in organizing it; they created larger fleets with larger ships and more people enrolled and a more permanent organization with a royal admiral was established. It seems more likely that sea warfare became less based on raids and turned into a well-organized royal strategy, especially from the early 14th century.

We do not know the number of ships that were on the Iberian Peninsula particularly well. Apparently, no attempt has been made to calculate how many ships the different towns along the Portuguese coast had to furnish for the yearly fossados. We know much more about the number of ships that came from the outside, because that is mentioned in the narratives of the large battles. Between 160 and 200 ships from northern regions in Europe took part in Afonso's conquest

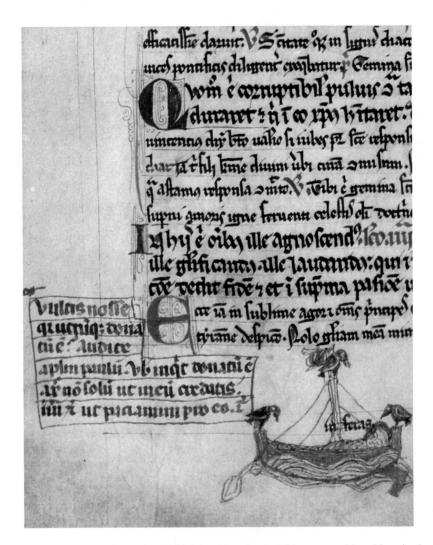

Figure 7.3 The mortal remains of St. Vincent arrive in Lisbon on a ship with only the ravens navigating it. In the margin of the Portuguese manuscript from the early 13th century, a scribe has added a quote from St. Paul's letter to the Philippians (1,29): "For unto you it is given in the behalf of Christ, not only to believe on him, but also to suffer for his sake." © University of Southern Denmark Press

of Lisbon in 1147. Genoa contributed sixty-three galleys in the battles of Almería and Tortosa in 1147 and 1148. Danish ships were amongst the approximately fifty-five to seventy-five ships which participated in the capture of Silves in 1189, and perhaps also amongst the 180 ships or so that contributed to secure Alcácer do Sal for Afonso II.[171]

The struggle for land and history 227

A more systematic enlargement of a navy with large ships under royal control seems to have taken place in 1179 or 1180, as can be seen from a series of charters to the towns, which had to supply men for the new fleet.[172] It would have been perceived as a landmark event at the time; this must be the explanation as to why the narrative of precisely this fleet was passed on and embellished. The legendary Admiral Fuas Roupinho was a powerful lord of a castle, who repelled the Moors when they crossed the Tagus in 1179 and 1180, and he took the defeated Muslim king to Coimbra and handed him to Afonso I. Lisbon was then attacked by a large Muslim fleet led by "a Moor by the name of Ioham Ferreiro Dalphamy";[173] judging by his name, he might have been a Christian apostate. Fuas received a royal order to clear and defend the coast and to equip a Christian fleet of galleys against the Muslim fleet. He was appointed Admiral of the fleet – a later narrative claims – even though the title of admiral is known only from 1288.[174] Afonso made sure Fuas had charts, and royal officials were told to give him anything he wanted. He now sailed as far as Algarve and attacked several Muslim ships, until he found the Muslim armada and defeated it completely. He then entered the harbour of Lisbon with all of his booty. The Muslims in Portugal now realized how great a danger they were in, and with the help from Muslims in Spain as well, they assembled a new fleet of fifty-four galleys. Fuas Roupinho joined the battle, and as a strong wind blew from behind, he sailed into the Muslim fleet with great speed. He fought gallantly but in vain. Because of the Muslim's superiority in numbers, it ended in a bloodbath where many Christians fell, among them Fuas Roupinho. "It happened on the 17th of October 1180," the late medieval narrative ends.[175]

Though fifty-four ships might sound like a medium-sized fleet, if they were the very latest, large galleys, it would have been a very large army. If this narrative from after 1400 can be used for anything at all regarding the late 12th century, the conclusion has to be that the navies of both the Portuguese Muslims and of the Portuguese Christians were very modern and were composed of large ships, cogs or galleys, that were becoming common in Northern Europe at the same time. Afonso initiated the founding of a new fleet of large ships in almost the same year as Valdemar the Great stood in Schleswig and watched his giant cog run ashore at its launch.

The importance of the navy for Portugal was fully recognized in contemporary sources. In the middle of the 14th century, the Portuguese chronicles explained that King Afonso Henriques had built galleasses and had them placed in Porto – and that his Porto galleasses had become the term for the country as such, *Portu-gal*.[176]

In both Denmark and Portugal, naval warfare was well regulated from the 12th century onwards, and the kings were able to command very large forces through the general conscription of the free population or through conscription from towns near the coast in Portugal. In both places, fleets were used in the crusades, both during the yearly and more regular raids and during very large operations. This is clear from the sources, but is also somewhat self-evident when seen from a comprehensive view of Denmark and Portugal in this period. Extensively militarized societies with such developed engagement in religious wars were unlikely to have had an extended naval organization without using it aggressively for crusades.

228 *The struggle for land and history*

During the final decades before 1200, it seems that ships became significantly larger in both countries; this fits with the general development in Europe at the time. It is part of a development, which might be termed an early military revolution. It was presumably a precondition for the Danish crusades being able to reach all the way to Estonia, and that the Portuguese ones could attack North Africa. At the same time, larger ships necessitated larger crews, perhaps a more professional crew, and probably also a permanent mobilization, where the ships were not laid up during wintertime.

Finally, ships combine a practical and a symbolic function. Both Denmark and Portugal were created when ships without crew or captain arrived, one of them with an infant, the other with the remnants of a dead saint on board. If the naval crusaders were aware of these stories, they might have felt as if they were taking part in the restaging of a religious narrative. They may not, in the usual medieval way, have distinguished between practical and symbolic. This is also the case for the other important means of transport and warfare during the crusades – the horse.

Horses – the Friesian and the jennet

The horse was the basis for the enormous striking force and prestige of the knights.[177] The most monumental and effective warhorses could cost vast sums of money; they were the finest of gifts between mighty princes, on a par with white falcons from the ice-covered lands in the North. Horses with lavish equipment were given to kings[178] and Popes, they were introductory gifts to abbots and deans, and a particularly fine stallion was even sent by ship all the way to the Mongol Great Khan of China in around 1300.[179]

Denmark was one of Northern Europe's most important horse breeding countries and had a large export market.[180] From Ribe alone, around 8,000 horses were shipped yearly during the 13th century,[181] others were shipped from other ports and most probably walked, led south along the Danish military road to cattle and horse markets in Holstein and in Northern Germany. When they passed through Schleswig, a duty had to be paid for them: six denarius for a riding horse and six denarius too for every horse that was pulled. If the rider was a cleric or a crusader, he was exempted from the duty.[182] Denmark was famous for its rich pastures and excellent horses in large measures, which made "the Danes as brilliant in warfare on horseback as from a ship deck."[183]

Horses were bred in studs, groups of half-wild horses in very large enclosures, which are still identifiable from many place names with "hestehave" – "horse grounds,"[184] or the horses were left on the many small islands off the Danish shores. The King owned studs all over the country.[185] The herd had to consist of at least twelve horses in order to qualify as a stud, and if they managed to escape the enclosure, they could cause much damage to fields and gardens, and they were difficult to catch again.[186] The Danish horse was known and praised for its strong neck and soft skin; its groin was high and its hue golden.[187] Yet compared to modern horses, it was not particularly large. The royal war stallions would have

The struggle for land and history 229

been around 1.5 metres high in the 12th century; more common horses were about thirty centimetres smaller.[188] These are average numbers and there would have been striking exceptions, giant horses that were traded for giant sums of money. Warhorses could reach prices as high as ten marks of silver.[189]

During the 12th century, a new institution entered horse breeding: the Cistercians. Their high level of organization and often aristocratic upbringing was a perfect basis for a systematic breeding programme. During the first years, the leadership of the order had second thoughts regarding this rather secular pursuit, but in time, their principles simply had to yield. In 1153, the General Chapter issued a direct ban on selling foals to anyone outside the Cistercian order.[190] In 1157, a development meant that the Cistercians could trade in wool and horses. It was established that the foals could be broken in with a harness but not with saddles, "so that they are trained in running." The idea must have been that the horses were to be used as workhorses only, not for racing, warfare or luxury. When the foals had replaced the first four teeth, they were to be sold before the rest were replaced. If that was not accomplished, the monastery was forced to keep the horses. Simultaneously, rules were issued stating that trading in foals was to take place on monastery land.[191]

However, the targeted breeding of warhorses became increasingly common amongst the Cistercians, and in 1184, the General Chapter had to abolish the ban. Instead, it was decided that the income from the sale of proper warhorses was to be transferred to the General Chapter so that it could be shared amongst the poor monasteries.[192] Monasteries could be poor for many reasons, but the Chapter may have had in mind the newly founded monasteries in the war-ravaged crusade territories that had not yet established a profitable agricultural production, and where it would have been all too risky to begin to breed expensive warhorses. The Cistercians in Esrom thus sold horses to noblemen of Zealand,[193] who waged crusades around Rügen, and they may have sent the money for the horses to the monasteries in Dargun, Eldena and Colbatz. The monasteries along the Baltic were perfect for further horse breeding, and, during the 13th century, it became a huge industry for the Cistercians, who exported luxury horses to Germany, Flanders, England and Italy.

During the 13th century, several other great institutions became involved in large-scale horse breeding, for instance the Hospitallers. When the *reconquista* moved further south during the 13th century, properties in Northern Spain were turned into stud farms that bred horses in large numbers. When the foals became young horses, they were led across the Pyrenees to the French monasteries under the order of St. John, where they were broken in and trained for war. Then, they were shipped to the Holy Land.[194]

What was the aim of the breeding programme? The source material is sparse; and archaeological material is not well suited to distinguishing between different breeds, so much is based on guess work and inference.[195] Nevertheless, it seems that the Cistercians in Denmark and Northern Germany worked with three breeds. The basic type would have been the heavy Friesian, which were bred together with stallions from Flanders to create a strong and persevering horse. This was

230 *The struggle for land and history*

then crossed with the Portuguese jennet, which contributed speed, flexibility and perseverance. The jennet is a much more slender horse, containing much that classifies an Arab horse; it has long legs and a much smaller head, compared to the body, than the Friesian horse.

If this reconstruction of horse breeding is correct, horse exports must have been amongst the important trade sources when, in 1157, Afonso exempted the Cistercians in Alcobaça from duties of all the goods they exported. In 1174, they received a similar privilege from Fernando II of León, who directly mentions horses as one of the items that are exempt from duty.[196]

The large horse gave force and weight to a direct attack, which could be decisive when meeting a more lightly equipped enemy. On the other hand, the large horse was weighed down and slowed down by the armoured rider; it was in order to be able to carry a warrior in full armour they had been bred in the first place. Whether the large horse was an advantage or not thus depended very much on the terrain. In the early 1150s, the Wends again invaded Zealand near Roskilde, where at first they were met by a small Danish force under the command of the heavily armoured knight Radulf. He was the first to reach the Wends because his horse was faster than the other horses, and he joined the battle with great flexibility. He avoided the stabbings and lashes of the Wends and attacked them repeatedly. However, every time he reached open terrain, the Wends' horses were too fast for him, simply because their riders were so much lighter. Radulf then drove the Wends into a grain field, where the horses had to make their way through the grain. The smaller Wendish horses were not nearly as good at this as his large, strong warhorse. Radulf caught up with the Wends, and then the rest of his men joined him. They attacked the Wendish army and killed many of the foot soldiers, while the light cavalry ran away. Many of the Wends panicked, rode out over the cliffs above the beach and were killed on the pebbles on the beach.[197]

Having the right horse was a question of life and death to the warrior, who prized his horse highly. This is related by one of the great crusaders, King Jaime I of Aragon, in his fascinating autobiography from the conquest of Mallorca in 1229.[198] Before a battle against heavily armed Muslims, he spoke to his vassals: "Noble men, our horses are precious to us in this land; we have only one horse each, and a horse is worth more than twenty Muslims."[199]

Heavenly horses

It must have been difficult for the medieval warriors to imagine a heaven without horses.[200] Luckily, there was no reason for that. A heavenly army on horseback is constantly ready to assist the warriors of God. This happened to Judas Maccabeus when he fought Timotheus in Gezer: "But when they were in the heat of the engagement, there appeared to the enemies from heaven five men upon horses, comely, with golden bridles, conducting the Jews: Two of them took Maccabeus between them, and covered him on every side with their arms, and kept him safe; but cast darts and fireballs against the enemy, so that they fell down, being both confounded with blindness, and filled with trouble."[201] The crusaders'

The struggle for land and history 231

urge to identify with the Maccabees is one explanation as to why they considered it perfectly natural to receive help from heavenly cavalry during the decisive battles. When the white horsemen came charging out of heaven during the siege of Antioch in 1098, the crusaders remarked that they had more right, in a way, to the support from them than the Maccabees. The Maccabees had fought for circumcision and pork, whereas the crusaders fought to cleanse the churches and spread the faith, and they spilled their blood to serve Christ.[202]

The last great battle on doomsday shall begin with the riders being set free, and Gog and Magog initiate the battle, as Ezekiel depicted it at the end of his prophecy,[203] and the Lord God calls on the wild birds and animals to feast on the flesh of fallen heroes and princes. The attack from the evil ones is depicted in one of the psalms that was quoted most often in a crusade context: "O God, the heathens are come into thy inheritance, they have defiled thy holy temple: they have made Jerusalem as a place to keep fruit. They have given the dead bodies of thy servants to be meat for the fowls of the air: the flesh of thy saints for the beasts of the earth. They have poured out their blood as water, round about Jerusalem and there was none to bury them."[204]

Yet, the most gruesome depiction of doom horsemen and presumably the best known in the Middle Ages was the Apocalypse of St. John, chapter 6: when the angel opened the first seal, the white horse with the rider with a bow and a crown arrived and went forth conquering that he might conquer. When the second seal was opened, the red horse arrived, and to him that sat thereupon it was given that he should take all peace from the earth so that men would kill each other, and he had a great sword. When the third seal was opened, the black horse with a rider with a pair of scales arrived. And the fourth seal was opened, and behold, a pale horse, and he that sat upon him, his name was Death, and hell followed him, and power was given to him over the four parts of the earth, to kill with sword, with famine and with death and with the beasts of the earth. These horsemen are the enemies of God, and those who were killed for the word of God – the crusaders, it would have been perceived from the 12th century onwards – lie in their white clothing under the altar and cries for justice.[205]

Justice arrives in the guise of a horseman: "And I saw heaven opened: and behold a white horse. And he that sat upon him was called Faithful and True: and with justice doth He judge and fight. And His eyes were as a flame of fire: and on His head were many diadems. And He had a name written, which no man knoweth but Himself. And he was clothed with a garment sprinkled with blood. And His name is called: The Word of God. And the armies that are in heaven followed Him on white horses, clothed in fine linen, white and clean."[206]

The crusaders' horses had very practical importance as instruments of war. Many crusaders probably also had a deeply personal relationship with their steed – the chivalric ballads carefully mention the names of the heroes' horses but not of their wives. At the same time, the warhorse was a status symbol of immense importance to the social status of the owner. But when the crusaders went out to fight evil, they also became players in the great doomsday battle. The crusaders and their horses became part of the heavenly army.

232　*The struggle for land and history*

Military orders and military saints

For the knights on their horses, the crusades offered a totally new opportunity for salvation which fitted their trade and temper. To the Church, warfare became accepted as a necessary means to protect the freedom of the church, and war was compared to the life in the monastery. These ideas amalgamated and gave rise 1) to a wholly new institution, the religious military orders, and 2) to stressing the military function of older saints, such as Santiago.

The temple and the hospital in Portugal

The Order of the Temple was the first formal military order.[207] It began in 1120 with a small group, nine individuals in total, under the leadership of Hugo de Payns, who in Jerusalem took a vow with the Patriarch to live a life within the rules; that means in poverty, celibacy and obedience. They were organized as canons at the Lord's Temple, the al-Aqsa Mosque on the Temple Mount; they received some revenue and were ordered to protect the pilgrimage roads to the holy places in Jerusalem. The Templars were the earliest order that combined religious life with active warfare, but the Hospitallers were quick to learn from them. In 1129,[208] a carefully planned synod was held in Troyes with the participation of papal legates and Bernard of Clairvaux. The Templars were given a rule, based on that of the Cistercians, and received papal recognition. The master of the Templars was able to return to the Holy Land with more knights for the order who could support the new kingdom militarily.

The Templars received land and revenue in donations, even before the synod in Troyes, from the counts of Anjou and Champagne and the dukes of Flanders, and soon others followed. The income from these donations was supposed to support the efforts of the order in the Holy Land, but very soon, the rulers on the other religious frontiers saw their potential and attempted to convince them to settle and fight the Muslims in their own lands. This was particularly successful on the Iberian Peninsula.

Already in 1128, Queen Teresa and several noblemen gave land and gifts to the Templars. The most important was probably the castle and the land around Soure, on the far side of the River Mondego, and the area between Coimbra and Leiria, which was still to be conquered from the Muslims.[209] This happened to support the Templar's defence of the Holy Sepulchre in Jerusalem.[210] The year after, Afonso Henriques gave the same gift to the Templars – a confirmation of the gift from his mother or a greatly needed attempt to mark his independence from her? Afonso's own reasoning is interesting: he donated because he "was a brother in your blessings and your confraternity."[211] Afonso did not give up his secular life or enter the order to live in obedience, poverty and celibacy, but he intended to demonstrate a close connection and support.

Afonso had inspirational models amongst his close neighbours. During the years of the establishment of the Templars, Alfonso I the Battler of Aragon fought the Muslims with great success. Between 1118 and 1120, Zaragoza and many other

The struggle for land and history   233

areas fell to his armies, actually such large areas fell that it was difficult to control and settle them with Christians afterwards. He established small, local knight-hoods and town militias – where the noblemen in a town organized themselves into religious confraternities in order to wage crusades – and he invited the Templars to settle in Aragon. In 1131, three years before his death, Alfonso the Battler, who had no sons, drew up a will, wherein he appointed his heirs: the whole king-dom of Aragon and all royal power was to be shared equally amongst the priest of the Holy Sepulchre in Jerusalem, the Knights of St. John and the Templars.[212]

When Alfonso the Battler died in 1134, no one outside this group of heirs ever considered keeping the stipulations detailed in the will. From Castile, Alfonso VII went in, captured Zaragoza and had himself proclaimed Emperor of all Spain the following year. The brother of Alfonso the Battler, Ramiro the Monk, left his monastery to marry Agnes, the sister of Guillaume VIII of Aquitaine. A daughter was born who had a strong claim to Aragon and immediately was engaged to Count Ramon Berenguer IV of Barcelona as early as 1137. Having done his duty, the father then returned to the monastery and resumed his life as a monk. Others appeared and grabbed other areas of Aragon.

Nevertheless, the Templars and the Hospitallers were not left out completely. Most of those who disregarded the stipulations of the will felt obliged to compen-sate the real heirs in some way. The orders received large donations of land and of castles. The father of the Count of Barcelona had been a full member of the Templars, Ramon Berenguer IV himself was attached to the order for one year in 1134, after which he was obliged to provide for ten knights of the order and to give it one tenth of all future conquest. There were thus different ways of being a Templar; the great princes could be attached or become temporary members, and were not bound by the vow of poverty, obedience and celibacy.

In Portugal, support for the Templars rose during the years after Afonso Henr-iques' donation and after he had apparently become an associated member in one way or the other. In 1145, the Bishop of Porto gave a hospital in the city to the Templars, and, in the following year, Afonso again gave them large gifts, this time in Braga.[213] The Templars became dominant in three areas of the Beira district: around Soure, around Tomar (where they built the impressive circular church pre-sumably just after the middle of the 12th century) and finally in several places in Beira Alta, the elevated frontier area to the Northwest, where the order built sev-eral spectacular castles, the ruins of which are still scattered across the landscape. The Templars' dominance in these areas shows that their task during the early part of the 12th century was to protect the royal crusade centre of Coimbra and to generally force the frontier further south by capturing land from the Muslims and holding on it. This is clear in 1147 when Afonso in the shadow of the second crusade initiated one of his greater offensives and, by using forced marches and a surprise attack at night-time, managed to capture Santarém on March 15, this time for good. In a letter of donation in April, he wrote that he had already vowed that he would give Santarém to God and the Templars, if he had the grace to capture the city, because they had a share in the conquest. Then he adds that he hopes that God in his piety will let him capture Lisbon.[214]

234 *The struggle for land and history*

The Templars did not play any great role in Alentejo to the south of the River Tagus, where the re-conquest became possible after the fall of Lisbon in 1147, and gained momentum in around 1170. There might be a particular reason for this. At that time, the military orders were becoming a local and royal instrument of power. In 1169, Afonso Henriques issued a document to the Templars. Its importance is obvious as it is addressed to none less than God, present and future Templars, the order's Master Gaufrido on this side of the ocean, the provincial Master Garcia Romero of Castile, the order's attorney Gualdino in Portugal and all their future successors. Afonso gives the order one third of all the land that he, with God's help, is able to capture and settle from the other side of the Tagus and further south. Afonso's condition is that the Templars must use everything that he gives them, now and in the future, "to serve God and him and his descendants as long as the war between the Saracens and the Christians lasts." Afonso continued, stipulating that none of the earlier property that he had given to the order could be used for the re-conquest to the south of the Tagus – but that all of it shall go to the Temple in Jerusalem and shall be kept there. Whereas the new property that he gives them, Afonso reiterates, must be spent on the war in the Kingdom of Portugal, as long as the Saracen war lasts.[215] Thus, there was a shift in royal policy towards the Templars in the year 1169, of which Afonso was quite aware and expressed clearly. It is connected to the vast region in Alentejo which was difficult to fortify with castles because it is so flat compared to the North.

If the Templars wished to be part of this new phase of the *reconquista*, they would receive large land holdings and large incomes, but only if they used everything in the service of the King in return. Apparently, this was not an attractive option to the Templars. They were even given land from Tomar all the way down to the north banks of the River Tagus around Vila-Nova-da-Barquinha,[216] presumably as a preparation for crossing the river in order to participate in the conquest. Nevertheless, they ended up staying to the north of the river. The re-conquest of Southern Portugal was taken over by the new local orders, primarily the Order of Avis, established in Évora in 1176, and the Order of Santiago, established in León in 1170. The new orders did not have a centre in the Holy Land to which they had any obligation. The royal policy shifted in 1169 towards establishing connections with local orders instead of international orders.

A similar shift took place elsewhere. When Alfonso II the Chaste became King of Aragon in 1162, he was supposed to have fulfilled his father's promises to the Templars from 1143. Ramon IV Berenguer had promised that they were to have one fifth of everything that the King captured in future wars against the Muslims. In practice, nothing came of this. The conquest of Southern Aragon by Alfonso was secured with the help of the newly established local orders, the Calatrave, founded in 1158, and Mountjoy, a military order founded in León in around 1173. They were given the castles and took part in the continuing re-conquest, whereas the Templars stayed at their former holdings in the North. To begin with, whether they received any compensation for the land to which they had a legitimate claim is not known. In practice, the problem was solved when the Order of Mountjoy

The struggle for land and history   235

was placed under the Order of the Templars, which then also took over its castles in Southern Aragon.[217]

The Knights of St. John, or the Hospitallers, in Portugal settled between Tomar and Beira Alta; they filled the gap between two Templar lands in the zone that was supposed to protect the area to the north of Mondego against Muslim attacks. It is not known for certain when the first Hospitallers arrived in Portugal, but it might have been simultaneous with the arrival of the Templars after the middle of the 1120s. One of the earliest known large donations was the monastery Leça do Balio just to the north of Porto, which was gifted by Afonso Henriques in March 1140.[218]

One of the Hospitallers' masters was Fernando Afonso, son of Châmoa Gomes. She became a widow in around 1129 and entered a convent, where she had a nobleman as a lover and gave birth to a son. When the lover died, she began a relationship with King Afonso Henriques and became the mother of Fernando. He was thus the eldest son of Afonso but was born outside of marriage; hence he could not succeed him as King. Fernando went into exile in León and entered the Templar order. At some point, however, he went over to the Hospitallers. In 1198, he was the master of all of the Iberian Peninsula, and in 1202, he became master of all of the order. After having partaken in the crusade against Constantinople in 1204, he continued to the Holy Land, but resigned his duties in 1205 in order to return to Portugal, where he died in 1207. Whether Fernando Afonso really aspired to the throne is a disputed point amongst Portuguese historians. In any case, his half-brother Sancho I donated large properties to the Hospitallers, thus it appears that relations between the King and the Hospitallers were close and good.[219]

The Hospitallers did not extend to the south of the River Tagus either. During the period 1187–1191, when the danger of attacks from the Almohads was imminent, Sancho donated several castles to the military orders to hold the frontier against the Muslims. The Order of Santiago had Alcácer, Palmela, Almada and Arruda in 1186; in 1187, the Order of Avis was given Alcanede, Alpedriz and, when it had been captured by the Christians, Juromenha in the easternmost region by the River Guardiana, and, in 1190, it was given Mafra as well. Thus, these two local orders were given castles to the north as well as to the south of the Tagus, but mostly to the south.[220] The Order of St. John was given land bordering the Tagus on its northern shore, where they built the castle of Belver, *The Beautiful Sight*, in 1194.[221] But they did not cross the river. Apparently, this only happened as late as in 1232, when the Hospitallers received Crato from Afonso III.[222]

The Templars and the Hospitallers played a significant role in the earliest period of Portugal, and they continued to be important in the North. In the South, however, they were replaced by local orders in the late 12th century. During the early period, the kings were almost only interested in the military aspect, which is reflected in the sources. Taking a wider view however, there was a decisive difference between the two orders. The Templars were focussed solely on fighting and gathering funds for further crusades, whereas the Hospitallers also had an important function as a hospital order. At the beginning of the 14th century, the Templars were condemned as heretics and the order was dissolved for many different

236   *The struggle for land and history*

reasons,[223] while the Hospitallers continued to fight in the crusade regions and to care for the sick in those areas that were no longer under threat from infidels and Muslims.

Saint James as a crusader

During the second half of the 11th century, the importance of Santiago de Compostela began to equal older pilgrimage sites, such as the tomb of St. Peter in Rome and the Holy Sepulchre in Jerusalem. St. James, the son of Zebedee, was among the most important of the disciples of Jesus, and as the first apostle, he died a martyr's death on the same day and hour as Jesus Himself. True, the date is not mentioned in the Bible, but it had been revealed in a vision to a believer, who had passed the information on to Pope Calixtus II.[224] The body of James was miraculously taken to Galicia by his followers; it washed ashore near the place where the cathedral and pilgrimage site were established later. The earliest written information claiming that the tomb of St. James was in Galicia, "at the outermost edge," stems from around 865.[225] In 874, Alfonso III of Asturia strengthened the cult of St. James immensely through the erection of new buildings and magnificent gifts to the church, among them a golden cross with the inscription "In this sign the enemy is defeated. In this sign the pious is protected."[226] Alfonso also gave large holdings of land to the church, land that he had received from defeated rebels as well as that captured from the Muslims. In his foundation charter, Alfonso referred to James as his special patron saint, who helped him to extend his territory. Apparently, active participation in warfare was not originally a part of his function as a saint.

In the 12th century it was believed that Santiago had taken active part in the battle of Clavijo in 844, where King Ramiro I of Asturia had been victorious thanks to his help and had liberated the Christians from having to pay a yearly tribute of 100 young virgins to the Caliph of Córdoba. In his gratitude for the victory, Ramiro donated an annual duty from everyone in Christian Spain to Santiago, and a fixed share of the land and booty that would be captured from the Muslims in the future – *votos de Santiago*, the votive offerings of Santiago. The chapter of Santiago could later present the document with the royal seal, issued by Ramiro. However, the letter is a forgery, produced in the middle of the 12th century by the canon Pedro Marcio; it is not included in the cathedral's index of letters from around 1130, and the chronology in the letter is confused. This did not prevent Pope Innocent III from confirming in 1199 that this votive offering had to be paid by all of Portugal.[227] Yet the forgery demonstrates how a tradition was invented in the 12th century which closely associated Santiago with the crusades against the Muslims, and placed the association far back in time as proof of the ancient status of the *reconquista* on the Iberian Peninsula. This is highlighted in the liturgy collected and written anew during the 12th century for use at rituals at Santiago's grave in the cathedral. Some of the liturgy referred to Santiago as "the experienced knight of Christ and illustrious standard bearer and most hardened warrior."[228]

Also outside his main cult centre, narratives about Santiago as a war leader against the Muslims begin to emerge. *Historia Silense* from the early 12th century tells the story of a Greek pilgrim who was poor in spirit as well as in money. He had arrived in Santiago de Compostela in 1064 and had heard King Fernando of León praying in the church for help to recapture Coimbra. The pilgrim thought it strange, as Santiago did not own a horse and had never even tried to sit on a horse. At night, Santiago appeared to the pilgrim in a vision, carrying keys in his hands and saying to him: "You laughed at me yesterday and believed that I had never been a strong knight." And while he said this, a brilliant horse of enormous stature went to the gates of the church. When the gates were opened, its brilliance was as radiant as snow and illuminated the whole church. The apostle mounted the horse, showed the pilgrim the keys, and said that on the next day he would give Coimbra to King Fernando at around the third hour of the day. That turned out to come true.[229]

Figure 7.4 The knight Domingos Joanes from Oliveira. Statue, presumably from his funeral church; 65 centimetres tall, 14th century. © University of Southern Denmark Press

238   *The struggle for land and history*

The order of Santiago

In 1170 a new military order was established in León with Santiago as its patron saint, *Militia Sancti Iacobi*.[230] Fernando II of León wanted a local order to protect the newly conquered Cáceres and to participate in the Leonese crusades. Already in 1171, the new order gained a very prominent member, the Archbishop Pedro Gudesteiz of Santiago de Compostela. He handed them Santiago's own banner and put them under obligation to protect Santiago and his lands against the Muslims. The order was recognized by Pope Alexander III in 1175 as a new instrument in the struggle against evil. "Just as many are knocked to the ground by the tail of the dragon, just so are many lost ones saved daily by returning to the Holy Spirit, and from the pits of hell, they are raised to search for heaven."[231] According to Martín, many noblemen on the Iberian Peninsula had given not just their earthly belongings but they had also put their lives in the greatest danger for the sake of the Lord. They joined together in an order and live in obedience under a master of the order as a religious society, with one restriction, however. Jesus did not decide for men only but also for women and wished that women should give birth and consort with men. Therefore, some lived in the order in celibacy, whereas others followed the word of St. Paul that virginity was not a commandment from the Lord, only advice, and in order to have offspring and to avoid being tempted, they shall continue to live in marriage and "use their wives" and together with them attempt to go from the vale of tears of this world and the earthly pilgrimage to the dwelling of the eternal fatherland – *patria*. The brothers of the Order of Santiago could choose to opt out of celibacy, and that might have been one reason for the popularity of the order.[232] Alexander also ruled that if one of the brothers died, the widow was to have permission from the master of the order to marry again with whomever she wanted. This also applied to the man, "because they are obliged by the same law."

In his charter to the Order, Pope Alexander continued by emphasizing that they could keep everything they captured from the Muslims without anyone else having a claim if it had been in Muslim possession "for longer than living memory." The wording is interesting as it is possibly only kings and churches that could make very old claims by referring to a distant past. Alexander thus protects the Order pre-emptively against claims from these institutions.

The purpose of the Order of Santiago was first and foremost to defend the Christians and to fight the Muslims, "not for worldly honour, not from a desire to spill blood, not from greed for earthly possessions, but only this one thing they shall strive for in their struggle, that the Christians shall be protected against attacks from the Muslims and that they try and call for the Muslims to follow the Christian faith." They shall also take care of pilgrims and the poor. Here, Alexander is probably referring to the pilgrims en route to Santiago de Compostela. The sign of the Order was a cross in the shape of a sword; warfare was thus a central element to the Order's self-perception. In 1172, the Order of Santiago admitted the Portuguese Order of Ávila, and there was a plan ready, as it appears from the merger agreement. When Santiago and Ávila had expelled the Muslims from the Iberian Peninsula, they would continue on to Morocco and lead the crusade through North Africa and towards Jerusalem to support the Holy City.[233] It took centuries still to reach Africa, and to Jerusalem they never came.

The Order of Santiago came to Portugal soon after its foundation; it immediately played a large part in the conquests and held strategically important castles. In 1172–1173, the Order received its first holdings in Portugal,[234] and in 1186 it took over the disputed and dangerous Alcácer, Palmela right on the other side of the Tagus at Lisbon and Almada and Arruda too.[235] Hence they gained possession of the largest salt mines in Portugal and received large incomes, which could be used in the continuing attempts to attract settlers to the troubled areas.[236] It happened in the honour of God and James the apostle, and over the coming years, it was followed by many more castles and properties. The Order of Santiago became one of the richest on the Iberian Peninsula and was militarily one of the most important in the first half of the 13th century.

The temple and the hospital in Denmark

The Templars never came to Denmark, or Norway or Sweden either. On the other hand, the Order was well known to Danish warriors and crusaders, and they would have been aware of what it stood for. The Cistercians' close connections with the Templars and Bernard's writings about them must have meant that Danish Cistercians would have told Danish noblemen and their own family members about how a true warrior of Christ should act. The ideals of the Templars were known, but whether the King tapped into their military strength is much more doubtful.

The Knights of St. John are mentioned for the first time in Danish material as witnesses in a letter issued by Absalon as Bishop of Roskilde, which stems from the period 1164–1178.[237] Valdemar I (also known as the Great) supposedly established the first Hospitallers convent in Antvorskov in 1170, but they might have been in Denmark decades before that. The Hospitallers enjoyed royal favours from the outset. Antvorskov was established on royal property, and Valdemar the Great gave the Hospitallers a tax of one denarius per year for every household in the realm, "which is called house farthing (huspenning)." It is emphasized that this tax is for the order's work in the Holy Land, and that it shall be paid *separatim* from the remaining contributions to the Holy Land and without any kind of "reduction." Apparently, the idea is that the Hospitallers in Denmark are not supposed to offset and keep any of the house denariuses for themselves if they have received particularly large, voluntary donations for the crusades. It is also suggested, although not mentioned directly, that it was supposed to be a permanent, yearly tax. It would have been mentioned if it had been an isolated tax for a limited number of years. Valdemar wished to ensure that both the tax and donations went directly to the Holy Land. We only know of this tax through its confirmation by his grandson in 1244[238] (the charter was renewed at least ten times by succeeding kings all the way up to 1527).[239]

240   *The struggle for land and history*

The Hospitallers tax was an unusually large favour to a military order at that early time. A possible explanation, as suggested by the historian Thomas Riis, could be that Valdemar I entered into a special relationship with the Hospitallers and put Denmark under the protection of the Order in a way that was supposed to be a parallel to the vassals of St. Peter's direct feudal relation with the Pope. This could explain two things. One is that Valdemar's father, Canute Lavard, was canonized on June 25 and had that day as his saint's day. June 25 would then have been the third day of celebration after the 23rd and 24th of June, which belonged to the Knights of St. John, and could thus serve to highlight the connection between them. The other is that the Danish flag – a white cross on red bunting – could be a copy of the mark of the Knights of St. John, and that Valdemar minted coins with a cross banner, which can be seen as either the Danish flag or as the mark of the Hospitallers.[240] The order seems to have had a broad, general appeal as well. Abbot Vilhelm of Æbelholt complained to Innocent III that some friars left his Augustinian convent in order to become members of the Order of St. John.[241]

One of the Order's important tasks during the early days was to collect money to support the work in Jerusalem. This became a success, so the Order was unable to satisfy the demand for crusade preachers and had to rely on less qualified, untrained personnel. This is the claim in a complaint sent by Bishop Absalon to Innocent III in 1198. The Hospitallers had used crude and simple laypeople to preach, as well as priests with outrageous conduct, who had put the cross on their chest but were toiling under drunkenness and greed, and who outraged both clergy and laypeople. Finally, it went wrong. In a church in Lund, which had been given to the Hospitallers by the former Archbishop, they stabbed the priest and defiled the church with bloodshed. And what was probably the worst – they had no respect for the Archbishop but referred to papal charters and refused to close the desecrated church for worship, and they admitted priests to the Order and let them perform the service, even though these priests had been suspended earlier by the Archbishop. And they lived with wives in their own houses and supported them with some of the money which they had collected. Innocent apparently believed Absalon's account and gave him far-reaching powers to excommunicate these individuals within the Order of St. John.[242]

It might not have been too bad after all, because the order remained in Denmark until the Reformation in 1536 and received considerable properties over the centuries. Antvorskov near Slagelse is probably the oldest, and at the time of the Reformation, it was the second largest monastery in Denmark, only surpassed by the Cistercian monastery in Sorø. The founding of St. John's monastery in Viborg soon followed; their church there was consecrated to both St. John the Baptist and the crusader saint St. James. The Hospitallers were in Odense before 1280, where their monastery grew during the Middle Ages and ultimately became an impressively large structure that was later taken over by the crown and used for local royal administration. The Hospitallers in Odense were given the church of Sankt Hans,[243] one of Denmark's only three churches with an outside pulpit, making it possible for large gatherings to hear the sermon – perhaps one of the popular crusade sermons?

The Hospitallers in Denmark collected money for the order's international work, but how many fighting knights there were in Denmark is actually not known. It is quite likely, however, that the order played a role in one of the culminating points of the Danish Baltic crusades, the conquest of the strong heathen fortress of Arkona on the island of Rügen in 1168. The Christian princes on Rügen later donated land to Antvorskov – the earliest evidence is from the beginning of the 14th century – and at some point, a Hospitallers monastery was established in Maskenholt on Rügen, possibly as late as at the beginning of the 15th century.[244] In the same way as with Rügen, we may imagine that the Hospitallers took part in the other culminating event in the Danish Baltic crusades, the capture of Tallinn in Estonia in 1219, but the sources let us down again.

How did King Valdemar get the inspiration to invite Hospitallers to his realm? There may be a connection to the Empire. In 1158, Fredric I Barbarossa took the Order under his protection, and in 1160, Margrave Albert the Bear founded a Hospitallers establishment in the town of Werben by the Elbe. This soon became the basis for several other Hospitaller convents in the North, stretching into the Slavic areas. They were united in the ballei of Brandenburg, which consisted of the Mecklenburg, Pommern, Lauenburg and at times parts of Poland, thus precisely the areas where the Danish crusades against the Wends in the 12th and 13th century took place.[245] In 1217, Count Niels of Halland together with the Counts Gunzelin and Henry of Schwerin gave the village of Sülstorf in Schwerin to the Hospitallers in Werben, to be used for the Order's work "at the other side of the sea" – that is, in the Holy Land.[246] There may be a connection between this gift and the fact that Count Niels a few years before had decided to go on a crusade to the Holy Land.[247] It shows that the links between the Danish royal family and the Order of St. John did not only extend to the houses, which were established within the borders of present-day Denmark.

The histories of the Templars and of the Hospitallers in Portugal are, despite certain details, largely parallel. Both enjoyed considerable royal support, both were very active castle-builders and participants in local crusades, even though the Templars only took part in the expansion to the south of the Tagus a little later. In Denmark, however, the histories of the two orders are very different. The Templars never came to Scandinavia. The Hospitallers, on the other hand, had special royal attention and received so many donations from several layers in society that they were the richest or the second richest order in Denmark at the time of the Reformation.

St. Canute and his confraternity

In 1170, Afonso Henriques had in practice distanced himself from the Templars and depended on the local military orders from then on. The same year,[248] King Valdemar the Great entered the Confraternity of St. Canute on Gotland and became a member of it. Valdemar employed more or less the same wording as Afonso had used on his entry into the Order of the Templars almost a generation before. Valdemar became a brother in Canute's confraternity in the same year that

242 *The struggle for land and history*

the Order of Santiago was founded in León. Is there a parallel? Was the Confraternity of St. Canute a military order?

Valdemar's father, Canute Lavard, had been Prefect of Schleswig and Prince of the Wendic Obotrites. On January 7, 1131, he was murdered by his cousin Magnus in Haraldsted forest, and soon after miracles happened at his tomb.[249] In 1135, his brother Erik Emune gave large gifts to the monastery in Ringsted and created a basis for the cult, which Erik supported for instance by commissioning the monk Robert of Ely to write a vita, a biography that was to be used as an argument for Canute being a saint.[250] From the outset, the idea of the crusade is introduced. We are told that Ringsted has its name because the sea is the same distance from the town no matter in what direction one travels – it surrounded it as a ring.[251] This is all that was needed for the medieval reader in the 1130s to immediately think of the centre of the world, the earthly Jerusalem, the place where Jesus died and was buried. After having placed Ringsted at the centre of the world, the earliest biography goes on to tell us that this is also why courts are held here.[252] The place of judgement is at the centre, just as the Last Judgement, when the time comes, shall be passed in Jerusalem.

Canute is depicted as the ideal of a just ruler, who is able to fight down robbers and men of discord, and who makes no difference between people. He hangs criminals, even if they are his own relatives, and if they try to get a lighter treatment by mentioning their relationship, they get the family treatment of being hanged in higher gallows than the other scoundrels. Canute is also described as a king keen on missionizing, who extended Christianity in the Wendic areas and brought peace – *pax* – to the heathens and the missionaries,[253] who built churches and equipped the new churches with priests, liturgical clothing and with another great rarity: books. "Even though he was not a book person, in this way he was as much a priest as he was a warrior."[254]

After his death, Canute performed miracles that were common for most saints.[255] Yet in addition, he performed two that distinguished him as a crusader saint. He freed a Swede who had been captured by the heathens and chained, and he saved a group of poor unarmed Christians who were attacked by a large band of heathens. They succeeded in defeating the heathens without a single Christian being wounded. In their gratitude, they gave a spear that had been thrown at them by the heathens to Canute's tomb in Ringsted. This miracle would have made a strong impression at the time immediately after Canute's death. It was only a little more than thirty years since a spear had saved the participants in the first crusade from a desperate situation, as they were besieged and outnumbered by a Muslim army at Antioch.[256] When Canute repeated the miracle, there would still have been many people alive who themselves had participated in the first crusade and experienced the discovery of the spear in Antioch and therefore would have been familiar with the story.

The crusader aspect of Canute was further elaborated in the extensive liturgy that was developed for his translation 1170. The very first page opens triumphantly with the words, "Blessed is the man, whose head the Lord crowns and surrounds with the wall of salvation, equips with the shield and sword of faith to defeat the

The struggle for land and history   243

heathens and all His enemies." Canute Lavard had played a significant role in the armed Christian mission. In this liturgy, Canute is described as the one who brought peace – *pax* – to both the Danes and the heathens, that is, he waged crusades, and as the one who forced the heathens to turn away from their empty and ungodly rituals. Canute had brought his people salvation, and he was an *athleta Christi*, a warrior of Christ. The life of Canute was thus increasingly described as the life of a crusader during the time between his death and his translation. The description of Canute's death developed along the same lines. According to the earliest biography, cousin Magnus lured Canute into an ambush by claiming that he had taken a vow to go on a crusade to the Holy Land. Therefore, he now asked Canute to take care of his wife and his children – which is what he wished to arrange in more detail with Canute in a dark and desolate forest. This explanation continues through the 12th century, but in the 1180s a new tradition emerges which turns it on its head.[257] It is now held that Canute went to meet Magnus "under the banner of the cross" *sub vexillo crucis*, which was the usual term for a person who had taken a crusading vow. Now it was Canute who was the crusader, not Magnus.

The best example of Canute's association with the crusades is the seal from the Confraternity of Canute in Schleswig, Canute's main city and the starting point of his missionary wars among the heathen Wends. The seal dates from around 1200 and depicts Canute on a horse in full armour, with a large sword and a banner. He rides at a gallop – with stretched legs – directly towards the enemy. He wears a helmet but apart from that particular detail, he is like a copy of the contemporary 12th-century pictorial depictions in Portugal and Galicia of Santiago. Both saints were crusader saints.

The earliest known statutes for the confraternity of St. Canute are from Flensburg from around 1200.[258] They are permeated with violence. The first rule states measures for when a non-member kills a member. The next decides what shall happen if a member kills another member. The following rules deal with cases where a brother kills someone outside of the confraternity. Then the other brethren must help him flee by giving him a horse or a boat. The rules predict cases where a member ravages the property of another brother, kills his men and rapes the women. It is forbidden during meetings to attack each other with an axe, a bench or a chair, at least not with so much force that blood is spilled. The rules reflect the social manners within a group where the members were armed and were used to weapons, and who were jealous of their honour. It is directly forbidden to say to another brother that he is lying. Additionally, there are rules that emphasize internal solidarity. All brothers shall intervene and help if a brother has been killed or if he has lost a ship or has been captured by the heathens.

The rules of the confraternity of St. Canute are very close to the regulations for the royal palace guard, the so-called Vederlov from the mid-1180s.[259] The reason why it is necessary to have such a rule, it is stated in the introduction, is that the Danish King rules many lands with very different customs, and they all send their young men to serve at the court of the King. In order to avoid strife and discord amongst them, established rules are needed. The young and proud warriors should

244 *The struggle for land and history*

unite as one single will, just as the limbs obey one head, and they should follow the King's command. Their swords and axes shall shine in gold, because the military crown is the sparkling shield bearings which follow the King everywhere. When the law was passed, the sound echoed from the goldsmiths in all towns, who forged the empty jewellery of vanity into magnificent hilts for the weapons. The moral distancing in the Vederlov to empty worldly splendour is reminiscent of Bernard of Clairvaux and his writing for the Templars. The Vederlov is ascetic and strict with regards to punishment, which even in the details are reminiscent of the earliest confraternity of St. Canute. It can be perceived as a type of rule for a religious confraternity, closely associated with the King. Even if the sources are sparse, taken together they can form the image of a type of local Danish military order, established on a royal initiative, coinciding with what happened on the Iberian Peninsula at the same time.[260]

When Valdemar entered the Guild of St. Canute in Gotland in 1170, a charter was issued, directed at all those who are engaged with the heathen problem: "Those who trade to procure goods, those who break the soil in the sweat of their face, and those who radiate with a warrior's belt."[261] The last group were the proper crusaders, and Valdemar addressed them with the same words that Urban II had employed at Clermont to the French noblemen.[262] But all three groups were equally important, if the war against the infidels were to lead to permanent conquests, settlement and conversion. And both the military action and the establishment of monasteries in the missionary areas happened in the name of St. Canute.

Rosendo, the Portuguese Canute?

Canute Lavard played a large role thus in Danish crusades, and he must have been a particularly important saint to Valdemar the Great, as the King's father. Why did Afonso apparently not try to get a member of the royal family canonized? Part of the explanation is that there were no signs of any cult for his father, who apparently did not perform any miracles. Besides, it must be taken into account that Afonso was well covered with regard to crusader saints. He had Santiago with his order to one side and St. Vincent of Lisbon to the other. One covered warfare on land, the other naval warfare.

There are, nevertheless, signs that Afonso actually participated actively in creating his own crusader saint, Rosendo, at almost exactly the same time as Valdemar succeeded in getting Canute canonized.[263] The Christian kingdoms on the Iberian Peninsula were under pressure during one of the most successful Muslim attempts at recapturing lost land, as Caliph Abu Yakub Yusuf himself led a new Almohad attack. In 1172, he reached as far north as Cuenca in Spain. Afonso Henriques, together with Fernando II of León and Alfonso VII of Castile, turned to the papal legate Hyacinth and asked for Rosendo to be canonized.[264] Hyacinth was a highly enthusiastic crusader and had personally given the cross to and led a whole army from Toledo during the defence against the Muslims a year earlier in 1172, but his engagement actually went all the way back to 1155, when he

The struggle for land and history 245

placed the cross on his own chest and offered to lead an army during a synod in Valadolid.

The request to Hyacinth was followed by a vita, newly written for the occasion, which described Rosendo's life and miracles in detail. He had founded the monastery of Celanova in the 10th century, and at a very young age, he became Archbishop of Mondoñedo on the north coast of Galicia. He saved all of Galicia from Norman attacks, allegedly during the years of 958–960, and at the same time he liberated his fatherland, Portugal, from Muslim attacks – *Portugalensium patriam diuina gratia ab incursu saracenorum liberauit.*[265] He thereby followed a proud family tradition, because his father had fought Muslims around Coimbra, which probably is not true either in a historical sense, but it fitted in well with the construction of Rosendo as a crusader saint. Among his many miracles were the usual ones regarding making the blind see and exorcizing demons, but he also liberated prisoners, awoke two people from the dead, and even had a nobleman split in two because he had attacked the monastery of Celanova.

In the vita, it was claimed that Rosendo was of royal descent, which strictly was not correct, but it would have made him even more attractive to the three kings who wanted him canonized.[266] In 1173, Hyacinth sent a canonization document to Archbishop João Peculiar of Braga. After he had become Pope as Celestine III, Hyacinth recognized his own earlier canonization of Rosendo.

The Portuguese King was thus involved in the canonization, not of a family member but a local saint with crusade affiliations nevertheless, which to a degree might have worked along the same lines as St. Canute in Denmark. The parallel must not be stretched too far, though. There were obvious differences; for instance, Canute had a whole order or confraternity organized around him, which Rosendo did not. Here, the comparison between Denmark and Portugal shows something else: how many ways crusader saints could be created and the different ways in which military orders could be spread and function in the crusades.

The warlike Mary

The cult of St. Mary reached a fervent high point during the 12th century, when great importance was attached to Mary's female aspects: tenderness, warmth, compassion, motherliness. Several theologians virtually wallowed in the image of the milk of salvation that dripped or sprang from her breasts directly into the mouth of the Christ Child.[267] Richard of St. Victor termed Mary's milk the Spring of Mercy in his commentary to the Song of Solomon when he reached the verse of the two breasts of the beloved which are like twin kids driven to graze amongst lilies.[268]

Sucking from Mary's breasts could be of help to a crusade preacher, who found it difficult to find inspiration to encourage a great war against Islam. It worked well and made him so eloquent that he ended up as a cardinal in Rome.[269] Or the milk could go directly into the mouth of Bernard of Clairvaux and heal him, during the time when he was preaching the second crusade and fell ill in Speyer, in 1146.[270] Such devoted motherliness meant that it was obvious that Mary would be

246 *The struggle for land and history*

very indignant of the infidels' deliberate rejection of her Son's divinity. Mary was thus – precisely as a loving mother – one of the effective saints to invoke during the crusades.

Mary's milk worked wonders, not only for Christians but for Muslims too. After a raid among the Christians, a group of Muslims in Spain returned home with much plunder, and the leader of the raid chose a picture of Mary and the child as his share of the booty. He hung it on his wall in his home and looked at it every day. Gradually he began to have doubts regarding God's incarnation, and finally he swore aloud that if God revealed himself, he would believe. Mary's breasts on the picture immediately began to grow and turn to flesh, and milk began to flow from them. The Muslim cried and converted from Islam to Christianity. The miracle was retold in several miracle collections, and, in the 13th century, it was put into verse and included in Cantigas de Santa Maria.[271]

Virgin Mary became the guardian saint of Toledo and all of Spain, and as the conquests continued, mosques were turned into churches and all of them consecrated to Mary.[272] She was depicted on a banner, which was carried in front during the battle of Las Navas de Tolosa in 1212. The banner miraculously crossed the frontline and waved amongst the enemies, and the Muslims were unable to take it or damage it with their stones and arrows. The banner was also depicted in the manuscripts, which described the battle.[273]

In the North, Virgin Mary became the guardian saint of the Teutonic Order, which was established in the 1190s in Acre in the Holy Land and received papal recognition in 1198. From around 1220, the order placed some of its activities in the Baltic region. In 1308, the order moved its headquarters to Marienburg in Prussia, and from then on it played a prominent role in the northern crusades, all the way up to the Lutheran Reformation in around 1530. The crusades of the Teutonic Order took place under the protection of Mary; they were at the time criticized for their brutality and for working against the conversion of the heathens by scaring them away.[274] Both members of the military orders and ordinary crusaders marched forth under the banner of the Virgin Mary. "They received hostages, entered the castle, called on the heathens to receive the faith, sprinkled the castle with holy water and raised Mary's banner from the top."[275]

The crusades also took place in a geographical space, which had the special attention of the Virgin Mary. As a prelude to the last great crusade plan of Innocent III, the indulgence for all other crusades other than for those going to the Holy Land was withdrawn in 1213, but Bishop Albert of Riga protested at the Fourth Lateran Council in 1215, explaining that Livonia around Riga was the Land of the Mother of God and that her own land was in danger pained her just as much as the fact that the land of the Son was in peril.[276] Where this idea originated, that a northern, ice-covered country inhabited by heathens was Mary's land, is not known, but Bishop Albert was certain, and his persuasive powers were not inconsiderable. At the Lateran Council, he succeeded in convincing Pope Innocent and the assembled clerics to reinstate the indulgence for those who fought in the crusades at Riga. Livonia and the Holy Land were equal and for a brief period were the only places to receive the crusader's indulgence.

The struggle for land and history   247

In Portugal, Mary's land is the designation for the area between Douro and Minho. It is presumably an old designation, but it cannot be dated with any certainty. It might have emerged during the 11th century, during the proto-crusades, as the earliest religious fighting took place in this very region, but it is possibly more likely that it happened in connection with the crusades of the 12th century.

The Queen of Heaven from the Revelations of St. John is dressed in the sun, with the moon underneath her feet and with a crown of twelve stars. While the fiery red, seven-headed, ten-horned dragon sweeps away one third of the stars in the sky, the woman gives birth to her son, who shall lead all nations with an iron sceptre. The sun became an image of Mary, *the sun of justice*, as she is called in the liturgy of St. Mary in Riga.[277] A star became another of the most widespread symbols of St. Mary, and, in the North, this led to an association with the sea – *stella Maria* could so easily be rendered as *stella maris*, the star of Mary to the star of the sea, and the two expressions were played out in several of the Mary ballads of the 12th and the 13th centuries. Mary became a protector of the sea that the crusaders crossed in order to fight in Mary's land around Riga, and the whole missionary region was known as "the land on the other side of the sea,"[278] just as the Holy Land was called Outremer.

Sometimes Mary could take rather strong measures against those threatening Riga. In 1221, King Valdemar the Victorious sent his envoy Gotskalk to Riga to take over the city. Livonians, Latvians and Germans protested, and the tradesmen established a commercial blockade in order to prevent it. The astonished Gotskalk withdrew and

> went out on the great, open sea, but without a helmsman the headwind threw him hither and thither. And perhaps because he had arrived in Livonia against the will of He who commands the winds, the winds rose against him with good reason, and the sun of justice did not shine over him. Because he disdained Mary, His mother, who is called the star of the sea, she did not show him a safe route. This knight was driven out of Livonia and returned to Denmark, and renounced thereafter any royal sovereignty over the land of the Blessed Virgin. Thus, thus protects the Mistress of the World and the Empress of all countries her own country always; thus, thus the Queen of heaven commands earthly kings. Was it not her who commanded when she descended upon many kings, who attacked Livonia? Did she not descend the great King Vladimir of Polotsk, when she struck him with sudden death when he came to Livonia with his army? And was it not her who immediately deprived the great King of Novgorod of his realm when he for the first time attempted to plunder Livonia, such that he was driven out by his people? And the second King of Novgorod, who was the other to plunder Livonia, she killed by the way of the Mongols.[279]

The catalogue of the Virgin Mary's effective interventions continues for a long time in the record. Swedes, who invaded the provinces that were placed under her banner, perish. The Danish King is captured by his vassal. The chieftains in

248 *The struggle for land and history*

the land of Treyden she kills with the plague. She annihilates the princes and the chieftains of the heathens from earth. What king – heathen or Danish or from any other nation – has ever fought against Livonia without perishing, Henry of Livonia asks in his chronicle. And he summarizes: "Behold, the mother of God, how tender she is towards her own, who faithfully serve her in Livonia, behold how she always defends them against all their enemies, and behold how cruel she is against those who invade her land or try to prevent the faith of her Son and the cult of Him in that land. Behold, which and how many kings she has descended upon. Behold, which heretic and heathen princes and chieftains she has annihilated from earth."

In Mary beauty and horror, awe and terror were united. The praises in the Song of Solomon of female beauty and the good shepherd's care for the kids in the lily fields passed into confusion and dread, the two emotions could not be separated.

> My beloved is gone down into his garden, to the bed of aromatic spices, to feed in the gardens, and to gather lilies.
>
> I to my beloved, and my beloved to me, who feedeth among the lilies.
>
> Thou art beautiful, O my love, sweet and comely as Jerusalem, terrible as an army set in array.
>
> Turn away thy eyes from me, for they have made me flee away.
>
> (The Song of Solomon 6, 1–4)

The Song of Solomon was used in the liturgy for the Assumption on August 15, one of the greatest feast-days for the crusaders devoted to the Virgin Mary. This was the day that Afonso Henriques chose in 1170[280] to knight his son Sancho and to have him crowned, so that he could continue the crusades in Portugal: "Thou art beautiful, O my love, sweet and comely as Jerusalem terrible as an army set in array." Later in the liturgy, the choir replies; "Who is she, who rises like the dawn, beautiful as the moon, splendid as the sun, terrible as an army set in array."[281] The Assumption was the perfect day for starting wars against the heathens. On that day, Fellin in Estonia fell to the crusaders in 1223, and this was the reason why the siege of the strong fortress of Dorpat was begun on the same date the year after.[282]

The saints illustrate the duplicity of tenderness and raw brutality so characteristic of the crusaders, which can be difficult to grasp today. Peaceful adherents of the Christian faith such as St. John the Baptist, St. James, St. Vincent and Bishop Isidore of Seville were assigned a role from around 1100 as leaders of bloody military battles against Muslims and heathens. They became guardian saints for the religious military order, a completely new phenomenon in Christianity, where warriors lived in religious communities and were praised as being particularly pious, at the same time as their main objective was to stay perpetually mobilized and to kill others. The unity of tenderness and brutality is most striking in the Virgin Mary figure, who is both the loving, nursing mother as well as the wrathful and avenging warrior goddess.

Warrior saints and the Mother of God were among the most important agents in the frontier areas, and they protected both the tangible church buildings that were

The struggle for land and history   249

consecrated in their names and the Church in general. Again, two aspects unite in the medieval perception, so that physical expression and institution and the Church as a pure concept become inseparable. It was impossible to speak of one without thinking of the other.

Notes

1 For the use of Charlemagne in the context of crusades in the Baltic area and for the attempt to depict Henry the Lion as a new Charlemagne, see Jeffrey Ashcroft, 'Konrad's Rolandslied, Henry the Lion, and the Northern Crusade', *Forum for Modern Language Studies* 22 (1986), pp. 184–207.
2 MUB: *Mecklenburgisches Urkundenbuch*, ed. Verein fur Mecklenburgische Geschichte und Altertumskunde (Schwerin, 1863–),1, no. 65, p. 56.
3 Julie A. Harris, 'Mosque to Church Conversions in the Spanish Reconquest', *Medieval Encounters* 3 (1997), pp. 158–172, pp. 167–169.
4 MUB 1, no. 65, p. 56.
5 Thomas Hill, 'Von der Konfrontation zur Assimilation. Das Ende der Slawen in Ostholstein, Lauenburg und Lübeck vom 12. bis zum 15. Jahrhundert', in: Michael Müller-Wille, Dietrich Meier und Henning Unverhau (eds.), *Slawen und Deutsche um südlichen Ostseeraum vom 11. bis zum 16. Jahrhundert. Archäologische, historische und sprachwissenschaftliche Beispiele aus Schleswig-Holstein, Mecklenburg und Pommern* (Neumünster, 1995), pp. 79–104.
6 Winfried Schich, 'Zum Ausschluss der Wenden aus den Zünften nord- und ostdeutscher Städte im späten mittelalter', in: Antoni Czacharowski (ed.), *Nationale, ethnische Minderheiten und regionale Identitäten in Mittelalter und Neuzeit* (Toruń, 1994), pp. 31–51.
7 Cistercians propagating crusade ideas, *The Second Crusade and the Cistercians*, ed. Michael Gervers (New York, 1992); Peter Dinzelbacher, *Bernhard von Clairvaux: Leben und Werk des berühmten Zisterziensers* (Darmstadt, 1998), pp. 284–307; Beverly Mayne Kienzle, *Cistercians, Heresy and Crusade in Occitania, 1145–1229. Preaching in the Lord's Vineyard* (York, 2001), pp. 64–67; William J. Purkis, *Crusading Spirituality in the Holy Land and Iberia* (Woodbridge, 2008), pp. 111–119; Anne E. Lester, 'A Shared Imitation: Cistercian Convents and Crusader Families in Thirteenth-Century Champagne', *Journal of Medieval History* 35 (2009), pp. 353–370. Cistercians in Denmark, Brian Patrick McGuire, *The Cistercians in Denmark. Attitudes, Roles, and Functions in Medieval Society* (Kalamazoo, 1982).
8 Generally, McGuire, *The Cistercians in Denmark.*
9 *Exordium magnum cisterciense* III, XXVII; also in SM II, 428–437.
10 DD 1:3, no. 32. Eskil writes "Porro insuper timemus ne nobilis regni uestri gloriam maculet. si auditum fuerit apud exteras nationes sic deliquisse in amicum dulcis Gallie abbates," which looks like a reference to the verses 1194 and 1210 of the *Chanson de Roland.*
11 DD 1:2, no. 114.
12 DD 1:2, no. 126.
13 DD 1:2, no. 122 and no. 126.
14 Christian Radtke, 'Die Entwicklung der Stadt Schleswig: Funktionen, Strukturen und die Anfange der Gemeindebildung', in: Erich Hoffmann and Frank Lubowitz (eds.), *Die Stadt im westlichen Ostseeraum: Vorträge zur Stadtgründung und Stadterweiterung im hohen Mittelalter* (Frankfurt a.M., 1995), pp. 47–91, here p. 68.
15 AD, p. 68, not in Annales Lundenses, AD, p. 54.
16 With yearly meetings in the general chapter of Cîteaux, the Danish and Portuguese abbots met face to face several times.

250   *The struggle for land and history*

17 Maur Cocheril, 'Abadias cistercienses portuguesas', *Lusitania Sacra* 4 (1959), pp. 61–92; Maur Cocheril, 'D. Afonso Henriques et les premiers cisterciens portugais', *Actas do 2º Congresso Histórico de Guimarães* 5 (1982), pp. 321–332; Maur Cocheril, *Routier des abbayes cisterciennes du Portugal*, nouvelle éd. par Gerard Leroux (Paris, 1986); dated 1140–1142 by Saul António Gomes, 'Entre memória e história: os primeiros tempos da Abadia de Santa Maria de Alcobaça (1152–1215)', *Revista de Historia da Sociedade e da Cultura* 2 (2002), pp. 187–256, here p. 201.

18 Cocheril, *Routier des abbayes*, p. 78.

19 Exordium monasterii S. Joannis de Tarouca.

20 José Mattoso, *Ricos-homens, infanções e cavaleiros: a nobreza medieval portuguesa nos séculos XI e XII* (Lisbon, 1982), pp. 188–190.

21 The text shifts between Adebert and Aldebert.

22 Exordium monasterii S. Joannis de Tarouca.

23 DMP I:1, no. 243, p. 297.

24 Stéphane Boissellier, *Naissance d'une identité portugaise: la vie rurale entre Tage et Guadiana de l'Islam à la reconquête (Xe-XIVe siécles)* (Lisboa, 1999), pp. 88ff.; Robert Durand, *Les campagnes portugaises entre Douro et Tage aux XIIe et XIIIe siècles* (Paris, 1982), pp. 59–66.

25 Boissellier, *Naissance d'une identité portugaise*, p. 100. José Mattoso, *Identificação de um país: ensaio sobre as origens de Portugal, 1096–1325*, vols. 1–2 (Lisbon, 1995), vol. 1, pp. 336–338 discusses *espírito de cruzada* and suggests a divide in the middle of the 12th century. Until then, the savage extermination of the other religion and massacres of women and children were not common, except when foreign warriors participated, for example the French knights in the 11th century. Then an exacerbation and brutalization took place; Mattoso suggests cautiously that it might have been a response to the contemporary intolerance of the Almohads, which had the Mozarabs suffer. A recent survey in English has taken over the idea of the intolerant foreign crusaders in Portugal: "This was a mixed blessing because the crusaders sometimes behaved brutally, plundering and committing atrocities like Viking raiders of old." A.R. Disney, *A History of Portugal and the Portuguese Empire. From Beginnings to 1807* (Cambridge, 2009), pp. 80–82, where the foreign crusaders are blamed for the massacres on Muslims at the conquest of Lisbon and Santarém.

26 One exception is E. Christiansen, *The Northern Crusades: The Baltic and the Catholic Frontier 1100–1525* (London, 1980), pp. 199–200, but he is significantly not brought up in the Danish tradition. A new generation has taken up war history and treats it from different angles; however, this is a new trend; Janus Møller Jensen, *Denmark and the Crusades, 1400–1650* (Leiden, 2007); Iben Fonnesberg-Schmidt, *The Popes and the Baltic Crusades 1147–1254* (Leiden, 2007).

27 Kurt Villads Jensen, 'The Blue Baltic Border of Denmark in the High Middle Ages: Danes, Wends and Saxo Grammaticus', in: David Abulafia and Nora Behrend (eds.), *Medieval Frontiers: Concepts and Practices* (Aldershot, 2002), pp. 173–193.

28 For Portugal, see Boissellier, *Naissance d'une identité portugaise*, pp. 88–109; A.H. de Oliveira Marques, *História de Portugal: Das Origens ao Renascimento* (Lisbon, 1997), vol. 1, pp. 125–129.

29 Kienzle, *Cistercians, Heresy and Crusade;* Mette Birkedal Bruun, *Parables. Bernard of Clairvaux's Mapping of Spiritual Topography* (Leiden, 2007), pp. 71–85.

30 Matthew 14, 1–11 and parallels.

31 John 1, 23, which refers to Isaiah 40, 3–4. The Cistercian monk would have felt like a voice of someone crying – as one who passes on the message of St. John the Baptist, just as St. John gave voice to Isaiah's cry, and Isaiah was the voice of God, to whom both Heaven and Earth must listen (Isaiah 1, 1).

32 Quoted from Birkedal Bruun, *Parables*, p. 72, note 68.

33 For example in Robert the Monk, *Historia Hierosolymitana*, PL 155; col. 672.

The struggle for land and history 251

34 *Urkundenbuch des Erzstifts Magdeburg*, vol. 1, no. 193, pp. 249–252, which closely follows Robert the Monk' version of Urban's sermon.

35 Kienzle, *Cistercians, Heresy and Crusade;* chapter 2 and 3.

36 Matthew 9, 38. Riccoldo da Monte di Croce, Libellus . . ., prohemium, where the harvest quote serves as a heading for all of his extensive missionary manual.

37 Mattoso, *Identificação*, vol. 1, pp. 196 ff.

38 Constance Hoffman Berman, *Medieval Agriculture, the Southern French Countryside, and the Early Cistercians, a Study of Fourty-Three Monasteries* (Philadelphia, 1986), is a classic on the economic role of the Cistercian order, focusing on Southern France and the early period; Lester K. Little, *Religious Poverty and the Profit Economy in Medieval Europe* (London, 1978) is more broad; criticized by Isabel Alfonso, 'Cistercians and Feudalism', *Past & Present* 133 (1991), pp. 3–30, for romanticizing the Cistercians as a kind of medieval American frontier farmers (p. 6), who broke new land in hostile surroundings. But that was what they actually did in a number of cases.

39 This was parallel to the privileges issued by kings to individuals and institutions wanting to establish themselves in the deserted frontier regions, for example DMP I:1, no. 12–17 and several later documents.

40 José Mattoso and Armindo de Sousa, *A Monarquia Feudal (1096–1480)* (Lisbon, 1993), pp. 197–200.

41 Ibid.; Mattoso, *Identificação;* pp. 255–256.

42 Saul António Gomes, 'Um Formulário Monástico Português Medieval: o Manuscrito alcobacense 47 da BNL', *Humanitas* 51 (1999), pp. 141–184, edition on pp. 159–184.

43 Fortunato de Almeida and Damiao Peres, *História da Igreja em Portugal* (Porto, 1967), p. 130.

44 Statuta O.C., *Statuta Capitulorum Generalium Ordinis Cisterciensis ab anno 1116 ad annum 1786*, ed. D. Josephus-Mia Canivez, vols. 1–8 (Louvain, 1933–1941), 1153, 25; 1157, 49; 1175, 16. In all three cases, it is forbidden to prevent the Muslims from being baptized, in the first and last case to buy them, in 1157 to sell them.

45 Gomes, 'Entre memória e história', pp. 222–223.

46 MUB 1, no. 111, p. 106.

47 MUB 1, no. 114, dated 1174; DD 1:5, no. 163 dated to after 1176.

48 On the huge rise in the international beer trade in around 1200, see Richard W. Unger, 'Beer: A New Bulk Good of International Trade', in: Lars Berggren, Nils Hybel and Anette Landen (eds.), *Cogs, Cargoes, and Commerce: Maritime Bulk Trade in Northern Europe, 1150–1400* (Toronto, 2002), pp. 113–127; for Danish trade in beer, see Nils Hybel and Bjørn Poulsen, *The Danish Resources ca. 1000–1550. Growth and Recession* (Leiden, 2007), passim.

49 MUB 1, no. 113, p. 109. Worwerk or Vorwerk is small plots of land, cf. Niels Skyum-Nielsen, 'Estonia under Danish Rule', in: Niels Skyum-Nielsen and Niels Lund (eds.), *Danish Medieval History, New Currents* (Copenhagen, 1981), pp. 112–135, here p. 117, but from the context here it could have been individuals working on fortification.

50 MUB 1, no. 147, p. 142.

51 Hans-Otto Gaethke, *Herzog Heinrich der Löwe und die Slawen nordöstlich der unteren Elbe* (Frankfurt a.M., 1999), pp. 234–235.

52 DOM vol 1, nr. 1.

53 DD 1:3, no. 64.

54 Helmold, 63.

55 KVJ: *Kong Valdemars Jordebog*, vols. 1–3, ed. Svend Aakjær (Copenhagen, 1926–1945), 1, 139–141, fol. 135v–136r, with the Fehmarn list, which includes both "the names of the towns on Fehmarn" as well as "the names of the Slavs' towns."

56 MUB 1, no. 122, p. 118; no. 125, p. 121.

57 DOM, vol. 1, no. 36.

58 According to a message from Professor Jens E. Olesen, University of Greifswald.

252 *The struggle for land and history*

59 J. Bolòs, 'Changes and Survival: The Territory of Lleida (Catalonia) After the Twelfth Century Conquest', *Journal of Medieval History* 27 (2001), pp. 313–329.

60 see generally *Historiographical approaches . . .* 2002.

61 DOM, vol. 1, no. 6.

62 Kienzle, *Cistercians, Heresy and Crusade;* chapter 2 and 3.

63 The only way before the introduction of modern maps, precisely described as 'verbal mapping', cf. Giles Constable, 'Frontiers in the Middle Ages', in: O. Merisalo (ed.), *Frontiers in the Middle Ages. Proceedings of the Third European Congress of Medieval Studes, Jyväskylä, 10–14 June 2003* (Louvain-la-Neuve, 2006), p. 9.

64 MUB 1, no. 114.

65 *Die Prüfeninger Vita Bischof Ottos I. von Bamberg nach der Fassung des Grossen Österreichischen Legendars*, ed. Jürgen Petersohn (Hannover, 1999), e.g. p. 132.

66 Bernard of Clairvaux, Sententiae III, 71; quoted in Birkedal Bruun, *Parables*, p. 77, note 83.

67 Birkedal Bruun, *Parables*, p. 77, discusses with Robert P. Harrison, *Forests: The Shadow of Civilization* (Chicago, 1992) whether Bernard's tree metaphors concern the heathens and an ancient heathen memory of sacred trees, or whether they were directed against all humans. They could presumably be used for both.

68 Saxo, 14.44.10.

69 Cocheril, *Routier des abbayes*, pp. 256–257.

70 Ezekiel 43, 10; Zechariah 2, 6; Revelation 21, 15.

71 2 Kings 21, 13.

72 Peter Donat, Heike Reimann, and Cornelia Willich, *Slawische Siedlung und Landesausbau im nordwestlichen Mecklenburg* (Stuttgart, 1999), p. 139.

73 McGuire, *The Cistercians in Denmark*, pp. 79–83.

74 DMA, xi–xii; Anne K.G. Kristensen, *Danmarks ældste Annalistik. Studier over lundensisk Annalskrivning i 12. og 13. århundrede* (Copenhagen, 1969).

75 Cistercians were not the only members of a monastic order who went out to cultivate the deserted missionary field. The Premonstratensians often arrived soon after. However, until the emergence of the mendicant orders in the 13th century, the Cistercians were the most numerous and best organized in the religious frontier lands, also in comparison with the Premonstratensians; see Tore Nyberg, 'Die skandinavische Zirkarie der Prämonstratenserchorherren', in: Gert Melville (ed.), *Secundum regulam vivere. Festschrift für P. Norberg Backmund O.Praem* (Windberg, 1978), pp. 265–279, here p. 268.

76 Bernard of Clairvaux, De laude.

77 Ibid., I, 1.

78 Ibid., III, 4.

79 Ibid., XIII, 31; see 118, 14.

80 Mattoso, *Ricos-homens*, pp. 48–49.

81 Gomes, 'Entre memória e história', pp. 218–219.

82 Helle Halding, *Thi de var af stor slægt. Om Hvideslægten og kongemagt i dansk højmiddelalder* (Ebeltoft, 2001).

83 Friedrich Benninghoven, *Der Orden der Schwertbrüder: Fratres milicie Christi de Livonia* (Köln, 1965).

84 Characteristically, on a map of the estates of the military orders in Portugal, A. H. de Oliveira Marques ('O poder e o espaço', in: Maria Helena da Cruz Coelho e Armando Luís de Carvalho Homem [eds.], *Nova História de Portugal* [Lisbon, 1996], vol. 3, p. 160) uses the same sign for the Knights Templars and the Order of Christ.

85 Kurt Villads Jensen, 'The Blue Baltic Border'; Kurt Villads Jensen, 'Knudsgilder og korstog', in: Lars Bisgaard and Leif Søndergaard (eds.), *Gilder, lav og broderskaber i middelalderens Danmark* (Odense, 2002), pp. 63–88.

86 On the Cistercians and the preaching of crusades and the role of Bernard, see e.g. *The Second Crusade and the Cistercians*; Jonathan Phillips, *The Second Crusade: Extending the Frontiers of Christendom* (New Haven, 2007), pp. 37–114; Purkis, *Crusading Spirituality*, pp. 86–119.

The struggle for land and history 253

87 Bernard, Opera, vol. 8, no. 457.
88 Edginton, 'The Lisbon Letter'; Phillips, 'St Bernard of Clairvaux'.
89 DD 1:2, no. 86.
90 Knytlinga saga, chapter 108.
91 Giles Constable, 'The Second Crusade as seen by Contemporaries', *Traditio* 9 (1953), pp. 215–279; Virginia G. Berry, 'The Second Crusade', *A History of the Crusades* 1 (1958), pp. 463–512; *The Second Crusade. Scope and Consequences*, ed. Jonathan Phillips and Martin Hoch (Manchester, 2001); Graham A. Loud, 'Some Reflections on the Failure of the Second Crusade', *Crusades* 4 (2005), pp. 1–14; Phillips, *The Second Crusade*, pp. 207–227.
92 From the life story of Bernard, see Geoffrey of Auxerre, *Vita Prima Bernardi*. Bernard's own defence of the second crusade in *De Consideratione Libri Quinque*, II, PL 182, esp. cols. 741–745.
93 Esp. Constable, 'The Second Crusade'.
94 Ane L. Bysted, *The Crusade Indulgence. Spiritual Rewards and the Theology of the Crusades c. 1095–1216* (Leiden, 2015).
95 H.-D. Kahl, 'Crusade Eschatology as seen by St Bernard in the Years 1146 to 1148', in: Michael Gervers (ed.), *The Second Crusade and the Cistercians* (New York, 1992), pp. 35–47; Bysted, *The Crusade Indulgence*; Fonnesberg-Schmidt, *The Popes*, pp. 152–153.
96 Bernard Epistula 64. 1–2; in Opera, vol. 8, no. 157–158.
97 Ekkehardus Uraugiensis, PL 154, col. 970.
98 Liber Sancti Jacobi, vol. 1, p. 302. In an edition of *Historia Turpini*, which is included in the manuscript with the cathedral's liturgy of St. James.
99 Hilário Franco Júnior, *Peregrinos, Monges e Guerreiros. Feudo-clericalismo e religiosidade em Castela medieval* (São Paulo, 1990), p. 94.
100 Hobsbaum, Eric, and Terence Ranger (eds), *The Invention of Tradition* (Cambridge, 1983); Helen Nicholson, *Love, War and the Grail* (Leiden, 2001), p. 14.
101 Liber Sancti Jacobi, vol. 1, p. 312.
102 *Chanson de Roland*, verse 1488.
103 Liber Sancti Jacobi, vol. 1, p. 325.
104 Liber Sancti Jacobi, vol. 1, p. 259.
105 Pilgrim's guide, vol. 2, p. 64.
106 Michael Müller-Wille, *Mittelalterliche Grabfunde aus der Kirche des slawischen Burgwalles von Alt Lübeck: zu dynastischen Grablegen in polnischen und abodritischen Herrschaftsgebieten* (Stuttgart, 1996), p. 47; Kurt Köster, *Pilgerzeichen und Pilgermuscheln von mittelalterlichen Santiagostrassen: Saint-Léonard, Rocamadour, Saint-Gilles, Santiago de Compostela* (Neumünster, 1983); Lars Andersson, *Pilgrimsmärken och vallfart. Medeltida pilgrimskultur i Skandinavien* (Stockholm, 1989); Christian Krötzl, 'Wege und Pilger aus Skandinavien nach Santiago', in: Robert Plötz (ed.), *Europäische Wege der Santiago-Pilgerfahrt* (Tübingen, 1990), pp. 157–169.
107 Ekkehardus Uraugiensis, PL 154, col. 970.
108 Phillips, *Defenders of the Holy Land*.
109 In Conrad's Rolandslied from between 1168 and 1172; see Ashcroft, 'Konrad's Rolandslied'.
110 Zrinka Stahuljak, *Bloodless Genealogies of the French Middle Ages: Translations, Kinship, and Metaphor* (Gainesville, 2005).
111 *Chanson de Roland*, verse 3534–3559.
112 Conversion Otgarii. The dating is from Knud Togeby, *Ogier le danois dans les littératures européennes* (Copenhagen, 1969), p. 20; he dates it to presumably the 11th century, perhaps early 12th century.
113 Apparently, there was a confusion with Bishop Faro of Meaux, who lived during the latter half of the 7th century.
114 Togeby, *Ogier le danois*, p. 34.

254   *The struggle for land and history*

115 The following treatment of narratives of Ogier the Dane is based on Ibid.
116 La chevalerie d'Ogier, vers 69.
117 Nicholson, *Love, War*, pp. 37–38. La chevalerie d'Ogier, vers 10420.
118 La chevalerie d'Ogier, verse 12342.
119 Ernst Robert Curtius, 'Le Chevalerie Ogier', *Romanische Forschungen* 62 (1950), pp. 125–157: "Unermüdlich vergiesst Ogier Blut und Hirn" (p. 132). "Man könnte im angloamerikanischen Detektivroman der Gegenwart ähnliche Unterschiede des Stils, des Geschmacks, der Leserschichten feststellen wie im französischen Epos um 1200. . . . Die Roheit des Ogier ist kein Anzeichen von Primitivismus, sondern von einer gesunkenen, kommerzialisierten Kunst, die auf niedere Instinkte spekuliert, besonders auf die Freude am Grässlichen und Widerwärtigen. Epische Kämpfe, die mit dem Mittel *sanc et cervele* wirken wollen, haben zu Heldentum und Rittertum keine seelische Beziehung mehr." (p. 138).
120 Togeby, *Ogier le danois*.
121 AD, p. 51. The vita of Erik Ploughpenny, which is not much younger, mentions Skokloster, urbi quiescit Holmgerus clarens miraculis, but mentions cautiously ut dicitur ("Skokloster, where Holmgerus lays buried and is famous for its miracles, as it is said"). VSD, p. 441, line 28–29.
122 Eyvind Fjeld Halvorson, 'Karlamagnus Saga', *KLNM* 8 (1956–1978), pp. 286–290, here p. 287.
123 Albert of Trois-Fontaines, ad 1210 (p. 891).
124 Saxo, 6.5.2. The story of Starkad continues all the way to 8.8.12, interrupted by several other stories.
125 Saxo, 8.8.6.
126 Saxo, 8.16.5.
127 Saxo, 9.4.26 and 9.4.25.
128 Saxo, 14.39.13.
129 Also in Helmold, 6.
130 E. Christiansen, 'The Place of Fiction in Saxo's Later Books', in: Karsten Friis-Jensen (ed.), *Saxo Grammaticus. A Medieval Author Between Norse and Latin Culture* (Copenhagen, 1981), pp. 27–37.
131 Inge Skovgaard-Petersen, *Da Tidernes Herre var nær. Studier i Saxos historiesyn* (Copenhagen, 1987), pp. 168–169.
132 Armando de Sousa Pereira, 'Motivos bíblicos na historiografia de Santa Cruz de Coimbra dos finais do século XII', *Lusitania Sacra* 2a sér 13–14 (2002), pp. 315–336, here p. 321; Armando de Sousa Pereira, *Representações da Guerra no Portugal da Reconquista (Séculos XI–XIII)* (Lisbon, 2003). Mattosso, *Ricos-homens*.
133 De expugnatione scalabis. Historical writing in Santa Cruz in the 1180s, see Pereira, 'Motivos bíblicos', for the library, Saul António Gomes, *In limine conscriptionis. Documentos, Chancelaria e Cultura no mosteiro de Santa Cruz de Coimbra (Séculos XII a XIV)* (Viseu, 2007), pp. 183–216.
134 Annales D. Alfonsi; Monica Blöcker-Walter, *Alfons I. von Portugal: Studien zu Geschichte und Sage des Begründers der portugiesischen Unabhängigkeit* (Zürich, 1966); Pereira, 'Motivos bíblicos'.
135 Miracula S Vincenti, lib. 1, cap. 1.
136 Indiculum.
137 Ibid., 3.
138 Ibid., 11.
139 Ibid., 7.
140 R. W. Chambers and C. L. Wrenn, *Beowulf. An Introduction to the Study of the Poem with a Discussion of the Stories of Offa and Finn* (Cambridge, 1967).
141 Rikke Malmros, 'Leding og Skjaldekvad. Det elvte århundredes nordiske krigsflåder, deres teknologi og organisation og deres placering i samfundet, belyst gennem den samtidige fyrstedigtning', *Aarbøger for Nordisk Oldkyndighed og Historie* 1985

The struggle for land and history   255

(1985), pp. 89–139; Niels Lund, *Lið, leding og landeværn. Hær og samfund i Danmark i ældre middelalder* (Roskilde, 1996).

142 JL, chapter 3.

143 Eriks Sjællandske, Lov, 3, XVIII.

144 expeditionis societas; Saxo, 16.4.5.

145 Slesvig stadsret, 7–8; DGK I, 5.

146 Gulathingslov, 305.

147 B. Holmberg, 'Maritime Place-Names', in: Ole Crumlin-Pedersen (ed.), *Aspects of Maritime Scandinavia AD 200–1200* (Roskilde, 1991), pp. 233–240; B. Holmberg and J. Skamby Madsen, 'Da kom en snekke . . . Havnepladser fra 1000- og 1100-tallet?', *KUML. Årbog for Jysk Arkæologisk Selskab* (1997/1998), pp. 197–225.

148 C.A. Christensen, 'Leidang', *KLNM* 10 (1956–1978), pp. 443–459.

149 Annals of Ryd and Annals of Ribe, in DMA, pp. 170, 232, 259.

150 Saxo, 10.9.3.

151 Saxo, 14.49.1.

152 J. H. Pryor, 'Transportation of Horses by Sea During the Era of the Crusades: Eighth Century to 1285 AD', *Mariner's Mirror* 68 (1982), pp. 9–27, 103–125; J.H. Pryor, *Geography, Technology, and War: Studies in the Marine History of the Mediterranean, 649–1571* (New York, 1988), especially pp. 112–134; J.H. Pryor, 'The Naval Architecture of Crusader Transport Ships and Horse Transports Revisited', *Mariner's Mirror* 76 (1990), pp. 255–273; J. H. Pryor, 'A View from a Masthead: The First Crusade from the Sea', *Crusades* 7 (2008), pp. 87–152. Larger ships in the Mediterranean during early 13th century, John E. Dotson, 'Ship Types and Fleet Composition at Genoa and Venice in the Early Thirteenth Century', in: John H. Pryor (ed.), *Logistics of Warfare in the Age of the Crusades* (Aldershot, 2006), pp. 63–75.

153 Malmros, 'Leding og Skjaldekvad', p. 95; Ole Crumlin-Pedersen, 'Ship Types and Sizes AD 800–1400', in: Ole Crumlin-Pedersen (ed.), *Aspects of Maritime Scandinavia AD 200–1200* (Roskilde, 1991), pp. 69–82, here p. 79; Anton Englert, *Large Cargo Vessels in Danish Waters AD 1000–1250*. Unpublished PhD dissertation, Kiel University (2000); Jan Bill, 'Castles at Sea. The Warship of the High Middle Ages', in: Anne Nørgard Jørgensen, John Pind, Lars Jørgensen and Birthe Clausen (eds.), *Maritime Warfare in Northern Europe. Technology, Organization, Logistics and Administration 500 BC–1500 AD* (Copenhagen, 2002), p. 51; Jan Bill, 'The Cargo Vessels', in: Lars Berggren, Nils Hybel and Anette Landen (eds.), *Cogs, Cargoes, and Commerce: Maritime Bulk Trade in Northern Europe, 1150–1400*, (Toronto, 2002), pp. 92–112.

154 James Craigie Robertson, *Materials for the History of Thomas Becket, Archbishop of Canterbury, Canonized by Pope Alexander III, A.D. 1173* (London, 1879), vol. 4.

155 Bill, 'Castles at Sea', p. 52.

156 Ibid., p. 50.

157 Henry of Livonia, *Henrici Chronicon Livoniae*, ed. Leonid Arbusow and Albertus Bauer (Hannover, 1955), 14, 1.

158 Saxo, 14.49.6.

159 Saxo, 14.49.4. Absalon might have been inspired by the great crusader Bishop Adhemar de Le Puy. During the struggle for Antioch in 1097, he paid the crusaders twelve denarius for each head of a Turk they could bring him. The heads were then put on long poles in front of the city wall to mock the Turks and rouse their anger. Guibert of Nogent, *Dei gesta per Francos et cinq autres textes*, ed. R.B.C. Huygens. Corpus Christianorum Continuatio Mediaevalis; 127A (Turnhout, 1996), 7, 23. See also Sini Kangas, *Deus vult: Images of Crusader Violence ca. 1095–1100*, Unpublished PhD-dissertation, Department of History, Helsinki University (2007), p. 111.

160 Saxo, 16.5.3.

161 Miracula S. Vincentii, 1, 8.

162 Mattoso and de Sousa, *A Monarquia*, pp. 254–255.

256　*The struggle for land and history*

163　Miracula S. Vincentii, 1, 16; 1, 17, a.o.
164　Caesarius of Heisterbach, 8, 66; J.F. O'Callaghan, *Reconquest and Crusade in Medieval Spain* (Philadelphia, 2003), p. 193.
165　La Chevalerie d'Ogier, verse 10373 and 10657.
166　DD 1:2, no. 89.
167　Odenius Oloph, 'Vincentius', *KLNM* 20 (1956–1978), pp. 88–89.
168　Miracula S. Vincentii, Introduction, 12–13.
169　A.H. de Oliveira Marques, *A expansão quatrocentista* (Lisbon, 1998).
170　PMH, Leges 1, 1, 634.
171　O'Callaghan, *Reconquest and Crusade*, p. 149.
172　Marques, 'O poder e o espaço', p. 57.
173　Duarte Galvão, *Crónica de el-rei D. Afonso Henriques* (Lisbon, 1995), cap. LV.
174　Marques, *A expansão*, p. 15.
175　Galvão, *Crónica*, LVI.
176　Isabel de Barros Dias, 'Cronística afonsina modelada em português: um case de recepção activa', *Hispania* 67 (2007), pp. 899–928, here pp. 919–920. *Crónica de 1344*, 1st and 2nd edition, one of the significant additions in the Portuguese translations of *Primera Crónica General de España*.
177　Ann Hyland, *The Medieval Warhorse from Byzantium to the Crusades* (Stroud, 1994); Charles Gladitz, *Horse Breeding in the Medieval World* (Dublin, 1997); Pryor, 'Transportation of Horses by Sea'; Pryor, 'A View from a Masthead', pp. 133–140.
178　In 1206, Bishop Albert of Riga gave an unusually fine destrier to Vladimir of Polotsk, Henry of Livonia, 10, 1.
179　Johannes Marignolli, *Relatio.*
180　Hybel and Poulsen, *The Danish Resources*, p. 211, p. 377.
181　Niels Skyum-Nielsen, *Kvinde og Slave* (Copenhagen, 1971), p. 312; Nils Hybel, 'Dansk eksport på det nordeuropæiske marked ca. 1200–1350', in: Per Ingesman og Bjørn Poulsen (eds.), *Danmark og Europa i senmiddelalderen* (Aarhus, 2000), pp. 183–197.
182　DGK I, 75.
183　Arnold of Lübeck, 3, 5.
184　Of which some may stem from a later age. It is rare that they are datable at all.
185　Poul Enemark, 'Hestehandel', *KLNM* 6 (1981), pp. 524–532.
186　Erik Oksbjerg, *Læsning i tekster fra Danmarks Middelalder. Jyske Lov. Sjællandske Krønike* (Viborg, 2002), pp. 128–129; JL III, 55.
187　Skyum-Nielsen, *Kvinde og Slave*, p. 156, refers to a letter by Stephan of Tournai.
188　Enemark, 'Hestehandel'.
189　DD 1:2, no. 42.
190　Statuta O.C. 1152, 18.
191　Statuta O.C. 1157, 37; 1158, 3; 1175, 27.
192　Statuta O.C. 1184, 7.
193　Count Niels decided to go on a crusade and sold land to Esrom, and received a very large part of the selling price in warhorses; DD 1:5, no. 7 and no. 8.
194　Jonathan Riley-Smith, *Hospitallers. The History of the Order of St John* (London, 1999), p. 47.
195　The sources are more plentiful from a slightly later period. An interesting study of horses and horse breeding of the Teutonic Order, but only from the late 14th century and the 15th century, is Sven Ekdahl, 'Horses and Crossbows: Two Important Warfare Advantages of the Teutonic Order in Prussia', in: Helen Nicholson (ed.), *The Military Orders*, vols. 1–2 (Aldershot, 1998), vol. 2, pp. 119–151.
196　Gomes, 'Entre memória e história', pp. 208–209. Barros, *História de administrão*, does not have any systematic source material regarding horse breeding before the latter half of the 14th century; vol. 4, pp. 90–99.
197　Saxo, 14.15.1–4.

The struggle for land and history   257

198 On Jaime's thoughts on God's support for his crusades, Damian J. Smith, 'The Abbot-Crusader: Nicholas Breakspear in Catalonia', in: Brenda Bolton and Anne J. Duggan (eds.), *Adrian IV The English Pope (1154–1159)* (Aldershot, 2003), pp. 29–40, here pp. 32–33.

199 James 1, cap. 60.

200 Or an earthly career except on horseback. One of the toughest punishments within the Calatrava order was a ban on horse riding, not so much because of the practical issues but rather because of the disgrace; Luis Rafael Villegas Diaz, 'La orden de Calatrava. Organización y vida interna', *Primeras Jornadas de Historia de las Órdenes Militares* (Madrid, 1997), pp. 29–54, here p. 39.

201 2 Maccabees, 10, 29–30.

202 Guibert of Nogent, 6, 9. Heavenly knights, R. I. Morris, 'Martyrs on the Field of Battle Before and During the First Crusade', in: Diana Wood (ed.), *Martyrs and Martyrologies* (Oxford, 1983), pp. 79–101; Christopher Holdsworth, 'An "Airier Aristocracy": The Saints at War', *Transactions of the Royal Historical Society* 6 (1996), pp. 103–122. Images and frescoes of the heavenly knights, Colin Morris, 'Picturing the Crusades: The Uses of Visual Propaganda, ca. 1095–1250', in: John France and William G. Zajac (eds.), *The Crusades and Their Sources. Essays Presented to Bernard Hamilton* (Aldershot, 1998), pp. 195–216. Crusaders and horsemen on Danish frescoes, Lise Gotfredsen, '. . . og jorden skælver, da de rider frem', *Århus Stifts årbog* 21 (1983), pp. 79–99.

203 Chapter 38 and 39, cf. chapter 6 and 50, with the horsemen from the north, destroying everything on their way.

204 Psalm 79 (Vulgata 78). Used by Urban II in his sermon at Clermont according to Baldric of Dole, Fulcher of Chartres, Robert the Monk, and Guibert of Nogent.

205 Revelation, 6, 1–11.

206 Revelations, 19, 11–18.

207 Malcolm Barber, *The New Knighthood: A History of the Order of the Temple* (Cambridge, 1994); Helen Nicholson, *The Knights Templar. A New History* (Thrupp, 2002).

208 Rudolf Hiestand, 'Kardinalbischof Matthäus von Albano, das Konzil von Troyes und die Entstehung des Tempelordens', *Zeitschrift fur Kirchengeschichte* 99 (1988), pp. 295–325.

209 DMP I:1, no. 77 and nos. 79–80.

210 Vita Martini, 11.

211 DMP I:1, no. 96; cf. Barber, *The New Knighthood*, pp. 32–33.

212 E. Lourie, 'The Will of Alfonso I, "El Batallador", King of Aragon and Navarre; A Reassessment', *Speculum* 50 (1975), pp. 635–651; E. Lourie, 'The Will of Alfonso I of Aragon and Navarre: A Reply to Dr Forey', *Durham University Journal* 77, 2 (1984–1985), pp. 165–172; A.J. Forey, *The Templars in the Corona de Aragon* (London, 1973); Clay Stalls, *Possessing the Land: Aragon's Expansion Into Islam's Ebro Frontier Under Alfonso the Battler, 1104–1134* (Leiden, 1995).

213 DMP I:1, no. 212, p. 261.

214 DMP I:1, no. 221, pp. 272–273.

215 DMP I:1, no. 295, p. 384.

216 DMP I:1, no. 297, p. 388.

217 Forey, *The Templars*, pp. 27–28.

218 Marques, 'O poder e o espaço', p. 23; Marques, *História de Portugal*, p. 122.

219 Mattoso and de Sousa, *A Monarquia Feudal*, p. 161.

220 DDS, no. 13, no. 14, no. 17, no. 65, and no. 73.

221 DDS, no. 73.

222 Marques, 'O poder e o espaço', p. 46.

223 Malcolm Barber, *The Trial of the Templars* (Cambridge, 1978).

224 Liber Sancti Jacobi, vol. 1, p. 296.

225 Richard A. Fletcher, *Saint James' Catapult: The Life and Times of Diego Gelmirez of Santiago de Compostela* (Oxford, 1984), p. 56.

258   *The struggle for land and history*

226 *Hoc signo vincitur inimicus. Hoc signo tuetur pius.* Fletcher, *Saint James' Catapult,*
     p. 69.
227 BP 56.
228 Christi miles emeritus, et signifer egregius, militia probissimus. Liber Sancti Jacobi,
     vol. 1, p. 248.
229 Historia Silense, cap. 191–192. The story is included in Vincent of Beauvais's col-
     lection of miracles of St. James, with a few details added. The pilgrim was a Bishop
     Stefan, and he cried out to the assembly: "Stupid peasants, do not call James a warrior
     but a fisherman." Miracula Sct. Jakobi, in PL 163, col. 1375.
230 Derek W. Lomax, *La Orden de Santiago, 1170–1275* (Madrid, 1965); José-Luis Mar-
     tín, 'Orígenes de la Orden Militar de Santiago (1170–1195)', *Anuario de estudios
     medievales* 4 (1967), pp. 571–590.
231 PL 200, cols.1024–1030.
232 Martín, 'Orígenes de la Orden', pp. 578–579.
233 O'Callaghan, *Reconquest and Crusade*, p. 54.
234 DMP I:1, no. 315 and no. 317.
235 DDS, no. 14; compare with no. 64 from 1193.
236 Lomax, *La Orden de Santiago*.
237 Erik Reitzel-Nielsen, *Johanniterordenens historie med særligt henblik på de nordiske
     lande* (Copenhagen, 1984–1991), vols. 1–2; Thomas Hatt Olsen, 'The Priory of Dacia
     in the Order of Saint John of Jerusalem', *Annales de l'ordre souverain militaire de
     Malte* 18,4 (1960), pp. 19–33; Tore Nyberg, 'Zur Rolle der Johanniter in Skandina-
     vien. Erstes Auftreten und Aufbau der Institutionen', in: Zenon Hubert Nowak (ed.),
     Die Rolle der Ritterorden in der mittelalterlichen Kultur (Toruń, 1985), pp. 129–144;
     DD 1:2, no. 163.
238 DD 1:7, no. 156.
239 Reitzel-Nielsen, *Johanniterordenens historie*, vol. 1, p. 367.
240 Thomas Riis, *Les institutions politiques centrales du Danemark 1100–1332* (Odense,
     1977), pp. 181–187.
241 BD, no. 24.
242 DD 1:3, no. 245.
243 DK 9:3, 1278–1281. The pulpit cannot be dated with certainty but may date back
     to the 13th century (p. 1278). Second outside pulpit also from a Hospitaller church,
     at Dueholm monastery on Mors (DK 12:1, 88). The third is late medieval and from
     Holmstrup, a popular pilgrimage church (DK 4:3, 1810).
244 Reitzel-Nielsen, *Johanniterordenens historie*, vol. 1, pp. 194–195.
245 Henning Floto, *Der Rechtsstatus des Johanniterordens. Eine rechtsgeschichtliche
     und rechtsdogmatische Untersuchung zum Rechtsstatus der Balley Brandenburg des
     ritterlichen Ordens St. Johannis vom Spital zu Jerusalem* (Berlin, 2003).
246 DD 1:5, no. 124.
247 DD 1:5, no. 7 and no. 8.
248 Dating 1170–1182; DD 1:3, no. 63 chooses 1177. It probably happened in connection
     with the translation of Canute Lavard in 1170.
249 Hermanson, *Släkt, vänner och makt*.
250 All biographies in VSD, pp. 167–247; *In festis*. See Michael Chesnutt, 'The Medi-
     eval Danish Liturgy of St Knud Lavard', *Bibliotheca Arnamagnæana* 42 (2003),
     pp. 1–160.
251 VSD, p. 240.
252 "Ringstad dicitur, quod habeat in circuitu circulatim terminos insulæ æquè distantes;
     ideo placitum generale ibidem est." VSD, p. 240.
253 Pacem Danis et paganis fidem sanctus contulit quos a uanis et prophanis ritibus
     recedere et in Cristum credere compulit sub pacis federe. VSD, p. 223; In festis 100.
254 VSD, pp. 236–237. These are the same basic facilities that the bishops in the Iberian
     frontier regions were praised for fitting the new missionary churches with; Barton,
     The Aristocracy, p. 189.

255 VSD, 242–245.
256 see J. Riley-Smith, *The First Crusade and the Idea of Crusading* (London, 1986), pp. 95–97.
257 Sven Aggesen, Brevis historia, cap. XIII.
258 *Danmarks Gilde- og Lavsskraaer fra Middelalderen*, ed. C. Nyrop, vols. 1–2. (Lyngby, 1977), vol. 1, pp. 6–17.
259 SM I, pp. 64–93.
260 Kurt Villads Jensen, 'Broderliste, Vederlov og Holger Danske', in: Janus Møller Jensen (ed.), *Broderliste, Broderskab, Korstog* (Odense, 2006), pp. 203–214.
261 "Sed quia deus . . . varietate rerum ac temporum determinauit negotia gentium, igitur siue mercimoniarum negotiis laborantibus, siue agriculturis desudantibus vel militiæ cingulo fulgentibus, æqua lance juris omnibus paterno tenemur affectu. DD 1:3, nr. 63. *Gentium* can be translated as the peoples in general, but in this context it makes sense to translate it as the heathens."
262 Accincti cingulo militiæ, Baldric of Dole, 1, 4.
263 Damian J. Smith, 'Saint Rosendo, Cardinal Hyacinth and the Almohads', *Journal of Medieval Iberian Studies* 1 (2009), pp. 53–67; also E.W. Kemp, 'Pope Alexander III and the Canonization of Saints', *Transactions of the Royal Historical Society* 27 (1945), pp. 13–28, here pp. 20–21.
264 In addition to the three kings, there were many clerics amongst the proposers, including the Prior of Santa Cruz in Coimbra.
265 Antonio García y García, *Estudios sobre la canonistica portuguesa medieval* (Madrid, 1976), p. 168.
266 Hyacinth refers to Afonso as King in his canonization document in 1173, even though he only gained the papal recognition of that title in 1179. This likely reflects Hyacinth's interest in strengthening the crusades and the princes who distinguished themselves during the crusades; see Smith, 'Saint Rosendo', p. 62.
267 Caroline Walker Bynum, *Jesus as Mother: Studies in the Spirituality of the High Middle Ages* (Berkeley, 1982), p. 132; Brian Patrick McGuire, *The Difficult Saint. Bernard of Clairvaux and His Tradition* (Kalamazoo, 1991), pp. 189–225.
268 McGuire, *The Difficult Saint*, p. 194.
269 Ibid., pp. 198–199. The preacher is Abbot Henri of Clairvaux, who died in 1179, but the story is only known from around 1300.
270 This story is only attested from around 1300, but may have been known in the 12th century. Around 1300 the story was widespread and also known, e.g. in Icelandic material.
271 Robert I. Burns, 'Christian-Islamic Confrontation in the West: The Thirteenth-Century Dream of Conversion', *The American Historical Review* 76 (1971), pp. 1386–1434, here p. 1429; illustration from Cantigas de Santa Maria on page 1414.
272 J.F. O'Callaghan, 'The Mudejars of Castile and Portugal in the Twelfth and Thirteenth Centuries', in: James M. Powell (ed.), *Muslims Under Latin Rule, 1100–1300* (Princeton, NJ, 1990), pp. 11–56.; Harris, 'Mosque to Church Conversions', p. 159.
273 O'Callaghan, *Reconquest and Crusade*, p. 191.
274 Christiansen, *The Northern Crusades;* William Urban, *The Teutonic Knights. A Military History* (Pennsylvania, 2003).
275 Henry of Livonia, 11, 6; 12, 3; 16, 4.
276 Ibid., 19, 7.
277 Ibid., 25, 2, notes.
278 Terra transmarina, Ibid., 15, 4.
279 Ibid., 25, 2.
280 The same summer as the young King Canute VI of Denmark and Henry the Young of England were crowned as co-regents.
281 Song of Solomon 6, 1–4. Antifon no. 5 in laudes for the Assumption, 15th of August, and the Benedictus antiphon on the same day. Thanks to Tore Nyberg for these references.
282 Henry of Livonia, 28, 4.

8 The rise and fall of the crusader kingdoms

Canute VI in Pomerania and Wendland

After the death of the great Valdemar in 1182 and of Afonso in 1185, the crusades continued in both countries, and the conquests of the two kings were followed up by their sons and later generations. New land came under the Cross, the victorious kings took new titles, local military expeditions were perceived in connection with the great crusades to the Middle East and probably coordinated with them and both Danish and Portuguese religious wars received reinforcements by crusaders from elsewhere. Charters for the new churches were negotiated or forced through with or without agreement of the Popes. During the second quarter of the 13th century, both the Danish and the Portuguese expansion reached their greatest extents, and then halted abruptly. Initially, this was probably down to purely political bad luck, both in Denmark and Portugal, where in one place the king was imprisoned and in the other deposed. Political accidents cannot explain it all, and religious warfare was typically resumed at a later point. However, that is outside the scope of this book, which ends in the middle of the 13th century, and the intention of the following chapter is only to try to show how the successors of the two great kings continued to wage crusades along the general lines.

When Valdemar died, his son Canute took over. He was not even twenty years old, but had his father's loyal advisors to assist him. He had already been crowned as a minor in 1170 in connection with the canonization of his grandfather, Canute Lavard.

In 1184, Canute went on an expedition to Estonia, allegedly because the crusader army was tired of peace and festivities and wished to return to the time of King Valdemar when there was warfare and heroic deeds almost all year round.[1] The army was not allowed to sit unengaged for long, however. After the death of Valdemar, Emperor Fredric initiated negotiations with Bugislav of Pomerania and talked him into becoming a vassal of his, which was marked by Bugislav by a surprise attack on Rügen with 500 ships. This happened in 1184, and Bugislav had so much faith in his forces and in victory that he sent a message to Fredric Barbarossa in advance, telling him that Canute would now have to subject himself to Bugislav, "which the Emperor was very glad to hear." Prince Jarimar of Rügen immediately sent a message to Bishop Absalon, who quickly organized a general

Rise and fall of crusader kingdoms   261

mobilization of Zealand, which included old and young warriors, warships and merchant vessels and ships that were to be scrapped, and the attack was repulsed.[2]

The victory was followed up by further attacks on Bugislav's possessions in Pomerania, and in the end he had to submit himself completely and provide hostages. Wolgast and Usedom were plundered, Wolin was levelled. Kammin was captured in 1185; it had long been Christian and an episcopal city. When Canute stood with his army facing the walls of Kammin, the townspeople walked in a procession, barefoot and with crosses, out to him and asked him to spare the city in the memory of his holy father and not to commit sacrilege by letting the holy Christian buildings of the city be burned down. Canute replied that he did not fight against God but against men and that his war was just and not a sacrilege. Yet in the end he did not burn down the city.[3] The Danish influence in Kammin after this is shown by the fact that the future bishops were Danish, even though the diocese continued to be directly under the Papal see.[4] The goal of the expansion during these years in Wendish territories was obviously to control the mouth of the River Oder, for which there were good strategic as well as mercantile reasons. During the 1180s, the result was that the Danish King by and large controlled the Wendish Baltic coast from Pomerania all the way to Holstein and the Ditmarshes in the West. Sometime before1190, he took the title of "King of the Danes and the Wends."

After the fall of Jerusalem: Odense, Acre, Finland and Estonia

Several attempts by the Kingdom of Jerusalem to try to get help from Western Europe during the critical years from the end of the 1160s did not come to anything substantial. The Kingdom remained exposed to Muslim attacks and was internally divided between several fractions of noblemen and mutually fighting military orders; the king was ill and his successor a minor. Under those circumstances the outcome was unavoidable: Jerusalem could not be held by the Christians, and what is odd is perhaps that it fell so late. In 1187, Saladin defeated a large royal army that had the support of the military orders in the battle of Hattin. In the extremely hot and arid territory, the Christians had managed to manoeuvre themselves into an untenable position without any water, and Saladin only had to wait. After the victory, several cities fell, including Jerusalem at the end of September.[5]

News of the fall of Jerusalem reached Denmark when Canute VI celebrated Christmas together with his court in Odense. During the festivities and the dinner, a messenger from Pope Gregory VIII arrived with the dreadful news of the fall of Jerusalem to Saladin. The head of the Christian religion and the place of death of God's only son, more magnificent than any other place, had been desecrated by the heathens. The letter from the Pope was read aloud by the messenger: "When I see enemies fall upon the Lord's City, I cannot bring myself to stop crying out. I cry out in the bitterness of my soul, urged by the adversities of agony that brings sadness, and while I write, a stream of tears ruins a page of the letter. Jerusalem has fallen. Listen, all earth and all who live there: Do not tolerate the assault on

262 *Rise and fall of crusader kingdoms*

Christ remaining unrevenged for long." The King and all his men broke into tears and deep sighs when they heard the Pope's proclamation, and they could not think of anything to say. They only sat, cheerless and silent.

Thus relates a narrative written only a few years after the event, perhaps during the 1190s.[6] It continues by recounting how Esbern Snare then rose up. He was the brother of Archbishop Absalon and one of the King's trusted advisors and also an eloquent speaker. First he praised the good old days with peace and exuberance, and encouraged everybody to follow the example of the forefathers and do heroic deeds. The Greeks and the Lombards knew that they were defeated by the Danes, the strength of Rome fell out of fear of our people, Normandy was plundered, Norway and England conquered, Finland and Sambia and the Slavic territories from Pomerania to Holstein were subdued. But even better than to fight for the sake of one's own name is to fight for religion, Esbern Snare concluded.

Fifteen noblemen decided to go and began to build ships, and at the same time the crusade was preached in all churches and at the things. Some deserted the cause during the preparations but seven did go. The noblemen probably had somewhere between 50 and 100 warriors each, so about 500 to 700 in total might very well have set off. After long preparations they went, and on the way, they picked up a companion in Norway. They suffered shipwreck and had to travel overland to Venice where they obtained passage to the Middle East. When they finally reached the Holy Land, it was all over. Richard the Lionheart and Saladin had concluded peace, and the Danes were able to visit the holy places, get relics and presumably other souvenirs as well, but not to do any heroic deeds. "As the quiet of peace forbade war, they decided to travel home."[7] This they did via the Greek imperial city of Constantinople, where they were well received and through connections in the Nordic Varangian guard – the imperial bodyguard – obtained passes with imperial seals to journey home through Hungary.[8]

This description of an expedition of noblemen is interesting, partly because it actually gives the names of several of the participants, and not least because the source gives a brilliant impression of the ideas and arguments that were employed to mobilize the politically important layers in the population for the long journey to the Holy Land. Many more, however, were seized by the movement and were persuaded by both the papal emissaries and the local crusade sermon; they decided to travel by sea, we know from other sources. In the Holy Land, two Christian kings were struggling for power. Conrad sat in Tyre while Guy de Lusignan had initiated a siege of Acre. In the autumn of 1189 he received support from a strong fleet from Friesland and Scandinavia with Norwegians, Danes and presumably Swedes. When the fleet arrived, it consisted of fifty large war cogs with 12,000 men in total. The siege lasted until July 12, 1291, when Acre finally fell to Richard the Lionheart of England and Philip August of France. At that point, only 100 survivors were left out of the Scandinavian army of 12,000 men. This contingent constituted an important contribution to the crusader army because the Danes, like the Frisians, had come from the harsh North and were mighty warriors due to "their long, supple limbs, an indomitable will and a fervent, burning faith."[9] Another group of Danish noblemen with 400 warriors in

Rise and fall of crusader kingdoms   263

their entourage later reached Acre; they were under the leadership of the *nepos* of the Danish King Canute – his nephew or perhaps his cousin, although his name is not mentioned.[10]

At the same time several crusades took place in the Baltic area; they were presumably large but the sources let us down completely. One of the annals reports that in 1191 "there was a great crusade to Finland, which was conquered by the Danes with a large force."[11] It was perhaps at this point that the Danes built two castles in Finland, whose current names stem from Danish and not from Swedish, as most other castles in Finland. They are Porvoo (from Danish Borgå) and Sipoo (from Danish Sibbesborg).[12] At the same time, Canute was heading several crusades to Estonia. The first one was in 1184 and was not large enough to warrant a mention in the short, laconic notices in the annals but is known from Saxo's depiction.[13] They were followed in the 1190s with something that must have been on a much larger scale, which also was commanded by Canute himself. It is placed in different annals under 1193, 1194, 1196 and 1197, but it might be down to uncertainties and errors in connection with the transcription rather than four different expeditions.[14] The crusades to Estonia took place in some form of co-operation with the Norwegian prince Eirik, who attacked Estonia in 1185 and was afterwards rewarded by King Canute with a ship.[15] The same Eirik was an experienced crusader who was likely to have been in the service of the Byzantine Emperor. He had also been to the Holy Land at some point before 1181. There he had managed, among other things, to dive into the River Jordan with a candle in his hand, which was still burning when he reappeared from the river. The miracle had many witnesses and was meant to prove that Eirik was a son of the Norwegian King Sigurd Munn.[16]

At the same time as the Danish and Norwegian expeditions against Estonia took place, a German mission began to take hold and penetrate into Lithuania. In 1184–1186 Bishop Meinhard persuaded a small group of crusaders to settle by Üxküll by the River Dvina, where they could defend themselves with modern crossbows and begin to build a fortress in stone. Despite continuous reinforcements from German crusaders, the position was quite exposed, and the new episcopal see was attacked again and again. In 1196, Meinhard gave up and wanted to move, and he considered transferring his activities to Estonia to be active in the Danish crusades there.[17] He died before anything materialized, but in 1197 Pope Celestine III issued a bull that placed crusades to Lithuania on an equal footing with those to the Holy Land and promised the participants the same indulgence that they could have earned by taking part in liberating Jerusalem.[18]

A large battle on July 24, 1198, with the participation of both Danish and German crusaders at the mouth of the Dvina, ended in a Christian victory, but the new Bishop, Bertold, fell in the fighting. This was one of the reasons for moving the episcopal see from Üxküll to the place where he had been martyred. In 1201, a completely new city, Riga, was founded. It was to be the future starting point of almost all crusades against Lithuania and Southern Estonia, and the city with its bishop became a very important partner and adversary of the Danish kings in their crusades into Estonia from the North, from the Gulf of Finland.

264 *Rise and fall of crusader kingdoms*

The Danish and Scandinavian crusades were thus directed against both the threatened crusader states in the Middle East and against the most distant regions of the Baltic. At the same time, the crusades on the Iberian Peninsula were resumed after a pause of a few years and as a direct consequence of the fall of Jerusalem to Saladin. One result of these crusades was the capture in September 1189 of the strong fortress Silves on the coast of Algarve, in which Northern European crusaders – including Danes – took part on their way from Scandinavia to the Holy Land. We shall return to this with more detail in a later chapter; for now it is important to keep in mind that the years 1188–1190 are another example of very large and well-coordinated crusades everywhere in Western Europe and the Middle East. Practical and spiritual matters still went hand in hand. After the great Christian defeat at the battle of Hattin in 1187, the Cistercians introduced a large liturgy in the memory of dead crusaders and to encourage new ones to follow them.[19] From 1190 onwards, the many Cistercian priests all over Christendom were to say a special mass of the Holy Spirit for crusaders and kings and princes on crusade.[20]

Further expansions by Canute and Valdemar the victorious

Over the following few years, King Canute faced two great problems, which he and his brother and successor had to deal with for the next twenty years, and which were to have significant influence on their options in European politics. One was a bishop who wished to be king. The other was a French king who was terror-stricken after having spent a wedding night together with a Danish princess.

Bishop Valdemar – a Melchizedek?

Valdemar the Great had first fought against, and then with, Canute, who was a son of his father's murderer, and King Valdemar was married to the sister of the same Canute. The son of Canute Magnussen was also called Valdemar and had, just as the troublesome relative Duke Buris had had, a reasonable claim to the Danish throne. Contrary to what happened to Buris, King Valdemar had him neither imprisoned nor mutilated but made sure that he had a good, solid education in Paris and was eased into an ecclesiastical career. In 1179, he was chosen as Bishop of Schleswig; he was then only twenty-one years old. That same year it was decided at the third Lateran council that the minimum age to become a bishop was thirty, which was not really the fault of Valdemar Canutesen.[21] After the death of King Valdemar the Great in 1182, he took over the position as Duke of Schleswig after Canute VI, who was now the sole King. This was from the outset considered a temporary solution, until Canute's younger brother, also called Valdemar, was old enough to take over the duchy. This he did in 1187, which apparently hurt Bishop Valdemar deeply. At least he later complained openly against the injustice perpetrated against him.[22]

In 1190, Emperor Fredric Barbarossa drowned in the River Saleph in outermost Anatolia, and, during the struggle to find a successor, Canute VI sided with the

Rise and fall of crusader kingdoms   265

candidate of the Welf family, the old Henry the Lion, who had returned from his long exile in England, and his son Otto. Bishop Valdemar sought to establish a connection to Fredric's son Henry VI of the Staufen family. These two great networks of noblemen were to clash in many different configurations during the following decades.[23] It first happened in 1192 in a large-scale move where Bishop Valdemar went ashore in Northern Jutland at the head of a Norwegian, Swedish and possibly Danish army, while the Staufen-friendly Count Adolf of Holstein crossed the Eider and attacked from the South.

Bishop Valdemar pronounced himself King of Denmark. This put him in an unusual position: he was consecrated and anointed as bishop and on the way to being consecrated and anointed as a king as well. Had he succeeded, he would have become a true Melchizedek, a priest–king in true Old Testament fashion, who in one person combined the highest ecclesiastical and the highest secular authority. The Mechizedek figure was often employed as an image by Pope Innocent III to illustrate the principal authority of the papacy, and a real doubly consecrated bishop-king supported by the Staufen would have been a nasty competitor to Innocent. It did not come to this, however. Bishop-King Valdemar was defeated by King Canute VI and was thrown into the stinking and unhealthy dungeon of the strong castle of Søborg, where he would die soon, if he did not get out, Pope Celestine III wrote on December 23 that year.[24] At that time, Bishop Valdemar had been in prison for six months. Fourteen years in total had to pass before he was set free.

When Innocent was elected Pope in 1198, he threw himself into the case of the imprisoned Bishop Valdemar with great energy but quickly discovered that the Danish King had the support of all of the Danish Church with Archbishop Absalon at its head. The case was complicated. Innocent could not on the one hand tolerate such an encroachment on the freedom of the Church – such a disdain of the episcopal dignity as it was to imprison a consecrated bishop. On the other hand, he had no warm feelings at all for Bishop Valdemar.

He said both openly: "If only he had never existed, this man, Bishop Valdemar of Schleswig, who disregarded the dignity of the episcopal office to unite royal power and priesthood, who became a many-headed monster and who conspired against King Canute of the Danes, to whom he was bound with an oath of fealty, and who rose against the one whose bread he ate."[25] "If only he had been turned into a pillar of salt when he took his hands off the plough of the Lord and looked back. Then he alone could have been washed away by the water, when he alone bewailed his own misfortune, because on the cheeks of the Church, there would not be a single tear. It would have been better if he had died by his own sword when he drew the secular sword." All the words of Innocent are echoes of strong Bible passages; the last sentence refers to Matthew 26,52, that those who take the sword shall perish by the sword, but through St. Augustine's interpretation: to take the sword means to use the secular sword, without it having been permitted or commanded by a superior authority.[26] Bishop Valdemar's offence was thus primarily that he had acted without authority. The punishment for this was death, but the Latin word from Matthew and Innocent is *pereo*, which can mean to die

Figure 8.1 Fighting between a Christian crusader and a heathen rider? Or two crusaders paying homage to the cross before they set out? Relief in granite above the entrance to the church of Nødager in Djursland, Denmark, around 1200.
© University of Southern Denmark Press

physically as well as to forsake one's eternal salvation, to be lost in the afterlife.[27] It is rather far-reaching, what Innocent wished for Bishop Valdemar.

Somewhat against his will, Innocent had to insist on having Bishop Valdemar set free, but this was to take some time. Only when the new King Valdemar II the Victorious married the young Dagmar from Bohemia did he consent to send Bishop Valdemar – in chains and heavily guarded – all the way to Rome, where Innocent could judge him and install a substitute as Bishop of Schleswig. There are several reasons why the King gave in to the Pope's pressure. One reason given in annals is that the new Queen had prayed for him, so that is presumably correct.[28] With this, Queen Dagmar entered popular history as the good Queen who had pity on the poor and on prisoners, but politically it was not a smart move. Another reason is that the King, by marrying Dagmar, secured a transport route to Rome through Eastern Europe and thus a long way from the French King Philip August and Philip of Swabia of the Staufen family, who would both have used the Bishop for their own political purposes.

A third reason is that in 1206, King Valdemar's great crusade to Estonia was to be launched after three years of preparations. It is difficult to imagine a crusade with indulgence and so forth for a king who had fallen out with the Pope.[29] Thus, the Bishop had to be despatched to the Curia. Despite all precautions, it went wrong. Bishop Valdemar managed to flee from Rome and back to the North, where he was elected Archbishop of Hamburg-Bremen with the support of Philip of Swabia, and yet again he became a military threat to King Valdemar the Victorious in Denmark. A few years passed by before the tension broke out in open warfare.

Queen Ingeborg of France – the lodge in the garden of cucumbers

In the years of entanglement with the Bishop of Schleswig, Canute VI and later Valdemar II were at the same time tied up in another, even more notorious case. In 1193, their young and shapely[30] sister Ingeborg had married the French King, Philip August. The offer of marriage had come from the French King and must have happened before or right after his return from his crusade to Acre together with Richard the Lionheart. The two young rulers had left at the same time and had had fine mutual relations en route, but on the way back, Richard had been taken prisoner by Leopold of Austria and Philip August had tried to take advantage of this. He was presumably interested in a marriage alliance with Canute VI in order to gain a share in the Danish royal family's hereditary claim to the English throne. Since 1066, it had not been too important for any of the Danish kings, but the claim was not forgotten; it was put forward on occasion during the rest of the Middle Ages, for instance during the Hundred Years War in the middle of the 14th century.[31] Philip August must surely also have been interested in support from the Danish fleet if he was by any chance to attack England, but Canute managed to avoid having to pledge direct military support to Philip August. Finally, an alliance between one of the most famous crusaders to the Middle East of the time and one of the great crusaders to the Baltic region must have seen quite natural.

The wedding was held in Amiens during the month of August. Even when Philip August walked up the aisle in the church, he began to shake and turn pale. The next morning, after the wedding night, Ingeborg was rejected and led away and was forbidden to show herself to her husband ever again. The case caused an enormous sensation at the time and great political difficulties for Philip August.[32] Initially he tried to have the marriage dissolved by claiming that he and Ingeborg were too closely related. After many court meetings where he produced genealogical tables, he suddenly changed his statement, almost ten years after the calamitous wedding night. He now claimed that Ingeborg had cast a spell over him on the wedding night and made him impotent.[33]

The sanctity of marriage was a leading issue for Pope Innocent and he entered the Ingeborg case with great zeal. One of his first letters as Pope was sent to Philip August and demanded that he release Ingeborg and show her the respect which a husband owes his wife. He was also to get rid of Agnes of Meran, whom he had married in the meantime instead of Ingeborg.[34] Innocent threatened to put all of France under interdict if Philip did not obey, and this actually happened in 1200. Philip at last seemed to have had enough. He agreed to negotiate with Canute and to send Agnes away, but he nevertheless dragged the proceedings out with legalistic hair-splitting for another year and a half. And finally, he put forward the accusation of witchcraft. The tone of Innocent's letter all of a sudden became much more cautious. It is obvious that this was an accusation which should be taken very seriously.

There has been much discussion amongst modern historians as to why Philip August sent Ingeborg away in the first place. Several political motives have been put forward, but it is difficult to see any rational cause for such a strange behaviour.

268   *Rise and fall of crusader kingdoms*

No matter what Philip August could have had by way of new political interests since the marriage was agreed, it would have been easier for him to reach them if he had kept Ingeborg as Queen and just ignored her and lived as he wanted to. The rejection was a provocation and was unnecessary – except in one case: that he had actually been frightened out of his mind after a night with Ingeborg. It is most logical to think that he actually believed that she was a witch. This would have been such a serious accusation against a member of strong royal family that he only laid the charge after many years and under very strong pressure. What the young Princess from Northern Europe actually might have done by way of strange rituals on her wedding night that could frighten a tough warrior such as Philip August, we shall never know, unfortunately.

Most important in this context, however, is that Pope Innocent III attached the Ingeborg case directly to his crusade policies regarding the Baltic region.[35] There seems to have been a close connection between King Valdemar II's crusader oaths and letters from Innocent to Philip August for the benefit of Ingeborg. Shortly before the crowning of her brother, Ingeborg wrote a touching letter to Innocent,[36] where she described her unfortunate position, kept in a prison, without sufficient food, without a priest to hear her confession or to comfort her with the words of God and without proper dresses suitable for a queen. The latter was not quite true; Philip August actually spent more money on Ingeborg's clothes than on the clothes of his new wife.[37] The reaction from Innocent was a strong letter to the French King, who was no longer called the special friend of the Church or a very Christian king, as the Popes had previously done. Innocent depicted the misfortune of the poor woman, rejected and lonely as a little sparrow, with cheeks furrowed by tears, and he compared her to a lodge in a cucumber garden. The latter image is taken from Isaiah 1,8 and only makes sense if interpreted from the most common and widespread Bible commentary of the time, *Glossa Ordinaria*. According to that, the lodge is empty because the guardian – who must be Philip August in this particular case – had taken away the fruit but left the lodge empty. The marriage had been consummated by sexual intercourse but had not led to the desired result, pregnancy.[38]

In the years leading up to Innocent becoming Pope, the crusades against Livonia were strengthened by two papal bulls that gave full indulgence to those who fought to defend the new missionary Church in Livonia.[39] This was confirmed by Innocent in 1199, who also gave permission to change crusader oaths for the Holy Land to join the fighting in the Baltic region instead.[40] Bishop Albert of the newly founded city of Riga travelled to Denmark in order to gain support from crusaders there and continued over the following few years to give sermons during tours of Germany.[41] In 1201, he dedicated all of his diocese and the Livonian missionary field to the Virgin Mary, and in 1202, he established the little but effective military order the Knights of the Sword.[42] When Valdemar was crowned on Christmas Day in 1202, he immediately began to prepare for a large crusade to the Baltics,[43] with additional support from the newly appointed Archbishop Anders Sunesen. The preparations took three years and had the support of Innocent; Anders was appointed missionary legate and received permission to install bishops in the

Rise and fall of crusader kingdoms 269

newly conquered lands according to his own choices. The crusade began in 1206 and captured the island of Ösel (Saaremaa), off the coast of Estonia. A fortress was built, but by the time winter arrived the Danish army withdrew after having burnt down their own fortress. Anders Sunesen did not go home, but spent the winter in Riga discussing the future of the mission.

Valdemar's crusade plans were public knowledge in the summer of 1203, and that same summer Innocent returned the effort by sending harsh letters to Philip August about Ingeborg. In December he sent letters to King Valdemar, further reminding him to release Bishop Valdemar of Schleswig from his almost twelve-year-long imprisonment. He wrote again to Philip August about Ingeborg, and three days later he wrote to Valdemar and called on him to support the Welf candidate Otto of Brunswick as emperor. In 1206, King Valdemar released Bishop Valdemar, the King went on the crusade to Ösel and Pope Innocent III appointed Anders Sunesen to legate, to papal plenipotentiary with special responsibility for the mission in the Baltic territories.

In October 1209, Innocent approved King Valdemar's plans for a new crusade against Prussia; he promised all the participants eternal rewards, and he wrote to Otto and forbade him from attacking Denmark while Valdemar was on crusade.[44] In January 1210, he again placed Denmark under papal protection for the same reason. This protection was repeated on May 7, 1210,[45] and on the very same day Innocent again wrote a comforting letter to Ingeborg. The context is obvious: when Valdemar promised to go on a crusade, Innocent dealt with the Ingeborg question more actively. The result of Valdemar's plans was a crusade to Sambia in Prussia, and one Polish prince, Mistwin, acknowledged Valdemar as his overlord and took an oath of fealty to him. Whether a church was founded on this occasion is uncertain.[46] On the other hand, the attempts of conquest in Prussia show that Valdemar deliberately attempted to extend his crusade territory further east, step by step. He had progressed quite far by 1210, and at that time, the Christian kings on the Iberian Peninsula began to reconsider crusades after a few years of standstill.

Sancho I's crusade against Muslims and heretic kings

Let us return to Sancho, who – after his father's disabling accident at Badajoz in 1168 – had been crowned in the summer of 1170 and in practice had taken on military leadership and was to carry the crusades further. For the first few years the effort was slow, also because Afonso Henriques had entered an eight-year-long truce with the Muslims. Yet, with the siege of Seville in 1178, a new wave of Portuguese crusades set in. This was probably the direct cause for Pope Alexander III to recognize Afonso Henriques as King with the bull *Manifestis probatum*,[47] which happened with direct reference to Afonso's many successful crusades over a long period.

This must have pleased Afonso Henriques during his last, difficult years before his death in 1185, but the delight would have been mixed. The new wave of Portuguese crusades had an unusually bad start. A large and successful Muslim

270   *Rise and fall of crusader kingdoms*

counterattack penetrated further north year by year in a determined attempt to reconquer lost Muslim territory. In October 1179, about a year after the Pope's great favour to Afonso, the castle of Abrantes was attacked by an army led by the son of the Caliph of Morocco,[48] and a siege began. Due to problems with supplies, the Muslim army had to end the siege as early as the fourth day and retreat, so perhaps the expedition was not that carefully planned after all. On the other hand, it was not just any raid into enemy territory, because the attacks grew stronger over the following years. Large groups of warriors on land were supported by naval forces, and Lisbon was under attack several times from large Muslim fleets.

Dom Fuas Roupinho was in charge of the Portuguese fleet that was assembled and equipped in order to take up the fight against the Muslims. He soon gained an almost legendary afterlife. While hunting he rode so fast through the mist that he almost rode over the edge of the cliffs at Nazaré, but he was warned by the voice of the Virgin Mary and escaped with his life. In a cave, he found the very wooden figure of the Virgin Mary that Joseph himself had carved. It had been hidden by the Christian king when the Muslims conquered the Iberian Peninsula in 711, but now the holy statue let itself be found again. Fuas Roupinho built a chapel on the spot, which is still one of Portugal's major pilgrimage sites.[49]

In 1184, Abu Yakub Yusuf, the Caliph of Morocco, arrived – "the Emperor of the Saracens who is called the donkey king because he always travels around riding on a donkey and is considered a prophet and a saint by all of his people. And he had then governed for 32 years."[50] After having conquered Morocco and several lesser kingdoms in that region, his heart was filled with arrogance, and he decided to conquer all of the Iberian Peninsula. After having built siege engines, he crossed the Straits of Gibraltar with a very large army, and on May 25, 1184, he attacked Seville. With support from local Muslim rulers on the Peninsula, he began a large raid against the North via Badajoz and across the River Tagus to Santarém, which was besieged and the surroundings plundered. "It was a mightily strong army that occupied the mountains and the valleys and all the surface of the earth, and only God alone would be able to count the numbers of the army, He who can count the drops of rain."[51]

The attack on Santarém was declared only the first step on the way to reconquering Lisbon and continuing on to Coimbra, after which the Caliph believed that the road to Toledo in Spain would be open. In order to attract as many soldiers as possible for the decisive expedition, Abu Yakub promised one year's supply of provisions to anyone who helped out. Sancho himself was encircled in Santarém and commanded the defences of the city. Fernando of León sent reinforcements, and the bishops of Porto and of Santiago headed the auxiliaries from Northern Portugal and Galicia. Against all odds they succeeded in splitting the Muslim army, and Yusuf was wounded during the fighting and died soon after, on July 28, 1184. The price had been high for the Muslim army; the Caliph had fallen but that only seemed to intensify the Almohads' lust for attack. Abu Yakub was succeeded by his son Abu Yusuf Yakub. During the great wars over the following fifteen years he earned the honourable epithet al-Mansur, "the victorious."[52]

Rise and fall of crusader kingdoms 271

The region had been hard pressed by Muslim attacks, and a large part of the Christian population had fled to the North. Santarém, Lisbon and Évora had received extensive charters in 1179 in order to keep their inhabitants and to make people settle in the desolate areas, but even this did not even seem sufficient any longer.[53] Things did not get any better when the old King Afonso Henriques died on December 6, 1185. Sancho then took over government in name as well, and he must have been worried about the threat from the Almohads. Some of his first acts were to secure himself militarily by giving charters and important castles south of the Tagus to the Order of Santiago, while the Order of Évora received the castle in Alcanede and Juromenha near Badajoz, too. The latter was subject to the order being able to capture it themselves.

The plan was obviously to protect Lisbon but also to create strongpoints in order to be able to counterattack. Sancho's plans of a military offensive were well prepared and they received unexpected and overwhelming support when his oldest son was born on April 23, 1186, on the saint's day of the popular crusader saint, St. George. The son was christened Afonso, like his famous and victorious grandfather, and was, right from the outset, intended for a career as a warrior. He ended up being too fat for that, to which we shall return shortly.

Abu Yusuf Yakub al-Mansur was under pressure from home, where two of his relatives rebelled and attempted to capture the throne, and, at the same time, local Muslim rulers on Mallorca and Minorca tried to win independence. Thus, there was no united front against the Christians, just as there had been none earlier.

After the fall of Jerusalem: Silves 1189

All of this happened while the Christians in the crusader states were under immense pressure and under the leadership of a child king and, in 1187, Jerusalem fell to Saladin. The news caused dismay all over Europe, from Odense to Coimbra. In both places it was immediately decided to intensify the crusade effort, and in Portugal, Sancho was personally deeply moved and shaken. This is how we must perceive the testament he wrote at some point after March 24, 1188,[54] presumably after having heard of the fall of Jerusalem. First, he gives a very large sum to the ransoming of prisoners, a total of 13,125½ morabituns. He then gives a large sum to Santa Maria in Coimbra – the cathedral – to Santa Maria in Alcobaça, Santa Maria in Lisbon, Santa Maria in Braga, Santa Maria in Porto, Santa Maria in Évora, Santa Maria in Viseu and Santa Maria in Lamego. "To the other hundred churches dedicated to Santa Maria I give one hundred marks, so that they can have one mark each and have a chalice made, and to the fifty churches dedicated to St. James I give fifty marks to have chalices made." Sancho had been crowned on the day of St. Mary's Assumption in 1170, and now he tried to secure support from the martial Mary to the best of his ability. All horses and armour and weapons and saddles and harnesses that belong to Sancho and all his Muslim slaves, men and women, shall go to the knight of Évora and of Alcácer if he dies, except his personal armour and sword, which "I leave to my son, who shall have the Kingdom." And with the exception of some particular horses and mules, which

272 Rise and fall of crusader kingdoms

are left to named individuals. The picture is clear. Sancho wished that all his personal belongings were to be left to two individuals, Mary the Mother of God and Santiago, the two most important saints in the Portuguese crusades. What was left should go to the local crusader confraternities, which held the most advanced positions to the south of the Tagus. Sancho was planning to go on a crusade, and he was planning for the eventuality that he would not return alive.

During the spring of 1189 a large fleet of Danish and Frisian crusaders assembled at Lisbon, from where it continued towards the Holy Land. En route, it laid siege to the Muslim fortress of Alvor on the coast of Algarve, which was captured quickly. We have no details as to how, but the result was a systematic massacre of the 5,600 inhabitants, a total destruction of the town and a tremendous booty of gold and silver. "They killed everybody in the town, large and small, men and women. May God reward their martyrdom on the day of resurrection," a contemporary Muslim commented.[55] The fleet was escorted all the way to Gibraltar by a Portuguese galley, which then returned to Lisbon with plunder and Muslim slaves. The Danish and Frisian fleet was presumably the fifty ships that arrived in Acre and joined the forces of Guy de Lusignan that autumn.[56]

In the summer of 1189, another large fleet with crusaders from the North arrived in Lisbon.[57] One of the participants was likely to have been a German and a priest, and he wrote a detailed account of the crusade against Silves. "In the year of 1187 after the incarnation of the Lord, the promised land was destroyed by the Sultan of Egypt, Saladin. Towns fell, inhabitants were killed or driven into captivity but the trumpet of the sermon sounded wide and far over the kingdoms of the Christians with the promise from the apostolic authority on indulgence and moved an immense multitude of people to make good the terrible loss."[58] The fleet set out from Bremen on April 22, 1189, and sailed via England and Brittany to Galicia and to Lisbon, which was reached on July 4.

They were received by Sancho I, who offered them an opportunity to take part in the capture of the strong Muslim fortress of Silves, which is close to the southern coast of Algarve. The crusaders were to have all silver, gold and provisions in Silves after the conquest, whereas the King himself was to have the sovereignty of town. They immediately sailed off together with the Portuguese forces and reached Silves on July 17 after three days at sea. When they had cast anchor off the coast, they sent messengers and made contact with the part of the Portuguese army that had travelled overland. Negotiations ensued and whether it was at all realistic to try and capture Silves was discussed. Several Portuguese leaders were of the opinion that they might as well give up beforehand and settle for other, smaller towns, but the crusaders from the North "trusted in God" and insisted on attacking Silves. They sailed as far up the river as possible and made a camp there. They were within sight of the town but could not get close because the water level was too low for the large cogs.

The town was well fortified with a wall and a moat, and there was not a single shed outside the walls to give shelter to the attackers. Everything had been cleared and made ready for war. The gates to the town were narrow and constructed with turns and twists, which meant that it would be easier to get above or through the

Rise and fall of crusader kingdoms 273

walls rather than to attack the gates. The towers of the town protruded so far from the wall that attackers could be fired upon from the walls if they were to attack the towers and from the towers if were they to attack the walls. The towers stood close, only a stone's throw from each other. The crusaders faced a difficult task.

The crusaders began to make ladders, and, after morning mass on July 21, the attack began. The ladders were placed against the walls, and the attackers were supported by a barrage of stones. They managed to quickly capture the lower part of the town. The defenders dropped their weapons and fled in panic, many were trampled to death inside the gate as they stampeded to get inside the upper fortress. Their bodies were thrown over the walls and into the inner town instead of being buried decently, which surprised the Christian crusaders. Perhaps it was punishment for leaving their positions and an attempt to heighten morale. This fits with the fact that the Muslim commander had the first refugees from the lower town decapitated as they arrived into the fortress.

On the next day, the crusaders' attack on the upper fortress met stiff resistance and they had to withdraw. They spent the time systematically setting fire to all houses in the lower town. This was a rather larger assignment than they had been used to at home, the people from the North remarked. The houses of Silves were not made from wood and with thatched roofs but built in brick, clay and cement and only very little wood. At the same time, they set fire to five Muslim ships, which had been drawn into the city to protect them from the crusaders' attack.

The crusaders now began to build siege towers and more ladders. King Sancho himself reached Silves on July 29 and was soon followed by the part of his army that carried heavy siege equipment and travelled more slowly.[59] Also the psychological warfare was intensified. The Christians executed the captured Muslims in front of the city wall to serve as a warning to the defenders. Two days later, on the Sunday, the Muslims hung three Christians by their feet and "then they stabbed them with swords and spears until they died." The wording suggests that it took some time. The crusaders were now even more eager to take the town.

The crusaders now began to build a siege engine, "which we call a hedgehog." It consisted of a large ram between two towers and was covered by a ship's sail with felt, earth and cement. The machine was pushed into position next to the wall, but the Muslim defenders managed to set fire to it and burn it down because it was too heavy to draw back into safety. "Therefore, there was great rejoicing among the heathens and great sadness among us."

With time, several towers and more areas of the city were captured, and in the end only the strongest part, the Almadina, held out. Attempts to dig mines underneath the walls were countered by a sortie by the Muslims, who set fire to the houses above the mine so that it burned and collapsed too early. Crusaders from Flanders began to hollow out the lowest part of the city wall that had been captured in order to make it possible to crawl through the hollowing to one of the towers. However, at night the defenders came out from the Almadina and tore down parts of the city wall so that it was no longer connected to the tower. The most effective weapon of the crusaders was possibly that they managed to cut off the water supply to the city. After this, increasing numbers of Muslims began to

274 *Rise and fall of crusader kingdoms*

desert at night and gave themselves up to the crusaders; they were spared and suffered no injury so that more defenders might be tempted to do the same.

At some point in August, Sancho decided to withdraw together with the Portuguese army. His excuse was that there were too few provisions for the horses and the men, but it must have been obvious to Sancho that Silves was about to fall. It was also obvious that the men from the North were unlikely to be able to complete the capture without Portuguese help. This put Sancho in a very favourable bargaining position, which he fully understood how to exploit. He let himself be persuaded by the crusaders from the North to wait a few more days in return for getting not just the city but all property within it. In return, the Nordic crusaders had to dig faster and employ more pressure in order to bring the siege to an end as quickly as possible. The new agreement about the sharing of the booty was entered on August 23, and, on September 1, the Muslim commander initiated negotiations about surrender. Sancho offered that all Muslims could leave safely with all their belongings and valuables. On the face of it, this sounds as if they got off lightly when considering that Sancho negotiated from a strong position and was more or less able to dictate the conditions. The explanation is probably that the constant fighting on the Iberian Peninsula, where the fortunes of war went back and forth, had created a particular pattern for surrenders. The population was quite often allowed to take their belongings when it finally gave up defending the town. It did not happen always but quite often, which, as far as it goes, was a rational conclusion of a war which could soon reignite with the other party as the winner. It was a reasonable solution from a Portuguese point of view, but it certainly did not appeal to the Nordic crusaders. Sancho now had to negotiate with them. He first promised them 10,000 then 20,000 gold pieces in compensation, but that was rejected as the money had to be brought from Portugal, presumably from Coimbra. They made a clear assumption that the transport could take quite some time and that the money could seep away en route. It was then agreed that the Muslims could only take the clothes they were wearing and had to leave everything else behind.

A long line of Muslims left the city on foot, but, out of fear of missing the plunder, the Nordic crusaders closed the city gate at night for a large group of them and tried to force the Muslims to tell them where their valuables were hidden by using violence. The yield was small and when the morning came, it became clear to the crusaders how bad the conditions had been inside the castle. The defenders were completely emaciated and could barely move their legs and many had to be carried or supported by the crusaders. Many lay half dead on the ground, and the stench of dead animals and humans was overpowering. Worst off were the Christian prisoners, who for four days had not had more than one eggshell full of water each. At night they had laid naked on the stones to absorb some moistness, and many had begun to eat wet earth. Out of 450 prisoners, fewer than 200 were still alive.

The tensions between the Nordic crusaders and the Portuguese King were not over yet. The King wanted the large store of grain that was still in the town because there had not been enough water to make it into bread. The Nordic crusaders had arranged that the plunder was to be shared inside the city so that nothing disappeared during transport to the camp outside. When that had been accepted, the Flemings in particular began to sell the grain in secret to the Portuguese, who were in desperate need of grain for their horses. When this was discovered, Sancho was furious and the Nordic crusaders became nervous and quickly left him the town with all its valuables. One of them remarked bitterly that the Portuguese warriors had neither worked nor fought but only incited the King against the Nordic crusaders. King Sancho gave them nothing, but treated them insultingly and they departed distrusting him. Besides, before the siege, the King had promised to give one tenth of the booty to the Holy Sepulchre in Jerusalem in order to persuade the Nordic crusaders to participate in the conquest of Silves, but the promise was never fulfilled, the Nordic crusader claims.[60]

Most of the foreign crusaders travelled on to the Middle East, but just as had been the case at Lisbon forty-two years before, some of them settled in the area around Silves. The great mosque was consecrated as a cathedral and Nicolas of Flanders was installed as Bishop in the city. A lord of the city was appointed by King Sancho and the defence was handed to the military orders. It is characteristic of the engagement of the Templars and the Hospitallers that they were excluded from the city soon after by Sancho, whereas the local order from Évora was handed military responsibility for the city. The conquest of Silves was considered a landmark event, and Sancho took the title "Dei gratia Portugalis, Silvii et Algarbi rex," "By the grace of God King of Portugal, Silves and Algarve,"[61] just as Canute, at almost the same time, extended his title to include "King of the Wends." Sancho had a new seal made, which depicted him with his victory banner on the front,[62] and he minted gold coins that still followed the Arabic morabitun in style and value but showed Sancho as a crusader with his sword drawn on the front.[63] The back of both seal and coins showed five shields forming a cross, the coat of arms of Portugal. In Santiago de Compostela, the capture of Silves was celebrated by adding a new passage to the liturgy, which described the miracle:

> *Behold, God's wonderful acts are happening again, as under the Maccabees*
> *And the sign of the ancient ones returns heavenly*
> *The people of Hagar perish and the righteous people triumph everywhere*
> *Under King Afonso, the miramolin fell*
> *And King Sancho, who is in the service of Santiago*
> *As his father before him, has been a loyal friend of the saint,*
> *The royal strength and the faithful act of service*
> *That stems from Santiago. In a twin kingdom*
> *The true faith rules. Silves is as the other sublime sceptre of the King*
> *To the palm of Spain the King's hand shall reach.*[64]

The victory seemed assured and there was reason to triumph, but it soon turned out that the rejoicing was to be brief.

The conquest of Silves was countered determinedly and energetically by Abu Yusuf Yakub al-Mansur with three large expeditions over the following couple

276   *Rise and fall of crusader kingdoms*

of years. One was aimed at recapturing Silves, the second was aimed at Évora and the third invaded the Tagus valley. Silves was besieged during the summer of 1190 and defended by English crusaders en route to the Holy Land, but, in July 1191, it was recaptured by the Muslims. There was much pillaging to the north of the River Tagus, the Templar castle in Tomar was besieged in July 1190 and the Templars' properties in the town and its surroundings were plundered and destroyed. Abu Yusuf Yakub al-Mansur withdrew from Tomar after six days of siege, which, in inscriptions and the later history of the order, was depicted as a great victory for the Templars. This is disputed, but one result was that the Templars rejoined the Portuguese *reconquista* more actively and from then on participated in the fighting to the south of the Tagus. How widespread the fear of Muslim attacks really was at the time is shown by the fact that the monastery of Santa Cruz in Coimbra asked for, and was granted, permission by King Sancho to move the mortal remains of his father away from the monastery, which was located outside of the city walls, to a safe place inside the city because of the danger from the Muslims.[65] Al-Mansur's forces did not get this far north, however, but the result of the offensive was that the frontier again followed the River Tagus.

Saladin's conquest of Jerusalem in 1187 led to a pronounced heightening of the crusade commitment. Several large expeditions set out from all areas of Europe. Local crusades were extended everywhere, which led to the conquests in Finland and Estonia and to the capture of Silves in Portugal. The Muslim opponents were well aware of the religious character of these new crusades. In an anonymous manuscript, which is today only known from one single copy, held at the Royal Library in Copenhagen, an Arab author wrote about the fall of Silves: "There came a large number of ships with Christians, who according to their custom travelled against Jerusalem, as it had been arranged by their religious leaders. They came each year to renew an oath they had taken to follow their faith and to free themselves from the oath and from the conditions, to which their religious leaders had subjected them."[66]

Crusades against Muslims and crusades against Christians: Portugal until 1212

In 1991, Abu Yusuf Yakub al-Mansur received a message from Saladin, who asked for assistance to completely drive out the Christians from the Holy Land. He emphasized the common obligation to wage a jihad against the Christians and to stand together, West and East, just as the Christians from the West had assisted their brothers in the East. However, Abu Yusuf declined.[67] He had his own jihad on the Iberian Peninsula. The appeal from Saladin shows how events in Portugal were followed with great excitement in both the Muslim and the Christian world, and the rejection shows that Abu Yusuf wished to use all his force to recapture the Iberian territories. Portugal and the other kingdoms were under pressure and had to arm themselves.

Sancho issued several charters to the military orders, which were to re-arm militarily and ideologically in order to wage crusades. In 1193, the Order of

Santiago was donated the royal properties in Santarém, "where there is the very tower through which my father, the lord King Afonso of good repute, entered Santarém."[68] In a brief glimpse, we get a small detail about the conquest of Santarém by Afonso Henriques in 1147. The tower was a suitable gift to a military order and a constant reminder to them of their task; it was given "for the service that you have given me and for the service that you are to give me in the future." The year after, Sancho gave a very large piece of land – Guidimtesta – to the north of the Tagus to the Hospitallers, with the express clause that they were to build a castle which was to be called Belver.[69] This happened soon after, and as early as 1210, a part of the royal treasure was kept in the new castle.[70] Sancho does not mention why it was important to him to decide on the name of the castle and why the name was to be Belver. It is quite possible that there is a connection to the fortress of Belvoir in the Holy Land. That castle had been transferred to the Hospitallers in 1168 and was strongly fortified after this. It is the first known example of a consistently concentric castle with a fortress inside a fortress. It was soon copied elsewhere and spread to Western Europe.[71] After the battle of Hattin in 1187, Belvoir withstood a siege by Saladin for eighteen months. Sancho would have wished to emphasize to the Hospitallers in Portugal that, with Belver, it was their duty to guard and hold the frontier to the north of the River Tagus in the same way as their brothers in the Holy Land had held Belvoir by the River Jordan.

Everybody had to help. The canons at the cathedral of Coimbra were exempted from all burdens and from participating in *fossatis* and *apelitis*, the regular raids and defence manoeuvres, "except if the enemy army is going to invade our land. Then they shall come to the defence of the realm and only let a few of the old and infirm stay at the church to hold service. And if we can lead a large army into the Muslim territories, the Bishop together with the dean and some of the canons are to follow us."[72] At some time during this period, before 1195, Sancho also confirmed the charters which a certain William of Cornibus with permission from Afonso Henriques had given to Frenchmen and Galicians who settled in Atourgia. This place is located near Peniche and had earlier been given – free of debt – to William because of his efforts during the capture of Lisbon in 1147.[73] Sancho emphasizes that they have to muster without delay when the King leads his army against the heathens. He adds that William used to defray their expenses to horses, which presumably implies that he intends to do the same, even though it is not mentioned directly.[74]

Sancho renewed several town charters during the same period or issued new charters, quite often with careful specifications of the military obligations. In Vila Franca, one third of the town knights were to muster for the expeditions against the Muslims whenever the King commanded, and two thirds had to stay home to defend the town. If a knight did not turn up, he was to pay a fine to the King. In return, he only had to participate in the royal expeditions once every year "or more, if he so wishes."[75] At the same time, Sancho attracted colonists from afar and gave them land, both Frenchmen and Flemings.[76]

It also seem to have fitted into Sancho's crusade plans that Alfonso IX of León, after the capture of Silves, became very interested in a marriage with Sancho's

278 *Rise and fall of crusader kingdoms*

daughter Teresa. They were married on February 15, 1191, even though they were cousins and the marriage was forbidden by the Church. Pope Celestine protested and excommunicated them both, without any great effect at the beginning. At the same time, Alfonso VIII of Castile was seriously worried about an alliance between Portugal and León, and Alfonso II of Aragon tried to mediate to make peace. The marriage was dissolved, probably in around 1195 and likely as a consequence of the complicated political game. In 1197, Alfonso IX of León married Berenguela, the daughter of Alfonso VIII of Castile, who was also his cousin. New excommunications followed, and Innocent III worked hard to have this marriage dissolved from the moment he took over as Pope in 1198.[77]

During these political entanglements, Abu Yusuf Yakub al-Mansur resumed warfare on the Iberian Peninsula after a pause due to illness and truce. He entered Castilian territory in 1195 and attacked the castle Alarcos by the River Guardiana, which Alfonso VIII of Castile recently had built as a defence against Muslim attacks. Alfonso had assembled a very large army in Toledo and had earlier obtained a papal crusade bull which secured the participants indulgence and martyrdom if they fell in the war.

On July 17, the battle of Alarcos was fought; it was to be the greatest Christian defeat in 100 years. The Muslims of North Africa heavily outnumbered the Christians, and they were professional warriors; Alfonso only just managed to slip away, and the territory to the south of Toledo was lost. Many of the castles of the Calatrava Order had to surrender. The number of Christian prisoners was huge, between 5,000 and 25,000.[78] The number of the fallen was unlikely to have been any less. Sancho had despatched a contingent of Portuguese knights to Alarcos, and they fell. So did the Grand Master of the Order of Évora, Gonçalo Viegas and the governor of Silves, Rodrigo Sanches. A whole generation of the best warriors of Castile and many from Portugal fell at Alarcos. In October that year, the Master of the Templars Gualdim Pais died; he was seventy-five years old, the founder of Tomar and almost a symbol of the crusades. Measured in men and measured in great men, 1195 was a tough year for the crusaders on the Iberian Peninsula.[79]

Abu Yusuf al-Mansur exploited his victory by crossing the River Tagus and making a forward thrust into Portuguese territory. Several areas were plundered and Alcobaça was attacked. The monks defended themselves as well as they could but many were killed. In other monasteries, the monks surrendered in order to save their lives.[80] Abu Yusuf then initially withdrew to Seville but during the spring of 1196, he attacked Castile again. This happened on an understanding with Alfonso IX of León, whom Abu Yusuf supported with both money and men.[81] Even though Alfonso was now divorced from Teresa of Portugal, Pope Celestine was far from enthusiastic about him, and the alliance with Abu Yusuf did not improve matters.

In 1196, the Pope put León under interdict; Alfonso IX was excommunicated again, and the archbishops of Toledo and Compostela were ordered to preach to the Leónese that they had been released from their oath of loyalty to their king. "For those who are reborn in the water of baptism there shall be one common faith in the mind and one common piety in the acts," and therefore, it pains the Pope to find errors with those "who should stand like a wall around the Lord's

Rise and fall of crusader kingdoms 279

house and fight those who try to destroy the Lord's vineyard." Just as a gangrenous limb must be cut off so as not to infect the whole body, so Alfonso IX had to be stopped. Therefore, the Pope could promise all who fought against Alfonso and his following the same indulgence as if they had fought the Muslims.[82] This probably contributed to Sancho I asking for papal support to fight his old son-in-law. On April 10, 1197, Celestine III issued a bull that promised everyone who fought Alfonso IX the same indulgence as to Jerusalem – including Alfonso's own vassals.[83] This was a remarkable step. It was quite unusual that a Pope went in to annul the loyalty oath of a whole people to its ruler, and it was the first time that a Pope directly promised full Jerusalem indulgence to fight a Western European ruler. Theologically, it was a reasonable development of the idea of the crusade. The Church was attacked and had to defend itself, not only against Muslims but also against those Christians who had become heretics by allying themselves with the Muslims. This extension of the concept of the crusade was used often from then on in papal theological policy. Celestine's crusade bull against Alfonso IX was issued in the same year as he gave full Jerusalem indulgence to those who participated against the crusades against the Lithuanians. The papal crusading policy was rearming.

In 1197, Abu Yusuf al-Mansur attacked Castile again and pillaged along the Spanish part of the River Tagus; destruction and fear was widespread. Cistercian abbots from the Iberian Peninsula were forgiven for not showing up at the order's annual general chapter "because of the incursion of the heathens."[84] It nevertheless ended with al-Mansur entering a ten-year truce with Alfonso VIII, and shortly afterwards, he returned to Morocco, where he died in 1199. Alfonso VIII was then free to attack León, which Sancho was at war with as well. Alfonso IX of León went to Seville and tried to obtain military assistance from Abu Yusuf but without any result. Alfonso was no longer a strong card, militarily speaking; he was excommunicated and had the threat of rebellion by his vassals – and of crusades directed against him – hanging over him.

In the end, Alfonso IX made peace with Alfonso VIII and married his daughter, which only contributed to upholding his excommunication. The alliance gave peace with Castile but not with Portugal. Several bloody battles ensued. Local Portuguese forces were supplemented by a group of crusaders from the North, mostly Danes, Germans and Englishmen. They were en route to the Holy Land as part of the crusade of the Holy Roman Emperor Henry VI, which petered out after the death of the Emperor in 1197. They were received in Lisbon by the Bishop and apparently agreed to fight against Alfonso IX under Sancho's leadership. They then continued to Silves, which "they snatched from the hands of the heathens and almost completely destroyed. They feared that if they handed it over to the Portuguese King, he would lose it to the Muslims, as he had done before."[85] Local military orders also took part in the fight against Alfonso IX. During the battle of Cidade Rodrigo in 1199, the new Master of the Portuguese Templars, Lopo Fernandes, fell.[86] Then the Portuguese-Leónese wars ended. The reason was likely that Sancho began to have domestic problems, both with rebellious noblemen and with the bishops of Porto and Coimbra. This is probably also the reason why the

280 *Rise and fall of crusader kingdoms*

Portuguese crusades against the Muslims seem to have been put on hold for the rest of Sancho's time, until his death in 1211, only just escaping excommunication because of his problems with the Church. This does not imply that there was peace and quiet. There was on the contrary great fear of Muslim attacks, which seemed to be confirmed by many supernatural events:

> In 1199 there was such an omen, which there has not been since the suffering of the Lord until this day. Between the 6th and 7th hour of the day, it suddenly became night, the sun turned darker than pitch and the moon and many stars became visible in the sky. When the night began to give way, the shadows followed, over which the sun with the power of its brilliance gained the upper hand. A large multitude of men and women, secular and religious, assembled in Santa Cruz in Coimbra in deep fear and expected nothing but sudden death, and they lamented and cried for help from God, and with great difficulty, the friars sang 'We praise you God' and the litany and prayed for divine mercy, and everybody was more dead than alive and struck with great wonder. And behold, to everyone's surprise, in the choir at Santa Cruz there were seven signs of a moon, one quarter or one fifth full, a sign that neither before or since has been seen at this place, but the moon signs were clear to all of Coimbra town, wherever the rays of the sun penetrated a little.[87]

The symbolism is obvious. The Christian sun fights against the Muslim crescent moon, day against night.

Las Navas de Tolosa 1212 and its consequences – Damietta, Alcácer do Sal and Tallinn

On July 16, 1212, one of the decisive battles of the *reconquista* was fought at Las Navas de Tolosa. The great Christian kings took part: Alfonso VIII of Castile with all his noblemen, Pedro II of Aragon with 3000 knights and a contingent of crossbowmen and Sancho VII of Navarre, who arrived a little later with his 200 knights. Then there was a larger number of Portuguese and Leónese and thousands of knights and foot soldiers from Southern France, who had crossed the Pyrenees during the hot summer to take part in the crusade. The military orders were present in large numbers, including the Portuguese Templars and Hospitallers and the Order of Santiago – "the penitents of the Virgin Mary, full of their heathen fanaticism," as one contemporary Muslim observer described them.[88] This international army had assembled at Toledo. During the preceding years, Pope Innocent III had issued crusade bulls intensively, with full indulgence to all who wished to fight the Muslims on the Iberian Peninsula. He had also encouraged ecclesiastics in Southern France to preach the crusade and to get the local noblemen to take part.

It was probably the largest crusader army ever assembled on the Iberian Peninsula, and in June it began to move slowly southwards from Toledo against the Almohad army under the command of Caliph Muhammad an-Nasir, who sat

Rise and fall of crusader kingdoms 281

during the decisive fighting with a sword in one hand and a Quran in the other and directed the battle, surrounded by his personal African bodyguard. It was a hot journey for the Christian army; most of the participants from the North went back home, but the soldiers from the Peninsula continued.[89]

After a few skirmishes, the battle was fought on July 16 at Las Navas de Tolosa on the plateau on the southern side of Sierra Morena. The battle swayed to and fro; at one point the Christians were hard pressed but then the three kings threw themselves into the battle with renewed determination and managed to turn the fortunes of the battle through a heroic effort that was depicted in great detail in later Spanish and Portuguese chronicles, historic literature and various images. The Christian victory was crushing, and the rest of al-Andalus lay open before them. In practice, a long time was to pass before the whole region became politically Christian, but at the time, the victory at Las Navas de Tolosa was justly proclaimed as one of the greatest victories in the history of the crusades since the liberation of Jerusalem in 1099. "They saved not only Spain but also Rome and all of Europe as well."[90]

The victory at Las Navas de Tolosa was one of the reasons why Pope Innocent III recalled all crusader indulgence on the Iberian Peninsula from the battles against the Muslims, in Southern France against the heretics and generally indulgence for all other places than the Holy Land itself. This might sound the wrong way round, but one reason was presumably that the Iberian kings had demonstrated that they could handle it themselves. Thus, there was no reason for indulgence to motivate warriors from elsewhere to take part. Besides, it coincides time-wise – probably accidentally – with one of Innocent's attempts to realize an old plan that he had had since the time that he took office as Pope back in 1198: to liberate Jerusalem and the Holy Land. This had led to the fourth crusade and to the conquest of the Christian city of Constantinople in 1204, an event that cast long shadows into the future and had effectively hindered new, great crusade initiatives for almost ten years. Now they were so far in the past that Innocent could start anew and concentrate his efforts – and all indulgence – on the Holy City itself.

Quia maior

With Innocent III's great crusade bull, *Quia maior*, from April 1213, everything was mobilized in order to prepare a new crusade to Jerusalem.[91]

> Because there is now more than ever a need to give help to the Holy Land and because there is now reason to hope that help will be of greater use than ever before, behold, I begin to cry out again – I cry out to you and I cry out for Him, who when He died cried with a loud voice on the cross, where He had been made obedient to God the Father, obedient until death on the cross – He cried to tear us from the torment of eternal death. He cries of Himself and says that if anyone wishes to follow me, he shall deny himself and take his cross and follow me.

282   *Rise and fall of crusader kingdoms*

At the same time, Innocent was optimistic and hoped and believed that fighting against Islam would make a difference. Muhammad's end was approaching, he thought, because the number of the Beast in the Apocalypse of St. John is 666, and of those, 600 had almost passed. The calculation makes sense if Innocent calculated from the establishment of Islam in 622, that is, from hijra: Muhammad's migration to Medina.

With Quia maior, crusade indulgence was withdrawn from the crusades on the Iberian Peninsula against the Muslims and from those in Provence against the Albigensian heretics,[92] partly because it had been limited to a certain period, which had now expired, partly because there was no longer any reason to wage crusades there. The Muslims were defeated and by the grace of God, there had been such progress in the fight against Muslims and heretics that there was no compelling need for help and indulgence right now. No more indulgence apart from crusades to Jerusalem, and it does seem that the crusades ceased everywhere in Europe. In the laconic form of the annals, it is noticed for 1213: "In this year there was no crusade in Denmark" – *expeditio in Dacia quieuit*.[93] This did not last for long. Innocent had wisely added in Quia maior that if the need arose for indulgence and crusades to other places than Jerusalem, he would assess the case and reconsider his verdict. It probably soon happened that rulers approached the Pope in order to have wars authorized as crusades. At least it happened at the fourth Lateran Council where, in front of the Pope and the cardinals, Bishop Albert of Riga argued that Riga was just as important as Jerusalem because Riga and all of Livonia had been dedicated to the Virgin Mary. "The Son loves His mother and just as He does not wish for His land to be lost, He does not wish her land to be in danger, either," Albert explained.[94] Innocent was persuaded, and after this there was again indulgence for those crusaders who wished to support Albert in the struggle against the heathen Livonians. Similarly, Spanish representatives turned up at the fourth Lateran Council and asked for indulgence for those who fought in Spain, but in vain.[95]

Quia maior contains an ideological programme and a declaration about uniting all of Western Christendom to fight against Islam and for the defence of Jerusalem. How this was to happen practically was outlined in the much shorter bull *Vineam Domini*, "The Lord's Vineyard," which at the same time called the general synod in the Lateran two and a half years later.[96] Each church province was obliged to nominate experts who could prepare to participate in the meeting and particularly to prepare for the participation of their region in a crusade, if the synod was to decide to initiate one. The bull was sent to archbishops and bishops all over Europe including Lund and Braga; it was sent to Armenia and to the Emperor and Patriarch of Constantinople, it was sent to the kings of France, Aragon, Navarre, Castile, León, Portugal, Cyprus, Norway, Sweden and others.[97]

John Lackland of England was not among the recipients as he was excommunicated at the time and, in 1211, had negotiated with Caliph Muhammad an-Nasir of Morocco over an alliance against France. He was assumed to have offered to convert to Islam at the time, but this sounds like pure slander and is almost certainly not true.[98] The German King and Holy Roman Emperor was not sent the bull

Rise and fall of crusader kingdoms   283

either; nobody knew at the time if he was Otto or Fredric II, even though developments favoured the latter. Finally, the Danish King Valdemar II the Victorious is missing from the list of recipients. It might simply be a mistake. Nothing indicates any disagreements between Valdemar and Innocent at the time. It could perhaps have something to do with Valdemar's relationship with Fredric II. After having swung to and fro between the candidates to the imperial throne during the first decade of the 13th century, Valdemar now supported Fredric, and he apparently had a good relationship with him. At the New Year of 1214–1215, Fredric issued the Golden Bull, wherein he gave Valdemar all land to the north of the Elbe and in Wendland as far east as West Pomerania and Hither Pomerania in gratitude of his support, which had contributed to the defeat of his rival Otto in one of the greatest and most decisive medieval battles, at Bouvines in July 1214.[99] All this is speculation, however. There is no positive proof that Innocent had anything against Valdemar and that he would not have sent *Vineam Domini* to him because of his relationship with Fredric. In practice, Valdemar became an eager and important crusader for Innocent.

Damietta in Egypt

As Innocent had hoped, the Fourth Lateran Council decided to initiate a new crusade to the Middle East. It was decided that Egypt should be targeted instead of the Holy Land itself on the strategic consideration that it would never be possible to hold on to Jerusalem and the Holy Land as long the Muslims there were able to receive reinforcements from Egypt. The crusade was now preached through the organization which had been built up all over Europe by the heads of the Church, who out of humbleness of heart and body had carried the words of the Cross and who had taken care to "lead the believers to revenge the injustice [that] has befallen the Crucified One."[100]

The preparations and the course of this crusade, later known as the fifth crusade, have been meticulously treated by James Powell, who also examined sources and literature to research the participants.[101] Only one single person is known from Portugal, the canon from Coimbra D., who took part in the month of July 1218 – what the D stands for is not even known.[102] Then there is Cardinal Pelagius, who was to play a rather large role in the complete military failure of the crusade. He was originally from Portugal but had been a cardinal and lived in Rome since 1206.[103] From Denmark, Niels Nielsen participated at some point. We know this because, for part of the financing needed for his participation, he gave a large donation of land to the Cistercian monastery of Esrom. At that point he states that his part in the crusade is by request of his mother and the King and with their approval.[104] Niels was a son of Niels of Halland, an illegitimate son of Valdemar I; thus, Niels Nielsen was a nephew of the King. It could hardly get any more distinguished than this, so Denmark was represented at the very highest level in the fifth crusade.

If we take a closer look at some of the other participants, we see that there was a very close link to the Danish royal house. Two great vassals of the Danish King

284 *Rise and fall of crusader kingdoms*

took part, Duke Kazimir II of Pomerania, who died in the Holy Land, and Count Henry of Schwerin, who unfortunately managed to get back home and in 1223 gained notoriety by imprisoning his overlord the King. Count Albert of Holstein had taken the cross but did not go.[105] Another of the early important crusaders was King András II of Hungary. In the spring of 1217, he journeyed towards the Holy Land after having his son Kálman crowned as his co-ruler. An important group in András's army was his elite archers, who were Turkish-speaking Cuman nomads from the Hungarian Puszta. They were Muslims, and it was presumably them who told the Arab traveller Yakut bin Abdulla in Aleppo that they had fought together with the Christian Hungarians and that their king had only waged war against the opponents of Islam. They thought they were on a jihad but had really fought in a crusade.[106] András had become related to the Danish royal house because his sister Constance had recently married Ottokar I of Bohemia, the father of Dagmar, becoming the first Queen of Valdemar II the Victorious.

By 1213, Dagmar was dead and, in May 1214, Valdemar was married to Berengaria of Portugal, daughter of King Sancho I and granddaughter of Afonso Henriques. She was the sister of Fernão, who had become Count of Flanders, with which Denmark had had good relations for more than a century. In the immediate circumstances, the Count of Flanders could have been a political counterweight to Philip August of France, with whom both Canute VI and Valdemar II had a rather strained relationship because of Philip August's treatment of their sister Ingeborg. In this context, an alliance with the greatest vassal of the French King and one of his great enemies, the Count of Flanders, would certainly have been of interest. If there had been such political considerations behind Valdemar's choice of spouse, he must have been terribly disappointed. During the battle of Bouvines on July 27 that year, Fernão was wounded and taken prisoner by Philip August and had to spend the next twelve years in a dungeon at the Louvre.[107]

Fernão was married to Jeanne of Hainaut and Flanders (1199/1200–1244), daughter of none other than the newly proclaimed Emperor of Constantinople, Baldwin I, the first Latin emperor after the fourth crusade's unfortunate conquest of the capital of the East Roman Empire in 1204. His maternal uncle was Count Phillip of Flanders, who died at Acre in 1191 and was buried in the Church of St. Nicholas outside the walls but was later brought back by his wife and buried in Clairvaux,[108] where the Danish Archbishop Eskil had also been recently laid to rest. Phillip had been married to Afonso Henriques' daughter Teresa of Portugal, who in Flanders went under the name Mathilde; thus, the Portuguese–Flemish connection stretched over a couple of generations.

The marriage of Valdemar and Berengaria in 1214 united two crusader dynasties, the Portuguese and the Danish. During the wedding dinner, the two brothers-in-law, Valdemar II of Denmark and Afonso II of Portugal, could conceivably have each arranged to go on crusades in their own region as part of the great international crusade, which they knew that Innocent was preparing. The kings probably did not meet in person at the wedding, but there would have been messengers who travelled between them frequently, and they would have been well oriented with each other's doings.

Rise and fall of crusader kingdoms 285

Figure 8.2 King Valdemar and Queen Berengaria on the morning after their wedding. Painting by Agnes Slott-Møller, 1931. © University of Southern Denmark Press

The crusade to the Holy Land was a drawn-out project, which was to be a huge failure eventually. The crusaders arrived at Acre in groups and did not manage to organize a large united attack; therefore, many gave up and returned home. András returned to Hungary as early as in the spring of 1218. The rest of the leaders of the Western European army held a council of war outside Acre and decided to attack Egypt and thus once and for all eliminate the most important Muslim power in the area. The siege of the strong fortress of Damietta, which dominated the entrance to the Nile, began in May 1218, and the castle fell in October the next year after one and a half years of attack.

One of the participants in the crusade was Francis of Assisi, who in the midst of the hostilities calmly walked into the Muslim camp and asked to speak to Sultan

286   *Rise and fall of crusader kingdoms*

al-Kamil, whom he tried to convert to Christianity.[109] He did not succeed, and
Francis was led back to the Christian army with full protection and veneration of
a group of Muslim soldiers. In later historical writing, Francis's surprising act was
interpreted as a criticism of the crusades but it was most likely not. Persuasion and
mission with words was a supplement to armed crusades, not an alternative.[110] The
story of Francis's offer to the Sultan was more likely spread at the time because it
emphasized that a crusade always had to be initiated with an offer to the opponent
that he could convert voluntarily.

Another important participant was the papal legate Pelagius, who arrived in Egypt
in the late summer of 1218 to take command of the army. He was a cardinal, Portuguese and exceedingly rigid. He bore the main responsibility for the turning down
of al-Kamil's repeated offers to hand over Jerusalem and several castles in the Holy
Land.[111] In 1221, he ordered the crusader army to march up along the Nile to attack
the new Egyptian fortress of al-Mansurah, where the crusaders were cut off from
provisions, surrounded on an island and flooded by the rising Nile. On August 26,
they decided to break up in secret in the middle of the night and fight their way back
to Damietta. Beforehand, the soldiers boosted themselves with wine which they
had brought and which they would otherwise have had to leave behind. When the
army began to move, it had to leave many behind because it was impossible to stir
them into action. Many staggered into ponds and ditches and drowned, and some
celebrated the whole thing by setting fire to their tents. The retreat was no longer a
secret, crusaders were killed in large numbers, and Pelagius and the King of Jerusalem, Jean de Brienne, had to enter an unconditional peace on the August 30, 1221.

Some historians have argued that Pope Innocent was lucky that he died in 1216
and did not live long enough to witness how his largest conceived and best planned
crusade turned into a failure. This is actually only correct if we perceive the crusade as only directed against the Middle East, and that angle is too narrow. After
the fourth Lateran Council, crusades were planned and prepared in other places as
well. In Portugal, Afonso II succeeded in capturing Alcácer do Sal, and in Denmark, Valdemar II the Victorious headed the crusade which managed to win the
final control over Tallinn and Estonia. Contrary to the Egyptian crusade, the two
others led to permanent conquests and to the christening of Muslim and heathen
lands, which would have appealed to Innocent, and they were carried through
before the Egyptian crusade descended into military disaster. The importance of
the Egyptian crusade lies elsewhere. The defeat led to strong criticism of both
Pelagius and the idea that ecclesiastics were to head crusades. They should leave
that to warriors and secular noblemen, the critics emphasized, and they spread
their ideas through the medium of troubadour ballads. After 1221, the crusades
began to be of a generally different nature. The Popes were just as involved in
planning and practical preparations as before, but the idea of ecclesiastic leadership of the fighting army was abandoned.

Alcácer do Sal 1217

Afonso II succeeded his father, Sancho, but he was most certainly not a warrior king. He suffered from an incurable disease – leprosy, traditional opinion

Rise and fall of crusader kingdoms   287

said – and he was tremendously fat, perhaps as a consequence of his disease.[112] In all of his short life, he was treated for both and was surrounded by a large corps of doctors, including Jewish and Muslim doctors. In a way it is ironic that it was Afonso II who was to become famous as one of the great crusader kings when he captured Alcácer do Sal in 1217.

Afonso was weak from birth. In 1200, when he was fourteen years old, Sancho gave a large gift to the church of Our Lady in Basto, where he "groaned his prayers amongst sighs and weeping to the Holy Virgin and she with her holy prayers had obtained Prince Afonso's salvation from the God the Lord Himself" when Afonso was close to death from illness.[113] Afonso succeeded to the throne in 1211. He concentrated on legislation and diplomacy and managed to build up one of the very earliest examples of a well-functioning royal administration in Western Europe. At the same time, his reign was plagued by in-fighting with his siblings and a difficult relationship with the large Church institutions. This might have been one of his reasons to enter a truce with the Muslims, presumably in 1211. Thus, the King was unable to take part in the fighting at Las Navas de Tolosa personally or with a royal army. However, he could let his noblemen decide for themselves whether they wanted to participate or not, and he could let the military orders take part.[114]

After the great Christian victory at Las Navas de Tolosa, the crusades were intensified on the Iberian Peninsula but only slowly in Portugal. Afonso gave charters to the military orders in order to make them build castles and fortify the frontier. For instance, he gave Cardosa north of the River Tagus to the Templars in 1214. Here they erected the castle of Castelo Branco, obviously an attempt to imitate the order's strong castle in Tripoli in the Holy Land, Chastel Blanc.[115]

In July 1217 a fleet of 200 ships arrived in Portugal on their way to Egypt. It was a German and Flemish fleet but with many Englishmen and Danes among the warriors. It would have been one of the earliest crusader fleets to set sail in order to follow the decision of the fourth Lateran Council to initiate yet another large crusade, but it was seriously delayed. The men "had toiled through four months to sail to Lisbon, where one can normally get to in fourteen days."[116] The fleet was under the command of Count Wilhelm of Holland and Friesland, a close ally of Fernão of Flanders. The crusader fleet had been hit by storms and troubles and had been forced to stop at the River Douro to repair the ships, and before this, the army had visited Santiago de Compostela. In Lisbon, they were met by the Bishop, Soeiro, who persuaded them to participate in an attempt to capture Alcácer do Sal, which had been retaken by the Muslims in 1191. The city was strongly fortified and was the starting point of constant raids into the Christian territories, where the Muslims were killing and hunting for slaves. This was so common that it had become a part of the taxation system: the people of Alcácer do Sal had to pay 100 Christian slaves to the Caliph annually and, additionally, they captured many for their own use.[117] This might be true, but it could very well be Soeiro's version in order to excite the crusaders from the North and persuade them to go on a Portuguese crusade.

The Portuguese arrived in great numbers to go against Alcácer do Sal: Bishop Soeiro of Lisbon, Bishop Soeiro of Évora, Abbot Fernandes of Alcobaça, the Master of the Order of Santiago and Templars and Hospitallers and many noblemen.

288   *Rise and fall of crusader kingdoms*

King Afonso, on the other hand, apparently did not contribute in any way. The crusader army from the North was split. The Frisians referred to the fact that Pope Innocent had revoked all crusade indulgence from the Iberian Peninsula after Las Navas de Tolosa in 1212, and they decided to continue to the Holy Land with eighty ships. The papal ban on indulgence weighed less heavily on the minds of the Portuguese bishops. They began to cross sign volunteers everywhere in their dioceses and in the whole realm, and they would not really have been able to do this without promising indulgence for fighting against the Muslims.[118]

The army reached Alcácer do Sal on July 30 after having sailed for three days on the River Sado. The castle was full of provisions and consisted of a concentric, double system of walls. The siege began immediately and passed in the usual way with assault and sorties, with mining and counter-mining. At the end of August, one of the outer towers collapsed, but this did not constitute any serious weakening of the castle. At the same time, the siege had dragged on for so long that a large relief army had been organized from Seville, Córdoba, Jaén, Jerez and Badajoz, which came ever closer. It was supposedly composed of 15,000 cavalry and 40,000 foot-soldiers, the most important Christian narrative on the battle reported.[119] It was unlikely to have underestimated the size of the enemy army and emphasized that the Christians had an unending supply of foot soldiers but only a little fewer than 300 cavalry. An open battle was unavoidable, and it took place on September 11. It only went well thanks to three miracles, which the crusaders carefully told the Pope about after the victory.

The day before the attack itself, the crusaders saw a miraculous omen of victory. A clear and brilliant cross appeared before them in the evening in the twilight sky. This strengthened them as much as the contingent of Templar knights that arrived around midnight under the command of the Spanish Master, Pedro Alvítiz. With him arrived yet more Hospitallers, Santiago knights and noblemen, even some from León. In total, 500 knights arrived during the night. During the attack of Alcácer do Sal, the crusaders invoked both Santiago and St. Vincent, he who had arrived in Lisbon about fifty years before in a ship without a captain.[120] When the outlook was most desperate, the crusaders were relieved by reinforcements from heaven; "their clothing shone as the sun and new, white snow and on their chests was a red sign of the cross. When the enemy saw this new army, they turned their backs and fled, the light blinded them and their hearts trembled."[121] The Muslim survivors, who had been captured, were scared and asked: "Where are the white knights who blinded us and defeated us?"[122] The Muslim army went into panic, and the Christian victory was total and bloody. The butchering of fleeing Muslims continued for three days. The fortress itself held out until October 21,[123] and then it had to surrender because of the extensive mining of two large defence towers. Most inhabitants were led away into slavery, some were baptized, among them the lord of the castle, Abu Abdallah. He was later captured in Muslim Seville and executed as an apostate from Islam.

The battle of Alcácer do Sal was famous all over Europe, not least because of the obvious miracles with the cross in the sky.[124] This was a sign that the Lord God was on the side of the crusaders; the Pope wept with emotion and gratitude when

Rise and fall of crusader kingdoms 289

he heard about it, he wrote in his letter of congratulations, in which he also called for prayers of thanksgiving and songs of praises.[125] On the other hand, there was less agreement as to where precisely God wished to support the crusades. The Portuguese asked Pope Honorius III to let the Nordic crusaders stay for one year in Portugal to help eradicate Islam once and for all from the Iberian Peninsula.[126] Count Wilhelm of Holland wrote to the Pope that the backing of the crusades on the Peninsula was enthusiastic and that most of the Muslims would now follow the example of Abu Abdallah and become Christians.[127] King Alfonso IX of León had now taken the cross together with Sancho VII of Navarre and truces with Muslims were cancelled; volunteers poured in to go on crusade. Wilhelm therefore asked the Pope to have his crusading vow changed so that he could fulfil it on the Iberian Peninsula rather than in the Holy Land. He was turned down on the grounds that the Lord God had let a small Christian army defeat a superior enemy; thus it was not the number of men that was important. Pope Honorius held on to the plan which had already been laid in order to fulfil the decision of the Lateran Council. He ordered the crusaders to travel on and in the month of March, they set sail from Lisbon and reached Acre in May 1218.

Papal policy was not immovable. When it turned out that the Archbishop of Toledo was actually able to head a new crusade and was able to make the kings of León, Castile and Navarre promise to take part, Pope Honorius gave permission to use Church income from Toledo and Segovia for the local crusades.[128] On March 15, 1219, he again gave indulgence to crusaders on the Iberian Peninsula and permission to commute a crusade oath to the Holy Land by fighting at home instead.

> The supreme one of the divine Council did not drive out the heathens from the countenance of the people of Israel at once but little by little, so that the thorn-bush shall not grow tall on earth or the wild beasts rise against them, that means against the Christians, who the people of Israel refers to, and He spread the infidel people and the enemies of God's name round and about so that the believers could be incited to practice what is good and not let the thorn-bushes and the thistles grow in the soil of their hearts but instead could fight the heathens for the honour of Christ and thus win forgiveness for their sins.[129]

The lull in the crusades had been going on for too long, Islam grew as the thistles and threatened to strangle the good seed, but the presence of the Muslims are at the same time part of God's plan for salvation and a penance for the believers. The privilege of crusade indulgence was renewed over the following years, despite the kings' difficulties in keeping peace between themselves, and led to some expeditions, especially against Valencia. Conquests were few and not lasting, and Portuguese participation was low or absent.[130]

King Valdemar's Cadaster and Afonso's inquirições

During the first half of the 13th century, both Denmark and Portugal reached a complex stage in administration, which made it possible to carry out a systematic

290   *Rise and fall of crusader kingdoms*

measuring and registering of royal land and income. This probably happened by mutual inspiration. King Valdemar of Denmark decided to initiate a record of his property in just the same way as his brother-in-law Afonso II of Portugal had done a few years earlier. They are some of the earliest examples in Western Europe of such developed administrative practice, and one of the most important objectives was to provide resources to wage religious wars of conquest.

In 1220, Afonso II initiated his *inquirições*, enquiries, where the King's representatives and the locals were to go through titles and rights: who held which properties or incomes, and did they have a royal charter validating it; which incomes was the King entitled to in the various regions of Portugal; and how were they solved. If the property owned by churches and local noblemen was recognized, they would receive a royal letter of confirmation. If not, it quite often happened that Afonso seized the property. These *inquirições* are, apart from the English Domesday Book from 1086, the first large and sustained attempt in Europe to create a comprehensive overview of royal income.[131]

The royal fact-finding committee was not welcome in all places. Some places they simply gave up trying to reach, after several of their predecessors were killed by robber barons in the mountains who did not wish to discuss property rights with anyone. "One killed the knight Romens, and the other killed Martin the Moor, and since then they have not dared to venture there."[132] In Ponte de Barca, the inhabitants in five out of twenty-six parishes fled "because of the unrest," other places were almost empty and in others only a hermit was left. The problems in Ponte de Barca were not caused by religious war with Muslims but by common strife. It shows how difficult it was to create a form of central administration in a region which had earlier been thoroughly militarized and organized for war.

Nevertheless, in most places it went well for the emissaries, and questions were asked in place after place about the king's income and how it was paid: wine, hens, chicken, fish at the coast and chestnuts in the mountains. In many places, the inhabitants gave *pro fossadeira* to be released from participating in the annual expeditions against the Muslims. This was mostly in the northern regions, furthest away from the religious frontier, where the crusades were beginning to be a thing of the past. Active participation had been replaced by taxation, which the King could use for wars further to the South. In Santa Maria de Tonguina, the King had one of his regular resting places for his journeys; it was a large location with cattle pens and slave farms, where the King's prisoners were chained up.[133] Region by region, a record was created of the King's income and its payment.

King Valdemar's Cadaster is a corresponding record of royal income from the 1230s with later additions. Even if it is often more succinct than the Portuguese *inquirições*, Valdemar may well have gained the idea of such a new administrative practice from his brother-in-law. The value of royal properties is estimated in *marcs* in gold and *marcs* in grain. Quite a few paid *kværsæde* in return for being allowed to remain at home when the crusades were being declared, corresponding to *pro fossadeira*. Honey, salmon and various sorts of grain were typical duties. In several places, the King had a right to stay overnight and to be fed, and in some places, he had himself and his entourage transported at the ferries. At

Rise and fall of crusader kingdoms 291

Dannevirke, the King was entitled to 120 marks in pure silver and provisioning for three nights in the summer for himself and his army when he was going on an expedition against the freedom-loving Frisians, "as he usually did."[134] One part of the Cadaster registered the many islands with game where Valdemar could visit and go hunting. The little island of Agersø off Skælskør was distinguished by having monkeys amongst the game. For obvious reasons, this has confused Danish historians and it might be a case of a writing error. However, it could also have been a princely gift from Afonso II to Valdemar II on the occasion of the wedding between Valdemar and Afonso's sister Berengaria. Maybe they were Barbary apes.

King Valdemar's Court Roll also includes the so-called Falster List, a mere four sheets of parchment with eight pages, filled only with place name after place name, village after village.[135] "*Egebjerg 1 bol, 3 marks; the King has 6 øre; Peter Benedictsen 12 øre and one ørtug; Peter Thrulsen 10 ørtug.*" For Korselitse with the Slavic name, it says: "*6 bol 6 marks. The Bishop has 2 marks; Frændi 10 øre; Peter Jukilsen ½ mark*" and so on. The style is lapidary and the interpretation uncertain, bit it may best be understood as a record of all the king's men who were obliged to go on crusade whenever the king ordered them to. The list of places shows where these permanent crusaders had their landed properties. The list consists of seventy-one individuals in the middle of the 13th century and, in addition, the Bishop of Odense.[136]

A list in King Valdemar's Court Roll concerning the island of Fehmarn[137] consists of a series of names of towns, which are divided into Christian towns and Slavic towns. Many of the Christian towns are named after individuals, and the list possibly shows that the island was conquered and colonized in the 12th century and that more than a hundred years later, the two population groups were still differentiated and thus it was likely to have remained a religiously mixed society. The King was entitled to income from ferries, from market stalls and from landed property. Some were placed directly under the King, others were given by him to several noblemen, presumably as a return for their effort during the crusade against Fehmarn, and they are carefully mentioned by name. Finally, the King was entitled to income from the Slavic towns.

There must have been other areas in the country, which had to be conquered under the leadership of the King and thus went to the King or his loyal men. It is difficult to follow in detail, but the King owned large parts of the southern parts of the island of Langeland, which suggests that the area had been conquered.[138]

Besides, King Valdemar's Court Roll contains a list of properties in the newly conquered crusade territory of Estonia. The names of the vassals and the size of incomes are listed, but the added comments convey a sad and resigned picture of the difficulties in maintaining control in the dangerous frontier region – for Valdemar, as it was for Afonso. "One kiligunda with 400 haken, which the Sword Bretheren have usurped, even though they have had no access to it."[139] Master Ywar owns in Haccriz parish the town of Tedau with fifteen haken and the town Orgiel and the farm Ryol with fifteen haken, Master Hælf other properties. Next to this information is the list of the displaced – Lændær, Arnold, Hermann, Wæzelin,

292   *Rise and fall of crusader kingdoms*

Johannes, Godefrith and Halworth. The list of "displaced" or "removed" is long, and judging from the names, they are the crusader vassals of the Danish King, who were forced to flee again and again, presumably because of attacks by the heathen Estonians. For the town of Kiulo no names are even mentioned – it says only "killed." Kiulo was later known by the German name *Fegefeur*, Hell's Fire.[140]

The earliest European attempts to carry out a thorough record of royal incomes and duties – apart from Domesday Book in 1086 – was King Afonso's inquirições and shortly after that King Valdemar II's Cadaster. Both provide a glimpse into the practical organization of a crusade society and into the dangers and problems found in such a society – it became more dangerous the further away one travelled from the centre under royal control. Both lists were made to get an overview of the incomes, parts of which could then be used to wage another crusade.

Sancho II: Crusader and rex inutilis

Afonso II died in 1223 from his illnesses, aged only thirty-seven years old. He was succeeded by his son Sancho. During his reign, the Portuguese crusades reached their greatest extent on the Peninsula, and the conquests led to the incorporation of Muslim territory into the realm of the Christian king. Sancho himself, however, only rarely participated in the crusades personally, and his reign was marked by clashes with the noblemen and the Church and, in the end, he was deposed as king.

In 1226, Alfonso IX of León initiated a crusade against Cáceres and Bedajoz; this happened with the understanding of Sancho II after a mutual peace agreement. The seventeen-year-old Sancho headed a Portuguese crusader army including most of the high ecclesiastics and an impressive line of noblemen. They attacked the Muslim town of Elvas and managed initially to destroy the town wall. Sancho himself only barely survived the siege. In the same year, he gave a large gift to Afonso Peres Saracins, who had saved Sancho during the siege with great risk to his own life.[141] To begin with, however, the Portuguese army had to retreat and was not able to hold the town. At the same time, an open feud broke out between some of the noble families; whether this was the reason for abandoning the siege or a result of it is not known. In any case, a group attempted to make Prince Afonso a new king instead of Sancho, his brother. It was staved off, after which Afonso moved to France and got the title of Duke of Boulogne through marriage. The feud between the noblemen continued.

The crusades were now intensified with the military orders in front.[142] In 1227, Mérida fell to Sancho's son Pedro, who was on a crusade for Alfonso IX of León. The Muslims of Elvas fled upon hearing of the fall of Mérida, and the Portuguese knights took it on behalf of Sancho. Sancho gave the town a charter in 1229 in order to attract new Christian settlers, just as he did with several other towns in the insecure frontier region. Nearby, Juromenha also surrendered and remained in Christian control after a long history of disputes where the town had changed hands several times. Portuguese knights also took part when Badajoz finally fell to Alfonso IX of León in 1230.

Rise and fall of crusader kingdoms 293

Then things went fast. One fortress after the other fell to the Portuguese. First on the far side of the Tagus: Serpa and Moura in 1232, Beja in 1232–1234, Aljustrel in 1234, Mértola and Alfajar da Pena in 1238. In 1239 the crusades began against the Muslim fortresses on Algarve, which fell one by one: 1240–1241 Alvor, 1242 Tavira and Castelo de Paderne. The very active crusader leaders were predominantly Paio Peres Corriea, leader of the Order of Santiago, who continued his successful and later very famous crusade career in Castilian service from around 1241, Afonso Peres Farinha, leader of the Hospitallers and Sancho's illegitimate half-brother Fernão de Serpa, who in only 1239 received no less than twelve crusade bulls from Pope Gregory IX supporting his crusades.[143]

Several of the bulls to Fernão de Serpa were standard crusade bulls that 1) placed the crusaders and their properties under papal protection, 2) promised the same indulgence to the crusaders under the command of Fernão as to the crusaders to Jerusalem or 3) gave absolution to those who had been excommunicated for attacking ecclesiastics, if they took the cross and defended the castle of Serpa, "because we shall fight the Saracens with all the strength that we possess."[144] In the same way, the Danish Archbishop Anders Sunesen received permission in 1204 to give absolution to a bailiff who had cut off the nose and tongue of a priest whom he had found in his wife's bed, in return for the bailiff supporting the crusades, either in the Holy Land or in the Baltic.[145]

Other bulls to Fernão reflect special circumstances. His castle Serpa lay amongst the Muslims and would have been under severe pressure. Together with his permission to wage crusades, Fernão also received permission to sell the booty he took from the Muslims back to the very same Muslims, with the exception of iron, horses, weaponry and timber for shipbuilding, which could be used in the war against the Christians. The money was to be used for the protection of the castle and to ransom Christian captives.[146] Sancho too received permission to sell to Jews and Muslims, but "it would probably be of more benefit to the royal honour if he sold to Christians," Pope Gregory added.[147] Relations between Christians and non-Christians were complicated and ambiguous. The King was openly criticized for preferring Jews and Muslims to Christians in public offices, in stark contradiction to the decisions of the fourth Lateran Council.[148] What this refers to exactly is not certain now.

On the other hand, Fernão de Serpa apparently had a group of Muslims to do very dirty jobs on his behalf. He sent the group to a church that belonged to the chapter in Lisbon, where they had plundered grain and wine, set the dean's house on fire and removed all his belongings. Fernão had several clerics killed – some he even beat with his own hands. Clerics were dragged out of churches and monasteries and from cemeteries where they had been hiding; they were beaten up and mistreated. Fernão now regretted all this and promised the Pope to do penance. During Lent he would neither shave nor wash his head and he would not dress in either silk, scarlet or golden brocades. During the whole of Lent, five poor men were to eat at Fernão's table, and he himself would make do with only one course and one servant. In Santarém, where he had ordered to kill the clerics, he was to walk barefoot and, with chains around his neck, he was to stand at the gates of the

294 *Rise and fall of crusader kingdoms*

churches, one by one. Here, he was to be received by a priest and to let himself be flogged. As part of the penance, he had to ransom thirty Christians from the Muslims and he had to promise never to support the Muslims against the Christians with either advice or action. Finally he had to promise to fight with all his might against the Muslims at the frontier for three years.[149]

There is no doubt that Fernão criss-crossed the religious frontier and enjoyed great political benefits from having his castle situated amongst the Muslims. That he now, finally in 1239, chose sides might very well be down to the simple fact that the Portuguese crusades had reached as far as the coast of Algarve. There was no secure future in supporting Muslim rulers, on the contrary, and this might be the explanation why Fernão became an eager crusader. To celebrate this, he became a vassal of St. Peter and swore solemnly on the gospels that he in the future would be loyal and obedient to St. Peter, the Holy Roman Church and Pope Gregory and the legitimate successors.[150] The formal vassal relationship was an important, mutual obligation between crusader and Pope of great political and religious importance; it was a quite natural part of the crusade preparations for a high-ranking prince. It is presumably for the same reason that the Danish King's son Valdemar III the Young became a vassal of St. Peter in 1216, the year before the Danish crusades to Estonia were resumed in earnest.[151]

It is the opinion of several historians that Sancho II did not take personal part in these crusades and mostly stayed in the background due to internal problems and criticism from the noblemen.[152] This is a qualified truth only. At least he benefited greatly from the crusades, also in political manoeuvring with noblemen and not least with the Church. As a crusader he was included in papal protection. In 1232, Pope Gregory IX issued a bull where he forbade the excommunication of Sancho as long as he fought the Muslims.[153] The year after he went as far as to give Sancho absolution in advance if he "in the army or some other place, not by the devil's prompting but during the disposing of the troops or from necessity to prevent an attack at time accidentally beat some ecclesiastics with a staff or with his hand."[154] Apparently, Sancho's desire for ecclesiastical company was not great, but ill will and even violence was accepted for the sake of the crusades. Again in 1234 and in 1241, the Pope issued bulls giving indulgence to those taking part in the crusades of Sancho II.

The opposition to Sancho nevertheless grew and received support from powerful Church forces such as the bishops of Coimbra and Guarda and the Archbishop of Braga. They approached Pope Innocent IV in 1245 and prevailed on him to issue a bull to Sancho, who was accused of being the cause of troubles and infighting, which he was ordered to put an effective end to. At the same time, Innocent was in touch with Afonso of Boulogne, whom he tried to persuade to go on a crusade to the Holy Land. Afonso replied that he would rather fight the Muslims on the Iberian Peninsula, and Innocent issued full crusade indulgence to those who followed Afonso.[155] This did not improve Sancho's chances with the Pope, and the desired reforms failed to materialize.

At the first council of Lyon in 1245, Innocent issued the bull *Grandi non immerito*, in which he named Sancho a *rex inutilis*, a useless king incapable of ruling, deposed him and appointed Afonso of Boulogne regent and defender of Portugal. This immediately led to three years of open warfare in Portugal, in which Sancho, based in Coimbra, defended himself against Afonso's troops, which had landed in Lisbon. The war was waged with new and underhanded methods as Raimundo Viergas de Pontocarreiro, the brother of the Archbishop of Braga, sneaked into Coimbra at night in 1246 and abducted Queen Mécia and took her to her own castle in Ourem, where he raped her so as to humiliate Sancho. The King demanded her release and laid siege to Ourem but was unsuccessful. Raimundo entered medieval Portuguese historical writing as the prime example of a disloyal vassal who betrays his lord. Lately, some historians have begun to wonder whether Mécia went on her own volition. At least she was allowed to keep her properties, even after the fall of Sancho.[156]

In 1247, Sancho defeated Afonso in a large battle at Leiria and although the situation remained rather fluid, he participated in the siege of distant Muslim Seville the following year. This might seem strange, but the explanation is probably that a great victory in a crusade would have given Sancho prestige and strengthened him politically. It turned out differently, however. At the end of 1247, Sancho gave up and went into exile in Toledo, where he died in January 1248. It was up to the new King Afonso III to complete the conquest of Algarve with the capture of Faro in 1249. The following year, Albufeira, Porches, Silves and the last remaining towns surrendered. The Portuguese crusades on land had now reached their final physical frontier. Future crusades were directed at North Africa or even further away, to Asia and later to America.

The conquest of Estonia 1219

Las Navas de Tolosa in 1212 had led to Innocent revoking indulgence from all crusades other than those who went to the Holy Land, and in 1213 "the crusade stopped in Denmark."[157] Yet it was only to be a short while before it was possible to lead armies against the heathens in the Baltic region again. Already by the end of 1215, Innocent wrote to all the faithful in Denmark that they should come to the rescue of the new Church in Livonia: "There are many who do not have the strength or the means for daring to put on the sign of the cross on their shoulders in order to help the Holy Land, and for the benefit of the remission of their sins we decide that if instead they will help fighting against the barbarian nations and for the new planting of the Christian faith with spiritual as well as material weapons, they shall receive gratitude in this life and in the following."[158] The wording is somewhat vague and does not actually convey complete equality between the Holy Land and the inherited land of the Virgin Mary, but it might have been perceived in that way. It was issued only two weeks after the great general crusade bull *ad liberandam terram sanctam* that went out to everybody in Western Europe and was to finally carry out the decisions of the fourth Lateran Council about a crusade.[159] In this way, the crusades in the Baltic became an alternative to the Holy Land after all.

One of those who took up the request was Count Albert of Orlamünde, a nephew of the Danish King and one of the great vassals of the realm, who possibly was to

296 *Rise and fall of crusader kingdoms*

prepare for the King's personal participation. He took part precisely to "receive absolution"[160] and thus perceived the papal privilege as sufficiently far-reaching. Albert arrived in Livonia in 1217 and was immediately involved in the war in Estonia together with the Sword Brothers and Bishop Albert of Riga. Albert of Orlamünde won one of the large battles in September 1217 against the Estonians, partly because of a huge war engine he had built. The defeated had to hand over a group of children as hostages, who were to be transferred to Riga and brought up in the Christian faith so they could later work as missionaries amongst their own people.[161] Albert of Orlamünde then returned to Denmark to make a report and to take part in a decisive assembly meeting in Schleswig in 1218.

Pope Honorius had more or less the same problem in the Baltic area as on the Iberian Peninsula – whether to direct all crusading efforts to the Holy Land or let them work locally. He chose to do both here as well. In February 1217, he sent detailed instructions on how the Lateran Council decision of a 5% crusade tax of all Church income was to be carried out. He explains in these instructions who can collect the tax, how it is to be signed for and how the money is to be passed on. And of course, the money is to be passed on to the Holy Land.[162] This happened in a general circular that also went to Lund. In May that same year he wrote to everyone in Germany, Bohemia, Moravia, Poland and Denmark who had taken the cross in order to help the newly converted Christians in Prussia. According to his instructions, they should assist the missionary Bishop Christian and, in general, support the conversion effort; they should not fight for personal economic advantages, which might scare the heathens away from the true faith.[163] At the same time, he ordered Archbishop Anders Sunesen to support the missionary efforts. The heathens in Prussia were like animals in their savagery: they killed all the baby girls except for one, and they sold their girls and wives into prostitution. Anders was therefore to buy up girls who would otherwise have been killed and have them brought up as Christians, and he should establish schools in Prussia to educate the boys as well. To support this project, he should immediately preach the crusade to those who do not have the strength or the means to go to the Holy Land – the same wording as Innocent applied three years before. Honorius had no second thoughts, however, and promised the same indulgence for these crusaders as to those who travel to Jerusalem.[164] The ground work had been laid for the greatest Danish crusade initiative of the High Middle Ages.

In "1218[,] King Valdemar II assembled all the noblemen of his kingdom, 15 bishops and three dukes and just as many counts and many abbots, and on the day of St. John the Baptist he gave his son Valdemar III the insignia of the kingdom in Schleswig. 1219. A crusade was called against the heathens in Estonia." In this way the Annals of Valdemar end their brief notices that all led up to the great crusade in Estonia.[165] What was discussed in Schleswig would have been a very important matter; it was one of the largest we know of from the Danish High Middle Ages. Albert of Orlamünde had arrived accompanying the Bishop of Riga, the Bishop of Estonia and the future Bishop of Semgallen. They took the opportunity and implored Valdemar to send his fleet to Estonia to prevent heathen Estonian and Russian attacks on the young Church in Livonia. When Valdemar had been

Rise and fall of crusader kingdoms 297

briefed on the situation, he promised to go to Estonia in the following year, "in the honour of the Holy Virgin as well for the remission of his sins. And the bishops rejoiced."[166]

Bishop Albert of Riga then travelled around, presumably in Northern Germany, and preached the cross and promised indulgence for those who went to Livonia and stood before the house of the Lord and the day of the battle and defended the new Church against heathen attacks. He spent the whole of the following year doing this, and he managed to persuade many to go. The idea was obviously to attack Estonia on two fronts, from the South via Livonia and from the sea. All this must have been arranged in Schleswig during the coronation of Valdemar the Young on June 24,[167] and on the following day the whole party could celebrate the feast day of King Valdemar's grandfather, the crusader saint Canute Lavard.

In 1219, Valdemar's army went to Estonia. The crusade was huge, according to a contemporary source, the fleet consisted of 1500 ships,[168] which in theory would have been possible to mobilize from Denmark but then they would have had to have scraped the barrel.[169] The castle of Lyndanise was demolished and a new one was quickly built called the Castle of the Danes, Tallinn.[170] A group of Estonian elders applied in person and received a friendly reception from Valdemar. They agreed to accept Christianity, were baptized and then returned to their own people. Three days later, however, they returned with large forces and attacked the Danish camp from five sides. This happened on June 15, the feast day of St. Vitus, and the very day when Arkona on Rügen had fallen fifty-one years before. The battle was chaotic; Bishop Theodoric was killed in his lavish tent because the Estonians believed that he was King Valdemar.

The Danish army was disintegrating but managed to hold, mainly thanks to the Danish contingent from Rügen under the leadership of Prince Wizlaw I. He assembled his men in the bay between the castle and the sea and was able to counterattack. He now fought for Valdemar the Victorious, whose father had defeated his father in a crusade and converted him to Christianity. Looking to the example of Wizlaw, the Danes stopped fleeing and fought back, and the fortunes of the battle were reversed. Now the Estonians were put to flight, and more than a thousand heathens were killed in the large battle. "The King and the bishops thanked God for the victory over the heathens that He had given them." This is what the contemporary narrative tells us. The victory belonged to God, and that can be put briefly. Later tradition, on the other hand, has extended the story drastically, just as it happened with the battle of Ourique in the Portuguese tradition, which ended up becoming a miracle where God Himself appeared to Afonso Henriques.

In the 1520s, two historians briefly relate that the Danish flag fell from the sky during the battle of Lyndanise.[171] One is the humanist and publisher Christian Pedersen, the other the Franciscan friar and collector of sources Peder Olsen. The latter tells us that the flag is one of the twelve wonders of Scandinavia, because it was a gift from heaven. He attributes it to a Danish crusade to Fellin in Estonia in 1208 but later mixed up his papers and thus connected the story to Tallinn in 1219. From these two, the story about the flag became very popular, in historical writing as well as in art, and it is still known by most Danes. It probably became

298   *Rise and fall of crusader kingdoms*

widespread because it was included in Huitfeld's history of Denmark, in a volume that was published in 1600. Huitfeld's history of Denmark had an unusually large readership despite its somewhat dry and repetitive style. He had many imitators, and thus all later Danish historians borrowed from him and were inspired by him. He includes many details from the battle of Lyndanise, the origin of which we have no idea but might very well go back to sources from the High Middle Ages. In some way, it would not be too strange if there had been a cross flag in the sky above Estonia – in 1208 or 1219 – just as there was a cross in the sky above Alcácer do Sal in 1217.

According to Huitfeldt, King Valdemar received reports about the Estonians gathering to attack the Christians in the area. He therefore assembled a mighty fleet consisting of 500 small ships and 500 long ships. On each of the small ships there were fifteen men, and on each of the large ones there were 120. Valdemar nevertheless became afraid when he saw how many heathens that had gathered, and he almost ordered a retreat. However, Bishop Peder of Aarhus stepped in and asked him to wait. He promised victory to Valdemar, providing that he would follow God closer than before and take care of his poor subjects and not trouble them with taxes and duties, such as Queen Berengaria had made him do, and that he would stop taking properties belonging to the cathedral of Aarhus. Bishop Peder's prediction was confirmed by Archbishop Anders Sunesen, who added that if a lord takes something from churches and monasteries, which had actually been given to the service of God, he only rarely gets something out of it. "The King promised that he would turn to both God and men/ and never follow the advice of Queen Berengaria." Everybody fell to their knees and prayed for luck to defeat the un-Christians, and the Archbishop promised that if they were victorious, all men in Denmark would, from their twelfth year for all their life, fast on water and bread on every Saint Lawrence Eve for all eternity. The battle began, and Huitfeldt writes about Anders Sunesen:

> It is written about him/ as of Moses/ Whether it is true or not/ God only knows/ That Bishop Anders stood on his knees/ On the mountain, praying to God/ And every time his hands reached to heaven/ The Danes were winning/ But as soon as his hands were lowered/ Because of his old age/ The un-Christians gained the upper hand/ Therefore, the other bishops and priests supported his arms/ As long as the battle was ongoing/ Piously they prayed/ That God would give victory to the Christians/ And convert the heathens to the confession of God.
>
> At the same time it supposedly happened/ that the Danes were beaten into flight/ And had lost the banner/ they should have followed/ Then out from heaven a banner supposedly fell down/ Of woven cloth/ Red on the field/ with a white cross/ they followed this/ Afterwards they defeated the enemies.[172]

Because Valdemar planted the Christian faith in Estonia, Denmark carries a white cross in its coat of arms, Huitfeldt continues. The flag is called Dannebrog and was for a long time considered sacred. Superstition arose claiming that the Danes

Rise and fall of crusader kingdoms 299

would always win if the Dannebrog was at their head, just as Emperor Constantine had a cross in his banner inscribed with "In this sign you will conquer." After having written all of this, Huitfeldt cautiously adds that it could have been a crusade banner which Valdemar had received from the Pope. And perhaps it did not fall from the sky after all. This explanation failed to gain much popularity before the latter half of the 19th century with the introduction of historical criticism: quite the contrary. A few years after the publication of Huitfeldt's history of Denmark, in 1625, King Christian IV had a vision of Christ appearing before him. Perhaps Christian too was inspired by Afonso Henriques and the miracle of Ourique, about which he could have read in the narratives from the Alcobaça monastery, because Christian IV was quite interested in what was happening in Portugal. As early as in 1591 he had begun to mint large gold coins with the cross of the Order of Christ, closely inspired by the Portuguese gold coins, minted in Portugal 1517–1557.[173] Narratives of crosses from heaven thus interested him very much.

The story of how the Dannebrog fell from heaven became very popular in the 17th century and received support from the highest places; during the Romantic period in the 19th century, it was a popular motif for historical paintings. Huitfeldt's history was a very important element in this development in the same way that he contributed to propagate the negative image of Berengaria. He wrote that, in 1220, "died Queen Berengara, whose real name was Bregenild/ But because of her malice known as Beengierd. . . . About her a ballad is sung until this day/ with this chorus/ Shame to her Beengierd/ The Lord God be with the King."[174]

Developments in the new Christian land were followed with care and worrying by the contemporaries. When Berengaria died in childbirth in 1221, it was considered an evil omen, coming so soon after the conquest of Estonia. "Some were of the opinion that the new Church, which had come into King Valdemar's power and was to give birth to spiritual children daily, would without a doubt perish during the King's reign. And that turned out to be the case."[175] The Church of Estonia lapsed, the Estonians rebelled. This was countered by large military forces; Valdemar himself went to Ösel together with his nephew, Albert of Orlamünde, and began the erection of a stone castle on the island at the same time as he entered agreements with the Bishop of Riga and the Knights of the Sword, which involved a division of the conquered territories, among other things. When the King returned to Denmark, the new castle was captured by the people of Ösel and completely demolished. The people from Ösel then toured all of Estonia, encouraging others to rebel and to cast off the Danish yoke and Christianity, and they taught other Estonians how to build siege engines.[176] In Sakkala, they captured the bailiff Ebbe and the other Danes; they were taken to their castle where they were tortured and killed, suffering "cruel martyrdom." They opened Ebbe's abdomen and pulled out his intestines, they ripped out his still beating heart, cooked it on the fire and shared it between themselves in order to gather strength against the Christians, and they gave his body to dogs and birds to gorge on.[177] They took back the women they had been forced to renounce when they became Christians, they dug up the dead from Christian cemeteries and gave them a heathen burial

300　*Rise and fall of crusader kingdoms*

and they scrubbed both themselves and their houses and fortresses using water and scrubbing brushes to wash off baptism and Christianity. "Then there was war all over Estonia," and with the help of God, the Estonians were put to flight, plundered and forced to surrender.

The Estonian Church was like a woman giving birth, who suffers great sadness and pain, and whose offspring is pursued by the dragon. The Church was still tender and weak, it was even persecuted by false mothers who wished to take possession of the daughter, especially the waste and barren Russian mother Church, Henry of Livonia wrote.[178]

Estonia was situated at the intersection of several powers. The Danish presence had to be secured with a robust military presence but with very long supply lines back to the Danish core areas. The Bishop of Riga and the Knights of the Sword entered from the South and from the East; Russian princes tried to gain influence. At the same time, in 1222, the earliest frightening rumours about the Mongols began to arrive; they drove the strong Turkish Cumans on the Hungarian steppe into panic, were soon to blanket most of Western Europe in terror and were already known as *tartari*, the hellish people, the people of doom. On the face of it, it seemed that King Valdemar the Victorious was facing a very difficult task, but on the other hand, he had very large forces. He had demonstrated his abilities as a general and a strategist with great success and his crusade had support in many places. Then on a spring evening, all of a sudden, the military and political situation changed when Valdemar and his son were taken prisoners by one of the king's great vassals.

Valdemar II: A crusader imprisoned

In May, Valdemar the Victorious and his son Valdemar met up with Count Henry I the Black of Schwerin and Boizenburg on the small island of Lyø south of Funen; they went hunting on the island, which was unusually rich in animals.[179] In the evening, Henry took the two kings prisoner and had them despatched quickly to castles in his county. Now, an extended round of negotiations began. Henry of Schwerin tried to sell off Valdemar to Emperor Fredric II, who was very interested and would be able to get him for a sum of 52,000 marks in silver, a new castle in Boizenburg with moat and palisades and several other specified services or payments. Fredric was of the opinion that Valdemar had violated the agreement from the Golden Bull of 1214 that acknowledged Valdemar's possessions to the north of the Elbe and that Valdemar had taken on imperial rights. Fredric now saw an opportunity to renegotiate the bull.[180] Before Henry and Fredric had managed to conclude the negotiations properly, the events took a new direction.

Pope Honorius III intervened directly and with great weight. He did so with a great and well-formulated papal bull that goes straight to the matter and begins with these words: "You have left a large and serious stain on your honour, which will burden you and your descendants for all time if you do not wash it off by offering compensation as soon as possible."[181] Henry did not only break the bond of vassalage to become an example to all rebels and thus abominable to all kings

Rise and fall of crusader kingdoms 301

and princes, he had set himself against God and the Roman Church. The Danish realm in particular belongs to the Church and therefore pays an annual tax to the Church, and King Valdemar is a special son and offers loyal support to the Church. Therefore, and especially because Valdemar has taken a vow to help the Holy Land with a large army, the Pope now intervened. Thus, Henry had imprisoned a crusader under the special protection of the Papal see and he had a month to release his prominent captives. Otherwise he would be excommunicated in all public places with bell-ringing and candle-lit processions; all churches in the diocese where the Valdemars were imprisoned would be closed and all religious services halted. The Pope would recommend the Emperor to go against Henry with arms and force him militarily. The last threat suggests that the Pope was unaware of Fredric's interest in buying Valdemar, or that Fredric had been double-dealing with Henry and negotiating with the Pope at the same time.

The long engagement in the crusades for more than 100 years was now bearing political fruit. Pope Honorius emphasized in other letters how both Valdemar and his predecessors always had been loyal and dedicated to the apostolic see. And furthermore, Valdemar had taken the cross, although he did not carry it in public, only hidden. This had happened by request of the Pope himself; Valdemar had promised that he or his son would sail to the Holy Land and take part in the imminent general crusade. If neither of them were able to take part personally, they would despatch 100 or at least 50 knights.[182]

It is not clear when the Pope persuaded Valdemar to take the cross, but it might well have been part of a greater plan. It is unlikely that Valdemar would have been able to tie himself into going to the Holy Land before his great crusade to Estonia in 1219 was concluded. He might have done it in 1220–1221, when the Church and military power were being established in Estonia and before the great rebellion broke out in 1222. Fredric had done more or less the same during that period. He had suddenly taken the cross on 1215 and, on the relics of Charlemagne in Aachen, he took an oath to liberate the Holy Land, but he hesitated to go. In 1218, he renewed the oath at a diet in Nuremberg and promised to send an army in the summer of 1219. This also failed to materialize. However, when he was crowned Emperor in 1220, he again promised to fulfil his pledge. Finally in April and June 1221, the first German troops sailed to Egypt with orders not to engage in battle until the Emperor himself was present. They arrived too late. On August 30, 1221, in the mud and ooze of the Egyptian delta, the crusader army had to give up and sign a peace treaty on eight points, which sealed a total defeat for the Christians.[183] This did not mean an end to the crusade plans, however, as they were continued unabated. In such a situation, Valdemar would have been an obvious prince for the Pope to have contacted and persuaded to go on a crusade. He had prestige after the conquest of Estonia, and his participation might even provoke Fredric to fulfil his crusade oath. In any event, it would engage Valdemar in the Middle East and remove one of Fredric's most important competitors in the North and thus make lame his excuse: that he had to stay at home in order to attend his interests in Northern Germany. Finally, some historians have suggested that although the truce with the Muslims was for a period of eight years, it was

302   *Rise and fall of crusader kingdoms*

implied that it would no longer apply as soon as a crowned king took the cross and put himself in charge of a crusader army.[184] Under such circumstances, it would have been quite feasible if Pope Honorius had intended an important role in the resumption of the failed, joint European crusade against Egypt.

The release of Valdemar was taking some time, however. In the summer of 1224, the first draft to an agreement on his release was made. King Valdemar had been transferred to the castle of Dannenberg at the Elbe, and a decisive figure in the negotiations was Emperor Fredric's envoy, the Grand Master of the Teutonic Order, Hermann von Salza. The centrepiece in the agreement was the crusades. Valdemar was to take the cross again and travel to the Holy Land in August 1226 with 100 ships, both large war cogs and long ships. He was to spend the winter in Spain, *Yspania*, which might very well have meant Portugal, and, during the spring of 1227, he was to arrive in the Holy Land. He should report to the King of Jerusalem and stay there for at least one year. In case he died or was prevented in any other way, he was to set aside a sum of 25,000 marks in silver to support the crusade. It was to be handed over to the Teutonic Order and the envoys of the King of Jerusalem in Lübeck on the day he was due to set out. Valdemar was also to surrender all territories on the far side of the Elbe and to take an oath of fealty with the Emperor. Finally, he was to pay large reparations to Henry of Schwerin and hand over hostages to ensure that the agreement was complied with.[185]

The counter proposal of the Danish noblemen was quite different. They omitted any mention of crusades and tried instead to make the agreement acceptable by increasing the ransom to include 100 large ward horses, magnificent clothing for 100 knights and, in addition, all the gold that had been part of Queen Berengaria's outfit except her crown.[186] This must refer to her regalia as a ruling Queen, but also include jewellery and personal belongings which she had brought with her from Portugal and everything Valdemar had presented to his wife, as both official and personal gifts. We do not know how Valdemar felt about the idea of being ransomed with Berengaria's jewellery or the idea that Berengaria's jewellery was to go to Henry of Schwerin. We do not even know whether Valdemar knew anything about it in advance or whether the noblemen's offer of all Berengaria's gold came as a surprise to him. The proposal of the Danish noblemen was not accepted initially, and the negotiations continued for more than a year. Finally, several items were agreed and were included in a treaty on November 17, 1225. Henry of Schwerin was to have 40,000 marks in silver, and he got all of Berengaria's gold – except her crown and whatever she had donated to monasteries as pious gifts before her death – 100 horses (of which half must be worth ten marks and half five marks per horse) and clothing for 100 knights. But there was no mention of crusades.[187] It does not seem that Fredric was included in the agreement, and it is doubtful whether it was ever officially sealed and ratified. Valdemar was set free soon after, presumably after having agreed to the treaty of November 17, although it is possible that he had to promise other things of which we know nothing today.

Valdemar now had a serious financial problem if he was to pay the huge ransom. The following summer, Pope Honorius solemnly put an end to it by releasing Valdemar from his obligation to pay, referring to the fact that if he was to pay he

Rise and fall of crusader kingdoms   303

would not be able to afford to go on a crusade.[188] This act of the Pope might again have been part of a larger plan. In July 1225 in San Germano, Fredric promised to go on a crusade. The pledge was carefully copied, clause by clause, from the first draft of a treaty to release Valdemar, which had been written the year before.[189] Fredric was not to arrive with ships, though, but with 1000 knights. Four months later, he was married to Yolanda, the heir to Jerusalem. This was a very promising alliance, which Hermann von Salza had been working on for several years. In the late summer of 1227, Fredric went on a crusade at last after having postponed it for twelve years. He became ill and had to give it up and was excommunicated. Of course, Honorius could not have known any of this in 1226.

When the Pope released Valdemar from his pledges to Henry of Schwerin in 1226, it was a real possibility that Valdemar and Fredric could have joined forces in a crusade with two large armies, at sea and over land. Not only would the two famous rulers have had a formidable force at their disposal, they would also have had prestige and political power to attract many other princes to the crusade. It was not to happen quite in this way. After his release, Valdemar attempted to retake his territories in Holstein and, in July 1227, he and his allies lost a large battle at Bornhøved. To begin with, this made impossible any participation in crusades to the Middle East and also meant that Valdemar now re-orientated his policies and no longer waged large-scale warfare, which had been a characteristic of his reign so far. The settlement of his debt to Schwerin took time but was reached eventually. Neither papal letters nor force of arms meant much, as Valdemar had been forced to let his three sons with Berengaria be imprisoned as hostages in return for the release of himself and his oldest legitimate son. Not until 1230 was the last instalment paid, and Erik, Abel and Christopher were released.[190]

The affair of Valdemar's imprisonment attracted much attention everywhere in Western Europe. The vassal's shocking treatment of his lord was condemned not only by the Pope but in the Danish annals as well. A commentary in the Annals of Ryd (from around 1250) has become famous and quoted ad infinitum, not least because it fits so well with the perceptions of Danish nationalism in the 19th century: "Take note, reader, that never or rarely have the Germans been successful or won any victories except by treason or deceit; it is in their nature, as has become obvious with the imprisonment of the two kings."[191] What prompted Henry to take such a drastic step is not entirely clear. Henry himself had participated in the fifth crusade and had been to Egypt when Valdemar was in Estonia. At some point a rumour arose claiming that Valdemar had used the opportunity to seduce Henry's wife, whom he had promised to guard. The imprisonment and humiliation of Valdemar was Henry's revenge.[192] This might be possible but appears to be a legend, which has been told about several Danish kings. Other reasons might have been more obvious. When Henry returned home from the Holy Land, he had lost half of his large fief. His brother's daughter, Oda, had been married to King Valdemar's illegitimate son Niels of Halland, who had died in 1220. Oda herself died in 1221 while Henry was away, and Valdemar was thus able to put himself forward as guardian of their young son. Then he could install his own men in half of the castles in Schwerin, and if the young heir was to die before he came of age,

304   *Rise and fall of crusader kingdoms*

all these properties would go to Valdemar. These dispositions were not only financially damaging to Henry but decidedly defamatory, and the meeting on Lyø was probably not just a nice hunting get-together. It must have been a political meeting and an attempt to reach a mutual understanding, which then broke down. It seems that Valdemar had taken a large part of the archive of the realm on the hunting trip, probably to be able to demonstrate his claims to the disputed territories. At least, it is striking how many original Danish medieval documents are held in the town archive of Schwerin today that originate from before 1223.

In Estonia, matters were tentatively regulated by the papal legate Wilhelm of Modena, who apparently tried to establish a form of an ecclesiastic dominion so that Estonia would be placed directly under the Pope.[193] In 1227, he handed the territory to the Knights of the Sword, and after they had been almost completely wiped out in 1236, at the battle of Saule, Lithuania, the Teutonic Order took control of Estonia. At that point, the Pope had apparently decided that large parts of Estonia were again to be placed under the King of Denmark,[194] but it was only put into effect a couple of years later with a settlement negotiated in the small village of Stensby in Southern Zealand. Here, Wilhelm of Modena met with King Valdemar; representing the Teutonic Order was the leader of its Livonian and Prussian branch, who was also named Hermann.[195] Valdemar's negotiating position was now much better than when he had faced Hermann von Salza. In the end, Valdemar gained control over the disputed provinces in Estonia and gave some to the Teutonic Order in return. At the same time it was agreed that they would support each other in the future, and everything captured in future crusades would be shared in such a way that Valdemar would receive two thirds and the Teutonic Order one third.

"Valdemar, the King of the Danes, was a hundred years old and he ruled for more than forty years. After having become old enough to carry weapons, he spent almost all the days of his life pursuing the infidels, both in Sithia and Frisia and Russia. He conquered six large dioceses and had just as many bishops consecrated."[196] Thus writes the contemporary and well-informed Matthew Paris from the monastery of St. Albans in England. He exaggerated Valdemar's age somewhat – he died in 1241, a little more than seventy years old and had governed as the sole king in almost forty years. Yet Matthew had included what was most important: Valdemar at his death was a crusader king of international renown, who had extended Christianity in his neighbouring territories in constant battles against the heathens. This was recognized at the time and it gave Valdemar a strong political profile as well. In 1240 it was even suggested that his oldest son with Berengaria, Erik Ploughpenny, ought to be the new emperor of the Holy Roman Empire, replacing the excommunicated Fredric.[197]

Three weeks after the death of Valdemar, on April 9, 1241, the Mongols were victorious in the battle of Liegnitz. Europe lay open before them, Hungary was removed from the map, and new crusades were called against the new danger in the East. Valdemar's three sons with Berengaria came to the Danish throne one by one, continuing the Baltic crusades, but at the same time, they fought each other. In 1250, Erik Ploughpenny was killed by Abel, who only two years later fell during an expedition against the Frisians, whereupon Christopher became King.

Rise and fall of crusader kingdoms   305

The fratricide and the struggle for the throne led to deep divisions between the families of Abel and Christopher, which left their marks on Danish politics both domestically and in relation to the crusades for many years. Valdemar's death is a traditional but well-chosen point to draw a line and conclude that part of Danish history, even though Danish crusades continued through the Middle Ages and, in the form of religiously motivated and meritorious war, lived on even after the Lutheran Reformation in 1536.[198]

Notes

1　Saxo, 16.4.3.
2　Saxo, 16.4.5.
3　Saxo, 16.8.5.
4　Ane L. Bysted, Kurt Villads Jensen, Carsten Selch Jensen, and John Lind, *Jerusalem in the North: Denmark and the Baltic Crusades, 1100–1522* (Turnhout, 2012), pp. 90–91.
5　For the events during the Battle of Hattin, see Helen Nicholson and David Nicolle, *God's Warriors: Crusaders, Saracens and the battle for Jerusalem* (Botley, 2005).
6　De profectione . . ., cf. Karen Skovgaard-Petersen, *A Journey to the Promised Land. Crusading Theology in the* Historia de profectione Danorum in Hierosolymam *(ca. 1200)* (Copenhagen, 2001).
7　Ibid., cap. 25.
8　Ibid., cap. 27.
9　Itinerarium peregrinorum, cap. 27.
10　Ibid., cap. 31.
11　Annales Lundenses; DMA, p. 60.
12　Bysted et al., *Jerusalem in the North*, p. 156.
13　Saxo, 16.4.3.
14　DMA 258 (1193), 168, 199, 230, 270 (1194), 19, 84, 110, 147, 168, 230, 278 (1196), 14, 60, 77, 103 (1197).
15　Sverri's Saga, chapter 113.
16　Ibid., chapter 59.
17　Henry of Livonia, *Henrici Chronicon Livoniae*, ed. Leonid Arbusow and Albertus Bauer (Hannover, 1955), 1, 11.
18　Ibid., 1, 12.
19　Christoph T. Maier, 'Crisis, Liturgy, and the Crusade in the Twelfth and Thirteenth Centuries', *Journal of Ecclesiastical History* 48 (1997), pp. 628–657, here pp. 634–635; Jessalynn Bird, 'Innocent III, Peter the Chanter's Circle and the Crusade Indulgence: Theory, Implementation and Aftermath', in: Andrea Sommerlechner (ed.), *Innocenzo III: urbs et orbis. Atti del congresso internazionale Roma, 9–15 settembre 1998*, 2 vols. (Rome, 2003), vol. 1, pp. 503–524; Amnon Linder, *Raising Arms. Liturgy in the Struggle to Liberate Jerusalem in the Late Middle Ages* (Turnhout, 2003), pp. 1–3, pp. 97–98 and passim.
20　O.C. Statuta, *Statuta Capitulorum Generalium Ordinis Cisterciensis ab anno 1116 ad annum 1786*, ed. D. Josephus-Mia Canivez, vols. 1–8 (Louvain, 1933–1941), 1190, 16; 1195, 9. Anne E. Lester, 'A Shared Imitation: Cistercian Convents and Crusader Families in Thirteenth-Century Champagne', *Journal of Medieval History* 35 (2009), pp. 365–366 discusses how the liturgical rearmament after Hattin was likely to have been continued on a local level through the first half of the 13th century by Cistercian nuns, who prayed and created the liturgical framework around local crusading families.
21　Valdemar Canutesen continued to act only as a chosen bishop for almost ten years, until he was installed in 1187/88, see the introduction to DD 1:3, no. 146.
22　DD 1:3, no. 175–177.

306   Rise and fall of crusader kingdoms

23 Hans-Otto Gaethke, *Herzog Heinrich der Löwe und die Slawen nordöstlich der unteren Elbe* (Frankfurt a.M., 1999), pp. 234–235.
24 DD 1:3, no. 175.
25 D 1:4, no. 83.
26 Augustinus, Contra Faustum, lib. 22, cap. 70; optaget i Gratians decretum, C. 23, q. 4, c. 36, i CIC I, 916.
27 Kurt Villads Jensen, 'Thi ath alle som tage swerd/ de skulle dø met swerd. Matt. 26, 52 hos Augustin, Innocens III og danske middelalderhistorikere', *Fønix* 24 (2000), pp. 66–78.
28 AD, p. 97.
29 Torben K. Nielsen and Kurt Villads Jensen, 'Pope Innocent III and Denmark', in: Andrea Sommerlechner (ed.), *Innocenzo III. Urbs et orbis, Atti del congresso internazionale Roma, 9–15 settembre 1998*, vols. 1–2 (Rome, 2002), vol. 2, pp. 1133–1168.
30 In truth, we do not know if she was particularly shapely, but it is certainly a possibility, as her mother *eximie pulchritudinis formam omni uenustatis artificio natura elaborauit. Nam in eius descriptione Tullii deficeret facundia, Nasonis exaresceret uena, Virgilii desudaret ingenium.* Sven Aggesen, Brevis historia, cap. XIX.
31 DD 3:5, no. 227 and following.
32 James W. Baldwin, *The Government of Philip Augustus. Foundations of French Royal Power in the Middle Ages* (Berkeley, 1986), pp. 82–87.
33 DD 1:4, no. 42, 43. Baldwin discusses whether Philip August had been infected with sweating-sickness and had had skin problems and loss of hair and had therefore become particularly neurotic, so that he might temporarily have been impotent when marrying Ingeborg (pp. 357–358).
34 DD 1:3, no. 226.
35 Nielsen and Jensen, 'Pope Innocent III'.
36 DD 1:4, no. 78.
37 Shown in Philip August's account books; oral communication from Professor John Baldwin.
38 DD 1:4, no. 79; Glossa Ordinaria III, 3.
39 Henry of Livonia, 1, 12 and 2, 3.
40 DD 1:3, no. 254.
41 Henry of Livonia, 3, 2.
42 Friedrich Benninghoven, *Der Orden der Schwertbrüder: Fratres milicie Christi de Livonia* (Köln, 1965).
43 Henry of Livonia, 10, 12, recounts that in 1206 Valdemar's army "had been assembled for three years."
44 DD 1:4, no. 162–164.
45 DD 1:4, no. 173.
46 AD, 98, 99.
47 *Manifestis probatum:* published in PL 200, cols. 1237–1238.
48 José Mattoso and Armindo de Sousa, *A Monarquia Feudal (1096–1480)* (Lisbon, 1993), p. 92, does not think he took part.
49 Duarte Galvão, *Crónica de el-rei D. Afonso Henriques* (Lisbon, 1995), cap. LIV–LVI. Roupinho received a prominent place in Portuguese national imagination by being mentioned in Camões, Os Lusíadas 8, 16–17.
50 Annales D. Alfonsi, era 1222.
51 Ibid.
52 Generally, see Mário Jorge Barroca, 'Da reconquista a D. Dinis', in: Manuel Themudo Barata and Nuno Severiano Teixeira (eds.), *Nova História militar de Portugal* (Lisbon, 2003), vol. 1, pp. 48–52.
53 For the town charters in 1179 and their connection with the emergence of Portugal as a kingdom, see Ana Maria Barrero García, 'Orden jurídico e identidad política en los albores de la recepción del derecho comun (sobre los forais de Coimbra, Lisboa y Santarém)', *Hispania* 67 (2007), pp. 827–848.

Rise and fall of crusader kingdoms 307

54 DDS, no. 31.
55 Charles Wendell David, 'Narratio de itinere navali peregrinorum Hierosolymam tendentium et Silviam capientium A.D. 1189', *Proceedings of the American Philosophical Society* 81, no. 5 (1939), p. 663.
56 Itinerarium peregrinorum, cap. 27.
57 According to Itinerarium peregrinorum it was the Danish-Frisian fleet that captured Silves and continued to the Holy Land, whereas De itinere navali describes a more mixed fleet with participants from several countries in the North. According to Annales Lamerti (MGH SS 16, p. 649) people from Cologne took part together with Frisians, Danes and Flemings. See also Bruno Meyer, 'El papel de los cruzados alemanes en la reconquista de la Península Ibérica en los siglos XII y XIII', *En la España Medieval* 23 (2000), pp. 41–66, pp. 48–53; and generally F. Kurth, 'Der Anteil Niederdeutscher Kreuzfahrer an den Kämpfen der Portugiesen gegen die Mauren', *Mitteilungen des Institutes für Österreichische Geschichtsforschung* Appendix 8 (1909), pp. 131–252.
58 David, 'Narratio de itinere navali', p. 610.
59 This is probably how we are to understand the expression "venit Portugalensis rex, et exercitus suus cum sarcinis lente subsequutus est." Ibid., p. 623.
60 Ibid., p. 632.
61 DDS, no. 41, December 1189. In the future, he only used the title 'King of Portugal and Algarve.'
62 Mattoso and de Sousa, *A Monarquia*, p. 93.
63 Ibid., p. 87.
64 Liber sancti Jacobi, vol. 1, 406–407; Luíz Gonzaga de Azevedo, *História de Portugal*, vols. 1–6 (Lisboa, 1935–1944), vol. 5, note 2.
65 Barroca, 'Da reconquista a D. Dinis', p. 51.
66 Quoted from David, 'Narratio de itinere navali', p. 666.
67 Jean Richard, *The Crusades ca. 1071– ca. 1291* (Cambridge, 1999), p. 226.
68 DDS, no. 64.
69 DDS, no. 73.
70 DDS, no. 194.
71 Hugh Kennedy, *Crusader Castles* (Cambridge, 1994), pp. 58–61, pp. 100–101; Adrian J. Boas, *Crusader Archaeology. The Material Culture of the Latin East* (London, 1999), 106–108; Ronnie Ellenblum, 'Frankish and Muslim Siege Warfare and the Construction of Frankish Concentric Castles', in: Michel Balard, Benjamin Z. Kedar and Jonathan Riley-Smith (eds.), *Dei gesta per francos. Etudes sur les croisades dédiées à Jean Richard* (Aldershot, 2001), pp. 187–198.
72 DDS, no. 72.
73 DMP I:1, no. 30.
74 DDS, no. 86.
75 DDS, no. 112.
76 DDS, no. 116 and no. 123.
77 Mattoso and de Sousa, *A Monarquia*, pp. 97–98.
78 James William Brodman, *Ransoming Captives in Crusader Spain. The Order of Merced on the Christian-Islamic Frontier* (Philadelphia, 1986), p. 1.
79 Barroca, 'Da reconquista a D. Dinis', p. 52.
80 Azevedo, *História de Portugal*, vol. 5, p. 25.
81 J.F. O'Callaghan, *Reconquest and Crusade in Medieval Spain* (Philadelphia, 2003), p. 62–63.
82 *Coelestin III*, Bull of 31.10.1196, ed. Fidel Fita and Ramón Riu, 'Noticias', *Boletín de la Real Academia de la Historia* 11 (1887), pp. 455–458.
83 Paptsurkunden, no. 154.
84 Statua O.C. 1197, 34.
85 Roger de Hoveden, Annales, to 1197.
86 Mattoso and de Sousa, *A Monarquia*, p. 98.

308   *Rise and fall of crusader kingdoms*

87 Chronicon Conimbricense, p. 325.
88 Quoted from Lomax, *La Orden de Santiago*, p. 10.
89 Charles Julian Bishko, 'The Spanish and Portuguese Reconquest, 1095–1492', *A History of the Crusades* 3 (1975), pp. 423ff.
90 Quoted from Peter Linehan, *The Spanish Church and the Papacy in the Thirteenth Century* (Cambridge, 1971), p. 5.
91 DD 1:5, no. 29.
92 For Innocent III and indulgence, see James M. Powell, *Anatomy of a Crusade, 1213–1221* (Philadelphia, 1986), pp. 20–21; Bird, 'Innocent III, Peter the Chanter's Circle'.
93 Annales Valdemarii, DMA p. 78.
94 Henry of Livonia, 19, 7.
95 Linehan, *The Spanish Church*, pp. 6–10; Elizabeth Siberry, *Criticism of Crusading 1095–1274* (Oxford, 1985), pp. 112–114.
96 DD 1:5, no. 32; BP 190.
97 Powell, *Anatomy of a Crusade*, pp. 16–17.
98 Mattæus Parisiensis, Chronica Majora 2, 559–566.
99 DD 1:5, no. 48.
100 The bull Pium et Sanctum, PL 216, col. 823; DD 1:5, no. 30.
101 Powell, *Anatomy of a Crusade*.
102 Ibid., p. 218.
103 Joseph P. Donovan, *Pelagius and the Fifth Crusade* (Philadelphia, 1950).
104 DD 1:5, no. 7.
105 Powell, *Anatomy of a Crusade*, p. 210, p. 216, p. 227. We also know of a Christian of Ribe (p. 217).
106 Nora Berend, *At the Gate of Christendom: Jews, Muslims, and "pagans" in medieval Hungary, ca. 100a. 1300* (Cambridge, 2001), pp. 56, 141.
107 Jean Dunbabin, *Captivity and Imprisonment in Medieval Europe 1000–1300* (Houndmills, 2000), p. 118.
108 PL 175, col. 1562.
109 John V. Tolan, *Le Saint chez le sultan. La Rencontre de Francois d'Assise et de l'Islam* (Paris, 2007).
110 B.Z. Kedar, *Crusade and Mission: European Approaches Toward the Muslims* (Princeton, NJ, 1984).
111 A History of the Crusades, vol. 2, pp. 376–428.
112 Veloso, *D. Afonso II*, argues that Afonso more likely suffered from a skin disease rather than from leprosy.
113 DDS, no. 130.
114 Azevedo, *História de Portugal*, vol. 5, p. 86.
115 Kennedy, *Crusader Castles*, pp. 138–141.
116 Honorio III, *La documentación pontificia de Honorio III (1216–1227)*, ed. Demetrio Mansilla (Rome, 1965), no. 95.
117 Azevedo, *História de Portugal*, vol. 5, pp. 87 ff.
118 O'Callaghan, *Reconquest and Crusade*, pp. 183–185.
119 Gosuino. The contemporary Caesarius of Heisterbach (8, 66) had been told by eyewitnesses that the Muslim army was 100,000 strong; Jaap Van Moolenbroek, 'Een wonder in Portugal. Caesarius van Heisterbach over de slag bij Alcácer do Sal (1217)', *Madoc* 13 (1999), pp. 102–110. Narratives from the German region on the battle; Kurth, 'Der Anteil Niederdeutscher Kreuzfahrer'; Meyer, 'El papel de los cruzados alemanes'.
120 Caesarius of Heisterbach, 8, 66; O'Callaghan, *Reconquest and Crusade*, p. 193.
121 Gosuino.
122 Honorio III, no. 95.
123 It was not on October 18, as claimed in several works; cf. Azevedo, *História de Portugal*, vol 5, pp. 96–97, note.

Rise and fall of crusader kingdoms 309

124 Maria Teresa S.F. Lopes Pereira, 'Memória cruzadística de Feito da Tomada de Alcácer (1217) (com base no Carmen de Gosuíno)', in: Camara municipal de Guimaraes (ed.), *Actas do 2° Congresso Historico de Guimarães* (Guimarães, 1996), vol. 2, pp. 319–358.
125 Honorio III, no. 134.
126 Ibid., no. 95.
127 Ibid., no. 96.
128 Ibid., no. 207.
129 Ibid., no. 209.
130 O'Callaghan, *Reconquest and Crusade*, pp. 81–83.
131 PHM Inq. 1–3; A.H. de Oliveira Marques, 'O poder e o espaço', in: Maria Helena da Cruz Coelho e Armando Luís de Carvalho Homem (eds.), *Nova História de Portugal*, vol. 3 (Lisbon, 1996), vol. 3, p. 103.
132 PMH, Inq. 1, 110.
133 PHM Inq. 1, 113.
134 KVJ: *Kong Valdemars Jordebog*, vols. 1–3, ed. Svend Aakjær (Copenhagen, 1926–1945), 1, 10, fol. 16r.
135 Ibid., 1, 131–137, fol. 129v–133r.
136 *Falsterundersøgelsen*, ed. Svend Gissel, vols. 1–2 (Odense, 1989), vol. 1, p. 230, pp. 250–251.
137 KVJ 1, 139–141, fol. 135v–136r.
138 Ibid., 1, 55, fol. 21r–21v.
139 Ibid., 1, 55, fol. 40r.
140 Ibid., 1, 57, fol. 41v; see commentaries in Ibid., 2, 371.
141 Barroca, 'Da reconquista a D. Dinis', p. 59.
142 Ibid., pp. 59–61.
143 Reg. Greg. IX: *Les Registres de Grégoire IX*, ed. Lucien Auvray, vols. 1–4 (Paris, 1896–1908), 4969–4974, 4976–4977, 4994–4996.
144 Ibid., 4973.
145 DD 1:4, no. 95.
146 Reg. Greg. IX, 4994.
147 Ibid., 5000, cf. 733.
148 Ibid., 5001.
149 Ibid., 5002.
150 Ibid., 4996.
151 DD 1:5, no. 74.
152 Barroca, 'Da reconquista a D. Dinis', p. 60; O'Callaghan, *Reconquest and Crusade*, p. 108; discussed in Mattoso and de Sousa, *A Monarquia*, p. 124.
153 Reg. Greg. IX, 926.
154 Ibid., 1385.
155 O'Callaghan, *Reconquest and Crusade*, p. 110.
156 José Mattoso, *A nobreza medieval portuguesa: A familia e o poder* (Lisbon, 1981), pp. 279–283.
157 Annales Valdemarii, DMA, p. 78.
158 DD 1:5, no. 61, 29th of December 1215.
159 BP 207, 14th of December 1215.
160 Henry of Livonia, 21, 1.
161 Henry of Livonia, 21, 1–7.
162 DD 1:5, no. 116.
163 DD 1:5, no. 139.
164 DD 1:5, no. 142; see also Iben Fonnesberg-Schmidt, *The Popes and the Baltic Crusades 1147–1254* (Leiden, 2007), pp. 138–144 about Honorius and indulgence in the Baltic crusades, pp. 144–149 about Honorius emphasizing the crusade to Holy Land as being more important than other crusades.

310   *Rise and fall of crusader kingdoms*

165 DMA, p. 79.
166 Henry of Livonia, 22, 1.
167 It was presumably in preparation for the coronation and the crusade that Valdemar the Young had become a vassal of Saint Peter in 1216; DD 1:5, no. 74.
168 Annals of Ribe and Annals of Ryd, in DMA, pp. 170, 232, 259.
169 Numbers are problematic. 1,500 ships have normally been considered unrealistic. With a max of forty men on each ship – most ships were unlikely to have held more than twenty to thirty men – the total army would have been 60,000 from all of Denmark and the Northern German territories. According to Saxo, Canute VI was able to mobilize 12,000 men on Rügen alone (Saxo, 16.7.1); and during the harsh winter of 1227, the Bishop of Riga led an army of almost 20,000 German and local crusaders across the ice to Ösel (Henry of Livonia, 30, 3). If these numbers are anything to go by, a fleet of 1,500 ships from whole Denmark is not totally unimaginable.
170 Henry of Livonia, 23, 2.
171 Christian Pedersen, *Danske Skrifter*, ed. C.J. Brandt, vols. 1–5 (Copenhagen, 1850–1856), vol. 5, p. 443; Peder Olsen in SM 1, pp. 459–460.
172 Arild Huitfeldt, *En Kaart Chronologia, forfølge oc Continuatz. 1. Part. Som indeholder Canuti VI. Historia . . .* (Copenhagen, 1600), p. 106.
173 Georg Galster, 'Danske efterligninger af fremmed mønt fra nyere tid', *Nationalmuseets Arbejdsmark* (1959), pp. 109–122.
174 Huitfeldt, *En Kaart Chronologia*, p. 109. *Beengierd* means skeleton.
175 Henry of Livonia, 24, 4.
176 Ibid., 26, 3.
177 Ibid., 26, 6.
178 Ibid., 28, 4. See Torben K. Nielsen, 'Sterile Monsters. Henry of Livonia and the Orthodox Church', in: A.V. Murray (ed.), *The Clash of Cultures on the Medieval Baltic Frontier* (Farnham, 2009), pp. 227–252.
179 KVJ 1, 31, fol. 33r.
180 DD 1:5, no. 214 and no. 217.
181 DD 1:5, no. 221.
182 DD 1:5, no. 222.
183 H.E. Mayer, *Geschichte der Kreuzzüge* (Stuttgart, 1995), pp. 194–201; A History of the Crusades, vol. 2, pp. 376–428.
184 Richard, *The Crusades*, p. 306.
185 DD 1:6, no. 16.
186 DD 1:6, no. 17.
187 DD 1:6, no. 42.
188 DD 1:6, no. 59.
189 DD 1:6, no.16.
190 DD 1:6, no. 109.
191 AD, p. 107.
192 Huitfeldt, *En Kaart Chronologia*, p. 113.
193 Gustav A. Donner, *Kardinal Wilhelm von Sabina. Bishop von Modena 1222–1234: Päpstlicher Legat in den nordischen Länder* (Helsinki, 1929).
194 DD 1:6, no. 212 and no. 215.
195 DD 1:7, no. 9.
196 Mattæus Parisiensis, Cronica Majora, vol. 4, 92.
197 DD 1:7, no. 52.
198 Janus Møller Jensen, *Denmark and the Crusades, 1400–1650* (Leiden, 2007).

9   Syncretism and regimentation

What was it all about? Why was so much energy and resources put into crusading? What was the danger to be opposed? The reform-eager Gregorian Church at the end of the 11th century reached a high point in the middle and late 13th century, and its efforts were directed against both infidels and against sinners within Christianity who brought the whole crusader movement into danger. It was, therefore, logical that it had to take action against those whom the theoreticians of the reform movement considered lukewarm and uncaring about the truth. These were different forms of blended religions, syncretism or even just a form of peaceful co-existence.

The Christians on the Iberian Peninsula under Muslim rule – the Mozarabs – had remained Christian and had, as peoples of the Book, a guaranteed right to practise their religion, but they adapted to the circumstances. They began to let themselves be circumcised, and even several of their bishops were circumcised. They began to consider certain types of food unclean and stopped eating pork, just as their Muslim neighbours. They began to dress in the common Muslim attire, many divorced and the Mozarab clerics were married. They began to use Arab names and used Arabic as their daily language, and there were so many Mozarabs in the Caliph's army that they were able to negotiate having Sunday off and not just the Muslim Friday. As faithful soldiers of the Caliph, they fought the Christians to the North. Among the Christians, several peculiar ideas emerged that seemed to suggest some form of syncretism, a blending of religions. There was an anti-Trinitarian movement that in principle held on to the different persons of the faith but rejected the trinity. Another great Iberian heresy was Adoptionism, which held that Jesus was not the real son of God: he was only adopted by Him. With this, the most important dogmatic difference between Christianity and Islam disappeared; Islam honours Jesus as one of the greatest prophets, but the Quran explicitly rejects the idea that Jesus is the son of God. Syncretism meant that the differences were erased and that more and more Christians ended up converting to Islam.[1]

When listed next to each other, this catalogue of deviation from the correct Christian teachings and way of life is lamentable, and this was the idea. The examples were collected by Christian polemists who lamented syncretism and regretted the peaceful co-existence on the Iberian Peninsula. These polemists

312 *Syncretism and regimentation*

wanted confrontation rather than *convivencia,*[2] and they emphasized that the confrontation was ancient and perennial. Alvarus and Eulogius actually succeeded in instigating an open rebellion against Islam in the middle of the 9th century, which, in a few years, produced fifty-four Christian martyrs.[3] However, this very intransigent attitude shows how desperate they really were on behalf of the faith. A very uncompromising attitude was necessary because most Christians were, by and large, quite comfortable and accepted living as a protected minority in a Muslim territory.

The Annals of Toledo from the early 12th century show small glimpses of this cultural blend in practice, even though they are unequivocally on the Christian side and celebrate victories over the Muslims. They go back a long way into the past and tell of when the Jews travelled from *Miecre*, which must be the Arabic *Misr*, Egypt. They also tell how Muhammad preached and "converted many people from idolatry to a faith in the Creator but not to the faith in Christ, because he does not believe in Trinity."[4] This wording more or less presupposes a close relationship between Christianity and Islam instead of an insurmountable contradiction, as most Roman Catholic theologians believed at the time.

The Mozarabs were apparently not severely persecuted by the Muslims until under the Almoravids, who were called in from North Africa in 1085. The situation only deteriorated under the more fanatical Almohads from around 1130. This is also the period during which several anti-Christian Muslim texts were issued, with arguments against the Christian faith or just simple pamphlets. Abn Abdun in Córdoba wrote in the 12th century that women should not be allowed to enter the abominable churches of the Christians, as their priest all were rakes, lechers and sodomites.[5] However, this kind of literature by Muslims about Mozarabs was rare and only emerged from the 12th century.

From the Roman Christian side, the tone turned harsh early on. One of Pope Gregor VII's most important reform objectives was not only to fight Islam but also, and in particular, to regiment the faith and to propagate the Roman liturgy everywhere. Here the old Mozarab form of Christianity was in the way. The most severe persecutors of the Mozarabs were to be the new, Roman-oriented Christian princes with family relations to France and sympathy for the reform movement of Cluny.

The Mozarab populations were large and could not be forced out of hand to become Roman, and many princes became invaluable helpers to the Christian crusaders. The conqueror of Coimbra in 1064 was a Mozarab with the Visigoth-sounding name Sisnando, the son of a man with the Jewish name David. He began his letters to his overlord, King Fernando of León or King Alfonso VI, in neat Arabic style with the words *glorificet illum deus – exaltet illum deus –* may God give him honour, may God exalt him.[6] Sisnando was sufficiently powerful – until his death in 1092 – to be able to prevent the Roman-oriented and Cluny-friendly Bishop Crescónio from introducing Roman liturgy in Coimbra, but in other places, the two versions of Christianity competed in the 11th century.[7]

A decision had to be made. It was an unusually harsh winter in the year 1077, stretching from Martinmas on November 11 until the following Easter, when,

Syncretism and regimentation   313

on Palm Sunday, two knights met to fight a duel on behalf of the Roman and the Mozarab liturgy, respectively. One was from Castile and one from Toledo. King Alfonso VI's knight won and in 1078 "the Roman liturgy was introduced into Spain." This is claimed by a couple of medieval annals.[8] The difference between the two types of Christianity was perceived as a duel in the Middle Ages, an ordeal by battle, in which God showed his will by letting the King's knight from Castile win. Later annals were thus able to honour Alfonso with the title *orthodoxus ispanus inperator*, the orthodox Spanish emperor.[9]

The Roman liturgy ended up victorious, but the victory was not achieved as quickly and as easily as the annals allege. There was a large uprising in Coimbra in 1111, which included a Mozarabic rebellion against the new Roman rulers.[10] The cathedral in Coimbra laid down a clear anti-Mozarabic line under Bishop Gonçalo, and by the time of his death in 1128, the diocese was Roman. In return, the monastery of Santa Cruz, established in 1135 in Coimbra, became a sanctuary where Mozarabic culture and scholarship survived to some extent. Yet even if the Mozarabs had deep roots in the region, they were gradually pushed aside and at times persecuted outright. A high point was the capture of Lisbon in 1147, when crusaders accidentally killed the Mozarabic bishop of the city. Consequently, many Mozarabs went over to the Roman rite, but many, perhaps even more, fled to the Muslim Miramolin of Morocco, "the Defender of the faithful," where they were able to practise their Christianity in peace. "The Mozarabs were forced to move to Morocco," it says directly under the year 1124 in the annals of Toledo.[11]

The Mozarabs represented a tradition that went back to the time before the Muslim conquest. They maintained a link with the early Church, and they had maintained the cult of Santiago and of Vincent, who became great crusader saints. There is no doubt that they were influenced by Arabic culture and language, but it is much more difficult to ascertain how much their Christianity was influenced by Islamic theology. However, this is a modern religious-historical consideration. They were clearly considered unorthodox and a danger to the true faith by the Roman Catholic knights, precisely because of the perception that they blended the religions. When Afonso Henriques returned from a raid far into Spain, he did so with a multitude of Mozarabic captives, who had lived under heathen rule and "who can almost not be said to follow the rites of Christianity." Afonso and his noblemen were therefore convinced that they could keep them as slaves, and only the threats from St. Teotónio about God's terrible anger finally made them set more than 1000 Mozarabs free. They were then settled on the lands of the monastery of Santa Cruz to cultivate the troubled frontier territories.[12]

Contamination of religion was not limited to the old Mozarabic populations; it was a danger to all Christians who came too close to Islam. In 1144, the Muslims attacked Soure and took "many mortals, both human and cattle" as booty. They were led to Santarém. Martin from the church in Soure then journeyed to Santarém and voluntarily went into "the fearful and foul-smelling dungeon" to the chained captives because, out of love for the Christians, he wished to teach them the gospel, "so that they would not be soiled – *commacularentur* – by the Moors' abominable rites."[13]

314 *Syncretism and regimentation*

The largest city in all of Europe at the end of the 11th century was Wolin, Adam of Bremen wrote.[14] This was an exaggeration, compared with Toledo and other mighty cities on the Iberian Peninsula. It was large, however, and characterized by the same cosmopolitan openness towards other religions as the great cities in the South. It also shared the impression of being ancient and of carrying a tradition that stretched further back than newly christened and missionary-eager countries, such as Denmark. In Wolin or Julin lived Slavs, barbarians, Greeks, Saxons and all other people. All were allowed to settle in the city "on equal terms with others, as long as they did not show their Christian faith for as long as they stayed there. For everyone there is still snared in the errors of heathendom."

Adam goes on to describe the many goods which were exchanged in Wolin, made possible by this policy of tolerance, especially exotic items from Scandinavia. The Christians would have lived as some form of a tolerated and protected minority amongst heathens, just as in many other places in the Baltic regions and in the Muslim cities by the Mediterranean. The Christians came from afar. In the early 1120s, a certain Bernhard from Spain attempted to missionize in Wolin. This did not go too well, however, as he looked so ragged and poor that the heathens were unable to take his God seriously. He withdrew to Bamberg, where he found pleasant company in the priest Heimo from the Church of St. James, with whom he discussed datalogy.[15]

In the Wendic territories there might have been a tradition for belonging to a Christian society that had roots back to the time before the Gregorian reform movement of the 11th century, or perhaps these traditions were invented during the crusader era in order to stand stronger against the crusaders. They could very well have blended syncretic elements from Christianity and heathenry. When the missionary Otto of Bamberg arrived in Wolin in the 1120s, he tells us about the local cult that it worshiped, a lance which had originally belonged to Julius Caesar, and thus their city was called Julin. When one of their "high priests" became angry because of Otto's success in converting heathens to Christianity, he ran towards him, wanting to pierce him with Caesar's lance, but when he lifted his arm, he was turned into stone.[16]

Otto of Bamberg managed to convince the local heathens about the truth of Christianity, and they abandoned their old gods and eagerly took part in the building of churches. However, they refused to cut down the old hazel trees even though Otto put much pressure on them. It was fine to give up the old faith, but not so much that the old sacred trees suffered.[17] When Otto returned a few years after his first journey, the new Christians had erected an altar for their old god inside the church next to the high altar.[18] This practice was obviously halted immediately, and the sacred building was cleansed and re-consecrated, but an altar for another god illustrates how differently the newly converted and the missionaries perceived things. The former heathens had no problem in combining elements from several religions, whereas the eager missionaries in the era of the crusades demanded the pure teaching.

The heathens nearest to the Danes in the 12th century were the Wends on the other side of the Baltic Sea, with whom they had had close connections for centuries.

Syncretism and regimentation   315

They had been the target for Christian missions several times before this, and their idol Svantevit must have been some kind of a representation of the missionary St. Vitus. To what degree they considered themselves Christians is impossible to know, but there are some indications that the Danish Christians recognized them not as heathens but as a type of Christian, although a wrong type. It is at the least suggestive that King Svend Grathe gave a golden cup to Svantevit in the 1150s. Perhaps it was in connection with negotiations concerning military assistance, but it would have had a religious significance nevertheless. "He preferred to deal with a foreign religion before his own, and the punishment for this sacrilege came later, which was to be his unhappy death," Saxo wrote.[19] Either Svend supported heathenry from sound political reasons, or he and his contemporaries would have had the impression that the Wendic cult on Rügen was some form of Christianity.

When Arkona fell in 1168 and its inhabitants surrendered, they had to promise to hand over their idol and the whole temple treasure, to free their Christian prisoners, to take part in King Valdemar's crusades in the future and to "receive all points of the true religion and to worship according to the Danish ritual."[20] To receive all points – *omnia monumenta* – emphasized that the people of Rügen had to take on the whole package; they were not allowed to have diverging or heretical views on particular elements of the faith. That they were to practise Christianity according to Danish ritual suggests that they had practised it before – only in a different and wrong ritual. Thus the Wends, as the Mozarabs, are an example of a people who practised a blended religion which could be tolerated no longer.

The Danish and Portuguese crusades of the 12th century were a continuation of the papal reform movement of the 11th century and its attempt to create uniform conditions within the Church. A mark was set to divide the old, when the difference between Christian and non-Christian was more difficult to define, from the new, uniform Christianity all over Europe. The contemporaries were fully aware of this division between past and present. From the time of Valdemar the Great, there is a list of the Danish kings: only the names, that is all. It is the earliest Danish source that includes the heathen kings: "they shall be divided into three groups, first the early ones who, although heathen, were kings nevertheless, second, the old Christian kings, third, the modern catholic kings."[21] The last old Christian King is Niels, who died in 1134; after that the kings are modern and Catholic. In the early 12th century, the *Historia Silense* distinguishes in exactly the same way between the orthodox Alfonso and his Mozarabic predecessors.[22] The Danish list of kings is from the same time as the Portuguese royal annals, which described Afonso Henriques as "a mighty warrior" and "entirely Catholic in his faith in Christ,"[23] and when Alexander III recognized Afonso as a king in 1179, he called him a "good son and Catholic ruler."[24]

On the Iberian Peninsula, the tradition of emphasizing the truly Catholic was actually even older. It went back to the 6th-century struggle between Arian and Catholic Christians that ended in 589 with a decision, at a synod in Toledo, to reject Arianism. After this, the term "the Catholic King" fell into disuse. However, in the 11th century, it could be transferred seamlessly to the struggle between Mozarabic and Catholic.[25]

316 *Syncretism and regimentation*

Another Danish list of kings from earlier in the 12th century does not include the heathen kings, but subdivides them into three groups nevertheless.[26] The first group contains only names and begins with Harald in 827 "as the first Danish king was baptized in Mainz." The second group contains "Names of the Catholic kings in Denmark, by the efforts of whom the Catholic faith has been spread, and who through love of religion built many churches and gave them royal gifts." It covers the kings from Svend Estridsen, whose rule began in 1044, up to and including King Niels, who died in 1134. The third group on the list must have been added later and counts the kings from Niels to Valdemar the Great. Again the idea is obvious. There is a dividing line between the kings who were just Christian and those who were Catholic, that is, universal, which means that they were part of the common Latin Christendom. The early list was probably right in dividing the list at Svend Estridsen, who warmly supported and took part in the reform movement of the 11th century.[27] The list is probably more or less contemporary with King Erik Emune's donation to the cathedral in Lund in 1135, where he confirms the earlier gifts of the "catholic kings" Svend Estridsen and his son, St. Canute, to the church.[28]

The later list moves the dividing line up to the death of King Niels in 1134. There are two good reasons for this; one is that the list was made at the time of Valdemar the Great, and he would have had a very direct interest in keeping a distance from Niels's part of the royal family and to mark his own as qualitatively different, as Catholic rather than old Christian. The other good reason is that the confrontation with the infidels at that very time had begun to predominate over the convivencia. The question of faith was now more important, the definitions more precise and the differences more sharply drawn than at the beginning of the 12th century. It is at this time that the word "Wend" went from being an ethnic term in the Norse skaldic epics to being a religious term simply meaning heathen.[29] During this transition phase it was important to make a mark in relation to the new dividing line between being only Christian and being Christian in the new way.

When Henry, the son of Henry the Lion, went on a crusade to the Holy Land and laid siege to the castle of Toron in 1197, the Muslims asked for a pause in the hostilities in order to negotiate with him. His people asked: "What is it that you wish to speak to him about, you who destroy peace and circumvent truth." The Muslims replied: "It is precisely about truth, that we wish to speak, and about concluding peace." It develops into a long speech about the relations between Islam and Christianity, put in the mouth of the besieged Muslims:

> We ask of you to show clemency and to have patience with us and to remember the Christian faith, which according to what you say, demands complete piety. This piety you, as religious people, should show to us now. We do not live without religion, even if we are not Christians, because we believe that we are Abraham's children and are called Saracens after his wife Sara. If one should truly believe that your Christ was truly God and man and saved you on the Cross, then you would be able to win glory by the mark of this Cross, and you can turn it against us. It is therefore a fact that even if the religion is

Syncretism and regimentation 317

different, we have one and the same Creator and one and the same Father, and it is therefore a fact that we are brothers, not in creed but as men.[30]

We cannot know for sure whether the Muslims in Toron really gave this speech of reconciliation, but the story shows that the problem was very real to Arnold of Lübeck, who wrote around 1209. In the Baltic region, the Middle East and on the Iberian Peninsula there were the same preoccupations concerning where the boundary lines lay between Christianity and heresy and heathenry, and how much could be tolerated if something was to be recognized as true Christianity. For how long could one hold on to the conviction of believing in the same god, and when would it be necessary to draw a line and distinguish between God and idol? With the Church reform of the 11th century and the crusades after the 12th century, the line was drawn sooner and with harsher means than before. Henry of course had to reject the Muslim argument and their offer and captured Toron violently.

Who started it? Medieval preaching and present-day acceptance of warfare

During the Middle Ages, both Christians and Muslims agreed that only a defensive war can be a just war. This idea has in a peculiar way had a form of afterlife amongst modern historians, who in both Portugal and particularly Denmark have developed a tradition which – often without much reflection – acquits the medieval warriors of their own land of guilt.

Danish historians have been convinced that their Danish ancestors could not have been fundamentally aggressive, and so the heathen Wends must have initiated the warfare. Saxo's depictions of a land laid waste by the plundering of the Wends have been repeated and believed as a matter of course. Historians on the Iberian Peninsula have had a double inheritance to administer. One strong tradition has emphasized the Christian population's ability and determination to defend Christianity; the other has stressed the tolerance of the mixed society and the cohabitation of the religions. The first explains the *reconquista* as a reasonable and just act of defence against constant Muslim attacks. The other tradition explains it as a form of Christian expansion, often initiated with help from the outside.

The Danish coast line was actually attacked by the Wends in the 12th century, also after the capture of Arkona on Rügen in 1168. In 1183, Bishop Svend of Aarhus bequeathed some properties on Djursland, "many in number but of low value because they are close to the coast and exposed to attack from the heathens."[31] Whether this was a general trait of all of the Danish coast is not known, perhaps the conditions on Djursland were special during those years. There is no reason to believe in the image that Saxo conveys: that Zealand was waste and barren to the East and the South, where the Wendish pirates had settled as if they were at home, and that there was no more than a little group of inhabitants left on Funen.[32]

The Wendish attacks were explained in two ways at the time. According to Saxo it is obvious that the divided Denmark with several kings fighting each

318 *Syncretism and regimentation*

other in 1146–1157 weakened the defences and left the country open to organized piracy. The Wends themselves had a different explanation. In 1156, Pribislav explained in Lübeck that the Wends had in principle nothing against converting to Christianity, but they could not afford to build churches and the like because they were so cruelly oppressed by the German knights and were squeezed hard for taxes. Conditions were the same in the nearby Wendish territories, and there was thus only one way out: to go to sea. "Is it our fault that we have been driven out of our fatherland and make the sea unsafe, and get our sustenance from the Danes and from the sailors who sail on the sea? It is the fault of the German princes, who force us away."[33] How widespread those attacks on the Danish coastline really were is difficult to measure. Forest historians have pointed to places, especially on Falster, where forests to this very day go all the way to the water's edge. This must be down to the devastation of the Wends, it is claimed. Why the forests haven't been cleared again and the coastal zone cultivated later is difficult to know. The argument is weak and must be based on a hunch, not more than this.[34]

The wars were fought with great cruelty, which have worried historians to a varying degree. Some have condemned it and reproached the medieval crusaders for their fanaticism and have excused the harshness of the war. Others have shown an almost astonishing understanding of the Christians' difficult circumstances. Despite regrettable bloodshed, it was nevertheless a good thing in the long perspective, as "Christianity and trade replaced Barbary and anarchy," as an American historian wrote in 1975 about the crusades in the Baltic.[35] Another argued in 1989 that the heathens lived in a violent and anarchic society, and that the Christians were forced to imitate the cruel warfare of the heathens, simply in order to survive.[36]

In these religious frontier societies, a particular type of literature emerged in the Middle Ages that reflects the constant wars and that was to justify them and make them understandable and acceptable, perhaps even necessary to the participants of the wars.

Not only were the Wends unmanly warriors, they were also fundamentally the opposite of good Danes. Their god Svantevit was a distortion of Christianity, as they had been christened by St. Vitus but had fallen from the faith and now worshipped him as an idol.[37] The heathens themselves were distortions of real humans and almost animal.[38] When the men from Rügen lay with their women, "it often happened to them, as it does for dogs, that they cannot separate again," and to mock them, they were hung across a beam and thus displayed.[39] The Wends were also treated accordingly. When Jamerik became king, he descended upon the Wends and hanged forty of them together with forty wolves.[40] The hanging of wolves was widespread in traditional societies and should probably be perceived as an expression of fear of werewolves, that is, inhuman brutes who had to be fought in every way possible.[41] Other contemporaries could tell of the suppression of women by the heathens. Unfaithful women were strangled and burned for their transgression, or they were undressed to the waist and attacked by all the good, virtuous women, who stabbed the unfaithful one with knives and drove her from village to village until she died from her wounds. And the Wends burned

Syncretism and regimentation 319

their widows alive. When a deceased man was laid on the pyre, the widow was supposed to throw herself on the fire and burn up together with him.[42] This has probably no truth to it, but it was an important element in the demonizing of the opponent.

It is almost impossible to estimate how widespread heathenism really was in this part of the Baltic region from the very biased sources in our possession. The religious landscape could presumably change rather quickly. When Canute Lavard was killed in 1131, Pribislav and Niklot obtained control of the Obotrites, Helmold of Bosau writes. They were like wild animals and bitter enemies of Christianity, and this led to a rise for heathenism. Several old gods were reintroduced, and the cult practice was tightened up. Every year, one Christian was sacrificed to Svantevit, the surrounding territories were ravaged and plundered from land as well as from the sea, and Christians were killed in a multitude of ways. Some were cut up, had their intestines drawn out and coiled up on a stick and were dragged around.[43] Others were nailed to crosses to suffer a slow death and to mock the Lord, and even prisoners who had been ransomed by their Christian families were first systematically tortured.[44]

Henry of Livonia tells of newly converted Livonians, who had relapsed in 1212 and were besieged by the crusaders in a castle. When a strong wind overturned one of the crusaders' siege towers, it was celebrated in a traditional heathen way by sacrificing dogs and goats from the town wall, and the sacrificial animals were thrown down on the crusaders in order to mock them and Christianity. At a later heathen uprising, Estonians tore out the still beating heart of the Danish bailiff Ebbe in Estonia and roasted and ate it.[45] Perhaps heathenism had turned harsher and more bloody as a reaction against the crusades, perhaps it is overstated. Anyway, the descriptions by Helmold and Henry have an obvious objective: to excite and to encourage crusades.

On the Iberian Peninsula, we find the same type of harsh, polemic literature, which became particularly conspicuous during the 13th century, especially with the mendicants' theological writings about Islam, but which had older roots.[46] During the 11th and the 12th centuries, much polemical literature by Christian Arab language authors was translated from Arabic into Latin, and it became widespread, with time also outside of the Peninsula. A particular genre within this literature was the depiction of the Prophet Muhammad as an inhuman brute, bloodthirsty and lecherous, so that it ought to be clear for all concerned that he in no way could be a prophet of God.[47] This led to fantastical stories of how Muhammad had originally been a Christian cardinal, who had lost a papal election and fled to Arabia, where he decided to create a new religion in order to take revenge on Christianity. There was no reason to hold back when describing Muhammad, because "it is safest to speak ill of him, because his evil supersedes any evil one might imagine," Guibert of Nogent wrote.[48] The descriptions of Muhammad's life developed into a whole genre, which fittingly has been termed "anti-hagiographical."[49] The aim of this kind of literature was to demonstrate that Islam was not a real religion and that Muslims were naïve or deliberately malignant if they could have belief in such a foolish religion. We do not know how widespread

320 *Syncretism and regimentation*

this kind of literature was in Portugal, but it must have been known in ecclesiastical circles and amongst crusaders if it was so common in nearby areas.

In the middle of the 12th century, Abbot Pierre of Cluny involved himself directly in the polemics against Islam by paying for a translation of the Quran, complete with critical commentary and a collection of polemical literature.[50] The translation was carried out by the English mathematician Robert of Ketton in Toledo and was finished in 1143. The result was a strongly polemical and personally biased translation, in which Robert chose as a matter of course the most negative variant, if there were several alternative translations possible. It was a spiteful paraphrase more than a translation.[51]

The translations were used by Pierre of Cluny as the basis for a treatise on Islam, titled *A Treatise against the Sect or Heresy of the Saracens*.[52] The idea is very clear: Islam was not an independent religion but a heresy within Christianity. The same basic idea lies behind all later medieval literature about Islam – and Judaism as well for that matter – and it springs from the conviction that the truth of Christianity is logically obvious and clearly revealed, not only in the Christian Bible but also implied in both the Quran and in the Talmud. If anyone still rejects truth, it must be deliberate and is thus a heresy.[53] In that case, to try and force the heretic back into the Church is not only legal according to canon law, it is a compassionate duty out of concern for the heretic himself, who would otherwise be lost. This conviction was expressed very directly in the short form of the annals; "1002: Almanzor died and was buried in hell."[54]

The narratives about the non-Christians are carried by indignation with the attacks of the infidels and their lack of will to believe the truth, but they are also permeated by the idea of martyrdom, of dying for the faith. Bishop Bertold of Livonia was successful in this respect in 1198, when he with only two men hurled himself on the heathen army and was killed. "We must believe that he has now been crowned with honour and glory, because he was burning in his desire to die."[55] Burning in his desire to die. This is not just a characterization of one of the most fervent crusaders, it is an ideal, a hero figure in these writings about fighting for the faith. The crusades almost turned into a competition, a contest of spirituality, of reaching the goal first. The goal was death and the triumphal wreath a martyr's crown. "Just as the first one wins the wreath of honour/he received as the first the reward of death," it was written about that same Bishop Bertold with a direct reference to 1 Corinthians (9,24 ff), where St. Paul wrote that everybody runs but only one receives the prize. This was the undying wreath of glory, which Pope Urban had also promised during his sermon in Clermont, and with which Bernard of Clairvaux allured his readers.[56]

In this mental universe, it does not make sense to begin to consider who initiated it, neither in Denmark nor in Portugal, nor who were most brutal. Militarily, both places were disputed frontier regions, where there had been warfare for centuries or perhaps even for millennia, and everyone could have always referred to an earlier episode, which made it necessary to defend against or to enact revenge. Ideologically, Christianity is sharpened up or clarified from the late 11th century onwards. This promoted martyrdom and made it natural and necessary to stress the difference from other faiths. However, similar movements existed within Islam during the same period and perhaps within the Nordic heathen religions as well – the latter we know too little about. It is also highly uncertain whether there is a direct connection between the changes in Christian theology and those in Islam and heathen religions. However, it is quite certain that it does not make sense to speak of a Christian theology as a simple reaction to increased pressure from Islamic or heathen quarters. The picture is too complicated and multifaceted for this.

Notes

1 Jose Goñi Gaztambide, *Historia de la Bula de la Cruzada en España* (Vitoria, 1958), pp. 8–13.
2 Thomas F. Glick, and Oriol Pi-Sunyer, 'Acculturation as an Explanatory Concept in Spanish History', *Comparative Studies in Society and History* 11 (1969), pp. 136–154; Maria Rosa Menocal, *The Ornament of the World: How Muslims, Jews, and Christians Created a Culture of Tolerance in Medieval Spain* (London, 2004). Critique of convivencia concept, Soifer, 'Beyond convivencia'. Similarly, Muslims complained that Muslims celebrated Christmas together with their Christian neigbours; Hanna E. Kassis, 'Muslim Revival in Spain in the Fifth/Eleventh Century. Causes and Ramifications', *Islam* 67 (1990), pp. 78–110, here p 85.
3 Kenneth Baxter Wolf, *Christian Martyrs in Muslim Spain* (Cambridge, 1988); Jessica A. Coope, *The Martyrs of Córdoba: Community and Family Conflict in an Age of Mass Conversion* (Lincoln, 1995).
4 Annales Toledanos, p. 401.
5 Quoted from Ricardo Luiz Silveira da Costa, *A guerra na Idade Média. Estudo da mentalidade de cruzada na Península Ibérica* (Rio de Janeiro, 1998), p. 91. Kassis, 'Muslim Revival', p. 89, links the anti-Christian Islamic writings from the 12th century with a fear in the Muslim societies of Muslims converting to Christianity.
6 For example LP 19, LP 21. Menédez Pidal y García Gómez, 'El conde mozárabe Sisnando Davídiz'.
7 José Mattoso and Armindo de Sousa, *A Monarquia Feudal (1096–1480)* (Lisbon, 1993), p. 29.
8 Chronicon Burgense 1178, p. 309; Annales Composellani 1177, pp. 320–321.
9 Historia Silense, cap. 118–119.
10 Luíz Gonzaga de Azevedo, *História de Portugal*, vols. 1–6 (Lisboa, 1935–1944), vol. 3, pp. 90–94; Mattoso and de Sousa, *A Monarquia Feudal*, pp. 42–43; José Mattoso, *Identificação de um país: ensaio sobre as origens de Portugal, 1096–1325*, vols. 1–2 (Lisbon, 1995), vol. 1, pp. 320–336.
11 Annales Toledanos, 1124, p. 388: "pasaron los Mozarabes à Marruecos ambidos, Era MCLXII."
12 Vita Theotonii, 17.
13 Vita Martini, 11.
14 Adam of Bremen, 2, 19. Taken over largely verbatim by Helmold, 2.
15 Vita Ottonis Ebbonis, 2, 1; Heimo . . . multa didicit de arte calculatoria. Władysław Filipowiak, 'Wolin – Jomsborg – Vineta', in: Michael Andersen (ed.), *Mare Balticum. Ostersøen, myte, historie, kunst i 1000 år* (Copenhagen, 2002), p. 32.
16 Vita Ottonis Prüfeninger, 2, 5; Vita Ottonis Ebbonis, 3, 1 and 3, 16. According to Helmold of Bosau, *Helmoldi presbyteri Chronica Slavorum*, ed. G.H. Pertz (Hannover, 1868) (cap. 2), Julin was founded by a Danish king.
17 Vita Ottonis Prüfeninger, 3, 11; Vita Ottonis Ebbonis, 3, 18.
18 Vita Ottonis Prüfeninger, 3, 5; Vita Ottonis Ebbonis, 3, 1.

322 Syncretism and regimentation

19 Saxo, 14.39.8.
20 "omniaque verae religionis momenta Danico ritu celebranda susciperent"; Saxo, 14.39.25.
21 Catalogus regum danie.
22 Historia Silense, cap. 118–119.
23 Anais de D. Afonso Henriques, 272v–273r, Annales D. Alfonsi, Era 1163.
24 "bonus filius et princeps catholicus"; *Manifestis probatum:* published in PL 200, cols. 1237–1238.
25 Amancio Isla, 'Warfare and Other Plagues in the Iberian Peninsula Around the Year 1000', in: Przemysław Urbańczyk (ed.), *Europe Around the Year 1000* (Warsaw, 2001), pp. 233–246.
26 Series regum danie.
27 Which might have been the reason for Adam of Bremen calling Svend Estridsen orthodox (3, 72), as the only one besides Emperor Louis the Pious (1, 38).
28 DD 1:2, no. 63.
29 Poul Grinder Hansen, *Venderne i Danmark. En diskussion af forskning og kilder om venderne i Danmark indtil omkring 1200.* Unpublished dissertation, University of Copenhagen, Copenhagen (1983).
30 Arnold of Lübeck, 5, 28.
31 DD 1:3, no 112.
32 Saxo, 14.15.5.
33 Helmold, 84.
34 *Falsterundersøgelsen*, vol. 1, p. 355.
35 William Urban, *The Baltic Crusade* (De Kalb, 1975), pp. xi–xii, p. 271 and later works by Urban; Peter P. Rebane, 'From Fulco to Theoderic. The Changing Face of the Livonian Mission', in: Andres Andresen (ed.), *Muinasaja loojangust omariikluse laveni. Pühendusteos Sulev Vahtre 75. sünnipäevaks* (Tartu, 2001), pp. 36–68, here p. 50.
36 Sven Ekdahl, 'Die Rolle der Ritterorden bei der Christianisierung der Liven und Letten', in: Pontificio Comitato di Scienze Storiche (ed.), *Gli Inizi Del Christianesimo in Livonia-Lettonia* (Citta del Vaticano, 1989), pp. 203–243, here note 100. However, Ekdahl has also polemicized directly against Urban's perception of the crusades as a peacekeeping mission; see Sven Ekdahl, 'Crusades and Colonisation in the Baltic: A Historiographic Analysis', XIX *Rocznik Instytutu Polsko-Skandynawskiego 2003/2004* 19 (2004), pp. 1–42, here pp. 8–9, pp. 28–29; and in a review against William Urban as "ein Apologeten des Deutschen Ordens," Sven Ekdahl, 'Review of William Urban, *The Teutonic Knights: A Military History* (Pennsylvania, 2003)', *Crusades* 4 (2005), pp. 193–195.
37 Helmold, 6; Saxo, 14.1.6.
38 Animales sunt et spiritualium penitus ignari donorum, about the Pomeranians. Vita Ottonis Ebbonis, 2, 1.
39 Saxo, 14.39.43.
40 Saxo, 8.10.5.
41 Martin Rheinheimer, 'Die Angst vor dem Wolf. Werwolfglaube, Wolfssagen und Ausrottung der Wölfe in Schleswig-Holstein', *Fabula* 36 (1995), pp. 25–78.
42 William of Malmesbury, *Gesta regum Anglorum* = The History of the English Kings, ed. R.A.B. Mynors, Rodney M. Thomson and Michael Winterbottom, vols. 1–2 (Oxford, 1998), vol. 1, p. 80.
43 Helmold, 52. Thematically but not verbally in accordance with Robert the Monk's (cap. 1) rendering of Urban II's description of the Muslim atrocities against Christians in Jerusalem. Coiling up of innards was apparently popular; Saxo tells of warriors from Julin who are tied to poles, get their abdomens sliced up and their intestines coiled up on a stick. "It was a dismal sight but very useful to our people," Saxo concludes (12.4.2).
44 Helmold, 52. At the same time, Helmold is able, almost as an aside, to suddenly praise the Wends on Rügen for their hospitality, their respect for their elders and their

Syncretism and regimentation 323

attention to the old and the infirm; Helmold, 108. That forms a part of their "natural good qualities," which Helmold probably added in order to stress more strongly the unnatural in their *odium Christiani nominis*, their hatred against the name of Christ.

45 Henry of Livonia, *Henrici Chronicon Livoniae*, ed. Leonid Arbusow and Albertus Bauer (Hannover, 1955), 16, 4; 26, 6.

46 Norman Daniel, *Islam and the West. The Making of an Image* (Edinburgh, 1960); Thomas E. Burman, *Religious Polemic and the Intellectual History of the Mozarabs* (Leiden, 1994); John V. Tolan, *Saracens: Islam in the Medieval European Imagination* (New York, 2002).

47 Kenneth Baxter Wolf, 'The Earliest Latin Lives of Muhammad', in: Michael Gervers and Ramzi Jibran Bikhazi (eds.), *Conversion and Continuity: Indigenous Christian Communities in Islamic Lands, Eighth to Eighteenth Centuries* (Toronto, 1990), pp. 89–101.

48 Guibert of Nogent, *Dei gesta per Francos et cinq autres textes*, ed. R.B.C. Huygens. Corpus Christianorum Continuatio Mediaevalis; 127A (Turnhout, 1996), 1, 3.

49 John V. Tolan, 'Anti-Hagiography: Embrico of Mainz's *Vita Mahumeti*', *Journal of Medieval Studies* 22 (1996), pp. 25–41.

50 James Kritzeck, *Peter the Venerable and Islam* (Princeton, NJ, 1964).

51 Ludwig Hagemann, 'Die erste lateinische Koranübersetzung – Mittel zur Verständigung zwischen Christen und Muslimen im Mittelalter?', in: A. Zimmermann und I. Craemer-Ruegenberg (eds.), *Orientalische Kultur und europäisches Mittelalter* (Leiden, 1985), pp. 45–58; Thomas E. Burman, 'Tafsir and Translation. Traditional Arabic Quran Exegesis and the Latin Qurans of Robert of Ketton and Mark of Toledo', *Speculum* 73 (1998), pp. 703–732; Thomas E. Burman, *Reading the Qur'ān in Latin Christendom*, 1140–1560 (Philadelphia, 2007).

52 *Liber contra sectam sive hæresim saracenorum*.

53 The intellectual renaissance of the 13th century with its stress on ratio was also used to classify Jews and Muslims as less logical than Christians; Anna Sapir Abulafia, *Christians and Jews in the Twelfth-Century Renaissance* (London, 1995).

54 "Mortuus est Almanzor, & sepultus est in inferno," Chronicon Burgense, 1002, p. 308. The quote would also have led the reader to think of the rich man in the story of Lazarus; "mortuus est autem et dives et sepultus est in inferno" (Luke 16, 22). From St. Augustine until the mendicants of the High Middle Ages, the rich man was perceived only negatively and interpreted as a figure of greed and injustice and as a persecutor of the poor; Jussi Hanska, *"And the Rich Man also died; and He was buried in Hell." The Social Ethos in Mendicant Sermons* (Helsinki, 1997), pp. 28–32.

55 Arnold of Lübeck, 5, 30.

56 Bernard, Epistola 1, 13, in Opera, vol. 7, no. 11.

10 Coordinated crusades in north and south?

There was a parallel development in Denmark and in Portugal – rulers and individuals in these two regions had a comparable mental background, they reacted in similar ways to the general European crusade movement and saw an advantage – or a duty – in utilizing its theoretical and theological apparatus in wars in their own local regions against their own heathens. The conquest of Jerusalem in 1099 created a template by which to understand later wars, also in the Baltic region and on the Iberian Peninsula, and the first crusade thus became a guiding principle or an ideal for religious wars in both places. Such parallel developments must presume a high degree of communication between the two regions, no matter what tangible traces we are left with today.

We do actually have quite a lot to back up such an assertion of intercommunication, both with regards to geographical information and dynastic connections. In addition, both places had the same international organizations in the form of monastic and military orders. From their respective centres, they maintained connections between their local chapters in both Denmark and Portugal, even though they did not write anything about it. It was taken as a matter of course and thus not worth mentioning specifically. Finally, there were most certainly good connections between the Churches in the two regions, directly and especially through third parties such as synods and via delegations in Rome.

Good connections between Denmark and Portugal in the 12th and early 13th century and thereby – by implication – between other countries in the geographical periphery of Western Europe have an implication. It means that the medieval crusade movement did not consist of simple expeditions with one or more contingents of participants, but it was a grandiose and coordinated plan that depended on the involvement of all Christians, including those in the periphery, at the frontier close to heathenism.

Who travelled?

There were good connections between Denmark and Portugal and Northern Spain during the decades around 1200. Sea-faring crusaders have been mentioned several times already, and they were the majority by far and presumably the most important in communicating both general impressions as well as acting

Crusades in north and south? 325

as messengers in specific negotiations. Unfortunately, we know next to nothing about how this worked in practice. However, we know much more about this in the case of two individuals who were centrally placed in mission and in European politics: St. Dominic and Bishop Gunner of Viborg.

The founder of the Dominican Order was originally a priest in Osma in Northern Spain. He was chosen to escort his Bishop, Diego, on several journeys within Europe. In 1203, the journey went north to negotiate the conditions for the marriage of the son of Alfonso VIII of Castile, possibly Fernando, who died in 1211. The bride-in-prospect was a princess who was a daughter of "the King of the March." In 1260, Dominican historians clarified that it was the King of Denmark.[1] It seems likely that Alfonso looked to the North in order to find a suitable crusader dynasty. His mother[2] was Richilde, a cousin to Valdemar the Great's Queen Sofie, and he himself was married to Eleanor of Aquitaine, a daughter of Henry II of England and a sister to Mathilde, who was married to the great crusader Henry the Lion, Duke of Saxony. Who the Danish princess was is less certain. She could have been one of Valdemar the Great's daughters, either Richiza, who was later married to the Swedish crusader and King Erik Knutson, or Sofie, who became the mother of Albert of Orlamünde, who led the Danish crusades against Livonia and Estonia from around 1210 to 1219.

This Spanish marriage did not materialize, but the attempt illustrates very well the span of the dynastic crusader connections of the centrally placed politicians and theologians. On his return journey from Denmark, Bishop Diego asked for Pope Innocent III's permission to continue eastwards to preach to the heathen Turkish Cumans on the Hungarian steppe. It was turned down; Innocent said that it was more important to fight heretics in the Toulouse region. Then Dominic settled there for a number of years, from 1205 to 1217, and established a community of friars, but he continued to dream of returning to Scandinavia. In 1219, he wished to go to "Prussia and other northern countries" to missionize.[3] Perhaps he imagined that he was to participate in the Danish crusade which conquered Estonia in 1219. There was also much goodwill towards missionizing friars in Scandinavia. Dominic's community received papal recognition in 1215, and one of the first places the Dominican order established new houses was in Lund under Archbishop Anders Sunesen in 1222.[4]

Another person who we know for certain travelled between Denmark and Portugal was the experienced Bishop Gunner of Viborg. He was abbot of Øm but was elected as Bishop of Viborg in 1222; he was then more than seventy years old. He was to officiate as bishop for almost thirty years, until he was 100 years old and died in 1251, when the natural warmth left his body.[5]

Gunner became bishop on the recommendation of his old study friend from Paris, the papal legate to Scandinavia, Gregorius Crescentio. Gunner was thus an experienced individual with many good, international connections. It was therefore obvious for King Valdemar the Victorious to choose Gunner, despite his advanced age, for a very important task: to go on the long journey to Portugal to escort the Portuguese princess who had been chosen to be his daughter-in-law and bring her back to Denmark. Leonora and her new husband, Valdemar the Young,

326 *Crusades in north and south?*

had great devotion for Gunner and loved him as if he were their own father, the monks in Øm wrote after the death of Gunner.[6]

We know of the princely marriages and the names of those who were to spend their future in a foreign land at the very top of society, such as Leonora and Berengaria before her. However, together with them came a large group which is unknown to us today – ladies' maids, serving noblemen, clerics and scholars and possibly cooks and kitchen staff as well. A wedding was a political manifestation and an opportunity to demonstrate power and splendour, and Berengaria's entourage must have been very large. Anything else would have been a blemish on the honour of Afonso II and an affront to King Valdemar II. But they have all disappeared from the frail memory of the sources, except one. In 1251, King Abel, who was one of Berengaria's sons, issued a charter to those circumnavigating the Danish peninsula of Jutland to trade in the Baltic. Among the witnesses was Martino Portagal, who had most probably come to Denmark in the entourage of one of the queens and ended in the highest circles around the king.[7]

We know very little of the events surrounding Berengaria's and later Leonora's wedding, but they were unlikely to have been any less magnificent than the wedding of Afonso Henriques' daughter Teresa had in 1183 with Count Filip of Flanders. Galleys from Flanders were sent to Portugal to fetch the princess. Afonso equipped her with a large entourage of knights, whom he had furnished with magnificent clothing embroidered with gold and silver and all kinds of precious stones. When the party reached Normandy, they were greeted by the knights of the English King, who provided them with everything they needed. King Henry II of England had applied much pressure to have the marriage arranged in order to weaken the King of France. The English knights followed Teresa and her Portuguese party to Flanders, where Filip awaited her in one of his strongest castles. When she approached, Filip rode out to greet her, also with a large and magnificently equipped entourage. He met up with her just outside his county so that he could marry her before she crossed the border and stepped on the land that had come into her possession as a countess.[8]

We do not have such detailed information about the Portuguese queens in Denmark. We know that they received large morning gifts, to the extent where Berengaria's had to be sent to Pope Innocent III to be approved.[9] Leonora received most of Southern Funen with the towns of Svendborg and Fåborg and more.[10] Berengaria must have been married and installed as Queen at a particularly solemn ceremony. She is the first queen of whom we know that was crowned, and her crown must have been exceedingly precious. When Valdemar was taken prisoner by Henry of Schwerin, Danish noblemen offered 45,000 marks in silver as a ransom in 1224 and 1225 and "all the gold that had been part of Queen Berengaria's outfit except her crown."[11] As Berengaria had been dead for several years, her crown must have had a special symbolic meaning when it was excluded from the ransom.

Many Portuguese must have come to Denmark for the occasion of Berengaria's wedding in 1214 and for Leonora's in 1229, and several of them must have ended up settling there. This means that several family ties must have been established between Denmark and Portugal apart from the royal ties, and that Portuguese in Denmark would have kept in contact with their families in Portugal for a long time.

The noblemen would have had a decisive role in communicating crusade ideas and concrete crusade plans between the countries. They were particularly suited for these two reasons. First, they were conscious of family ties and lineages and kept the memory of those for generations. Second, they saw it as their mission in life to fight and to fight for the faith. Therefore, they often travelled to countries with religious frontiers and crusades. One of the earliest genealogies of noblemen in Europe is the Portuguese *Livro velho de linhagens*, The Old Family Book. It was written to the Riba de Vizela family in 1286–1290[12] and opens with the proud words: "Now, my friends, if it pleases you, we shall sing about the family lineages of the noblemen in the realm of Portugal, of those who were sons of somebody, of those who had to arm themselves and do something and go to war to guard the realm of Portugal. And those, my friends, were divided into five groups. The first was Uffo Belfagers, from whom the Sousas descend from directly. The second was Alam."[13] *Livro velho* enumerates the five great families from the 12th century that created the realm and went on crusades, and even though it is from the late 13th century, it has an impressive grip on the family relations, as far as it has been possible to control the information from other material. We must assume that noblemen everywhere in Europe felt the same and were interested in the history of their family.

That this was the case in Denmark too, we can glimpse from the oldest preserved non-royal genealogical table. *The Genealogical Table of Archbishop Absalon and his relations* is from 1283–1289,[14] almost the same years as *Livro velho de linhagens*. It is rather brief but also opens with crusades and christening: "The genealogical table of Lord Absalon and his brothers' and male relatives. Absalon was the venerable Archbishop of Lund, the Primate of Denmark and Sweden and at the same time, by special papal permission, the administrator of the church in Roskilde, and by his magnificent effort and heroic strength, an island in the East [Rügen] was won for Christ, where earlier since the creation of the world, men had sacrificed to gods and demons. Slau was the heathen who founded Slagelse, which is named after him, and he is buried in a mound next to the town. He was the father of Toke Trylle [the Magician], who became a Christian and father to Skjalm Hvide." Then the list continues by mentioning all the great crusaders and warriors over the following 200 years who were related to Absalon through Slau.

The free movement of the fighting warriors was crucial to enable crusades to take place, but the ability to exchange ideas concerning the crusades was also a necessity. This happened through a variety of groups that had mutual connections and knew of each other's viewpoints. Most religious orders were entirely internationalized; the members met regularly and exchanged their experiences, most had some kind of training internally in the order and a particular literature of the order, which was usually completely free of any national characteristics. For instance the Cistercians, whose fight against evil was best fought in the wilderness and preferably in the missionary fields themselves as soon as the crusades had secured

328　*Crusades in north and south?*

some measure of security for the monks. This was most certainly the case with the mendicants at the end of our period. It goes for the great military orders, such as the Templars and the Hospitallers. Also outside the orders, common ecclesiastics could travel far. In 1181, Absalon's priest was on his way back to Denmark from Santiago de Compostela – his name and his errand, apart from being on a pilgrimage, is unfortunately not known to us.[15]

The common parish church structure left room for local traditions but was at the same time well suited to bring out the same message everywhere in the Christian Latin world. With Pope Innocent III's bull *Quia maior* from 1213 it was decided that all High Masses were to be concluded with a crusade sermon, and we can tell from surviving material that people received more or less the same sermon everywhere in Europe. Via the Church structure, the idea of the crusade penetrated to the most distant parts of Europe and created a common world of ideas everywhere.

The great institutions of education – the cathedral schools and during the 12th century, the predecessors of the universities, the schools in Paris – trained individuals for the highest Church offices, to become royal advisors and advisors for that elite which managed theology and historical writing. This again created a certain uniformity that left its traces in the treatment of the past. Everywhere in Western Europe, the history of the realm became a crusade history during the 12th century; Denmark's Saxo is only one example among many others.

There has been a tradition in modern historical writing to assume that communication was slow during the Middle Ages, that communication across large distances was not particularly common and something that only a tiny upper class would engage in, whereas the majority were isolated in local communities whose interests and horizons did not extend much further than the parish border and whose only concern was to subdue the earth to produce that little yield that would keep starvation at bay. If this is the perception of the Middle Ages, it will lead to a particular type of historical writing. If we attempt to turn it upside down and claim that communication levels were high and uniform, leading to common knowledge and perceptions everywhere in Europe among high and low, it must necessarily lead to a different way of writing history.

Different historical writing?

When looking at Denmark's or Portugal's history during the Middle Ages, it is easy to dig down into the material from the individual country and get lost in the many well-written descriptions of the past. It is impossible to get around the tradition when one goes to the source material. The tradition is a key to understanding and a necessary framework, but it can also turn into a limited, too-narrow framework that is almost impossible to break through. If one is trained as a historian of the Danish Middle Ages, there are many questions about which one has to make up one's mind because all one's predecessors have done this. And there is a multitude of questions one never gets to ask because they were not considered interesting to the predecessors. How does one perform the difficult exercise to be

Crusades in north and south? 329

initially trained as a historian of medieval Denmark in order to get the necessary background and knowledge about the tradition, only to then forget all that one has learnt to make it possible to go to the sources again with a new perspective?

It is probably impossible to do this completely, but the comparison of Denmark and Portugal has been an attempt to become a historian of the Portuguese Middle Ages, as well as possible, in order to return to the Danish material and to look at it through Portuguese glasses. It is difficult to keep matters apart and to split oneself into two persons in this way, but I believe that it might bring about some novel and different ways to perceive history – ways that also happen to be more accurate and give a better understanding of those sources we do actually possess.

The history of Denmark has often been written in a closed and self-reliant way, as if Denmark did not have any connections to the surrounding world during the Middle Ages. This is also the case with Portuguese historical writing, although less so. If the crusades are chosen as a starting point, it becomes obvious that both Denmark and Portugal participated in a joint European project in completely the same way as most other countries in Western Europe. If one takes a closer look at the individual institutions – practical as well as ideological ones – that were developed in the context of the crusades, it is also obvious that a massive exchange of knowledge and attitudes took place across the current national borders. One can demonstrate this and support it with references to good source material, and then one has found something new that can be added to the sequence of perceptions of national medieval history. However, this is not just a new discovery on par with others; it is not just a new, little piece added to the big jigsaw puzzle. Insisting on breaking the national historic frame work has to – if we consider this through – shake the very foundation on which we base our understanding of history.

Traditional, national, historical writing did not cross the borders and did not see any connections, or at least no decisive connections, between what happened in Denmark and in the rest of Europe. Therefore, all changes in the history of Denmark had to be explained with something Danish, with inner developments and tensions and continuations of motives and actions. Put briefly, all changes in the history of Denmark have been explained by some previous event in the history of Denmark. Historical writing has always been diachronic and moved along a time line. This time line has had a direction, to lead on to the next decade and the next century and all the way up to our own time, because the historian knew of the events in advance and knew what it ended up with. The diachronic historical writing must almost necessarily get a touch of predestination to it. History could not evolve in any different way, and the historical agents, real living individuals through time, become pieces in a game. In general histories of Denmark one rarely gets the sense that they could have acted differently, and one rarely gets a sense of their motives and considerations.

Life was not like this in the Middle Ages if seen from the perspective of the crusades. This is not particularly odd. Crusades are about warfare, life and death. When it comes to practical warfare, the agents do not primarily look back to their past and their earlier history. It becomes a matter of life and death to follow

330 *Crusades in north and south?*

contemporary technological developments and to learn and copy from wherever wars are being fought. It becomes necessary to follow diplomatic and political twists, which decides who fights who and when. Actually, it stands to reason that the history of warfare should not be perceived diachronically but synchronically, so that Denmark at all times must be compared to other countries and not with an older Denmark. This then is also the case with the most important aspect of warfare: the ideological or theological side. How to defend killing other people, and how do people make themselves do it in practice? It has at all times been possible to refer to one's own glorious past, as Esbern Snare did at the Christmas meeting in Odense in 1187. However, this does not work in a national vacuum either. Everywhere in Europe, historical writing was used as a justification to wage crusades, and the historians at the time knew of one another and were often trained at the same places. They also followed theological developments, and themes from the theologians' intricate discussions regarding justification were presented in a brief and pithy format and made useful in liturgy such as in Santiago de Compostela during the 12th century or in historical writing such as with Saxo in around 1200.

When thinking synchronically instead of diachronically, it also becomes more obvious that all acts in the past arose from choices. We can follow the results of the choices and witness how ideas of justification and reform of the Church and the individual Christian during the 11th century are combined with ideas of war in the service of good, and it all develops into crusades, which became a huge success and spread everywhere very quickly. It is futile to ask what would have happened if single individuals in the past had chosen differently. It cannot be answered with any degree of certainty, but it is sufficient to keep in mind that they did actually choose. That history is open and does not follow a predetermined pattern or any inevitability.

The idea of dynamic interaction is really medieval. Jerusalem was the centre of the world and Denmark and Portugal were at the very edge of the world. However, the further out into the periphery and heathendom one travelled, the closer one came to heaven and the possibility of miracles and martyrdom. The countries in the periphery became their own Jerusalem, and Livonia became the hereditary land of the Virgin Mary. Comparing Denmark and Portugal really ought to be a small contribution to the attempt at writing a different history of the crusades, which encompasses all countries, including those in the geographical periphery, and a different history of Europe that operates with a little more advanced understanding of the dynamism of history rather than just a mechanistic conception of cultural transmissions from centre to periphery.

Finally, one might consider what all this means to our understanding of the role of the papacy in crusade history and thus in European history. The comparison of Denmark and Portugal is supposed to support the assertion that it really was possible to coordinate large military expeditions across Europe and wage crusades simultaneously in the Middle East, the Baltic and on the Iberian Peninsula. There was simultaneous development of crusade institutions and ideas across Europe; there were Europe-wide institutions such as religious orders and Church structure;

Crusades in north and south? 331

and at times there were actually crusades at precisely the same time in the three regions. They must have been organized in concert in some way or the other, and it must have been done directly or indirectly through the Papal see, which in principle was the only body that could authorize a war as a true crusade and promise the participants indulgence and martyrdom if they fell in the struggle for the faith. When comparing Denmark and Portugal with the rest of Europe it also becomes obvious that the Popes coordinated charters to different rulers, took crusader kings under papal protection to advance the crusades at certain times, promised indulgence or revoked indulgence according to changing priorities and tied other political and theological problems to the crusades, for instance in the case of the Danish Princess Ingeborg who was rejected as the Queen of France. The Papal see – either the Popes as individuals or the Curia with its cardinals and advisors – played a decisive role regarding the crusades. It contributed through the large network of many different bodies to coordinate the large crusades that included all of Europe.

Notes

1 Gerardus de Fracheto, *Vitae Fratrum*; Jarl Gallén, *La Province de Dacia de l'Ordre des Frères-Precheurs* (Helsinki, 1946); Jarl Gallén, 'Les voyages de S. Dominique au Danemark. Essai de datation', in: Faymundus Creytens O.P. et Pius Kunzle O.P. (eds), *Xenia Medii Aevi Historiam illustrantia oblata Thomae Kaeppeli O.P.* (Rome, 1978), pp. 73–84; Iben Fonnesberg-Schmidt, *The Popes and the Baltic Crusades 1147–1254* (Leiden, 2007), pp. 156–162.
2 Alfonso VII of Castile was married to Richilde, a daughter of Wladislaw II of Poland. Sofie was a daughter of Richiza, and Richiza and Wladislaw were siblings and children of Boleslaw III of Poland.
3 Acta Sanctorum; Berthold Altaner, *Die Dominikanermission des 13. Jahrhunderts. Forschungen zur Geschichte der kirchlichen Unionen und der Mohammedaner- und Heidenmission des Mittelalters* (Habelswerdt, 1924), p. 4; Jarl Gallén, 'Les voyages de S. Dominique au Danemark', pp. 73–84.
4 Gallén, *La Province de Dacia*.
5 Vita Gunneri, XIII.
6 Ibid., IX.
7 DD 1:2, no. 50.
8 Luíz Gonzaga de Azevedo, *História de Portugal*, vols. 1–6 (Lisboa, 1935–1944), vol. 4, pp. 149–151.
9 DD 1:5, no. 82.
10 D 1:6, no. 98.
11 D 1:6, no. 17 and no. 42, item 1.
12 José Mattoso, *Identificação de um país: ensaio sobre as origens de Portugal, 1096–1325*, vols. 1–2 (Lisbon, 1995), vol. 1, p. 135. For Livros de linhagens, see L. Krus, *A Concepção Nobiliárquica do Espaço Ibérico (1280–1380)* (Lisbon, 1994); Bernardo Vasconcelos e Sousa, 'Linhagen e identidade social na nobreza medieval portuguesa (séculos XIII–XIV)', *Hispania* 67 (2007), pp. 881–898. Livros velhos was presumably an attempt from the Portuguese noblemen to counter demands of control from a strong king by asserting an independent identity as those who created the realm by waging crusades; see Krus, *A Concepção*, pp. 57–70. It is tempting to view Absalon's genealogical table in the same light as the Hvide family's emphasizing their great importance, precisely at a time when several of the family's members were under pressure

332 *Crusades in north and south?*

after the murder of Erik Glipping in 1286 and Erik Menved's imprisonment of Jens Grand on the 9th of April 1294.

13 *Livros velhos de linhagens*, the introduction, p. 23–24.
14 *Genealogia Ansalonis*. Jens Grand is listed as a rural dean, not yet an archbishop.
15 DD 1:3, no. 83.

11 Conclusion

Everything discussed earlier has had something to do with centre and periphery, which is not so strange if one lives as a Dane in modern-day Europe. However, it has also been an attempt to depict a fluid, changeable world where the wars of kings and noblemen surged back and forth for generations while they themselves crossed back and forth across the religious frontier according to their political senses and inner religious convictions. A world where theologians created fixed categories of infidels and faithful, and those who were categorized possibly would not have recognized the category as a legitimate perception of themselves. This was a world where the historian played a decisive role in his attempt to find or create a pattern in the chaos of reality.

This is a different way to understand this part of the Middle Ages from the traditional, national and romanticizing historical writing in which it was almost a given that Valdemar and Afonso would turn out as great kings and create the modern nation states of Denmark and Portugal. However, they could not have known this themselves. The type of historical writing where everything leads up to the present and known result is simply too easy. The past reality was much more multitudinous. It might be easier to see this now than it was 100 years ago. It is not primarily because developments are faster than before, as many claim, because most people have thought since the dawn of time that everything went much faster than it used to. Development and its speed are relative phenomena, not absolutes, and the acts of individuals do not depend on how fast development goes but on how fast individuals feel that it goes.

On the other hand, time today is possibly more fleeting than only a few generations ago: it has become more open to change. When I was a student, I had a job as a night watchman in a corporation where the workers had their portraits painted and displayed in a large memorial hall after forty years of employment. There were many of them, but there will not be any more. No one sees it as an ideal to be in the same company for forty years, but many did so until the 1970s. Transition and changeability have also captured such an important area as the medium in which we express our thoughts. The printed, unchanged word in rows of beautiful books in a well-ordered library has been replaced by electronic texts which we do not know how to find and which change web addresses or are discontinued or quietly revised, rewritten, added to so that one is never quite sure whether they are the same texts one returns to the next time.

334   *Conclusion*

That the world is fleeting has probably always been a basic condition for human beings, but it has become more recognized and accepted also amongst historians lately than it was for most of the 20th century. The world consists and consisted of a network of associations and connections through which one can move about and create meaning in many ways – in the same way as we surf the internet. This does not mean that the world and history are arbitrary and open to any interpretation, but it makes it possible and acceptable to admit that history has a personal meaning. That it is uninteresting if it does not treat great existential questions such as nation, land, war, faith, how these questions gave meaning to people in the past and what we might learn from their experiences and opinions. This also means that it has become more acceptable to admit that the historian's obsession with great existential questions of decisive importance to all might have been set in motion by rather small, personal experiences and emotions.

This whole narrative actually began on a quiet afternoon in the church of Sankt Bendt in my new hometown of Ringsted. I had visited the church several times before and now stood again looking at the remnants of Berengaria's plait, which is exhibited inside the church in a vitrine. To protect the plait, a fine, soft piece of blue cloth was placed over the vitrine. When one, in the quiet of the church, pulls the cloth to the side, one can see the plait lying there, almost 800 years old. It is a strange feeling. It says more than a multitude of pages of written sources from the time: possibly because it does not actually say anything at all. It can therefore be a springboard for one's wildest imagination, without any petty critical considerations. One is allowed to be moved. This happened to the great nationalist Danish poet Valdemar Rørdam in 1915.

XX
En Glug i Væggen er jeg standset ved –
et Glasskrin holder jeg i mine Hænder,
mit Hjerte hamrer, gråd mit Øje blænder –

XX
I am standing at a peephole in the wall –
I am holding a glass chest in my hands,
My heart beats, my eyes are blinded by tears

XXI
I dette Glasskrin, adskilt kun ved Glaret
her fra min Hånd, ligger en Kvindes Hår,
en fyldig Fletning, underfuldt bevaret
hos Død og Mulm i syvsindhundred År,
blot sælsomt sprød og som et Tovværk
  bleget –
Med denne Fletning har Kong Volmer
  leget.

XXI
In this chest, only separated by the glass
From my hand, lies the hair of a woman,
A thick plait, wonderfully preserved
With death and darkness for seven hundred
  years,
Only strangely brittle and bleached as
  rope –
With this plait King Valdemar has played.

XXII
Tit har han løsnet disse tunge Knuder
Snoning for Snoning ved Alkovens Væg
og tynget lykkelig de hvide Puder,
idet han sænkede sit gyldne Skæg,
sin røde Mund dybt ned i Lokke-Mulmet,
for sødt at finde, hvad derunder
  svulmed.

XXII
Often he loosened these heavy knots
Twist by twist by the wall of the bed
And happily laid on white pillows
As he lowered his golden beard,
His red mouth deep into the dark of the hair,
To sweetly find what filled it underneath.

XXIII

Det er den skønne Berengarias Fletning,
den onde Dronning Beengjærds
   Ravnelok,
lig Hampen bleget af den lange
   Tvætning
i Dødens Flod – dog endnu mægtig nok.
Den Fletning har jeg her i mine Hænder
og græder ved det, græder, så det brænder.

XXIV

For Skønheds Fald de første hede Tårer;
de springer frem som Bloddryp for et
   Stik.
For Elskovs Død. Vi kysser og vi kårer,
og Kraniet venter med sit hule Blik.
Dog siden smerter dybere et andet:
At Skønhed er en Gift, vor Lyst
   forbandet.

XXV

Se, denne Fletning, der tilforn
   omsnoede
Kong Volmers Vilje med sin sorte Pragt,
hans Stammes Storværk rev den op med
   Rode,
hans egen Lov ved den blev ødelagt.
Af Frugten sås, hvad der var dulgt i
   Blostret:
I Beengjærds hvide Skød blev Orme
   fostret.

XXVI

Den fletning knuged sine Slangebugter
om Danmarks lykke. Vi slog
   Kæmpeslag –
ormædte faldt selv vore Sejres Frugter
for Hertugsvig og Brodersplid og Nag.
Sten efter Sten er tabt, Guldkronen
   brusten.
Men så vort Sværd da? – Tys! Dèr
   graver Rusten.

XXVII

Os øder ikke nu den store Skæbne,
der af de tre blå Strømmes Styrkebånd
har lagt os Lænker. Den som vil, kan
   væbne
sit Væsens Frihed, selv med ufri Hånd.
Og den som ærligt holder ud i Striden,
kan bøje Skæbnen bort og modstå
   Tiden.

XXIII

It is the plait of the lovely Berengaria,
The raven hair of the evil Queen Beengjærd,
Like hemp dyed by the long washing
In the river of death – yet still mighty.
This plait I hold here in my hand
And cry, cry until I burn.

XXIV

For the fall of beauty, the first warm tears;
They spring forward as blood drops from a
   stab wound.
For the death of love. We kiss and we
   choose,
And the skull waits with its hollow gaze.
Though since something else hurts more:
That beauty is poison, our desire is cursed.

XXV

Behold, this plait, which formerly twirled
   around
King Valdemar's will with its black splendour,
The achievement of his tribe it tore up by
   its root,
His own law was ruined by it.
From the fruit it was seen what was hidden
   amongst the petals:
In Beengjærd's white womb, worms were
   nurtured.

XXVI

This plait held its snake twirls
Around the destiny of Denmark. We battled
   mightily –
Even the fruits of our victories fell, worm-
   eaten,
For treason of dukes and division and
   resentment amongst brothers.
Stone after stone is lost, the golden crown
   broken.
But what about our sword? – Quiet! There
   rust is working.

XXVII

We are not now destroyed by the great fate,
Which by the strong bonds of the three blue
   streams
Have put us in irons. He who wants can arm
The freedom of his spirit, even with an
   un-free hand.
And he who honestly holds out in the struggle,
Can deflect fate and withstand time.

Conclusion

XXVIII	XXVIII

Nej; det er indefra, vi lægges øde.
Nu, da den store Skæbnetime slår,
nu har vi træt gjort op med vore Døde
og valgt at visne under Trællekår.
Saga sit Stenbryst over Konger
   Hvælver.
Men tom står Kirken; og dens
   Grundvold skælver.
	No; it is from within we are destroyed.
	Now that the great hour of fate rings out,
	Now that we wearily have settled with our
	   dead
	And chosen to wither in slavery.
	Saga with her stony breast arches over
	   kings.
	But the church stands empty; and its
	   foundation shakes.

Valdemar Rørdam's poem is not really a homage to Berengaria. In her white womb, worms were nurtured, that is Erik, Abel and Christopher. Valdemar Rørdam was not fond of foreigners and of foreign cultures; during the Second World War he got so carried away by hyper-nationalism and Nazism that he had his official honours taken away after the war. He was excluded from the Danish Author's Society and died a bitter and lonely man. To Rørdam, nationalism became isolating, something that divided Danish culture from other cultures to an assertion of what was peculiarly Danish. Rørdam went too far, but his basic perception is neither unusual nor necessarily wrong in itself, that which is Danish is something in itself, and in its changeability it is something special despite all the similarities with other countries and cultures. Rørdam's implications, then, is that contact with the foreign, the Southern and the sexual destroyed what was manly and Nordic, and that had to be avoided. Otherwise it would go wrong. That conclusion, on the other hand, is nonsense.

Poor Berengaria had a negative posthumous reputation in Denmark. One of the first times I was shown around in the church of Sankt Bendt in Ringsted, the churchwarden stopped by her tomb in reverence. In a low voice, he told a story that he had heard from his predecessor, who had heard it from his predecessor, and so on. A long time ago, the church was haunted, and during Mass all the candles were all of a sudden blown out at once. This happened repeatedly in Mass after Mass, until a clever priest figured out that it was Berengaria who was haunting the place. The tomb was then opened and her skull removed from the rest of the skeleton so that she could no longer blow out the lights, and a large stone was put in its place. Since then, the candles have never gone out during services in the church. Perhaps it is true that she haunted the church. When modern archaeologists opened her tomb again in 1855, they found to their astonishment a large stone where the head ought to be. The skull, which they described so thoroughly, almost lovingly, was placed at the side, slightly above the left shoulder. Perhaps the story of the haunting was only invented after the opening of the grave in 1855 to explain the strange position of the remains, perhaps it does go back to medieval times. In any case, it had the same function through the 20th century: to stress that the Southern is different and dangerous, such as Rørdam described it.

c

Figure 11.1 The plait of Berengaria, now on display in the church in Ringsted. © Worsaae, *Kongegravene* . . . , 1858.

338 *Conclusion*

Several Portuguese historians have had the same idea about the difference of cultures as Rørdam and Danish historians, but many of them nevertheless reached the opposite conclusion. They believe that it is during the meeting of cultures, by the blending of North and South, that sparks fly and something happens. This is a completely different attitude to foreign phenomena. This might be due to Portugal's long and glorious history as a colonial power; it could be because the religious frontier continued to exist in the expanding Portuguese realm, whereas it disappeared in Denmark. It could be because of the temperament and horizon of Portuguese historians. Whatever the reason, I believe that it is an attitude that Danish historians could learn something from and use to reach a better understanding: not only of Portuguese and European history, but of Danish history as well.

In 1984, the great Portuguese historian of the Middle Ages, José Mattoso, wrote about Berengaria and her bones and skull, which excited the anthropologists so much in 1855. He ended thus: "Berengaria is a female symbol par excellence: With a beauty that her mortal remains reveal and hide at the same time, a carrier of fertility and death, a messenger of connections between two nations so far away from each other, so exotic in each other's eyes. In truth, a symbol of difference but at the same time a seductress and someone who disturbed everything that divides man and woman, North and South, cold and warmth."[1]

Note

1 Mattoso in the introduction to Luciano Cordeiro, *Berengela e Leonor rainhas da Dinamarca* (Lisbon, 1984).

Literature

Abbreviations

AD: *Annales Danici Medii Ævi*, vol. 1–2, ed. Ellen Jørgensen (Copenhagen, 1920).

APL: *Acta processus litium inter regem danorum et archiepiscopum lundensem*, ed. Alfred Krarup et William Norvin (Copenhagen, 1932).

ASV, Reg. Vat.: Archivum Secretum Vaticanum, Registra Vaticana.

BD: *Bullarium Danicum. Pavelige aktstykker vedrørende Danmark 1198–1316*, ed. Alfred Krarup (Copenhagen, 1931–1932).

BP: *Bulário Português. Inocêncio III (1198–1216)*, ed. Avelino de Jesus da Costa e Maria Alegria F. Marques (Coimbra, 1989).

CIC: *Corpus Iuris Canonici* vol 1–2, ed. Aemilius Friedberg (Graz, 1959) [1879].

COD: *Conciliorum Oecumenicorum Decreta*, ed. G. Alberigo, Joseph A. Dossetti, Pericles Joannou, Claude Leonardi, and Paul Prodi (Bologna, 1973).

DD: *Diplomatarium Danicum*, ed. Det Danske Sprog- og Litteraturselskab (Copenhagen, 1938–).

DDS: *Documentos de D. Sancho I (1174–1211)*, ed. Rui de Azevedo, Avelino de Jesus da Costae Marcelino Pereira (Coimbra, 1979).

DF: *Danmarks Folkeviser: Et Hundrede udvalgte Danske Viser*, vol. 1–2, ed. Jørgen Lorenzen (Copenhagen, 1974).

DgF: *Danmarks gamle Folkeviser*, vols. 1–13, ed. Svend Grundtvig, Axel Olrik, and Iørb Piø (Copenhagen, 1853–1965).

DGK: *Danmarks Gamle Købstadslovgivning*, vols. 1–5, ed. Erik Kroman and Peter Jørgensen (Copenhagen, 1951–1961).

DgL: *Danmarks gamle Landskabslove med Kirkelovene*, vols. 1–10, ed. Det danske sprog- og litteraturselskab (Copenhagen, 1933–1951).

DK: *Danmarks Kirker*, ed. the National Museum (Copenhagen, 1933–).

DMA: *Danmarks middelalderlige annaler*, ed. Erik Kroman (Copenhagen, 1980).

DMP: *Documentos medievais portugueses*, ed. Academia Portuguesa da Historia (Lisbon, 1940–).

DOM: *Urkunden und erzahlende Quellen zur deutschen Ostsiedlung im Mittelalter*, vols. 1–2, ed. Herbert Helbig and Lorenz Weinrich (Darmstadt, 1984) [1968].

DR: *Danmarks Runeindskrifter*, vols. 1–3, ed. Lis Jakobsen and Erik Moltke (Copenhagen, 1941–1942).

DS: *Diplomatarium Svecanum*, ed. Kungl. Vitterhets Historie och Antikvitetsakademien och Riksarkivet (Stockholm, 1829–).

IF: *Islenzk Fornrit*, ed. Hid islenzka fornritafelag (1933–).

JL: *Den Jyske Lov*, ed. Peter Skautrup (Aarhus, 1941).

340   *Literature*

KLNM: *Kulturhistorisk Leksikon for Nordisk Middelalder fra vikingetid til reformation-stid*, vols. 1–20 (Copenhagen, 1956–1978).

KVJ: *Kong Valdemars Jordebog*, vols. 1–3, ed. Svend Aakjær (Copenhagen, 1926–1945).

LP: *Livro Preto. Cartulario de Se de Coimbra*, ed. Manuel Augusto Rodrigues (Coimbra, 1999).

LPV: *The Letters of Peter the Venerable*, vols. 1–2, ed. Giles Constable (Cambridge, MA, 1967).

LS: *Livro Santo de Santa Cruz. Cartulário do Sec. XII*, ed. Leontina Ventura e Ana Santiago Faria (Coimbra, 1990).

Manifestis probatum: published in PL 200, cols. 1237–1238.

MGH: Monumenta Germaniae historica.

MUB: *Mecklenburgisches Urkundenbuch*, ed. Verein fur Mecklenburgische Geschichte und Altertumskunde (Schwerin, 1863–).

PL: *Patrologia Latina*, vols. 1–221, ed. Jacques-Paul Migne (Paris, 1844–1855).

PMH: *Portugaliae monumenta historica a saeculo octavo post Christum usque ad quintumdecimum*, ed. Acedemia Scientiarum Olisiponensis (Lisbon, 1856–1888).

Reg. Greg. VII: *Das Register Gregors VII*, vols. 1–2, ed. Erich Caspar (Berlin, 1967) [1920].

Reg. Greg. IX: *Les Registres de Grégoire IX*, vols. 1–4, ed. Lucien Auvray (Paris, 1896–1908).

RHC: *Recueil des historiens des Croisades*, ed. Académie des inscriptions and belles-lettres (Paris, 1841–1906).

SM: *Scriptores minores historia danica medii avi*, vols. 1–2, ed. M.Cl. Gertz (Copenhagen, 1917–22).

SRD: *Scriptores Rerum Danicarum medii avi*, vols. 1–9, ed. Jacob Langebæk (Copenhagen, 1772–1878).

Statuta O.C.: *Statuta Capitulorum Generalium Ordinis Cisterciensis ab anno 1116 ad annum 1786*, vols. 1–8, ed. D. Josephus-Mia Canivez (Louvain, 1933–1941).

VSD: *Vitae sanctorum danorum*, ed. M.Cl. Gertz (Copenhagen, 1908–1912).

Sources

Abd Allah, *El siglo XI en 1a persona: Las "Memorias" de Abd Allah, último Rey Zirí de Granada destronado por los Almorávides (1090)*, traducidas par E. Lévi-Provençal y Emilio García Gomez (Madrid, 1980).

Acta Sanctorum Aprilis 5, ed. Joh. Pinio, Guilielmo Cupero, Joanne Stiltinge (S.J.) (Antwerp, 1741).

Adam of Bremen, *Adami Gesta Hammaburgensis ecclesiae pontificum*, ed. J.M. Lappenberg (Hannover, 1876).

Albert of Aix, *Historia Expeditionis Hierosolymitanae*, PL 166, cols. 389–716. RHC, Historiens Occidentaux, IV, pp. 300–713.

Albert of Trois-Fontaines, *Alberici monachi Triumfontium Chronicon*, ed. G.H. Prutz. MGH, Scriptores, 23 (Hannover, 1874), pp. 631–950.

Alcuin, *Vita sancti Willibrordi*, i *Monumenta Alcuiniana*, ed. Wilhelm Wattenbach and Ph. Jaffé (Berlin, 1873), pp. 39–61. *Anais, crónicas e memórias avulsas de Santa Cruz de Coimbra*, ed. António Cruz (Porto, 1968).

Anais do D. Afonso, rei dos portugueses, in Fr. António Brandão, *Monarquia Lusitana*, vol. 3. Also published as *Annales D. Alfonsi Portugallensium regis.*

Annales Compostellani, in *Espana Sagrada* 23, pp. 317–324.

Literature 341

Annales D. Alfonsi Portugallensium regis, in Monica Blöcker-Walter, *Alfons I. von Portugal: Studien zu Geschichte und Sage des Begründers der portugiesischen Unabhängigkeit* (Zürich, 1966), pp. 151–161.

Annales Magdeburgenses, hrsg. Georg Waitz. MGH Scriptores; 16 (Hannover, 1859), pp. 105–196.

Annales Toledanos. Annales Toledanos I, in *España Sagrada* 23, pp. 381–400; *Annales Toledanos* II, in *España Sagrada* 23, pp. 401–409.

Annalista Saxo, in MGH, Scriptores, 6.

Anónimo de Sahagún, in *História del Real Monasterio de Sahagun*, ed. Romualdo Escalona (Madrid, 1782).

Arnold of Lübeck, *Arnoldi Chronica Slavorum*, ed. J.M. Lappenberg. MGH Scriptores; 14. (Hannover, 1868).

Augustinus, *Contra Faustum Manichaeum*, PL 42, cols. 207–518.

Augustinus, *De doctrina christiana*, PL 34, cols. 15–122.

Augustinus, *Tractatus in Ioannis Evangelium*, PL 35, cols. 1379–1976.

Baldric of Dole, *Baldrici episcopi Dolensis Historia Jerosolimitana*, RHC, Historiens Occidentaux, IV, pp. 1–146.

Beowulf, ed. and transl. John Porter (Norfolk, 2000).

Bernard of Clairvaux, *De Consideratione Libri Quinque ad Eugenium tertium*, PL 182, cols. 727–808.

Bernard of Clairvaux, *De laude nove militie*, i *Sancti Bernardi opera*, vol. 3, pp. 213–239.

Bernard of Clairvaux, *In circumcisione Domini*, PL 183, cols. 131–282.

Bernard of Clairvaux, *Opera*, vols. 1–8, ed. Jean Leclercq and Henri Rochais (Rome, 1955–77).

Bernard of Clairvaux, *Sermones in Cantica canticorum*, PL 183, cols. 785–1198.

Biblia latina cum glossa ordinaria, vols. 1–4, ed. princeps Adolph Rusch 1480/81 [Facsimile ed. Turnholt, 1992].

Caesarius of Heisterbach, *Dialogus miraculorum*, vols. 1–2, ed. J. Strange (Cologne, 1851).

Cartulaire de Cluny, *Recueil des chartes de l'abbaye de Cluny*, vols. 1–6, ed. A. Bernard and A. Bruel (Paris, 1876–1903).

Catalogus regum dacie, in SM, vol. 1, pp. 159–160.

Christian Pedersen, *Danske Skrifter*, vols. 1–5, ed. C.J. Brandt (Copenhagen, 1850–1856).

Chronica Adefonsi Imperatoris, in A. Maya Sánchez, *Chronica Hispana saeculi XII.* Corpus Christianorum Continuatio Medievalis 70 (Turnhout, 1990), pp. 109–248.

Chronica Gothorum, part 1 published in Pierre David, *Études historiques sur la Galice et le Portugal du VIe au XIIe siècle* (Lisbon, 1947), pp. 291–302; part 2 as *Annales D. Alfonsi* and *Anais do D. Afonso* (ut supra).

Chronicon Burgense, in *España sagrada* 23, pp. 307–310.

Chronicon Conimbricense, in *España Sagrada* 23, pp. 330–356; and in PMH, Scriptores 1.

Chronicon ex historia compostellana codice, in *España sagrada* 23, pp. 325–328.*Chronicon Roskildense*, in SM 1, pp. 1–33.

Coelestin III, Bull of 31.10.1196, ed. Fidel Fita and Ramón Riu, 'Noticias', *Boletín de la Real Academia de la Historia* 11 (1887), pp. 455–458.

Conversio Otgarii duplex, i Passiones vitaeque sanctorum aevi merovingici, ed. B. Krusch and N. Levison. MGH Scriptores rerum merovingicarum; 5 (Hannover, 1910), pp. 203–206.

Crónica Najerense, ed. Antonio Ubieto Arteta (Zaragoza, 1985) [1966]. *Danmarks Gilde- og Lavsskraaer fra Middelalderen*, vols. 1–2, ed. C. Nyrop (Lyngby, 1977) [1895].

342 Literature

Das Itinerarium peregrinorum: Eine zeitgenossische englische Chronik zum dritten Kreuzzug in ursprunglicher Gestalt, ed. Hans Eberhard Mayer (Stuttgart, 1962).

De Camões, Luís, *Os Lusíadas* (Lisbon, 1572).

De Expugnatione Lyxbonensi = *The Conquest of Lisbon*, ed. and transl. Charles Wendell David; reissued by Jonathan Phillips (New York, 2001) [1936].

De expugnatione scalabis, PMH, Scriptores, 1, pp. 93–95.

De Itinere navali, 'Narratio de itinere navali peregrinorum Hierosolymam tendentium et Silviam capientium A.D. 1189', ed. Charles Wendell David. *Proceedings of the American Philosophical Society*, 81, no. 5 (1939), pp. 592–675.

De Profectione Danorum in Hierosolymam, in SM 2, pp. 444–492.

Die Prufeninger Vita Bischof Ottos I. von Bamberg nach der Fassung des Grossen Österreichischen Legendars, ed. Jürgen Petersohn (Hannover, 1999).

Die Urkunden Kaiser Alfons VII von Spanien, ed. Peter Rassow, *Archiv fur Urkundenforschung* 10 (1928), pp. 327–468; 11 (1929), pp. 66–137.

Diplomatarium Norvegicum, ed. Kommisjonen for Diplomatarium Norvegicum/ Riksarkivet (Kristiania/Oslo, 1847–).

Duarte Galvão, *Crónica de el-rei D. Afonso Henriques* (Lisbon, 1995) [1986].

DuCange, Ch. Du Fresne, *Glossarium mediae et infimae latinitatis*, vols. 1–10 (Paris, 1937–1938) [1678].

Dudo, *Dudonis de moribus et actis primorum Normanniae ducum*, PL 141, cols. 609–758.

Ekkehardus Uraugiensis, *Chronicon universale*, PL 154, cols. 497–1059. Also in *Frutolfs und Ekkehards Chroniken und die anonyme Kaiserchronik*, ed. and transl. Franz-Josef Schmale and Irene Schmale-Ott (Darmstadt, 1972).

Epistolae pontificum romanorum ineditae [edidit] S. Loewenfeld, ed. Samuel Loewenfeld (Graz, 1959).

Eriks Sjællandske Lov, in DgL, vol. 5, pp. 3–366.

Ermoldus Nigellus, *In honorem Hludovici elegiacum carmen*, ed. Edmond Faral (Paris, 1932).

España Sagrada, 56 vols., ed. Henrique Florez et al. (Madrid, 1749–1961).

Exordium magnum cisterciense. Conradus Eberbacensis, *Exordium magnum cisterciense sive narratio de initio cisterciensis ordinis*, ed. Bruno Griesser. Corpus Christianorum Continuatio Mediaevalis; 138 (Turnhout, 1997).

Exordium Monasterii Cara insula, i SM 2, pp. 158–264.

Exordium Monasterii S. Joannis de Tarouca, PMH, Scriptores 1, pp. 88–90.

Fragmentary Annals of Ireland, ed. Joan Newlon Radner (Dublin, 1978).

Fulcher of Chartres, *Historia Iherosolymitana . . . auctore domno Fulcheri Carnotensi*, RHC Historiens Occidentaux III, pp. 311–485.

Galberti Brugensis, *De vita et martyrio beati Caroli*, PL 166, cols. 943–1046.

Gallus Anonymus, *Chronik und Taten der Herzoge und Fursten von Polen*, ed. Josef Bujnoch (Styria, 1978).

Genealogia Absalonis Archieepiscopi & cognatorum ejus, SRD 4, pp. 545–551.

Geoffrey of Auxerre, *Vita Prima Bernardi*, PL 185, cols. 301–368.

Gerardus de Fracheto O.P., *Vitae Fratrum ordinis praedicatorum necnon cronica ordinis ab anno MCCIII usque ad MCCLIV*, ed. Benedictus Maria Reichert. Monumenta ordinis fratrum pradicatorum historica; 1 (Rome, 1897).

Gesta Francorum et aliorum Hierosolimitanorum, The deeds of the Franks and the other pilgrims to Jerusalem, ed. by Rosalind Hill (London, 1962).

Gosuino, *Quomodo fuit capta Alcaser a Francis*, PMH, Scriptores 1, pp. 101–104.

Gualterus Tarvanensis, *Vita Caroli Boni*, PL 166, cols. 901–943.

Guibert of Nogent, *Dei gesta per Francos et cinq autres textes*, ed. R.B.C. Huygens. Corpus Christianorum Continuatio Mediaevalis; 127A (Turnhout, 1996).

Literature 343

Guibert of Nogent, *Opusculum de virginitate*, PL 156, cols. 579–608.

Gulathingslov, in *Norges gamle Love indtil 1387*, vols 1–5, ed. R. Keyser et al. (Oslo, 1846–1895) vol. 1, pp. 3–118.

Gutalagen, in *Svenske landskapslagar. Tolkade och forklarade for nutidens svenskar*, vols. 1–5, ed. Åke Holmbäck och Elias Wessén (Stockholm, 1933–1946), vol. 4, pp. 203–290.

Hákonar saga Hákonarsonar, etter Sth. 8 fol., AM 325 VIII, 4:o og AM 304,4, udg. Marina Mundt (Oslo, 1977).

Heimskringla, see Snorri Sturluson.

Helmold of Bosau, *Helmoldi presbyteri Chronica Slavorum*, ed. G.H. Pertz (Hannover, 1868).

Henry of Livonia, *Henrici Chronicon Livoniae*, ed. Leonid Arbusow and Albertus Bauer (Hannover, 1955).

Historia Compostellana, ed. Emma Falque. Corpus Christianorum Continuatio Mediaevalis; 70 (Turnhout, 1988).

Historia Silense, ed. Justo Perez de Urbel and Atilano González Ruiz-Zorrilla (Madrid, 1959).

Honorio III, *La documentación pontificia de Honorio III (1216–1227)*, ed. Demetrio Mansilla (Rome, 1965).

Huitfeldt, Arild, *Danmarckis Rigis Krønnicke från Kong Dan den første oc indtil Kong Knud den 6.* (Copenhagen, 1978) [1603].

Huitfeldt, Arild, *En Kaart Chronologia, forfølge oc Continuatz. 1. Part. Som indeholder Canuti VI. Historia . . .* (Copenhagen, 1978) [1600].

Indiculum fundationis monasterii S. Vincentii, PMH, Scriptores 1, pp. 90–93.

In festis Sancti Canuti Ducis ad Horas et Missam, in Michael Chesnutt, 'The Medieval Danish Liturgy of St Knud Lavard', *Bibliotheca Arnamagnæana* 42 (2003), pp. 1–160, edition pp. 79–160.

Islandske Annaler indtil 1578, ed. Gustav Storm (Oslo, 1888).

Itinera Hierosolymitana Crucesignatorum (saec. XII–XIII), vols. 1–4, ed. S. de Sandoli (Jerusalem, 1978–1984).James 1. *The Book of Deeds of James I of Aragon. A Translation of the Medieval Catalan* Llibre dels Fets, ed. Damian Smith and Helena Buffery (Aldershot, 2003).

Johannis Marignolli, *Relatio*, in *Itinera et relationes Fratrum Minorum saeculi XIII et XIV*, ed. Anastasius van den Wyngaert; *Sinica Franciscana* 1 (Quaracchi-Firenze, 1929), pp. 513–560.

Knytlingesagaen, in *Danakongunga Sogur*, ed. Bjarni Guðnason, IF; 35 (Reykjavik, 1982).

La Chanson d'Antioche, vols. 1–2, ed. Suzanne Duparc-Quioc (Paris, 1977–1978).

La Chevalerie d'Ogier de Danemarche. Canzone di gesta, ed. Mario Eusebi (Milan, 1963).

Liber Sancti Jacobi, Codex Calixtinus, vols. 1–2, ed. Walter Muir Whitehill (Santiago de Compostela, 1944).

Liutprand (?), *Adversaria*, PL 136, cols. 1133–1180.

Livro de Linhagens do Conde D. Pedro, vols. 1–2, ed. José Mattoso, PMH, nova séria (Lisbon, 1980).

Livros velhos de linhagens, ed. Joseph Piel e José Mattoso, PMH, nova séria I (Lisbon, 1980).

Lundeårbøgerne, AD, pp. 44–129; DMA, pp. 21–70.

Magnúss saga blinda ok Haralds gilla, in Snorri Sturluson, *Heimskringla*, IF 28, pp. 278–302.

Magnúss saga ins góda, in Snorri Sturluson. *Heimskringla*, IF 28, pp. 3–67.*Magnussona saga*, in Snorri Sturluson. *Heimskringla*, IF 28, pp. 238–277.

Mattaus Parisiensis, *Matthaei Parisiensis Monachi Sancti Albani Chronica Majora*, vols. 1–7, ed. H.R. Luard (London, 1872–1883).

344   *Literature*

Miracula S. Thomae auctore Willelmo Cantuariensi, ed. J.R. Robertson (London, 1875).

Miracula S. Vincentii, i S. Vicente de Lisboa e seus milagres medievais, ed. Aires Augusto Nascimento and Saul António Gomes (Lisbon, 1988).

Missa de hostibus, in *Le Liber ordinum en usage dans l'Église wisigothique et mozarabe d'Espagne du cinquième siècle*, ed. Marius Ferotín (Paris, 1904).

Papsturkunden in Portugal, ed. Carl Erdmann (Berlin, 1927).

Peter Tudebodis, *Petri Tudebodi seu Tudebovis sacerdotis Sivracensis historia de Hierosolymitano itinere*, RHC Historiens Occidentaux III, pp. 1–117.

Petrus Comestor, *Historia scolastica*, PL 198, cols. 1049–1720.Petrus Venerabilis, *De laude dominici sepulchri*, in Giles Constable, 'Petri Venerabilis sermones tres', *Revue Benedictine* 64 (1954), pp. 224–272; edition pp. 232–254.

Petrus Venerabilis, *De miraculis libri duo*, PL 189, cols. 851–954.

Petrus Venerabilis, *Liber contra sectam sive haresim saracenorum*, in James Kritzeck, *Peter the Venerable and Islam* (Princeton, NJ, 1964), pp. 220–291.

Pomniki Dziejowe Polski = Monumenta Poloniae historica, vols. 1–6, ed. August Bielowski (Lwow, 1864–1893).

Radulphus Niger, *Radulfi Nigri chronica – The Chronicles of Ralph Niger*, ed. Robert Anstruther (London, 1851).

Raymund of Aguilers, *Historia Francorum qui ceperunt Iherusalem*, ed. John Hugh Hill and Laurita Lyttleton Hill (Philadelphia, 1968).Riccoldo da Monte di Croce, *Libellus ad nationes orientales*, ed. Kurt Villads Jensen, http://www1.sdu.dk/Hum/kvj/Riccoldo/index.html

Rimbert, *Vita Anskarii*, ed. Georg Waitz (Hannover, 1977).

Ritual de Santa Cruz de Coimbra, ed. Joaquim O. Bragança (Lisbon, 1976).

Robert Monachus, *Historia Hierosolymitana*, PL 155, cols. 667–758.

Rodrigo Ximenes de Rada, *Roderici Ximenii de Rada Historia de rebus Hispanie sive Historia gothica*, ed. Juan Fernández Valverde. Corpus Christianorum Continuatio Mediaevalis; 72 (Turnhout, 1987).

Roger de Hoveden, *Annales Comprising the History of England and of Other Countries of Europe from A.D. 732 to A.D. 1201*, vols. 1–2, ed. Henry T. Riley (London, 1853).

Roskildekrøniken, Chronicon Roskildense, in SM 1, pp. 1–33.

Saxo, *Gesta Danorum. Danmarkshistorien*, vols. 1–2, ed. Karsten Friis-Jensen, transl. Peter Zeeberg (Copenhagen, 2005).

Series regum danie ex necrologio lundensi, in SM 1, pp. 157–158.

Skånske Ledingsret, in DgL 1.

Skånske Lov, in DgL 1, pp. 1–199.

Snorri Sturluson, *Heimskringla*, vols. 1–3, ed. Bjarni Aðalbjarnarson. IF; 26–28 (Reykjavik, 1939–1951).

Song of Roland, Chançon de Roland, ed. Gerard Moignet (Paris, 1985).

Sven Aggesen, *Brevis historiae regum dacie*, in SM 1, pp. 94–141.

Sven Aggesen, *Lex castrensis sive cvrie*, in SM 1, pp. 64–93.

Sverris Saga etter Cod. AM 327 4o, ed. Gustav Indrebo (Oslo, 1920).

Torquato Tasso, *Gerusalemme conquistata*, ed. Luigi Bonfigli and Angelo Solerti (Bari, 1934) [1581].

Torquato Tasso, *Gerusalemme liberata*, ed. Luigi Bonfigli (Bari, 1930) [1581].

Urkundenbuch des Erzstifts Magdeburg, ed. Friedrich Israël and Walter Möllenberg (Magdeburg, 1937–).*Valdemars Sjællandske Lov*, DgL 8, pp. 3–104.

Vincent of Prag, *Vincentii Pragensis Annales*, ed. Wilhelm Wattenbach, MGH Scriptores; 17 (Hannover, 1861), pp. 654–684.

Vita Gunneri episcopi Vibergensis, in SM 2, pp. 265–278.

Vita Ottonis Ebbonis, Ebbonis Vita Ottonis episcopi Babenbergensis, ed. G.H. Pertz, MGH Scriptores; 12 (Hannover, 1856), pp. 822–883.

Vita Ottonis Herbordi, Herbordi Vita Ottonis episcopi, ed. G.H. Pertz, MGH; Scriptores 12 (Hannover, 1856), pp. 746–822.

Vita Ottonis Prüfeninger, Die Prüfeninger Vita Bischof Ottos I. von Bamberg nach der Fassung des Grossen Österreichischen Legendars, hrsg. Jürgen Petersohn (Hannover, 1999).

Vita Sancti Martini Sauriensis, PMH, Scriptores 1, pp. 60–62.

Vita Sancti Theotonii, PMH, Scriptores 1, pp. 79–88.

Vitae sanctorum danorum, ed. M.Cl. Gertz (Copenhagen, 1908–1912).

Widukind, *Widukindi Rerum gestarum saxonicarum libri tres*, ed. Georg Waitz (Hannover, 1882).

William of Malmesbury, *Gesta regum Anglorum* = The History of the English Kings, vols. 1–2, ed. R.A.B. Mynors, Rodney M. Thomson and Michael Winterbottom (Oxford, 1998).

William of Tyre, *Willelmi Tyrensis archiepiscopi Historia rerum in partibus transmarinis gestarum*, in RHC Historiens occidentaux 1–2.

Literature

Abulafia, Anna Sapir, *Christians and Jews in the Twelfth-Century Renaissance* (London, 1995).

Abulafia, David, 'Introduction. Seven Types of Ambiguity, c. 1100–c. 1500', in: David Abulafia and Nora Berend (eds.), *Medieval Frontiers: Concepts and Practices* (Aldershot, 2002), pp. 1–34.

Abulafia, David, and Nora Berend (eds.), *Medieval Frontiers: Concepts and Practices* (Aldershot, 2002).

Adriansen, Inge, *Nationale symboler i det danske rige 1830–2000* (Copenhagen, 2003).

Albrectsen, Esben, '700–1523', in: Carsten Due-Nielsen, Ole Feldbæk and Nikolaj Petersen (eds.), *Dansk Udenrigspolitiks Historie* (Copenhagen, 2001), pp. 10–215.

Alemparte, Jaime Ferreiro, *Arribadas de normandos y cruzados a las costas de la Península Ibérica* (Madrid, 1999).

Alfonso, Isabel, 'Cistercians and Feudalism', *Past & Present* 133 (1991), pp. 3–30.

Allen, C.F., *Haandbog i Fædrelandets Historie med stadig Henblik på Folkets og Statens indre Udvikling* (Copenhagen, 1840).

Allen, W.E.D., *The Poet and the Spae-Wife. An Attempt to Reconstruct Al-Ghazal's Embassy to the Vikings* (London, 1960).

Almazán, Vicente, 'Vikingerne i Galicien', in: Christopher Bo Bramsen (ed.), *Vikingerne pa Den Iberiske Halvø*, udg. Christopher Bo Bramsen (Madrid, 2004), pp. 41–51.

Almeida, Fortunato de, and Damiao Peres, *História da Igreja em Portugal* (Porto, 1967).

Altaner, Berthold, *Die Dominikanermission des 13. Jahrhunderts. Forschungen zur Geschichte der kirchlichen Unionen und der Mohammedaner- und Heidenmission des Mittelalters* (Habelswerdt, 1924).

Amaral, Diego Freitas do, *D. Afonso Henriques. Biografia* (Lisbon, 2000).

Andersen, Harald, 'The Graves of the Jelling Dynasty', *Acta Archaeologica* 66 (1996), pp. 281–300.

Andersen, Hellmuth H., *Danevirke og Kovirke. Arkæologiske undersøgelser 1861–1992* (Aarhus, 1998).

346　*Literature*

Andersen, Maria Josefina, 'Princesas portuguesas D. Berengária e D. Leonor, Rainhas da Dinamarca', in: Comissão Executiva dos Centenários (ed.), *Congresso do Mundo Português* II (Lisbon, 1940).

Andersen, Per, *Legal Procedure and Practice in Medieval Denmark* (Leiden, 2011).

Anderson, James M., *The History of Portugal* (London, 2000).

Andersson, Lars, *Pilgrimsmärken och vallfart. Medeltida pilgrimskultur i Skandinavien* (Stockholm, 1989).

Antunes, Jose, 'A versão portuguesa do "Tratado" de Tui (1137). Uma interpretação diferente da de Paoulo Merêa e de outros historiadores', *Actas do 2º Congresso Histórico de Guimaraes* 4 (Guimarães, 1996), pp. 33–43.

Arbusow, Leonid, 'Ein verschollener Bericht des Erzbischofs Andreas von Lund a.d. Jahr 1207 über die Bekehrung Livlands', *Sitzungsberichte der Gesellschaft für Geschichte und Altertumskunde der Ostseeprovinzen Russlands aus dem Jahre 1910* (1910), pp. 4–6.

Arruda, José Jobson, and José Manuel Tengarrinha, *Historiografia Luso-Brasileira Contemporânea* (Bauru, 1999).

Arup, Erik, *Danmarks historie* 1 *(til 1282)* (Copenhagen, 1925).

Arup, Erik, 'Kong Svend 2.s Biografi', *Scandia* 4 (1931), pp. 55–101.

Ashcroft, Jeffrey, 'Konrad's Rolandslied, Henry the Lion, and the Northern Crusade', *Forum for Modern Language Studies* 22 (1986), pp. 184–207.

Azevedo, Luíz Gonzaga de, *História de Portugal*, vols. 1–6 (Lisbon, 1935–1944).

Azevedo, Rui Pinto de, 'A expedicão de Almançor a Santiago de Compostela em 997, e a de piratas normandos à Galiza em 1015–16', *Revista Portuguesa de História* 14 (1973), pp. 73–93.

Baldwin, James W., *The Government of Philip Augustus. Foundations of French Royal Power in the Middle Ages* (Berkeley, 1986).

Baranowski, Shelley, 'The 1933 German Protestant Church Elections. *Machtpolitik* or accommodation?', *Church History* 49 (1980), pp. 298–315.

Barber, Malcolm, *The Trial of the Templars* (Cambridge, 1978).

Barber, Malcolm, *The New Knighthood: A History of the Order of the Temple* (Cambridge, 1994).

Barrero García, Ana Maria, 'Orden jurídico e identidad política en los albores de la recepción del derecho comun (sobre los forais de Coimbra, Lisboa y Santarém)', *Hispania* 67 (2007), pp. 827–848.

Barroca, Mário Jorge, 'Da reconquista a D. Dinis', in: Manuel Themudo Barata and Nuno Severiano Teixeira (eds.), *Nova História militar de Portugal*, vol. 1 (Lisbon, 2003), pp. 22–161.

Barros, Henrique da Gama, *História de administrão publica em Portugal nos seculos XII a XV* (Lisbon, 1885–1922).

Bartlett, Robert, and Angus MacKay (eds.), *Medieval Frontier Societies* (Oxford, 1989).

Bartlett, Robert, *The Making of Europe: Conquest, Colonization, and Cultural Change, 950–1350* (London, 1993).

Barton, Simon, *The Aristocracy in Twelfth-Century Leon and Castile* (Cambridge, 1997).

Barton, Simon, 'A Forgotten Crusade: Alfonso VII of Leon-Castile and the Campaign of Jaen (1148)', *Historical Research* 73 (2000), pp. 312–320.

Becker, C.J., 'Magnus den Godes Hedeby-mønter – De første danske erindringsmønter', *Nordisk Numismatisk Unions Medlemsblad* 1983 (1983), pp. 42–47.

Literature 347

Beirante, Maria Ângela, 'A "reconquista" cristã', in: Jean Pierre Leguay, Antonio Henrique R. de Oliveira Marques and Maria Ângela V. da Rocha Beirante (eds.), *Nova história de Portugal*, vol. 2 (Lisbon, 2003), pp. 253–263.

Benninghoven, Friedrich, *Der Orden der Schwertbrüder: Fratres milicie Christi de Livonia* (Cologne, 1965).

Bentley, Michael, 'General Introduction: The Project of Historiography', in: Michael Bentley (ed.), *Companion to Historiography* (London, 1997), pp. xi–xix.

Berend, Nora, *At the Gate of Christendom: Jews, Muslims, and "pagans" in Medieval Hungary, ca. 100a. 1300* (Cambridge, 2001).

Berend, Nora, 'Preface', in: David Abulafia and Nora Berend (eds.), *Medieval Frontiers: Concepts and Practices* (Aldershot, 2002), pp. x–xv.

Berman, Constance Hoffman, *Medieval Agriculture, the Southern French Countryside, and the Early Cistercians, a Study of Fourty-Three Monasteries* (Philadelphia, 1986).

Berry, Virginia G., 'Peter the Venerable and the Crusades', in: G. Constable and J. Kritzeck (eds.), *Petrus Venerabilis, 1156–1956, Studies Commemorating the Eighth Centenary of his Death, Studia Anselmiana* 40 (1956), pp. 141–162.

Berry, Virginia G., 'The Second Crusade', *A History of the Crusades* 1 (1958), pp. 463–512.

Bill, Jan, 'The Cargo Vessels', in: Lars Berggren, Nils Hybel and Anette Landen (eds.), *Cogs, Cargoes, and Commerce: Maritime Bulk Trade in Northern Europe, 1150–1400* (Toronto, 2002), pp. 92–112.

Bill, Jan, 'Castles at Sea. The Warship of the High Middle Ages', in: Anne Nørgard Jørgensen, John Pind, Lars Jørgensen and Birthe Clausen (eds.), *Maritime Warfare in Northern Europe. Technology, Organization, Logistics and Administration 500 BC–1500 AD* (Copenhagen, 2002).Bird, Jessalynn, 'Innocent III, Peter the Chanter's Circle and the Crusade Indulgence: Theory, Implementation and Aftermath', in: Andrea Sommerlechner (ed.), *Innocenzo III: urbs et orbis. Atti del congresso internazionale Roma, 9–15 settembre 1998*, 2 vols. (Rome, 2003), vol. 1, pp. 503–524.

Birkedal Bruun, Mette, *Parables. Bernard of Clairvaux's Mapping of Spiritual Topography* (Leiden, 2007).

Bisgaard, Lars, *Tjenesteideal og fromhedsideal. Studier i adelens tankemåde i dansk senmiddelalder* (Aarhus, 1988).

Bisgaard, Lars, 'Det religiøse liv i senmiddelalderen. En tabt dimension i dansk historieskrivning', in: Per Ingesman and Jens Villiam Jensen (eds.), *Danmark i Senmiddelalderen* (Aarhus, 1994), pp. 342–362.

Bishko, Charles Julian, 'Liturgical intercession at Cluny for the King-Emperors of Leon', *Studia Monastica* 3 (1961), pp. 53–76.

Bishko, Charles Julian, 'Count Henry of Portugal, Cluny, and the Antecedents of the Pacto Succesorio', *Revista Portuguesa de História* 13 (1971), pp. 155–188.

Bishko, Charles Julian, 'The Spanish and Portuguese Reconquest, 1095–1492', in: *A History of the Crusades* 3 (1975), pp. 396–456.

Bishko, Charles Julian, 'Fernando I and the Origins of the Leonese-Castilian Alliance with Cluny', in: C.J. Bishko (ed.), *Studies in Medieval Spanish Frontier History* (London, 1980), pp. 1–136 [1968/69].

Bishko, Charles Julian, 'Portuguese Pactual Monasticism in the Eleventh Century: The Case of São Salvador de Vacariça', in: Homenagem a A.H. de Oliveira Marques (eds.), *Estudios de História de Portugal*, vol. ecs. X–XV. (Lisbon, 1982), pp. 139–154.

Bisson, Thomas, *Tormented Voices* (Cambridge, MA, 1998).

348　　*Literature*

Bloch, Marc, 'Toward a Comparative History of European Societies', in: F.C. Lane and J.C. Riemersma (eds.), *Enterprise and Secular Change. Readings in Economic History* (Homewood, IL, 1953), pp. 494–521 [1928].

Blöcker-Walter, Monica, *Alfons I. von Portugal: Studien zu Geschichte und Sage des Begründers der portugiesischen Unabhängigkeit* (Zürich, 1966).

Blomkvist, Nils, *The Discovery of the Baltic. The Reception of a Catholic World-System in the European North (AD 1075–1225)* (Leiden, 2005).

Blöndal, Sigfús, *The Varangians of Byzantium* (Cambridge, 1978).

Blumenthal, Uta-Renate, *Gregor VII. Papst zwischen Canosa und Kirchenreform* (Darmstadt 2001).Boas, Adrian J., *Crusader Archaeology. The Material Culture of the Latin East* (London, 1999).

Bøgh, Anders, 'Mellem modernisme og middelalder. Dansk middelalderhistorie før og nu', in: E. Christiansen and J.C. Manniche (eds.), *Historiens Ansigter* (Aarhus, 1991) pp. 35–52.

Bøgh, Anders, 'Korståge? Om den nyere korstogsbevægelse i dansk historieskrivning – samt en anmeldelse', *Historie* 108 (2008), pp. 175–187.

Boissellier, Stéphane, *Naissance d'une identité portugaise: la vie rurale entre Tage et Guadiana de l'Islam à la reconquête (Xe–XIVe siécles)* (Lisbon, 1999).

Bolòs, Jordi, 'Changes and Survival: The Territory of Lleida (Catalonia) After the Twelfth Century Conquest', *Journal of Medieval History* 27 (2001), pp. 313–329.

Bonde, N., and K. Christensen, 'Trelleborgs alder. Dendrokronologisk datering', *Aarbøger for Nordisk Oldkyndighed og Historie* 1982 (1984), pp. 111–152.

Borgolte, Michael, 'Perspektiven europaischer Mittelalterhistorie an der Schwelle zum 21. Jahrhundert', in: Michel Borgolte (ed.), *Das europäische Mittelalter im Spannungsbogen des Vergleichs* (Berlin, 2001), pp. 13–27.Braembussche, A.A. van den, 'Historical Explanation and Comparative Method: Towards a Theory of the History of Society', *History and Theory* 28 (1989), pp. 1–24.

Brandão, António, *Terceira parte da Monarchia lusitana* (Lisbon, 1632).

Breide, Henrik, 'Itinerariet. Det historiska dokumentet – en översikt', in: Gerhard Flink (ed.), *Kung Valdemars Segelled* (Stockholm, 1995), pp. 11–23.

Brodman, James William, *Ransoming captives in Crusader Spain. The Order of Merced on the Christian-Islamic Frontier* (Philadelphia, 1986).

Bronisch, Alexander Pierre, *Reconquista und Heiliger Krieg. Die Deutung des Krieges im christlichen Spanien von den Westgoten bis ins frühe 12. Jahrhundert* (Münster, 1998).

Bronisch, Alexander Pierre, ' "Reconquista und Heiliger Krieg". Eine kurze Entgegnung auf eine Kritik von Patrick Henriet', *Francia Forschungen zur westeuropäischen Kultur* 31 (2004), pp. 199–206.

Brundage, James A., 'Cruce Signari: The Rite for Taking the Cross in England', *Traditio* 22 (1966), pp. 289–310.

Brundage, James A., *Medieval Canon Law and the Crusader* (Madison, 1969).

Bruun, Chr., 'Berengaria af Portugal, Valdemar II Sejers Dronning. En Historisk Undersøgelse', *Aarbøger for nordisk Oldkyndighed og Historie*, II, 8 (1893), pp. 46–120.

Buc, Philippe, 'La vengeance de Dieu. De l'exégèse patristique à la réforme écclésiastique et à la première croisade', in: D. Barthélemy, Francois Bougard and Regine Le Jan (eds.), *La vengeance 400–1200* (Rome, 2006), pp. 451–486.

Buchwald, Vagn Fabritius, *Iron and Steel in Ancient Times* (Copenhagen, 2005).

Buchwald, Vagn Fabritius, *Iron, Steel and Cast Iron Before Bessemer* (Copenhagen, 2008).

Buescu, Ana Isabel, *O Milagre de Ourique e a História de Portugal de Alexandre Herculano. Uma Polemica Oitocentista* (Lisbon, 1987).

Literature 349

Bull, Marcus, *Knightly Piety and the Lay Response to the First Crusade: The Limousin and Gascony, ca. 97a. 1130* (Oxford, 1993).

Bull, Marcus, 'Overlapping and Competing Identities in the Frankish First Crusade', in: André Vauchez (ed.), *Le concile de Clermont de 1095 et l'appel à la croisade* (Rome, 1997), pp. 195–211.

Burman, Thomas E., *Religious Polemic and the Intellectual History of the Mozarabs* (Leiden, 1994).

Burman, Thomas E., 'Tafsir and Translation. Traditional Arabic Quran Exegesis and the Latin Qurans of Robert of Ketton and Mark of Toledo', *Speculum* 73 (1998), pp. 703–732.

Burman, Thomas E., *Reading the Qur'ān in Latin Christendom*, 1140–1560 (Philadelphia, 2007).Burns, Robert I., 'Christian-Islamic Confrontation in the West: The Thirteenth-Century Dream of Conversion', *The American Historical Review* 76 (1971), pp. 1386–1434.

Burns, Robert I., 'The Significance of the Frontier in the Middle Ages', in: Robert Bartlett and Angus MacKay (eds.), *Medieval Frontier Societies* (Oxford, 1989), pp. 307–330.

Bynum, Caroline Walker, *Jesus as Mother: Studies in the Spirituality of the High Middle Ages* (Berkeley, 1982).Bysted, Ane L., *The Crusade Indulgence. Spiritual Rewards and the Theology of the Crusades c. 1095–1216* (Leiden, 2015).

Bysted, Ane L., Kurt Villads Jensen, Carsten Selch Jensen, and John Lind, *Jerusalem in the North: Denmark and the Baltic Crusades, 1100–1522* (Turnhout, 2012).

Caetano, Marcelle, *História do direito portugues: Fontes – direito publico (1140–1495)* (Lisbon, 1992).

Cahen, Claude, *Orient et Occident au temps des croisades* (Paris, 1983).

Cahen, Claude, *The Formation of Turkey. The Seljukid Sultanate of Rūm* (Harlow, 2001) [1988].

Cambell, J., *The Hero with a Thousand Faces* (Princeton, NJ, 1949).

Cámera Municipal de Guimarães e Universidade do Minho (ed.), *Actas do 2º Congresso Histórico de Guimarães*, vol. 1–7(Guimarães, 1996).

Carelli, Peter, *En kapitalistisk anda. Kulturella förändringar i 1100-talets Danmark* (Stockholm, 2001).

Carver, Martin (ed.), *The Cross Goes North. Processes of Conversion in Northern Europe, AD 300–1300* (London, 2003).

Castello Branco, Jose Barbosa Canaes de Figueiredo, 'Apontamentos sobre as relações de Portugal com a Syria no seculo 12', *Memorias da Academia real das sciencias de Lisboa. Classe de sciencias moraes, politicas e bellas lettras, nova serie*, tom. 1, parte 1 (1854), pp. 49–97.

Cate, James Lea, 'The Crusade of 1101', *A History of the Crusades* 1 (1958), pp. 343–367.

Catroga, Fernando, and P.A. de Carvalho, *Sociedade e Cultura Portuguesas*, vols. 1–2 (Coimbra, 1996).

Chambers, R.W., and C.L. Wrenn, *Beowulf. An Introduction to the Study of the Poem with a Discussion of the Stories of Offa and Finn* (Cambridge, 1967).

Chekin, Leonid S., *Northern Eurasia in Medieval Cartography: Inventory, Text, Translation, and Commentary* (Turnhout, 2006).

Chenu, M.-D., *Nature, Man and Society in the Twelfth Century. Essays on New Theological Perspectives in the Latin West* (Chicago, 1968).

Chesnutt, Michael, 'The Medieval Danish Liturgy of St Knud Lavard', *Bibliotheca Arnamagnæana* 42 (2003), pp. 1–160.

Christensen, Aksel E., 'En feudal periode i dansk middelalder?', *Scandia* 16 (1944), pp. 45–68.

350   *Literature*

Christensen, Aksel E., *Kongemagt og aristokrati. Epoker i middelalderlig dansk statsopfattelse indtil unionstiden* (Copenhagen, 1945).

Christensen, Aksel E., *Vikingetidens Danmark på oldhistorisk baggrund* (Copenhagen, 1969).

Christensen, C.A., 'Leidang', *KLNM* 10 (1956–1978), pp. 443–459.

Christiansen, E., *The Northern Crusades: The Baltic and the Catholic Frontier 1100–1525* (London, 1980) [New ed. 1997].

Christiansen, E., 'The Place of Fiction in Saxo's Later Books', in: Karsten Friis-Jensen (ed.), *Saxo Grammaticus. A Medieval Author Between Norse and Latin Culture* (Copenhagen, 1981), pp. 27–37.

Christiansen, Tage E., 'Trelleborg og Pine Mølle', *Aarbøger for nordisk Oldkyndighed og Historie* 89 (1989), pp. 9–98.

Ciggar, Krijnie, 'Denmark and Byzantium from 1184–1212. Queen Dagmar's Cross, a Chrysobull of Alexius III and an 'ultramarine' Connection', *Mediaeval Scandinavia* 13 (2000), pp. 118–143.

Cipollone, Giulio (ed.), *La liberazione dei 'captivi' tra cristianitá e islam. Oltre la crociata e il ğihād: Tolleranza e servizio umanitario* (Vatican City, 2000).

Cocheril, Maur, 'Abadias cistercienses portuguesas', *Lusitania Sacra* 4 (1959), pp. 61–92.

Cocheril, Maur, 'D. Afonso Henriques et les premiers cisterciens portugais', *Actas do 2º Congresso Histórico de Guimarães* 5 (1982), pp. 321–332.

Cocheril, Maur, *Routier des abbayes cisterciennes du Portugal*, nouvelle éd. par Gerard Leroux (Paris, 1986).

Collins, R., *The Arab Conquest of Spain 710–797* (Oxford, 1989).

Constable, Giles, 'The Second Crusade as seen by Contemporaries', *Traditio* 9 (1953), pp. 215–279.

Constable, Giles, 'Medieval Charters as a Source for the History of the Crusades', in: Peter Edbury (ed.), *Crusade and Settlement: Papers Read at the First Conference of the Society for the Study of the Crusades and the Latin East and Presented to R.C. Smail* (Cardiff, 1985), pp. 73–89.

Constable, Giles, 'The Place of the Crusader in Medieval Society', *Traditio* 29 (1998), pp. 377–403.

Constable, Giles, 'The Place of the Magdeburg Charter of 1107/08 in the History of Eastern Germany and of the Crusades', in: Franz J. Felten and Nikolas Jaspert (eds.), *Vita religiosa im Mittelalter: Festschrift für Kaspar Elm zum 70. Geburtstag* (Berlin, 1999), pp. 283–299.

Constable, Giles, 'The Historiography of the Crusades', in: Angeliki E. Laiou and Roy Parviz Mottahedeh (eds.), *The Crusades from the Perspective of Byzantium and the Muslim World* (Washington, DC, 2001), pp. 1–22.

Constable, Giles, 'Frontiers in the Middle Ages', in: Outi Merisalo (ed.), *Frontiers in the Middle Ages. Proceedings of the Third European Congress of Medieval Studes, Jyväskylä, 10–14 June 2003* (Louvain-la-Neuve, 2006), pp. 3–28.

Constable, Giles, 'The Historiography of the Crusades', in: Giles Constable (ed.), *Crusaders and Crusading in the Twelfth Century* (Aldershot, 2008), pp. 3–44.

Coope, Jessica A., *The Martyrs of Córdoba: Community and Family Conflict in an Age of Mass Conversion* (Lincoln, 1995).

Cordeiro, Luciano, *A Condessa Mahaut* (Lisbon, 1899).

Cordeiro, Luciano, *Berengela e Leonor, rainhas da Dinamarca* (Lisbon, 1984) [1893].

da Costa, Ricardo Luiz Silveira, *A guerra na Idade Média. Estudo da mentalidade de cruzada na Península Ibérica* (Rio de Janeiro, 1998).

Literature 351

la Cour, Vilhelm, *Danske borganlæg til midten af det trettende århundrede*, 1–2 (Copenhagen, 1972).

Cowdrey, H.E.J., 'The Peace and Truce of God in the Eleventh Century', *Past and Present* 46 (1970), pp. 42–67.

Cowdrey, H.E.J., 'Two Studies in Cluniac History, 1049–1126', *Studi Gregoriani* 11 (1978), pp. 1–298.

Cowdrey, H.E.J., 'Pope Gregor VII's "Crusading" Plans of 1074', in: B. Kedar, H.E. Mayer and R.C. Smail (eds.), *Outremer* (Jerusalem, 1982), pp. 27–40.

Cowdrey, H.E.J., *Pope Gregory VII, 1073–1085* (Oxford, 1998).

Cowdrey, H.E.J., 'Christianity and the Morality of Warfare During the First Century of Crusading', in: Marcus Bull and Norman Housley (eds.), *The Experience of Crusading*, vol. 1 (Cambridge, 2003), pp. 175–192.

Crumlin-Pedersen, Ole, 'Ship Types and Sizes AD 800–1400', in: Ole Crumlin-Pedersen (ed.), *Aspects of Maritime Scandinavia AD 200–1200* (Roskilde, 1991), pp. 69–82.

Cruz, António, *Santa Cruz de Coimbra na cultura portuguesa da Idade Media* (Porto, 1964).

Curtius, Ernst Robert, 'Le Chevalerie Ogier', *Romanische Forschungen* 62 (1950), pp. 125–157.

Cushing, Kathleen, 'Anselm of Lucca and the Doctrine of Coercion: The Legal Impact of the Schism of 1080?', *Catholic Historical Review* 81 (1995), pp. 353–372.

Cushing, Kathleen, *Papacy and Law in the Gregorian Revolution. The Canonistic Work of Anselm of Lucca* (Oxford, 1997).

Dahan, Gilbert, *L'exégèse de la Bible en occident médiéval* (Paris, 1999).

Damsholt, Nanna, *Kvindebilledet i dansk højmiddelalder* (Copenhagen, 1985).

Daniel, Norman, *Islam and the West. The Making of an Image* (Edinburgh, 1960).

Danstrup, John, 'Træk af den politiske magtkamp 1131–82', in: Astrid Friis og Albert Olsen (eds.), *Festskrift til Erik Arup* (Copenhagen, 1946), pp. 67–87.

David, Charles Wendell, 'Narratio de itinere navali peregrinorum Hierosolymam tendentium et Silviam capientium A.D. 1189', *Proceedings of the American Philosophical Society* 81, 5 (1939), pp. 592–675.

David, Pierre, *Études historiques sur la Galice et le Portugal du VIe au XIIe siècle* (Lisbon, 1947).

Davidsen, Helle Munkholm, *Litteratur og Encyklopædi. Semiotiske og kognitive aspekter af den litterare teksts mening* (Odense, 2006).

Davidson, Ellis, *The Viking Road to Byzantium* (London, 1976).

Dawkins, R.M., 'The Later History of the Varangian Guard: Some Notes', *The Journal of Roman Studies* 37 (1947), pp. 39–46.

Dehaisnes, Chrétien César Auguste, *Les annales de Saint-Bertin et de Saint-Vaast: suivies de fragments d'une chronique inédite, pub. avec des annotations et les variantes des manuscrits, pour la Société de l'histoire de France* (Paris, 1871).

DeVries, Kelly, 'God and Defeat in Medieval Warfare: Some Preliminary Thoughts', in: Donald J. Kagay and L.J. Andrew Villalon (eds.), *The Circle of War in the Middle Ages. Essays on Medieval Military and Naval History* (Woodbridge, 1999), pp. 87–97.

Dias, Isabel de Barros, 'Ares, Marte, Odin . . . ', in: A. Ward (ed.), *Teoria y practica de la historiografía medieval* (Birmingham, 2000), pp. 80–93.

Dias, Isabel de Barros, *Metamorfoses de Babel. A istoriografia ibérica (secs. XIII–XIV): Construções e estratégias textuais* (Lisbon, 2003).

Dias, Isabel de Barros, 'Cronística afonsina modelada em português: um case de recepção activa', *Hispania* 67 (2007), pp. 899–928.

352 *Literature*

Dinzelbacher, Peter, *Bernhard von Clairvaux: Leben und Werk des berühmten Zisterziensers* (Darmstadt, 1998).

Disney, A.R., *A History of Portugal and the Portuguese Empire. From Beginnings to 1807* (Cambridge, 2009).

Dobat, Andres Minos, 'A contested heritage – the Dannevirke as a mirror and object of military and political history', in: Michael Bregnsbo and Kurt Villads Jensen (eds.), *Schleswig Holstein – Contested Region(s) Through History* (Odense, 2016), pp. 193-218.

Donat, Peter, Heike Reimann, and Cornelia Willich, *Slawische Siedlung und Landesausbau im nordwestlichen Mecklenburg* (Stuttgart, 1999).

Donner, Gustav A., *Kardinal Wilhelm von Sabina. Bishop von Modena 1222–1234: Päpstlicher Legat in den nordischen Länder* (Helsinki, 1929).

Donovan, Joseph P., *Pelagius and the Fifth Crusade* (Philadelphia, 1950).

Dotson, John E., 'Ship Types and Fleet Composition at Genoa and Venice in the Early Thirteenth Century', in: John H. Pryor (ed.), *Logistics of Warfare in the Age of the Crusades* (Aldershot, 2006), pp. 63–75.

Doxey, Gary B., 'Norwegian Crusaders and the Balearic Islands', *Scandinavian Studies* 68 (1996), pp. 139–160.

Duedahl, Poul, 'Når begreber dræber. En begrebshistorisk analyse af racebegrebet', in: Per H. Hansen and Jeppe Nevers (eds.), *Historiefagets teoretiske udfordring* (Odense, 2004), pp. 107–127.

Dujčev, Ivan, 'Les Normands a Byzance et dans la peninsule des Balkans', in: Knud Hannestad, Knud Jordal, and Ole Klindt-Jensen (eds.), *Varangian Problems. Report on the First International Symposium on the Theme "The Easter Connections of the Nordic Peoples in the Viking Period and the Early Middle Ages"* (Copenhagen, 1970), pp. 201–208.

Dunbabin, Jean, *Captivity and Imprisonment in Medieval Europe 1000–1300* (Houndmills, 2000).

Durand, Robert, *Les campagnes portugaises entre Douro et Tage aux XIIe et XIIIe siècles* (Paris, 1982).

Eco, Umberto, *The Role of the Reader* (Bloomington, 1979).

Edginton, Susan B., 'The Lisbon Letter of the Second Crusade', *Historical Research* 69 (1996), pp. 336–339.

Edginton, Susan B., 'Albert of Aachen, St Bernard and the Second Crusade', in: Jonathan Phillips and Martin Hoch (eds.), *The Second Crusade. Scope and Consequences* (Manchester, 2001), pp. 54–70.

Edinton, Susan B., 'The First Crusade in Post-War Fiction', in: Marcus Bull and Norman Housley (eds.), *The Experience of Crusading, Western Approaches*, vol. 1 (Cambridge, 2003), pp. 255–280.

Edson, Evelyn, *Mapping Time and Space. How Medieval Mapmakers Viewed Their World* (London, 1997).

Eichenberger, Thomas, *Patria. Studien zur Bedeutung des Wortes im Mittelalter (6.-12. Jahrhundert)* (Sigmaringen, 1991).

Ekdahl, Sven, 'Die Rolle der Ritterorden bei der Christianisierung der Liven und Letten', in: Pontificio Comitato di Scienze Storiche (ed.), *Gli Inizi Del Christianesimo in Livonia-Lettonia* (Vatican City, 1989), pp. 203–243.

Ekdahl, Sven, 'Horses and Crossbows: Two Important Warfare Advantages of the Teutonic Order in Prussia', in: Helen Nicholson (ed.), *The Military Orders*, vols. 1–2 (Aldershot, 1998), vol. 2, pp. 119–151.

Literature 353

Ekdahl, Sven, 'Crusades and Colonisation in the Baltic: A Historiographic Analysis', XIX *Rocznik Instytutu Polsko-Skandynawskiego 2003/2004* 19 (2004), pp. 1–42.

Ekdahl, Sven, 'Review of William Urban, *The Teutonic Knights: A Military History* (Pennsylvania, 2003)', *Crusades* 4 (2005), pp. 193–195.

Ellenblum, Ronnie, 'Frankish and Muslim Siege Warfare and the Construction of Frankish Concentric Castles', in: Michel Balard, Benjamin Z. Kedar and Jonathan Riley-Smith (eds.), *Dei gesta per francos. Etudes sur les croisades dédiées à Jean Richard* (Aldershot, 2001), pp. 187–198.

Enemark, Poul, 'Hestehandel', *KLNM* 6 (1956–1978), pp. 524–532.

Engels, Odilo, *Reconquista und Landesherrschaft. Studien zur Rechts- und Verfassungsgeschichte Spaniens im Mittelalter* (Paderborn, 1989).

Englert, Anton, *Large Cargo Vessels in Danish Waters AD 1000–1250.* Unpublished PhD dissertation (Kiel University, 2000).

Epp, Verena, *Fulcher von Chartres: Studien zur Geschichtsschreibung des ersten Kreuzzuges* (Düsseldorf, 1990).

Erdmann, Carl, *Das Papsttum und Portugal im ersten Jahrhundert der portugiesischen Geschichte* (Berlin, 1928).

Erdmann, Carl, *O papado e Portugal no primeiro século da História Portuguesa* (Coimbra, 1935).

Erdmann, Carl, 'Der Kreuzzugsgedanke in Portugal', *Historische Zeitschrift* 141 (1930), pp. 23–53.

Erdmann, Carl, *Die Entstehung des Kreuzzugsgedankens* (Stuttgart, 1935).

Erdmann, Carl, *A Idea de Cruzada em Portugal* (Coimbra, 1940).

Erkens, Franz-Reiner, 'Vicarius Christi – sacratissimus legislator – sacra majestas. Religiöse Herrschaftslegitimierung im Mittelalter', *Zeitschrift der Savigny Stiftungfür Rechtsgeschichte: Kanonistische Abteilung* 89 (2002), pp. 1–55.

Erslev, Kristian, *Danmarks Riges Historie*, vol. 2 (Copenhagen, 1898–1905).

Erslev, Kristian, 'Europæisk Feudalisme og dansk Lensvæsen', *Historisk Tidsskrift* 7. Rk. 2 (1899), pp. 247–305.

Erslev, Kristian, *Vort Slægtleds Arbejde i dansk Historie. Rektortale ved Københavns Universitets Aarsfest 16. November 1911* (Copenhagen, 1922).

Ewald, P., 'Die Papstbriefe der Brittschen Sammlung', *Neues Archiv der Gesellschaft für ältere deutsche Geschichte* 5/2 (1880), pp. 277–596.

Fabricius, A., *Forbindelserne mellem Norden og den Spanske Halvø i ældre Tider* (Copenhagen, 1882).

Feldbæk, Ole (ed.), *Dansk Identitetshistorie*, vols. 1–4 (Copenhagen, 1991–1993).

Ferreiro, Alberto, 'The Siege of Barbastro 1064–65: A Reassessment', *Journal of Medieval History* 9 (1983), pp. 129–144.

Filipowiak, Władysław, 'Wolin – Jomsborg – Vineta', in: Michael Andersen (ed.), *Mare Balticum. Ostersøen, myte, historie, kunst i 1000 år* (Copenhagen, 2002), pp. 21–34.

Fischer, Mary, 'The Books of the Maccabees and the Teutonic Order', *Crusades* 4 (2005), pp. 59–71.

Fletcher, Richard A., *Saint James' Catapult: The Life and Times of Diego Gelmirez of Santiago de Compostela* (Oxford, 1984).

Fletcher, Richard A., 'Reconquest and Crusade in Spain ca. 1050–1150', *Transactions of the Royal Historical Society* 37 (1987), pp. 31–47.

Fletcher, Richard A., *The Quest for el Cid* (Oxford, 1989).

Fletcher, Richard A., *Moorish Spain* (London, 1992).

354 Literature

Flint, Valerie I.J., 'The Hereford Map: Its Author(s), Two Scenes and a Border', *Transactions of the Royal Historical Society* 6. ser. 8 (1998), pp. 19–44.

Flori, Jean, *Croisade et chevalerie: XIe-XIIe siécles* (Bruxelles, 1998).

Flori, Jean, *La guerre sainte. La formation de l'idée de croisade dans l'Occident chrétien* (Paris, 2001).

Floto, Henning, *Der Rechtsstatus des Johanniterordens. Eine rechtsgeschichtliche und rechtsdogmatische Untersuchung zum Rechtsstatus der Balley Brandenburg des ritterlichen Ordens St. Johannis vom Spital zu Jerusalem* (Berlin, 2003).

Floto, Inga, 'Erik Arup og hans kritikere', *Historisk Tidsskrift* 78 (1978), pp. 474–498.

Folda, Jaroslav, 'Art in the Latin East, 1098–1291', in: J. Riley-Smith (ed.), *Oxford Illustrated History of the Crusades* (Oxford, 1995), pp. 141–159.

Fonnesberg-Schmidt, Iben, *The Popes and the Baltic Crusades 1147–1254* (Leiden, 2007).

Forey, A.J., *The Templars in the Corona de Aragon* (London, 1973).

Forey, A.J., 'The Second Crusade: Scope and Objectives', *Durham University Journal* 86 (1994), pp. 165–175.

Forey, A.J., 'The Military Orders and the Conversion of Muslims in the Twelfth and Thirteenth Centuries', *Journal of Medieval History* 28 (2002), pp. 1–22.

Forey, A.J., 'The Siege of Lisbon and the Second Crusade', *Portuguese Studies* 20 (2004), pp. 1–13.

Forey, A.J., 'Henry II's Crusading Penances for Becket's Murder', *Crusades* 7 (2008), pp. 153–164.

Forte, Angelo, Richard Oram, and Frederik Pedersen, *Viking Empires* (Cambridge, 2005).

France, John, *Western Warfare in the Age of the Crusades, 1000–1300* (Ithaca, 1999).

France, John, 'Holy War and Holy Men: Erdmann and the Lives of the Saints', in: Marcus Bull and Norman Housley (eds.), *The Experience of Crusading, Western Approaches* (Cambridge, 2003), pp. 193–208.

Franco Júnior, Hilário, *Peregrinos, Monges e Guerreiros. Feudo-clericalismo e religiosidade em Castela medieval* (São Paulo, 1990).

Frandsen, Karl-Erik, *Vang og tagt. Studier over dyrkningssystemer og agrarstrukturer i Danmarks landsbyer 1682–83* (Esbjerg, 1983).

Frank, Roberta, 'King Cnut in the Verse of His Skalds', in: Alexander R. Rumble (ed.), *The Reign of Cnut: King of England, Denmark and Norway* (London, 1994) pp. 106–124.

Franklin, Simon, and Jonathan Shepard, *The Emergence of Rus, 750–1200* (London, 1996).

Frantzen, Ole L., and Knud J.V. Jespersen (eds.), *Danmarks Krigshistorie*, vols. 1–2 (Copenhagen, 2008).

Fritzbøger, Bo, 'Esrum Klosters landskaber', in: Søren Frandsen, Jens Anker Jørgensen and Chr. Gorm Tortzen (eds.), *Bogen om Esrum Kloster* (Frederiksborg, 1997), pp. 79–97.

Fryde, Natalie, Pierre Monnet, and Otto Gerhard Oexle (eds.), *Die Gegenwart des Feudalismus* (Göttingen, 2002).

Gaethke, Hans-Otto, *Herzog Heinrich der Löwe und die Slawen nordöstlich der unteren Elbe* (Frankfurt a.M., 1999).

Gallén, Jarl, *La Province de Dacia de l'Ordre des Frères-Precheurs* (Helsinki, 1946).

Gallén, Jarl, 'Les voyages de S. Dominique au Danemark. Essai de datation', in: Faymundus Creytens O.P. et Pius Kunzle O.P. (eds.), *Xenia Medii Aevi Historiam illustrantia oblata Thomae Kaeppeli O.P.* (Rome, 1978), pp. 73–84.

Gallén, Jarl, *Det "danska itinerariet." Franciskansk expansionsstrategi i Östersjön* (Helsinki, 1993).

Galster, Georg, 'Danske efterligninger af fremmed mønt fra nyere tid', *Nationalmuseets Arbejdsmark* (1959), pp. 109–122.García, José Manuel Rodriguez, 'Historiografía de las Cruzadas', *Espacio, Tiempo y Forma*, Ser. 3, H.a Medieval 13 (2000), pp. 341–395.

Literature 355

García-Guijarro Ramos, Luis, 'Expansion economica medieval y cruzadas', in: Luis García-Guijarro Ramos (ed.), *La primera cruzada, novecientos años despues: el concilio de Clermont y los orígenes del movimiento cruzado* (Madrid, 1997), pp. 155–166.

García y García, Antonio, *Estudios sobre la canonistica portuguesa medieval* (Madrid, 1976).

Gaudemet, Jean, *Le mariage en occident: les moeurs et le droit* (Paris, 1987).

Gaudio, Michael, 'Matthew Paris and the Cartography of the Margins', *Gesta* 39 (2000), pp. 50–57.

Gaztambide, Jose Goñi, *Historia de la Bula de la Cruzada en España* (Vitoria, 1958).

Gelting, Michael H., 'Europæisk feudalisme og dansk 1100–1200-tal', in: Poul Enemark (ed.), *Kongemagt og Samfund i middelalderen. Festskrift til Erik Ulsig* (Aarhus, 1988), pp. 3–17.

Gelting, Michael H., 'Det komparative aspekt i dansk højmiddelalderforskning. Om Familia og familie, Lid, Leding og Landevarn', *Historisk Tidsskrift* 99 (1999), pp. 146–188.

Gervers, Michael (ed.), *The Second Crusade and the Cistercians* (New York, 1992).

Gissel, Svend (ed.), *Falsterundersøgelsen*, vols. 1–2 (Odense, 1989).

Gladitz, Charles, *Horse Breeding in the Medieval World* (Dublin, 1997).

Glick, Thomas F., *Islamic and Christian Spain in the Early Middle Ages* (Leiden, 2005).

Glick, Thomas F., and Oriol Pi-Sunyer, 'Acculturation as an Explanatory Concept in Spanish History', *Comparative Studies in Society and History* 11 (1969), pp. 136–154.Goetz, Hans-Werner, *Moderne Mediavistik. Stand und Perspektiven der Mittelalterforschung* (Darmstadt, 1999).

Gomes, Saul António, *Introdução á história do castelo de Leiria* (Leiria, 1995).

Gomes, Saul António, 'A produção artesanal' and 'Grupos étnico-religiosos e estrangeiros', in: Maria Helena da Cruz Coelho and Armando Luís de Carvalho Homem (eds.), *Nova História de Portugal*, vol. 3 (Lisbon, 1996), pp. 309–383, 476–486.

Gomes, Saul António, 'Coimbra: centro das Religiões Abraâmicas', *Semente em Boa Terra. Raizes do Cristianismo na Diocese de Coimbra. Do século IV a 1064* (Coimbra, 2000), pp. 120–133.

Gomes, Saul António, 'Um Formulário Monástico Português Medieval: o Manuscrito alcobacense 47 da BNL', *Humanitas* 51 (1999), pp. 141-184, edition on pp. 159-184.

Gomes, Saul António, 'Entre memória e história: os primeiros tempos da Abadia de Santa Maria de Alcobaça (1152–1215)', *Revista de Historia da Sociedade e da Cultura* 2 (2002), pp. 187–256.

Gomes, Saul António, *In limine conscriptionis. Documentos, Chancelaria e Cultura no mosteiro de Santa Cruz de Coimbra (Séculos XII a XIV)* (Viseu, 2007).

González Fernández, Fidel, 'El contexto historico de la 'reconquista' española y la Orden trinitaria (Ordo Sanctae Trinitatis et Captivorum)', in: Giulio Cipollone (ed.), *La liberazione dei 'captivi' tra cristianità e islam. Oltre la crociata e il ğihād: Tolleranza e servizio umanitario* (Vatican City, 2000), pp. 131–159.

Gotfredsen, Lise, '. . . og jorden skælver, da de rider frem', *Århus Stifts årbog* 21 (1983), pp. 79–99.

Gotfredsen, Lise, and Hans Jørgen Frederiksen, *Troens Billeder. Romansk kunst i Danmark* (Copenhagen, 2003) [1987].

Guiance, Ariel, 'To Die for Country, Land or Faith in Castilian Medieval Thought', *Journal of Medieval History* 24 (1998), pp. 313–332.

Guincho, Maria dos Anjos Brandão Maurício, 'Le premier roi de Portugal, prisonnier de ses premiers mots: essay d'analyse du recit *De expugnatione scalabris*', in: Danielle Buschinger (ed.), *La Guerre au moyen age: Réalité et fiction* (Amiens, 2000), pp. 69–81.

356   Literature

Hagemann, Ludwig, 'Die erste lateinische Koranübersetzung – Mittel zur Verständigung zwischen Christen und Muslimen im Mittelalter?', in: A. Zimmermann and I. Craemer-Ruegenberg (eds.), *Orientalische Kultur und europäisches Mittelalter* (Leiden, 1985), pp. 45–58.

Halding, Helle, *Thi de var af stor slægt. Om Hvideslægten og kongemagt i dansk højmiddelalder* (Ebeltoft, 2001).

Halvorson, Eyvind Fjeld, 'Karlamagnus saga', *KLNM* 8 (Copenhagen, 1956–1978), pp. 286–290.

Hammerich, Fr., *Danmark i Valdemarernes Tid (1157–1375). En historisk Skildring* (Copenhagen, 1860).

Hannestad, Knud, *Korstogene. Et møde mellem to kulturer* (Copenhagen, 1963).

Hannestad, Knud, Knud Jordal, and Ole Klindt-Jensen (eds.), Varangian Problems. Report on the First International Symposium on the Theme "The Easter Connections of the Nordic Peoples in the Viking Period and the Early Middle Ages" (Copenhagen, 1970).

Hansen, Poul Grinder, *Venderne i Danmark. En diskussion af forskning og kilder om venderne i Danmark indtil omkring 1200.* Unpublished dissertation, University of Copenhagen (Copenhagen, 1983).

Hanska, Jussi, *"And the Rich Man also died; and He was buried in Hell." The Social Ethos in Mendicant Sermons* (Helsinki, 1997).

Harris, Julie A., 'Mosque to Church Conversions in the Spanish Reconquest', *Medieval Encounters* 3 (1997), pp. 158–172.

Harrison, Robert P., *Forests: The Shadow of Civilization* (Chicago, 1992).

Hatt Olsen, Thomas, 'The Priory of Dacia in the Order of Saint John of Jerusalem', *Annales de l'ordre souverain militaire de Malte* 18, 4 (1960), pp. 19–33.

Haupt, Heinz-Gerhard, and Jurgen Kocka, 'Historischer Vergleich: Methoden, Aufgaben, Probleme. Eine Einleitung', in: Heinz-Gerhard Haupt and Jürgen Kocka (eds.), *Geschichte und Vergleich. Ansätze und Ergebnisse international vergleichender Geschichtsschreibung* (Frankfurt a.M., 1996), pp. 9–45.

Head, Thomas, and Richard Landes (eds.), *The Peace of God. Social Violence and Religious Response in France Around the Year 1000* (Ithaca, 1992).

Hehl, E.-D., *Kirche und Krieg im 12. Jahrhundert. Studien zu Kanonischem Recht und Politischer Wirklichkeit* (Stuttgart, 1980).

Heiberg, Steffen, *Christian IV og Europa: Den 19. Europarådsudstilling Danmark 1988* (Copenhagen, 1988).

Hemmingsen, Lars, 'Middelaldergeografien og Historia Norwegie', in: Inger Ekrem, Lars Boje Mortensen and Karen Skovgaard-Petersen (eds.), *Olavslegenden og den latinske historieskrivning i 1100-tallets Norge* (Copenhagen, 2000), pp. 26–53.

Hemptinne, Thérèse de, 'Les épouses des croisés et pèlerins flamands aus XIe et XIIe siècles: L'exemple des comtesses de Flandre Clémence et Sibylle', in: Michel Balard (ed.), *Autour de la première croisade. Actes du Colloque de la Society for the Study of the Crusades and the Latin East (Clermont-Ferrand, 22–25 juin 1995)* (Paris, 1996), pp. 83–95.

Henriet, Patrick, 'Hagiographie et politique à Leon au début du XIIIe siécle: Les chanoines réguliers de Saint-Isidore et la prise de Baeza', *Revue Mabillon* 69 (1997), pp. 53–82.

Henriet, Patrick, 'L'idéologie de guerre sainte dans le haut moyen âge hispanique', *Francia Forschungen zur westeuropäischen Kultur* 29 (2002), pp. 171–220.

Herculano, Alexandre, *História de Portugal desde o começo da monarquia até o fim do reinado de Afonso III* (Lisbon, 1980) [1846–53].

Hermanson, Lars, *Släkt, vänner och makt. En studie av elitens politiska kultur i 1100-tallets Danmark* (Göteborg, 2000).

Literature   357

Hiestand, Rudolf, 'Reconquista, Kreuzzug und heiliges Grab. Die Eroberung von Tortosa 1148 im Lichte eines neuen Zeugnisses', *Gesammelte Aufsätze zur Kulturgeschichte Spaniens* 31 (1984), pp. 136–157.

Hiestand, Rudolf, 'Kardinalbischof Matthäus von Albano, das Konzil von Troyes und die Entstehung des Tempelordens', *Zeitschrift fur Kirchengeschichte* 99 (1988), pp. 295–325.

Hiestand, Rudolf, 'The Papacy and the Second Crusade', in: Jonathan Phillips and Martin Hoch (eds.), *The Second Crusade. Scope and Consequences* (Manchester, 2001), pp. 32–53.

Hill, Thomas, 'Von der Konfrontation zur Assimilation. Das Ende der Slawen in Ostholstein, Lauenburg und Lübeck vom 12. bis zum 15. Jahrhundert', in: Michael Müller-Wille, Dietrich Meier and Henning Unverhau (eds.), *Slawen und Deutsche um südlichen Ostseeraum vom 11. bis zum 16. Jahrhundert. Archäologische, historische und sprachwissenschaftliche Beispiele aus Schleswig-Holstein, Mecklenburg und Pommern* (Neumünster, 1995), pp. 79–104.

Hofstadter, Richard, *The Progressive Historians. Turner, Beard, Parrington* (London, 1969).

Holdsworth, Christopher, 'An "Airier Aristocracy": The Saints at War', *Transactions of the Royal Historical Society* 6 (1996), pp. 103–122.

Holm, Poul, 'The Slavetrade of Dublin, ninth to twelfth Century', *Peritia* 5 (1988), pp. 317–345.

Holmberg, B., 'Maritime Place-Names', in: Ole Crumlin-Pedersen (ed.), *Aspects of Maritime Scandinavia AD 200–1200* (Roskilde, 1991), pp. 233–240.

Holmberg, B., and J. Skamby Madsen, 'Da kom en snekke . . . Havnepladser fra 1000- og 1100-tallet?', *KUML. Årbog for Jysk Arkæologisk Selskab* (1997/1998), pp. 197–225.

Holmqvist-Larsen, Niels Henrik, 'Saxo Grammaticus in Danish Historical Writing and Literature', in: Brian P. McGuire (ed.), *The Birth of Identities. Denmark and Europe in the Middle Ages* (Copenhagen, 1996), pp. 161–188.

Homem, Armando Luís Carvalho, 'O medievismo em Liberdade: Portugal, Anos 70 / Anos 90', *Signum* 3 (2001), pp. 173–207.

Housley, Norman, *Contesting the Crusades* (Oxford, 2006).

Huizinga, Johan, *The Waning of the Middle Ages: A Study of the Forms of Life, Thought and Art in France and the Netherlands in the Fourteenth and Fifteenth Centuries* (Harmondsworth, 1955) [1919].

Huntington, Samuel P., 'The Clash of Civilizations?', *Foreign Affairs* 72, 3 (1993), pp. 22–49.

Huntington, Samuel P., *The Clash of Civilizations and the Remaking of World Order* (London, 2002) [1996].

Husmann, Heinrich, 'Sinn und Wesen der Tropen veranschaulicht an den Introitustropen des Weihnachtsfestes', *Archiv für Musikwissenschaft* 16 (1959), pp. 135–147.

Hybel, Nils, 'Dansk eksport på det nordeuropæiske marked ca. 1200–1350', in: Per Ingesman and Bjørn Poulsen (eds.), *Danmark og Europa i senmiddelalderen* (Aarhus, 2000), pp. 183–197.

Hybel, Nils, and Bjørn Poulsen, *The Danish Resources ca. 1000–1550. Growth and Recession* (Leiden, 2007).

Hyland, Ann, *The Medieval Warhorse from Byzantium to the Crusades* (Stroud, 1994).

Ilkjær, Jørgen, *Illerup Ådal* (Højbjerg, 2000).

Ingesman, Per, 'Radikalisme og religion i dansk middelalderforskning. En fagtraditions magt i historiografisk lys', *Fønix* 16 (1992), pp. 45–62.

358   *Literature*

Ingesman, Per, and Thomas Lindkvist (eds.), *Norden og Europa i middelalderen. Rapporter til Det 24. Nordiske Historikermøde, Århus 9–13. August 2001* (Aarhus, 2001).

Isla, Amancio, 'Warfare and Other Plagues in the Iberian Peninsula Around the Year 1000', in: Przemysław Urbańczyk (ed.), *Europe Around the Year 1000* (Warsaw, 2001), pp. 233–246.

Jaspert, Nikolas, *Stift und Stadt. Das Heiliggrabpriorat von Santa Anna und das Regularkanonikerstift Santa Eulàlia del Camp im mittelalterlichen Barcelona, 1145–1423* (Berlin, 1996).

Jaspert, Nikolas, 'Die Ritterorden und der Orden vom heiligen Grab auf der iberischen Halbinsel', *Militia Sancti Sepulcri: idea e istituzioni; atti del colloquio internazionale* (Vatican City, 1998), pp. 381–410.

Jaspert, Nikolas, 'Capta est Dertosa, clavis Christianorum: Tortosa and the crusades', in: Jonathan Phillips and Martin Hoch (eds.), *The Second Crusade. Scope and Consequences* (Manchester, 2001), pp. 90–110.

Jaspert, Nikolas, 'Frühformen der geistlichen Ritterorden und die Kreuzzugsbewegung auf der Iberischen Halbinsel', in: Klaus Herbers (ed.), *Europa an der Wende vom 11. zum 12. Jahrhundert. Beitrage zu Ehren von Werner Goetz* (Stuttgart, 2001), pp. 90–116.

Jaspert, Nikolas, 'Vergegenwärtigungen Jerusalems in Architektur und Reliquienkult', in: Dieter Bauer, Klaus Herbers and Nikolas Jaspert (eds.), *Jerusalem im Hoch- und Spätmittelalter. Konflikte und Konfliktbewältigung – Verstellungen und Vergegenwärtigungen* (Frankfurt a.M., 2001), pp. 219–270.

Jensen, Bernhard Eric, *Historie – livsverden og fag* (Copenhagen, 2003).

Jensen, Carsten Selch, 'Valdemar Sejr, korstogsbevægelsen og den pavelige reformpolitik i 1200-tallets første halvdel', *Historisk Tidsskrift* 102 (2002), pp. 23–54.

Jensen, Janus Møller, 'Danmark og den hellige krig. En undersøgelse af Korstogsbevægelsens indflydelse på Danmark ca. 1070–1169', *Historisk Tidsskrift* 100 (2000), pp. 285–328.

Jensen, Janus Møller, 'War, Penance, and the First Crusade. Dealing with a "Tyrannical Construct"', in: Tuomas M.S. Lehtonen and Kurt Villads Jensen with Janne Malkki and Katja Ritari (eds.), *Medieval History Writing and Crusading Ideology* (Helsinki, 2005), pp. 51–63.

Jensen, Janus Møller, *Denmark and the Crusades, 1400–1650* (Leiden, 2007).

Jensen, Janus Møller, 'King Erik Emune (1134–1137) and the Crusades. The Impact of Crusadig Ideology on Early Twelfth-Century Denmark', in: Kurt villads Jensen, Kirsi Salonen and Helle Vogt (eds.), *Cultural Encounters during the Crusades* (Odense, 2013), pp. 91–104.

Jensen, Jørgen, *Danmarks oldtid*, vols. 1–4 (Copenhagen, 2001–2004).

Jensen, Kurt Villads, 'Bellum Iustum i 1200-tallets vesteuropæiske tænkning og kirkens fred', *Historisk Tidsskrift* 93 (1993), pp. 30–46.

Jensen, Kurt Villads, 'Den hvide race og den danske jord', *Historie* (1998), pp. 92–103.

Jensen, Kurt Villads, 'Denmark and the Crusading Movement. The Integration of the Baltic Region into Medieval Europe', in: A.I. Macinnes, T. Riis and F.G. Pedersen (eds.), *Ships, Guns and Bibles in the North Sea and the Baltic States, ca. 1350-c.1700* (East Linton, 2000), pp. 188–205.

Jensen, Kurt Villads, 'Korstogstanken i dansk senmiddelalder', in: Per Ingesman and Bjørn Poulsen (eds.), *Danmark og Europa i Senmiddelalderen* (Aarhus, 2000), pp. 39–63.

Jensen, Kurt Villads, 'Thi ath alle som tage swerd/de skulle dø met swerd. Matt. 26,52 hos Augustin, Innocens III og danske middelalderhistorikere', *Fønix* 24 (2000), pp. 66–78.

Literature 359

Jensen, Kurt Villads, 'The Blue Baltic Border of Denmark in the High Middle Ages: Danes, Wends and Saxo Grammaticus', in: David Abulafia and Nora Behrend (eds.), *Medieval Frontiers: Concepts and Practices* (Aldershot, 2002), pp. 173–193.

Jensen, Kurt Villads, 'Knudsgilder og korstog', in: Lars Bisgaard and Leif Søndergaard (eds.), *Gilder, lav og broderskaber i middelalderens Danmark* (Odense, 2002), pp. 63–88.

Jensen, Kurt Villads, 'Introduction', in: Tuomas M.S. Lehtonen and Kurt Villads Jensen with Janne Malkki and Katja Ritari (eds.), *Medieval History Writing and Crusading Ideology* (Helsinki, 2005), pp. 16–33.

Jensen, Kurt Villads, 'Broderliste, Vederlov og Holger Danske', in: Janus Møller Jensen (ed.), *Broderliste, Broderskab, Korstog* (Odense, 2006), pp. 203–214.

Jensen, Kurt Villads, 'Bring dem Herrn ein blutiges Opfer. Gewalt und Mission in der dänischen Ostsee-Expansion des 12. und 13. Jarhunderts', in: H. Kamp and M. Kroker (eds.), *Schwertmission. Gewalt und Christianisierung im Mittelalter* (Paderborn, 2013), pp. 139–157.

Jørgensen, Claus Møller, 'Patterns of Professionalization and Institutionalization in Denmark from 1848 to the Present', in: Frank Meyer and Jan Eivind Myhre (eds.), *Nordic Historiography in the 20th Century* (Oslo, 2000), pp. 114–148.

Jørgensen, Ellen, 'Fra svenske Biblioteker', *Kirkehistoriske Samlinger* 5. Rk., 5. Bd. (1909–1911), pp. 771–786.

Jørgensen, Ellen, *Historiens Studium i Danmark i det 19. Aarhundrede* (Copenhagen, 1943).

Jørgensen, Poul Johs., *Dansk Retshistorie. Retskildernes og Forfatningsrettens Historie indtil sidste Halvdel af det 17. Aarhundrede* (Copenhagen, 1940).

Kahl, H.-D., 'Crusade Eschatology as seen by St Bernard in the Years 1146 to 1148', in: Michael Gervers (ed.), *The Second Crusade and the Cistercians* (New York, 1992), pp. 35–47.

Kangas, Sini, *Deus vult: Images of Crusader Ciolence ca. 1095–1100*, Unpublished PhD-dissertation, Department of History (Helsinki University, 2007).

Kantorowicz, Ernst, 'The "King's Advent": And the Enigmatic Panels in the Doors of Santa Sabina', *The Art Bulletin* 26 (1944), pp. 207–231.

Kantorowicz, Ernst, 'Pro Patria Mori in Medieval Political Thought', *American Historical Review* 56 (1951), pp. 472–492.

Kassis, Hanna E., 'Muslim Revival in Spain in the Fifth/Eleventh Century. Causes and Ramifications', *Islam* 67 (1990), pp. 78–110.

Kedar, B.Z., *Crusade and Mission: European Approaches Toward the Muslims* (Princeton, NJ, 1984).

Kedar, B.Z., 'The Jerusalem Massacre of July 1099 in the Western Historiography of the Crusades', *Crusades* 3 (2004), pp. 15–75.

Kemp, E.W., 'Pope Alexander III and the Canonization of Saints', *Transactions of the Royal Historical Society* 27 (1945), pp. 13–28.

Kennedy, Hugh, *Crusader Castles* (Cambridge, 1994).

Kennedy, Hugh, *Muslim Spain and Portugal: A Political History of al-Andalus* (London, 1996).

Kienzle, Beverly Mayne, *Cistercians, Heresy and Crusade in Occitania, 1145–1229. Preaching in the Lord's Vineyard* (York, 2001).

Kline, Naomi Reed, *Maps of Medieval Thought. The Hereford Paradigm* (London, 2005).

Knappen, M.M., 'Robert II of Flanders in the First Crusade', in: Louis J. Paetow (ed.), *The Crusades and Other Historical Essays Presented to Dana C. Munro by His Former Students* (New York, 1928), pp. 79–100.

360 Literature

Knoch, Peter, 'Kreuzzug und Siedlung. Studien zum Aufruf der magdeburger Kirche von 1108', *Jahrbuch für die Geschichte Mittel- und Ostdeutschlands* 23 (1974), pp. 1–33.

Koch, Hal, *Kongemagt og Kirke 1060–1241* (Copenhagen, 1963).

Kocka, Jürgen, 'Comparison and Beyond', *History and Theory* 42 (2003), pp. 39–44.

Koht, Halvdan, 'The Dawn of Nationalism in Europe', *The American Historical Review* 52 (1947), pp. 265–280.

Koselleck, Reinhart, *Zeitschichten. Studien zur Historik* (Frankfurt a.M., 2000).

Kossinna, Gustaf, *Ursprung und Verbreitung der Germanen in vor- und Frühgeschichtlicher Zeit* (Berlin, 1926).

Köster, Kurt, *Pilgerzeichen und Pilgermuscheln von mittelalterlichen Santiagostrassen: Saint-Léonard, Rocamadour, Saint-Gilles, Santiago de Compostela* (Neumünster, 1983).

Kristensen, Anne K.G., *Danmarks ældste Annalistik. Studier over lundensisk Annalskrivning i 12. og 13. århundrede* (Copenhagen, 1969).

Kritzeck, James, *Peter the Venerable and Islam* (Princeton, 1964).

Krogh, Knud J., *Gåden om kong Gorms grav. Historien om nordhøjen i Jelling* (Herning, 1993).

Kromann, Anne, 'Finds of Iberian Islamic coins in the Northern lands', in: Mario Gomes Marques and D.M. Metcalf (eds.), *Problems of Medieval Coinage in the Iberian Area. A Symposium held by the Sociedade numismática scalabitana and the Instituto de Sintra on 4–8 October, 1988* (Santarem, 1988), pp. 243–253.

Krus, L., *A Concepção Nobiliárquica do Espaço Ibérico (1280–1380)* (Lisbon, 1994).

Krus, L., *Passado, Memoria e Poder na Sociedade Medieval Portuguesa* (Redondo, 1994).

Kræmmer, Michael, *Den hvide klan. Absalon, hans slægt og hans tid* (Copenhagen, 1999).

Kræmmer, Michael, *Kongemordernes slægt* (Copenhagen, 2007).

Krötzl, Christian, 'Wege und Pilger aus Skandinavien nach Santiago', in: Robert Plötz (ed.), *Europäische Wege der Santiago-Pilgerfahrt* (Tübingen, 1990), pp. 157–169.

Kuhn, Thomas S., *The Structure of Scientific Revolutions* (Chicago, 1970).

Kurth, F., 'Der Anteil Niederdeutscher Kreuzfahrer an den Kämpfen der Portugiesen gegen die Mauren', *Mitteilungen des Institutes für Österreichische Geschichtsforschung* Appendix 8 (1909), pp. 131–252.

Landes, Richard, *Relics, Apocalypse, and the Deceits of History. Ademar of Chabannes, 989–1034* (Cambridge, 1995).

Landes, Richard, Andrew Gow, and David van Meter (eds.), *The Apocalyptic Year 1000. Religious Expectation and Social Change, 950–1050* (Oxford, 2003).

Larsen, Inge M., *Sem Poder et sem Renome. Den parallelle nationale diskurs i Portugal – dens opståen, udvikling og kulmination hos* Renascenca-*generationen*. Unpublished PhD-dissertation, University of Copenhagen (1998).

Lattimore, Owen, *Nomads and Commissars. Mongolia Revisited* (Oxford, 1962).

Lattimore, Owen, *Studies in Frontier History. Collected Papers 1928–1958* (Oxford, 1962).

Lay, Stephen, 'The Reconquest as Crusade in the Anonymous *De expugnatione Lyxbonensi*', *Al-Masāq* 14 (2002), pp. 123–130.

Leclercq, J., *The Love of Learning and the Desire for God. A Study of Monastic Culture* (London, 1978) [1957].

Lehtonen, Tuomas M.S., *Fortuna, Money, and the Sublunar World. Twelfth-Century Ethical Poetics and the Satirical Poetry of the Carmina Burana* (Helsinki, 1995).

Lehtonen, Tuomas M.S., and Kurt Villads Jensen with Janne Malkki, and Katja Ritari (eds.) *Medieval History Writing and Crusading Ideology* (Helsinki, 2005).

Lester, Anne E., 'A Shared Imitation: Cistercian Convents and Crusader Families in Thirteenth-Century Champagne', *Journal of Medieval History* 35 (2009), pp. 353–370.

Literature   361

Lévi-Provencal, Évariste, *Histoire de l'Espagne musulmane*, vols. 1–3 (Paris, 1950–1967).

Liebs, Detlef, *Lateinische Rechtsregeln und Rechtssprichwörter* (Munich, 1998).

Lind, John, 'De russiske ægteskaber. Dynasti- og alliancepolitik i 1130'ernes danske borgerkrig', *Historisk Tidsskrift* 92 (1992), pp. 225–263.

Linder, Amnon, *Raising Arms. Liturgy in the Struggle to Liberate Jerusalem in the Late Middle Ages* (Turnhout, 2003).

Linehan, Peter, *The Spanish Church and the Papacy in the Thirteenth Century* (Cambridge, 1971).

Linehan, Peter, 'Religion, Nationalism and National Identity in Medieval Spain and Portugal', in: Stuart Mews (ed.), *Religion and National Identity* (Oxford, 1982), pp. 161–199.

Linehan, Peter, *History and the Historians of Medieval Spain* (Oxford, 1993).

Linehan, Peter, 'Utrum reges Portugalie coronabantur annon', *Actas do 2º Congresso Histórico de Guimarães* 2 (1996), pp. 387–401.

Little, Lester K., *Religious Poverty and the Profit Economy in Medieval Europe* (London, 1978).

Livermore, Harold V., *A History of Portugal* (Cambridge, 1947).

Livermore, Harold V., 'The 'Conquest of Lisbon' and Its Author', *Portuguese Studies* 6 (1990), pp. 1–16.

Lomax, Derek W., *La Orden de Santiago, 1170–1275* (Madrid, 1965).

Loud, Graham A., 'Some Reflections on the Failure of the Second Crusade', *Crusades* 4 (2005), pp. 1–14.

Lourie, E., 'A Society Organized for War: Medieval Spain', *Past and Present* 35 (1966), pp. 54–76.

Lourie, E., 'The Will of Alfonso I, "El Batallador", King of Aragon and Navarre; A Reassessment', *Speculum* 50 (1975), pp. 635–651.

Lourie, E., 'The Will of Alfonso I of Aragon and Navarre: A Reply to Dr Forey', *Durham University Journal* 77, 2 (1984–1985), pp. 165–172.

Lubac, Henri, *Exégèse Médiévale*, vols. 1–2 (Paris, 1959).

Lund, Niels, *Lið, leding og landeværn. Hær og samfund i Danmark i ældre middelalder* (Roskilde, 1996).

Lund, Niels, 'Horik den Førstes udenrigspolitik', *Historisk Tidsskrift* 102 (2002), pp. 1–20.

Lund, Niels (ed.), *Kristendommen i Danmark for 1050* (Roskilde, 2004).

Lund, Niels, 'Leding and crusading', in: Birgitte Fløe-Jensen and Dorthe Wille-Jørgensen (eds.), *Expansion – Integration? Danish-Baltic Contacts 1147–1410 AD* (Vordingborg, 2009), pp. 39–43.

Magoun, Francis P. Jr., 'The Pilgrim-Diary of Nikulas of Munkathvera: The Road to Rome', *Mediaevel Studies* 6 (1944), pp. 314–354.

Maier, Christoph T., 'Crisis, Liturgy, and the Crusade in the Twelfth and Thirteenth Centuries', *Journal of Ecclesiastical History* 48 (1997), pp. 628–657.

Malmer, Brita, 'Kristna symboler på danske mynt ca. 825–1050', in: Niels Lund (ed.), *Kristendommen i Danmark for 1050* (Roskilde, 2004), pp. 75–85.

Malmros, Rikke, 'Leding og Skjaldekvad. Det elvte århundredes nordiske krigsflåder, deres teknologi og organisation og deres placering i samfundet, belyst gennem den samtidige fyrstedigtning', *Aarbøger for Nordisk Oldkyndighed og Historie* 1985 (1985), pp. 89–139.

Manniche, Jens Chr., 'Historieskrivningen 1830–1880', in: Aksel E. Christensen, H.P. Clausen, Svend Ellehøj, and Søren Mørch (eds.), *Danmarks historie*, vol. 10 (Copenhagen, 1992), pp. 199–266.

Manzano Moreno, Eduardo, *La frontera de al-Andalus en época de los Omeyas* (Madrid, 1991).

362 Literature

Manzano Moreno, Eduardo, 'The Creation of a Medieval Frontier: Islam and Christianity in the Iberian Peninsula, Eighth to Eleventh Centuries', in: Daniel Power and Naomi Standen (eds.), *Frontiers in Question: Eurasian borderlands, 700–1700* (New York, 1999), pp. 32–54.

Markowski, M., 'Crucesignatus: Its Origin and Early Usage', *Journal of Medieval History* 10 (1984), pp. 157–165.

Marshall, Christopher, *Warfare in the Latin East, 1192–1291* (Cambridge, 1992).

Martín, José-Luis, 'Orígenes de la Orden Militar de Santiago (1170–1195)', *Anuario de estudios medievales* 4 (1967), pp. 571–590.

Martínez, Carlos de Ayala, 'Hacia una comprension del fenómeno cruzado: las insuficiencias del reduccionismo económico', in: García-Guijarro Ramos (ed.), *La primera cruzada, novecientos años después: el concilio de Clermont y los orígenes del movimiento cruzado* (Madrid, 1997), pp. 167–195.

Martínez, Carlos de Ayala, Pascal Buresi, and Philippe Josserand (eds.), *Identidad y representation de la frontera en la España medieval (siglos XI–XIV)* (Madrid, 2001).

Martins, Joaquim Pedro de Oliveira, *História de Portugal*, vols. 1–2 (Lisbon, 1886).

Mattoso, José, *A nobreza medieval portuguesa: A familia e o poder* (Lisbon, 1981).

Mattoso, José, *Ricos-homens, infanções e cavaleiros: A nobreza medieval portuguesa nos séculos XI e XII* (Lisbon, 1982).

Mattoso, José, 'Sobre o problema do feudalismo em Portugal (Reposta a Robert Durand)', *Revista Portuguesa de História* 21 (1984), pp. 13–19.

Mattoso, José, 'Portugal e a Europa', *Communio. Revista internacional católica* 3 (1985), 114–125, in: José Mattoso, *A Escrita da Historia. Teoria e Métodos* (Lisbon, 1997), pp. 129–141.

Mattoso, José, 'A realeza de Afonso Henriques', *Histórica & Crítica* 13 (1986), 5–14, in: José Mattoso, *Fragmentos de uma Composição Medieval* (Lisbon, 1993), pp. 213–232.

Mattoso, José, ' "O feudalismo português", Lecture at the Academia Portuguesa de História 19th of July 1985', in: José Mattoso (ed.), *Fragmentos de uma Composição Medieval* (Lisbon, 1987), pp. 115–123.

Mattoso, José, *Portugal Medieval. Novas interpretações* (Lisbon, 1992).

Mattoso, Jose (ed.), *História de Portugal*, vols. 1–8 (Lisbon, 1993).

Mattoso, José, *Identificação de um país: ensaio sobre as origens de Portugal, 1096–1325*, vols. 1–2 (Lisbon, 1995).

Mattoso, José, *A Identidade Nacional* (Lisbon, 1998).

Mattoso, José, *D. Afonso Henriques* (Lisbon, 2006).

Mattoso, José, and Armindo de Sousa, *A Monarquia Feudal (1096–1480)* (Lisbon, 1993).

Mayer, H.E., *Geschichte der Kreuzzüge* (Stuttgart, 1995) [1965].

McGuire, Brian Patrick, *The Cistercians in Denmark. Attitudes, Roles, and Functions in Medieval Society* (Kalamazoo, 1982).

McGuire, Brian Patrick, *The Difficult Saint. Bernard of Clairvaux and His Tradition* (Kalamazoo, 1991).

Meier, Kurt, *Kreuz und Hakenkreuz. Die Evangelische Kirche im Dritten Reich* (Munich, 2001).

Melve, Leidulf, *Inventing the Public Sphere: The Public Debate During the Investiture Contest (ca. 1030–1122)* (Leiden, 2007).

Menédez Pidal, R., *Los españoles en la historia y en la literatura* (Madrid, 1947).

Menédez Pidal, R., and E. García Gómez, 'El conde mozárabe Sisnando Davídiz y la Política de Alfonso VI con los taifas', *Al-Andalus* 12 (1947), pp. 27–41.

Menocal, Maria Rosa, *The Ornament of the World: How Muslims, Jews, and Christians Created a Culture of Tolerance in Medieval Spain* (London, 2004).

Merêa, Paulo, *Introdução ao problema do feudalismo em Portugal* (Coimbra, 1912).

Merêa, Paulo, *O poder real e as Cortes* (Coimbra, 1923).

Meyer, Bruno, 'El papel de los cruzados alemanes en la reconquista de la Península Ibérica en los siglos XII y XIII', *En la España Medieval* 23 (2000), pp. 41–66.

Mill, John Stuart, *A System of Logic: Ratiocinative and Inductive, Being a Connected View of the Principles of Evidence and the Methods of Scientific Investigation*, vols. 1–2 (London, 1872) [1843].Miller, Konrad, *Weltkarte des Arabers Idrisi vom Jahre 1154* (Stuttgart, 1981) [1928].

Mínguez, Jose Maria, *La Reconquista* (Madrid, 1989).

Molbech, Christian, 'Om Historiens nationale Betydning og Behandling: Om historiske Arbeider og Formaalene for en historisk Forening i Danmark', *Historisk Tidsskrift* 1 (1840), pp. 1–41.

Montesquieu, *De l'esprit des lois* (Genève, 1748).

Mordhorst, Mads, and Jes Fabricius Møller, *Historikeren Caspar Paludan-Müller* (Copenhagen, 2005).

Morris, Colin, *The Papal Monarchy: The Western Church from 1050 to 1250* (Oxford, 1989).

Morris, Colin, 'Picturing the Crusades: The Uses of Visual Propaganda, ca. 1095–1250', in: John France and William G. Zajac (eds.), *The Crusades and Their Sources. Essays Presented to Bernard Hamilton* (Aldershot, 1998), pp. 195–216.

Morris, Colin, *The Sepulchre of Christ and the Medieval West. From the Beginning to 1600* (Oxford, 2005).

Morris, R.I., 'Martyrs on the Field of Battle Before and During the First Crusade', in: Diana Wood (ed.), *Martyrs and Martyrologies* (Oxford, 1983), pp. 79–101.

Muldoon, James, *Popes, Lawyers, and Infidels. The Church and the Non-Christian World 1250–1550* (Philadelphia, 1979).

Müller-Wille, Michael, *Mittelalterliche Grabfunde aus der Kirche des slawischen Burgwalles von Alt Lübeck: zu dynastischen Grablegen in polnischen und abodritischen Herrschaftsgebieten* (Stuttgart, 1996).

Murray, Alan V. (ed.), *From Clermont to Jerusalem: The Crusades and Crusader Societies, 1095–1500* (Turnhout, 1998).

Murray, Alan V., 'Might Against the Enemies of Christ: The Relic of the True Cross in the Armies of the Kingdom of Jerusalem', in: John France and William G. Zajac (eds.), *The Crusades and the Sources. Essays Presented to Bernard Hamilton* (Aldershot, 1998), pp. 217–238.

Murray, Alan V., *The Crusader Kingdom of Jerusalem: A Dynastic History 1099–1125* (Oxford, 2000).

Naumann, Hans-Peter, 'Nordische Kreuzzugsdichtung', in: Hans-Peter Naumann, Magnus von Platen and Stefan Sonderegger (eds.), *Festschrift für Oskar Bandle zum 60. Geburtstag am 11. Januar 1986* (Basel, 1986), pp. 175–189.

Nedkvitne, Arnved, 'Why Did Medieval Norsemen Go On Crusade?', in: Tuomas M.S. Lehtonen and Kurt Villads Jensen with Janne Malkki and Katja Ritari (eds.), *Medieval History Writing and Crusading Ideology* (Helsinki, 2005), pp. 37–50.

Nicholson, Helen, *Love, War and the Grail* (Leiden, 2001).

Nicholson, Helen, and David Nicolle, *God's Warriors: Crusaders, Saracens and the Battle for Jerusalem* (Botley, 2005).

Nielsen, Herluf, 'Peterspenge', *KLNM* 13 (1956–1978), pp. 249–252.

364 Literature

Nielsen, Leif Chr., 'Hedenskab og kristendom. Religionsskiftet i vikingetidens grave', in: Peder Mortensen and Birgit M. Rasmussen (eds.), *Høvdingesamfund og Kongemagt* (Aarhus, 1991), pp. 245–267.

Nielsen, Torben K., 'Sterile Monsters. Henry of Livonia and the Orthodox Church', in: Alan V. Murray (ed.), *The Clash of Cultures on the Medieval Baltic Frontier* (Farnham, 2009), pp. 227–252.

Nielsen, Torben K., and Kurt Villads Jensen, 'Pope Innocent III and Denmark', in: Andrea Sommerlechner (ed.), *Innocenzo III. Urbs et orbis, Atti del congresso internazionale Roma, 9–15 settembre 1998*, vols. 1–2 (Rome, 2002), vol. 2, pp. 1133–1168.

Nors, Thyra, 'Ægteskab og politik i Saxos Gesta danorum', *Historisk Tidsskrift* 98 (1998), pp. 1–33.

Nors, Thyra, 'Slægtsstrategier hos den danske kongeslægt i det 12. århundrede. Svar til Helge Paludan', *Historie* 2000 (2000), pp. 55–66.

Nyberg, Tore, 'Kreuzzug und Handel in der Ostsee zur dänischen Zeit Lübecks', in: O. Ahlers et al. (eds.), *Lübeck 1226. Reichsfreiheit und frühe Stadt* (Lübeck, 1976), pp. 173–206.

Nyberg, Tore, 'Die skandinavische Zirkarie der Prämonstratenserchorherren', in: Gert Melville (ed.), *Secundum regulam vivere. Festschrift für P. Norberg Backmund O.Praem.* (Windberg, 1978), pp. 265–279.

Nyberg, Tore, 'Deutsche, swedische und dänische Christianisierungsversuche ostlich der Ostsee im Geiste des 2. und 3. Kreuzzuges', in: Zenon Hubert Nowak (ed.), *Die Rolle der Ritterorden in der Christianisierung und Kolonisierung des Ostseegebietes* (Toruń, 1983), pp. 93–114.

Nyberg, Tore, 'Zur Rolle der Johanniter in Skandinavien. Erstes Auftreten und Aufbau der Institutionen', in: Zenon Hubert Nowak (ed.), *Die Rolle der Ritterorden in der mittelalterlichen Kultur* (Toruń, 1985), pp. 129–144.

Nyberg, Tore, *Die Kirche in Skandinavien. Mitteleuropäischer und englischer Einfluss im 11. und 12. Jahrhundert. Anfange der Domkapitel Børglum und Odense in Dänemark* (Sigmaringen, 1986).

Nyberg, Tore, 'The Danish Church and Mission in Estonia', *Nordeuropaforum* 1 (1998), pp. 49–72.

Nyberg, Tore, '*Monasticism in North-Western Europe, 800–1200* (Aldershot, 2000).

Nørgård Jørgensen, Anne, 'Naval Bases in Southern Scandinavia from the 7th to the 12th Century', in: Anne Nørgård Jørgensen, John Pind, Lars Jørgensen, and Birthe L. Clausen (eds.), *Maritime Warfare in Northern Europe* (Copenhagen, 2002), pp. 125–152.

Nørlund, N.E., *Trelleborg* (Copenhagen, 1948).

Nørlund, N.E., *De gamle danske Længdeenheder* (Copenhagen, 1955).O'Callaghan, J.F., 'The Mudejars of Castile and Portugal in the Twelfth and Thirteenth Centuries', in: James M. Powell (ed.), *Muslims Under Latin Rule, 1100–1300* (Princeton, NJ, 1990), pp. 11–56.

O'Callaghan, J.F., *Reconquest and Crusade in Medieval Spain* (Philadelphia, 2003).

Odenius, Oloph, 'Vincentius', *KLNM* 20 (1956–1978), pp. 88–89.

Oksbjerg, Erik, *Læsning i tekster fra Danmarks Middelalder. Jyske Lov. Sjællandske Krønike* (Viborg, 2002).

Olesen, Martin Borring, 'Trelleborg eller ej? – om den skånske trelleborgs tilknytning til de danske ringborge', *KUML. Årbog for Jysk Arkæologisk Selskab* 2000 (2000), pp. 91–111.

Oliveira Marques, A.H. de, *Ensaios de historiografia portuguesa* (Lisbon, 1988).

Oliveira Marques, A.H. de, 'O "Portugal" islâmico', in: Jean Pierre Leguay, António Henrique R. de Oliveira Marques and Maria Ângela V. da Rocha Beirante (eds.), *Nova História de Portugal*, vol. 2 (Lisbon, 1993), pp. 121–249.

Literature 365

Oliveira Marques, A.H. de, 'O poder e o espaço', in: Maria Helena da Cruz Coelho and Armando Luís de Carvalho Homem (eds.), *Nova História de Portugal*, vol. 3 (Lisbon, 1996), pp. 11–163.

Oliveira Marques, A.H. de, *História de Portugal: Das Origens ao Renascimento*, vol. 1 (Lisbon, 1997).

Oliveira Marques, A.H. de, *A expansão quatrocentista* (Lisbon, 1998).

Olsson, Sven-Olof (ed.), *Medeltida danskt järn. Framställning av och handel med järn i Skåneland och Småland under medeltiden* (Halmstad, 1995).

Ottosen, Knud, and Michael H. Gelting, 'Kong Gorms mulige begravelse', *Svundne tider* 10 (2007), pp. 42–48.

Paravicini, Werner, 'Rittertum im Norden des Reichs', in: W. Paravicini (ed.), *Nord und Süd in der deutschen Geschichte des Mittelalters* (Sigmaringen, 1990), pp. 147–191.

Partner, Peter, *God of Battles. Holy Wars of Christianity and Islam* (London, 1997).

Paulus, Nikolaus, *Geschichte des Ablasses im Mittelalter*, vols. 1–3 (Paderborn, 1922–1923).

Pedersen, Morten, *Det tidlige kirkebyggeri og sognedannelsen på Falster.* Unpublished dissertation, University of Southern Denmark (Odense, 1999).

Pereira, Armando de Sousa, 'Motivos bíblicos na historiografia de Santa Cruz de Coimbra dos finais do século XII', *Lusitania Sacra* 2a sér. 13–14 (2002), pp. 315–336.

Pereira, Armando de Sousa, *Representações da Guerra no Portugal da Reconquista (Séculos XI–XIII)* (Lisbon, 2003).

Pereira, Maria Teresa S. F. Lopes, 'Memória cruzadística de Feito da Tomada de Alcácer (1217) (com base no Carmen de Gosuíno)', in: Camara municipal de Guimaraes (ed.), *Actas do 2º Congresso Historico de Guimarães*, vol. 2 (Guimarães, 1996), pp. 319–358.

Phillips, Jonathan, *Defenders of the Holy Land. Relations Between the Latin East and the West, 1119–1187* (Oxford, 1996).

Phillips, Jonathan (ed.), *The First Crusade. Origins and Impacts* (Manchester, 1997).

Phillips, Jonathan, 'St Bernard of Clairvaux, the Low Countries and the Lisbon Letter of the Second Crusade', *The Journal of Ecclesiastical History* 48 (1997), pp. 485–497.

Phillips, Jonathan, 'Papacy, Empire and the Second Crusade', in: Jonathan Phillips and Martin Hoch (eds.), *The Second Crusade. Scope and Consequences* (Manchester, 2001), pp. 15–31.

Phillips, Jonathan, *The Second Crusade: Extending the Frontiers of Christendom* (New Haven, 2007).

Pirenne, Henri, 'Un appel à une croisade contre les Slaves adresse à l'évêque de Liège, au duc de Lotharingie et au comte de Flandre au commencement du XIIme siècle', in: *Mélanges Camille de Borman. Recueil de Mémoires relatifs à l'histoire, a l'archéologie et à la philologie offert au Baron de Borman et publié par ses amis et admirateurs* (Liège, 1919), pp. 85–90.

Poulsen, Bjørn, 'The Widening of Import Trade and Consumption Around 1200 A.D.: A Danish Perspective', in: Lars Berggren, Nils Hybel and Anette Landen (eds.), *Cogs, Cargoes, and Commerce: Maritime Bulk Trade in Northern Europe, 1150–1400* (Toronto, 2002), pp. 31–52.

Powell, James M., *Anatomy of a Crusade, 1213–1221* (Philadelphia, 1986).

Power, Daniel, and Naomi Standen (eds.), *Frontiers in Question: Eurasian Borderlands, 700–1700* (New York, 1999).

Powers, James F., *A Society Organized for War. The Iberian Municipal Militias in the Central Middle Ages, 1000–1284* (Berkeley, 1987).

Price, E.H., 'Voltaire and Montesquieu's Three Principles of Government', *Publications of the Modern Language Association of America* 57, 4 (1942), pp. 1046–1052.

366 *Literature*

Pryor, J.H., 'Transportation of Horses by Sea During the Era of the Crusades: Eighth Century to 1285 AD', *Mariner's Mirror* 68 (1982), pp. 9–27, 103–125.

Pryor, J.H., *Geography, Technology, and War: Studies in the Marine History of the Mediterranean, 649–1571* (New York, 1988).

Pryor, J.H., 'The Naval Architecture of Crusader Transport Ships and Horse Transports Revisited', *Mariner's Mirror* 76 (1990), pp. 255–273.

Pryor, J.H., 'A View from a Masthead: The First Crusade From the Sea', *Crusades* 7 (2008), pp. 87–152.

Purkis, William J., *Crusading Spirituality in the Holy Land and Iberia* (Woodbridge, 2008).

Queller, Donald E., and Thomas F. Madden, *The Fourth Crusade: The Conquest of Constantinople* (Philadelphia, 1997).

Radtke, Christian, 'Die Entwicklung der Stadt Schleswig: Funktionen, Strukturen und die Anfange der Gemeindebildung', in: Erich Hoffmann and Frank Lubowitz (eds.), *Die Stadt im westlichen Ostseeraum: Vorträge zur Stadtgründung und Stadterweiterung im hohen Mittelalter* (Frankfurt a.M., 1995), pp. 47–91.

Radtke, Christian, 'Kommune og gilde i Slesvig i højmiddelalderen', in: Lars Bisgaard and Leif Søndergaard (eds.), *Gilder, lav og broderskaber i middelalderens Danmark* (Odense, 2002), pp. 41–62.

Ramos, L. García-Guijarro (ed.), *La Primera cruzada, novecientos años después: el concilio de Clermont y los orígines del Movimiento cruzado* (Madrid, 1997).

Ranke, Leopold von, *Weltgeschichte*, vols. 1–9 (Leipzig, 1881–1888).

Rassow, Peter, 'La cofradía de Belchite', *Anuario de historia del derecho español* 3 (1926), pp. 220–226.

Rebane, Peter P., 'From Fulco to Theoderic. The Changing Face of the Livonian Mission', in: Andres Andresen (ed.), *Muinasaja loojangust omariikluse laveni. Pühendusteos Sulev Vahtre 75. sünnipäevaks* (Tartu, 2001), pp. 36–68.

Reilly, Bernard F., *The Kingdom of Leon-Castille under King Alfonso VI, 1065–1109* (Princeton, NJ, 1988).

Reilly, Bernard F., *The Contest of Christian and Muslim Spain 1031–1157* (Oxford, 1992).

Reilly, Bernard F., *The Kingdom of Leon-Castille Under King Alfonso VII, 1126–1157* (Philadelphia, 1998).

Reitzel-Nielsen, Erik, *Johanniterordenens historie med særligt henblik på de nordiske lande*, vols. 1–2 (Copenhagen, 1984–1991).

Reynolds, Susan, *Fiefs and Vassals. The Medieval Evidence Reinterpreted* (Oxford, 1994).

Rheinheimer, Martin, 'Die Angst vor dem Wolf. Werwolfglaube, Wolfssagen und Ausrottung der Wölfe in Schleswig-Holstein', *Fabula* 36 (1995), pp. 25–78.

Riant, Paul, Letters in the Royal Library, Copenhagen, in the collections *Add* 611a; *NKS* 3681; *NBU* 11.1.1863.

Riant, Paul, *Expéditions et pèlerinages des Scandinaves en Terre Sainte au temps des Croisades* (Paris, 1865).

Richard, Jean, *The Crusades ca. 1071– ca. 1291* (Cambridge, 1999).

Riis, P.J., and Thomas Riis, 'Knud den Helliges ørnætappe i Odense Domkirke – et forsøg på nytolkning', *KUML 2004* (2004), pp. 259–273.

Riis, Thomas, *Les institutions politiques centrales du Danemark 1100–1332* (Odense, 1977).

Riis, Thomas, *Das mittelalterliche danische Ostseeimperium* (Odense, 2003).

Riis, Thomas, *Einführung in die Gesta Danorum des Saxo Grammaticus* (Odense, 2005).

Riley-Smith, Jonathan, *The First Crusade and the Idea of Crusading* (London, 1986).

Literature 367

Riley-Smith, Jonathan, 'Family Traditions and Participation in the Second Crusade', in: Michael Gervers (ed.), *The Second Crusade and the Cistercians* (New York, 1992), pp. 101–108.

Riley-Smith, Jonathan, 'The Crusading Movement and Historians', in: J. Riley-Smith (ed.), *Oxford Illustrated History of the Crusades* (Oxford, 1995), pp. 1–12.

Riley-Smith, Jonathan, *The First Crusaders, 1095–1131* (Cambridge, 1997).

Riley-Smith, Jonathan, *Hospitallers. The History of the Order of St John* (London, 1999).

Riley-Smith, Jonathan, 'Some Modern Approaches to the History of the Crusades', in: Torben Kjersgaard Nielsen and Iben Fonnesberg-Schmidt (eds.), *Crusading on the Edge. Ideas and Practice of Crusading in Iberia and the Baltic Region, 1100–1500* (Turnhout, 2016), pp. 9–27.

Roberts, Geoffrey (ed.), *The History and Narrative Reader* (London, 2001).

Robertson, James Craigie, *Materials for the History of Thomas Becket, Archbishop of Canterbury, Canonized by Pope Alexander III, A.D. 1173* (London, 1879).

Rodrigues, José Honório, 'D. Henrique e a abertura da Fronteira Mundial', *Revista Portuguesa de História* 9 (1960), pp. 45–62.

Rodríguez García, José Manuel, 'Cruzados y fronteros. Discusión sobre el carácter cruzado de la guerra en la frontera, 1214–1314', in: Francisco Toro Ceballos and José Rodríguez Molina (eds.), *III Estudios de Frontera. Convivencia, Defensa y comunitatión en la Frontera* (Alcala la Real, 2000), pp. 569–585.

Roesdahl, Else, *Vikingernes verden* (Copenhagen, 1993) [1987].

Rosa, Maria de Lurdes, 'O corpo do chefe guerreiro, as chagas de Cristo e a quebra dos escudos: caminhos da mitificação de Afonso Henriques na Baixa Idade Média', *Actas do 2º Congresso Histórico de Guimarães*, vol. 3 (Guimarães, 1996), pp. 85–91.

Rüsen, Jörn, *Grundzüge einer Historik*, vols. 1–3 (Göttingen, 1983–1989).

Russell, F.H., *The Just War in the Middle Ages* (Cambridge, 1975).

Schich, Winfried, 'Zum Ausschluss der Wenden aus den Zünften nord- und ostdeutscher Städte im späten mittelalter', in: Antoni Czacharowski (ed.), *Nationale, ethnische Minderheiten und regionale Identitäten in Mittelalter und Neuzeit* (Toruń, 1994), pp. 31–51.

Schieffer, Rudolf, 'Gregor VII und die Könige Europas', *Studi Gregoriani* 13 (1989), pp. 189–211.

Seegrün, Wolfgang, *Das Papsttum und Skandinavien* (Neumünster, 1967).

Sewell, William H. Jr., 'Marc Bloch and the Logic of Comparative History', *History and Theory* 6 (1967), pp. 208–218.

Sheils, W.J. (ed.), *The Church and War* (Oxford, 1983).

Siberry, Elizabeth, *Criticism of Crusading 1095–1274* (Oxford, 1985).

Silva, António Martins da, 'A ideia de Europa no período entre as duas guerras. O Plano Briand e o posicionamento português', *Revista de História da Sociedade e da Cultura* 2 (2002), pp. 85–151.

Skovgaard-Petersen, Inge, 'Saxo. Historian of the Patria', *Medieval Scandinavia* 2 (1968), pp. 54–77.

Skovgaard-Petersen, Inge, 'Oldtid og Vikingetid', in: Aksel E. Christensen, H. P. Clausen, Svend Ellehøj, and Søren Mørch (eds.), *Danmarks Historie*, vol. 1 (Copenhagen, 1977), pp. 15–209.

Skovgaard-Petersen, Inge, *Da Tidernes Herre var nær. Studier i Saxos historiesyn* (Copenhagen, 1987).

Skovgaard-Petersen, Inge, 'Wendenzüge – Kreuzzüge', in: Michael Muller-Wille (ed.), *Rom und Byzanz im Norden. Mission und Glaubenswechsel im Ostseeraum während des 8.–14. Jahrhunderts*, vol. 1 (Stuttgart, 1997), pp. 279–289.

368 *Literature*

Skovgaard-Petersen, Karen, *A Journey to the Promised Land. Crusading Theology in the* Historia de profectione Danorum in Hierosolymam *(ca. 1200)* (Copenhagen, 2001).

Skyum-Nielsen, Niels, *Kvinde og Slave* (Copenhagen, 1971).

Skyum-Nielsen, Niels, 'Estonia under Danish Rule', in: Niels Skyum-Nielsen and Niels Lund (eds.), *Danish Medieval History, New Currents* (Copenhagen, 1981), pp. 112–135.

Skyum-Nielsen, Niels, *Fruer og Vildmand* (Copenhagen, 1997).

Smalley, Beryl, *The Study of the Bible in the Middle Ages* (Oxford, 1952).

Smith, Damian J., 'The Abbot-Crusader: Nicholas Breakspear in Catalonia', in: Brenda Bolton and Anne J. Duggan (eds.), *Adrian IV The English Pope (1154–1159)* (Aldershot, 2003), pp. 29–40.

Smith, Damian J., 'Saint Rosendo, Cardinal Hyacinth and the Almohads', *Journal of Medieval Iberian Studies* 1 (2009), pp. 53–67.

Soares, Torquato de Sousa, 'Review of Carl Erdmann: A idea de cruzada em Portugal', *Revista Portuguesa de História* 1 (1941), pp. 305–311.

Soifer, Maya, 'Beyond Convivencia: Critical Reflections on the Historiography of Interfaith Relations in Christian Spain', *Journal of Medieval Iberian Studies* 1 (2009), pp. 19–35.

Soto Rabános, Jose Maria, '¿Se puede hablar de un entramado político religiose en el proceso de independencia de Portugal?', *Hispania* 67 (2007), pp. 795–826.

Sousa, António Caetano de, *História Genealógica da Casa Real Portuguesa* (Lisbon, 1748).

Sousa, Bernardo Vasconcelos e, 'Linhagen e identidade social na nobreza medieval portuguesa (séculos XIII–XIV)', *Hispania* 67 (2007), pp. 881–898.

Sousa Viterbo, Francisco Marques de, *O mosteiro de Sancta Cruz de Coimbra* (Coimbra, 1914).

Spengler, Oswald, *Der Untergang des Abendlandes. Umrisse einer Morphologie der Weltgeschichte* (Munich, 1922).

Sprandel, R., *Das Eisengewerbe im Mittelalter* (Stuttgart, 1968).

Stahuljak, Zrinka, *Bloodless Genealogies of the French Middle Ages: Translations, Kinship, and Metaphor* (Gainesville, 2005).

Stalls, Clay, *Possessing the Land: Aragon's expansion into Islam's Ebro frontier under Alfonso the Battler, 1104–1134* (Leiden, 1995).

Steenstrup, Johannes C.H.R., *Danmarks Riges Historie*, vol. 1 (Copenhagen, 1898–1905).

Stone, Lawrence, 'The Revival of Narrative. Reflections on a New Old History', *Past and Present* 85 (1979), pp. 3–24.

Svenstrup, Thyge, *Arup – En biografi om den radikale historiker Erik Arup, hans tid og miljø* (Copenhagen, 2006).

Sybel, Heinrich von, *Geschichte des ersten Kreuzzugs* (Düsseldorf, 1841).

Szacherska, Stella Maria, 'The Political Role of the Danish Monasteries in Pommerania 1171–1223', *Medieval Scandinavia* 10 (1977), pp. 122–155.

Taha, 'Abdulwahid Dhanun, *The Muslim Conquest and Settlement of North Africa and Spain* (London, 1989).

Throop, Susanna, 'Vengeance and the Crusades', *Crusades* 5 (2006), pp. 21–38.

Tiemroth, Jens Henrik, 'Professionalisering og demokrati 1880–1991', in: Aksel E. Christensen et al. (eds.), *Danmarks Historie*, vol. 10 (Copenhagen, 1992), pp. 267–285.

Tobias, Ruth, *Der Sebastianismo in der portugiesischen Literatur des 20. Jahrhunderts: zur literarischen Konstruktion und Dekonstruktion nationaler Identität am Beispiel eines Erlösermythos* (Frankfurt a.M., 2002).

Togeby, Knud, *Ogier le danois dans les littératures européennes* (Copenhagen, 1969).

Literature 369

Tolan, John V., 'Anti-Hagiography: Embrico of Mainz's *Vita Mahumeti*', *Journal of Medieval Studies* 22 (1996), pp. 25–41.

Tolan, John V., *Saracens: Islam in the Medieval European Imagination* (New York, 2002).

Tolan, John V., *Le Saint chez le sultan. La Rencontre de Francois d'Assise et de l'Islam* (Paris, 2007).

Torgal, Luís Reis, José Amado Mendes and Fernando Catroga, *História da história em Portugal. Séculos XIX-XX*, vols. 1–2 (Lisbon, 1998).

Torres Sevilla-Quiñones, Margarita C., 'Cruzados y peregrinos leoneses y castellanos en Tierra Santa ss. XI-XII', *Medievalismo* 9 (1999), pp. 63–82.

Toswell, M.J., 'St Martial and the Dating of Late Anglo-Saxon Manuscripts', *Scriptorium* 51 (1997), pp. 3–14.

Toubert, Pierre, 'Le concept de frontière. Quelques réflexions introductives', in: Carlos de Ayala Martínez, Pascal Buresi and Philippe Josserand (eds.), *Identidad y representación de la frontera en la España medieval (siglos XI-XIV)* (Madrid, 2001), p. 1–4.

Toynbee, Arnold J., *A Study of History*, vols. 1–12 (London, 1935–1961).

Turner, Frederick Jackson, *The Frontier in American History* (New York, 1921).

Tyerman, Christopher, 'Were There Any Crusades in the Twelfth Century?', *English Historical Review* 110 (1995), pp. 553–577.

Tyerman, Christopher, *The Invention of the Crusades* (Houndmills, 1998).

Tyerman, Christopher, *God's War. A New History of the Crusades* (London, 2006).

Tyermann, Christopher, *The Debate on the Crusades, 1099–2010* (Manchester, 2011).

Unger, Richard W., 'Beer: A New Bulk Good of International Trade', in: Lars Berggren, Nils Hybel and Anette Landen (eds.), *Cogs, Cargoes, and Commerce: Maritime Bulk Trade in Northern Europe, 1150–1400* (Toronto, 2002), pp. 113–127.

Unger, Richard W., 'The Northern Crusaders: The Logistics of English and Other Northern Crusader Fleets', in: John H. Pryor (ed.), *Logistics of Warfare in the Age of the Crusades* (Aldershot, 2006), pp. 251–273.

Urban, William, *The Baltic Crusade* (De Kalb, 1975).

Urban, William, 'The Frontier Thesis and the Baltic Crusade', in: Alan V. Murray (ed.), *Crusade and Conversion on the Baltic Frontier 1150–1500* (Aldershot, 2001), pp. 45–71.

Urban, William, *The Teutonic Knights. A Military History* (Pennsylvania, 2003).

Van Moolenbroek, Jaap, 'Een wonder in Portugal. Caesarius van Heisterbach over de slag bij Alcácer do Sal (1217)', *Madoc* 13 (1999), pp. 102–110.

Vellev, Jens, 'Jernfremstilling', in: Else Roesdahl (ed.), *Dagligliv i Danmarks middelalder. En arkæologisk kulturhistorie* (Copenhagen, 1999), pp. 221–226.

Veloso, Maria Teresa Nobre, *D. Afonso II. Relações de Portugal com a Santa Sé durante o seu reinado* (Coimbra, 2000).

Villegas Diaz, Luis Rafael, 'La orden de Calatrava. Organización y vida interna', *Primeras Jornadas de Historia de las Órdenes Militares* (Madrid, 1997), pp. 29–54.

Virgili, Antonio, '*Angli cum multis aliis alienigenis*: crusade settlers in Tortosa (Second Half of the Twelfth Century)', *Journal of Medieval History* 35 (2009), pp. 297–312.

Warren, W.L., *Henry II* (London, 1973).

Wasserstein, David, *The Rise and Fall of the Party-Kings: Politics and Society in Islamic Spain 1002–1086* (Princeton, NJ, 1985).

Weber, Gerd Wolfgang, 'Saint Olafr's Sword. Einarr Skulason's *Geisli* and Its Trondheim Performance AD 1153 – A Turning Point in Norwego-Icelandic Scaldic Poetry', in: Gerd Wolfgang Weber (ed.), *Mythos und Geschichte – Essays zur Geschichtsmythologie Skandinaviens in Mittelalter und Neuzeit* (Trieste, 2001), pp. 145–151.

370 Literature

Weibull, Curt, 'Saxos berättelser om de danska vendertågen 1158–1185', *Historisk Tidsskrift* 83 (1983), pp. 35–70.

Werner, Michael, and Bénédicte Zimmermann, 'Beyond Comparison: Histoire Croisée and the Challenge of Reflexivity', *History and Theory* 45 (2006), pp. 30–50.

Westerdahl, Christer, 'Transportvägar. Itinerariet och forntida transportsystem', in: Gerhard Flink (ed.), *Kung Valdemars Segelled* (Stockholm, 1995), pp. 24–32.

White, Hayden, *Metahistory: The Historical Imagination in the Nineteenth Century in Europe* (Baltimore, 1973).

Williams, John, 'The Making of a Crusade: The Genoese Anti-Muslim Attacks in Spain, 1146–48', *Journal of Medieval History* 23 (1997), pp. 29–53.

Wolf, Kenneth Baxter, *Christian Martyrs in Muslim Spain* (Cambridge, 1988).

Wolf, Kenneth Baxter, 'The Earliest Latin Lives of Muhammad', in: Michael Gervers and Ramzi Jibran Bikhazi (eds.), *Conversion and Continuity: Indigenous Christian Communities in Islamic Lands, Eighth to Eighteenth Centuries* (Toronto, 1990), pp. 89–101.

Wolf, Kenneth Baxter, *Making History: The Normans and Their Historians in Eleventh-century Italy* (Philadelphia, 1995).

Wood, Ian, *The Missionary Life: Saints and the Evangelisation of Europe, 400–1050* (Harlow, 2001).

Worsaae, J.J.A., *Kongegravene i Ringsted Kirke aabnede, istandsatte og dækkede med nye Mindestene ved Hans Majestæt Kong Frederik Den Syvende* (Copenhagen, 1858).

Ziese, Jurgen, *Wibert von Ravenna, der Gegenpapst Clemens III (1084–1100)* (Stuttgart, 1982).

Index

Aachen 112, 208, 301
Aarhus 161–2, 298
Abd Allah 52
Abd al Malik 52
Abd al-Rahman II 75, 78
Abd al-Rahman III 51
Abel 303–5, 326, 336
Abraham 60, 216, 316
Abrantes 151, 270
Absalom 662
Absalon, Bishop of Roskilde/Archbishop
of Lund 26, 90, 123, 153, 157, 160–2,
164, 170, 173, 180, 190, 202, 213,
223, 239–40, 255, 260, 262, 265,
327–8, 331
Abu Abdallah 288, 289
Abu Yakub Yusuf 244, 270
Abu Yusuf Yakub al-Mansur 270–1,
275–6, 278–9
Achaia 100
Acre 19–20, 97, 99, 211, 246, 261–3, 267,
272, 284–5, 289
Adalbert, Archbishop of Hamburg/Bremen
53, 62
Adam of Bremen 57, 62–3, 65, 97, 100,
102, 215, 314, 322
Adebert 192, 250
Adelaide, German Empress 71
Adele of Flanders, Danish Queen 81, 139
Adele of France 81
Adhemar, Bishop of Le Puy 255
Ad liberandam terram sanctam 295
Adolf of Holstein 155, 162, 265
Æthelred 63
Afonso I Henriques 31, 35, 36, 130–9,
142–53, 155, 166–8, 171–2, 174–8,
183, 191–4, 205, 216–18, 224–5, 227,
230, 232–5, 241, 244, 248, 259–60,
269–71, 275, 277, 284, 297, 299, 313,
315, 326, 333

Afonso II 1, 3, 152, 226, 284, 286–92,
308, 326
Afonso III 235, 294–5
Afonso Peres Farinha 293
Afonso Peres Saracins 292
Agersø 291
Agnes of Aquitaine, German Empress 64,
71, 233
Agnes of Meran 267
Alarcos 278
Albert, Bishop of Riga 223, 246, 256, 268,
282, 296–7
Albert, Bishop of Szczecin 141
Albert of Aix 16, 106–7
Albert of Holstein 284
Albert of Orlamünde 295–6, 299, 325
Albert of Stade 97
Albert of Trois-Fontaines 212
Albert the Bear, Margrave of Brandenburg
141, 241
Albufeira 295
Alcácer do Sal 77, 147–50, 224, 226, 280,
286–9
Alcácer Quibir in Morocco 35
Alcanede 235, 271
Alcobaça monastery 31, 169, 191–3,
195–6, 201–6, 230, 271, 278, 287, 299
Aldebert *see* Adebert
Aleppo 138, 284
Alexander II, Pope 53, 68, 74
Alexander III, Pope 151, 161, 171–5, 206,
208, 238, 269, 315
Alexander the Great 100, 104, 152–3
Alfajar da Pena 293
Alfonso I of Aragon 131–2, 23233
Alfonso II of Aragon 234, 278
Alfonso III of Asturia 236
Alfonso VI of León-Castile 53–6, 70–2,
78, 81, 84, 88, 107, 119, 122, 131, 138,
163, 167, 183, 312–13

372   *Index*

Alfonso VII of León-Castile 133–5, 137, 140, 149, 168, 180, 233, 244, 315, 331
Alfonso VIII of Castile 278–80, 325
Alfonso IX of León 149, 277–9, 289, 292
Algarve 225, 227, 264, 272, 275, 293–5, 307
Al-Idrisi 101
Ali Ibn Yussuf 131
Aljustrel 293
Allen, C.F. 23
All Saints monastery, Lund 63
Almada 235, 239
Almería 140, 226
Almohads 85, 140, 148, 171, 235, 244, 250, 270–1, 280, 312
Almoravids 55–6, 73, 85, 107–8, 122, 125, 131, 140, 148, 312
Alpedriz 235
Als 167
Alvarus 312
Alvastra monastery 189
Alvor 99, 272, 293
Amadeus III of Savoy 139
Amarelo Mestaliz 78
Ambure 209
Anders Sunesen, Archbishop of Lund 26, 210, 268–9, 273, 293, 296, 298, 325
András I of Hungary 80
András II of Hungary 284–5
Angantyr 58
Anselm of Lucca 45
Antioch 80, 99, 105, 110, 146, 231, 242, 255
Antvorskov 239–41
Apulia 69, 81, 216
Aristo, Bishop of Ratzeburg 65
Aristotle 6, 10
Arkona 117, 142, 159, 171–3, 214, 216, 241, 297, 315, 317
Arnald of Aerschot 143
Arnold 291
Arnold of Lübeck 317
Arruda 235, 239
Arup, Erik 12–13, 21, 24–7, 31, 46–7
Astorga 111
Atourgia 277
Augustine 10, 167, 265, 323
Augustus, Emperor 163, 213
Aversa 69
Azevedo, Luíz Gonzaga de 40, 111

Babylonia 100
Badajoz 52, 56, 73, 148, 150–2, 171–2, 217, 224, 269–71, 288, 292

Baldric of Dole 16–18
Baldwin, Flemish count 81
Baldwin I, Emperor of Constantinople 284
Baldwin I, King of Jerusalem 15, 108, 110
Baldwin II, King of Jerusalem 182
Baldwin of Flanders 211
Barbastro, 1064 Battle 53–4, 84
Bari 69, 100
Barosa River 191
Bartlett, Robert 96
Basto 169, 287
Beatrice of Upper Lothringia 67
Beelphegor 113
Beira Alta 191, 233, 235
Beja 148, 150, 293
Belin 208, 210
Belleisle 98
Belver 235, 277
Belvoir 277
Benedict, friend of Ogier the Dane 209
Benevento 69, 172
Berengaria, Queen of Denmark 1–3, 9, 36, 284–5, 291, 298–9, 302–4, 326, 334–8
Berenguela of Castile-León 278
Bergen monastery 202
Bergson, Henri 38
Bermudo II of León 89
Bermudo Peres 132
Bernaldo, Archbishop of Toledo 54, 104
Bernard, Archbishop of Toledo 54, 128
Bernard II, Count of Barcelona 70
Bernard of Clairvaux 84, 139–42, 147, 149, 178, 188–93, 200, 202–7, 232, 239, 244–5, 252–3, 320
Bernhard, Spanish missionary in Wolin 314
Berno, Bishop of Schwerin 196, 200
Bertold, Bishop of Üxküll/Livonia 263, 320
Bethlehem 80, 99
Bjernede 204
Bjørn, peasant 27
Bjørn Ironside 76
Blekinge 57, 99
Blicher, Steen Steensen 31
Bloch, Marc 7
Blót Svend 115
Bodil, Danish Queen 109–10, 126
Bodil, nurse of Sofie 156
Bohemund 16, 81, 110
Boizenburg 300
Boleslaw III, Duke of Poland 116, 331
Borgå 263
Bornhøved, 1227 Battle 303

Index 373

Bourges 139
Bouvines, 1214 Battle 283–4
Braga 77–8, 85, 111, 121, 132–3, 140, 169, 192, 233, 245, 271, 282, 294–5
Brandenburg 66, 112, 141, 188, 241
Bremen 53, 62–3, 65–6, 74, 197, 266, 272
Brito 191–2
Brittany 17, 97–8, 208, 272
Brügge 112
Bruno 198
Brunswick 197, 269
Bruun, Christian 1, 9, 29, 36
Bugislav I of Pomerania 90, 173, 260–1
Buiça, Manuel 37
Burgos 71, 121
Burgundy 55–6, 64, 69, 81–2, 106–8, 125, 188, 208
Buris 162, 264

Cáceres 150, 238, 292
Cádiz 78, 148
Caesar 153, 314
Caesarius of Heisterbach 308
Cairo 36
Calabria 69
Calatrava 140
Calatrava Order *see* Order of Calatrava
Calixtus II 56, 120, 236
Camões, Luís de 34–5, 37, 41
Canute II the Great 53, 63–5, 67, 71, 81, 87, 102
Canute IV the Holy 69–70, 80–1, 105, 108–10, 139, 175, 316
Canute VI the Young 165, 174, 190–1, 259, 260–1, 263–5, 267, 275, 284, 310
Canute Lavard 116–18, 121–2, 153–5, 163, 174–5, 190, 196, 204, 240–5, 258, 260, 297, 319
Canute Magnussen 141–2, 155–7, 190, 205, 264
Canute the Furry 190
Cape Colony 37
Cape Finis Terre 75
Cape of Good Hope 35
Cape Town 36
Capo São Vincente 224
Carauel 211
Cardosa 287
Carl of Flanders 81
Carlos of Portugal 37
Carquere monastery 130
Carthage 100, 207
Castello Branco, Jose Barbosa Canaes de Figueiredo 38

Castelo Branco 287
Castelo de Abrantes 151
Castelo de Monsanto 151
Castelo de Paderne 293
Celanova 245
Celestine III 245, 263, 265, 278–9
Celorico de Basto 169
Ceuta 122
Châmoa Gomes 235
Charlemagne 81, 96, 102, 104, 167, 187, 207–9, 211–12, 214–15, 224, 249, 301
Charles Martel 51, 57
Chartres 209
Chastel Blanc 287
Christ *see* Jesus Christ
Christensen, Aksel E. 26, 47–8
Christian, Bishop of Prussia 296
Christian IV 106, 299
Christian Pedersen 297
Christopher I 303–5, 336
Cidade Rodrigo, 1199 Battle 279
Cilicia 108
Cincfal 97
Cîteaux 188–9, 249
Civitate, 1053 Battle 69
Clairvaux 92, 188–90, 192, 259, 284
Clavijo, 844 Battle 844 236
Clermont 16, 18, 20, 82, 84, 104, 110, 114, 144, 165, 194, 212, 244, 257, 320
Cluny 52–3, 56–7, 63, 67, 70–1, 74, 81, 105, 108, 116, 125, 128, 134, 140, 188, 312, 320
Coimbra 37–8, 55, 73, 78, 85, 104, 110–12, 118–20, 123, 126, 131–3, 135, 138, 148, 150–1, 164, 167–9, 195, 210, 216, 227, 232–3, 237, 245, 259, 270–1, 274, 276–7, 279–80, 283, 294–5, 312–13
Colbatz monastery 191, 202, 229
Cologne 100, 112, 142–3, 146–7, 208, 218, 307
Conrad, prince 253
Conrad I of Jerusalem 262
Conrad II, Emperor 63–4
Conrad III of Germany 139, 149, 155, 205
Constance of Hungary 284
Constantinople 16, 38, 79–80, 100, 212, 235, 262, 281–2, 284
Consuega, 1097 Battle 1097 107
Cooper, James Fenimore 93
Copenhagen 1, 25, 46, 48, 88–9, 103, 223, 276
Cordeiro, Luciano 1, 9, 36
Córdoba 52, 75, 77, 122, 236, 288, 312

374 *Index*

Cornegainha 169
Cortesão, Jaime 42
Corvey 112, 214
Coryn 199
Costa, Alfredo 37
Cour, Vilhelm la 23
Covadunga, 722 Battle 51
Crato 235
Crescónio, Bishop of Coimbra 312
Crete 100
Cuenca 107, 244
Cuzis 198
Cyprus 110, 282

Dagmar of Danmark 266, 284
Dalmatius Geret from Cluny 56
Damascus 100, 103, 138–9, 205
Damietta 280, 283, 285–6
Dannenberg 302
Dargun monastery 191, 196–8, 200–2, 204, 229
Dartmouth 97–8, 142–3
David, Old Testament king 16, 62, 70, 138, 165, 222
Díaz, Osorio 89
Didago 79
Diego, Bishop of Osma 325
Diego, mythical hero 55
Diego, Spanish nobleman 119
Diego Gelmírez, Archbishop of Santiago de Compostela 120–1, 132–3
Diocletian 224
Djursland 266, 317
Doberan monastery 198, 202
Dobin 138, 141–2, 155, 205
Dona Zalamiz 79
Dorpat 248
Douro River 52, 55, 77–8, 111, 169, 191, 195, 247, 287
Duarte Galvão 137
Dueholm monastery 258
Dvina River 263

Ebbe, bailiff in Estonia 299, 319
Ebbe Sunesen 204
Ebo, Archbishop of Reims 58
Ebro River 52–3, 140
Edessa 138–41, 148, 204
Edgar of England 63
Egas Moniz 130, 191–2
Eider 180, 265
Eirik of Norway 263
Ekkehard 105, 124
Elbe River 58, 66, 141, 197, 241, 283, 300, 302

el Cid 52, 55, 107–8, 125, 171
Eldena monastery 198, 202, 229
Eleanor of Aquitaine 325
Elvas 292
Elvira of León-Castile 82
Engels, Friedrich 6
Erdmann, Carl 39–40, 50, 119, 138
Erik, monk in the monastery of Silos 78
Erik I the Good (Ejegod) 44, 108–11, 115, 117–18, 126
Erik II Emune 109, 111, 117–18, 127, 129, 153–4, 242, 316
Erik III Lamb 141
Erik IV Ploughpenny 239, 254, 303–4, 336
Erik V Glipping 332
Erik VI Menved 332
Erik Gonçalves 79
Erik Knutson 325
Ermengold III of Urgell 53
Erslev, Kristian 23, 42, 46
Esbern 78
Esbern Snare 157, 175, 190, 223, 262, 330
Escalon 100
Eskil, Archbishop of Lund 92, 116, 128, 154, 161–2, 173, 189–90, 203, 205, 215, 249, 284
Eskil, Bishop of Aarhus 161
Eskil, Danish nobleman 134
Esrom monastery 109, 163, 171, 189–92, 196, 202–3, 206, 229, 256, 283
Estonia 26, 28, 99, 174–5, 213, 222, 228, 241, 248, 260–1, 263, 266, 269, 276, 286, 291–2, 294–301, 303–4, 319, 325
Estrid 25, 63
Ethiopia 100
Eude I of Burgund 56, 82, 106, 108, 125
Eugenius III 204
Eulogius 312
Évora 54, 150–1, 203, 231, 271, 275–6, 278, 287
Evulus of Roucy 54
Ewald, Johannes 35, 50
Ezekiel 100, 231

Fåborg 326
Fabricius, A. 29
Falster 65, 201, 291, 318
Faro 295
Faro, Bishop of Meaux 210, 253
Farrol 97
Fehmarn 198, 251, 291
Fellin 248, 297
Fernandes, abbot of Alcobaça 287
Fernando, Prince of Castile 325

Index 375

Fernando I of León-Castile 52–3, 70–1, 166–7, 237, 312
Fernando II of León 149–51, 171, 230, 238, 244, 270
Fernando Afonso 235
Fernão de Serpa 293–4
Fernão Gonçalves 150
Fernão of Flanders 284, 287
Fernão Peres de Trava 132–3
Feron monastery 209–10
Filip of Flanders 326
Flanders 3, 16, 36, 64, 80–2, 97, 100, 108, 110, 112, 114, 139, 142, 197, 208, 211, 229, 232, 273, 275, 284, 287, 326
Florina of Burgundy 82, 106–7
Fortuna 35, 50
Fotevig, 1134 Battle 117–18, 128, 153–4
Foz do Sousa 169
Franciscan Order 297
Francis of Assisi 285–6
Frederic, Archbishop of Tyre 172
Frederic VII 1
Frederik, Bishop of Schleswig 161
Fredric I Barbarossa, Emperor 139, 156, 161, 174, 209, 241, 260, 264–5
Fredric II, Emperor 283, 300–4
Friis, Astrid 25
Frode Fredegod / Frotho 213, 219
Fuas Roupinho 227, 270
Fulcher of Chartres 15–16, 257
Fulko, missionary bishop 175

Galicia 17–18, 55–6, 74, 76–9, 82, 97, 99–100, 107, 111, 119, 131–4, 139, 207, 236, 243, 245, 270, 272, 277
Galicia-Ulf *see* Ulf Jarl
Gandelbodus of Friesland 208
García III of Navarre 53
García of León-Castile 55
Garcia Romero 234
Garrett, Almeida 31
Gaufrido 234
Gayferus of Bordeaux 208
Genoa 17, 140, 226
Geoffrey of Anjou 209
Georgios Maniakes 80
Geraldo Geraldes "the Fearless" 150, 171–2
Gerhoch af Reichersberg 140
Gering, Bishop of Meissen 199
Gertrude of Flanders 81
Ghazal, Al- 75–7, 89
Gibraltar 51, 57, 77, 97, 148, 270, 272
Gilbert, Bishop of Lisbon 147, 149

Gloriande 211
Godefrith 292
Godfrey of Bouillon 80, 82, 104, 106–7, 114, 125, 143
Godfrey of Lorraine 80
Godfrey of Lower Lorraine 112, 114
Godfrey the Bearded 82
Gog and Magog 100, 231
Golgotha 91
Goliath 222
Gomes Nunes 134
Gonçalo of Navarra 53
Gonçalo Pais, Bishop of Coimbra 313
Gonçalo Sanches 77
Gonçalo Viegas 278
Gorm 59–60, 86, 190
Gotland 223, 241, 244
Gøtrik *see* Gudfred of Denmark
Gotskalk 65, 68–9, 74
Gotskalk, envoy to Riga 247
Grandi non immerito 294
Grathe Moor, 1154 Battle 158, 163
Greenland 53
Gregorius Crescentio 325
Gregory VII 21, 47, 53–4, 67–70, 91, 84, 88
Gregory VIII 261
Gregory IX 293–4
Greifswald 202
Grønsund 201
Guadalquivir River 75
Gualdim Pais 278
Gualdino 234
Guarda 294
Guardiana River 140, 235, 278
Gudfred of Denmark 102, 211, 214
Guhtkepole 200
Guibert of Nogent 17–18, 113, 212, 257, 319
Guidimtesta 277
Guido, papal legate 137
Guillaume V (VII) of Aquitaine 64
Guillaume VI (VIII) of Aquitaine 53, 233
Guillaume "Carpenter", crusader 18
Guimarães 73, 79, 130, 133, 191
Gundered 77
Gundisalvus, Bishop 76
Gunhild, German Empress 64, 71
Gunhild, married to Svend 1. Tveskæg 66
Gunner, Bishop of Viborg 325–6
Gunzelin 241
Guy de Lusignan 211, 262, 272

Haakon Sigurdson 62
Haccriz 291
Hadrian IV 138, 149, 178

376   *Index*

Hælf 291
Hagar 275
Halland 57, 169–71, 241, 283, 303
Halworth 292
Hamburg 65, 76
Hamburg-Bremen 53, 62–3, 65–6, 74, 197, 266
Harald, Ingvar's brother 90
Harald Klak 58, 316
Haraldsted forest 117, 242
Harald the Brutal (Hardrada) 80
Harald the Good (Bluetooth) 59–60, 62–3, 66, 78, 86
Hasting 76–7, 89
Hattin, 1187 Battle 211, 261, 264, 277, 305
Havelsberg 66, 112
Heimo, priest in Bamberg 314
Hekla Mountain 154
Helmold of Bosau 117, 141–2, 147, 155, 160, 215, 319, 321–3
Henrik Gotskalksen 67, 73, 114, 117
Henri of Clairvaux 259
Henrique 55–7, 69, 81–2, 85, 107–8, 110–11, 119, 121, 125–6, 130–2, 138, 169, 176, 192
Henry, knight from Cologne 218
Henry, son of Henry the Lion 317
Henry I, Count of Schwerin 241, 284, 300–4, 326
Henry I of France 80–1
Henry II, Emperor 71
Henry II, King of England 172, 174–5, 185, 209, 325–6
Henry III, Emperor 64, 71
Henry IV, Emperor 88, 104, 109–11, 126, 139, 265
Henry V, Emperor 113
Henry VI, Emperor 279
Henry of Livonia 248, 319
Henry the Lion 141, 155, 159–60, 162, 174, 187, 197, 209, 249, 265, 317, 325
Henry the Young 172, 184, 259
Herbert of Clairvaux 189
Herculano, Alexandre 30–3, 36, 38–40, 42, 50, 137, 179
Hermann 291
Hermann, Livonian Master 304
Hermann von Salza, Grand Master of the Teutonic Order 302–4
Herrisvad monastery 189, 191, 215
Hildesheim 189
Himmelbjerg 57
Hitler, Adolf 40

Hollingsted 156
Hollywood 93
Holme monastery 189
Holmstrup 258
Honorius III 289, 296, 300–3, 309
Horik I 58, 75–6, 89
Hospitallers *see* Order of St. John
Hubaldus, Cardinal 205
Hugh, Abbot of Cluny 56, 67, 71, 81
Hugh, Bishop of Jabala 139
Hugh I of Burgund 56
Hugo de Payns 232
Huitfeldt, Arild 34, 127, 298–9
Huizinga, Johan 6
Hungary 80, 92, 111, 262, 284–5, 304
Huntington, Samuel 6, 12, 94
Hyacinth, papal legate 244–5, 259
Hybel, Nils 29

Ibn Aisha 107
Ibn Bassam 183
Ibn Qasi 148–9
Ibn Yasin 55
Ibsen, anatomist 1
Iceland 47, 53, 102, 104, 109–10, 124, 154, 212, 214, 259
Ingeborg, Queen of France 267–9, 284, 306, 331
Ingemann, B. S. 31, 219
Ingvar 90
Innocent II 177
Innocent III 124, 152, 206, 236, 240, 265–9, 278, 280–4, 286, 288, 308, 325–6, 328
Innocent IV 294–6
Ioham Ferreiro Dalphamy 227
Ireland 77, 89, 188, 213
Isabella of Urgell 53
Isidor, monk in Silos 78
Isidore of Seville 248
Ismar 135–6
Ivar the Boneless 63

Jabal Tariq 51
Jaén 140, 178, 288
Jaime I of Aragon 230, 257
Jarimar I of Rügen 202, 260
Jean de Brienne of Jerusalem 286
Jeanne of Hainaut and Flanders 284
Jelling 59–63
Jens Grand, Archbishop of Lund 332
Jerez 288

Index 377

Jericho 15
Jerusalem 3–4, 7–8, 14–21, 39–40, 42, 44, 59, 65, 80, 82, 91, 96, 98–101, 104, 106–16, 118–21, 124, 126–7, 129, 133, 135, 139, 141–3, 146, 148, 161, 164–5, 171–2, 175, 182, 189–90, 199, 201, 204–8, 211–12, 231–4, 236, 239–40, 242, 248, 261, 263–4, 271, 275–6, 279, 281–3, 286, 293, 296, 302–3, 322, 324, 330
Jesus Christ 16, 23, 31, 44, 54, 59–65, 100–1, 105, 112–13, 116, 120–2, 133, 136–7, 141, 143, 145, 147, 151–3, 164, 167–8, 194, 201, 203–4, 206, 209–10, 216–17, 226, 231, 236, 238–9, 242–3, 245, 252, 262, 289, 299, 311–12, 315–16, 323, 327
João VI of Portugal 30
João Cirita, abbot 191–2
João Gondesendes 123
João Peculiar, Archbishop of Braga 140, 245
Johannes from Scotland, Bishop in Mecklenburg 65
Johannes in Estonia 292
John IX 59
John Lackland 282
John Paul II 152
John the Baptist 133, 150, 194, 224, 240, 248, 250, 296
John the Evangelist 100, 167, 231, 247, 282
Jørgensen, Ellen 22
Joshua 15
Judah 60, 62
Judas Maccabeus 165, 230
Julin 314, 321–2
Juromenha 150, 235, 271, 292

Kade 27
Kálmán, King of Hungary 104, 284
Kalmar 115–16, 128
Kammin 261
Kanhave Canal 58
Karakos 211
Karenz 161
Karlot 211
Kazimir I of Pomerania 173, 196–7, 200
Kazimir II of Pomerania 284
Keld of Viborg 141
Kilij Arslan (Sultan Soliman) 106–7
Kiulo 292
Koch, Hal 27

Kolberg 196
Kongshelle 115, 118
Königslutter 163
Korselitse 291
Kossinna, Gustaf 25
Kunigunde or Gunhild 71

Ladebow 198
Lændær 291
Lamego 111, 166, 191–2, 195, 271
Las Navas de Tolosa, 1212 Battle 246, 280–1, 287–8, 295
Lattimore, Owen 93–4
Lauenburg 241
Leça do Balio 235
Leipzig 199
Leiria 135, 138, 169, 192, 232, 295
Leo IX 69
León 52–6, 64, 70–2, 78, 81, 88, 119–21, 131–3, 140, 149–51, 163, 166, 171, 195, 230, 234–5, 237–8, 242, 244, 270, 277–80, 282, 288–9, 292, 312
Leonora, Danish Princess 1, 325–6
Leopold of Austria 267
Lérida 140
Letold 125
Libya 100
Liegnitz, 1241 Battle 304
Limoges 64
Líria 134
Lisbon 1, 31, 36–8, 54–6, 75, 77–8, 97, 99, 107–8, 122, 124, 132, 138, 142–4, 146–50, 171, 192–4, 205, 217–18, 224–7, 233–4, 239, 244, 250, 270–2, 275, 277, 279, 287–9, 293, 295, 313
Lopo Fernandes, Master of the Templars 279
Lordemanos 78
Lordemão 78
Lorraine 16, 80–1, 105, 112, 114, 139, 143
Lorvão 119–20
Lothar, Duke of Supplinburg *see* Lothar III, Emperor
Lothar I, Emperor 58
Lothar III, Emperor 117, 163
Louis VII of France 139, 147, 149, 172, 174–5, 189, 208
Louise 35
Louis the Pious, Emperor 322
Lourie, E. 94
Lübeck 67, 141, 154, 160, 187, 197, 302, 318
Lucho 196

378   *Index*

Luís Filipe 37
Luke the Evangelist 111
Luna 77
Lund 47, 59, 63, 86, 104, 111, 114, 116,
    124, 127–8, 161, 165, 171, 174, 197,
    202, 212, 224, 240, 282, 296, 316,
    325, 327
Lundby, H. V. 35
Lüneburg 100, 188
Lüneburger Heide 100
Lyndanise 297–8
Lyø 300, 304
Lyon 294
Lyrskov Heath, 1043 Battle 65

Maccabees 168, 182, 231, 275
Mafra 235
Magdeburg 109, 112–15, 119, 187–8,
    194, 205
Magnus Nielsen of Denmark 115–17,
    153–5, 242–3
Magnus of Denmark 64–5, 67
Mahaut 36
Maia 79
Mainz 58, 87, 316
Malaga 122
Malagón 108
Mallorca 122, 230, 271
Manifestis probatum 171, 174, 269
Mansur, al- 79, 89, 270
Mansurah, al- 286
Manzikert, 1071 Battle 69, 80
Maqqari, al- 183
Markús Skeggjason 110, 126
Martín, José-Luis 238
Martin, prior 112, 119
Martin, son of el Cid 123
Martin from Soure 313
Martin Muniz 112, 119
Martino Portagal 326
Martins, Oliveira 32, 42
Martin the Moor 290
Marx, Karl 6
Maskenholt monastery 241
Mathilde of Flanders (Teresa) 36, 248,
    284, 326
Mathilde of Savoy 139
Mathilde of Saxony 325
Matthew Paris 304
Matthew the Evangelist 265
Mattoso, José 250, 338
Maurício, Cardinal Bishop of Porto (in
    Italy) 119
Maurício Burdino 111
Mauritanians 77

May, Karl 93
Mayer, H. E. 19
Meaux 210–11, 253
Mécia of Portugal 295
Mecklenburg 65, 160, 174, 191, 197–8,
    202, 241
Meinhard, Bishop of Üxküll 263
Meissen 112, 156, 159, 199
Melchizedek 264–5
Mendo Goncalves 77
Mercedars / Friars of Our Lady of
    Mercy 124
Mérida 292
Merseburg 112
Mértola 148, 293
Mieszco, Duke of Poland 66
Milde River 156
Minho River 56, 77–8, 107, 169, 247
Minorca 140, 271
Miranda do Corvo 131
Mirok 223
Mistivoi 66
Mistwin 269
Moabites 113, 119, 143
Molbech, Christian 46
Mondego River 55, 120, 131–2, 135, 167,
    232, 235
Mondoñedo 76, 111, 245
Montaigne, Michel de 210
Montanchez 150
Montelius, Oscar 32
Montemor-o-Velho 131
Morocco 35, 55, 76, 131, 135, 148, 172,
    239, 270, 279, 282, 313
Mors 258
Moses, Patriarch 298
Mosul 138
Mount of Olives 110
Moura 293
Mozarabs 51, 131, 144, 147, 167, 195,
    224, 250, 311–13, 315
Mstislav Vladimirovich 153
Muhammad, Prophet 52, 168, 209,
    215–16, 312, 319
Muhammad an-Nasir, Caliph 280–1
Mumadona Dias 73, 79
Muno, spansk stormand 119

Nájera 71
Naumburg 112
Nazaré 270
Nicea 181
Nicolas of Flanders 275
Nicomedia 81
Nidaros *see* Trondheim

Niels, Count of Halland 190, 241, 256, 283, 303
Niels, King of Denmark 113–18, 153–4, 205, 315–16
Niels, Marshal 123
Niels Nielsen 283
Niels Pribislavsen 197
Niklot 159–60, 181, 319
Nikulás af Munkathvera 102
Noah 225
Novgorod 247
Nud, Queen of Denmark 76
Nuño, Spanish nobleman 119
Nyberg, Tore 29, 128, 259
Nybow 198
Nydala monastery 189

Óbidos 192
Obotrite 66–7, 73, 117, 159, 242, 319
O'Callaghan, Joseph F. 41
Oda of Halland 303
Oddar, Dean 66
Odense 59, 81, 109, 126, 141, 205, 240, 261, 271, 291, 330
Oder River 64, 261
Odilo, Abbot of Cluny 70
Odin 225
Odinkar, Bishop of Schleswig 62
Ogier the Dane 36, 81, 207–15, 224, 254
Olav II (Saint Olav) 62, 64–5, 77–80, 90, 115, 121
Olav Tryggvason 62
Oldenburg 66, 159–60
Oliveira Marques, A. H. de 41
Øm monastery 161, 325–6
Order of Calatrava 203, 234, 257, 278
Order of Santiago 151, 234–5, 238–9, 242, 271, 276–7, 280, 287–8, 293
Order of St. Canute 162, 204, 241–5
Order of St. John 29, 133, 162, 171, 229, 232–3, 235, 239–41, 258, 275, 277, 280, 287–8, 293, 328
Order of the Holy Trinity 124
Order of the Knight Templars 134, 151, 203–6, 211, 232–5, 239, 241, 244, 252, 275–6, 278–80, 287–8, 328
Orgiel 291
Orkney Islands 77
Ösel 269, 299, 310
Osma 121, 325
Otto, Bishop of Bamberg 105, 124, 127, 141, 200, 314
Otto I, Emperor 59, 71
Otto II, Emperor 66
Otto IV, Emperor 265, 269, 283

Ottokar I of Bohemia 284
Ourem 295
Ourique 36, 135, 217, 299
Ourique, 1139 Battle 31, 135, 137, 151, 297
Outremer 116, 211, 247
Ovid 156
Oviedo 78
Ozsyari *see* Ogier the Dane

Paio Peres Corriea 293
Palmela 74, 78, 148, 151, 235, 239
Paludan-Müller, Caspar 6
Pamplona 167
Paschal II, Pope 38, 87, 111, 119–20, 129
Paschal III, Antipope 208
Peder, Bishop of Aarhus 298
Peder Bodilsen 189
Peder Olsen 297
Pedro, son of Sancho I 292
Pedro I of Aragon 53
Pedro II of Aragon 280
Pedro Alvítiz 288
Pedro Engelbertiz 71, 78
Pedro Gudesteiz, Archbishop of Santiago de Compostela 238
Pedro Henriques 142
Pedro Marcio 236
Pedro Pitões, Bishop of Porto 143, 146
Pelágio 51
Pelagius, Cardinal 283, 286
Pelagius Eriquez 78
Pene River 196
Peniche 277
Peter Benedictsen 291
Peter Engelbrektsen *see* Pedro Engelbertiz
Peter Jukilsen 291
Peter of Poitiers 140
Peter Palaiz 123
Peter the Venerable, Abbot of Cluny 71, 105, 116, 120, 128, 140
Peter Thrulsen 291
Peter Tudebodis 16
Petrus Comestor 84
Philip I, King of France 110
Philip II August, King of France 262, 266–9, 284, 306
Philip of Swabia, King of Germany 266
Pirenne, Henri 114
Pisa 17, 145
Pium et sanctum 308
Poitiers 51, 57, 140, 208
Poland 24, 66, 92, 116–17, 241, 296, 331
Pomerania 90, 116–17, 128, 141, 173, 175, 188, 196, 198, 260–2, 283–4

380 *Index*

Ponte de Barca 290
Poppo, Missionary priest 59
Porches 295
Porto 37, 111, 143, 145–6, 169, 227, 233,
    235, 270, 271, 279
Porto (in Italy) 119
Portocarreio 203
Porvoo 263
Powell, James 283
Powers, James F. 94
Priapus 113
Pribislav 154, 318–19
Pripegala 113
Prislav 159
Prussia 22, 26, 30, 100, 128, 191, 203,
    246, 269, 296, 304, 325

Quantum predecessores 139
Quia maior 281–2, 328

Radulf, Bishop of Ribe 87
Radulf, Knight 230
Radulphus Niger 160
Raimund IV Saint-Gilles 82
Raimundo of Galicia 55–6, 73, 82, 107–8,
    131, 133, 139, 176
Raimundo Viergas de Pontocarreiro 295
Ramiro I, King of Asturia 74, 76, 236
Ramiro I of Aragon 53, 70
Ramiro II the Monk, King of Aragon 233
Ramon Berenguer IV, Count of Barcelona
    140, 233–4
Ranke, Leopold von 6, 106
Raol 142, 218
Ratzeburg 65, 187, 197
Raymund of Aguilers 16
Raymund of Saint-Gilles 69
Regner Lodbrog 76
Reinald, Count of Ditmarshes 162
Reuter, Fritz 31
Rhineland 142
Rhine River 100, 214
Rhodes, Cecil 36–7
Riant, Paul 28–9, 106
Ribe 97–8, 221, 228, 308
Richard, Duke of Normandy 77
Richard of Aversa and Apulia 69
Richard of Capua 69
Richard of Saint Victor 245
Richard the Lionheart 170, 211, 262, 267
Richiza, daughter of Boleslaw 116, 331
Richiza, daughter of Valdemar I the
    Great 325
Riga 223, 246–7, 256, 263, 268–9, 282,
    296–7, 299–300, 310

Riis, Thomas 29, 240
Rinaldo 106
Ringsted 1–2, 117–18, 122, 154, 163, 242,
    334, 336–7
Robert I, Duke of Burgundy 81, 105
Robert II, Count of Flanders 81–2, 112,
    114, 139
Robert I the Frisian, Count of Flanders
    80–1
Robert Crespin of Normandy 53
Robert Guiscard 69
Robert of Ely 242
Robert of Ketton 320
Robert the Monk 20, 43, 91, 106, 113–14,
    148, 251, 322
Rodrigo, Bishop of Toledo 124
Rodrigo Esberniz (Esbernsen) 78
Rodrigo Peres Veloso 134
Rodrigo Sanches 278
Roger Bursa 81
Roger Guiscard 53
Roland 209–10, 215
Roliung 215
Rollo, Duke of Normandy 64
Rome 54, 63–4, 67–70, 77, 91, 96, 100,
    102, 111, 141, 152, 161, 211, 214, 236,
    245, 262, 266, 281, 283, 324
Romens 290
Roncevalles 209, 212
Rørdam, Valdemar 334, 336, 338
Roskilde 25, 47, 59, 62, 157, 160–2, 168,
    173–4, 190, 202, 230, 239, 327
Rügen 28, 114, 117–18, 127, 141–2, 154,
    159, 161–3, 171–5, 202, 214–15, 222,
    229, 241, 260, 297, 310, 315, 317–18,
    322, 327
Ryd monastery 190
Ryol 291

Saaremaa *see* Ösel
Saint Albans monastery 304
Saint Albanus 224
Saint Benedict of Nursia 196, 210
Saint Bertin monastery 81
Saint Dominic of Osma 325
Saint George 271
Saint Isidor 78
Saint James *see* Santiago
Saint Martial, Apostle? 64
Saint Martial monastery 64
Saint Michael monastery 63, 87, 190
Saint Nicholas 109, 284
Saint Olav *see* Olav II
St. Omer 81
Saint-Patrice 212

Saint Paul 54, 226, 238, 320
Saint Peter 54, 63–4, 68–72, 81, 88, 104, 137, 152, 236, 240, 294, 310
Saint Rosendo 244–5
Saint Sylvester 224
Saint Teótonio 313
Saint Vincent 122, 217–18, 224–6, 244, 248, 258, 288, 313
Saint Vitus 117, 173, 214, 297, 315, 318
Saladin 19, 172, 211, 261–2, 264, 271–2, 276–7
Salazar, António de Oliveira 37
Saleph River 264
Salzwedel 198
Sambia 262, 269
Samsø 58
Samson, Duke of Burgundy 208
Sancho, monk from Mallorca 122
Sancho I, King of Portugal 165, 171, 184, 235, 248, 269–80, 284, 286–7
Sancho II, King of Portugal 292–5
Sancho I Ramirez, King of Aragon 53, 70, 81
Sancho II of Castile 71
Sancho III of Castile 149, 151
Sancho III the Great, King of Navarra 52, 60, 70
Sancho IV of Navarre 54
Sancho VII of Navarre 280, 289
Sancho of León-Castile, Brother of Alfonso VI 55
Sancho of León-Castile, Son of Alfonso VI 131
San Germano 303
Santa Cruz convent 111, 133, 138, 164, 168–9, 183, 216–17, 259, 276, 280, 313
Santa Maria de Tonguina 290
Santarém 31, 55–6, 73, 107–8, 124, 131, 143, 148, 166–7, 183, 193, 216–17, 233, 250, 270–1, 277, 293, 313
Santiago 122, 135, 167, 208, 217, 224, 232, 236–8, 243, 244, 272, 275, 288, 313
Santiago de Compostela 18, 75–9, 99, 107, 111, 121–2, 132, 133, 143, 167, 207–13, 236–8, 270, 275, 287, 328, 330
Santiago Order *see* Order of Santiago
São João de Tarouca monastery 191
São Mamede, 1128 Battle 133, 135
São Pedro do Sul 151
São Salvador de Vacariça monastery 73–4
Sara 316
Saraiva, José 42
Saule 304

Saxo 22, 34–5, 41, 46, 94, 107, 109–10, 117–18, 128, 141–2, 153, 155–61, 164, 168, 173, 180–2, 194, 213–16, 219–23, 263, 310, 315, 317, 322, 328
Scania 57, 59, 61–2, 86, 123, 157, 189, 215
Schleswig 24, 62–3, 65, 115, 117, 154–7, 161–2, 180, 190, 222, 227–8, 242–3, 264–7, 269, 296–7
Schwerin 196–7, 241, 284, 300, 302–4, 326
Sebastião 35–6
Segeberg 154
Seine River 210
Semgallen 296
Sens 161
Serpa 150, 293
Serra Estrela 55, 195
Setúbal 74, 225
Sevilla 52
Sibbesborg 263
Sicily 69, 80, 97, 100–1, 105, 211
Sierra Morena 281
Sigurd Jorsalfarer (the Crusader) 111, 115–16, 118, 120, 127–8, 131–2, 176
Sigurd Munn 263
Silos monastery 78
Silves 75, 77, 97, 99, 148–9, 226, 264, 271–9, 295, 307
Sintra 55, 132, 144, 148
Sipoo 263
Sisnando, Bishop of Santiago de Compostela 77
Sisnando Davidiz, Mozarab Count 55, 167, 312
Skjalm Hvide 117, 327
Skokloster 254
Slangerup 109
Slau 327
Sluis 97
Småland 112, 115–16, 128
Soares, Torquato de Sousa 39–40
Søborg 161, 265
Soeiro, Bishop of Évora 287
Soeiro Viegas, Bishop of Lisbon 287
Sofie, Daughter of Valdemar I the Great 325
Sofie of Denmark 156, 325, 331
Soliman *see* Kilij Arslan
Solomon, Old Testament king 165, 245, 248
Søndervinge Stone 27
Sorø monastery 170, 190–1, 203–4, 240
Soure 131, 232, 233, 313
Sprogø 158

382 Index

Stamford Bridge, 1066 Battle 80
Starkad 213–15, 254
Steenstrup, Johannes 25, 31
Stefan, Greek bishop 258
Stiklestad, 1030 Battle 62, 80
Suger, Abbot of Saint Denis monastery
    147, 182
Sülstorf 241
Sus 172
Svantevit 159, 173, 184, 215, 315,
    318–19
Svend, Bishop of Aarhus 161–2, 317
Svend, Bishop of Viborg 134
Svend, Prince of Denmark 82, 106–8
Svend I Forkbeard, King of Denmark
    62–3, 66, 221
Svend II Estridsen, King of Denmark
    25, 47, 65–70, 72, 74, 81–2, 88, 106,
    316, 322
Svend III Grathe, King of Denmark
    141–2, 154–60, 180, 205, 315
Svend Aggesen 156, 216, 219
Svendborg 326
Svold, 1000 Battle 62
Sybel, Heinrich von 106
Szczecin 116, 141, 202

Tacitus 93
Tagus River 55–6, 74, 132, 135, 144,
    146–8, 150–1, 164, 169, 224, 227,
    234–5, 239, 241, 270–2, 276–9,
    287, 293
Taicha Mountain 192
Tallinn 99, 241, 280, 286, 297
Tariq 51
Tarouca 191–2
Tarsus 108
Tasso, Torquato 106
Tavira 293
Tedau 291
Templars see Order of the Knight Templars
Teotónio 111, 133
Teresa, Daughter of Afonso I Henriques
    see Mathilde of Flanders
Teresa, Daughter of Sancho I 278
Teresa, Queen of Portugal 56, 82, 130,
    132–3, 138, 176, 232
Teutonic Order 94, 246, 256, 302, 304
Theoderik of Ardenne 212
Theodoric, Bishop of Estonia 297
Thetlev 157–8
Thierry II of Lorraine 81, 139
Thomas Becket, Archbishop of Canterbury
    172, 174, 222

Thor, Pagan God 116
Tierri, Duke of Aragon 209
Timotheus in Gezer 230
Toager 170
Toke Trylle 62, 86, 327
Tola 90
Toledo 52, 54–6, 71, 76, 78, 104, 107–8,
    111, 121–2, 128, 131, 140, 149, 163,
    167, 244, 246, 270, 278, 280, 289, 295,
    312–15, 320
Tomar 233–5, 276, 278
Toron 316–17
Toronho 134
Tortosa 140, 178, 226
Toulouse 82, 325
Tove 66, 86
Tovi 27
Toynbee, A.J. 6
Trancoso, 1140 Battle 191–2
Transdouro 55
Trava see Fernão Peres de Trava
Treyden 248
Trondheim 62, 65, 111, 115, 121, 224
Troy 100
Troyes 232
Tudela 56
Tummatorp 115
Turner, Frederick Jackson 92–4
Turpin 167, 208, 210
Tuy 77, 111, 121, 134
Tvis monastery 189
Tyerman, Christopher 20, 44
Tyre 100, 172, 262

Uclès 131
Uffo Belfagers 327
Ulf Jarl (Galicia-Ulf) 63, 78, 126
Umar al-Mutawakkil of Badajoz
    54–6, 73
Umayyads 51–2
Uppsala 91
Urban II 14, 16–18, 20–1, 34, 54, 82, 84,
    104, 110, 113–14, 118–19, 127, 129,
    139, 144, 163, 165, 194, 203, 206, 210,
    212, 244, 251, 257, 320, 322
Urraca, daughter of Afonso
    I Henriques 149
Urraca, daughter of Henrique 132
Urraca of Asturia 75
Urraca of Galicia / Aragon 56, 82,
    131–2, 176
Usedom 261
Uto 66, 73
Üxküll 263

Index 383

Valdemar, Bishop of Schleswig 264–6, 269, 305
Valdemar I the Great, King of Denmark 107, 118, 131, 133, 153–66, 168, 171–5, 190, 202, 214, 216, 221–2, 227, 239–42, 244, 260, 264, 283, 315–16, 325, 333
Valdemar II the Victorious, King of Denmark 1, 3, 28, 97, 99, 153, 171, 221, 247, 264, 266–9, 283–6, 289–92, 296–306, 325–6, 334–5
Valdemar III the Young, King of Denmark 294, 296–7, 300–1, 310, 325–6
Valdemar IV Atterdag, King of Denmark 46
Valdevez, 1141 Battle 134, 137
Valencia 52, 55, 107, 224, 289
Vandkær 198
Vartislav, Duke of Pomerania 117
Vasco da Gama 35
Vatalandi 108
Vedel, Anders Sørensen 34, 106
Vederlov 243–4
Veila Gonçalves 79
Vends 159
Venice 17, 262
Vetheman 162, 223
Viborg 134, 141, 155, 158, 180, 240, 325
Viken 62
Viktor IV 161
Vila Franca 277
Vila-Nova-da-Barquinha 234
Vila Pouca de Aguiar 169
Vila Real 169
Vilhelm, Abbot of Æbelholt 240
Vilhelm, Bishop of Roskilde 25
Vineam Domini 282–3
Viseu 111, 130, 133, 166, 191, 271
Vitskøl monastery 158, 190
Vizelin 154
Vladimir of Polotsk 247, 256

Wæzelin 291
Walcheren 97

Wampen 198
Wellington, Arthur Wellesley 30
Wends / Wendland 26–7, 92, 94–5, 110, 115–18, 121, 141–2, 155, 158–62, 168, 173–4, 187–90, 194, 196–8, 200–1, 203, 205, 221, 223, 230, 241–3, 260–1, 275, 283, 314–18, 322
Werben 241
Weser River 197
Widukind, Saxon chronicler 59
Wieck 198
Wilfred, Bishop of Narbonne 53
Wilhelm, Count of Holland and Friesland 287, 289
Wilhelm of Modena, legate 304
William I Bravehead, Duke of Burgundy 56, 69
William of Cornibus 277
William of Malmesbury 17–18
William of Tyre 106, 181
Willibrord, Frankish missionary 58
Wizlaw I of Rügen 297
Wladislav II of Bohemia 141, 331
Wladislaw II of Poland 331
Wolgast 162, 168, 261
Wolin 62, 175, 261, 314
Wurzen 199

Ximena 107

Yakut bin Abdulla 284
Yding Skovhøj 57
Yolanda, Queen of Jerusalem 303
Yre 27
Ysoré, giant 210
Yussuf Ibn Tashufin 55
Ywar 291

Zaida, Princess of Seville131
Zamora 133, 137
Zaragoza 52, 55, 122, 208, 232–3
Zealand 35, 59, 61–2, 117, 153, 155, 157–8, 161–2, 204, 220, 229–30, 261, 304, 317
Zenghi, Imad ad-Din 138, 148